Practical Counseling in the Schools

Practical Counseling in the Schools

Second Edition

Gary S. Belkin
Long Island University

wcb

Wm. C. Brown Company Publishers
Dubuque, Iowa

wcb
group

Wm. C. Brown, **Chairman of the Board**
Mark C. Falb, **Corporate Vice President/Operations**

wcb

WM. C. BROWN COMPANY PUBLISHERS, COLLEGE DIVISION

Lawrence E. Cremer, **President**
Raymond C. Deveaux, **Vice President, Product Development**
David Wm. Smith, **Assistant Vice President/National Sales Manager**
David A. Corona, **Director of Production Development and Design**
Matthew T. Coghlan, **National Marketing Manager**
Janis Machala, **Director of Marketing Research**
William A. Moss, **Production Editorial Manager**
Marilyn A. Phelps, **Manager of Design**
Mary M. Heller, **Visual Research Manager**

BOOK TEAM

Susan J. Soley, **Editor**
Joyce S. Oberhausen, **Production Editor**
Don Hedeman, **Designer**
Faye Schilling, **Visual Research Editor**
Mavis M. Oeth, **Permissions Editor**

To my parents

Contents

Preface

The reader of this second edition of *Practical Counseling in the Schools* will notice substantial changes, both in content and organization, from the first edition. The second edition has been extensively rewritten and reorganized to make it more consistent with the content and emphasis of school guidance and counseling courses in the 1980s. Topics that were treated briefly in the first edition are given more extensive coverage in this edition, including such important topics as counseling the exceptional student, adolescent counseling (including drug and alcohol abuse), counseling women in the 1980s, counseling minority clients, the school counselor and social problems (such as child abuse prevention, the single parent family), innovative techniques in school counseling (such as horticultural counseling and transactional analysis), values clarification counseling.

Several helpful suggestions regarding the strengths and weaknesses of the first edition were taken into account in the revision. Some readers felt there was too much "philosophizing" about counseling in the first edition, a reflection no doubt of my own biases. While I thought that many of these philosophical sections were interesting, they were not, I realized upon subsequent readings germane to most introduction to school counseling courses. These have been cut out of the second edition. Several reviewers of the first edition pointed to a brevity in the explication of elementary and secondary school counseling applications, and the coverage of this important material has been doubled in this revision (see chapters 9 and 10). You will note, too, that in this edition there is greater focus throughout on the actual school setting, including detailed coverage and many examples of the types of challenges and situations the school counselor is most likely to face.

While the specific changes from the first edition are too numerous to detail, the following major changes have been made:

> *Full* chapter coverage of key topics in *school* counseling has been added—including assessment and appraisal; counseling the exceptional student; counseling in the elementary school; counseling

in the secondary school; group counseling in the schools; values clarification counseling

All of the major theories of counseling are presented *concisely* in one chapter.

Behavioral counseling is developed in a separate chapter, with emphasis on how behavioral techniques can be applied in the school setting.

There is an increased use of examples, including case material and brief transcriptions of counseling interactions.

Many new and up-to-date references are included; over 50 percent of the references cited were not in the earlier edition.

I am indebted to a number of individuals who gave generously of their time and talent in helping me prepare this book. My editor at Wm. C. Brown Company Publishers, Bill Fitzgerald, provided me with encouragement, guidance, and an enthusiasm for the project. A number of my graduate students at Long Island University read sections of the manuscript and offered valuable criticisms, suggestions, and comments. My counseling colleagues who reviewed the manuscript—Alan P. Milliren, Illinois State University; John J. Pietrofesa, Wayne State University; and Calvin L. Stoudt, University of Wisconsin-Stout—were of enormous assistance in providing direction and a balanced perspective. The members of my department at Long Island University were supportive of my work and offered many valuable suggestions in their respective areas of expertise. I thank them all.

Introduction

The second half of the 1970s saw many exciting changes in the counseling profession, especially in the school counseling setting. The passage by Congress in 1975 of Public Law 94–142, the Education for All Handicapped Children Act, opened the way for the school counselor to become a central force in working with the exceptional child, both directly and as a consultant to the teaching and administrative staffs. The remnant philosophy of the social change movement that swept our campuses in the late 1960s and early 1970s became the working credo of counselors, who came to view themselves as integral elements of social change. Important new research efforts toward understanding the special needs of minority group clients led to valuable new counseling strategies and to a new awareness by counselors of their roles. Also on the plus side, a powerful impetus toward the licensing and credentialing of counselors gave everyone in the profession an important new subject for analysis; sometimes cause for debate; and finally, a call to action. On the minus side, many school districts across the country, beset by the ravages of inflation, cut their counseling staff beyond what any reasonable person would say was the absolute minimum for effective services.

The 1980s will, no doubt, bring many changes of equal magnitude. Counseling is, after all, an evolving profession—continually in search of new meanings to guide it, of new ways of proving socially beneficial to an expanding public, and of new relationships with its sister disciplines in the mental health profession. As I mentioned in the earlier edition of this book— and affirm now more strongly—the field is changing so quickly, its growth is so rapid and often unpredictable, that it is almost impossible at any given time to pinpoint with accuracy the nature, scope, and basic methods of counseling.

The profession of counseling will be surveyed in depth in the fifteen chapters that comprise this book and together we will examine the actual work of the counselor in the school setting. Two key themes will recur throughout—in the text, in the examples, and in the organization. First, it will be emphasized time and again that the person of the counselor is the instrumental force in the counseling process. It is not so much theories of counseling or abstract ideas that define counseling; it is, rather, the people engaged in the process. Counseling can only be as effective as the counselor is effective.

Second, we will note as we look at applied counseling practices that the tens of thousands of pages of empirical research, of published project reports, of enlightened individual observations and comments are eminently useful to the counselor and the student of counseling. The well-known injunction, those who cannot learn from history are condemned to repeat it, can be rephrased for counseling: counselors who do not look at the published literature that presents itself in counseling journals now are doomed to do less than their best in the future. It has been my aim throughout the book to draw from the professional journals' timely and relevant reports and research findings, and to indicate how these can be used in providing the most up-to-date and effective counseling services for clients.

Chapter 1, "The Contexts of School Counseling," sketches the historical background and philosophical underpinnings of the counseling profession and details where contemporary school counseling fits into the counseling picture. Chapters 2 and 3 cover all the major theories (or schools) of counseling, including psychodynamic, humanistic-existential, Gestalt, transactional analysis, reality therapy, and rational-emotive (in chapter 2), and the behavioral approaches (in chapter 3). Chapters 4 and 5 focus directly on the counseling relationship and the counseling process, which are, we shall see, inextricably intertwined in practice.

The working roles and functions of the school counselor are the subject of chapter 6, "The School Counselor in Perspective." In this chapter we will note how clients, teachers, counselors, and other individuals may, at times, have very different expectations and perceptions about what the school counselor should do and about what the counselor actually does do. To clarify the function of the school counselor, two valuable and very practical school counseling applications will be examined in depth in chapter 7, "Values Clarification Counseling" and in chapter 8, "Career Counseling in the Schools."

It will be noted that while everything covered up to this point is equally applicable to all school levels, there are certain adaptations that have to be made when working on either the elementary or the secondary level. These adaptations are usually the consequence of age-related problems, such as the child abuse problem on the elementary level or the drug abuse problem on the secondary level. In chapters 9 and 10 we look at client problems and counseling strategies geared specifically to the elementary level (in chapter 9) and to the secondary school level (in chapter 10).

From the inception of school counseling, the paired tasks of assessment and appraisal have been associated with the role of the school counselor. These are covered in chapter 11.

The counselor's relationship with the exceptional learner in the schools has not yet been fully defined, especially in light of the Education for All Handicapped Children Act of 1975, which promises some important changes. The counselor should, it is generally agreed, have a working knowledge of conditions that are exceptional and some tentative idea of his or her role in providing an optimal (or, as it is called, "least restrictive") environment for the exceptional learner. Chapter 12, "Counseling the Exceptional Person," examines some possible new roles of the school counselor in the area of the exceptional learner and explicates the major categories of exceptionalities generally recognized in the profession. Chapter 13, "Group Counseling in the Schools," while not focusing directly on the exceptional learner, provides an introduction to the important modality of group work, which has gained prominence as an economical and practical counseling resource.

Many clients come to counseling because they are in the midst of a crisis situation. In chapter 14, "Crisis Counseling in the Schools," we look first at the general principles of crisis intervention and then at some specific types of crises with which the school counselor is likely to deal: grief crisis, anxiety crisis, suicidal crisis, rape crisis, and problem-pregnancy crisis.

Finally, in chapter 15 we consider the needs of the special population client—women, minorities, and children from nonintact family situations. Although general counseling principles do apply for each of these types of clients, there are certain recognitions and adaptations required on the part of the counselor that warrant separate coverage.

We will begin by setting the stage for examining the contexts of school counseling.

Practical Counseling
in the Schools

The Contexts of School Counseling

There is in the counseling profession much confusion about the functional and theoretical differences between *guidance, counseling,* and *psychotherapy.* This semantic confusion extends to misunderstandings about the roles of the guidance counselor, the school psychologist, the psychological (or clinical) counselor, the psychotherapist, and of other ancillary job titles and functions. The lay public, and to a large extent, the helping professional, cannot say with certainty at which point the purview of the one ends and the other begins. For the most part, the confusion is born of knowledge and practical experience, not of ignorance. For as those familiar with the intimate workings of these specialties know, the terms do overlap, and in many instances the same practitioner will think nothing of switching from one designation to the other. The result is that over the years there has arisen a semantic equivalency between guidance and counseling, and between counseling and psychotherapy. For example, in the school setting the school counselor may speak of his or her guidance position and may even be called a guidance counselor, while in the clinical setting the mental health counselor may view himself or herself as practicing therapy and may even be designated as a psychotherapist.

Moreover, as one engages in the practice of guidance, counseling or psychotherapy, or any combination of the three, it becomes even more striking how much the terms have in common in relation to their moment-to-moment interactions; how many parallels of purpose and technique there are between them. It could be argued, and indeed it has been, that to differentiate between them is simply nit-picking. Yet there is a compelling reason to do just this; a reason that becomes emphasized, however, only after the differences between them have become clearly determined. The reason is this: because the human organism is highly complex and specialized, both physically and psychologically, the range of problems and situations that the organism encounters is also complex and specialized. In the psychological realm, for example, problems run the gamut from deeply emotional conflicts to basic decision making; to interpersonal relationships;

to minor conflicts; to learning problems; to vocational problems; and to a score of other types of problems. To deal effectively with this legion of interlocking problems, there evolved over a period of many years specialists of different skills and backgrounds, each equipped to handle expertly one or more categories of problems, yet able to have insight into all of the areas.

These specialists work under a variety of professional titles. They are called psychologists, psychiatrists, psychiatric social workers, counseling psychologists, family counselors, pastoral counselors, psychotherapists, psychoanalysts, learning disabilities specialists, vocational counselors, school counselors, guidance counselors, and so on. Each is equipped to handle his or her own specialized range of problems, yet each is acutely aware of the other specialists' responsibilities, and the possibility of referral and consultation is always in the foreground.

In practice, as we shall soon see, it is probably not theory that distinguishes one helper from another; nor is it title or training. Nor does the professional designation of the helper determine the quality and value of the help given. Rather, it is a matrix of factors involving, among other variables, the personalities of the client and the helper; the setting; the presenting problems and underlying conflicts; the length of time available for treatment; and client motivation.

The school counselor, with whom we are primarily concerned in this textbook, practices an amalgam of guidance, counseling, and psychotherapy within the context of a school setting. The school counselor is also a referral person, whose familiarity with the allied mental health specialties makes possible the initiation of appropriate referrals where he or she believes that a particular client's difficulties can best be dealt with by an adjacent area of expertise. It is imperative, therefore, not only that he or she understand the distinctions among the guidance role, the counseling role, and the psychotherapeutic role, but also that the relationships among the three roles and the relationship to other specialized roles within the broad professional ranks be understood. Because guidance, counseling, and psychotherapy have different origins, because they have vastly different orientations, different axiomatic bases, different resources, the counselor's understanding of the differences among them not only helps in the understanding of the three types of approaches available but also helps to define his or her function comprehensively and understand the rightful place in the mental health profession hierarchy. By looking at the three terms as three distinct phases of the mental health effort, the school counselor is better able to gain a working perspective of his or her role in the treatment of individual difficulties.

The purpose of this chapter, therefore, is not to clear up a semantic problem or to set up arbitrary distinctions with which a counselor can feel comfortable, but rather to begin to clarify and to define the factors that contribute to our description of the complex job of the school counselor. Let us begin by examining the origins of the guidance and counseling movement, noting particularly the forces that are integral in providing a historical, cultural, and contextual perspective for understanding contemporary school counseling.

THE ORIGINS OF THE COUNSELING MOVEMENT

The counseling profession, as we know it today, derives from six basic sources: laboratory psychology, brought over from Europe; innovative approaches to the treatment of the "insane," leading to the inception of the "talking cure"—psychoanalysis; the mental hygiene movement and the mental testing movement, both originating in the United States; the influence of humanistic psychology; and the vocational guidance movement, which sprung up during the early part of this century. We could add the influence of sociology, progressive education, and other psychological and sociocultural influences, sprinkled in among the basic sources. Let us consider each of these individually and then together.

Laboratory Psychology

The beginning of modern laboratory psychology is usually traced to 1879 when Wilhelm Wundt set up the first experimental psychology laboratory in Leipzig, Germany. When Wundt began his research, he was already familiar with the physiological studies of E. H. Weber, Johannes Müller (who is sometimes called "the father of experimental psychology"), and Hermann von Helmholtz. These three researchers had discovered a mass of evidence about nervous reflexes, about sensation, about nerve impulses, and about the relationship between physical and mental states. Wundt's contribution was to focus his efforts on the mind, or consciousness per se, while still using the scientific method of the physiolgical researchers.

Wundt attempted to study the structure of the mind by using the method of introspection. This method involves the subject's self-reflection and verbalizing to the experimenter what he or she is experiencing. The experimenter then records it, and studies how images and sensations and thoughts are connected in consciousness. The problem with this method, of course, is that experiments cannot be replicated and there is too much room for subjectivity. Also, the scope of any investigation that focuses on the structure of mind is somewhat limited by the possibility of human error. In the United States, William James modified Wundt's *introspectionist* psychology, attempting instead to simply study the structure of the mind to discover its functions. He and his followers became known as *functionalists.* While their initial efforts were much like the efforts of the introspectonists, they gradually developed new experimental designs to study perception, attention, responses to stimuli, habit patterns, and so on—with the idea of understanding *why* the mind functions as it does.

While this introspectionist-functionalist argument was raging, a new force in laboratory psychology—one that was destined to become the most important force as far as counseling was concerned—began to develop in the United States. It was called *behaviorism,* and it sprung up in 1912, subjecting the introspectionists, and to some extent the functionalists, to a barrage of critical analysis from which they would never fully recover.

The behaviorists' major criticism of the introspectionists rests on their emphasis on consciousness, an untenable concept for the behaviorists because of its intangibility. "From the time of Wundt on," Watson (1930), the founder of American behaviorism, argues, "consciousness becomes the keynote of psychology. . . . It is a plain assumption just as unprovable, just as unapproachable, as the old concept of the soul. And to the behaviorist the two terms are essentially identical, so far as concerns their metaphysical implications" (p. 14). Instead of building a psychology of consciousness and instead of using introspective techniques, the behaviorists suggested, use something that would be subject to scientific measurement and experimental replication: namely, observable and measurable behavior. With this as their working premise, behavioristic psychologists attempted to formulate, through systematic observation and experimentation, the generalizations, laws, and principles that underlie the individual's behavior (Watson, 1919).

The rift between these two early schools of psychology is indicative of the schism that divides the ranks of the mental health professionals today. "Are we," ask practitioners, "to be primarily concerned with feelings, perceptions, associations, and other manifestations of consciousness, or are we to focus our attention on symptoms, actions, learning, and other observable and quantifiable forms of behavior?" Should the counselor be primarily concerned with the client's condition of consciousness—his or her subjectivity—vague as this concept is, or should the counselor deal primarily with the client's behavior, which is observable and empirically modifiable (trainable)? These fundamental questions still challenge counselors, and it is the responsibility of each counselor as he or she enters the profession to decide which premises are right for him or her, which assumptions will guide him or her in practice. We shall see later how the influence of psychoanalysis from Vienna—combined with the European experimental psychology movement; combined with behavioral psychology and public efforts in mental health; combined with the American psychometric movement—became the germ of the contemporary counseling movement.

New Approaches to Treating Emotional Problems

Despite all the efforts to come to grips with the complexities of the human psyche, there were no early psychological attempts to treat emotional problems to "cure" emotional illnesses. In fact, no such discipline arose until the mid-nineteenth century when a number of disparate movements took hold and individually attempted to treat mental and emotional illness in a humane, constructive, and scientifically valid manner. Before that, the problem of healing was strictly in the purview of magical healers, of priests, of medicine men, who often applied their art in a most bizarre and unscientific fashion. Yet, their work ultimately led to the psychological treatment of emotional disorders. As Ehrenwald (1976) dramatically emphasizes,

> If mental healers were to be summoned to the patient's bedside in the order of their appearance in history, the magician or medicine man would be the first one to answer the call. He would be followed by the philosopher-priest . . . who would, in turn, yield his place to the scientifically oriented psychotherapist. There would be a world of difference between their underlying philosophies and the way they minister to their patients' needs. But their goal would be the same: to cure psychological (and sometimes physical) ills essentially by psychological means. (p. 17)

Prior to that time, victims of mental illness were treated either as prisoners, avatars of the Devil, or persons who were chronically and hopelessly incurable. "The insane," Thomson (1968) points out, "were regarded simply with fear and disgust, and were thrust into prison-like asylums to be left to the mercy of brutal and ignorant keepers. . . . The typical European asylum contained naked, ill-fed wretches who slept on straw in filthy, unventilated and unlit cells. The quarters resembled dungeons, and the more disturbed patients were frequently chained. In England, lunatics were often exhibited like animals in a side-show for the amusement of the public" (p. 194).

In France in 1793, a young psychiatrist, Dr. Philippe Pinel, was given charge of the notorious Bicêtre asylum. Pinel instituted a program of reform, based on the principle that the job of an asylum was to restore the inmate to functional mental health. Such a simple principle, yet one so revolutionary in its time that it met with much opposition from the community and from the national government. But Pinel persisted, at Bicêtre and later at Salpêtrière, and he deserves credit as the first pioneer in the mental health movement.

After Pinel's death, another psychiatric innovator, Jean Martin Charcot, emerged at Salpêtrière. He was a distinguished neurologist, with a special interest in psychosomatic diseases, who had spent several years diagnosing and treating patients who believed they were suffering from a form of paralysis or epilepsy, but who actually had nothing physically wrong with them. Charcot labeled this disorder *hysteria* and formulated a detailed clinical description of it, distinguishing it from closely related symptomatic disorders. He pioneered the use of hypnosis as a clinical tool in the diagnosis of hysterical disorders, suggesting that hypnosis itself was a form of "artificial" hysteria.

It was a colleague of Charcot's, another neurologist named Pierre Janet, who discovered a method to treat this newly diagnosed disorder. Charcot had used hypnosis as a *diagnostic* tool in working with hysterical patients; Janet took this one step further and began to use hypnosis as a *curative* agent as well. He discovered through trial and error that hysteric persons were able under hypnosis to recall memories and feelings from the past. As the hypnotist helped the hysteric person remember those buried memories, the patient suddenly began to experience a rapid alleviation of the debilitating symptom, a "miraculous" cure. Janet used the term *catharsis* to describe this sudden freeing of the dammed-up memories, and he laid the groundwork upon which a later student would revolutionize the field of treatment. This student was named Sigmund Freud.

Freud was deeply impressed by the works of Charcot and Janet. A poor young man, he managed to obtain a scholarship in 1885 in order to travel to France to study under Charcot, who was internationally renowned at the time. Studying during the day and reviewing and critically examining these studies at night, Freud returned from his sojourn in France full of new and exciting ideas. He shared these ideas with a colleague, Dr. Josef Breuer, and the two collaborated to use the cathartic-hypnotic treatment in working with hysterical patients. This marked the beginning of what was to emerge a few short years later as the psychoanalytic movement (see chapter 2, pp. 37–40).

The Mental Hygiene Movement

At the same time in the United States, mental illness, while not regarded quite as primitively as in pre-Pinel France, was still viewed without the slightest sophistication or optimism. No national policy, no prominent physicians, no humanitarian organizations watched out for the interests of the mentally ill. On the contrary, the mentally ill person was at best a pariah— an emotional leper—who had to be separated from society, for both his good and for the general welfare. This attitude was pervasive in the United States during the same period that the guidance movement was in its flowering stages.

What was needed was someone to bring to the attention of a public long motivated by humanitarian and progressive instincts the enormity and seriousness of the problem. Such a man, ironically enough, was Clifford Beers, a minor clerk in the financial district of New York City. Beers, who suffered from schizophrenia, spent many of his years in mental institutions, outraged by the conditions but helpless to do anything about them. Finally, recovering enough to function, he wrote a book about his experiences, *A Mind That Found Itself* (1956), which became an influential bestseller. The book, with its graphic detail of the Dantean plight of the institutionalized, shocked the American public. Even more important, the book, a subtle combination of personal experiences and rhetoric that called for reform, instigated rapid and sweeping changes in the field of mental health care. Beers ultimately became a social activist and crusader, helping to found the Society for Mental Hygiene. While Freud made its conception possible, men like Beers made possible the implementation of modern mental health treatment, which did so much to change the relationship of the mentally ill to the greater society.

Once the American public became aware of the need for mental health reform, the innovations of Freud and his contemporaries were quickly imported and put into practice here. From the 1920s onward, psychoanalysis and its derivative approaches (especially Adlerian therapy) began to make an impact on the counseling movement. Combined with the burgeoning vocational guidance movement, something of a specific shape was forming; the winds of change were in the air.

The laboratory work of Watson, Skinner, and the other behavioral psychologists also began to make an impact on the counseling movement. Most new movements in the social and behavioral sciences attempted to "legitimize" themselves by formulating their own nomenclature, by setting up their own disciplinary rules and formulae, and claiming privilege by invoking the good name of *science*. How tempting it was for the early followers of the counseling stance to seize the quantifiable findings of the behaviorists and apply these to counseling problems.

The Testing Movement

In quick time, counselors and counselor educators began to recognize the value of testing, and the testing movement became a significant part of counseling from its very beginnings. From the late nineteenth century, when the British scientist Sir Francis Galton attempted to devise a simple measure of intelligence, through Alfred Binet's landmark development of the first IQ tests, through Lewis M. Terman's administration of the test to a large population, through E. L. Thorndike's myriad contributions to the American testing movement, the profession of counseling became intricately entwined with and influenced by the testing and measurement movement. Quantitative tools were developed to help assess the client's needs, to measure his or her abilities, aptitudes, and problems, and to evaluate the outcomes of the counseling encounter more accurately. By the 1950s there was no area of counseling that had not been profoundly influenced by the testing movement.

Together, behavioral laboratory psychology and the use of empirical and quantitative methods (testing and statistics) offered a scientific dimension to counseling. This side of counseling, still important today, has its advocates and its critics. Clearly, one cannot fail to acknowledge that it has had a profound effect upon the development of contemporary counseling.

The Humanistic Influence

Perhaps the most notable reaction to the quantitative influence in counseling was begun by a young psychologist who had been trained in the psychoanalytic method, but who found that method too depersonalizing. Arguing that each patient had to be viewed as a total, distinct, and important individual, not as a proof for some tentative theory of behavior, learning, or psychosexual development, Carl R. Rogers initiated what he then called "nondirective psychotherapy," but which today bears the eponymous title, *Rogerian therapy* (see chapter 3). Rogers's ideas have had a more significant impact upon the development of counseling than has any other system of psychotherapy. Rogers's belief in the dignity of the individual and in the ultimate worth of the client was compatible not only with the attitudes of professionals in the guidance field but also with the attitudes of many prominent psychotherapists as well. Rogers's influence upon the counseling movement is incalculable, and the tradition he established set the stage for the merging of the terms *counseling* and *psychology* as we know them today.

As the terms were joined in happy matrimony, new possibilities unfolded to develop further each of the functions embodied within the rubric. Most importantly, the burgeoning philosophy of *existentialism*, which states that people are free agents, seeking meaning in their lives through their voluntary actions, and which was popular during the 1950s and 60s, began to wield its weight within the movement. It was not uncommon to hear of existential approaches to vocational counseling, to job training, to personnel work, to rehabilitation counseling, as well as to psychotherapy. Even in such practical areas as student personnel work and vocational counseling, existential ideas have made an impact.

The Vocational Guidance Movement

By the first decade of this century, the revolution in helping that was taking place here was the indigenous vocational guidance movement, which was springing up throughout the country. This socially progressive educational movement, which was designed to help individuals find themselves through their work, was originated by Frank Parsons, a Boston educator. Its goals of self-fulfillment made it compatible with the impending counseling movement. Cremin's (1964) description of Parsons's thinking accurately reflects its relationship to counseling—that is, to helping the individual fulfill his or her capacities:

> The key to Parsons' ultimate goal . . . lay in his notion of "the useful and happy life." Parsons, a significant figure in the history of American reform, believed not only that vocational counseling would lead to greater individual fulfilment, but that people suited to their jobs would tend to be active in the creation of a more efficient and humane industrial system. Intelligently practiced, the craft of vocational guidance would serve not only the youngsters who sought counsel, but the cause of social reform as well. (p. 13)

The influences that were brought to bear on the formation of the guidance movement are direct consequences of the events of the time. The closing decade of the nineteenth century most precisely pinpoints the birth of the vocational guidance movement. It was a time of change in America, a time of massive building and rapid technological innovation, a time of increasing immigration from Europe and of migration from rural America into the cities. A predominantly homogeneous agrarian society was in the process of being transformed into a primarily heterogeneous urban society as the great swell of European immigrants and American country folk flocked to the great urban centers, heating up the classical melting pot that was to play so great a part in twentieth-century American cultural and social history. The consequences of this demographic tipping were staggering. The cities became kaleidoscopes of ethnic idiosyncracies as each of the assimilating groups gently, but often painfully, began to make its presence felt in its new homeland.

Other changes were also making themselves felt at this time. Barry and Wolf (1963) cite "industrialization, specialization, urbanization, the changing role of women, the growing need for education, rising enrollments, expanding curricula, rising secularism, the desire for useful education, and new educational theories as some of the changes and developments that created or intensified the need for guidance-personnel work" (p. 16). To this list, we must also add other, sometimes subtle, social changes that were beginning to bear profoundly on individual lives by the 1890s. Five years before this decade, the first electric railroad, the prototype for urban mass transportation, was opened in Baltimore, signaling the massive influence electricity was to play on the course of history. Ironically, in the year 1890, William Kemmler earned the dubious distinction of becoming the first man in history to be executed by electricity, at Sing Sing Prison in Ossining, New York. That same year, Ellis Island replaced the antiquated Castle Garden as the reception point for the hundreds of thousands of immigrants who flocked to our shores. A strike at the Carnegie Steel Mills in 1892, which resulted in a violent and fatal confrontation between management and labor, emphasized the rising antagonism between the classes—a problem that would plague this country for many years. Massive unemployment swept the country, and 20,000 Americans marched on Washington in 1894 to protest the precarious condition of the economy. These were important national events, newsworthy and duly recorded. But meanwhile, unannounced and unbeknownst to most people, seemingly minor isolated events in different parts of the country were the first manifestations of the guidance movement, as it would be known many years later.

The most significant work was Parsons's, but he had important protégés. In 1895, Parsons began to offer informal vocational counseling to indigent youth in Boston. Emphasizing "choosing a vocation rather than merely looking for a job, he urged young people to acquire a wide knowledge of occupations so as to avoid falling into the first convenient job opening" (Tolbert, 1978, p. 60). At about the same time, George Merrill instituted the first systematic vocational guidance program at the California School of Mechanical Arts in San Francisco. This resulted in the Vocational Bureau of Boston, which he opened with Meyer Bloomfield in 1908. This new movement quickly gained prominence throughout the country: in Grand Rapids, Jesse B. Davis organized the first large-scale school guidance program; Frank P. Goodwin instituted a similar effort in Cincinnati; Parson's seminal work, *Choosing A Vocation,* the first guidance textbook, was published posthumously in 1909. A year later, the first national conference on vocational guidance was held in Boston. The first doctoral dissertation in guidance was accepted at Columbia University in 1914, one year after the National Vocational Guidance Association (NVGA) was founded; Eli Weaver of Boys' High School in Brooklyn began to systematically advise his students about their career plans and future education, and provided summer work opportunities for them; William Wheatly of Middleton, Connecticut, introduced special school courses on vocations and added a unit on vocations to the social studies curriculum. These are but a few of the notable events; similar efforts were blossoming throughout the country.

Two important insights about contemporary guidance and counseling can be gleaned from these events. First, it is clear that counseling, as we know it today, evolved in part from the vocational guidance movement, which was brought about largely by the changing social and demographic forces that played so crucial a role in shaping America at the turn of the century. Second, it is evident that underlying all these innovative gestures was a strong commitment to the principles that marked the beginnings of this country: namely, the belief in the individual, the humanitarian spirit, the inalienable relationship between the individual and society. Taken together, we see the guidance movement as an inevitable consequence of the American spirit that has so forcefully shaped our national destiny, and an inexorable force in the shaping of contemporary counseling ideology.

COUNSELING—IN SEARCH OF IDENTITY

Counseling, as it exists today then, is the fusion of many influences. It brings together the compassionate treatment of mental problems began in mid-nineteenth century France, the psychodynamic insights of Freud and psychoanalysis, the scientific scrutiny and methodology of the behavioral approach, the quantitative science of psychometrics, the humanistic perspective of client-centered therapy, the philosophical bases of existentialism, and the practical insights and applications evolved from the vocational guidance movement. With this, has come a recent merging of other concerns indigenous to the social work and helping professions: the treatment and prevention of child abuse, health counseling, family counseling, and the like. We can see, then, that the profession of counseling is not some well-established entity, but rather it is a dynamic movement still in its flowering stages.

Perhaps it is characteristic of a blossoming discipline, or perhaps it is peculiar to counseling alone, but in either case it is safe to say that counseling, in its slow process of gestation and development, is going through a confusing time of doubt and self-examination, a period of finding itself and defining itself intelligently. An entire issue of *The Counseling Psychologist* (Vol. 7, No. 2, 1977) attempted in over one hundred double-column pages, written by many of the acknowledged leaders in the field, to come to grips with the question of what the professional identity of counseling as a discipline is today. In his presidential address to Division 17 of the American Psychological Association (the Division of Counseling Psychology), Norman Kagan (1977) compared the role of counselors to primary care physicians, who are "broadly skilled and have a holistic approach to the individual." The role, as he conceptualizes it, is preventive as well as ameliorative:

So-called "normal" people no longer are content to seek help only when they are vocationally uncertain, depressed, grieving or unable to grieve, preorgasmic or impotent. They want prevention and enrichment. They want the wherewithal to anticipate and deal with the many major personal and interpersonal events of living—they want a tool kit along with the car, so that they themselves are able to effect maintenance and repairs when things don't run smoothly. There is a need and a demand for self-directed personal and vocational exploration programs, personal and marital enrichment programs, mental health checkups and preventative maintenance programs. (p. 5)

Counseling, in this respect, is a dynamic approach toward the prevention and amelioration of human problems, as Kagan suggests. It represents a comprehensive attempt to help the individual deal with the myriad challenges of living.

When we speak about counseling movement, then, we are not inquiring about a fixed and static concept, one that can be precisely defined and explicated. Hardly! In fact, when we speak of counseling, it must be clear from the outset that we are speaking about a growing, evolving, continually changing concept, responsive to a nexus of interlocking pressures and concerns. "Counseling in the 1970s," Bradley (1978) points out, "[is] in a state of change and innovation from without and within" (p. 42). We are dealing with a movement dedicated to the growth and change of individuals, and which itself is still in the process of growing and changing, of defining itself.

In attempting to understand the contemporary framework of counseling, one of the key points is understanding the differences and the similarities, both functionally and theoretically, between guidance, counseling, and psychotherapy. This is a confusing question, one that has been the source of much contention in the professions. Asking, and still asking, "Where does the guidance function end and the counseling function begin?" or "Where does counseling end and psychotherapy begin?" counselors went busily about their work, with barely enough time to answer their questions.

But this question of the differences between guidance, counseling, and psychotherapy is an important question—one that must be answered. It is surrounded by myths and misconceptions, in part perpetuated by an establishment with vested interests. It is to this question that we shall now turn our attention.

GUIDANCE, COUNSELING, AND PSYCHOTHERAPY

The differences between guidance, counseling, and psychotherapy are in part revealed in their historical origins. When we consider the roots of these disciplines, and the social contexts that brought them about, it helps us better understand the functional contemporary definitions.

This guidance movement, of course, has changed dramatically since its beginnings almost ninety years ago. No longer is guidance simply vocational or educational guidance; on the contrary, the term *guidance* has become linked almost automatically with its partner, *counseling*. This was a natural evolution as vocational guidance personnel began to realize that what they were doing was more than merely providing guidance, or advice. They were helping individuals resolve difficulties in their lives, sometimes very complex and deeply rooted, and treating the problems in a way that was different from psychotherapy. The narrow emphasis on vocational needs and interests began to broaden into an emphasis on human adjustment, which required more far-ranging skills than information giving alone. Nowadays, Moser and Moser (1963) point out, "guidance is a term with many meanings. It is a point of view; it is a group of services; it is a field of study" (p. 8). This broadness is borne out if we examine some of the contemporary definitions of guidance. McDaniel and Shaftel (1956), for example, describe the guidance function comprehensively:

> Guidance in the modern school contributes in two broad areas to the concept that education is an individual process. . . . Guidance represents a pattern of services, which includes *orientation, individual inventory, educational and occupational information, counseling, placement, and follow-up.* (p. 17, italics added)

Kirby (1971) views guidance within the context of the total educational process:

> Guidance is an *incremental* process of education that is particularly cognizant of those aspects of educational, vocational, and social development not generally or specifically planned for in the curriculum. The guidance function, being incremental, is concerned with marginal changes; it is cognizant of those "critical incidents" in development common to most tasks of the emerging adult, and is primarily concerned with assisting in day-to-day decision making. (p. 596)

Downing (1968) presents a point of view along similar lines, emphasizing the adjustment of the individual:

> Guidance is an organized set of specialized services . . . an integral part of the school environment designed to promote the development of students and to assist them toward a realization of sound, wholesome adjustment and maximum accomplishments commensurate with their potentialities. (p. 7)

And, finally, Sprinthall (1971), in his superb book *Guidance for Human Growth*, suggests that the teaching function and the guidance function serve as a team to liberate the individual through education. He suggests a "dual curriculum to develop the individual's cognitive capacities and his personal development simultaneously."

> The dual curriculum implies a frame of reference with distinct but related priorities—learning to learn with a priority on subject matter mastery, and learning to learn with a priority on mastery and competence as a person. Such a dual curriculum for education makes requisite a collaboration of the two priorities. (p. 16)

In this sense, the guidance function and the teaching function work in harmony for the total development and growth of the individual.

The distinction between counseling and psychotherapy is even more of a fine-line distinction when we look at their historical origins. Albert (1966) finds no general differentiation between the two terms, and Ard (1966) concedes that "a fine-line distinction between counseling and psychotherapy is admittedly difficult if not impossible to draw" (p. vi). Curran (1968) too sees the terms as almost synonymous, separated in meaning by only a slight shade of connotation, "the main difference perhaps now being that counseling tends to refer to an educational, family, or pastoral setting and psychotherapy has a more clinical tone" (p. 4). Kirman (1977), tackling the problem from a different point of view but arriving at much the same conclusion, makes the important point that if the client has a problem, and has come to treatment to deal with this problem, it makes no *practical* difference whether we call that treatment counseling or whether we call it psychotherapy. Kirman says,

> When we perceive the helping process from the point of view of the counselee, the differentiation between counseling and psychotherapy becomes meaningless. We take from each helping relationship what it has to offer though we may have hoped for more. We give in each helping relationship what we are able regardless of the definition of role. (p. 22)

This is certainly a pragmatic statement: one that goes right to the heart of the client's perceptual world and attempts to come to grips with a very complex theoretical question as practicably as possible. It also offers strong support to the argument that the terms *counseling* and *psychotherapy* can be used interchangeably.

Despite these well-articulated positions, however, there are several strong arguments against them. In fact, the range of literature reflects a remarkable diversity of opinion on this subject, and much of what has been written has important ramifications in the counseling setting. We have considered briefly the position that counseling and psychotherapy are synonymous terms. In this section, we will examine the representative positions that maintain that counseling differs from psychotherapy by the seriousness of the client-patient's problems and the emotional "depth" or "intensity" of the treatment, and that it differs from psychotherapy in its theoretical foundation, in practical concerns, and in discrepant historical origins.

The "Difference of Degree" Argument

The "difference of degree" argument asserts that counseling and psychotherapy differ in the consideration of their concerns or the depth of their approaches. Every major American dictionary differentiates between the two terms. *Webster's Third New International Dictionary* (1976), for example, defines counseling as "a practice or professional service designed to guide an individual to a better understanding of his problems and potentialities by utilizing modern psychological principles and methods especially in collecting case history data, using various techniques of the personal interview, and testing interests and aptitudes."[1] The same dictionary offers a much more elaborate definition of psychotherapy. It reads as follows:

> 1: treatment of mental or emotional disorder or maladjustment by psychological means, especially involving verbal communication. . . . 2: any alteration in an individual's interpersonal environment, relationships, or life situation brought about especially by a qualified therapist and intended to have the effect of alleviating syndromes of mental or emotional disturbance. 3: the process whereby a patient or other subject becomes aware of the content and mechanisms of his unconscious mind through free association.[2]

Aubrey (1967) and Bordin (1968) both assert that what distinguishes counseling from psychotherapy is the degree of the client's disturbance; that in counseling, the client is an "adequately functioning individual," and in psychotherapy, the patient is "neurotic and pathological." This type of distinction is popular, and it is hard to find fault with it. Like the dictionary definitions, it does seem to accurately describe what is generally perceived as the reality of the situation: the *is* rather than the *should be.* In practice, however, many cases are not so clearly defined, either in terms of the personality level of the client-patient or in terms of the problems under treatment, that we can specify the condition of the client in his or her totality. Just where counseling ends and psychotherapy begins, if we view the two terms on a continuum, is still not clear.

1. By permission. From *Webster's Third New International Dictionary* © 1976 by G. & C. Merriam Co., Publishers of the Merriam-Webster Dictionaries.
2. See note 1 above.

Hansen, Stevic, and Warner (1977), reflecting much of the current thinking, view counseling and therapy along a continuum:

> In examining this situation, let us concede that indeed there is a continuum between counseling and psychotherapy. While they appear at opposite ends of the continuum, they are neither dichotomous nor mutually exclusive ways of helping people in need. Nevertheless, the counselor and psychotherapist generally operate at different ends of that somewhat mystical continuum. (p. 13)

They go on to explain a continuum built on a model developed by William G. Perry, and conclude that "counseling is concerned with helping individuals learn new ways of dealing with and adjusting to life situations. It is a process through which people are helped to develop sound decision-making processes either in an individual or group setting. . . . Counseling does not attempt to restructure personality, but rather to develop what already exists" (p. 15).

This point of view, then, is that the differences between counseling and psychotherapy are differences in *degree* and *emphasis*. On the whole, this is the most substantiated argument. Perry et al. (1955), in an ambitious undertaking, analyzed the discrepancies between counseling and psychotherapy in terms of process differences, rather than product differences alone. Their report, based on analyses of therapist and counselor activities, is often cited in the literature. It concludes, after much exposition, that,

> Counseling looks more often toward the interpretation and development of the personality in the relations characteristic of specific role-problems, while psychotherapy looks more often toward the reinterpretation and reorganization of malignant conflictual elements within the personality through the relation with the therapist. (p. 11)

When we look at Perry's conclusions, as illustrated in figure 1.1, we seem to be approaching a consensus about the differences in common usage between the terms *counseling* and *psychotherapy.*

Practical Differences and Historical Influences

There are a number of practical differences between counseling and psychotherapy, and these differences are to a large extent a result of the diversity of historical influences and in basic underlying theory. We can summarize the major positions regarding these practical differences as follows: counseling is directed toward one set of problems while psychotherapy

figure 1.1 Psychotherapy and counseling continuum

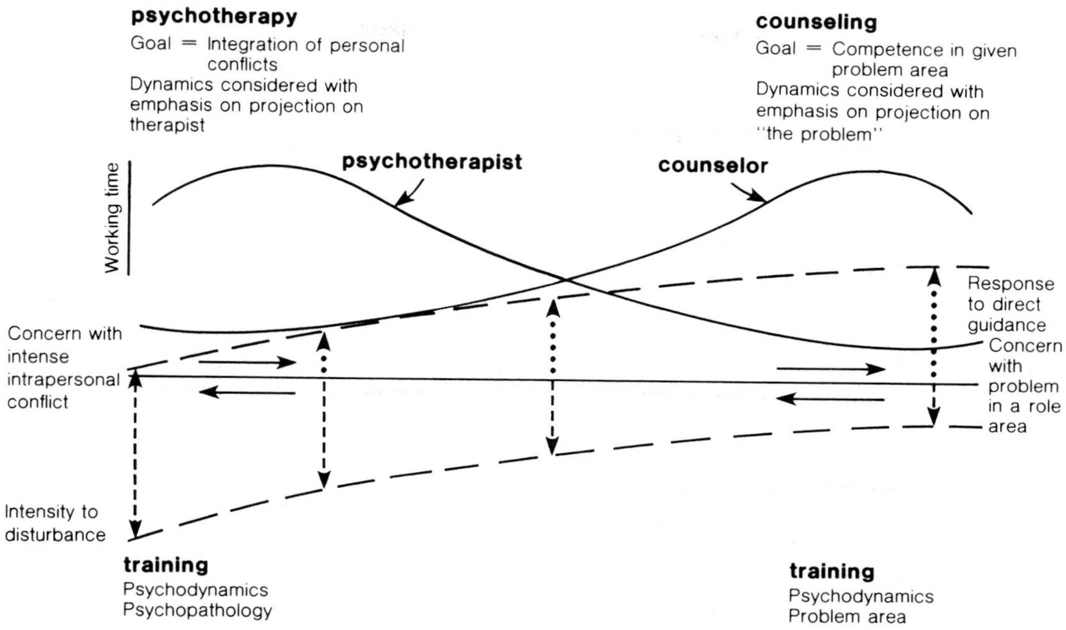

psychotherapy
Goal = Integration of personal
conflicts
Dynamics considered with
emphasis on projection on
therapist

counseling
Goal = Competence in given
problem area
Dynamics considered with
emphasis on projection on
"the problem"

psychotherapist   counselor

Working time

Concern with
intense
intrapersonal
conflict

Response
to direct
guidance
Concern
with
problem
in a role
area

Intensity to
disturbance

training
Psychodynamics
Psychopathology

training
Psychodynamics
Problem area

Note: From "On the Relation of Psychotherapy to Counseling" by W. G. Perry, Jr., Annals, New York Academy of Sciences, 1955, 63, 396–407. Used by permission of New York Academy of Sciences.

is directed toward another set; counseling uses one set of methods, while psychotherapy uses another; counseling emphasizes the rational, environmental forces, while psychotherapy emphasizes the dynamic, inner-dimensions of experience. We get the sense, throughout these different arguments, that the thrust of counseling is upon helping clients deal with their immediate problems and improve their life situations, and that the attitude of the counselor is that of one individual interacting with another, on more or less equal footing. Counseling also emerges as a more comprehensive approach than psychotherapy in that it is not concerned specifically with the client's problems, but rather with the client himself or herself.

Different theories and axioms about people influence the perceptions of the psychotherapist and the counselor. These are to a large extent based on historical factors. The counselor sees the client, existing in the here and

figure 1.2 Two perceptions

the psychotherapist's view of the patient   **the counselor's view of the client**

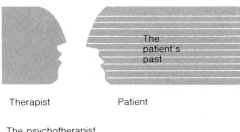

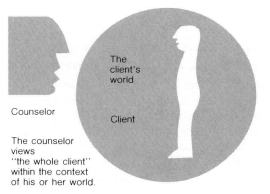

Therapist   Patient   Counselor   Client

The psychotherapist
views the "persona"
of the patient
as the uppermost layer
of his or her past.

The counselor
views
"the whole client"
within the context
of his or her world.

Note: From *Developmental Counseling* by Donald H. Blocher. Copyright © 1966 by The Ronald Press Company, New York. Used by permission.

now, as a responsible, developing individual. This is largely the result of the influences of progressive education, where the early counseling movement flourished, and the Rogerian counseling surge, which helped mark the break between nondirective counseling and psychoanalysis. The psychotherapist, on the other hand, generally views the client as a product of his or her past, whether that past be viewed in terms of conditioning experiences (influence of behaviorism) or psychosexual stages (influence of Freudianism). The counselor, in viewing the client, is more interested in the *total* person, while the psychotherapist is more interested in certain areas of the personality, particularly those areas that are symptomatic of emotional disturbances. This again reflects a counseling's debt to the vocational guidance movement and to testing, and psychotherapy's derivation from the medical disciplines. Admittedly, these distinctions are not valid for all counselors and all psychotherapists, since many straddle a middle ground.

There are also theoretical differences that translate into practice. A theory of psychotherapy generally consists of an underlying theory of personality, a theory of psychopathology, and a body of clinical techniques. Counseling, on the other hand, is built more upon a philosophical foundation, and although it may be structured along the lines of scientific reasoning, *it emphasizes one's innate dignity, one's individuality and uniqueness, one's world that is known through the senses.* Theories that attempt to explain human actions, feelings, and thoughts, therefore, can be divided between theories of counseling and theories of psychotherapy by the way they go about their reasoning.

COUNSELING IN THE SCHOOLS

What we have discussed so far does not fully explain the scope of counseling in the school setting, although it does give us some context in which to understand it. In fact, the school counselor's role is not always clearly defined, and he or she may well be perceived differently by each of the people with whom he or she interacts during the typical workday in the school setting, as we will see in chapter 6. And we should also note that in the school setting there may be some conflict or confusion about what the school as an institution expects and what the counselor sees as the legitimate counseling role.

Zerface and Cox (1971) discuss the difficulty the counselor experiences in trying to break away from the school's point of view. Counselors are either explicitly or implicitly agents of the school, and they are often caught in conflicts between what they believe they should do and what the school demands of them. As the studies cited in chapter 6 demonstrate, there is a sharp discrepancy between the role as the counselor sees it, as it is defined in training, and as the counselor experiences it in the school situation.

Landy (1963) raises the question, Who does what in the guidance program? This is a legitimate question that challenges the coordination of counseling functions and, indirectly, the relationship between the work of the counselor and the work of other school personnel. This must be clarified. Roles should be defined from the beginning in order to prevent subsequent misunderstandings.

An allied issue, which will be discussed in this text, is the question of the counselor's professionalism. As long as the counselor conducts himself or herself as a professional person working in a highly sensitive and very important position, he or she is more likely to be able to effect the changes wished for. In order to be professional, counselors have to be sure of themselves, or their abilities, and they must also be confident in what their jobs entail. Arbuckle (1970) discusses this point:

> A professional individual, of course, in a school as elsewhere does not ask his employer "What do you want me to do?" It is not a case of the individual being fitted to the job, but rather are the particular skills and capacities of the individual such that he can be effective in a certain task. If they are, he

might consider accepting the position, if they are not, he obviously should not accept the position even if it were offered to him. It is difficult for me to believe that any professional school counselor, if asked by a potential employer, "Do you accept the responsibility of utilizing your authority to compel certain students to change their behavior?" would answer any other way than, "No, I do not." On the other hand, it would seem equally logical that a school administrator, if asked the same question, might respond, "Well, I hope we never have to compel a student to do anything, but if his behavior is disruptive, and counter to school policy, then yes, I might have to compel him to change his behavior or leave the institution." (p. 122)

While all counseling efforts must inexorably challenge these difficult predicaments, such challenges are especially important for the practical counselor, whose work stresses fundamental unity of the individual with the school, the school with society, the part with the totality, the theory with the praxis.

The counselor's role definition is a crucial phase of his or her professional activity because it influences profoundly everything that is done. The job of role defining can be made somewhat simpler if the counselor can communicate to associates in the school the multifaceted, integrative approach he or she is willing to use. The counselor need not and should not emphasize either the therapeutic, the informational, the appraisal, the consultative, or the administrative functions, but rather should show the other staff members that he or she is integrating all these functions together to improve the total service program for the student population as well as for the benefit of the professional staff. Such as integration will not only be appreciated by the others, but it—more than anything the counselor can say—will help them understand the practical application of counseling and the essential role of the practical counselor.

The Counseling Team

Much of the work of the school counselor is carried out in conjunction with other members of the counseling team, along with parents, community people, and other interested parties who have the benefit of the student population at heart. Counseling is always an interactive activity, not only between the counselor and the counselee but between the counselor and other concerned people as well. Leviton (1977) found, for example, that in addition to the counselor, other concerned people to whom students go for help when they have problems included relatives, especially parents, friends, and at times, teachers. Most interestingly, as we see in figure 1.3 (from Leviton, 1977), the person sought for help depends much on the type of problem. By and large, parents were most important for resolving career

figure 1.3 Summary of where students go for help with various types of problems

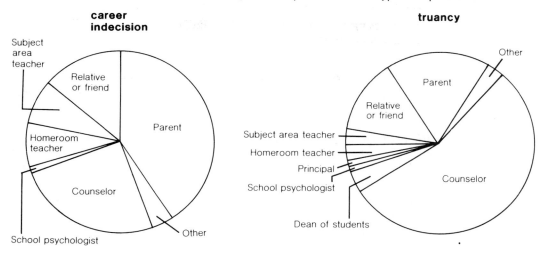

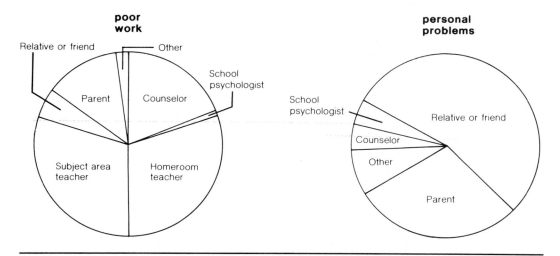

Note: From "Consumer Feedback on a Secondary School Guidance Program" by H. S. Leviton, *Personnel and Guidance Journal,* 1977, *55* (5), p. 243. Used by permission.

indecisions, while the school counselor was important in dealing with truancy problems. Note too that while 54 percent of the students would seek out a relative or friend to discuss a personal problem, only 4 percent would seek out the counselor. Later in this book, when we look at the role of the school counselor, we will see that this disparity is important, but now we should keep in mind that the counselor as a consultant or team member can be much more responsive to a wider range of client problems than could a counselor acting alone. In this section we will look at some approaches to the coordinated counseling function and examine the specific role of the counselor as a consultant.

The counseling team typically consists of the counselor, the teacher, the school psychologist or social worker, the consulting psychiatric specialist, medical and paramedical personnel (physicians, nurses, etc.), community personnel, and other specialists in the mental health and educational professions. We shall examine individually, constructive modes of professional interaction between the counselor and the teacher, between the counselor and the school psychologist, and between the counselor and other members of the team. As we do so, we should keep in mind that the contributions of these other team members are equal to the contributions brought to the team by the counselor. The teacher contributes an intimate knowledge of the client in the classroom setting; the school psychologist brings specialized psychological skills, including diagnostic ability, psychometric information, and the like; other members of the team contribute in their own ways.

The Counselor and the Teacher

Probably the single most important member of the counseling team, in addition to the counselor, is the teacher. Helpern (1964) describes ways in which the counselor can effectively assist teachers in the performance of their duties and in expediting the comprehensive counseling function:

> Since he is concerned with on-going developmental processes and with a continuous study of the individual needs of all children as they progress through group situations, his [the teacher's] work must necessarily take the form of frequent communication and consultation with teachers. Teachers . . . frequently need additional help if they are to assess accurately the needs of children and of themselves. They need further information about child growth and development, about how children learn, about what constitutes normal behavior, about the importance of individual methods of response, about the exploded myths of the past (as the over-emphasis on the I.Q.) and about the new experiments currently being conducted. They need this type of continuing cognitive experience but need above all . . . the opportunity

to talk about how *they* feel about what is happening in the classroom, in the school, about their reactions to the children, about their own anxieties and frustrations in their teaching roles, about their own interpersonal relationships and expectations. . . . Such opportunities for discussion may be offered in one-to-one teacher-counselor relationships or may be extended to discussion groups, to child-study workshops or to in-service training courses. (pp. 17–18)

According to this view, *the counselor functions as a facilitator of the teacher's growth and development as well as in a consultative capacity.* The counselor's two-fold function—facilitator and consultant—illustrates the complexity of the balance that must be maintained so delicately as she or he deals with the teacher, most likely to be seen on a day-to-day basis.

Lundquist and Chamley (1971) also view the counselor as both a counselor and a consultant in his or her relationship with the teacher. They list six counseling functions that define the facilitating aspect of the relationship with the teacher:

1. Help the teacher or teachers to develop an increased awareness of their affective domain and how it relates to their professional identity and fulfillment of their roles as teachers.
2. Help the teacher or teachers to develop an awareness of how their intrapersonal feelings effect [sic] and influence their roles in the educative process with children.
3. Help the teacher or teachers to learn to identify and express the intrapersonal feelings they own.
4. Help the teacher or teachers to develop more positive attitudes about the feelings they possess so that they may function more effectively with students in the total learning environment.
5. Help teachers to learn to relate to other professional people in more effective ways.
6. Help teachers by providing personal and professional support in crisis situations. (p. 364)

Other writers have supported this role of the counselor (Dinkmeyer, 1968; Tyler, 1969; Brown & Srebalus, 1972), and it is generally accepted in the profession that the effective counselor must work with teachers as well as with students at the school. Some writers, such as McClain and Boley (1968), emphasize the "complementary" nature of the counseling and the consultation function.

If we look at the counselor's relationship with the teacher in terms of this dichotomy—counselor and consultant—we can better appreciate how the counselor and the teacher form a constructive team that enhances the potentials of the educative process. The counselor supports the teacher, and the teacher utilizes this support to become more proficient in relationships with the student. Thus, the student-client benefits from the efforts of two people, working together on his or her behalf.

Munson (1970, pp. 121–129) describes this complex relationship in some detail. The consulting relationship, he points out, is one that "builds continually from the first contact." He differentiates between *first-level, second-level,* and *third-level* consulting relationships. The first-level relationship usually deals with external matters that are not personally threatening or emotionally intense to the teacher, matters such as curriculum, dealing with a discipline problem, and the like. The second-level relationship is more intense and dynamic:

> It is at this second-level of consultation that the more creative, innovative practices can be encouraged. Assuming that the consultant is aware of and concerned about his relationship with the consultee, he can begin to intervene in ways which can result in a positive influence on the learning environment. . . . He functions very much as he would in the counseling relationship. He reads feelings, he encourages the expression of feelings, he is aware of attitudes. He is involved with the teacher. He is concerned with her growth. He cares. (p. 124)

The third-level relationship is simply an extension of the second-level. It is a relationship of the same quality and intensity, continued in time. Munson does not suggest, however, that the counselor use this phase of the relationship to commence a psychotherapeutic relationship because this might well entail a number of difficulties. The counseling relationship, however, should continue to progress and develop.

Lauver (1974) has developed what he calls a "systematic approach" for consulting with teachers. This approach consists of seven steps:

Step 1 Identify a problem situation in which a need for change may exist.

Step 2 Identify what constitutes a desirable outcome in operational terms—terms that will allow you to know whether or not the outcome has been achieved.

Step 3 Observe the situation for relevant information about relationships among important people, objects, and actions.

Step 4 Identify encouragers for desirable behavior and discouragers for undesirable behavior.

Step 5 Devise a plan for using encouragers and discouragers to achieve the desired outcomes.

Step 6 Try out the plan.

Step 7 Observe the results and compare what has actually happened with what was desired.

In many cases such a structured approach may prove helpful—especially to the beginning counselor who has not yet found an individual style.

The Counselor and the School Psychologist

Unfortunately, many instances of conflict between the counselor and the school psychologist have prevented these two related specialties from achieving the harmony and concordance they so much need in order to work effectively. Sources of conflict between the counselor and the school psychologist usually are a result of failure to adequately define their roles or the relationships between their respective roles, or failure of communication, which invariably leads to misunderstandings. Where the two are able to work together—as is sometimes the case—the consequences are most advantageous to the students.

A number of writers have scrutinized the coordination between the counseling and school psychology functions (Johnson et al., 1961; Mathewson, 1962; Patterson, 1962; Byrne, 1963; Gray & Noble, 1965). Gray and Noble, who have reviewed the literature, point out that "working together always demands some compromises and some giving up of cherished functions," and they argue that both the school psychologist and the school counselor must recognize this in order to work together effectively. Perhaps the simplest solution to the difficulties that divide the professions is for school counselors and school psychologists to engage in mutual consultation, in which each utilizes the expertise of the other for the benefit of the student. The psychologist may be more adept at testing and statistical interpretation, while the counselor may prove to be a more skillful interviewer. By combining their talents and skills, it is inevitable that the student-client will benefit in the long run.

Consulting with Parents

There are three major reasons for conscientiously consulting with parents. First, the counselor is meeting an ethical obligation to parents, who are, after all, citizens and taxpayers responsible for the counselor's salary. Second, and more important, consultation with parents can and should help them become more responsible family members and able to deal more effectively with whatever difficulties in the home are manifesting themselves in the school setting. Third, and most important, parents becomes active members of the counseling team. By definition, they are working *with* the counselor to improve the life situation *for* the student-client, whom the counselor is directly interested in helping.

Consultation with parents reflects a specialized skill of the counselor's. He or she must understand how to communicate effectively with a parent in a manner and style that is open and straightforward, yet not threatening nor accusatory. At all times, unnecessary nomenclature should be avoided; parents respond best to language that they are readily able to understand. When the counselor begins to flaunt technical vocabulary at the expense of clarity, although it may impress parents, it does little to promote a feeling of trust and rapport between the counselor and parents.

Parents can also serve as resource persons for the counselor. Rothney (1972) discusses this aspect of the counselor-parent interaction:

> Parents can make contributions that no one else can provide to the information needed about a counselee. They can describe patterns of their child's development; reactions to norms and pressures he has met; frustrations and opportunities he has experienced; persons to whom he has showed strong attachment or repulsion; and the models which through imitation and introjection he has adopted. Only parents can provide dependable information about financial matters when expenditure of funds is required to further the counselee's plans. (pp. 90-91)

Approaches to Consultation

Consultation is an art of its own. Simply meeting with a teacher, parents, or a professional colleague is not in itself necessarily consultative. What determines consultation is the approach used by the counselor in meetings with others. Technically, _consultation is meeting of counselor and another person (third party) to discuss a client._ There are a number of guidelines the counselor may find useful in consultative endeavors. These guidelines are admittedly general and would at times have to be modified to meet the special needs of particular situations:

1. In a consultative capacity, the counselor must conduct himself or herself in a fully professional manner, recognizing limitations and strengths, aware of ethical and legal responsibilities, and sensitive to philosophical and theoretical axioms that underlie his or her work and support a commitment.

2. As a consultant, the counselor always recognizes that the primary responsibility to the client dictates the substance and spirit of this third-party intervention.

3. In providing advice or information to others, the counselor must always attempt to present it objectively and unbiasedly: to show the other person, when it is appropriate, that there may be more than one way to look at a situation, that there may be legitimate points of view different from

the one the counselor favors. In short, the person with whom the counselor consults always has a right to know and to choose.

4. Consultation implies cooperation. It is the counselor's obligation, more than anyone else's, to work toward this cooperative spirit. At times this may require compromise; at times, retreat. The counselor must be willing to sacrifice at times the needs of his or her ego to the demands of the situation.

5. Goals of consultation should be mutually established by the consultant and the consultee. Misunderstandings can often be avoided when there is a mutual reason for sharing a consultative session.

6. When the person consulting with the counselor is overly impressed by professionals (as parents often are), the counselor must take extra care to impress upon the consultee that the counselor is not infallible and is as likely to make errors as anyone else.

Models of Counseling Teamwork

Mahoney (1972), using a catchy phrase, makes the point that "action is the product of guidance teamwork." This is quite true, and in this section we will examine some ways in which the counseling team can become effectively coordinated and accomplish those actions that are productive, therapeutic, and in accord with the goals of counseling.

What is a team? *Webster's New World Dictionary of the American Language* defines a team, in the sense that we wish to use it, as "a group of people working together in a coordinated effort."[3] The coordinated efforts in this case are toward the facilitation of learning and the prospect of emotional growth, with the resolution of those barriers that work against these efforts. Since the processes of growth and development in the school situation comprise both educational and psychological components (see chapter 6 for a fuller discussion of this relationship), the counseling team will coordinate the efforts of the learning specialists with the mental health specialists. It is important that the counselor be at the heart of this coordinating effort, that he or she become the primary administrator of the coordinated counseling services. Yet the counselor must scrupulously avoid becoming bogged down in administrative, bureaucratic, and organizational trivia. The counselor is working with the organization—but working for the client. As Tyler (1969) most aptly states it, "To make use of organizations without becoming an 'organization man,' to make use of bureaucracy without becoming a bureaucrat—that is the course a counselor must try to follow."

Fazzaro and Gillespie (1972) describe six different models of guidance program organization. The *traditional bureaucratic model* is the one we are

---

Consultation is an important part of the counselor's role.

all so painfully familiar with. It is an inflexible model, "usually found in those schools that are organized to provide a more traditional program" (p. 155). In the *differentiated role model,* each member of the counseling team has a specific role to perform. "For example, if there are four members on the counseling staff, then one counselor would be responsible for all testing, another for community service liaison, another for job and college placement services, and perhaps another for providing individual counseling for specific students" (p. 155). This is a particularly viable model for the counselor to use in implementing the coordination between counseling and other student personnel functions.

The *laissez-faire model* "is one which allows the student to select the counselor of his choice at the time his services are needed" (p. 156). For this model to be effective, the authors point out, "there must be complete agreement regarding professional matters between various members of the counseling and guidance staff." If we translate this model into a broad counseling application, we would have to assume that the student could adequately discriminate between the different functions of the student personnel team, which is not likely the case. Because this is not the case, the counselor must act as a source of referral when other services are needed.

The *task group model* "is one in which counselors and other specialists are grouped together in order to accomplish a specific objective or task" (p. 156). This is a particularly constructive model when a serious problem requires consultation, cooperation, and coordination between several specialists. The counselor, school psychologist, and school nurse may work together under this model, for example, to deal with drug problems in the school (see chapter 10).

The *objectives model,* which has recently been gaining wide popularity, works by stating specific objectives to be met and the methods by which the team will try to meet these objectives. "The focus of this particular model is on performance" (p. 156). The *performance contracting model* "also stresses the defining of specific objectives, then contracting with a private agency to meet these objectives" (p. 157). What would be more useful to us, however, is the idea of the couselor's contracting with other members of the student personnel team to carry out the objectives that have been defined. For example, having determined that there is a serious problem of teen-age gangs causing chaos in the school environment, the counselor can contract with the psychologist, with teachers, with administrators and supervisors, with parents, and with law enforcement personnel, each to assume a part of the total burden dealing with this problem. In many ways, such performance contracting is similar to the task group model just discussed.

These six different models of organizational counseling should help the counselor better understand some of the possibilities of the team counseling approach. "The staff of guidance programs that have achieved recognition and praise," Shertzer and Stone (1971) point out, "have high morale and work cooperatively. . . . Cooperation among personnel marks the good guidance program." To achieve this facilitative level of cooperation, the counselor must take the initiative of organizing the guidance program in such a way that the skills of a variety of members of the counseling team are utilized.

SUMMARY

It is appropriate at this point to summarize the topics that have been covered in this chapter, and to arrive at some conclusions that can guide us through the remainder of our long journey into the multidimensional field of school counseling. First, we surveyed the diverse influences on counseling, focusing on how counseling evolved, its historical roots, and how it has been in search of a professional identity for many years. Next, we turned to the question of what differentiates guidance and counseling from psychotherapy, or if in fact they are interchangeable terms. Our findings were:

1. There is a difference in common usage and connotative meaning between the three words, as indicated by the dictionary, by speakers of the language, and by practitioners.
2. However, there is much disagreement about what the differences are—especially between counseling and psychotherapy—how they affect practice, and how they can be operationally demonstrated.
3. We also considered the position that counseling differs from psychotherapy by the degree of the problem treated (its severity), and the differences in emphasis in the treatment process. This notion was related to the history of each movement, and we saw that the origins of counseling and psychotherapy revealed a great deal in this respect.

The chapter ended with a detailed look at the contexts of school counseling. It was pointed out that the school counselor is a member of the counseling team—including the teacher, school psychologist, parents, community members, and other interested parties. As a member of the team, the counselor will spend much time in consultation, and we examined some models of counseling teamwork and consultation with parents and others in a professional capacity.

Major Theories of Counseling

In the preceding chapter, we examined the background sources and roots of school counseling, and considered some basic questions that challenge the school counselor today. We began by determining the concerns of the counseling profession, both in theory and in practice, and particularly the contexts and scope of counseling in the school setting. Now, it is time to turn our attention to the specific theories that currently dominate the field of counseling—the well-known "schools" of counseling, or counseling approaches, many of which have important applications in the school setting.

It is more than coincidental that the terms *theories* and *schools* are used interchangeably to describe counseling approaches. Each counseling approach is built on an underlying *theory*—a view of the individual—and each has practitioners—partisans of the theory—that *apply* the theory in clinical, agency, and educational settings and teach it to others; hence, the alternate term *school*. We shall, in this chapter, survey each approach by examining first its origins and then its view of the individual; its underlying theories of personality, of behavior, and of what makes the person what he or she is. The sections in this chapter will explicate the ways in which practitioners of a particular position look at the human condition in general and the way they look at the individual client in particular.

We will consider the role of the counselor in each counseling approach and examine ways in which the client is expected to contribute to the process. We will see that what is expected from the client varies from one approach to another, and that the counselor's job varies directly with the role of the client. We will also see that with some very little is required of the client, other than that he or she come to sessions. But, we also note how other approaches require the client to engage in some risk taking and early commitments to courses of action.

We will also examine the techniques and goals of each approach. Here we penetrate the crux of the counseling process. What specifically does the counselor do (and for what reasons) in order to help the client overcome whatever difficulties he or she came into counseling to work out? Finally, we will briefly evaluate each position and examine its applications in the school counseling setting.

In organizing the many theories of counseling into a workable scheme, I have relied on the paradigm developed by David H. Frey (see especially Frey, 1972; Raming & Frey, 1974), who has done important work in constructing a taxonomy of counseling approaches. I have modified the paradigm somewhat to make it more relevant for the beginning student, eager to see a clear rationale behind the diverse approaches. Specifically, I have divided the approaches into four categories: psychodynamic, humanistic, rational, and behavioral. This division, while debatable on theoretical levels, does clearly emphasize the similarity of goals and techniques under each rubric.

As the counselor considers each of these schools of therapy, he or she should be asking, "What parts of each approach are relevant to *my* needs, aptitudes, and interests? What parts are compatible with *my* personality?" Not every counselor is cut out for the emotional dissection required by the psychodynamic approaches, just as not every counselor can maintain the scientific objectivity necessary for the behavioral approaches. Most counselors fall somewhere in between, and in their practices they are probably more eclectic than they would like to admit. But, as each counselor comes to recognize what he or she can draw from each position, that counselor will be better able to extract from his or her own emotional and intellectual reservoir. This will inevitably serve as the counselor's first step in efforts to establish and perfect individual counseling techniques, held together by his or her own personal "theory" of counseling.

We will begin with the psychodynamic approaches, which are most penetrating of the inner core of the personality, but which have found least acceptance in the school setting. Next, we will move on to the rational approaches, which have in recent years enjoyed wide acceptance in the schools. Finally, we will look at humanistic counseling, still probably the most widely used counseling approach in the schools. The behavioral approaches to counseling will be considered separately in chapter 3 because of the complexity and detail required for adequate coverage.

PSYCHODYNAMIC APPROACHES

As we saw in chapter 1, psychoanalysis played an important part in the evolution of all Western psychotherapies and, indirectly, in the development of the counseling movement in the United States. While both its partisans and its critics are sometimes intemperate in their bold assertions and their blanket denunciations, a dispassionate assessment of psychoanalysis reveals some significant strengths as well as some glaring weaknesses. Many of the weaknesses of the Freudian legacy, interestingly enough, have encouraged new therapy and counseling approaches that began as reactions to classical psychoanalysis. Many of the acknowledged strengths have been incorporated into these new schools, making them derivative forms, often referred to as neo-Freudian or psychodynamic approaches. While the psychodynamic approaches are not at this time widely used in the school setting, the impact they have made on all forms of counseling cannot be minimized. In this section we will survey the psychodynamic approaches and evaluate the application of different psychoanalytic principles to short-term and long-term school counseling.

Background

Psychoanalysis evolved during the 1880s from the research conducted by Sigmund Freud and Josef Breuer in the treatment of hysteria. When Freud returned from Paris where he had been studying hypnosis with Charcot, Dr. Joseph Breuer, a colleague, reported to him a fascinating case that had preoccupied his attention for some time. He had been treating a young woman named Bertha Pappenheim, who had been suffering from a variety of ailments that together were diagnosed as hysteria. Breuer discovered that as Bertha began to remember things that had happened to her in the distant past, often under the influence of a mild trance he induced, her symptoms began to disappear. He began to use hypnosis to help her talk freely, and as she talked, the symptoms lessened.

Using this case as a starting point, Freud and Breuer discovered that the physical symptoms of hysteria could be alleviated as the patient, under hypnosis, recalled and verbalized unpleasant forgotten memories, thereby releasing psychic energy bottled up inside the body. They published the case as "The Case of Anna O," now considered the first case in psychoanalysis. The sudden freeing of the repressed material was called a *catharsis* (purging), and this type of treatment was called a cathartic treatment.

Freud gradually abandoned the use of hypnosis. In its place, he encouraged the patient into a state of mental relaxation in which the patient was able to produce spontaneous verbalization, without regard to proprieties and tact. Through analysis and interpretation, these verbalizations led to the repressed memories. This technique came to be known as the method of *free association*. [*free association*]

The discovery of the free association method marked the beginning of *talking* as a therapeutic strategy. For the first time in history, physical symptoms produced by psychological disorders were being treated medically and scientifically by no other means than the direct use of the patient's

Sigmund Freud, the founder of psychoanalysis

verbalization. The articulation of feelings into language in a controlled, analytical setting was replacing the use of hypnosis, water treatments, exorcisms, and drownings, which characterized the treatment of mental illness in earlier periods. The patient talked and got well—how remarkable this must have seemed to those who heard of it! Despite all of the subsequent rebellions and reactions to psychoanalysis over the years, this simple principle of a "talking cure," as Freud called it, was to remain the guiding principle for most subsequent psychotherapies.

Over the next few years, by studying the free associations of his patients, Freud discovered the significance of childhood sexuality upon the development of personality and the importance of dreams as a way of understanding the sexual feelings that are repressed in the unconscious. Freud referred to dreams as "the royal road to the unconscious," because they revealed the person's deepest wishes in symbolic and disguised form.

Psychoanalysis emerged as a major social force during the 1920s. In addition to its popularity as a form of treatment for emotional disorders, its influence was clearly felt in literature and the arts. By this time, a number of Freud's closest pupils—most notably, Alfred Adler and Carl Gustav Jung—had broken away from the fold and were developing their own derivative theories. Adler emphasized the individual's struggle for power; the fight against feelings of inferiority; his or her style of life; and the relationship to the society in which he or she lives. Rejecting Freud's notion of the primacy of the sexual instinct as a basis for all human motivation, Adler suggested that the person instinctively strives for perfection in the attempt to compensate for feelings of inferiority through his or her striving toward superiority (the terms *inferiority complex* and *superiority complex* are from Adler's writings). Moreover, Adler considered social striving as equivalent in intensity, importance, and pervasiveness to Freud's ubiquitous sexual instincts.

De-emphasizing the Freudian psychosexual stages, Adler (1958) developed in its place a comprehensive scheme of people and their actions, dominated by alternative social and psychological motivations, feelings, intuitions, and strivings. Adler, and his followers, call his approach *individual psychology,* and although it is a derivative of Freudian psychoanalysis, it is not psychoanalytic in the truest sense. Adler was the first of the psychoanalysts to show a direct interest in child guidance. In 1920 he established child guidance clinics in Vienna, where difficult children as well as normal ones were offered counseling, conducted at joint sessions with their teachers and parents.

Another disciple of Freud's who subsequently broke ranks with him to found his own approach—which is called *analytical psychology*—was Carl Gustav Jung. Jung, like Adler, believed that Freud placed too much emphasis on sexuality. While he is in agreement with many of Adler's points, he differs from Adler on many crucial practical and theoretical issues. Although Adler and Jung expressed a similar disinclination to the Freudian method, they took off in different directions, each pursuing the specific area of psychology that he knew best and that to him explained most clearly the complexities of the human psyche (Whitmont & Kaufman, 1973).

Jung contributed a number of specific ideas for which he earned fame. He introduced the concepts of *introversion* and *extraversion*, which are still widely used terms today. He rejected Freud's assumption of a single unconscious, arguing instead that we have two unconsciouses: a *personal unconscious* and a transpersonal or *collective unconscious.* The personal unconscious closely resembles Freud's version, consisting of everything that has been repressed during one's development. The collective unconscious, his unique contribution to the theory of psychoanalysis, consists of *archetypes*—innate predispositions derived from the cumulative experiences of the race. The Adlerian counseling approach is especially helpful in working with elementary school-age children. In chapter 9 we will look at the key concepts of Individual Psychology and examine Adlerian child counseling as a special application of the psychodynamic model.

Karen Horney is another important figure in neo-Freudian psychoanalysis. Horney became disillusioned with the narrowness of some of Freud's ideas. In her writings (1937, 1939, 1950), she stresses the social and environmental factors that influence the personality development of the individual. Her theory of neurosis is a vividly detailed theory of intrapsychic conflicts, with different systems of the psyche "at war" with each other. Cantor (1967) points out that while Freud emphasized the early sexual fixation, Horney spoke of the current conflicts between systems of the psyche. Consequently, her treatment strategies differ in many ways from that of Freud. Horney sees as the primary task of the analyst eliciting constructive forces in the client's life and helping the client mobilize these forces to resolve his or her problems and conflicts. Although early childhood experiences are significant in both systems, they play less of a role in Horneyan therapy than in Freudian.

The Development of Modern Psychoanalysis

During the 1950s and 1960s, a number of practicing psychoanalysts conceded the weaknesses of classical (Freudian) psychoanalysis as a form of treatment. From the 1940s to the present, the thrust of new psychoanalytic developments has been in the treatment of seriously disturbed patients, particularly schizophrenics. Freud disqualified from psychoanalysis a large portion of the population whom he deemed "analytically unfit" because they were isolated from interpersonal relations by what he termed the "stone wall of narcissism." These patients, many of whom have the greatest need for therapy, do not respond to the interpretative method advocated by Freud. Moreover, a large percentage of neurotic patients are not fully treatable because their underlying "narcissism"—a concomitance to most problems in life—would not respond to the traditional psychoanalytic methods.

To overcome these serious deficiencies, Hyman Spotnitz (1963, 1968, 1976), an innovative psychoanalytic psychiatrist, introduced a variety of new psychodynamic treatment techniques that did not require that the patient be emotionally or intellectually capable of understanding interpretations. As Spotnitz's following grew during the late 1960s, his influence began to be felt throughout the country. The Manhattan Center for Advanced Psychoanalytic Studies (MCAPS) was founded in 1973 in New York City by the leading practitioners of modern psychoanalysis, including Benjamin D. Margolis (a founder, along with Theodore Reik, of the prestigious National Psychological Association for Psychoanalysis), Phyllis W. Meadow (the first Dean of MCAPS), and William J. Kirman, a pioneer in the area of emotional education. By 1979, there were affiliated centers for the study of Spotnitz's new approach to psychoanalysis in Boston, Philadelphia, Tampa, and other places throughout the United States.

Under the rubric of *modern psychoanalysis,* Spotnitz and his colleagues have developed treatment techniques for dealing with many problem areas traditionally closed off to psychoanalysis. Moreover, during the past decade, modern psychoanalytic counseling has begun to make an impact in the classroom setting (Kirman, 1977). We shall look at some of the specific applications of modern psychoanalytic counseling later.

Hyman Spotnitz, the originator of the modern psychoanalytic movement

The Psychodynamic View of the Person

Freud viewed people as inherently instinctual creatures, driven by their strivings for infantile gratification. Throughout life, individuals are strongly motivated to seek out satisfaction of their primitive instinctual drives—sex and aggression—often beclouding in the process their perceptual and emotional awareness of self and others. According to the Freudian theory, we distort the reality of the world around us by utilizing defense mechanisms that protect the ego by allowing us to block out and subjectively redefine that which we cannot accept. While this does protect the ego, it alters our world and our relationships in that world significantly, so that what we see, think, and feel consciously is only a fraction of the wide range of possibilities within us.

What makes us different from lower animals is our ability to transform all of our brute lust into such socially productive forces as art, politics, education, medicine, humanitarian projects, and the like. This process, by which man rechannels his instincts into socially constructive actions that benefit humankind, Freud called *sublimation.*

The Psychosexual Stages

The Freudian theory of personality is a deterministic one, which proposes that by the time the child is five years old the basic foundation of his or her personality is already well-established and that experiences of the later years are relatively unimportant in effecting changes on the deeper, dynamic level of the mind. Freud divides the early years of development into five stages, each of which has its own characteristics and problems. Each of the first three stages is named after the part of the body that is most sexually stimulating to the child during that stage—the primary erogenous zone. These are the *oral, anal,* and *phallic stages.*

The oral stage is the first psychosexual stage, extending from birth to about the middle of the second year of life. It is a critical period during which the child's awareness of reality (the *ego*) begins to develop. During this period, the mouth is the primary erogenous zone, thus giving the stage its name. The main source of gratification during this period is incorporation of, or eating—the taking in of nourishment. If, as the child passes through this stage, enough oral gratification is not received, or if there is too much gratification (that is, if the mother is overstimulating), he or she may become fixated at the oral level, maintaining in later years emotional characteristics that are more appropriate to the infant. Because the oral child is completely dependent on the mother for nourishment and security, deprivations may also result in lifelong feelings of inadequacy, overdependency, and worthlessness.

At approximately eighteen months of age, there is a shift of erotic activity from the mouth to the anus, marking the beginning of the anal stage. During this period, children receive erotic pleasures from the act of defecation, and they express their will, their *individuality,* through the retention or expulsion of feces. Society in general, and parents in particular, reinforce the child's interest in anal behavior in many ways. At this age, much attention is focused on toilet training and children learn that they can exert control over parents through the manipulation of this natural bodily function. If the parent is overly strict in toilet training, the child may hold back feces and become constipated. This might show itself later in such adult traits as hoarding, stinginess, excessive neatness, or obstinacy.

The phallic stage follows the anal stage. At about the beginning of the third year, the genital area itself becomes the primary erogenous zone. During this stage, genital masturbation is not uncommon, nor is an intense interest in the genitals of the opposte sex. The stage is notable for the introduction of two controversial concepts—castration anxiety and penis envy, both of which have become the subject of heated debate in recent years.

The Oedipus Complex

The Oedipus complex period derives its name from the famous Greek legend of Oedipus, the king of Thebes, who unwittingly killed his father and married his mother. When he discovered what he had done, he blinded himself in an agony of remorse. Freud suggests that in the Oedipal conflict the child falls in love with the parent of the opposite sex and develops feelings of rivalry and hostility toward the parent of the same sex, who is the "rival parent." The boy wants to possess his mother, although he does not have full-formed ideas of sexuality. He views the father as the prime competitor and wishes to remove him. The girl, likewise, desires her father and wishes to remove the mother.

A healthy resolution of the Oedipal conflict requires the boy to identify with the father and the girl to identify with the mother. Through this identification, the child takes on characteristics of adults of the same sex, and this contributes not only to emotional development, but to social development as well. Irene Josselyn (1948), an interpreter of the classical psychoanalytic position who is noted for her practical applications of Freud's more technical ideas, explains that the resolution of the boy's conflict is "to identify with the father and incorporate the father's goals and standards into his own pattern of behavior" For the girl "to advance toward healthy emotional maturation, she must find gratification and security in the feminine role. To do this she identifies with her mother" (p. 58). In both cases, we see that _identification_ is the key word.

Latency

The successful resolution of the Oedipus complex leads into the latency period: a time when the sexual strivings remain dormant and the child concentrates primarily on socialization. It is during this period that the child enters the elementary school and the important processes of school socialization begin. It is also during this period that the counselor or teacher will have an opportunity to observe directly the strengths and weaknesses of the child's earlier development.

Although the Freudian position is controversial and not directly supported by empirical evidence, many of its insights have proven useful in understanding and dealing with children and adult clients (Anna Freud, 1935). While a totally Freudian perspective may be an exaggeration of the child's complex social and interpersonal reality, there is no doubt that many children's interests, inclinations, fantasies, and pathologies are amenable to a Freudian explanation. Moreover, one of the truly important contributions of this approach is to emphasize the vital, dynamic influence of childhood sexuality, often obscured in the myths and presuppositions of childhood innocence that permeate our cultural outlook. Freud may have been extreme in one direction, but many of his insights have nevertheless served his opponents well by counterbalancing their opposite positions. Later, in chapters 9 and 10, in which we look at counseling applications on the elementary and secondary school levels, we will focus on a more socially oriented psychodynamic personality theory, that of Erik Erikson.

The Unconscious

Freud's view of the person is deeply influenced by his notion of the unconscious. Our personality and our actions, argues Freud, are in a large part determined by the thoughts and feelings contained in the unconscious. These thoughts and feelings are not directly accessible to consciousness, cannot be readily recalled, and are consequently outside the individual's field of awareness, observation, and self-reflection. In *The Psychopathology of Everyday Life* (1901/1961), he demonstrates how the repressed content of the unconscious inadvertently slips through in our words and deeds, resulting in what is commonly called the Freudian slip. The belief that most activities are governed by the unconscious indicates that the individual may have a limited responsibility for his actions. It is not so much that Freud views man as the victim of circumstances but rather as the victim of one's own past.

Psychopathology

According to Freud, each person is fixated to varying degrees at different stages of development, and the result of these fixations determines to a large part his or her adult conduct and abilities to react in situations. A person who is stingy and stubborn is not that way by choice nor because he or she has evaluated all of the options, but rather because during the anal stage of development, certain difficulties arose that were never adequately resolved. An overly timid woman who has difficulties dealing with people around her, according to Freud, might be suffering from repressed Oedipal fixations of which she is unaware. The implications of this type of reasoning are clear: *we are enslaved to our past to the degree that our past repeats itself in our present situations.*

Role of the Psychoanalytic Counselor

Clients who are receiving treatment from a psychoanalytic counselor are expected to bring all their thoughts and feelings into the counseling session and to verbalize them through the use of free association. It is expected that clients, no matter how eager they are for treatment, will resist the analysis because of their unconscious fears. This resistance can take many forms, including missing appointments, refusing to speak, telling jokes, falling asleep, and so on. The purpose of resistances is to avoid anxiety by protecting the ego from feelings that it cannot accept.

Most important of the resistances therapeutically is *transference.* Transference can be defined as transferring onto the person of the counselor feelings that were once attached to emotionally significant figures early in life. Originally, Freud considered transference an obstacle to treatment; but eventually he realized that it was the phenomenon of transference that made the treatment and the cure possible. As the client transfers feelings onto the counselor, he or she is able to re-experience emotionally the early life conflicts from which the present difficulties arise. Through this transference neurosis, as it is called, the counselor is able to learn directly of the client's childhood.

Consider, for example, the case of a man who has developed a transference relationship with his counselor. He begins to experience the counselor as being rejecting and ungratifying in the same way he unconsciously experienced his parents many years earlier. If he communicates these transference feelings to the counselor, as he should, and if the counselor is perceptive enough to see them, as he or she hopefully is, the counselor will then have an understanding of the client's early childhood that could not be provided by the client himself since he is not consciously aware of these feelings. Clients often reveal, in fact, many of their unconscious wishes, fears, distortions, and conflicts through the transference relationship. Whenever the counselor feels that he or she is being perceived as some other person, it is reasonably certain that transference is at work.

The Modern Psychoanalytic Counselor

In discussing the role of the psychoanalytic counselor, a clear discrepancy exists between the classical conception of the Freudian analyst and the more expansive ideas of modern psychoanalytic counseling. Typically — or stereotypically, as the case may be — the psychoanalyst is viewed as extremely passive and detached, offering little of himself and repeatedly responding with his famous "Um hum." This image is not entirely accurate, however. True, the classical psychoanalyst, as defined in Freud's writings, is one who maintains an attitude of objective neutrality, of "evenly suspended attention" (Freud, 1912/1958), who refrains from responding positively or negatively to any of the client's expressions, and studies with detachment the meaning of the client's associations, communications, and dreams. But even during Freud's own time, this passive image of the analyst began to change. Sandor Ferenczi (Eng. trans., 1950), one of Freud's most influential colleagues, proposed what he called "active psychotherapy," in which the analyst became a responsive contributing member of the treatment team. Other innovators, such as Otto Rank, began to expand the original doctrine to make it more relevant for a wider client population. The work of such innovators served as a theoretical beginning for a future generation of psychoanalysts who recognized the therapeutic significance of the analyst's active participation in the treatment.

Hyman Spotnitz, leading the modern psychoanalytic movement, made important inroads into the active psychodynamic approach. Arguing that the analyst relies on his or her own *countertransference* feelings to formulate appropriate therapeutic responses, Spotnitz and the other modern analysts have extended the scope of psychodynamic therapy beyond the analytic setting, and well into the purview of counseling. While the theory is somewhat beyond the scope of this book, we can summarize its contributions in four basic principles, which at the same time will show its relevance for school counseling: a relevance that has often been neglected in discussing psychoanalysis:

1. Each person comes to the counseling setting with unmet maturational needs: deep emotional needs that arose at a specific period of life and that were not adequately met then. As a result, the client does not know how to go about satisfying these needs now.
2. Resistances to solving one's problems can be divided into two categories: Oedipal and pre-verbal. The former are rooted in the Oedipal period of development, while the latter, more difficult, more stubborn resistances, are from the period of life before we learned to speak.
3. The psychodynamic counselor relies on his or her objective countertransference feelings to understand the feelings that the client is unconsciously communicating. "The objective countertransference refers to those feelings that the counselor experiences toward the client which are a function of the client's ego. These *induced feelings* were felt toward the client by other significant people in his past. . . . or, they may reflect feelings the client has for himself" (Kirman, 1977, p. 75).
4. The main job of the counselor is to help the client learn how to meet his or her maturational needs. This does not necessarily involve the classical technique of interpretation. Dr. Spotnitz (1976) describes the role of the analyst as a "maturational agent, helping people . . . resolve whatever obstacles to personality maturation they have experienced" (p. 16).

While modern psychoanalytic techniques were originally developed to be used with severely disturbed patients, recent efforts to apply these principles to neurotics and to clients showing behavioral problems indicate a significant trend in the psychoanalytic profession: a trend that may have great implications for the counseling profession in future years.

In any case, the most important therapeutic task of the modern analytic counselor is still to help the client resolve resistances that disrupt treatment and prevent him or her from living maturely. In classical psychoanalysis, this is accomplished by interpreting his or her unconscious to the client. Modern psychoanalysis, however, differs from the classical approach by concentrating on those deeply imbedded resistances that do not respond to interpretation. The modern analytic counselor uses reflective and mirroring techniques in addition to interpretation, in order to *help the client resolve resistances*—to enable the client to experience them emotionally—instead of explaining them to him or her.

Whenever an analytic counselor works with a client over a period of time, it is inevitable that the counselor will develop some feelings about the client. These are called *countertransference feelings.* According to the modern analysts, whether or not these feelings are positive or negative is not as important as whether they are realistic, objective responses to the way the patient is feeling about the analyst. When the counselor's feelings are objective, they are productive in the treatment. When, on the other hand, they are subjective—neurotic distortions by the analyst—they are counterproductive to the goals of the treatment. Thus, if the client is inducing positive feelings in the counselor and the counselor in turn feels positive toward the client, this is said to be an objective countertransference. If the client is expressing a great deal of invisible hostility, and the counselor begins to pick up these negative feelings from the client, this is also objective countertransference. In both cases, the counselor's feelings, as long as they are *objective* responses to the client's feelings, serve as an indicator of what the client is feeling unconsciously. Thus, the countertransference serves the same purpose to the counselor as the X-ray machine serves to the physician: to reveal those parts of the client that are hidden from view.

Theodore Reik (1948), a disciple of Freud's, describes the concept of "listening with the third ear." The counselor does this by associating with the client, experiencing his or her own relevant feelings as the client talks. The counselor, naturally, is not daydreaming while the client is speaking, but rather is allowing the client's words to stimulate feelings and ideas that are relevant to the communications that the client is offering. This is a further use of countertransference, whereby the counselor relies on his or her own feelings to understand and empathize with the feelings of the client.

We can best clarify the role of the psychoanalytic counselor by stating five cardinal rules that would probably be acceptable to most psychoanalytic practitioners, regardless of their specific orientation. These rules are:

1. Never offer personal information about yourself, unless there is a specific and compelling therapeutic reason for doing so.
2. Analyze resistances as they appear. Do not try to quash or minimize a resistance; confront it head-on, interpreting or reflecting as may be necessary.
3. Learn about the patient not only by listening to what she or he is saying, but by examining your own feelings about the patient, which are responses to the patient's communication.

4. Give priority to freeing the unconscious over making the patient feel comfortable. Avoid interjections and interpretations which are solely designed to reduce anxiety, and emphasize those communications that are compatible with the long-range goals of the treatment.

5. Consider all comments, requests, and other communications from the client within the total context of the treatment, rather than as isolated instances. This not only helps the counselor understand the implications of specific material in the client's mind but helps unify and structure the treatment in a progressively curative manner.

Applications of Psychoanalysis to School Counseling

Psychoanalysis has often been minimized as a technique applicable to the school counseling setting. Its critics argue that it places too much emphasis on the unconscious and that as a counseling approach it requires too much time and an impractical frequency of sessions; that it does not deal directly with the behavior; that it brings to the surface more repressed material than is necessary; and that it only works for certain kinds of clients. While many of these criticisms are justified and essentially valid, the modern psychoanalytic approach does in fact have much to offer the school counselor and is fully adaptable to the counseling perspective.

Kirman, in his seminal paper, "Modern Psychoanalytic Counseling," addresses himself to this point. "The modern psychoanalytic point of view," he argues (1976, pp. 84,89), "sees counseling as a specialized application of modern psychoanalytic psychotherapy. . . . School and vocational problems are seen as occurring in the context of a total and integrated personality." He goes on to expand this idea, offering numerous specific applications of school problems that can be adequately dealt with by the modern psychoanalytic approach. This would lead us to conclude that while classical psychoanalysis may not be fully appropriate for the school setting, the modern analytic approach has hardly begun to be exploited.

RATIONAL APPROACHES TO SCHOOL COUNSELING

Three indigenous American schools of therapy that have made considerable impact in school counseling are rational-emotive therapy (RET), reality therapy, and transactional analysis. Although there are substantial differences among these three approaches, they all rely on the client's mobilization of logical faculties to overcome his or her emotional difficulties. Since the three of them, with their emphasis on the cognitive dimensions of emotional conflicts, integrate a variety of dynamic and behavioral constructs into counseling practice, we call them "rational approaches."

Rational-Emotive Counseling

The person associated with rational-emotive therapy is Dr. Albert Ellis, its founder and leading spokesperson. Ellis was originally trained in the traditional classic psychoanalytic method, which he practiced for a number of years during the late 1940s and early 1950s, but became disillusioned with the confines of the psychoanalytic approach when he realized that "no matter how much insight [the] clients gained, nor how well they seemed to understand the events of their early childhood and to be able to connect them with their present emotional disturbances, they rarely lost their presenting symptoms . . . and when they did, they still retained tendencies to create new troubling symptoms" (Ellis, 1973b, p. 168). Exploring this problem, he discovered that the source of his clients' emotional difficulties and psychological misperceptions were not simply a result of what had happened in the past, but were also a reflection of an active, ongoing process in their lives.

In working out his theoretical position, Ellis undertook a number of experimental strategies with his patients. He discovered, in his own words,

> that people are not exclusively the products of social learning (as the theories of the psychoanalysts and the behavior psychologist emphasize) but that their so-called pathological symptoms are the result of *bio*social learning. That is to say, *because they are human* . . . they tend to have several strong, irrational, empirically unvalidatible [sic] ideas; and as long as they hold on to these ideas . . . they will tend to be what we commonly call "neurotic," "disturbed," or "mentally ill." (1973b, p. 169)

During the middle 1950s, Ellis began to abandon the psychoanalytic approach and concentrate his enormous energies on his newly discovered rational-emotive psychotherapy. In 1959 he organized the Institute for Rational Living, a non-profit scientific and educational organization in New York City. Nine years later, a state-chartered training institute, The Institute for Advanced Study in Rational Psychotherapy, was founded to train rational-emotive therapists. During the following decade, thousands of RET therapists were trained for work in the clinical, agency, and school settings.

Ellis is a prolific writer and has written many important books and articles outlining, explicating, or defending his position. His most important works

Albert Ellis, the father of rational-emotive therapy

are *Reason and Emotion in Psychotherapy* (1962), *The Art and Science of Love* (1969a), *Growth Through Reason* (1971), *A Guide to Rational Living*, coauthored with Robert A. Harper (1961), and *Rational-Emotive Therapy: A Handbook of Theory and Practice* (with R. Grieger, 1977). A journal, *Rational Living,* is published to bring up to date the research in this field.

View of The Person

The rational-emotive view of personality is dominated by the principle that emotion and reason—thinking and feeling—are intricately and inextricably entwined in the psyche. As a person thinks about things, she or he distorts and generalizes according to preconceptions and misguided ideas: "Humans, in other words, are highly suggestible, impressionable, vulnerable, and gullible" (Ellis, 1958, p. 34). This strong statement, in effect, becomes the RET theoretical basis for the connection between the individual's feelings and ideas.

In the process of growing up, he suggests, children are taught to think and feel certain things about themselves and others. Those things that are associated with the idea, This is good! argues Ellis (1958), become positive human emotions, such as love or joy, while those associated with the idea, This is bad! become negative emotions, with painful, angry, or depressive feelings. Neurotic behavior, he goes on to point out, is illogical and irrational, associating, This is bad! with things that really are not. He offers as an example the etiology of a phobia, in which an individual experienced an early life disturbance upon discovering that he had strong death wishes against his father. Because he thought such wishes were bad, he felt that he should be blamed and punished for having these feelings. As a result of this incongruity, he developed a neurotic phobia against dogs (because dogs reminded him unconsciously of his father, who loved to hunt). "Later on," Ellis (1958) continues,

> this individual may grow to love or be indifferent to his father, or his father may die and be no more of a problem to him. His fear of dogs, however, may remain: not because, as some theorists would insist, they still remind him of his old death wishes against his father, but because now he hates himself so violently for *having* the original neurotic symptom—for behaving, in his mind, so stupidly and illogically in relation to dogs—that every time he thinks of dogs his self-hatred and fear of failure so severely upset him that he cannot reason clearly and cannot combat his illogical fear. (p. 39)

The rational-emotive view of the person emphasizes that we are born with the potential to be rational and logical, but become illogical and influenced inordinately by "crooked thinking" because of distortions during childhood and the contemporary repetitions of these distortions. "The central theme of RET," Ellis (1962) explains, "is that man is a uniquely rational as well as uniquely irrational animal; that his emotional or psychological disturbances are largely a result of his thinking illogically or irrationally; and that he can rid himself of most of his mental or emotional unhappiness, ineffectuality, and disturbance if he learns to maximize his rational and minimize his irrational thinking" (p. 36).

The RET Counselor

In rational-emotive counseling the client is responsible for engaging in an ongoing *dialogue* with the therapist: a dialogue that is dynamic, reactive, introspective, and at times, painful and provocative. Clients in rational-emotive counseling function much as a learner does in the educational setting, and their ability to improve is contingent upon their motivation and cooperation in the learner's role. They must be willing, specifically, to recognize and deal with those feelings or beliefs that they once considered logical and natural and that now they are discovering are illogical and unhealthy. The rational-emotive counselor is unequivocally directive, and intentionally attempts to "lead" the client to a "healthier" perspective.

The counselor, according to Ellis (1962), devotes his or her efforts toward distinguishing what is seen as the difference between understanding and a deeper level of involvement on his or her part. "That the therapist should normally understand his patient's world and *see* the patient's behavior from

his patient's *own* frame of reference," he points out, "is highly desirable."
But, Ellis goes on to point out,

> That the therapist should literally *feel* his patient's disturbances or *believe* in his irrationalities is, in my opinion, usually harmful rather than helpful to the patient. Indeed, it is precisely the therapist's ability to comprehend the patient's immature behavior *without* getting involved in or believing in it that enables him to induce the patient to stop believing in or feeling that this behavior is necessary. (p. 115)

Thus, the RET counselor does not indiscriminately accept any and all feelings; he or she deals with them as paralogical systems.

Ellis sees no reason why counselors should not be able to inject their own values into the counseling encounter when such experience dictates that this course is advisable. After all, he argues, the counselor's values are presumably healthy values, and there is no logical reason why the client should not be exposed to healthy values—or at least values that are healthier than his or her own. Like Glasser, whose ideas we will examine later in the chapter, Ellis believes that the counselor's values are a legitimate therapeutic tool.

Techniques and Goals

Rational-emotive counseling consists largely of what we might call "teaching techniques," but teaching techniques that synthesize the cognitive and emotional facets of the clients's existence. The content of the RET experience, Ellis and Harper (1961) point out,

> largely consists of *teaching* the patient effective self-analysis: How, specifically, to observe his own feelings and actions, how to evaluate them objectively instead of moralistically and grandiosely, and how to change them, by consistent effort and practice, so that he may achieve the things he most wants to do in this brief span of human existence while, simultaneously, not interfering seriously with the preferences of others. Self-analysis, in this sense of the term, is not merely an important but actually a requisite aspect of successful psychotherapy. (p. 101)

We see, then, that the ultimate goal of rational-emotive teaching is that the clients become capable of introspectively analyzing and correcting their distortions of the world.

Ellis (1973b) divides the counseling process into three basic modes, each comprising a set of techniques: *cognitive, emotive,* and *behavioristic.* "Cognitive therapy," he explains, "teaches [the client] how to find his *should, oughts,* and *must;* how to separate his rational . . . from his irrational beliefs" (p. 182). This is the level of rational-emotive counseling that is most indicative of its emphasis on the importance of logic and reason in human thought. The second level, which focuses on the emotive aspects of thinking and behavior, integrates this cognitive emphasis with aspects of the more dynamic approaches. "Emotive-evocative therapy," Ellis goes on to explain,

> employs various means of dramatizing truths and falsehoods so that he [the patient] can clearly distinguish between the two. . . . The therapist may employ *role-playing,* to bring forth to the client exactly what his false ideas are and how they affect his relations with others; *modeling,* to show the client how to develop different values; *humor,* to reduce some of the client's disturbance—creating ideas to absurdity; *unconditional acceptance* of the client, to demonstrate to him that he is acceptable, even with his unfortunate present traits; . . . *exhortation,* to persuade him to give up some of his crazy thinking and replace it with more efficient notions. (p. 183)

This is the level of RET counseling that is most overtly dramatic and that is generally associated with the showy side of the rational-emotive approach. It is important for the counselor to remember, however, that this is only one phase of the process—not the entire course of counseling, as some lay people and a number of critics would lead us to believe.

Behavior therapy methods are employed "to help the client change his dysfunctional symptoms and to become habituated to more effective ways of performing, and to help him radically change his *cognitions* about himself, about others, and about the world" (Ellis, 1973b, p. 183). These behavioristic methods may include giving clients homework assignments, encouraging them to take risks, or having them intentionally fail at some effort in order to learn to cope with the feelings of failure.

The RET counselor uses what Ellis calls the *A-B-C theory of personality* as the underlying basis and rationale for his or her technique. "A" stands for the activating event; "B" is the belief system; and "C" stands for the emotional and behavioral consequences. It is the job of the therapist, Ellis (1971) argues, to show the client the A-B-Cs of his or her disturbances: "RET . . . shows the individual that whenever he upsets himself at point C (the emotional consequence), it is not . . . because of what is happening to him at point A (the activating event). Rather it is because of his own irrational and unvalidating suppositions at point B (his belief system). More precisely, when a person feels depressed at point C, it is not because he has been rejected by someone or has lost a job at point A, but because he is convincing himself, at point B, of both a rational and an irrational hypothesis" (p. 6).

We see from these remarks that the rational-emotive approach comprises a variety of different types of techniques, all clustered around the central goal—to correct the client's illogical beliefs and irrational feelings. The goals of the counseling are therefore specifiable in terms of the ideas and thoughts that are to be corrected.

Evaluation and Application of RET

In recent years, the rational-emotive counseling approach has come to enjoy a wide acceptance in many different settings, including the schools. While its critics have not been shy to speak their minds and vent their objections, Ellis has consistently rejoined attacks with a hearty spirit and a veritable cornucopia of empirical evidence (i.e., Ellis, 1975a, 1976a, 1977). He has maintained firmly in his writings that the effects of RET are pervasive and deep enough in the client's life to make long-lasting and significant changes (Ellis, 1975a). The wide application of RET, promulgated by Ellis and others, attests to this.

RET has been widely adopted in the school setting, for example. Ellis (1969b) has fully discussed the application of rational-emotive techniques for teaching emotional education in the classroom. Lafferty, Dennerll, and Rettick (1964) have applied rational-emotive techniques to a school mental health program. They offer an example of how Ellis's approach was used to study human behavior in the classroom. Hauck (1967) has even suggested that RET is useful not only as a model for teachers but as a model for parents looking for the best way to raise their children.

Studies evaluating the efficacy of RET, while mixed, have been generally positive. Di Giuseppe, Miller, and Trexler (1977), in a comprehensive review of these studies, conclude cautiously:

1. The studies of RET efficacy are "increasing [in] quantity and improving in quality."
2. "Rational-emotive therapy appears to have earned some scientific credibility as a relatively effective form of treatment."
3. A large research project recently found that RET ranked second in efficacy among the ten types of therapy examined. It was led only by systematic desensitization.
4. "While the results, as we see them now, appear generally positive and promising, they remain far from conclusive." They acknowledge that some of the earlier objections to RET efficacy studies are still valid. (p. 70)

This exhaustive and impartial review sums up aptly the current state of research on the efficacy of RET.

Reality Therapy

Reality therapy, which was originally developed and made famous as an approach for working with institutionalized delinquent girls, has enjoyed much attention in the school setting during the past two decades. It is now considered one of the staples of counseling approaches, with advocates and practitioners at every end of the spectrum.

Background

Reality therapy is largely the product of a single man, Dr. William Glasser. Glasser was trained in the psychoanalytic approach, with which he became discouraged late in his training. He objected primarily to the concepts of neurosis and mental illness, arguing instead that the patient is weak, not ill, and that if his or her abilities were strengthened, he or she would be a more fit member of society.

Through experimentation, Glasser found that in treating clients it was not necessary to explore their past histories in any detail. What counted most was what was happening at the present time, not what had transpired in the past. Second, he also rejected the Freudian notion of transference, arguing that the patient perceived the therapist as another human being, a real person, and not as some imagined figure of the past. Thirdly, he rejected the very important Freudian idea that to be mentally healthy one had to have insight into one's unconscious mind.

In 1962 Glasser joined the staff of the institute for wayward adolescent girls at Ventura, California. Three years later he published *Reality Therapy: A New Approach to Psychiatry,* which outlined the details of his therapy and offered rich examples of its use at the Ventura school. In 1969 he published *Schools Without Failure,* which applied the principles of reality therapy to the school setting. He has lectured widely in recent years on the application of reality principles to educational psychology and school counseling.

View of the Person

The reality counselor, like the behaviorist, views the individual largely in terms of his or her behavior. But rather than examining behavior in terms of the stimulus-response model, as the behaviorist does, or looking at the individual's behavior phenomenologically as the client-centered counselor does, the reality therapist considers behavior against an objective standard of measurement, which he or she calls "reality." This reality may be a practical reality or a moral reality. In either case, the reality couselor sees the individual as functioning in consonance or dissonance with that reality.

"When a man acts in such a way that he gives and receives love, and feels worthwhile to himself and others, his behavior is right and moral,"

William Glasser, the founder of reality therapy

argues Glasser (1965, p. 57). Throughout his thinking, the criterion of "right" plays an important role in determining the appropriateness of behavior. He uses such terms as *satisfactory, improved, good,* and *moral* to describe behavior, and his view of mental health is directly related to how well one's behavior meets these standards of measurement. The reality counselor's view of the person is continually shadowed by the normative points of these higher goals.

Glasser sees as the main motivation in people's behavior their attempts to fulfill their needs. He suggests that there are two basic psychological needs: the *need to love and be loved* and the *need for "achievement of self-worth,* the feeling that you are worthwhile as a person both to yourself and to others" (1971). In a later paper (Glasser & Zunin, 1973), he reduces this to one basic need that synthesizes these two: *the need for personal identity.* When individuals are frustrated in satisfying this need, they may lose touch with the objective reality and lose their ability to perceive things as they are. "In their unsuccessful effort to fulfill their needs," Glasser (1965) argues, "no matter what behavior they choose, all patients have a common characteristic: they all deny the reality of the world around them."

It is in our strivings to satisfy these basic needs, argues Glasser, that the patterns of our behavior are determined. A person's sense of responsibility for himself or herself helps to change and modify behavior, to arrive ultimately at more acceptable and satisfactory standards that, in turn, enable her or him to gratify needs more successfully.

Thus, the reality counselor attaches direct values to behavior, measuring a person's success or failure in counseling against these values enumerated and determining how well they have been met. Responsibility serves as a foundation concept; a value in itself, against which all other values are measured. It is not so much that the individual is taught to be responsible, but rather that responsibility becomes the means utilized for the therapeutic end.

The view of the individual, then, can be summarized as follows: the healthy person is a responsible being in the process of satisfying basic life needs (to love and be loved; to feel worthwhile), which together give the individual a sense of experiential unity, of personal identity, of purpose in life.

The Reality Couselor

The primary job of the client in reality counseling is to learn to make appropriate choices, to develop a sense of responsibility, to be able to interact constructively with others, and to understand and accept the reality of his or her existence. Although this appears on the surface to be identical to the role of the existential client, it differs in two important aspects: the reality client, unlike the existential client, is not in the process of creating his or her own existence and own destiny through choices; but rather, the client is conforming to the counselor's notions of reality; secondly, the reality client's sense of responsibility is defined as "the ability to fulfill one's needs, and to do so in a way that does not deprive others of the ability to fulfill their needs" (Glasser, 1965, p. 13).

The basic technique of reality counseling is a teaching technique; specifically, to teach the client the meaning of reality and to show him or her how to act responsibly within the context of that reality. Prior to this teaching, the counselor must first gain the necessary involvement with the client, for "unless the requisite involvement exists between the responsible therapist and the irresponsible patient, there can be no therapy" (Glasser, 1965, p. 21). After the reality therapy counselor gains the necessary involvement, he or she begins to point out to the patient the unrealistic aspects of his or her irresponsible behavior. "If the patient wishes to argue that his concept of reality is correct," Glasser points out, "we must be willing to discuss his opinions, but we must not fail to emphasize that our main interest is his behavior rather than his attitude."

Evaluation of Reality Counseling

Since the publication of Glasser's first book in 1965, reality therapy has gained many adherents in the counseling ranks and has had an especially powerful impact on the practice of school counseling. A spate of research projects (summarized by Bassin, Bratter & Rachin, 1976) have shown the tangible value of reality counseling in a number of diverse settings. Glasser's own works have emphasized its value in the school setting, and dozens of papers appear annually about effective reality counseling efforts on the elementary and secondary levels.

Transactional Analysis

Transactional analysis (TA) has the distinction of being the only counseling approach that has had its two seminal books on the national best-seller list for longer than a year. These two landmark works, Eric Berne's *Games People Play* and Thomas A. Harris's *I'm OK — You're OK* are but two of the several books on TA that have achieved wide public recognition and popularity, bringing to millions the basic ideas of TA, and in the process, making TA one of the most popular therapeutic modalities. As of this writing, there are half a dozen institutes of transactional analysis, a professional organization devoted solely to its study and propogation, and over two hundred book titles relating directly or indirectly to it. While TA has achieved professional recognition as an important modality of individual counseling, by far its greatest impact has been in the areas of group counseling, in organizational psychology, and in the educational and school counseling settings.

Background

The individual primarily responsible for developing transactional analysis was Eric Berne, a medical doctor by training. Berne, like Glasser and Ellis, began in the Freudian tradition. And like them, recognizing many of the limitations of the classical method in which he was trained, Berne sought a more "rational" approach, less dependent on the unconscious. Many of his ideas evolved from his experiences in conducting group therapy during the war and afterwards. Berne's ideas were explained in his early professional publications, such as his first technical paper on TA, "Ego States in Psychotherapy," published in 1957, several years before his approach would achieve public recognition. His important books include *Transactional Analysis in Psychotherapy* (1961) and *The Structure and Dynamics of Organizations and Groups* (1963) and his most popular works *Games People Play* (1964) and *What Do You Say After You Say Hello?* (1972).

Eric Berne died in 1970 in Carmel, California, where he was practicing transactional psychiatry.

Eric Berne, best-selling author known for the development of transactional analysis

The TA View of the Person

In exploring the foundations concepts of TA, we should look at it first as a way of understanding the person and, second, as a way of helping people overcome their problems. These two viewpoints converge in the underlying theory.

Central to TA are the concepts of *transaction* and *ego states.* A transaction is the most basic unit of social interaction. A transaction occurs whenever one person acts as a stimulus for another, and the other responds to the first. What makes TA unique in its analysis of human transactions is that people are not viewed as uniform bodies. Rather, each person is viewed in terms of his or her *ego states,* "which are coherent systems of thought and feeling manifested by corresponding patterns of behavior" (Berne, 1972, p. 11). As we analyze transactions, then, we are actually diagramming the communications between two person's ego states.

Each of us has three ego states, which together, constitute our personality. These states are designated Parent (P), Adult (A), and Child (C).

The Parent is "a huge collection of recordings in the brain of unquestioned or imposed external events perceived by a person in his early years" (Harris, 1973, p. 40). The Parent ego state is filled with values, injunctions, shoulds and oughts, goods and bads. "In this state," Berne (1972) suggests, the individual "feels, thinks, acts, talks and responds just as one of his parents did when he was little. This ego state is active, for example, in raising one's children. Even when we are not actually exhibiting this ego state in our transactions, it influences our behavior as the 'Parental influence,' performing the functions of a conscience" (pp. 11-12). The Parent is roughly equivalent to Freud's "superego."

The Adult state is the most rational, reality-oriented ego state. It is "principally concerned with transforming stimuli into pieces of information, and processing and filing that information on the basis of previous experience" (Berne, 1972, p. 93). Unlike the Parent, the Adult reacts to the situation as it is actually experienced, rather than to the way it was programmed in the past. Berne uses the metaphor of the Adult state as a computer, processing information without introducing distortion or neurotic bias. This state is roughly equivalent to Freud's concept of a fully developed or mature ego.

The Child state is conceptualized as the little boy or girl within us, "who feels, thinks, acts, talks, and responds just the way he or she did when he or she was a child of a certain age." Berne (1972) goes on to make an important distinction:

> The Child is not regarded as "childish" or "immature," which are Parental words, but as childlike, meaning like a child of a certain age, and the important factor here is the age, which may be anywhere between two and five years in ordinary circumstances. It is important for the individual to understand his Child, not only because it is going to be with him all his life, but also because it is the most valuable part of his personality. (p. 12)

This concept of ego states, which helps explain how transactional analysts view personality, plays an integral part in the therapy process, and in the development of therapy goals.

The Four Life Positions

Analyzing our relationships with others is a central part of transactional analysis. When do we function well with others and when do we function poorly? Unlike Freudian theory, which relies on its psychopathology (built on its underlying personality theory) to help explain the strength and weaknesses of interpersonal relationships, the contribution of TA is most dramatically represented in its concept of the *four life positions,* which replace an explicit psychopathology. They are designated (Harris, 1973):

I'M NOT OK—YOU'RE OK

I'M NOT OK—YOU'RE NOT OK

I'M OK—YOU'RE NOT OK

I'M OK—YOU'RE OK

These "positions" are shorthand ways of describing the way we feel in our relations with others. They describe four types of human transactions, and at the same time they show developmentally how such transaction evolved. They can also be represented schematically:

$$(-,+)$$
$$(-,-)$$
$$(+,-)$$
$$(+,+)$$

The bottom position, "I'm OK—You're OK" $(+,+)$, is the healthy one—the goal of therapy. All of them, however, help us analyze how we interact (and did interact!) with the people that are (and were) most important to us.

These positions are developmental. They are associated with growth. The infant's earliest response to the world is "I'm not OK—You're OK," $(-,+)$. This means that the infant feels inadequate, incompetent, or in Adlerian terms, inferior. But it also means that the infant recognizes the world outside as more competent, as superior, as able to provide an emotional nurturance, which transactional analysts call *stroking,* even if it is not fully satisfying. As Harris (1973) describes this infantile view of the world,

> In the first position the person feels at the mercy of others. He feels a great need for stroking, or recognition, which is the psychological version of the early physical stroking. In this position there is hope because there is a source of stroking—YOU'RE OK—even if the stroking is not constant. The Adult [in this position] has something to work on: What must I do to gain their strokes, or their approval? (p. 68)

As the infant attempts to become more autonomous, he or she may evolve into the second position, "I'M NOT OK—YOU'RE NOT OK" $(-,-)$. The cause of this is the increasing lack of and independence from stroking by the parents. This is a most difficult life position, one characterized by feelings of hopelessness. Were the person to remain in this position, as unfortunately many do, life would be almost impossible. "A person in this position gives up. There is no hope" (Harris, 1973, p. 70). Unfortunately where no opportunities for growth and warmth exist, the child may become stuck in the third position.

The next position is also pathological. "A child who is brutalized long enough by the parents he intially felt were OK will switch positions to the third, or criminal, position: I'M OK—YOU'RE NOT OK." This type of person suffered from not receiving enough stroking early in life; from not developing the trusting relationships with loved ones that is so necessary to feel OK about oneself. As a result, the child develops a feeling of distrust for all those around him, and survives only by acceding to this position, which in effect saves him or her. Harris explains,

> For this child the I'M OK—YOU'RE NOT OK position is a life-saving decision. The tragedy, for himself and for society, is that he goes through life refusing to look inward. He is unable to be objective about his own complicity in what happens to him. It is always "their fault." It's "all them." . . . The ultimate expression of this position is homicide, *felt* by the killer to be justifiable (in the same way that he felt justified in taking the position in the first place). (p. 73)

Finally, we come to the position of hopefulness, of health: "I'M OK—YOU'RE OK" $(+,+)$. This differs from the other three positions in an important way. While the first three positions are all unconscious, arising at an early period of life as a result of the child-parent interactions, this position is conscious, rational, verbal. "The first three positions," Harris (1973) maintains, "are based on feelings. The fourth is based on thought, faith, and the wager of action" (p. 74).

This fourth position is expressed behaviorally through our ability to have successful interpersonal relationships, to feel good about ourselves, to feel we deserve the best, and to be capable of getting the best for ourselves. It is roughly equivalent to Freud's ideal of full psychosexual development and sublimation. In the following section, we will look more closely at how this life position can be developed through the TA therapy process.

The TA Counseling Process

"The basic interest of transactional analysis," Eric Berne (1972) suggests, "is the study of ego states" (p. 11). Most of the theory and techniques of TA counseling revolve around this process, which is called *structural analysis*. The methods of TA were developed in order to facilitate the analysis of ego states. The process is diagrammatic and presumably precise.

The process of analysis is simple. For convenience, a diagrammatic representation is used in figure 2.1 to illustrate the three ego states.

Transactions between two people may be complementary or crossed. They are complementary when the lines representing the transaction are parallel, as shown in figure 2.2.

figure 2.1 The ego states: Parent (P), Adult (A), and Child (C)

Note: From Belkin, Gary S., *An Introduction to Counseling.* © 1980 Wm. C. Brown Company Publishers, Dubuque, Iowa. Reprinted by permission.

figure 2.2 Complementary transactions are represented by parallel lines. The top line represents the stimulus communication and the bottom line the response. For example, in (*a*), Parent to Parent, a husband tells his wife he will take her out to her favorite restaurant for dinner and she responds that he treats her very well—he is a good husband. In (*b*), Adult to Adult, Jack asks Jerry who won the ball game, and Jerry answers that the Pirates won, 3 to 1. In (*c*), Child to Child, Paula tells Joy she wants to cut school and Joy says, "That's a great idea. Let's hang out at the park today."

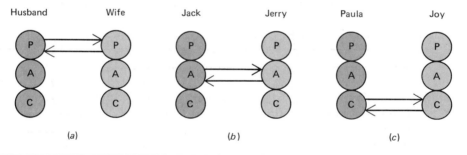

Note: From Belkin, Gary S., *An Introduction to Counseling.* © 1980 Wm. C. Brown Company Publishers, Dubuque, Iowa. Reprinted by permission.

This type of interaction indicates that a person is responding on the level from which he or she is being addressed. But a transaction may also be crossed; that is, the person responds on a level other than that on which he

figure 2.3 A crossed transaction occurs when the stimulus communication and the response are not parallel. Here we see a crossed transaction between Bob and Gene.

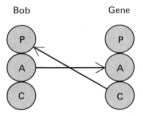

Note: From Belkin, Gary S., *An Introduction to Counseling.* © 1980 Wm. C. Brown Company Publishers, Dubuque, Iowa. Reprinted by permission.

figure 2.4 In this crossed transaction, Sue's Parent addresses Lydia's Child, and Lydia's Adult then responds to Sue's Adult.

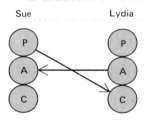

Note: From Belkin, Gary S., *An Introduction to Counseling.* © 1980 Wm. C. Brown Company Publishers, Dubuque, Iowa. Reprinted by permission.

or she is addressed. If Bob's Adult addresses Gene's Adult ("I'll be happy to loan you this book when I'm done with it"), and Gene responds through his Child ("Oh sure, you always have to read everything first so you're up one on me."), it would look like the illustration in figure 2.3. On the other hand, if Sue's Parent addresses Lydia's Child ("You always think you can get away with things, but just wait . . . everyone gets what they deserve in the end."), and Lydia's Adult response in turn to Sue's Adult ("My observation is that people don't always get what they deserve."), it would look like the illustration in figure 2.4.

The TA counseling process begins by examining all the transactions and determining what level they are on. Are they complementary or crossed? Does the person have a particular pattern that permeates his or her interactions with others? From this, a great deal of information can be attained and used to help the client reach more mature functioning; i.e., more Adult-Adult interactions.

Strokes, Games, and Scripts

Three important TA concepts in understanding the counseling interaction are *strokes, games,* and *scripts.*

On its most superficial level, a stroke is a unit of recognition, such as saying hello to someone. But more significantly, on its deeper level, stroking is the process through which a parent cares for an infant. Stroking is a sign of concern, of caring for another.

Throughout our lives, we are stroked by others through their recognition and treatment of us. If we are not sufficiently stroked, we suffer from one of the NOT-OK positions discussed above.

The concept of games helps us better understand stroking. As the structural analysis is being conducted, the transactional analyst tries to figure out what kind of games the patient is playing. The concept of game is of prime importance: it reveals how people are communicating and what they are trying to get out of their relationships. Goldhaber and Goldhaber (1976) explain the transactional concept of games this way:

> A game is a complementary, ulterior transaction leading to a payoff. The complementary transaction enables the game and its communication to continue until completion. The ulterior transaction enables the game players to hide their real meanings. And the payoff enables the players to justify their reasons for playing. (pp. 137–138)

In short, then, a game is a way of cooperatively interacting on a superficial level, for the purpose of concealing the real meaning of the interaction on a deeper level.

If the game is a way of understanding the short-term interaction, a more long-ranging analysis is done through explicating the script, or *life script.* "A script," according to Berne (1972), "is an ongoing program, developed in early childhood under parental influence, which directs the individual's behavior in the most important aspects of his life" (p. 418). Scripts contain many cultural and familial elements—as if each script were written by many coauthors, each putting in his or her individual say. For instance, a script may contain many cultural characteristics ("Democracy is good, so I am to be a democratic person in my dealings with others.") which combine with personal characteristics, learned from the parents ("I am a good boy").

People play out their scripts through the many different games they play. There is always a central theme to the person's script, and this theme reveals the nexus of a person's life choices and problems. The transactional analyst then addresses himself or herself to these problems, trying to help the patient rewrite the script, making it better for his or her life.

Goals

If we look for the specific goals of transactional analysis as a counseling approach, we find them expressed through the concepts we have just described.

First, the transactional analyst analyzes the structural interactions. Diagrams may be made of how the person is relating to the other through the P-A-C paradigm.

Second, these structural analyses are interpreted in terms of the client's unique life script. This may include such things as the need for stroking. Games are pointed out as they are played, and their implication in the person's life script is explored. Transactional analysts have given commonly played games their own names, (such as "RAPO"), to quickly identify a series of transactions.

Finally, the client, through his or her script analysis, is taught how to function on the mature adult level. This involves making the client more aware of how he or she is functioning, followed by cognitive-affective restructuring through the changing of certain essential elements in the script.

We see then as we look at TA in these conceptual terms that it is clearly a cognitive-dynamic counseling approach in that it holds to the axiom that a certain level of rational functioning (expressed by the interaction AA-AA) is the epitome of psychological health, and the goal of the therapy.

Evaluation of TA

TA offers several advantages as a counseling application in the school setting. It is conducive to short-term interactions; works effectively for many school-related problems; can easily be adapted to group counseling; and helps the client quickly get a new type of understanding of his or her personality. Most important, from a practical point of view, is the fact that even counselors who do not view themselves primarily as practitioners of transactional analysis can integrate many aspects of it into their practices. Mellecker (1976) points out that TA offers all counselors, regardless of orientation, "rewarding techniques for graphing characterizations of [their] counselees which can serve as baselines for charting progress as it occurs" (p. 197).

HUMANISTIC COUNSELING

Humanistic counseling has its roots in Europe and in the United States, mainly as a reaction to the determinism of psychoanalysis and to the alleged mechanistic impersonality of the behavioral psychologies. Its major proponents in the United States are Carl Rogers, Eugene Gendlin, Rollo May, Eric Fromm, Victor Frankl, Frederick Perls, Abraham Maslow, and Gordon Allport. In Europe, existentialists such as Ludwig Binswanger and Medard Boss translated the philosophy of existentialism into a practical psychology. There are substantial differences in origin and purpose between the European existential movement and the American self-actualization psychologies; but each acknowledges the influence of the other, and they are generally compatible. As we examine the origins of humanistic counseling we will see how so many of its fundamental concepts are reactions to the theories and practices of psychoanalysis and behavior modification therapy.

The major spokesmen for the humanistic, or *"third force,"* positions are Carl Rogers, Abraham Maslow, and Gordon Allport. Since we will cover Rogers in depth in the following section, we will focus our discussion now on the ideas of Maslow and Allport.

Maslow begins with the assumption that psychology should start by studying the normal, healthy personality rather than the "pathological," unadapted personality. "If one is preoccupied with the insane, the neurotic, the psychopath, the criminal, the delinquent, the feebleminded," Maslow (1954) argues, "one's hopes for the human species become perforce more and more modest, more and more 'realistic,' more and more scaled down: one expects less and less from people." To break away from the traditional constraints of the first two forces (psychoanalysis and behavioral psychology), he abandoned in part the scientific facade of detachment and total objectivity, and used in its place a subjective, personal perspective. As Goble (1970) points out,

> Maslow was convinced that we can learn a great deal more about human nature through consideration of the subjective as well as objective. . . . Maslow felt that a comprehensive theory of behavior must include the internal or intrinsic determinants of behavior as well as extrinsic or external and environmental determinants. Freud had concentrated on the first, the Behaviorists on the second. Both points of view needed to be combined. An objective study of human behavior was not enough; for complete understanding the subjective must be considered as well. We must consider people's feelings, desires, hopes, aspirations in order to understand behavior. (p. 16)

This attitude (and methodology) which characterizes all the attempts at formulating a humanistic psychology becomes the basic assumption of the humanists' position. In some respects it parallels an approach that developed in Europe as a reaction to Freudianism, which we now call existential psychology.

The Existential Position

Existential psychology and *existential counseling* derive from the philosophy of existentialism, which was originated by Sören Kierkegaard, a nineteenth-century Danish theologian and philosopher. Although Kierkegaard did not call his philosophy *existentialism* (the word was applied to his work some years after his death), he did lay down the basic framework upon which all later existentialist thinking was built; namely, that each person carves his or her own destiny and that one's *essence,* one's inner being, is the product of one's actions. Kierkegaard, however, shaped his philosophy in the context of theology. It was not until seventy years after his death that existentialism took hold as a distinct philosophical movement, with the publication of major works by Martin Heidegger and Jean Paul Sartre, the German and French existential leaders.

The merging of existentialism, psychotherapy, and counseling was inevitable. Throughout its history, counseling has always been deeply influenced by the social, cultural, and intellectual trends of the time. All that was required was for practitioners to translate the principles of existential philosophy to psychotherapy and counseling.

Victor Frankl (1967), an Austrian born psychiatrist, developed *logotherapy,* a specialized form of existential analysis. Frankl, who was incarcerated in a German concentration camp for several years, studied the psychology of people under severe stress and hardship, concluding that many of the insights about these extreme cases could be applied to neurotic and psychotic patients he later encountered in his practice. Specifically, in addition to an analysis of being, Frankl was concerned with an analysis of meaning in the patient's life. Unlike the Freudian contention of the organism's will to pleasure or the Adlerian contention of the will to power, Frankl sees the will to meaning as the underlying essence of man's authentic existence.

Rollo May, probably the most famous existentialist in the United States, may be the single person most responsible for the popularity of humanistic-existential counseling today. May articulated some of the more practical applications of existential thought. In his writings, he emphasizes each person's individuality and the need for counselors to separate themselves from preconceived diagnostic categories in attempting to understand and help their clients.

Existential View of the Person

The convenient catch phrase that expresses the basic tenet underlying all the philosophies and theologies found under the rubric of existentialism is *existence precedes essence.* In its most simple form, this means that what a person does with his or her life—the way one lives it—determines what and who one is. We are not born to be anything in particular, argues the existentialist, but we become what we are through our actions and our commitments to those actions. We make choices between alternatives, exercising our free will and judgment, and then accept complete responsibility for the choices we have made. In this way, we govern our own lives, shape our destinies, and develop our "essential" nature.

Heidegger introduced the concept of *authenticity,* in which a person, seriously engaged in projects that are meaningful to his or her life, exhibits deep concern for the projects, commitment to the goals, and responsibility for the results. This notion pretty well sums up the feelings of all existentialists regarding the importance of meaningful activities in one's life. We cannot simply live our lives as if they were parts in a play, prearranged and inevitable; but rather, we must actively participate in making our lives something special—that which we desire. Paul Tillich, the existential theologian, calls this vigor of character "the courage to be."

The existential concept that influences all aspects of existential counseling is the notion of *choice and commitment,* which function as a single action. The individual—as a free agent—is constantly choosing between possibilities of action. We alone are responsible for our choices and for the consequences of these choices. Since whatever choices we make help determine our existence, and hence *who* we are, choosing is an essential part of being. The validity of our choices is not determined by how successful the choices are in executing the ends (as they would be in pragmatism), but in how willing we are to accept the consequences of the choices as our own being— as a part of ourselves.

The existentialist's view of the person can be summed up in five basic tenets that underlie the philosophy:

1. Existence precedes essence: what we do determines who we are.
2. We are free to choose and are responsible for the consequences of our choices—our existence.
3. Our life is always lived with a *view-toward-death.* Our authenticity derives from our ability to be aware of this, and to courageously confront our existence.
4. Our existence is never completely separate from the existence of others and the world, and the existence of the world is never completely separate from our existence.

5. Perception is more valid when we try to understand another person from his or her subjective point of view. ✗

The Existential Counselor

The existential counselor has three basic tasks in the counseling relationship: to help clients discover valid meanings in their existence; to help them develop the freedom to govern their own destiny; to help them deal more effectively in their encounters with others. In many ways, the function of the existential counselor is to provide the right attitude that will enable the client to accomplish these things. Dreyfus (1971) states it most explicitly:

> Existential counseling . . . is not a system of techniques but an underlying attitude toward counseling. . . . The method employed by the existentially oriented counselor is . . . concerned with the immediate, existing world of the client at the moment. He is concerned with the raw data offered by the client. Hence the approach is ahistorical in the sense that the counselor does not attempt to actively delve into the client's past. The past is important only insofar as the client introduces it into the present. . . . The point of departure during the counseling hour is the conflict which brought the client to the counselor, not that which led up to the conflict. (p. 416)

The existential counselor can only be successful to the extent that he or she is able to understand the client in terms of the client's philosophy. In practice, this means examining many of the client's feelings as philosophical ideas.

Kemp (1971) points out that in existential counseling, *"technique follows understanding. . . .* the existential counselor's primary goal is to understand the counselee as a person, a being, and as a being-in-the-world. This does not mean that he has low respect for technique, but rather the technique takes its legitimate place in a new perspective" (p. 18).

When techniques are employed, however, existential counselors differ markedly in the kinds they use. Many of them, trained in the classical Freudian approach, rely heavily on free association and interpretation, while others whose background is in the client-centered approach deal more with active verbal interactions with the client. In either case, it is likely that the existential counselor—more perhaps than any other type of counselor—will rely most on whatever techniques are most compatible with his or her personality. For in existential counseling, the "being" of the counselor is always a dynamic force in the counseling interaction, with the consequence that far greater emphasis is placed on the meaningfulness of the relationship than on the particular application of techniques.

It would be wrong, however, to give the impression that existentialists have some type of aversion to techniques. Frankl, for example, discusses an important technique that he calls *paradoxical intention.* The counselor uses paradoxical intention when he tells the client to wish for something, attempt to do something, or think intensely about something, that something representing the client's worst fears. He gives the example of a phobic male client who had a fear of sweating and was encouraged by the therapist to show people whom he met how much he was able to sweat. "A week later he returned to report that whenever he met anyone who triggered his anxiety, he said to himself, 'I only sweated a liter before, but now I'm going to pour out at least ten liters!'. . . After suffering from this phobia for four years, he was quickly able, after only one session, to free himself of it for good by this new procedure" (Frankl, 1967, p. 146). It is not immediately clear, however, if this type of dynamic technique is a basis for Frankl's existential approach, or incidental to it.

Goals

The goal of existential counseling, if we may speak of a singular goal, is to help the client find and develop meanings in life. This is generally accomplished in two stages. First, the client must be shown his or her condition as a *free agent,* capable of choosing both that which is right for him or her and that which is not. Some clients believe that they can only make choices that repeat the early choices that their parents taught them. After clients realize the myriad possibilities they are capable of exploring, they must begin to understand how the consequences of these different choices have profound ramifications in their existence.

Client-Centered Counseling

Client-centered counseling was conceived and nurtured from the work of a single man, Carl R. Rogers, and consequently it is sometimes referred to as Rogerian counseling, or therapy. Rogers too became dissatisfied with the psychoanalytic approach to therapy. His early thinking, particularly, is a pronounced reaction to the Freudian position. First, he objected to the use of the word *patient* because of its connotations of debility. In its place, he substituted the word *client* to convey "one who comes actively and voluntarily to gain help on a problem, but without any notion of surrendering his own responsibility for the situation" (Rogers, 1951, p. 79). Next, he reacted against the directiveness of Freudian therapy. Recognizing that the initiative for change in therapy must come from the client, Rogers began to conceptualize his client-centered point of view, referring to it at the time as *nondirective counseling.* Finally, where Rogers totally parted company with the

Carl Rogers, the founder of client-centered therapy

psychoanalytic approach was at the point where he rejected the principle of the unconscious, attempting in its place what we now call a *phenomenological* view of the client: that is, accepting the client's feelings and world view as they are presented, rather than looking for hidden meanings underneath. This important step enabled Rogers to take a new, uncolored view of the client and, consequently, to evolve his new form of treatment.

Rogers has been a prolific author. He published his first book, *The Clinical Treatment of the Problem Child,* in 1939, but most of his early theoretical concepts, along with a verbatim transcript, were first presented in *Counseling and Psychotherapy,* published in 1942. In 1951, having revised some of his views—the revisions based in part on his experience at the counseling center of the University of Chicago where he practiced from 1945 to 1957— he published *Client-Centered Therapy.* In this book, Rogers outlines a comprehensive statement of his theory, including the change of the name of his therapy from nondirective to client-centered.

During the 1950s, Rogers and his colleagues doggedly pursued their research, attempting in a number of ways to isolate those factors that contributed most substantially to therapeutic efficacy. Several important studies and position papers (Rogers & Dymond, 1954; Rogers, 1957a, 1957b, 1959a, 1959b, 1967) emerged from this research. Rogers then began to explore the possibilities of client-centered counseling as an approach in dealing with psychotic patients, with mixed results. These were published in 1967 under the title, *The Therapeutic Relationship and Its Impact.*

In his recent book (Rogers, 1970), on encounter groups and on marriage, he translates a number of the client-centered principles into practical, helpful concepts for living. While client-centered therapy seems to have lost some of its influence in recent years (to the newer therapies, such as transactional analysis and Gestalt Therapy), it is still one of the most popular forms of therapy in the counseling profession and has gained wide acceptance in group work.

View of The Person

The client-centered counselor perceives the individual as essentially good in nature, inherently capable of fulfilling his or her destiny and living life in a peaceful, productive, and creative way. The forces that interact to impede this type of natural growth are not intrinsic to an individual's personality; but rather they represent an amalgam of interacting social and psychological forces that work against the realization of his or her potentialities. In the Rogerian philosophy, people are seen as having the capacity to deal with their own conflicts, but are limited in doing so insofar as they lack knowledge about themselves.

Rogers developed his view of the person within the context of the counseling situation. One of Rogers's clearest and most direct statements on the subject is found in his response to those writers who have discussed his "view of man":

> My views of man's most basic characteristics . . . include certain observations as to what man is not, as well as some description, of who he is. . . .
>
> I do *not* discover man to be well characterized in his basic nature by such terms as fundamentally hostile, antisocial, destructive, evil.
>
> I do *not* discover man to be in his basic nature, completely without a nature, a *tabula rasa* on which anything may be written, nor malleable putty which can be shaped into any form.
>
> I do *not* discover man to be an essentially perfect being, sadly warped and corrupted by society.
>
> In my experience I have discovered man to have characteristics which seem inherent in his species, and the terms which have at different times seemed to me descriptive of these characteristics are such terms as positive, forward-moving, constructive, realistic, trustworthy. (Rogers, 1957b, p. 199)

We might also add that Rogers's philosophy has an "existential flavor— man choosing himself, man the architect of himself" (1965, p. 4). We see from these comments that Rogers's view is an integral part of his counseling ideology.

The Client

The client is expected to learn to deal with conflicts, to order and direct the forces of his or her life, to come to grips with problems, and to "overbalance the regressive and self-destructive forces" (Rogers, 1951, p. 122) that are the source of his or her difficulties. Most succinctly stated, the client's job is to cure himself or herself through constructive relationship with the counselor, from whom he or she is able to gain support, encouragement, and understanding.

What clients are actually engaged in as they undergo counseling is a process of self-exploration, which leads to the eventual understanding of and coming to grips with one's essential freedom. Clients' task within the counseling context is to explore their feelings and behavior, to discover, with a sense of wonder, new aspects of themselves, and to blend these new aspects into the image of self that holds together the range of their perceptions.

The client may not, however, be immediately capable of this difficult task. Because of previous experiences with a counselor or therapist, or because of erroneous preconceptions about counseling, the client may regard the counseling experience as "one where he will be labeled, looked upon as abnormal, hurt, treated with little respect, [or] look upon the counselor as an extension of the authority which has referred him for help" (Rogers, 1951, p. 66). He or she may feel threatened by the counseling setting, self-conscious, ashamed. In such a case, it is the counselor's job to communicate to the client the nonjudgmental, warm, and accepting reality of the situation. This type of communication will help clients begin to help themselves.

The Client-Centered Counselor

The primary job of the client-centered counselor is to develop a facilitative relationship with the client. This is accomplished not by formal techniques and procedures, but rather by the counselor's total attitude toward the client and toward the counseling interaction.

The client-centered counselor must enter the subjective personal world of the client and experience along with the client his or her manifold feelings and perceptions. As Rogers describes it, the counselor's task is to assume "the internal frame of reference of the client, to perceive the world as the client sees it, to perceive the client himself as he is seen by himself, to lay aside all perceptions from the external frame of reference while doing so, and to communicate something of the empathic understanding to the client" (Rogers, 1951, p. 29). By doing so, the counselor helps the client overcome his or her frightening and negative feelings about the counseling situation, engenders a feeling of trust and rapport with the client, and helps the client begin to reorganize and restructure his or her own subjective world wherever it is *incongruent* (defined as the discrepancy between the individual's experience and his or her distorted perception of the experience).

Rogers emphasizes above all else the need for open communication, for *dialogue,* as the prerequisite for all counseling (and, for all interpersonal relationships). He calls his concern with communication the "one overriding theme in my professional life. . . . From my very earliest years it has, for some reason, been a passionate concern of mine. I have been pained when I have seen others communicating past one another" (Rogers, 1974, p. 121). Rogers suggests that the counselor establishes communication not so much through what he or she does, but rather through what he or she is. It is the personal qualities of counselors that make them effective or ineffective.

Three of the most important qualities that Rogers considers essential for the client-centered counselor are *genuineness, empathy,* and *unconditional positive regard.* This trinity of traits has become the signature of the Rogerian counselor, and the bulk of Rogers's research during the 1950s and 1960s has been designed to operationally define and evaluate these conditions and to test their validity as counseling variables. The significance attached to these qualities is based on the principle that,

> constructive personality growth and change comes about only when the client perceives and experiences a certain psychological climate in the relationship. The conditions which constitute this climate do not consist of knowledge, intellectual training, orientation in some school of thought, or techniques. They are feelings or attitudes which must be experienced by the counselor and perceived by the client. (Rogers, 1962, p. 422)

Genuineness simply means that the counselor be himself or herself in the relationship, avoid presenting a facade or acting with contrivance because he or she is the therapist. The counselor must be able to accept all of his or her own feelings, even those that may be inappropriate to the relationship. "Genuineness," Rogers (1957a) says,

> means that within the relationship he [the counselor] is freely and deeply himself, with his actual experience accurately represented by his awareness of himself. It is the opposite of presenting a facade, either knowingly or unknowingly. . . . It should be clear that this includes being himself even in ways which are not regarded as ideal for psychotherapy. His experience may be "I am afraid of this client" or "My attention is so focused on my own problems that I can scarcely listen to him." If the therapist is not denying these feelings to awareness, but is able freely to be them (as well as being his other feelings), then the condition (of genuineness) is met. (p. 97)

Empathy, a condition that has probably been investigated more thoroughly than any other condition, constitutes the central focus of the counselor's perception of the client. Rogers's (1962) description of empathy demonstrates its importance dramatically:

> The second essential condition in the relationship . . . is that the counselor is experiencing an accurate empathic understanding of his client's private world, and is able to communicate some of the significant fragments of that understanding. To sense the client's inner world of private, personal meanings as if it were your own, but without ever losing the "as if" quality. . . . To sense his confusion or his timidity or his anger or his feeling of being treated unfairly as if it were your own . . . this is the condition I am endeavoring to describe. (p. 419)

"Over the years," Rogers (1975) points out in a recent paper, reaffirming the importance of empathy, ". . . the research evidence keeps piling up, and it points strongly to the conclusion that a high degree of empathy in a relationship is possibly the *most* potent and certainly one of the most potent factors in bringing about change and learning" (p. 3).

Unconditional positive regard occurs when the counselor accepts the client and all of his or her experiences, without judgment, without evaluation, and without any conditions. This has been criticized as a condition of client-centered counseling, inasmuch as it is nearly impossible to accept another person so totally. But as Rogers explains, this is the optimum level of acceptance to be strived for.

In short, we can say that the client-centered counselor acts as an *empathic ear and an invisible guiding hand.* Through listening, they empathize along with their client's feelings and experiences. Their communications to the client act as a catalyst for growth and are not intended to impose changes upon the clients' lives. They help their clients guide themselves to better understanding by their nondirective and unobtrusive attitudes. Counselors are there, as Rogers says, primarily to motivate and support their clients in their personal quests for answers to their difficulties.

Goals of Client-Centered Counseling

The main goal of client-centered counseling is *congruence,* the concordance between the client's perceptions of experiences and the reality of those experiences. In one respect, congruence is the ability to accept reality. This requires a critical reorientation of the sense of self in interaction with the environment. Clients must come to understand themselves and care about themselves differently from the way they did when they began the counseling.

Rogers (1959a) describes specifically some of the changes he expects successful counseling to produce:

> The person comes to see himself differently.
> He accepts himself and his feelings more fully.
> He becomes more self-confident and more self-directing.
> He becomes more the person he would like to be.
> He becomes more flexible, less rigid, in his perceptions.
> He adopts more realistic goals for himself.
> He behaves in a more mature fashion.
> He changes his maladjustive behaviors, even such a long established one as chronic alcoholism.
> He becomes more acceptant of others.
> He becomes more open to the evidence, both to what is going on outside of himself, and to what is going on inside himself.
> He changes in his basic personality characteristics in constructive ways. (p. 232)

We see from this description the relationship between the Rogerian philosophy of counseling and the desired goals. Rogers's criteria for successful counseling reflect his deep concern for the self-actualization processes of the individual client and this highlights his general idea of what a healthy life should be like.

Gestalt Counseling

Gestalt counseling derives from the school of the same name in the psychology of perception, which originated in Europe in the years prior to the first world war. The Gestalt movement instituted a new kind of analysis: one which began with the perceptual field as a whole, differentiating it into figure and background, and then examining the relative properties of each of these and their interrelationship to each other. The word gestalt, which is roughly equivalent to the English word pattern, expresses the basic meaning of the movement, namely, that all perceptions are dependent upon a number of distinct stimuli that are organized by consciousness into a perceptual whole, a total pattern.

Unfortunately, Gestalt psychology remained essentially an academic theory of perception, limited in its ability to account for the activity of the human organism as a whole. "The academic Gestalt psychologist," Wallen (1957) points out, "never attempted to employ the various principles of gestalt formation . . . to organic perceptions, to the perceptions of one's own feelings, emotions, and bodily sensations" (p. 8). It is in this area that *Gestalt Counselling* Frederick (Fritz) Perls made his contributions that subsequently blossomed into the birth of Gestalt therapy and Gestalt counseling.

Fritz Perls, whose dynamic personality helped make
Gestalt therapy one of the most popular therapy
approaches

Perls received his medical degree from Friedrich Wilhelm University in Berlin in 1921 and continued his training in psychoanalysis at the Psychoanalytic Institute of Berlin, Frankfort, and Vienna. Forced to flee Germany in 1933, he settled in Amsterdam where he worked in private practice until the specter of Nazism drove him to South Africa in 1935. In 1947 he published *Ego, Hunger, and Aggression,* the first statement of his principles of Gestalt psychology applied to personality development. In 1946, he moved to the United States and set up a private practice. Between 1964 and 1969, he conducted training workshops in Gestalt therapy in the Esalen Institute in California. His publications include *Gestalt Therapy: Excitement and Growth in the Human Personality* (1951, with Ralph Hefferline & Paul Goodman) and *Gestalt Therapy Verbatim* (1969).

Perls developed a systematic therapeutic approach that utilizes the large body of literature in Gestalt psychology, in psychoanalysis, in experimental psychology, and the practical insights and experiences of a working therapist.

Gestalt View of the Person

The Gestalt counselor considers the individual's perceptions (and this means perceptions of oneself, one's feelings, one's relationships, etc.) in terms of the *figure-ground* dichotomy. Gestalt counselors believe that a healthy personality exists when a person's experiences form a meaningful whole, when there is a smooth transition between those sets of experiences that are immediately in the focus of awareness (what they call the *figure*) and those that are in the background (which they call the *ground*). "The basic premise of Gestalt psychology," Perls (1973) writes, "is that human nature is organized into patterns or wholes, that it is experienced by the individual in these terms, and that it can only be understood as a function of the patterns of wholes of which it is made." Proper functioning is dependent upon one's abilities to continually shift the figure-ground relationship.

The key word in understanding the Gestalt conception of psychological health and proper functioning is *growth.* Harman (1974) points out that "from the Gestalt therapy point of view, growth occurs when a person is willing to make contact with people, objects, and situations in the environment" (p. 363). Supporting this position, Carmer and Rouzer (1974) suggest that the "Gestalt conception of healthy functioning is derived from certain premises about the nature of living organisms and their relationship to the surrounding environment" (p. 20). These premises are that the individual must be able to differentiate between the more prominent and less prominent stimuli in the environment at any given time, and be flexible in his or her interaction with the environment. "The organism/environment interaction," Carmer and Rouzer continue, "is regulated according to the principle of homeostasis. From a relative stage of equilibrium, needs arise which must be met to restore the balance." The healthy individual is able to meet these needs by accommodating his or her perceptions accordingly.

Although the Gestalt view of the person tends to be humanistic, there are a number of explicit values underlying the philosophy. Naranjo (1970) has listed nine important "moral injunctions" implicit in Gestalt therapy. They are:

1. Live now. Be concerned with the present rather than with the past or future.
2. Live here. Deal with what is present rather than with what is absent.
3. Stop imagining. Experience the real.
4. Stop unnecessary thinking. Rather, taste and see.
5. Express rather than manipulate, explain, justify, or judge.
6. Give in to unpleasantness and pain just as to pleasure. Do not restrict your awareness.
7. Accept no *should* or *ought* other than your own. Adore no graven image.
8. Take full responsibility for your actions, feelings, and thoughts.
9. Surrender to being as you are. (pp. 49-50)

In many ways, these nine principles are existential, and it would be difficult to distinguish these from the basic tenets of existentialism, even though the language in which they are expressed may differ at points. The Gestalt view of the person, like the existential position, looks at the individual in continuous interaction with others and with his or her environment, striving for authentic engagements and commitments, actualizing, as he or she lives life meaningfully, fulfilling his or her potential.

The Gestalt Counselor

The Gestalt counselor believes that the client ultimately changes through his or her own activities. "The task of the counselor," Ponzo (1976) suggests, "is to operate in a way that increases both the client's and counselor's awareness of the situation and communicates a caring, honest, and competent atmosphere" (p. 415). The counselor, in this respect, serves as a "catalyst" . . . or "helper" (Raming & Frey, 1974).

The Gestalt client is asked to *experience* rather than simply to intellectualize. Whereas in some forms of counseling it is sufficient for clients to verbalize their feelings, in the Gestalt approach it is imperative that clients be willing to expose themselves to a direct experiential reliving of their feelings. This is true in the Gestalt method of interpreting dreams, in confronting resistances, in coming to grips with the repressed past.

The Gestalt counselor's main job is restoring a personality to its *gestalt,* its organized whole. One method of doing this is to help clients better understand the relationship between themselves and their environment. The Gestalt counselor may use several types of exercises, also called "experiments," "games," and "gimmicks," to help clients redefine and integrate themselves within the environment. The Gestalt counselor may also use principles from the Gestalt psychology of perception insofar as he or she helps patients understand the *patterns* of their lives. Within the framework of Gestalt therapy, *patterning* functions as the equivalent to diagnosis (Fagan, 1970).

The Gestalt counselor is interested in finding out as much as possible about the client's life. While the client may remain unaware of the underlying and embedded conflicts that are the source of his or her problem,

> some dissociation or other is bound to become manifest in the first interview. Some anxiety, some talking around the subject will provide the opportunity to show him [the client] the existence of unrealized conflicts. (Perls, 1948)

As the counselor discovers these conflicts, he or she attempts to help the client resolve them by enabling her or him to identify with all vital functions— to accept herself or himself as a total, functioning organism, a whole entity. The counselor does this by emphasizing (and at times insisting on) the "here and now"—the immediacy of the counseling situation.

One method of accomplishing this is to "provoke" the client into coming to grips with his or her feelings. Provocation, therefore, is a legitimate, integral part of the Gestalt repertoire of techniques. The Gestalt counselor plays provocative games with the client, games that are intended to force the client to confront and acknowledge the feelings that he or she has been so arduously trying to avoid. One of the main purposes of the Gestalt games is to help the client become more aware. "Awareness," Harman (1974) points out, "means being in touch with, being aware of, what one is doing, planning and feeling" (p. 259).

Goals

The goal of Gestalt counseling, like the goal of psychodynamic counseling, is the integration of the personality.

> The treatment is finished when the patient has achieved the basic requirements: a change in outlook, a technique of adequate self-expression and assimilation, and the ability to extend awareness to the verbal level. He has then reached that state of integration which facilitates its own development, and he can now be safely left to himself. (Perls, 1948, p. 585)

This is all to be accomplished, however, without the need for intensive probing into the psychological past of the client.

EVALUATION OF HUMANISTIC APPROACHES

The Client-Centered Approach

Despite the popularity of client-centered counseling, and despite the spate of studies that have demonstrated its efficacy, there are certain limitations and criticisms that should be addressed. In part, the popularity of this approach may be attributed to the optimistic attitude of the underlying philosophy, to the simplicity of its techniques, and to a number of other factors. In any case, it is quite clear that at the present time, and probably for some time to come, many prospective counselors will be using the client-centered approach in their practices.

There are some inherent difficulties in the client-centered approach. Most notably, it requires an attitude by the counselor that in fact many counselors are unable to maintain. While it is theoretically desirable to speak of unconditional positive regard, total acceptance, warmth, and empathy, in the real world of counseling these fine feelings are frequently the farthest thing from the counselor's mind.

On the other hand, client-centered counseling can be practiced successfully with a minimum of academic training. Because it relies more on the feelings and personality of the counselor than on his or her technical know-how, it offers many possibilities to the counselor who has not had an opportunity to study intensively the more directive and technique-oriented therapeutic approaches. Confronted by the complex and sometimes overwhelming forces that disrupt many clients' lives, it is sometimes more expedient as well as more facilitative to offer the client appropriate feelings and genuine concern rather than to attempt to treat the unconscious, repressed factors underlying his or her problem.

Speaking of Rogers's total contribution, which is reflected throughout his writings, Farson (1974) points out what is probably his greatest accomplishment.

> In effect he managed to *demystify* the practice of therapy. He showed how it really works. And he did this so convincingly and helpfully that thousands were encouraged to try to develop such relationships with their own clients, patients, students, employees, customers, or inmates. His demystification of therapy not only made extensions into other fields possible, but it encouraged many other workers to further uncover the mystifying practices of psychotherapists. (p. 198)

Such a statement eloquently reflects Rogers's contribution not only to counseling and psychotherapy but to the quality of life in general.

Existential Counseling

Existentialism has much to offer the counselor. Its philosophic basis is relevant to the needs of young people, who are often in a state of turmoil and change, confusion and flux, growth and evolution. Its emphasis on individuality and self-development are helpful to the counselor working with the middle-aged and geriatric clients, confused about who they are and what their roles are in life. Many nonhumanistic counselors find it particularly helpful to use such existential concepts as phenomenological perception and free choice to understand the activities of their clients in a new light.

Existential counseling has proven valuable in a variety of settings. Historically, existentialism has been used in the treatment of every classic disorder from neurosis to psychosis, to perversion, to psychopathy (May, Ellenberger, & Angel, 1959). In recent years, existentialism has even found some application in the school and agency settings.

Gestalt Counseling

Gestalt therapy offers counselors a number of ideas and techniques that may prove applicable to their work in a variety of settings. The emphasis on the "here and now" is especially attractive to the counselor whose limitations of time may demand direct intervention into the immediacy of the client's situation. The Gestalt therapist's concern with the *wholeness* of his client expresses an intuitive belief that is already held by many counselors on a personal level. Furthermore, the Gestalt emphasis on body language proves a fruitful resource to the counselor, who has a rich opportunity to study the body language of his or her clients, even during a short period of time.

Gannon (1972) has found that Gestalt group work proved helpful to a group of high-school students in improving their openness and interpersonal relationships. Passons (1972) has suggested some ways of using Gestalt interventions during group counseling sessions. Bunt (1970) has suggested that the Gestalt approach be used for the diagnosis and treatment of early childhood psychopathology. Foulds (1972) has discussed the experimental-Gestalt growth group, detailing and clarifying some of the techniques that the counselor may wish to employ. Raming and Frey (1974) point out that Gestalt techniques have been widely adopted in school counseling, personnel work with college students, industrial counseling, growth groups, and marriage counseling (p. 179).

Behavioral Counseling

3

The behavioral approaches to counseling differ substantially from the other counseling approaches we have examined. In fact, there is considerable debate as to whether the behavioral approach, in the strictest sense of the word, can legitimately be considered a counseling approach at all. It may be more of a retraining, a reeducation, a learning procedure than a form of counseling. For unlike the other approaches we looked at in the preceding chapter, behavioral counseling does not utilize as the fundamental principle the axiom that the client improves by talking; nor does it emphasize the importance of the counseling relationship. Instead, behavioral counseling comprises a body of related approaches held together by the common belief that *emotional, learning, and adjustment difficulties can be treated through a variety of prescriptive, mechanical, usually nondynamic techniques and procedures.* While the other modalities we have looked at could be called either "internalistic," focusing as they do on the inner person, or "rational," focusing on objective parameters of logic and reality, the behavioral approaches could be called "external determinism," focusing as they do on the environmental factors that shape the individual's behaviors (Mahoney, 1977). In this chapter we shall explore the origins of behavioral counseling and survey its present applications, particularly in the school counseling setting.

BACKGROUND

The various (and sometimes conflicting) approaches that make up behavioral counseling were each introduced by an important and innovative seminal thinker who was disturbed by the status quo. While the philosophical and psychological premises of the behavioral approach can be traced back to the empirical philosopher John Locke, the important psychological foundation of the behavioral approach—the groundwork that led to the subsequent systematic exposition of the theory—was set down at the beginning

John B. Watson, the founder of behavioral psychology

of this century in the United States. Two of its important figures who should be acknowledged are John B. Watson and Edward L. Thorndike.

Much of contemporary behavioral counseling derives from the system of psychology called *behaviorism,* which was expounded by an American psychologist, John B. Watson, in 1913. Watson was attempting to develop what he called an "objective psychology": one that would deal only with the observable behavior of the organism and avoid probing into what he considered to be the "subjectivity" of mental activity, which he felt deprived psychology of its scientific basis. He considered objective observation of the organism the only valid method of psychological investigation.

Watson (1913) begins by arguing that the dominant psychology of his time (Wundt's introspectionism) is too bound up with philosophy and religion; that it is lacking the scientific integrity necessary to make it an effective and practical study. He goes on to suggest that for psychology to become truly scientific it must rely solely on observable behavior as its subject matter, and it must "attempt to formulate, through systematic observation and experimentation, the generalizations, laws, and principles which underlly man's behavior" (Watson, 1924).

"As a science," he continues, "psychology puts before herself the task of unravelling the complex factors involved in the development of human behavior from infancy to old age, and of finding the laws for the regulation of behavior." To help formulate these laws, he explicates the concepts of *stimulus* and *response* and the law that from any given stimulus we can deduce a predictable response. This idea—that each stimulus is linked up to a response—has become the basic rule of behavioral psychology and behavioral counseling.

Watson applied the principles of experimental psychology to human behavior problems. In 1920, Watson and his associate Rosalind Raynor reported a clinical example of a phobia being induced by methods of conditioning. They took an eleven-month-old boy, Albert, and taught him to be fearful of white rats. They did this by emitting a loud, frightening noise whenever Albert reached out to touch the rat, which he was not initially frightened of. After a few of these trials, the boy developed a fear whenever he saw the rat, even if the noise was no longer emitted. Ultimately, he acquired a phobia for all furry objects, apparently generalizing the fear of the rat to these other objects as well.

Experiment which showed that if some one is conditioned they can be reversed

What is most important about this experiment is that if such a fear can be instilled through conditioning, then it can also be removed by conditioning. In fact this is exactly what happened. Four years later, Mary Cover Jones used these same principles in reverse to cure a phobia of a three-year-old boy, thus providing the first clinical example of behavioral principles applied to the treatment situation.

A decade earlier, Edward L. Thorndike had conducted a series of important experiments in psychology that influenced Watson's thinking and the course of behaviorism. In one famous study, he put a hungry male cat into a cage that was constructed in such a way that the cat could trigger a mechanism to allow him access to food that was immediately outside the grating of the cage. At first the cat tried to force his way out of the cage in order to get at the food. He struggled in vain, continually repelled by the inflexibility of the steel grating. Finally, by accident he triggered the mechanism which allowed him to leave the cage and obtain the food. After a brief interval, he was placed back in the cage and the situation was repeated. Thorndike observed that the cat gradually learned the relationship between triggering the mechanism, leaving the cage, and obtaining the food. After many such repetitions, the cat could immediately trigger his release after he was placed in the cage.

Experiment of condition cat.

Thorndike called the principle that was at work here the *law of effect.* Simply, this law states that an act that is reinforced positively will tend to be repeated, and an act that is reinforced negatively will tend to be avoided. Thorndike developed and refined this law into his comprehensive *connectionist psychology,* which stated that the individual makes connections between external and internal events and that these connections lead to goal-directed behavior.

Although the research of Thorndike and Watson became the groundwork for behavioral psychology, it wasn't until the landmark laboratory work of

B. F. Skinner, who is widely recognized for his work in operant conditioning

B. F. Skinner that behavioral psychology—and particularly behavior modification—became as important as it ultimately did.

Skinner was born in Susquehanna, Pennsylvania, in 1904. He came from a middle-class family, and from his earliest years was an avid reader. He had his heart set on becoming a poet and writer when he set off for Hamilton College in upstate New York. He showed considerable talent in that field, but after undergraduate school, as his plans to write professionally were frustrated, his interest turned increasingly to psychology. In 1928, after living the Bohemian life in New York's Greenwich Village, Skinner was accepted at the Harvard Graduate School of Psychology. Thus began the career that would influence the course of American psychology for almost half a century.

During the 1930s, Skinner set forth some assumptions that would influence his thinking for the next fifty years. He strongly rejected the psychoanalytic notion that behavior problems were the result of unconscious conflicts, arguing instead that drive and motivation are not intrinsic to the person but the result of outside stimulation and training. Skinner also expounded the basic idea of *operant conditioning,* a method through which the subject is conditioned by changing the consequences of his or her behavior. As positive behavior is rewarded and negative behavior punished, argued Skinner, the subject learns to behave more positively. Skinner conducted a series of animal experiments, usually with rats as subjects, and he is well known for his invention of the Skinner box, which is actually a training maze. His novel, *Walden Two* (1966), attempts to portray a utopian social system, based on his principles of learning and conditioning. In 1976, he published the first volume of his autobiography, *Particulars of My Life.*

BEHAVIORAL VIEW OF THE PERSON

To the behavioral counselor, the individual is a product of conditioning. The behaviorist speaks of the S-R paradigm as the basic pattern of all human learning. Each person reacts in a predictable way to any given stimulus, depending on his or her training. "Behavioral counselors . . . are not concerned with inner states but rather with how the integrated organism behaves. Change to the behaviorist means change in *behavior.* . . . Understanding the nature of the problem is not enough; clients must arrange with the counselor step-by-step processes to change responses or to develop new responses" (Ewing, 1977, p. 336). Behavioral counselors realize, of course, that observable behavior itself does not adequately explain the *totality* of human nature, so they have set forth a number of concepts to explain the legion of processes through which learning and behavioral change take place. The key word underlying their view of the person is *conditioning.* Although there are several types of conditioning, there are two basic classes that are usually discussed: *classical* (respondent) *conditioning* and *operant* (instrumental) *conditioning.*

Classical Conditioning

Classical conditioning always involves the pairing of stimuli. One of the paired stimuli elicits a response, which either has already been learned or one that doesn't have to be learned. For instance, if you are given a shock and you jump up, this is a response that never had to be learned: it is autonomic. But we may also have a stimulus, such as an obscene word, which causes you, upon hearing it, to wince (or to feel uncomfortable). This response was learned many years ago, but is now natural and much like the autonomic response of jumping to a shock. In either case, this stimulus elicits a natural immediate response. We call this stimulus the *unconditioned* ‑ natural response *stimulus,* commonly abbreviated UCS. The response it elicits is called the *unconditioned response,* or UCR. The term *unconditioned* is used since the stimulus and response are natural, and require no training.

But as I stated, in this type of conditioning there are always two stimuli *paired* together. The other stimulus in this pair is neutral and elicits either no specific response or a response that is different than the UCR. This is called the *conditioned stimulus,* commonly abbreviated CS. Levis (1970)

figure 3.1 Classical (respondent) and operant (instrumental) conditioning

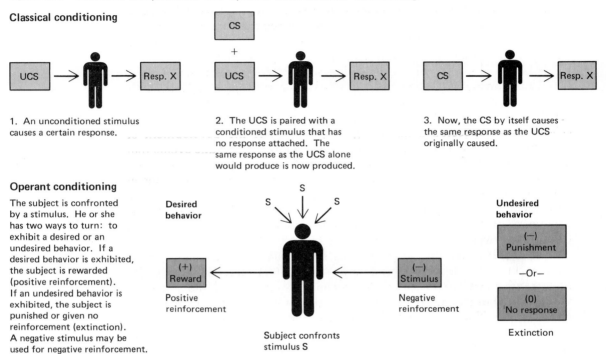

Classical conditioning

1. An unconditioned stimulus causes a certain response.

2. The UCS is paired with a conditioned stimulus that has no response attached. The same response as the UCS alone would produce is now produced.

3. Now, the CS by itself causes the same response as the UCS originally caused.

Operant conditioning

The subject is confronted by a stimulus. He or she has two ways to turn: to exhibit a desired or an undesired behavior. If a desired behavior is exhibited, the subject is rewarded (positive reinforcement). If an undesired behavior is exhibited, the subject is punished or given no reinforcement (extinction). A negative stimulus may be used for negative reinforcement.

Note: From Belkin, Gary S., and Jerry L. Gray. *Educational Psychology: An Introduction.* © 1977 Wm. C. Brown Company Publishers, Dubuque, Iowa. Reprinted by permission.

clearly explains the classical conditioning paradigm and how it differs from operant conditioning:

> Descriptively, the classical conditioning paradigm differs from the instrumental procedure in that the sequence of events presented is *independent* of the subject's behavior. This sequence consists of an unconditioned stimulus (UCS), a stimulus known to evoke a regular and measurable response (UCR), and the conditioned stimulus (CS), a stimulus which at the outset of the experiment does not evoke the UCR. The usual order of the sequence is to present the CS followed closely in time by the UCS. The regular and measurable response elicited by the UCS is called the unconditioned response (UCR). If conditioning occurs, the CS presentation will elicit a conditioned response (CR) which resembles the UCR and which occurs prior to or in the absence of UCS presentations. (p. 15)

This is the type of conditioning illustrated in Pavlov's famous experiment with the dog. As you may recall, Pavlov discovered, while studying digestion in animals, that if a bell rang immediately before a dog was fed, after a time the ringing of the bell itself would cause the dog to salivate. The pairing of the ringing bell (conditioned stimulus) and the feeding (unconditioned stimulus) caused the dog to respond to the bell by salivating.

Experiment of classical conditioning

Likewise, a number of the basic learning experiences of the average individual can be explained through the classical conditioning paradigm. Most important of these experiences, from the counselor's point of view, are the maladaptive or neurotic learning experiences. Eysenck and Rachman (1965) have suggested a three-stage explanation of the development of abnormal behavior. The first stage involves a series of traumatic events that produce autonomic reactions in the individual. These autonomic reactions are considered as unconditioned responses, which in turn may result in neurotic behavior patterns. The second stage utilizes the classical conditioning paradigm directly. This stage is particularly useful in explaining the generalization of anxiety to unhealthy proportions. The final stage involves instrumental avoidance of painful or anxiety-provoking situations. Let us consider as an example a boy who has developed a fear of dogs. It may have begun with a traumatic incident in which he was bitten by a dog. The trauma of being bitten (unconditioned stimulus) produced an immediate body reaction (pain-autonomic response), which set the stage for the development of the phobia. Now, whenever the boy sees a dog (conditioned stimulus) he associates this with the traumatic event and runs away (conditioned response). Running away from dogs and avoiding them (operant avoidance) produces a relief of his original anxiety that was brought about by the traumatic event in the first place. Thus, the phobia and avoidance serve as a *reinforcing stimulus*.

Example

As we see from this description (and this is only one of many paradigms the behaviorists use to explain neurotic behavior), the mechanics of learning neurotic behavior can be quite complex. But the resultant behavior is always explained by the processes of learning, which are descriptive and predictable and which, in the classical conditioning models, always involves the pairing of stimuli.

Operant Conditioning

The second major class of conditioning is operant or instrumental conditioning. The terms can be used interchangeably. This is the type of conditioning generally associated with the work of B. F. Skinner. The term *operant* comes from combining the words *operate* and *environment*. In this type of conditioning, the person's actions produce a consequence that either increases or decreases the probability of the behavior reoccuring. The term *reinforcement* is used to describe this process.

> The standard distinction between operant and reflex behavior is that one is voluntary and the other involuntary. Operant behavior is felt to be under the control of the behaving person and has traditionally been attributed to an act of will. Reflex behavior, on the other hand, is not under comparable control. (Skinner, 1974, p. 44)

Consider, for example, what happens in a simple Skinner box. In this contraption, an animal is taught to push a lever and is rewarded with food (*positive reinforcement*). This pattern of behavior eventually becomes learned. The learning principle behind operant conditioning is that new learning occurs as a result of positive reinforcement, and old patterns are abandoned as a result of the lack of reinforcement, or because of punishment.

It would be unfair to imply that the entire behavioral view of the person is dominated solely by these mechanistic learning theories. True, the concepts of reinforcement and stimulus pairing play a key role in the explanation of how human behavior is learned; but the behaviorists also recognize that other factors play a vital role as well. Carter and Stuart (1970), in responding to a highly critical assessment of the behavioral approach, argue that "the common accusation that behaviorists explain all behavior in terms of learning history is inaccurate. Behaviorists [also] recognize as well the impact of physiology and contemporary events" (p. 44).

The criticism of the "empty organism"—the argument that in behavioral counseling the "totality" of the client as a person is not considered—often lodged against behaviorists, such as Skinner, is frequently unsupported when we look directly at their work. Behavioral counselors, as much as anyone else, recognize the human side of clients; but they approach the problems besetting clients from an objective, scientific, empirical standpoint. Speaking in an interview, for example, Skinner (1976b) makes clear how his position goes beyond the constraints of S-R psychology, while still maintaining its scientific credibility:

> Let me emphasize first that I do not consider myself an S-R psychologist. As it stands, I'm not sure that response is a very useful concept. Behavior is very fluid: it isn't made up of lots of little responses packed together. The stimulating environment is important among the variables of which behavior is a function, but it is by no means the only one. It is a mistake to suppose that there are no internal stimuli and to try to formulate everything as S-R psychology. . . . I think, however, that the problem goes deeper than that. If the "O" represents the organism, then the question arises, How important

is the O? I guess I'm even more opposed to postulating the influence of O than I am to the strict S-R formulation. As I see it, psychology is concerned with establishing relations between the behavior of an organism and the forces acting upon it. Now the organism must be there. . . . I don't really believe in an "empty organism." (p. 85)

In an important article about the role of the counselor, Thoresen (1969) conceptualizes the counselor as an "applied behavioral scientist." This means that the counselor is both a behavioral scientist, who sets out to "draw upon the propositions and findings of *all* approaches and to set about empirically and experimentally validating specific techniques," and is, at the same time a "disciplined romantic," who exercises "ingenuity and creativeness in his concern for his wholeness and totality. We can and should be disciplined romantics and critical humanists" (p. 843).

In a more recent discussion, Thoresen (1973) expands the concept of what he calls "behavioral humanism." He points out that "we can benefit from the work of behaviorists and humanists if we act to reduce the confusion and ambiguity about contemporary behaviorism and humanism and if we develop and use new scientific methods tailored to the study of human phenomena" (p. 385). He shows specifically how the traditional concerns of the humanists can be translated into compatible behavioral terms, and outlines the beginnings of "a synthesizing perspective that draws from a variety of sources and avoids insidious dichotomies—humanist versus behaviorist" (p. 414). Thoresen's conciliatory attitude reflects a growing trend in the counseling profession. Mahoney (1977) also points out that there seems to be emerging a "partial reconciliation" between the behavioral and humanistic positions. "Although it is seldom acknowledged in print," he argues, "I think the proponents of each perspective may have come to recognize some of their ideological and practical inadequacies" (p. 6).

THE ROLE OF THE BEHAVIORAL COUNSELOR

Before we can appreciate the role of the behavioral counselor, we must understand the responsibilities of the client (which differ from the client's expected role in other approaches) and the full meaning of the term *behavior modification.* Let us consider each of these individually.

The Client

The primary task of the client in behavioral counseling is to learn new responses to old situations. The client may be asked to do a number of things. For example, he or she may be asked to provide the counselor with a list of the stimulus situations that provoke the greatest anxiety. In order to be conditioned to respond in a healthy and appropriate way to anxiety-evoking stimuli, it may at times be necessary for the client to expose himself or herself directly to those stimuli, no matter how painful the anticipation of exposure may be. A young woman who has difficulty asserting herself may be taught to do so in the counseling setting and then rewarded for her successful attempts (positive reinforcement).

The role of the behavioral counselor is confined primarily to dealing with the client's *observable* behavior. Unlike the psychodynamic and humanistic counselors that have been discussed, the behavioral counselor makes little attempt to probe and explore the "inner reaches" of the psyche. On the contrary, she or he avoids such excursions, considering them irrelevant to the task at hand. Michael and Meyerson (1962) emphasize the point that to the behavioral counselor, "Conceptual formulations such as ego-strength, inferiority feelings, or self-concept are not behavior but simply ways of organizing and interpreting observable behavior by referring it to an inner determiner" (p. 395).

Although the behavioral counselor is limited to dealing with observable behavior, it is agreed that much of this observable behavior will touch upon the realm of feelings. But the counselor's manner of approaching feelings—and changing them—requires direct interventions in the behavior itself. These interventions are known as behavior modification approaches.

The Modification of Behavior

Behavior modification can be broadly defined as any procedure or set of procedures designed to change an individual's behavior through the use of any of the conditioning or modeling paradigms. This definition suggests that the *goal* of any behavior modification program is to change behavior. Does this mean that the individual has to act differently after the program than he or she did before? Yes and no. We would expect that if the problem that the individual entered the program with is a behavioral problem, then the specific behavior will be changed by the end of the program. On the other hand, if we are trying to teach children to be less aggressive, not only would we expect their behaviors to change, but also we would expect their attitudes, beliefs, and feelings to change as well. In such a situation, we would be speaking about more than behavior itself; we would be speaking about feelings, perceptions, cognitions.

Most simply, behavior modification is a way of "influencing" a person. The sphere of influence may extend only to behavior, or far beyond behavior into other realms. The single factor that holds behavior modification together is the belief that the present environment is a greater force on the person than are past experiences (Skinner, 1975). The scientific manipulation of variables in the environment becomes the art of behavioral psychology. "Most behavior modification procedures are based on the general principle that people are influenced by the consequences of their behavior. Behavior modification assumes that the current environment is more relevant in affecting an individual's behavior than most early life experiences, enduring intra-psychic conflicts, or personality structure. Insofar as possible, the behaviorally oriented mental health worker limits the conceptualization of the problem to observable behavior and its environmental context" (Stolz, Weinckowski, & Brown, 1975, p. 1028).

The important point in thinking about any kind of behavior modification program is that it is a *planned* intervention, with a specific goal stated at the outset. The fact that we happen to do something, and as a result of our action the person's behavior changes, does not necessarily make our intervention behavior modification. On the contrary, the most essential element of behavior modification is lacking in such a case: the *planned goal* of the intervention.

John D. Krumboltz, a leading proponent of the behavioral counseling approach, makes two important points regarding the role of the behavioral counselor. First, he suggests that "the central purpose of counseling is to help each client resolve those problems for which he requests help" (1965). This involves the setting up of a contract and the statement of goals. Second, he suggests that when operant conditioning is in use, the counselor's ability to time the reinforcements maximally can be the critical variable between success and failure. Krumboltz (1966) also emphasizes the important principle that "we learn to do those things which produce certain kinds of desirable conditions . . . [and] the attention and approval of a counselor might have reinforcing effects for a client, especially if the client feels that the counselor understands his problem and can do something to help" (Introduction).

While many of the behavior modification procedures may on the surface seem mechanistic, it should be pointed out that within the total role of the behavioral counselor lies the responsibility for correcting neurotic behavior. In this respect, one of the main tasks of the behavioral counselor is "to find an acceptable response pattern which is antagonistic to the neurotic activity of the patient and to substitute this adaptive behavior for the non-adaptive neurotic behavior" (Rachman, 1967). He or she does this by exploring with the client the constellation of situations that provoke the anxiety. Behavioral counselors, while they do give credence to the client's perceptions and insights into what causes anxiety, rely most heavily on their direct observations of changes in the client's behaviors. Considering the emphasis on observable behavior, this priority seems perfectly logical.

TECHNIQUES OF BEHAVIORAL COUNSELING

Behavioral counseling is clearly the most technique-oriented of all the counseling approaches we have studied. Because the quality of the counseling relationship is de-emphasized, and because the main priority is on the resolution of the client's symptoms, the behavioral counselor relies heavily on a repertoire of empirical techniques to deal with each specific problem. It should also be mentioned that although in other systems the counselor's technique may be considered a part of the counselor's personality or emotional disposition (see chapter 4 for a full discussion counseling technique), in behavioral counseling the employment of a technique is independent of the counselor's feelings, beliefs, and personality. Behavioral techniques are prescriptive operational procedures designed to achieve certain specifiable ends.

The behavioral techniques are all derived from models in learning theory, under the assumption that emotional growth requires new learning patterns. As we examine each of these techniques, therefore, we will note that there is at work a learning principle applied to a psychological-behavior problem.

CLASSICAL CONDITIONING TECHNIQUES

Techniques using respondent conditioning always involve the pairing of stimuli, as described earlier in the chapter. In the counseling setting, the counselor's job is to decide which stimuli to pair in order to effect the desired changes. This may require innovative apparatus or may be direct and simple. In a landmark experiment, Mowrer and Mowrer (1938) treated a case of enuresis (bed-wetting) using classical conditioning methods. Willis and Giles (1976) summarize the procedure used:

> Treatment was based on Pavlovian or classical conditioning principles. The goal was to associate waking up with a full bladder. To accomplish this association, a special mattress pad was developed which basically consisted of two pieces of bronze screening separated by a piece of absorbent cloth. When wet, however, the pad became a good conductor and closed a circuit that included a battery and an electric doorbell.
> The bell served as an unconditioned stimulus for awakening. When the pad was placed on the child's bed, the ringing of the bell coincided with the beginning of bed-wetting and with a relatively full bladder.
> The child was instructed to get up when the bell rang and go to the bathroom. In theory, a full bladder, which occurs at the same time as the ringing bell, would become a conditioned stimulus for awakening.

The apparatus was used nightly until seven successive dry nights occurred. Then the child was given one or more cups of water more than normal just before going to bed. When seven more consecutive dry nights occurred, use of the apparatus was discontinued. (p. 27)

We see from this example how the basic classical conditioning model, unaltered, can be used to change an unhealthy condition. In practice, however, there are more sophisticated applications of the classical conditioning paradigm. One of the most widely used is systematic desensitization.

Systematic Desensitization

Systematic desensitization is a form of classical conditioning in which anxiety-evoking situations are paired with inhibitory responses. Wolpe (1961) describes the process this way:

> The desensitization method consists of presenting to the imagination of the deeply relaxed patient the feeblest item in a list of anxiety-evoking stimuli — repeatedly, until no more anxiety is evoked. The next item in the list is presented, and so on, until eventually, even the strongest of the anxiety-evoking stimuli fails to evoke any stir of anxiety in the patient. (p. 191)

The technique of systematic desensitization is based upon the learning principle of _reciprocal inhibition_, which was developed by Wolpe (1958). Reciprocal inhibition means that if a relaxing response is paired with an anxiety-producing stimulus, a new bond develops between the two so that the anxiety-provoking stimulus no longer provokes anxiety. The idea is that we can't have two opposite responses at the same time. For example, let us say that a young man has a fear of flying on a plane. If every time this client thinks of flying in a plane, he is relaxed and made to feel comfortable by the therapist, ultimately the stimulus (of flying on a plane) will fail to elicit the anxiety it once did.

The systematic desensitization approach "is essentially characterized by a treatment package which includes relaxation training, construction of hierarchies of anxiety-eliciting stimuli via imagery with relaxation" (Unikel, 1973, p. 4). The young man discusses the components of his fear with the counselor in order to construct a list of anxiety-evoking stimuli in order of intensity (e.g., driving to the airport, waiting in the lounge, boarding the plane, taking off, being in the air, etc.). The stimuli are dealt with, one at a time, until the most anxiety provoking is no longer capable of generating anxiety. This approach comprises, in other words, cumulative, sequential — hence, systematic — processes of desensitization.

Some forms of behavior require the hypnotic relaxation of the patient.

Garvey and Hegrenes (1966) offer an example of how a school psychologist used systematic desensitization to treat a child suffering from school phobia, a disorder that responds well to this technique. The client, a ten-year-old boy, was unable to get into the car that was to take him to school in the morning. The desensitization consisted of twelve stages. During the first stage, the psychologist sat with the boy in the car that was parked in front of the school. When the boy finally felt comfortable in this situation, the next step was applied, and so on until the final step was taken. The following eleven steps were then taken:

example
systematic desensitization

1. getting out of the car and approaching the curb;
2. going to the sidewalk;
3. going to the bottom of the school steps;
4. going to the top of the steps;
5. going to the door;
6. entering the school;
7. approaching the classroom a certain distance each day down the hall;
8. entering the classroom;
9. being present in the classroom with the teacher;
10. being present in the classroom with the teacher and one or two classmates; and
11. being present in the classroom with a full class.

We note in this example how systematic desensitization slowly builds up, step-by-step, to the highest anxiety-producing situation. This necessitated, according to the authors, twenty treatments, involving a total of ten to twelve hours of the therapist's time. Of course, the time and success will vary directly with the kind of problem, the cooperation of the client, and the design of the program.

Implosive Therapy (IT)

Implosive therapy is a modified form of the classical conditioning paradigm. Although IT has not yet been as widely adopted as systematic desensitization, it has much unexplored potential in the counseling setting for all kinds of problems: sexual dysfunctioning; rehabilitation counseling; the behavioral treatment of phobia; school-related problems, including test anxiety; marriage and family counseling; hysterical and obsessional neuroses.

The theory underlying implosive therapy combines the basic model of *extinction* (figure 3.2) with elements of classical conditioning. It resembles systematic desensitization, but aims for the same result in the opposite way. Both require the subject to bring to mind the anxiety-evoking stimuli. But with IT, the subject is *not* given simultaneous anxiety-inhibiting stimuli. Rather, the client, by intensely concentrating on the fearful stimulus, is taught to associate "neutral stimuli" with the anxiety-evoking ones.

figure 3.2 Flow chart for extinction

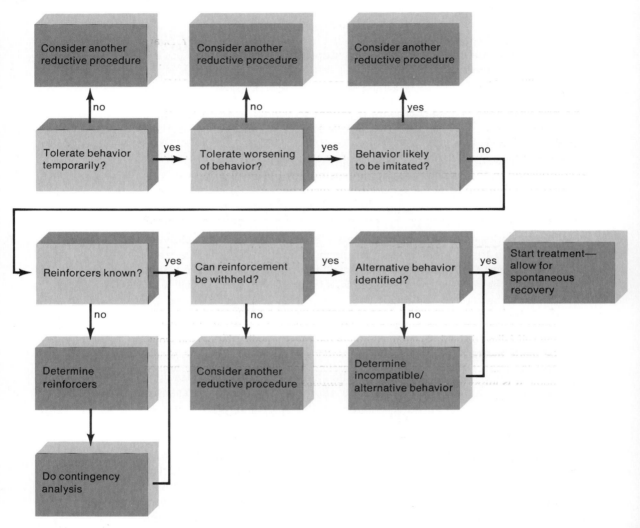

Note: From "Extinction: Guidelines for Its Selection and Use" by R. B. Benoit and G. R. Mayer, *Personnel and Guidance Journal,* 1974, *52,* 291. Used by permission.

Implosive therapy is based on the "two-factor model of avoidance learning." Thomas Stampfl (1970), the originator of this approach, explains the underlying theoretical model this way:

> The two-process model . . . assumes that . . . when "neutral" stimuli are associated with unconditioned or conditioned positive reinforcers, positive affect is acquired. If the neutral stimuli are associated with unconditioned or conditioned aversive reinforcement, negative affect is acquired. (p. 184)

The principle here is that the client is taught to vividly imagine the thing that he or she most fears (this process is called *flooding*), and while imagining it is shown that there are no consequences attached. The client, in a sense, becomes "desensitized" to the previously frightening stimulus; but this is accomplished in the opposite way from systematic desensitization.

Implosive therapy is indicated wherever disturbed avoidance behavior is the symptom, as in the case of a phobia. During the first interviews, the counselor "seeks to answer [these] questions: What is the patient avoiding? What might he be avoiding? What is he afraid of? What might he be afraid of?" (Stampfl, 1970, p. 195). Once the counselor is able to answer these questions, the procedure is then set up. Hogan (1966) describes its implementation in the clinical counseling setting:

> An acrophobic (person with a fear of heights) would be requested to imagine himself falling off a high building or cliff, or perhaps be instructed to picture himself falling through space in complete darkness. Ideally, the person would be made aware of his feelings and sensations while falling. Then he should feel the impact of his body with the ground and view his crushed, broken body. It is important that the therapist emphasize how the person looks and feels throughout the scenes. If the client should recall an actual traumatic experience, the clinician should center succeeding imagery around that experience. (p. 26)

In recent years, IT has been used to treat a number of problems, ranging from sexual dysfunctioning to the emotional conflicts of retardates. Curtis et al. (1976) have found the flooding technique of IT very effective in alleviating a phobic response. Hogan (1975) reports the successful treatment of a case of frigidity, using IT. Silvestri (1974) has shown its use in the treatment of emotionally disturbed retardates. It should also be noted that a related technique, called *covert sensitization,* or *covert conditioning,* has been developed by Joseph R. Cautela (see Cautela, 1969, and Cautela, 1977, for good discussions of the technique and its applications). With covert sensitization, the client is taught to vividly imagine unpleasant, noxious experiences, such as nausea or pain, each time he or she thinks of or approaches stimuli that lead to abnormal behaviors. As a general rule of thumb, counselors can use the less aversive technique of covert sensitization wherever they would use IT.

OPERANT CONDITIONING TECHNIQUES

Operant conditioning, in its various forms, is probably the single most popular behavior modification paradigm. Whereas in classical conditioning it is the *pairing* of stimuli that elicits new responses from the subject, in operant conditioning, it is the *reinforcement* that follows the subject's responses that determines the new behaviors that are to be formed. Some of the client's responses (behaviors) are reinforced; that is, they are strengthened. Others are not. The combination is what changes behavior.

Broadly, a reinforcer is anything that increases the probability of a response. Sometimes called a reinforcing stimulus, the reinforcer is some kind of reward that either strengthens a response or increases its frequency of occurrence. "A reinforcing stimulus," Lindsley (1971) points out, "is the powerful thing which builds behavior." He goes on to suggest that we can think of reinforcers in terms of *accelerating* or *decelerating* responses. In this way, we see directly their relationship to behaviors.

Before we look at different types of reinforcement, let us consider what happens when reinforcement is withheld.

Extinction

"When a learned response is repeated without reinforcement the strength of the tendency to perform that response undergoes a progressive decrease" (Dollard & Miller, 1950). This is the simplest definition of *extinction*. Let us say that a teacher has been giving a star to each student who hands in a neat homework assignment. When the teacher's supply of stars runs out, he or she forgets to buy a new box. After a period of time, according to the theory of extinction, the students will be less likely to hand in neat assignments because the reinforcement they had been receiving for so doing is no longer there. "The rate of extinction," Bandura (1969) points out,

> is governed by a number of factors, among them the irregularity with which the behavior was reinforced in the past, the amount of effort required to perform it, the level of deprivation present during extinction, the ease with which changes in conditions of reinforcement can be discerned, and the availability of alternative modes of response. Because of the diversity of the controlling variables, a number of different theoretical conceptualizations of extinction have been proposed. (p. 355)

The theory of extinction becomes much more complicated than the simple definition first given. Calvin, Clifford, Clifford, Bolden and Harvey (1956) have shown, for example, that the time interval between extinction trials influences the rate of extinction. Bandura (1969, pp. 356-423) cites over a hundred different studies of different factors that influence the rate of extinction.

Benoit and Mayer (1974) have discussed the uses of extinction as a classroom behavior modification technique. They point out the critical questions that the counselor must answer before deciding whether extinction is the appropriate technique: Are the reinforcers of the behavior that is to be extinguished known? Can these reinforcers be withheld? Have alternative behaviors been identified? Can an increase in the negative behavior be tolerated? They also point out the important difference between simply ignoring a behavior and having it extinguished. Extinction requires that the reinforcement for a particular behavior be withheld; it may well be, they suggest, that the reinforcement for a specific behavior is not always apparent on the surface. For example, the client may be getting pleasure out of some fantasy associated with the behavior rather than with any overt response.

Answering these kinds of questions will help the counselor decide if he or she can use extinction, or whether it will be necessary to find an alternative technique, such as desensitization or operant conditioning.

It is especially important to note that in using extinction, the negative behavior is likely to get worse before it gets better. Consider, for example, the situation in which a counselor calls the child-client's mother into the office every time the child has a temper tantrum. This, of course, would reinforce the child's inappropriate behavior by showing that such behavior brings a reward, the presence of the mother. The counselor decides to use extinction; to cut out the reinforcement. At first, the child's rate and intensity of tantrums increases as the child tries to provoke the counselor into acting-out and calling in the mother. The counselor must be able to withstand this pressure if the extinction is to be successful. On a more subtle level, if the counselor shows disgust for the child's behavior, this in itself may be enough reinforcement for the child to continue. In such a situation, the child may develop a different reinforcer for the same behavior, and if the counselor is not aware of it, she or he cannot extinguish it.

This is why it is so important in using extinction to decide at the outset which reinforcers actually can be withheld and which cannot.

Reinforcement Programs

Operant conditioning progams always involve instrumental learning. "The essential feature of the instrumental learning paradigm," McLaughlin (1971) points out, "is that the response is instrumental in the achievement of a

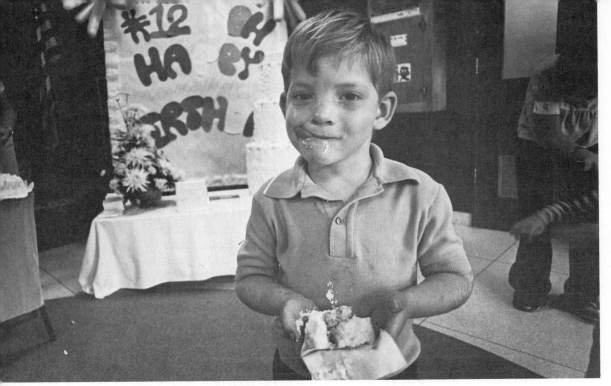

Primary reinforcers can be determined by learning what the individual likes.

goal. If a hungry organism is offered a choice of equally attractive responses, only one of which leads to food, the tendency will inevitably be to make the response that leads to food once the consequences of each response are known" (p. 52). The subject operates on the environment (hence, operant), and his or her choices result in certain predictable consequences. This is the fundamental principle underlying all operant conditioning reinforcement programs.

The ultimate success or failure of any operant conditioning program is determined by the kind of reinforcers used, the planned intervals of reinforcement, and the consistency of reinforcement. Let us consider each of these important areas.

Since a reinforcer must serve to strengthen behavior, it is imperative that the counselor selects a reinforcer that will have precisely this effect on the subject. Let's say that the counselor wants John and Ellen to do certain tasks which he or she does not feel they would be willing to do. To encourage each one, John is offered a ticket to the Ram's game and Ellen is offered a ticket to the ballet as reward for performing the tasks. This may be well and good if John likes football and if Ellen likes ballet, but it just so happens that John is an avid ballet aficionado and Ellen a passionate football fan.

We see that inappropriate reinforcers were chosen for each of them—that the counselor was incorrectly influenced by sex-role stereotypes—and that therefore the likelihood of either performing the task is greatly diminished. The point is this: *it is important that the correct reinforcer be selected for any individual—the reinforcer that will be most appropriate for him or her.*

I used this example of a ticket for an event. A candy bar, a dinner at a French restaurant, money, or any other concrete thing that directly gives pleasure could also have been chosen. These are called *primary reinforcers.* In many cases, however, a reinforcer that is so direct is not used, but rather something like praise, a smile, an encouraging remark. These are called *secondary reinforcers.* They have value insofar as they have been associated in the past with primary reinforcers, and retain this value for many years. If you recall that your parents gave you candy when they said you were good, then being told, "You are good" will have a positive effect, even if no candy is given, many years later. In both cases, it is necessary to select the correct reinforcer for the individual. With primary reinforcers it is easier to determine exactly what the individual likes: John could have been asked if he prefers a ballgame or a ballet, as could have Ellen. With secondary reinforcers, however, it is sometimes more difficult to determine the appropriate reinforcement of an individual. As Krumboltz and Thoresen (1969) point out, "Words of praise or approval cannot be used with the assurance that they will always be effective reinforcers" (p. 26). It is necessary, they go on to suggest, that counselors test their reinforcers, since the selection of reinforcers is of critical importance in effectively strengthening or weakening certain behaviors. One of the most direct ways of doing this is by asking the client what will best serve as a reward or punishment.

Positive Reinforcement

Positive reinforcement is probably the most widely used and the most successful of all the behavior modification techniques. This approach simply involves providing a reward for a positive behavior. The reward (positive reinforcer) can be anything ranging from a token that can be used to purchase goods, to a star in one's book, to a verbal compliment, to a smile. The principle underlying positive reinforcement is that the tendency to repeat a response to a given stimulus will be strengthened as the response is rewarded.

The counselor who wishes to use positive reinforcement is confronted at the outset by a number of questions. Which behaviors should be rewarded? What type of reward and how frequently should it be dispensed? Should the positive reinforcement be combined with another technique, such as extinction, punishment, or modeling? What is probably most important for counselors to remember is that positive reinforcement is used all the time, even if they are not aware that they are using it. So long as counselors respond with a variety of responses they are reinforcing some behaviors more than others.

Negative Reinforcement and Punishment

The terms *negative reinforcement* and *punishment* are often used interchangeably. They are not the same however. It is important to understand the distinction between them because they are used in different ways, for different purposes. Greer and Dorow (1976) describe negative reinforcement as "the process whereby the removal of an ongoing event acts to increase a behavior" (p. 66). They go on to give the example of "the seat belt warning buzzer [an unpleasant stimulus] which continues to sound until the seat belt is buckled [the desired behavior]." In general, a negative reinforcer is any unpleasant stimulus presented to a person in order to encourage a desirable behavior that is designed to escape or to avoid the unpleasant stimulus.

example <

Punishment, on the other hand, is used after a behavior has occurred. Whereas negative reinforcement involves the *removal* of a negative stimulus, punishment involves the presentation of it. If the parent scolds the child when she or he is caught stealing from the cookie jar, this would be a form of punishment. Skinner (1974) offers a clear differentiation between the functional roles of punishment and negative reinforcement:

> Punishment is designed to remove behavior from a repertoire, whereas negative reinforcement generates behavior. Punishing contingencies are just the reverse of reinforcing. When a person spanks a child or threatens to spank him because he has misbehaved, he is presenting a negative reinforcer rather than removing one, and when a government fines an offender or puts him in prison, it is removing a positive reinforcer . . . rather than presenting a negative one. (p. 69)

In many cases, negative reinforcement and punishment are used in tandem to increase the probability of eliminating undesirable behaviors. Most studies have shown that positive reinforcement, combined with punishment, is more effective than punishment alone.

OTHER BEHAVIORAL COUNSELING TECHNIQUES

Shaping

Shaping is a technique sometimes used by behavioral counselors. It involves reinforcing behavior that approximates the desired goal. "In shaping," Patterson (1973) points out, "the experimenter at first reinforces behavior that is only similar to the behavior that is ultimately desired but does not exist at the present." Through gradual changes in the pattern of reinforcement, the desired behavior is finally reached. In a sophisticated operant conditioning program, where the desired behaviors require the coordination of a number of complex responses, shaping would probably be useful in building up response repertoires.

Modeling

Modeling is another important technique used by behavioral counselors. With this technique, the subject models himself or herself after another's behavior or actions. It may not be necessary for the client to perform in any particular way in order to learn from modeling; merely observing the model's behavior is often sufficient. "When a person observes a model's behavior," Bandura (1969) suggests, "but otherwise performs no overt responses, he can acquire the modeled responses while they are occurring only in cognitive, representational forms." This constitutes a form of sensory conditioning.

In its most obvious form, modeling is learning by example. If the example is a positive one, then positive behavior will be the likely outcome; if, on the other hand, the example is a negative one, then undesirable behavior will be the outcome. Thus, the child who models himself or herself after the best behaved child in the class (perhaps because of the teacher's attitude toward this "good" child) will try to behave well, while the other child who uses the class troublemaker as a model (perhaps because the teacher gives this troublemaker special attention) will tend toward similar disruptive behavior.

Time-Out (TO)

Time-out is a simple procedure in which the individual is removed from the area in which the inappropriate behavior is reinforced. It is similar to extinction in that in both situations the behavior is changed because of a lack of consistent reinforcement, but differs in one basic way: "The chief difference between extinction and time-out," Benoit and Mayer (1976) point out, "is that in extinction reinforcement is withheld for a particular behavior, while in time-out the client is denied access to all sources of reinforcement through either transferring him or her to a nonreinforcing situation or removing the source of reinforcement from the present situation."

Patterson, Cobb, and Ray (1973) have written about a multifaceted behavior modification program in which parents of aggressive boys were trained to be behavior therapists. One of the main techniques they used was time-out. "Most of the studies," they point out, " . . . indicated that the effect of repeated applications of TO was to produce rapid decreases in the rate of coercive social behaviors in children" (p. 178). In this experiment time-out was used as an alternative to the parents' previously unhealthy method of dealing with the child's aggressiveness; namely, beating the child. "The parent learned to observe, to apply TO, and to reinforce pro-social behaviors as alternatives to beating the child." Time-out allowed the parent an opportunity to "cool off," as well as allowing the child the opportunity to find alternative, more productive behaviors. In this sense, time-out served a dual purpose.

GOALS OF BEHAVIORAL COUNSELING

While most of the counseling approaches I discussed in the preceding chapter are oriented to theoretical goals ("integration" in psychoanalysis; "self-actualization" in the client-centered; the "will to meaning" in existentialism), the goal of behavioral counseling depends entirely on the type of problem for which the client has sought treatment. Krumboltz (1966) argues that "it is the counselor's job to help the client translate his problem into a behavioral goal that the client wants to attain and that the counselor believes will contribute to the welfare of his client." In behavioral counseling the aim is directed always to the presenting problem, and the removal of that problem is the goal of the counseling process.

In general, the goal of most behavioral counseling—particularly with the method of desensitization—is the elimination of neurotic anxiety, or its manifest symptoms. The behavioral counselor believes that this anxiety acts as an inhibiting factor against healthy, adaptive behavior.

Bandura (1969) has stated this goal of behavioral counseling quite succinctly: "The patient has a repertoire of previously learned positive habits available to him, but these adaptive patterns are inhibited or blocked by competing responses motivated by anxiety or guilt. *The goal of therapy, then, is to reduce the severity of the internal inhibitory controls, thus allowing the healthy patterns of behavior to emerge*" (italics added).

EVALUATION AND APPLICATIONS

Ironically, what has often been cited as the greatest fault of behavioral therapy proves to be its greatest advantage in the counseling setting, namely that it deals directly with the symptom. Most of the difficulties that the counselor is confronted with take the form of behavioral problems. Individuals do not generally seek counseling for long-term self-insight, but rather because they are troubled by a specific, symptomatic problem. These are problems in role areas of functioning: in the client's relationship with others, in successfully carrying out his or her work, and so on. Or, they are problems involving inordinate degrees of anxiety (neurotic anxiety), which interfere with the client's living. In this respect, behavioral counseling, with its emphasis on the symptom itself, offers a practical bonus to the counselor.

However, by focusing so emphatically on change in the client's behavior, the behavioral approach has come to be viewed by a wary public and sometimes skeptical professional audience as either immoral, amoral, or against our "natural inclinations." As Lazarus (1977), a partisan of behavioral therapy, recently pointed out:

> Behavior therapy and behavior modification have acquired a bad press. To receive funding, many hospitals and community agencies have had to drop the label *behavior* from their program proposals. In several quarters, the term *behavior modification* is an adrenalin-raiser that evokes unfortunate stereotypes. One grows weary of explaining that behavior therapists do not deny consciousness, that they do not treat people like Pavlovian dogs, that they are not Machiavellian and coercive, that aversion therapy (except in the hands of a lunatic fringe) has always been a minor and relatively insignificant part of our armamentarium, and that we are not ignorant of the part played by mutual trust and other relationship factors among our treatment variables. (p. 553)

Lazarus's remarks reflect an unfortunate truth: that behavior therapy and behavioral counseling, despite their merits, do not always fare well in the public eye. The essence of this criticism, however, involves more than public relations. It involves some very real ethical questions that underlie the entire behavioral modification movement: How far can we go in shaping the way a person really is by modifying his or her behavior? Under what circumstances and to what degree must there be *voluntary* consent? Who is primarily responsible for establishing goals? Davison and Stuart (1975) attempt to deal with each of these questions from an ethical point of view; evaluate any possible conflicts between behavior therapy and civil liberties. They conclude that when these questions are satisfactorily resolved—which they can be—behavior therapy can make "valuable contributions to pluralism by generating a body of data describing the operation of influence processes and their consequences. Thus, if people are to make their own decisions about how to conduct their lives, is it not reasonable to provide as much knowledge as possible about how behavior is developed, maintained, and changed" (p. 762)?

Behavioral counseling has also been criticized for its lack of emphasis on the human qualities of the client and the counselor. It reduces the complexities of human interactions, its critics suggest, to simple equations that, although they may adequately explain the individual's ostensible behavior, do not take into account the motives behind it, the feelings accompanying it, and other crucial factors. Sprinthall (1971) has argued that "it [behavioral counseling] virtually ignores developmental stages: stages of moral development, personal development, epistemological development—so much so that we may have inadvertently left the human being out of the process" (p. 66).

One can see, however, how some behavioral concepts—such as desensitization, extinction, reinforcement, shaping, and time-out—in conjunction with the warmth and acceptance of the Rogerian, the probing of the pyschoanalyst, and the exploration for meaning of the existentialist, can add to the full dimension of counseling and to the counselor's understanding of the client.

Applications of the behavioral counseling approaches in the schools are legion. In fact, behavior modification has become the treatment modality of choice in the many counseling settings, not only in the schools (Goldman, 1978). The most popular single paradigm is still Skinnerian operant conditioning (Herrnstein, 1977), especially through the token economy programs, although modeling, systematic desensitization and time-out are all widely used. The counselor can be a valuable resource person by teaching the teachers and parents how to implement a behavioral change program. The research is plentiful in this area. Greer and Dorow (1976) have shown in detail how different behavioral techniques can be used to solve a wide range of school-related problems, both by the classroom teacher and by the school counselor. They describe the successful application of the principles of behavioral conditioning that were used to increase the cooperative behaviors of disruptive hyperactive children. A token economy system was introduced. The child was initially reinforced with candy and verbal approval, then candy and check marks (which were exchangeable for tangible goods such as candy bars, comics, small toys, etc.). Bursts of disruptive behavior resulted in mandatory time-out, which consisted of isolation from the playroom. The frequency of cooperative play behaviors increased in fifteen days from an average of 45 percent to an average of 90 percent. Jeffrey (1976) has critically evaluated the use of operant conditioning techniques in modifying hyperactive and aggressive behavior, which despite some criticisms, have found wide-scale success.

Behavior mod programs have proven effective in treating language and communication disorders, especially stuttering (Ryan, 1974), in which it has an extremely high treatment success rate. Other research has shown behavior modification effective in the treatment of alcoholism, juvenile delinquency, drug addiction, sexual dysfunctions, reduction of neurotic anxiety, and many other conditions. It has been used successfully in the hospital setting, for rehabilitation counseling, in special education, and in the prison setting. On the whole, there is more research supporting the effectiveness of behavior modification than any other group of approaches.

SUMMARY

In this chapter we examined some of the major models of behavioral counseling, including classical conditioning, operant conditioning, systematic desensitization, implosion therapy, and modeling. Behavior modification, we indicated, developed from the behavioral psychology of John B. Watson in the early years of this century. Behaviorism emphasized using observable, measureable behavior as the basis of psychology, and introduced the stimulus-response relationship in interpreting behavior patterns. Using many of the early principles, B. F. Skinner then formulated the basic principles of operant conditioning and Joseph Wolpe the process of systematic desensitization.

The behavioral counselor views the individual as a product of his or her conditioning. The two main types of conditioning are classical (respondent) and operant (instrumental). Classical conditioning involves the pairing of an unconditioned with a conditioned stimulus, so that the response associated with the former becomes associated with the latter. Operant conditioning requires that the subject respond to a stimulus, and that the response then be reinforced. Behavioral counselors, it was pointed out, do not necessarily hold a mechanistic view of the person, and Skinner particularly has argued against the restrictive view of the client as an "empty organism."

The behavioral counselor's main job is to design a program through which specified target behaviors will be modified. The classical conditioning techniques used to this end include systematic desensitization (which involves the client imagining anxiety-evoking stimuli in a hierarchical order, while the therapist presents relaxing, anxiety-inhibiting stimuli at the same time) and implosive therapy (where the subject vividly fantasizes anxiety-evoking images until they are neutralized); and extinction (breaking an established response pattern by not reinforcing it). Specific types of operant conditioning models (reinforcement approaches) were also discussed. Three other techniques—shaping, modeling, and time-out—were covered briefly.

The Helping Process 4

In the preceding two chapters, we examined in some depth the major theories, or schools as they are sometimes called, of counseling today. In this chapter we focus on the face-to-face interaction between the counselor and client engaged in individual counseling—the helping process itself. We will begin by looking in some detail at the initial counseling interview, to consider ways that the counseling process can get off to a most promising start. We will also briefly look at how to terminate the counseling process on a positive note. We shall then explore some of the general techniques available to the counselor, to see how these are evolved, how they are implemented, and what results they produce. Finally we shall look at the goals of counseling in more depth, paying particular attention to how the client and counselor formulate counseling goals for growth and change, how expectations of counseling affect the process, and how a variety of forces interact to become a part of the counseling relationship. By the conclusion of this chapter, you will have acquired, subject to the limitations of the printed medium, a "feel" for how the counseling process facilitates growth and change and in particular, for the myriad complexities and diversities of the counseling process.

THE INITIAL INTERVIEW

Initiating the counseling process is critical to the ultimate success or failure of the entire course of the counseling. The very continuity and integrity of the counseling experience attests to the importance of the beginning phase. When we look at the initial interview, therefore, we should keep in mind that our discussion transcends the narrow time limitations of a single session and extends throughout the course of the counseling experience. Moreover, we will note that the operational definition of the term *interview* tells us a great deal about what should happen at the first interview.

First, we raise the question, What is an interview and how does it differ from other encounters between two people, such as ordinary conversation?

Kadushin (1972) suggests that an interview differs from conversation in that it has a central purpose that is agreed to by the participants. "The interaction is designed to achieve a consciously selected purpose. The purpose may [even] be to establish a purpose for the interview" (p. 8). Gorden (1975) also makes the point that an interview always has a central purpose and this is what distinguishes it from conversation. Schubert (1971) expands these ideas, citing the concepts of "mutuality and purposeful talking" as central to the structure of an interview. He raises the following basic questions that help us define an interview and determine its structure:

> Who does the talking? How is the purpose determined? How is mutuality achieved? The rather unsatisfactory answer to these questions is that "it depends"—it depends on a complex constellation of factors that have to do with the nature of the problem or task at hand, the person who feels some concern about it, the auspices under which help is being offered, the psychological, cultural, and social attributes of the person involved in the interview, and the physical setting in which the interview takes place. (p. 1)

This emphasizes the point that the counselor makes an ordinary encounter an interview by his or her actions and by the setting in which the encounter takes place.

The moment the client enters the counselor's office for the first time, a number of things should be going through the counselor's mind. Under what circumstances was this appointment arranged? Was it voluntary or was it made under some type of compulsion: required by a teacher, by the court, by the parents of the client, and so forth? How does the client appear as he or she walks through the door? Does body language reveal anything to the counselor? Does his or her face indicate any particular indications of attitude? What might his or her expectations be at this moment? The counselor recognizes that because this is the client's first appointment he or she is most likely nervous, unsure of what to expect, and probably in the throes of some type of conflict. "The beginning interview," Porter (1950) argues,

> presents certain problems to the counselor that are in part different from subsequent interviews. It is likely that the beginning interview will be more demanding of the counselor for several reasons. The counselor and the client are new to each other and the relationship which is established at the outset will color a great deal of what follows. The counselor must be prepared to adapt himself to the mode of expression the client develops: the counselor is not going into the interview with a set routine. It is in the first interview that the client will begin to reveal himself. The counselor's reactions are correspondingly important. Errors in understanding the client may result in his hasty withdrawl. And usually it is in this interview that the client decides whether the counseling relationship is the method he will use in his attempts to work out his difficulties. (p. 88)

Porter's comments highlight the difficulties as well as the importance of the first interview. From these comments, as well as from common sense, it might be discerned that the beginning interview is best used by the counselor as a time to study the client, to learn about her or him and decide on the way the treatment is likely to proceed, to weigh expected results, and so on. Bell (1965) points out that the initial interview can be used productively as a factor in determining instances of significant changes in the client's behavior.

Eisenberg and Delaney (1977) cite as the goals of the first interview "stimulating, open, honest, and full communication about the concerns needing to be discussed and the factors and background related to those concerns; working toward progressively deeper levels of understanding, respect, and trust between helpee and helper; providing the helpee with the view that something useful can be gained from the helping sessions; identifying a problem or concern for subsequent attention and work; and establishing the "gestalt" that counseling is a process where both parties must work hard to understand the client and his or her concerns" (p. 99). This set of goals is theoretically ideal, but at times difficult to implement. There are many factors, some of which are seemingly extraneous, that work against open communication during the initial interview. These have to be dealt with before the goals of counseling can move forward.

Vontress (1973) points out, for example, some of the cultural barriers between counselor and client that may impede progress at the beginning. These include racial and socioeconomic class differences. Sue (1977), carrying this point even further, suggests that counselor's white, middle-class biases may confuse their "role behaviors" during the first interview and "predispose us to assume that a client's initial expectations and requests are not indicative of real needs" (p. 221). Factors beyond the counselor's control may also influence what transpires. Cash, Begley, McCowen, and Weise (1975) have found that clients perceive physically attractive counselors more positively in many dimensions than they do physically unattractive counselors. Stone and Morden (1976) found that the physical distance between counselor and client affects the client's ability to produce verbal material (they suggest 5 feet as the optimum distance). Newton and Caple (1974) found that clients that come into counseling with a personal problem perceived the same counselor differently than those who came for help with vocational-educational problems, indicating that clients' needs influence their perceptions. All of these things need be taken into account during the initial counseling interview.

To meet the multifaceted and interacting demands of the initial interview, the beginning counselor might do well to have a tentative, but very flexible, routine worked out so that he or she feels comfortable conducting the interview. The counselor must find a compromise between total spontaneity and preparedness. Tyler (1956) suggests three aspects of the initial interview that are generally applicable: assessing the foundation for the relationship, identifying the client's psychological realities, and structuring the counseling situation. This is not to suggest that counselors act in a mechanical way during the first interview, but rather that they have an overall structure from which they may freely deviate as the need arises. The counselor should have a repertoire of possible responses available to meet the specific needs of the client during the initial interview. He or she should have a tentative structure planned. This structure may include any or all of the following components: eliciting a personal history from the client, beginning the counseling relationship, helping the client feel comfortable, frankly discussing alternative possibilities to counseling, and establishing a contract if the client indicates he or she wishes to continue with the counselor. This last point requires some clarification.

A contract in counseling differs from the use of the word in its legal context. A counseling contract is an unwritten but usually explicit agreement between the counselor and the client about what the treatment should do, how many sessions are expected, what general rules and guidelines will be followed, and so forth. It is not intended to rigidly fix the course of the counseling, but to assure both the counselor and the client that an understanding exists between them and that any deviations from this understanding should be mutually agreed upon by both of them. Some counselors, particularly behavioral counselors, use the contract to establish the particular goals of the treatment, while other counselors use the contract to explore the range of ideas to be examined during the course of treatment. Ezell and Patience (1972) have suggested that the use of the contract is itself a counseling technique.

Shertzer and Stone (1971) offer as guidelines for the initial interview *establishing rapport with the [counselee], providing some structure, helping the counselee talk, remaining alert to the counselee's feelings, and smoothly terminating the interview.* We shall discuss each of these in some detail.

Rapport is demonstrated when the counselor offers an accepting, open attitude, when she or he shows interest in what the client has to say, and everything possible is done to make the client feel comfortable. Tyler (1969) offers some helpful remarks on how to communicate positively with the client at the outset, avoiding the dangers of premature interpretations:

> We must recognize that the people who consult us may have mixed feelings about being understood. They must be sure that understanding can in no way constitute a threat before they can welcome it. Many of us are afraid that

someone will "see through us," uncovering our hidden weaknesses. We have put up strong defenses against this. Much of what we say, many of the things we do, are designed to hide rather than to reveal our underlying motives and traits. For this reason if it happens that the counselor shows by some penetrating remark that he has seen through a new client's defenses, the person may very well retreat in panic from the whole situation. It is only when he has become certain of a thorough-going unshakable acceptance that he can run the risk of trying to make his real feelings understood. (pp. 49–50)

In order to establish rapport, therefore, it is important that the counselor not probe too deeply into the hidden recesses of the client's psyche; that he or she not manipulate to bring too much too quickly. The establishment of rapport requires patience and understanding.

Counselors provide structure during the initial interview by translating into practice their concepts and beliefs about counseling. "Providing some structure for the interview," Shertzer and Stone (1971) point out, "means that the counselor must have clearly in his mind the concept of counseling." The Rogerian counselor will structure the interview far differently from that of the psychoanalytic, reality, existential, or behavioral counselor. In general, however, the client's moves toward structuring the interview should have priority over the counselor's.

Helping the counselee talk is often the most difficult part of the initial interview. The silent client, who sits and stares blankly at the counselor, the client who is silent out of fear is a challenge to most counselors. There are a number of gentle, appropriate ways of helping the client speak. These include asking questions, suggesting things that the client may wish to speak about, asking if he or she is comfortable, and so on. A general guideline is that the counselor should only say those things that are intended to act as a catalyst for the client in his or her efforts to communicate. Rarely does the situation occur in which the counselor makes the client feel comfortable and the client is still unable to speak.

Remaining alert to the client's feelings and providing for his or her needs is the first distinctively therapeutic part of the counseling process. The counselor wants to get a *sense of the client,* an appreciation of the client's unconscious reservoir of feelings. Typically, the client will demonstrate certain needs during the session. She or he may request information, vocational advice, or assistance in working out a personal problem. He or she may explain the need for "just someone to talk to," or the wish for sympathy for some predicament about which he or she has been unable to find someone to speak to. He or she may be seeking punishment and chastisement for an action that he or she considers "bad" or "evil." While the client may not directly comment on such needs, she or he usually offers a number of subtle indications of what is being presented or will be looked for during the course of the counseling treatment.

Termination

The skillful termination of the counseling interview (and counseling process) has also been the subject of much research and discussion. We know that the conclusion of the initial interview is important, both in bringing the client back again (when required) and in shaping his or her judgment about the entire session. Moreover, the skillful termination of the counseling interview helps the client feel more positive about the experience as well as increasing the likelihood of his or her returning if the need arises. Brammer and Shostrom (1968) suggest what they call "capping techniques," which consist of changing the subject to something less intense, "yet still propelling the interview forward." I would agree too with the suggestion that it is important to end the initial interview on a calm level, rather than in the midst of a highly emotional interchange.

The skillful termination of the counseling process is of equal importance, of course. Termination may be viewed as temporary, since there is always the possibility that the client will return at some later point. Eisenberg and Delaney (1977) suggest that the goals of the termination session are to "(1) reinforce the client's behavior changes in the direction of the goal as stated by the client; (2) make sure the client has no other pressing concerns; and (3) help the client realize that he may seek the counselor's aid at any time in the future, as the 'door is always open' " (p. 199). There are several ways of doing this.

First, the counselor should encourage the client to discuss openly his or her feelings (which are probably ambivalent) about termination. On the one hand, the client may be pleased about the progress made; but on the other hand, the client may feel a sense of loss about not seeing the counselor again. The counselor can be reassuring to the client that he or she can return to visit whenever the need is felt. It is only through actual experiences, however, that the counselor gets a sense of how to terminate an interview— or the counseling process—in a manner that is most in accord with the counselor's own personal style.

Any of the following statements by the counselor (in context) may serve as an adequate closing of the interview:

> Well, I think we have a number of things to discuss in our next session.
>
> So, our next appointment is Thursday at noon. I'll see you then.
>
> I hope you'll decide to call for another appointment. I would like to explore this further with you.

Each of these conveys to the client a distinct sense of continuity.

VARIETIES OF COUNSELING TECHNIQUES

The relationship between the counselor and his or her techniques changes as the counselor becomes more experienced, more confident of his or her abilities, more mature as a person, more comfortable in the counseling situation, and more aware of the client as a person. At first the counselor is likely to hold onto techniques as a person who cannot swim holds onto a life preserver: they not only provide the ability to stay afloat, but they continually support her or him and conserve efforts. As the counselor gains experience and confidence, however, he or she gradually becomes less dependent upon techniques and more reliant upon a personal counseling sense of intuition. The counselor may continue to use the same techniques with the same frequency as she or he did before, but the techniques are now at the service of the counselor. Soon the counselor begins to modify techniques to suit his or her own idiosyncratic nature; the counselor gives the bland, objective, impersonal techniques a personal touch.

It is at this point that counselors often become troubled by conflicts that arise between their theoretical orientation (and the techniques dictated by that theory) and the feelings they are experiencing in the immediacy of the counseling setting. A client-centered counselor, for example, may be unable to feel positive regard for a certain client. In spite of what he or she believes should be done in a specific situation, the feelings being experienced are communicated to the client above and beyond the application of the technique being employed. At this point in the interview, the "style" of the counselor becomes more prominent than the technique. A counseling style integrates the counselor's feelings and techniques and has a dramatic impact on the client's ability to communicate (Hawes, 1972).

This compatibility evolves slowly and requires flexibility and openness on the part of the counselor. The counselor must be willing to study herself or himself in the counseling situation to learn where capabilities and weaknesses lie, where she or he has much to offer the client and where little to offer, where personal needs might conflict with the client's needs, and where his or her personality might inadvertently distort perceptions of the client. While evidence does not indicate either that feelings have priority over techniques or that techniques are more important than the counselor's feelings, it is clear from the research that techniques and feelings are interrelated and that each is to some extent functionally dependent upon the other. For this reason most counselors, knowingly or unknowingly, draw from many different schools of counseling to discover the techniques that work for them. Counselors who draw from different schools in their choice of techniques are said to be eclectic.

Eclectic Counseling

Counseling eclecticism, according to Thorne (1973), its originator and chief proponent, "involves the selective application of basic science methods using the most valid current knowledge available for specific clinical situations according to indications and contraindications. It is not committed to any parochial view of man." Like the "applied behavioral scientist" conception of the counselor presented by Thoresen, the eclectic counselor utilizes a scientific approach to the problems of treatment in which he or she selects and combines, through careful planning, "compatible elements from diverse sources, even from otherwise incompatible theories and systems" (Thorne, 1973).

Brammer (1969), in a paper on eclecticism, traces the development of learning and personality theory in psychology and maintains that "there is a need for an eclectic position that avoids indiscriminate picking and choosing and leads to a consistent and comprehensive synthesis of theory unique to the individual counselor" (p. 193). Brammer not only contends that "there is room for the emerging eclectic position elaborated in this paper" but also suspects that "an empirical study of counselor practices would reveal it is the most dominant, though unexpressed, point of view." He asserts that "each counselor must grapple with the task of developing his own comprehensive point of view. A counselor cannot in good professional conscience go to the literature on theories of counseling and psychotherapy to find a ready made one for himself" (p. 193).

Brammer tells us that to develop this eclectic view "it is necessary to resist emphasizing theory exclusively." The counselor "must sharpen his powers of behavioral observation in the best scientific tradition . . . adopt a behaviorist stance in the broad meaning of the term . . . trust his powers of observation, criticism and experimental technique . . . know his own personality. The counselor must be aware of his values, deed-distorted perceptions, and potentials and limitations with particular kinds of clients" (p. 195). Sometimes, then, a counselor is able to reach a point where he "transcends both person and method to develop a creative, innovative, approach to behavior change."

The basic organizing principle used by the eclectic counselor is an objective evaluation of the client. Rather than approach the client with clinical biases (such as a predetermined view of personality or a predetermined conception of what the clinical goal of the treatment should be), the eclectic practitioner adapts the course of counseling, as well as his or her own strategies, to the particulars of the client's situation. In this section, we shall examine some of the techniques that may be used by an eclectic practitioner, as well as by practitioners in almost any particular school. Thorne (1950,

1967) emphasizes that the selection of these techniques requires some organization, and the beginning counselor should keep this admonition in mind.

As a rule, the technique is named after the type of response the counselor offers to the client. Some of the techniques to be mentioned are applicable only to one or two schools of counseling, while others are used extensively by all of the schools. Seven of the most common—and most useful—counselor techniques (responses) are offered below, with a brief illustration of each:

Specific Techniques

Clarification

Clarification is intended to make clear, either for the counselor or for the client, the meaning of the client's communications. In addition to achieving cognitive understanding of information, it may help the client to understand ambiguities or confusions in his or her thinking.

> **Client** I can't get along with Mr. Jones or Buzzy, so I don't go to class.
>
> **Counselor** In what way does going to class require you to interact with Buzzy or with Mr. Jones?
>
> **Client** Well since Buzzy sits in front of me . . . you know, it's pretty hard to avoid him . . . especially since he's always starting up something with me. And since Mr. Jones always takes his side, I always get caught in the middle.

Reflection

"Reflection consists of bringing to the surface and expressing in words those feelings and attitudes that lie behind the interviewee's words" (Benjamin, 1974, p. 117). It is not so much a restating in words what the client has expressed as it is an empathic mirroring of the feelings behind the words. The counselor never expresses his or her judgment in a reflective statement; but, rather, captures the emotional perspective of the client, reflecting back perceptions of a situation. Because it is a communication of feeling rather than words, it is difficult to illustrate its impact in transcript form.

> **Client** I've been feeling badly lately . . . like I've done something bad.
>
> **Counselor** Like you've done something bad? (*asked empathically*)
>
> **Client** Yes. Like I deserve to be punished.
>
> **Counselor** You feel that you should be punished. (*said empathically*)

The counselor captures the emotional perspective of the client.

Probing

The counselor, through the use of questions, attempts to encourage the client to expressions of greater depth and to a personal awareness of deeper understanding and self-insight. The probing questions should never be overwhelming to the client.

Client	I find that I just can't study, even if I know that I'm going to fail the test.
Counselor	What happens when it gets down to study time?
Client	I get blocked. I can't concentrate.
Counselor	What are your feelings at such a time?
Client	I feel like I'm going to fail.

Silence

Although it is sometimes not recognized as a skillful, facilitative response, silence is one of the most helpful expressions that the counselor can offer to the client. It is particularly useful when the client is engaged in self-analysis, which can be helpful to the ultimate success of the counseling process.

Client   Why do you think I'm so upset about this test? Intellectually, I know I can pass it, but emotionally. . . .

Counselor   (*Silence*)

Client   Why do I feel this tenseness whenever I have to take a test?

Counselor   (*Silence*)

Interpretation

The counselor explains to the client a hidden meaning behind his or her statements or actions. From the psychoanalytic point of view, interpretation means making what was once unconscious now fully conscious. But other approaches use interpretive statements to increase the client's awareness in a variety of areas.

Client   I'm sorry that I'm laughing at you—don't take it personally. I can't help it, but I find you very funny looking. Whenever I think of you, I laugh.

Counselor   Perhaps it is really feelings of anger that you are experiencing.

Empathic Response

The counselor shows that he or she accepts the client and understands emotionally what the client is attempting to communicate. It is important that the counselor be able to differentiate between sympathy and empathy. The former is an expression of pity, while the latter is an acknowledgment that the counselor, too, has these same feelings. Empathy is a positive, active commitment on the part of the counselor.

Client   I feel like such a stupid idiot . . . such a failure. Everyone has a date for the party except me. No one has asked me . . . and I know nobody is going to.

Counselor   I, too, have felt left out at times . . . like I was some kind of freak . . . an object of ridicule. I thought at the time I could never survive, never show my face again. But I have survived, and so will you.

Investigating Alternatives

This has two purposes: to assist the client in making choices and to help in an understanding of the reasons underlying whatever choices he or she is disposed to. This technique is particularly helpful in terms of the client's reality orientation.

Client   Since I wasn't able to get into any college, I guess I'm going to be a failure.

Counselor   What are some other possibilities you might consider?

Client   Well, I guess I could pursue carpentry. I do love working with wood.

Counselor   How would you get a job in that field?

Client   I guess I could ask my Uncle Al. He's in the union, you know.

These represent only a handful of the many counseling techniques. They have been selected because they are the most general in scope and the most widely used. Another that should be mentioned is the open-ended question that allows the client flexibility of response because of the question's lack of structure. These types of questions—"Tell me about yourself," for instance—are particularly helpful during the first interview.

THE HELPING DIMENSION

If counseling were only technique, of course, there would actually be very little need for counselors. It would simply be a mechanistic process. In reality, there is much more to the counseling experience than the counselor's use of techniques: there is the human dimension of the interaction, and this dimension comes through, without exception, in every counseling interview. This is beyond explanation and can only be experienced in person, in the "here and now" of the interaction. It is called the "helping dimension."

There are two significant variables in the counseling process: the counselor and the client. To learn about the process and to discuss it intelligently, we break down these two variables into subvariables, such as age, sex, race, background, motivation, personality, and so forth. One variable not yet mentioned is what Gendlin (1961) calls "experiencing." He describes it this way:

> (1) Experiencing is *felt,* rather than thought, known, or verbalized. (2) Experiencing occurs in the *immediate* present. It is not generalized attributes of a person such as traits, complexes, or dispositions. Rather, experiencing is what a person feels here and now, in this moment. Experiencing is the changing flow of feeling which makes it possible for every individual to feel something any given moment. (p. 234)

Gendlin sees this variable as significant because it affects the client's ability to change and grow. In fact, the quality of experiencing is central to every counseling interview, and the congruence between the client's experiencing and the counselor's is an important contributor to a successful outcome.

We can now focus more closely on the key facet of the entire counseling process: the helping dimension. Rogers (1961) lists the questions that circumscribe this dimension.

> Can I *be* in some way which will be perceived by the other person as trustworthy, as dependable or consistent in some deep sense? . . . Can I be expressive enough as a person that what I am will be communicated unambiguously? . . . Can I let myself experience positive attitudes toward this other person? . . . Can I be strong enough as a person to be separate from the other? . . . Am I secure enough within myself to permit his separateness? . . . Can I let myself enter fully into the world of his feelings and personal meanings and see these as he does? . . . Can I receive him as he is? (p. 50–54)

The answers to these questions and several others like them lead Rogers to the "process conception" of client-centered counseling that was discussed in chapter 2. This conception examines the various movements of the client toward growth as she or he experiences the facilitative communications of the counselor.

Responding to the Client

Much of the emotional learning—and hence, growth—that takes place in counseling is the result of the way the counselor responds to the client. In their taxonomy of the affective domain, in which they outline the hierarchical stages of emotional learning, Krathwohl, Bloom, and Masia (1964) cite *responding* as the second level of affective development, immediately following *receiving* (awareness) and preceding *valuing*. The precondition for any kind of responding, they point out, is that the individual be aware of the world around her or him; that she or he be willing to and capable of "receiving" the world, of attending to it. Immediately after this receiving of the world—and of others in the world—the individual is able to respond to it—and to others!—and from there is able to develop values about things. This sequencing is relevant to our discussion of the counselor's responding to the client, for the counselor must first be open to receive what the client is communicating before he or she can respond to the client. Another way of saying this is that sensitivity is a precondition for empathy, which itself is a precondition for effective communication. This will become more meaningful as we look at Krathwohl's breakdown of what the level of responding comprises. This level is divided into three stages: acquiescence in responding; willingness to respond; and satisfaction in response. A brief description of each stage should clarify what responding entails.

Acquiescence means passive agreement, and indeed this level involves a compliant individual—one who responds passively to the stimuli around. At this level, the individual "makes the response, but he has not fully accepted the necessity for doing so" (p. 179). This would be characteristic of a counselor who is only half listening to what the client has to say, who is picking up the words but not the feelings behind the words. Such a counselor is, in effect, saying to the client, "I am willing to hear your words, but not to feel what you are feeling."

Next, the emotionally developed individual develops what Krathwohl (Krathwohl et al., 1964) calls a "*willingness to respond,*" at which point he or she feels a commitment to a certain response. It is at this point that the counselor not only hears what the client is saying but also feels compelled to react to what the client is communicating. The counselor at this level is saying to the client, "I not only hear your words, but they are having an effect on me . . . causing me to act a certain way, to feel a certain way."

Finally, at the third level, *satisfaction in response,* the individual derives "a feeling of satisfaction, an emotional response, generally of pleasure, zest, or enjoyment," from the response. The difference between this stage and the two that precede it can be illustrated in the difference between reading a book because it is required and reading a book for pleasure. Not only is the qualitative experience different but the quantitative experience (of learning, of what is gained) also differs because of the increased motivation that characterizes the second level. A counselor at this satisfaction level responds to the client because he or she is really involved with the client, is experiencing along with the client.

Cognitive Restructuring

Thus, appropriate responding requires empathic understanding. But this is only the beginning. How can counselors assure that their response is facilitative for the client: *that they are responding to what the client is communicating in such a way that the client will be helped.* It is not enough for counselors to simply respond according to their feelings. A counselor may have good intentions, but lack the knowledge needed to make a facilitative response. Every response should have a purpose, and this purpose should extend beyond the demands of the moment. Schmidt (1976) makes the point that "If we are truly going to make a difference, we must not only listen to feelings or reinforce specific verbal statements and behaviors, we also must develop strategies that will give our clients new skills that they can use away from the counseling relationship" (p. 71). He goes on to discuss an approach he calls "cognitive restructuring," which is becoming an increasingly important guideline in helping counselors decide how to respond to clients. "Cognitive restructuring," he points out, "is any therapeutic technique that employs the change of "self-thoughts" in order to alter emotional reactions and behaviors toward more favorable outcomes." He offers some examples of how this works in the counseling setting:

> In general, what happens in the treatment goes something like the following: a self-defeating thought, for example, "It is terrible to make mistakes," is challenged by a counterthought, "Everybody makes mistakes." This counterthought is positively reinforced in that the ensuing emotion and behavior are pleasant and more productive. Furthermore, these counterthoughts can be positively reinforced more intentionally by asking clients to engage in reinforcing thoughts or activities immediately following each counterthought. For example, after using the counter, "Everybody makes mistakes," a client can fantasize a pleasant scene for thirty seconds. In a similar manner, negative self-thoughts can be punished by instructing clients to engage in unpleasant fantasies following such thoughts. (p. 72)

As we see from this description, *cognitive restructuring* as a technique—as a form of responding to the client—embodies the principles we are suggesting are necessary for all categories of responses to the client. In cognitive restructuring, the taxonomic stages of affective functioning are recapitulated: first, the counselor becomes aware of what the client needs; second, he or she feels compelled to respond to these needs, and finally, the counselor feels a pleasure in helping the client get over the obstacle. Although other methods differ from cognitive restructuring in substance, they embody the same principles in different forms.

A good example of a related type of technique—in fact, a visual variant of cognitive restructuring—is what Pyke (1979) calls cognitive templating. Cognitive templating involves having the client reexamine his or her life experiences from the social-learning-theory perspective, and then the presenting of the counselor's analysis of the client's experiences and perceptions to the client in diagrammatic form (called the cognitive template). The purpose of this is to facilitate the client's cognitive restructuring. The counselor uses his or her response, through the medium of the visual diagram, to reach the client's subjective world.

For example, Pyke (1979) uses the technique for helping women reexamine some of their sex-typed behaviors and gender-related feelings about themselves. In one case, a young lady named Carol tended to overemphasize her negative experiences and minimize her accomplishments and positive experiences. Figure 4.1 shows the first phase of the template prepared by Carol's counselor in a session with Carol. We see visually how much more emphasis is accorded the negative than the positive. This is explored with Carol in another session. Figure 4.2 then shows the second phase in which

figure 4.1 Cognitive template showing emphasis on negative experiences

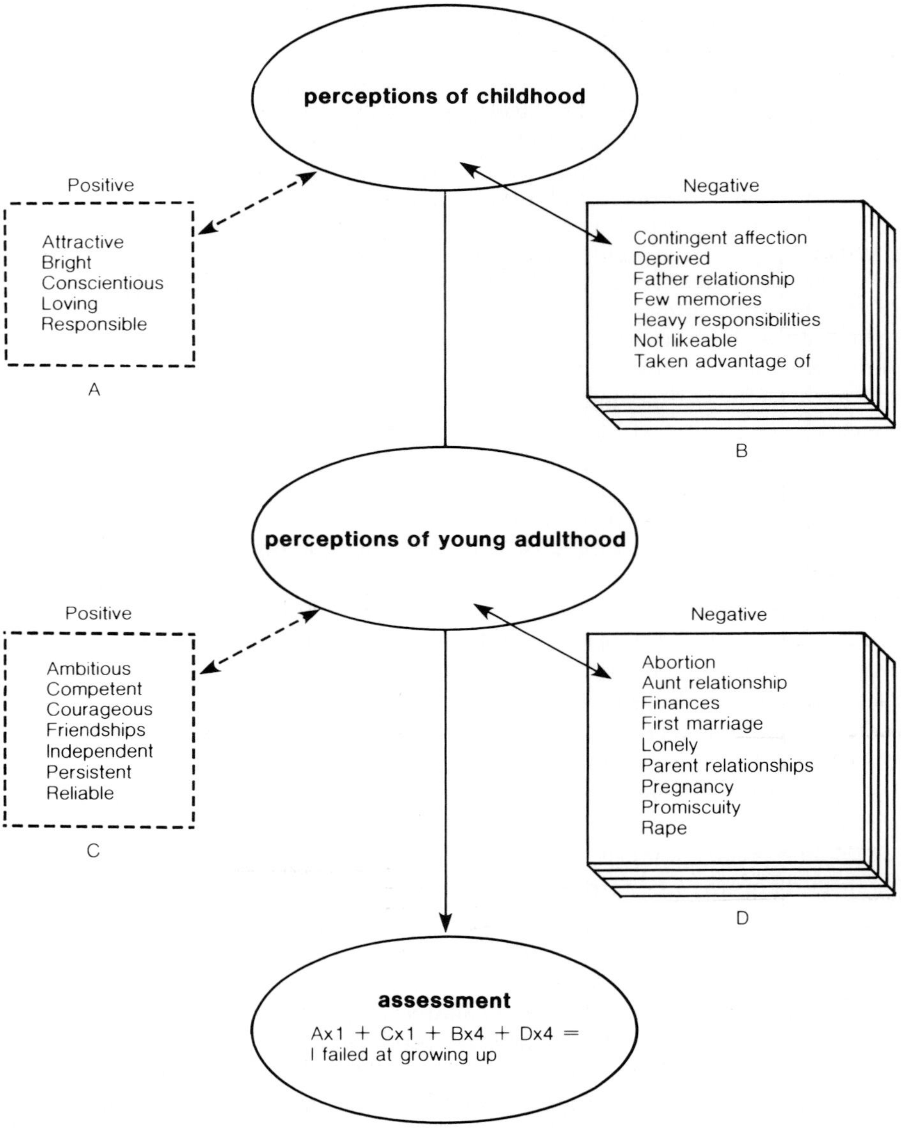

perceptions of childhood

Positive

Attractive
Bright
Conscientious
Loving
Responsible

A

Negative

Contingent affection
Deprived
Father relationship
Few memories
Heavy responsibilities
Not likeable
Taken advantage of

B

perceptions of young adulthood

Positive

Ambitious
Competent
Courageous
Friendships
Independent
Persistent
Reliable

C

Negative

Abortion
Aunt relationship
Finances
First marriage
Lonely
Parent relationships
Pregnancy
Promiscuity
Rape

D

assessment

Ax1 + Cx1 + Bx4 + Dx4 =
I failed at growing up

Note: From ''Cognitive Templating: A Technique for Feminist (and Other) Counselors'' by S. W. Pyke, *Personnel and Guidance Journal,* 1979, *57* (6), 317 Used by permission.

figure 4.2 Cognitive template showing reassessment of experiences

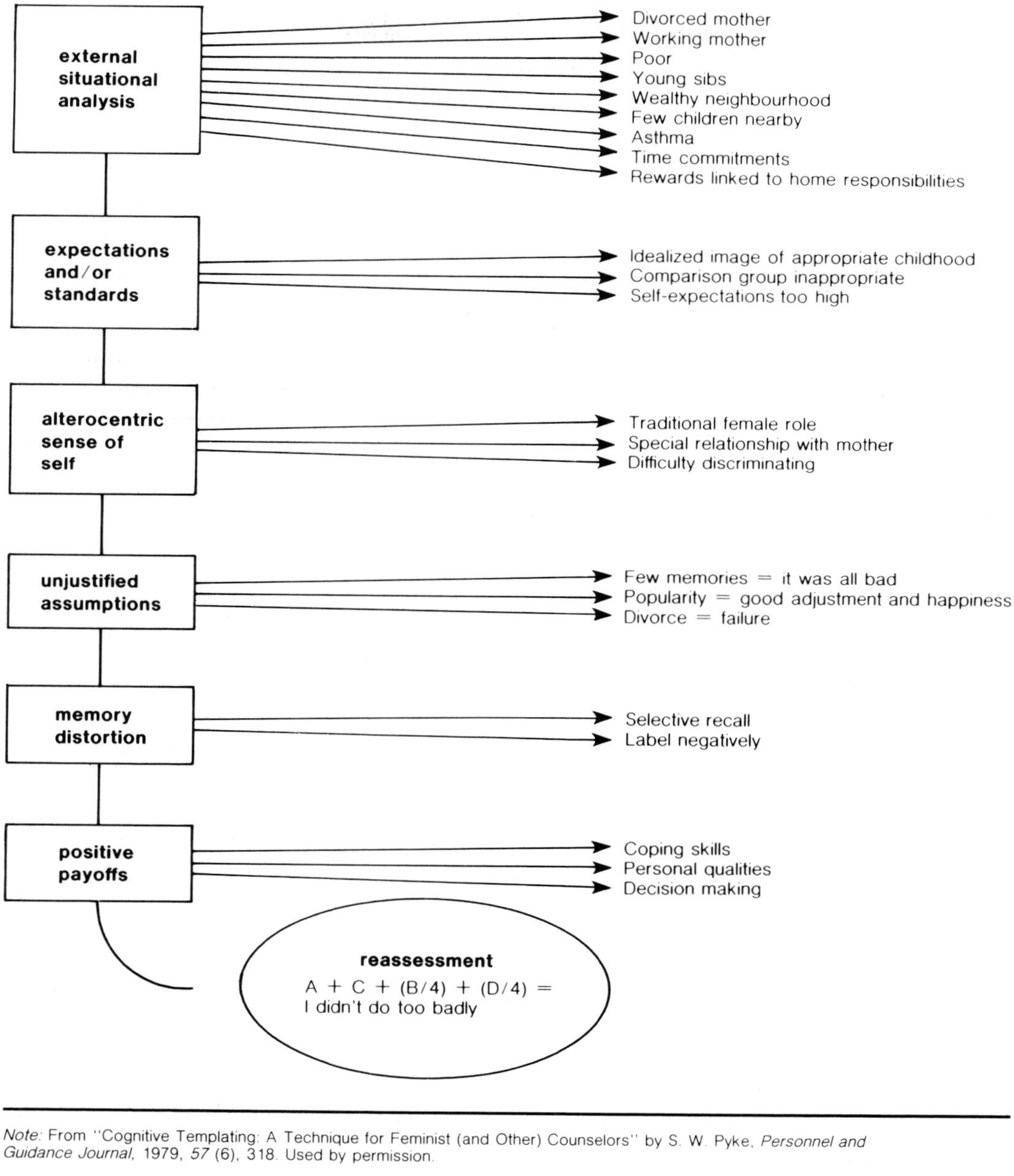

external situational analysis
→ Divorced mother
→ Working mother
→ Poor
→ Young sibs
→ Wealthy neighbourhood
→ Few children nearby
→ Asthma
→ Time commitments
→ Rewards linked to home responsibilities

expectations and/or standards
→ Idealized image of appropriate childhood
→ Comparison group inappropriate
→ Self-expectations too high

alterocentric sense of self
→ Traditional female role
→ Special relationship with mother
→ Difficulty discriminating

unjustified assumptions
→ Few memories = it was all bad
→ Popularity = good adjustment and happiness
→ Divorce = failure

memory distortion
→ Selective recall
→ Label negatively

positive payoffs
→ Coping skills
→ Personal qualities
→ Decision making

reassessment
A + C + (B/4) + (D/4) =
I didn't do too badly

Note: From "Cognitive Templating: A Technique for Feminist (and Other) Counselors" by S. W. Pyke, *Personnel and Guidance Journal*, 1979, *57* (6), 318. Used by permission.

the counselor makes "an attempt to depict some significant factors neglected in Carol's analysis and indicates how these variables force a restructuring of perceptions" (p. 317). In reality almost all counseling techniques, in one way or another, use some of the learning principles underlying cognitive templating, although not always visually.

To see how this works, let us consider two aspects of counselor response: the counselor's values and answering clients' questions.

Valuing

Recall that we mentioned that the level next to responding in the taxonomy is *valuing.* In the taxonomy, valuing is used in its common meaning, referring to the attribution of worth to a thing, a behavior, a goal or purpose, and so forth. Valuing is clearly a process that influences the forming of goals in the counseling setting. The question of what the counselor values, then, has an important influence on how the counselor helps the client formulate the goals of counseling.

We will talk later about how being nonjudgmental is a quality associated with effective counseling. Even so, it is necessary that the counselor be committed to some values in order that he or she be able to maintain a sense of meaningfulness in life. The core question we are concerned with is this: to which types of values, to which logical biases, should the counselor commit himself or herself? The answer to this crucial question becomes abundantly clear when we look at the literature and consider the issues at hand. The primary value to which the counselor must be committed is *freedom,* the value from which all other values are derived. Peterson (1970), in his thorough study of counseling and values, calls freedom the "valuational basis for counseling." Viewing the ultimate task of the school counselor as "helping the individual to become the free person that he potentially is," as I have been suggesting throughout this book, Peterson goes on to speak of the counselor's own values of freedom:

> The essential quality of freedom is that it allows man room to be himself, to be creative, to make choices and be responsible for them. Freedom allows man to choose higher values if he desires. It allows him to follow his own quest for truth, to develop his own philosophy of life. Freedom is a matter of degree. We must talk in terms of *more* or *less* rather than of *presence* or *absence.* Freedom involves man in his individual functioning, in his functioning with others, and in his search for meaning. It has many facets, and man is confronted by choices involving them. Freedom can be at least part of a base from which one can examine and evaluate practice. (p. 182)

As a value from which the counselor works, freedom is an ideal that propels the individual to certain types of actions. Freedom guides the individual in the direction in which to move; it always entices the individual. "Rather than command, dictate, or affirm, freedom as an ideal attracts. It pulls man, for it offers enhanced possibility for fulfillment. It is always out of reach in an absolute sense but at the same time is within reach to a relative degree" (p. 186).

It is easier to speak about freedom as a concept than to experience it as a condition. Many of us, unfortunately, are unable to experience freedom because of constraints within us as well as because of forces from the outside. One factor that might influence the degree of freedom an individual can experience is his or her upbringing. There are also forces exerted upon us by the system: the fact, for example, that a counselor may be required to maintain a professional facade in the agency setting may alter his or her choices as well as the opportunity to choose meaningfully and responsibly.

It is imperative, then, that the counselor be consciously aware of the values to which he or she subscribes. Different types of values require different types of examination. Rosenthal (1955) points out that particularly in the areas of sex, aggression, and authority the moral values of the counselor are important because they touch directly upon the issues typically involved in the client's conflicts. We would agree with these categories, and add race—sex—age stereotyping as equally important.

In conclusion, we should say again that the recognition of freedom as a primary value helps the counselor to help the client develop goals for counseling: goals that will enable the client to function more freely in living. Now, let us look at ways of answering clients' questions.

Answering Clients' Questions

A systematic analysis of the typical counseling interaction will undoubtedly reveal that one of the major forms of communication between counselor and client is the question. The question is a viable and productive medium of communication because it requires an answer and therefore promotes the interactive nature of the relationship between the counselor and client. Questions asked by the counselor are dealt with often in the area of techniques. In this section, we will examine some of the ways in which the counselor might answer questions posed by the client.

First, we must ask, What kinds of questions does the typical client pose to the counselor? There are four basic types: information questions, questions of value, direction questions, and personal questions. Let us examine each individually.

Information questions may be either objective or subjective. What colleges offer degrees in forestry? is an objective question. So are the questions, Where can I find an abortion clinic in this city? What kind of work do you think I am best suited for? and, What were the results of the test I took last month? When such a question is asked, certainly all the counselor has to do is give an answer. This will satisfy the client and provide types of information that may help with his or her plans. But what if the counselor does not know the answer—what should be done then? Might the client not lose confidence because she or he doesn't know?

The solution to this problem is simple. The counselor must acknowledge that she or he does not have the answer. For it is only when the counselor is truthful with the client (as well as with herself or himself) that the client can develop the respect that is a prerequisite for a successful counseling relationship. "If the client asks a question regarding facts," Darley (1950) points out, "and you don't have the facts, it is better to say 'I don't know' rather than to run with a lot of vague generalities or in some other way try to cover up your own ignorance. The client is likely to have more confidence in the interviewer who does not hesitate to admit his ignorance. It would be desirable for the counselor to get these facts later, and to tell the client where to get them."

Felker (1972) takes a different tack. She feels that in many cases when approached with questions the counselor cannot answer, he or she must "turn the table back to the obstinate inquirer." She gives a number of examples:

> The first response you could try is bold-faced and direct. It consists of the counter question, "What do you think the answer is?" A second alternative response builds in a bit of reinforcement for the questioner, and while he basks in the compliment he may decide not to persist in seeking an answer. It goes something like this: "I can see that you devoted a good deal of thought to this issue, and since you seem to be a very critical thinker, let me get your views first." The third approach is one I recommend when you want to bolster your own ego or position. . . . You say something like this: "I've spent a good deal of time thinking about that very question, let me see if your opinions are similar to mine." (p. 684)

Felker's manipulative methods may be adequate for dealing with a hostile questioner who is out to prove how ignorant you are. We include them here not to advocate their unlimited use with sincere clients, but because these methods may be useful with certain types of clients whose needs are not for information, but rather for challenge and confrontation. Moreover, these types of responses are often used inadvertently or unintentionally by counselors who do not feel comfortable when they don't know the right answer.

There is no shame in not knowing, but there is shame in using tricks to cover up one's ignorance unless the intentions or the questioner are objective and provocative.

Benjamin (1969) probably sums up the middle position best when he says, "We ought to supply the information requested when it is feasible and appropriate to do so, but we should always be open to the possibility that there is something behind and beyond the question which is worth getting at" (p. 75). What this means in practice is that we take each question as it appears—receiving and *then* responding—and subjugate the general rule to the specific instance.

Subjective information questions refer to personal information about the client. Why am I feeling this way? or, Is there something wrong with me? are typical questions requiring information that is subjective, interpretive, or downright speculative. These are not, in the technical sense, questions for information but merely assume the form of such questions. "Questions are often disguises for more penetrating and deep concerns," suggest Dimick and Huff (1970). "It is the job of the counselor to assess the nature of the questions—to 'hear' what is meant. . . . When a legitimate request for information is 'heard', then the counselor responds with whatever data resources he may have. When some other request is 'heard', he responds to that need."

Clients often ask for value judgments from the counselor. Particularly in areas where their own value orientation is fuzzy, the client may seek a resolution for a moral dilemma by eliciting from the counselor an evaluative response. But because the counselor may be perceived as an authority figure—or at least an *authoritative* figure—his or her value judgments will be weighed more heavily by the client than they should be. Therefore, the appropriate response in such a situation is to help the client arrive at his or her own moral decisions, rather than imposing moral or value decisions.

When a client seeks information regarding the direction he or she should take (what choice to make, what approach to use, etc.), there is ever present a strong temptation on the counselor's part to tell him or her, particularly if the counselor feels that she or he knows the best answer to the client's problems. This should generally be avoided, however, inasmuch as the client will gain strength if allowed to make his or her own judgments. Certainly, one of the most important goals of counseling is to enable clients to make better decisions, and part of this process may require that the counselor become an active agent in the decision-making process. But to answer a client's decision oriented question with a specific, close-ended answer diminishes significantly the possibility that the client will grow enough to make decisions.

To do this, the counselor should respond to the client's directional questions with questions of his or her own, questions that are designed to help the client arrive at solutions. For example,

Client   Which college do you think I should apply to? Harvard, where I don't have much of a chance of getting accepted, or State, where I can probably get a scholarship?

Counselor   Well, how would you feel about going to Harvard and how would you feel about going to State?

Or,

Client   I'm not sure if I should enroll in that special weight-watchers' program or not. What do you think?

Counselor   What are your feelings about that program?

Note how the counselor, through questioning, is helping the client make his or her own decisions: decisions that are very important for the client's future growth, development, and above all, independence as a person. Giving the client the appropriate response helps the client learn how to answer key decision-making questions.

When the client asks the counselor personal questions—How old are you? or, Are you married?—they are often a source of confusion to the beginning counselor. There is no absolute rule here, and much depends on the kind of question asked. Very personal questions (Do you enjoy oral sex with your wife?) require a different kind of evaluation than seemingly more innocuous questions such as, Where did you go to graduate school? In both cases, however, there is usually more to the question than appears on the surface, and it is the counselor's job to find out what lurks underneath.

Each counselor has to decide for himself or herself how much personal information he or she is willing to give out, but a good rule of thumb is that before answering any personal questions the counselor should have a good idea of why the client is asking them, and what the question really means. This deeper level is not always clear at the outset. As Sue (1979) points out,

> There are many subjective emotional components to even a question such as "How old are you?" The client might actually be asking "Are you competent and qualified, or do you have enough experience to work with me?" Also, questions that are subjective or which ask for personal self-disclosure on the part of the counselor are very sticky. For example, in cross-cultural counseling a question often asked of white counselors from a culturally different client might be "How do you feel about interracial relationships." The question, while it might appear innocuous, is a very loaded one.

Often clients ask personal questions not so much because they desire information but because they feel that if they are willing to share their personal selves with the counselor, the counselor should be willing to share his or her personal self with the client. This may be a fair request, at least on the surface, and yet the position of withholding most personal information seems to have some practical advantages.

In conclusion, then, the counselor should answer questions for information if the answers are helpful to the client, give some personal information, and acquaint the client with resources he or she can use for further answers to questions. The counselor should avoid answering moral or value judgment questions or directional questions and encourage the client to arrive at his or her own answers to these questions.

The section that follows will illustrate how the counselor's use of questions can yield practical benefits in the counseling setting.

Practical Considerations

A counselor's skillful use of questions is demonstrated in this transcription taken from an individual counseling session between Dr. Cirillo (DR) and Mrs. Jackson (MJ). The meeting was conducted in an urban social agency setting. Mrs. Jackson and her three boys, aged 14 (Alonzo), 11 (Willi), and 9 (Stan), have been in family counseling with Dr. Cirillo, and now Mrs. Jackson has entered individual counseling with Dr. Cirillo, as well. This is her second session of individual counseling. There are several things we should observe in the interaction. First, note how this young man allows the emotional tone and the objective content of the session to be determined by the client. He allows the client to "lead the way," and he follows her lead with his response. She is the determiner of change; he the catalyst.

Second, we should note how skillfully he parries questions when necessary, avoiding some of the obvious pitfalls. You will see too that he answers questions directly when this is helpful to the client, and when he feels that he understands the intent behind the question. Finally, note how Dr. Cirillo combines all the qualities of counselor sensitivity and counselor effectiveness with the perspicacity of a keen mind, and how he helps the client "discover" parts of herself as she works to resolve the entrenched family conflict. Deletions are indicated by ellipses.

MJ (*Out of breath, panting*) I'm sorry I'm late, Doctor, but my car wouldn't start on the way over here, and then the lady who comes to take care of Stan didn't come over. Guess I'm lucky that I got over here at all.

DR (*Gesturing to the chair*) Why don't you have a seat?

MJ Thank you. Say, I don't remember if I asked you last time about that note.

DR Note?

MJ The one for the school. I think that the principal said she needed it. I promised Alonzo's teacher that I'd bring it in with me when I go up to see him, and he said that was good and that I didn't have to have Alonzo bring it with him to school.

DR No, I don't believe we discussed this.

MJ I just need a note that Alonzo is coming to see you so that the principal can know. She said a note from you would be enough, and that she could get the information.

DR I am a bit confused about this. What do you want me to say in the note? Does Alonzo know about the note?

MJ Oh, just to say that Alonzo is seeing you and that . . . (*she hesitates*) . . . that he needs extra work for school. Tell the principal that he needs a tutor for school.

DR I see. You want a note that Alonzo is seeing me for counseling and that he needs a tutor for school. Is that it?

MJ Oh yes, that would be good. And if you write it, I'll take it with me, and give it to Alonzo's teacher when I see him. He said he would take it to the principal for me.

DR Well, I'm a little confused. I don't believe we discussed anything about tutoring. Why does the principal want this note?

MJ Oh, I see, . . . the note. You see, Mrs. Flynn (the social worker assigned to the Jackson family) said she could get me the money for the tutor if the principal gives her a letter. So when I asked her she said that I needed to get a note from you first.

DR I see. If I write the note, you will receive extra money in your check. The note has to say that Alonzo needs extra tutoring.

MJ That's it. Then they pay sixteen dollars extra for the tutor. See, if you write the note, then we can get the money.

DR Oh, I'm beginning to understand now. The note will help you get sixteen dollars extra every two weeks.

MJ That's it.

DR How will you use that money? The extra sixteen dollars.

MJ You see, I'll buy things for the family. We need more money for food. Why I hardly have enough to even buy a meat dinner on Sundays. We also need clothes. Willi needs a new winter coat, and Stan has to have his shoes fixed.

DR So the money will not actually be used for tutoring, then?

MJ Oh, you see, I could spend the money on that too. Sure, that's a good idea.

DR Have you mentioned this to Alonzo? I don't recall our discussing it when we were all together.

MJ Oh, yeah, I'm going to tell Alonzo. Soon as I get the note I'm going to tell him.

DR So in other words, you will tell him *after* you have the note. Not before.

MJ Oh, I could tell him if you wanted me to. I don't know what's the difference.

DR Well, we should consider the possibility that Alonzo may resent having his name used in a note when he doesn't directly benefit from it. And when he hasn't given us permission to use his name. Maybe we should discuss it with him when we are all together. I believe that will be this Thursday.

MJ Oh, good. That's a good idea.

MJ So, if I go to work, then I have to leave the kids all night. There just isn't any day job I could take, and I don't think that they can be on their own all night. I told you what happened to my aunt's children when she left them alone, and I don't want that to happen to mine.

DR That certainly makes sense. I get the impression that you feel you are protecting your children by staying with them. Is my impression correct?

MJ Yes. I think that I am keeping them out of trouble. And I know that I am.

DR How does that make you feel as a mother?

MJ *(Pauses, thinking)* I don't know what you mean.

DR Well, what I want to know is how you feel being so devoted a mother. After all, you have mentioned a few times that many of your friends, and even your aunt, don't pay nearly as much attention to their children as you do. How do you feel being so devoted to your children.

MR Why, I feel real good. Why shouldn't I?

DR No reason. I just wanted to know. How do the children make you feel? Do they appreciate what you do for them?

MJ *(Hesitantly)* I guess so. You know how kids are. They're too busy trying to have a good time that they don't know what you're doing for them. So long as it gets done. I don't know.

DR *(Not pressing the point, but reinforcing the client)* I think that you show many fine qualities as a mother, Mrs. Jackson. Probably even more than you realize.

There are two things that should be pointed out at this time. In the first segment, note how the counselor probed Mrs. Jackson's reason for the request for the principal's note until he found out the "real" purpose behind her request: her stipend would be increased as a result of writing the note. He sensed that this might be subtly unfair to Alonzo. It should be mentioned that in the family meetings Alonzo often expressed the feeling that his mother took advantage of him; that she made him do chores for the neighbors and then kept the money he earned. Mrs. Jackson's rationale was that it wasn't good for a young boy to have too much money. Dr. Cirillo felt that he might be getting involved in this conflict before there was an opportunity to fully explore it, and he therefore suggested that it be saved for the family session. His response to the request (to the question) was made only after fully considering all of its implications. He could have easily agreed at once to write the note, but that may have caused many hard feelings later on.

In the second segment, we see an example of how the counselor "retreated" from his probing when he realized that he was treading on ground that the client was not yet emotionally ready to explore. He began to allude to a subtle theme that he had noticed during the family sessions: that Mrs. Jackson felt her children did not appreciate her or what she was doing for them. Dr. Cirillo believed that this unexpressed feeling was at least in part responsible for her taking advantage of them economically. He got the sense, as he approached this subject, however, that the client was not ready to talk about it, and he let her gently lead him away from it, on to safer ground.

MJ So the problem, Doctor, is that if I don't go to work I'm just not going to have enough money to take care of my children. And, you know what. . . .

DR What?

MJ That Mrs. Flynn don't believe me. She thinks we have enough to live on. I told her, "Why don't you just try living on my check." That's what I told her!

DR So Mrs. Flynn gives you the feeling that you should be "making do" with what you've got. She can't understand how difficult it is for you.

MJ You bet she can't. What do you think I should do? How am I going to get enough money to take care of my family? I don't like to talk about this in front of the kids. I think it gets them upset.

DR So you try to protect them from the problems you are having. You don't want them to worry with you. *(Long pause, during which the counselor reflects to himself, experiencing the client's feelings)* You want to carry your problems all by yourself.

MJ It won't do no good for them to worry. Won't do no good at all.

DR But maybe it will help them understand what *you're* going through. I notice that you try to protect them. They're big boys now—especially Alonzo—and maybe it wouldn't hurt for them to know what you're going through for them.

MJ They sure don't know now.

DR How do you think they would react if they knew all the difficulties you have to face? How would they feel?

MJ I don't know. I guess they would be mad at me.

DR Mad?

MJ For not being a better mother, you know. For not giving them a good home.

DR So by not telling them your problems, you feel they will think you are a better mother.

MJ I guess so.

In this segment, the counselor, by responding facilitatively to the client's communications, helps the client gain an insight into how she feels. Later on in the treatment, Mrs. Jackson realizes that her feelings about sharing her problems with the boys are ambivalent. On the one hand, she tries to protect them by refusing to share her problems with them. On the other hand, she resents having to carry the burden alone. Her recognition of this will take time, but today she has made an important first step.

Finally, let us look at the close of this session. As Mrs. Jackson stands up to leave, a short exchange takes place between her and Dr. Cirillo. This brief exchange illustrates how the counselor's appropriate responses makes growth for the client a realistic possibility.

MJ Look, Doc. I'll talk to Alonzo before Thursday. I'll explain to him all about the note.

DR That will be fine, Mrs. Jackson. Also, you might keep in mind that you are asking me to lie in the note.

MJ Lie? How?

DR You want me to say that Alonzo needs tutoring. We haven't even discussed that. I don't know that he needs tutoring.

MJ You know, I never thought of it that way. I really don't want you to lie, so I don't know why I asked that. We never did talk about it, did we?

DR No, we haven't. Does he need tutoring?

MJ *(Laughs).* To tell you the truth, Doc, I don't know. I'm going to talk to that boy when I get home, and if he does need tutoring, I'm going to see that he gets it. If he don't, then we can forget about the note.

SUMMARY

In this chapter we looked at the helping process in some detail, and a few of the main interventions and techniques that are widely used were outlined. We focused first on the initial counseling interview, and considered ways in which that interview could be used constructively. We also examined some of the difficulties the counselor faces in working out a termination procedure, either for the initial interview or for the entire counseling process. In both cases, it was noted how the opportunity for future contact between client and counselor should be maintained through closing statements. Next we looked at seven of the commonly used eclectic counseling techniques: clarification, reflection, probing, silence, interpretation, empathic response, and investigating alternatives.

Next, we considered some of the ways of facilitating client growth and change: the essential core of the helping process. First, we considered how the counselor responds to the client. We began by looking at "responding" as a level on the taxonomy of affective development, and considered its implications as part of the affective counseling interaction. I pointed out the technique "cognitive restructuring," which embodies many of the principles of facilitative response to the client. We also looked at "valuing," the following level, and asked, How does the counselor's process of valuing influence the formulation of counseling goals?

We then turned our attention to the issue of answering clients' questions. Different viewpoints on this matter were presented, and some case examples were examined. We noted that it is important that, before the counselor responds to a question, he or she understand the full implication of what the client is asking. We then considered effective types of responses.

Finally, we looked at some case material to see how these principles of counselor response translate into action. We noted how a mother of three boys learned to express some of her ambivalent feelings in the counseling setting. The counselor used a synthesis of techniques and personal characteristics in helping the client gain insight and in responding to her requests.

The Counseling Relationship

The quality of the counseling relationship is the most critical variable in all counseling efforts. Without a "facilitative" relationship—one that provides a climate for growth and for self-exploration—there can be little or no success in counseling. We can define a *facilitative relationship* as one that offers a connection between the emotional elements necessary for growth and change. This involves certain specific personality qualities (empathy, genuineness, etc.) as well as certain kinds of communications inside the relationship—called facilitative responses—which make free expression of feelings easier to articulate.

In the previous chapter, we explored some of the ways that the counseling process can get off to a promising start and looked at a few of the main counseling interventions and techniques, as well as some representative case material. In the following chapter, we will look in more detail at the role and function of the school counselor. In this chapter, however, to establish a point of orientation from which we can proceed, we shall focus our attention exclusively on the behavioral and dynamic components of the counseling relationship, paying special attention to how these components affect the counseling process.

We shall begin by asking how the counselor can find and develop those qualities that have been shown to be most related to successful counseling outcomes. Next, we will consider some practical counseling guidelines counselors can use, integrating their own personal feelings. While I would maintain that the counselor's feelings have priority over his or her actions, I want to point out that there are some important principles underlying what the counselor does, and that the counselor should be aware of exactly how what he or she does affects the client.

THE EFFECTIVE COUNSELOR

Probably no question has received more attention in counseling theory and research than the question, What qualities are indicative of the *potential* and *actual* effectiveness of the counselor? The attention this question has received is justified for several reasons: first, it helps us better understand the connection between the subtle factors that contribute to counseling success; second, it is important to counselor educators who must make crucial decisions in the selection and training of students of counseling; third, it encourages aspiring counselors to find within themselves and strengthen those qualities that have been indicated as predictors of successful counseling; fourth, it helps in developing techniques and strategies that are derivatives of effective counselor qualities; and finally, it assists trainers and researchers in determining the likely outcome of specific counseling interactions, based on tested criteria of counseling effectiveness.

Unfortunately, despite the abundance of research and exposition (or perhaps because of it), this very important question is still surrounded by much confusion, contention, and obscurity, and it is not entirely clear at this point exactly what qualities make one counselor more effective than another. We will examine the semantic problems that make this research difficult and the findings of some contemporary research on this subject, and summarize the consensus of thinking to date.

Language Problems: A Source of Confusion

The language problem is one of the major obstacles in tackling the question, What makes a counselor effective? When we attempt to describe an effective counselor—or, more precisely, when we attempt to enumerate those qualities we believe make the counselor effective, we are forced to rely on multidimensional words to condense and encapsulate the multifaceted behavioral and emotional matrices we wish to describe. Words such as *genuine, sincere, nonpossessive, honest, warm, empathic, accepting,* and so on are the closest we can come to pinpointing the very human, idiosyncratic, and complex qualities that contribute to counseling success.

But words inevitably fail to define effective counseling, and more importantly, to differentiate effective counseling traits from ineffective counseling traits. There are too many words with too many overlapping meanings, and not enough specific, descriptive meanings of the words we use to prove of much help in answering our questions. Before we can confidently approach the question of what qualities make an effective counselor, we must come to grips with this problem of language and decide at the outset what we are going to do to make words work for us.

Our problem can be stated simply as follows: if we call X the quality associated with effective counseling, what can we do to determine whether a counselor demonstrates this quality? The question is not easily answered. Let us say X is empathy, and we want to determine if Counselor A has empathy for the client. We could, of course, administer an empathy-rating scale and look at the score. But what does this actually tell us? Certainly we would not want to define empathy solely as such-and-such a score on the test. And what is empathy? Can we formulate an objective definition of empathy that will separate empathic counselors from nonempathic counselors? This has been a refractory problem that has plagued not only research in empathy but almost all studies on counselor qualities in counseling effectiveness.

Kurtz and Grummon (1972), in reviewing the issue of empathy, for example, have found much semantic confusion in the studies: "These studies have used several different ways of conceptualizing and measuring empathy, but it is not altogether clear whether they deal with one variable or several different variables employing the same label" (p. 106). They speak of an ambiguity that exists in the literature; an ambiguity that is the result of not being able to clearly define empathy in terms of empirical evidence. Gellen (1970) tackles the problem in a different way. Suggesting at the beginning of his paper that "empathy is measured by the counselor's capacity to express affect rather than by the extent to which he is able to communicate his perceptions of another person's feelings and attitudes," he goes on to measure empathic response physiologically by measuring finger blood volume. In this way he is able to establish empirical criteria for empathy: "If a counselor's finger blood volume level approaches 'Q' while listening to a specific taped dramatic dialogue, he can be said to be exhibiting the quality we shall call empathy." While such a method does allow us to be objective about what is essentially a subjective quality, it still does not explain what the quality is. It is helpful in this respect to keep in mind Ralph Waldo Emerson's idea that "Words are also actions, and actions are a kind of words." In all our efforts to describe the qualities of an effective counselor, we must attempt to link the words to some type of specifiable actions that give meaning to the words.

Another word that gives us trouble is *effective*. We must be able to define accurately and objectively what we intuitively mean by *effective counseling* in order for us to evaluate seriously its component qualities. The term sounds good, but what does it actually mean? Do we mean that counseling effects a change in the client? Do we mean *counseling efficiency*, the ability to accomplish a wide range of objectives over a brief period of time? Do we evaluate effectiveness by the client's impressions and feelings about the treatment, or do we allow the counselor to be the primary judge of its success or failure? Possibly we determine effectiveness by the degree of mitigation of the so called "presenting symptoms" or "behavioral problems." This issue is far from resolved, and over the past few years there has appeared a growing sentiment, matched by a more persistent effort, among counselor educators and researchers to define this term *effectiveness* more accurately and unambiguously.

Heikkinen and Wegner (1973) provide a comprehensive review of studies utilizing the Minnesota Multiphasic Personality Inventory, a standardized personality test, as a measure of characteristics indicative of counselor effectiveness. Cattell, Eber, and Tatsuoka (1970) have attempted to predict counselor effectiveness from scores on the Sixteen Personality Factor Questionnaire (16PF), and Shelton (1973) has used the 16PF as an indicator in a later study. Walton and Sweeney (1969), in an oft-quoted paper, offer a survey of studies that attempt to pinpoint predictors of counseling effectiveness. They conclude that there are no clear and decisive definitions of counselor effectiveness. In most of the studies they investigated, counselor effectiveness was measured by such unquantifiable and unverifiable ratings as supervisor ratings, peer ratings, and administrator ratings, without any uniform criteria. A widely used instrument, The Counselor Evaluation Rating Scale (CERS), has been shown to be an accurate standardized instrument for measuring the effectiveness of counselor trainees in practicum or internship settings (Loesch & Rucker, 1977).

Even before we confront the equally difficult problem of measuring a quality once it has been adequately defined, we must tackle the problem of language. To deal with this, I will attempt throughout this chapter to describe each characteristic as precisely and in terms of as many observable and measurable behavioral objectives as is feasible.

The Commonsense Bias

A second problem that confronts us at the start of our discussion is what we call the "commonsense bias." This bias asserts that some positions are ipso facto logical and sensible; for when we speak of common sense, we imply that some things are obvious even before logical scrutiny, that they are irrefutable or at least assumed to be true until proven otherwise. In reality, however, common sense is always a culturally relative term. What may be commonsensical to a middle-class counselor may be nonsensical or downright wrong to a person from a different culture.

Common sense is a term that is in fact weak but that implies a strong sense of verification. The commonsense bias includes value judgments, culturally-based perceptions, and intuitive beliefs. To humanistic counselors, for example, there is a commonsense position that acceptance, warmth, empathy, and genuineness are positive counseling characteristics. This may or may not be true—there is evidence to support both the affirmative and negative positions—but in any case, it would be best not to prejudge any specific quality or set of qualities until the evidence is assembled and evaluated. The only way to avoid the commonsense bias is to assume that nothing is true until it is proven to be true!

The Problem of Generalization

Finally, we face what we call the problem of _generalization_. Is there in fact such a thing as an effective counselor, or are different counselors effective for different reasons to different degrees with different clients? There is some evidence to support both positions. While some studies have shown that there are universally important counselor qualities, other studies have indicated that certain traits work well with some clients but not with others. We shall keep in mind, as we explore the literature, that to generalize from a single study to a universal proposition is often an unsound policy.

Conclusions

Despite these persistent problems, a good deal has been learned about qualities that contribute to effective counseling outcomes. Certainly we can offer some valid generalizations that would most likely be met with hearty agreement by those in the profession and that would also stand up to experimental scrutiny. We know, for example, that the counselor's personal traits play a vital part in the counseling interaction and are determinants of counseling effectiveness. We know, too, that there is no positive correlation between counseling knowledge and counseling effectiveness (Joslin, 1965). We know that a counselor's abilities to communicate effectively, to act maturely, to listen attentively, to work as a role model all exert a significant influence upon the counseling outcome. But what does all of this tell us? How can we translate such statements into behavioral equivalents? Again, we are left without a clear answer to our questions.

So we shall examine some empirical research as well as theoretical models that attempt to clarify the question, What qualities are related to successful counseling outcomes? As we do this we should keep in mind the problems just outlined, but at the same time recognize the importance of considering this question and all of its ramifications. We shall see that although the body of evidence is not conclusive and is at times confusing, there is enough information to indicate those qualities that are most likely related to effective counseling.

WHAT MAKES COUNSELING EFFECTIVE: AN OVERVIEW

Predictably, many of the qualities that we intuitively associate with effective counseling have been borne out in the experimental studies. The value of these studies is that they confirm empirically what our philosophical premises imply are the qualities of an effective counselor. It would seem evident, for example, that an effective counselor would be less prejudiced than an ineffective counselor, and Milliken (1965) has indeed confirmed this in a study. We would also assume that the counselor's attitudes exert a crucial influence on the ability to deal effectively with clients. Jackson and Thompson (1971) have supported this contention in a study in which effective counselors were found to be more positive in their attitudes toward self, most clients, and toward counseling itself. Their conclusions were that the most important factor contributing to counselor effectiveness "is the feeling that the other person is a human being who is friendly, able, and worthy, and an approach to the counseling situation that is freeing, altruistic, and important." Allen (1967) too found that "the effective counselor is a person who is on relatively good terms with his own emotional experience and that the ineffective counselor is one who is relatively uneasy in regard to the character of his inner life." Similar findings have been obtained in other studies, and research has supported the idea that counselor effectiveness is a specific set of counselor qualities that professionals agree about. For example, Trotzer (1976), in investigating how people involved in the counseling field perceive counseling effectiveness, found that "all groups associated with the counseling profession view counselor performance in much the same light" and that this includes those traits supported by the research.

However, the research on counseling effectiveness, we must point out, has not been consistent. Rowe, Murphy, and DeCsipkes (1975), in a thorough review and evaluation of the empirical evidence, found that it was virtually impossible to establish significant relationships between specific counselor characteristics and measures of counselor effectiveness. Loesch, Crane, and Rucker (1978), continuing the work of the earlier study, confirmed these conclusions. This is why much of the important findings in this area involves not measures of counselor qualities and counseling outcomes per se, but rather more indirect indices.

Truax and Lister (1970), for example, in a controversial study concerning the employment of paraprofessional counseling aides at a residential vocational rehabilitation center, found some startling results that bear upon the issue of counseling effectiveness. In attempting to assess how paraprofessionals should be deployed, they set up three conditions for the treatment of cases that ranged from personality disorders to mental retardation. Under the first condition, the experienced counselor worked alone with the client in the traditional manner; under the second condition, the counselor was assisted by a counselor aide who worked under maximum supervisory conditions; under the third condition, the counselor aide functioned autonomously as a counselor, utilizing the experienced counselor only in a supervisory role. All clients were randomly assigned in order to assure that each condition included clients of varying degrees of severity. Progress was evaluated by the use of a rating scale that measured the client's evidence of rehabilitation in his or her work efforts.

When the results were tabulated and analyzed, a most interesting anomaly emerged. To their surprise, the experimenters found that the clients who made the greatest improvement were those who were treated by the untrained counselor aides alone; next in order of improvement were the clients treated by the experienced counselor alone; lowest in improvement were those treated conjointly by the experienced counselor and the untrained aide.

To explain these results and their conclusion "that the effectiveness of counseling and psychotherapy, as measured by constructive change in client functioning, is largely independent of the counselor's level of training and theoretical orientation," they suggested that the untrained aides fared better because they were "innately more health engendering than the professional counselors." While they do not fully explain what is meant by "health engendering," they refer to such counselor qualities as "empathic understanding, non-possessive warmth, and genuineness." The important point here is that *counselor knowledge and counselor training had no positive effect on counseling outcome;* on the contrary, it seemed to minimize the effects of the counseling. What did emerge as important was the attitude and feelings of the practitioners—their warmth and genuineness.

Because of the controversial nature of these findings, this study was followed by a criticism (McArthur, 1970; and Sieka, Taylor, Thomson, & Muthard, 1971), that contested the experimental integrity of the study and the validity of the conclusions, and a rejoinder (Truax, 1972). On the whole, however, Truax's and Lister's findings appear to hold their own weight and are in accord with other studies (Poser, 1966) that have arrived at similar conclusions.

One of the most important contributors to the literature on qualities of counselor effectiveness is Robert Carkhuff, who, along with his collaborators, Bernard Berenson and Charles Truax, have published prolifically in this area. Truax and Carkhuff (1967) have found a common thread that runs through all of the divergent theories of counseling and psychotherapy:

> In one way or another, all have emphasized the importance of the therapist's ability to be integrated, mature, genuine, authentic, or congruent in his relationship with the patient. They have all stressed also the importance of the

therapist's ability to provide a nonthreatening, trusting, safe or secure atmosphere by his acceptance, nonpossessive warmth, unconditional positive regard, or love. Finally, virtually all theories of psychotherapy emphasize that for the therapist to be helpful he must be accurately empathetic, be "with" the client, be understanding, or grasp the patient's meaning. (p. 25)

As the research undertaken by Carkhuff and his associates progressed, new dimensions were discovered and counselor rating scales for these additional qualities were developed. The core conditions currently associated with Carkhuff's work are empathy, respect, warmth, genuineness, self-disclosure, concreteness, confrontation, and an immediacy of relationship.

Tyler (1969) has suggested, and we would agree, that "the qualities most essential for counselors are the basic attitudes that make it possible to accept and understand other people." While this is a general description, in many ways it is more precise than the complex adjectival descriptions that are confusing in their ambiguity and redundancy.

Carl Rogers's Contribution

One of the most important researchers in this area is Carl Rogers, a man whose persistence and tenacity have earned him a well-deserved following and the respect of even his harshest critics. For the past thirty years, Rogers has been doggedly attempting to evaluate, in a precise, empirical manner, the qualities of an effective counselor, what he has called the "conditions of therapy." His well-known terminology includes *empathy, genuineness,* and *unconditional positive regard* as its key words. In a massive research effort, Rogers and his colleagues (Rogers et al., 1967) have attempted to test thoroughly his assumption that,

> regardless of what method or technique the therapist uses . . . effective therapy would take place if the therapist fulfilled the following three "conditions": a.) The therapist responds as the real person he actually is in this relationship at the moment. He employes no artificial front. . . . b.) The therapist senses and expresses the client's felt meaning, catching what the client communicates as it seems to the client. This condition was termed "empathy." c.) The therapist experiences a warm and positive acceptance toward the client. (p. 10)

Rogers was attempting to test out, in other words, the hypothesis, that effective counselor personality factors, what he refers to as "the conditions for therapy," outweighed all other considerations in contributing to the therapeutic efficacy in the counseling process. With such findings, we would be able not only to see which qualities are important but also to understand in which specific way each quality contributes to the client's improvement. Rogers's study attempted to resolve this very complex issue once and for all, and in many ways it has succeeded in its goal. Unfortunately, there were a couple of serious problems that limit its application, and these problems should be presented first.

First, the subjects in his study were divided between institutionalized "schizophrenics" and "normals" who were recruited from various community and social organizations. The experiment, therefore, involved a rather specialized population, atypical of those who seek the help of a counselor. Second, as in all studies of therapeutic efficacy, there are many serious questions regarding the validity of the experiment in relation to what it attempts to measure. Finally, despite all of Rogers's positive results, he was compelled by the evidence to conclude that "in many respects the therapy group taken as a whole showed no greater evidence of positive outcome than did the matched and paired control group" (p. 80).

These considerations aside, however, Rogers's research did shed light on what qualities are important to the counselor. The crux of his findings are found in the following excerpt:

> In spite of the subtlety of the variables being measured, in spite of the crudity of the instruments used in measuring them, there appears to be substantial evidence that *relationships rated high in a sensitively accurate empathic understanding and high in genuineness as perceived by the patient, were associated with favorable personality changes and reductions in various forms of pathology,* particularly in schizophrenic pathology. (p. 86, italics added)

It is clear from these findings that qualities of the counselor, such as empathy, genuineness, and positive regard, do play an important role in counseling, but it is still unclear how these qualities work toward effecting whatever we determine to be the "goal" in the treatment.

Probably the most successful way to consider the question of effective counselor characteristics is to recognize the simple principle that counseling situations are not separate and distinct from our everyday activities. Carkhuff (1966) explains the relationship this way:

> Counseling and psychotherapy . . . are simply additional instances of all interpersonal processes. . . . There is no evidence to suggest that these helping processes are any more or less critical than parent-child, teacher-student, and other significant human relationships. . . . The direct implication of this proposition is that *the same dimensions which are effective in the other instances of human encounters are effective in the counseling and therapeutic processes.* (p. 424, italics added)

It may well be, as Carkhuff suggests, that the very qualities that make us likeable and effective persons in everyday life are the same qualities that contribute to counseling effectiveness. Let us consider for a moment the implications of such a statement: first, it implies that effective counselors are also effective (or successful) as spouses, parents, and citizens. For if the qualities that Rogers, Carkhuff, and others have suggested are important for counselors are evaluated carefully, they are clearly desirable in all human beings. Secondly, it emphasizes the priority of counselor qualities over counselor technique in respect to positive growth and change in the client. This would require us to look at the "counselor as a person" over the "counselor as a practitioner." The counselor's personality and spirit would take precedence over degrees and formal training: we are compelled to ask, Who are you—what are you?, rather than, What degree do you have from which school? Finally, it implies that counselors who do not possess these personal qualities are at a disadvantage in working with their clients.

The question then reduces itself to this: What is it about a person—counselor or otherwise—that contributes to his or her ability to help others, to relate meaningfully with others, to add to the lives of one's fellow people? To approach this very difficult question, we have divided the traditional counselor qualities into three major headings: *knowing oneself, understanding others,* and *relating to others*—and we shall look at each of these broad categories to study the relationship among the specific qualities subsumed under each.

KNOWING ONESELF

^{understanding yourself}

Before a counselor can attempt to understand a client, before the counselor is able to reach out and touch another, she or he must have an objective and satisfying understanding of herself or himself. Counselors must be able to recognize and accept strengths and limitations, to understand in which areas success is likely to be found and which area is more open to failure. To help the counselor better understand ways of assessing himself or herself with respect to counseling effectiveness, we have listed the three personality characteristics most essential to effective counseling: security, trust, and courage.

Security *self-confidence / self respect.*

The prerequisites to security are self-confidence and self-respect. The types of feelings that these create within individuals are inevitably communicated to all with whom they come in contact. The secure counselor must be free from fear and anxiety, must maintain an objective and flexible view of himself or herself. Milliken and Kirchner (1971) found that "the more anxious counselors were less accurate in their ability to recall words spoken and feelings expressed in simulated interviews" (p. 14). Anxiety can only be reduced when one feels good about oneself—when one likes oneself—and recognizes the irrational nature of the anxiety.

Insecure counselors tend to act more defensively with their clients than do secure counselors. They fear the client's anger and rejection and consequently attempt more to *please* than to *help* the client. Insecure counselors may also take advantage of their clients, manipulating a client into meeting the unhealthy needs of the counselor. Secure counselors, on the other hand, know their own ground and feel comfortable standing on it: they are unshakable and strong; a healthy model for the client.

Security, as a personal quality, also offers counselors a strategic advantage in the performance of their duties. If counselors know who they are and are comfortable with the knowledge, they are then more likely to allow clients to be themselves. Secure counselors have no need to shape clients in their own images; they are confident enough to allow clients to develop at their own rates and in their own directions.

Trust

Trust is a basic quality that develops during the early stages of life. To be able to trust another, in its simplest form, is to be able to give to another, to receive from another, and to depend upon another. To be able to trust and to be trustworthy are different sides of the same coin: people who experience difficulty trusting others are usually themselves untrustworthy.

The counselor who is suspicious, who questions every person's motives, whose cynicism colors all interactions is unlikely to relate to clients in a manner that contributes to growth and adjustment. All too often untrusting counselors attribute feelings and ideas to clients not because the client has expressed them, but rather because the counselor considers such ideas and feelings common to all people. The distrustful counselor might say, for example, "I am certain that this client doesn't pay the slightest bit of attention to what I say." When asked the reason for feeling this way, it turns out that she or he believes most people do not listen to others, do not trust others.

Trust, unfortunately, is a quality that is difficult to learn. So deeply rooted is it in the personality that the quality of trust must be considered one of the foundations of all subsequent personality development. Counselors who are not trusting would do best to seek their own individual counseling to resolve the problems in this area of their emotional development.

The Courage to Counsel

feelings directed towards counsel. (is) anger.

Counseling demands a special kind of courage. While each of us wants to be liked, to be admired, to be respected—to be loved—counselors must at times place many of their own feelings aside; they must remain ungratified in order for clients to prosper and grow. The committed counselor must be willing to bear the often unjustified brunt of the client's anger—an anger that, although self-inspired, inevitably becomes directed toward the counselor during the course of the treatment. The counselor must be willing to feel a profound and distressing sense of "aloneness" as the client, progressing during the treatment, grows away, becomes autonomous.

The courage required of counselors is much like the courage required of parents. In both cases, stronger persons—powerful forces in another's life—must be emotionally capable of relinquishing their strength and allowing the other to become stronger. The courageous counselor finds that she or he has enough self-confidence, enough self-belief, enough security in her or his job and person, that she or he does not retreat in the face of adversity, does not waver in the heat of anger.

The true courage of the counselor is found in a willingness to give away a part of self without recompense, knowing that inner sources will always bring strength. Counselors are courageous insofar as they are able to confront the challenges before them, bravely and with dedication and hope.

UNDERSTANDING OTHERS

Open-Mindedness

Open-mindedness in the counseling setting may be defined as freedom from fixed preconceptions and an attitude of open receptivity to that which the client is expressing. Open-minded counselors are able to accommodate clients' values, insights, feelings, and perceptions that are different from their own. Moreover, they are able to experience and interact with the client throughout a wide breadth and range of feelings, since this flexible frame of reference does not find itself restricted by set expectation. Open-mindedness, in its sense of combined accommodation and receptivity, produces the second important quality of the effective counselor: *perceptiveness*.

The quality of open-mindedness also implies the ability to listen, to respond, to interact with the client, free from the constraints of imposing value criteria.

Listen respond and react with client.

A Nonjudgmental Attitude

The open-minded counselor is also *nonjudgmental.* This does not mean that he or she has no personal values, or is anomic or amoral; on the contrary, the effective counselor should have a well thought-out and meaningful sense of values with which he or she feels comfortable. The quality of being non-judgmental "means that the counselor (refrains) from judging the guilt or innocence of the *client;* it does not mean that the counselor may not objectively judge the *attitudes, standards or actions* of the client. The client is hurt when *he* is judged; he is not necessarily hurt if his behavior is evaluated" (Biestek, 1953). As Sue (1979) conceptualizes it, in terms of a level of counselor functioning within the total context of the counseling interaction,

There are three levels of human behavior interaction. First, there is a level of observation *(descriptive)* where a person describes behaviors. For example, a counselor who sees a client avoid eye contact can describe it behaviorally and even quantify it. The second level is an *interpretive* one of which the counselor attempts to add meaning to what he or she observes. For example, the counselor can assume that avoidance of eye contact is due to shyness, unassertiveness, or sneakiness. Motivation is imputed on to the behavior. The third level which is most damaging, is that of *evaluation/judging.* A judgmental act is one where the avoidance of eye contact and whatever motives it implies are presented as bad. It is the imputing of "badness" or "goodness" [to behaviors] which is damaging and tends to cause inability to establish rapport.

The nonjudgmental counselor is able to participate effectively in a counseling interaction, in a relationship of therapeutic benefit in which the client holds a differing set of values, and to accept the client as she or he is, for what he or she is. Acceptance, according to Blocher (1966), means simply, "a belief in the worth of the client," and this belief can only become operative when the counselor is open-minded enough to accept the client without restrictive value judgments.

The importance of openness in the counseling setting, and its manifestation as a counselor personality characteristic, has been discussed by Combs (1976), who makes the point that the secure counselor, through his or her personal openness, helps the client improve in different areas of growth:

Openness . . . is a function of an attitude, which regards the confrontation of life as, not only possible but, even, enjoyable and rewarding. We have talked much in the theory of counseling about the importance of the counselor's remaining unshockable and demonstrating for his client his own willingness to look at events without fear or hesitation. Mostly we have sought these goals because it made it more possible for the client to look at his problems. But the counselor's demonstration of openness to experience is much more than a technique for the facilitation of talking. It is a most important teaching technique which provides the client with an experience which may add considerably to his strength and stature. (pp. 48–49)

Sensitivity

Sensitivity is a prime factor in contributing to counselor effectiveness. While open-mindedness makes possible a comprehensive and accurate view of the client, sensitivity—a cognitive as well as an emotional response to the client as a total individual—makes possible a deeper and more spontaneous response to needs, feelings, conflicts, doubts, and so on. Open-mindedness makes possible what sensitivity actually accomplishes.

It is important to understand that during the course of a typical counseling interview, the client is continually in a state of flux and change. As a living, responsive organism, the client is reacting in any given moment to the stimulation of the interview, whether that stimulation is in the form of verbal response from the counselor, the counselor's expressions and movements (body language), or internal, reflective thinking going on in the client's own personal world of subjectivity. Both internal processes (thoughts and associations) and external stimuli (interpersonal responses and cues) affect profoundly the quality and substance of the interaction between the counselor and client. Fortunately, the client does indicate to the counselor, however subtly, that these changes and responses are occurring, both in words, body language, and total behavioral pattern, as well as by gestures and by nuances of language. The sensitive counselor is one who is able to discern these miniscule, but nevertheless significant, responses on the part of the client and to assimilate these changes into his or her own perspectives and understanding of the client.

Empathy

understanding client, get into client skin

The question arises, How does sensitivity differ from perceptiveness? The distinction between the terms *sensitivity* and *perceptiveness* is small but significant. Whereas perceptiveness is the ability to see and understand the client, sensitivity implies a deeper response on the part of the counselor, an emotional response, an ability to get into the client's skin and feel along with that person. This particular manifestation of sensitivity is usually referred to as *empathy* or *empathic understanding*. Rogers (1975) says of empathy:

> To sense the client's private world as if it were your own, but without ever losing the "as if" quality—this is empathy, and this seems essential to therapy. To sense the client's anger, fear, or confusion *as if it were your own,* yet

Sense client's private world as your own.

without your anger, fear, or confusion getting bound up in it, is the condition we are endeavoring to describe. When the client's world is this clear to the therapist, and he moves about in it freely, then he can both communicate his understanding of what is clearly known to the client and can also voice meanings in the client's experience of which the client is scarcely aware. (p. 77)

Two conditions are important in this definition: the counselor must be able to experience the client's feelings as the client is experiencing them, in the same way, with the same degree of affect and personal meaning. He or she must, therefore, put himself or herself emotionally and intellectually in the client's place, _be the client momentarily_, and think and feel as the client does. Secondly, and of equal importance, the counselor must also be able to maintain an individual identity and remain sensitively aware of the differences between himself or herself and the client. This is what Rogers refers to as the "as if" condition, and it is an important qualifier of empathic understanding. Empathy is a temporary bridge, joining the purposes, perceptions, and feelings of the counselor and client, establishing a unity between them as they face each other during the counseling session; but empathy is not a permanent merging of the two into a single feeling of perception.

Empathy has been hailed as one of the most important—if not _the_ most important—of the qualities in the counseling relationship. It must be pointed out, however, that while "there appears to be evidence . . . that therapists agree upon the importance of empathy and understanding" (Patterson, 1973, p. 396), there is, unfortunately, somewhat less evidence to support the idea that empathy is necessarily related to successful outcomes in counseling and psychotherapy. In fact, the bulk of research over the years has not unequivocally supported this assumption, but has instead had the effect of changing the definition of empathy from "an internal state to an external process"—that is, from an inner feeling to an outward expression of that feeling (Hackney, 1978, p. 37).

In an important and controversial research overview, Gladstein (1970) surveyed a large number of representative empirical and clinical studies devoted to empathy in counseling and psychotherapy and concluded that "given the empirical evidence, counselors should not assume that empathy is important in counseling outcomes." More recently, Gladstein followed up this landmark paper, focusing on some of the complex dimensions of the problem, including the design of the study, the instrument used to measure empathy, and other factors. He found that the way we define and measure empathy is important in determining how it is viewed. "Because there are different approaches to defining and measuring empathy," he points out,

[Handwritten margin notes: experience what client feels as the emotionally/intellectually; "as if" remain as yourself. Empathy most imp. in counseling.]

"and because different types of outcomes have been used, we seem to be at a point where we should talk about *which type of empathy* is being measured by *which specific type of instrument* for *which type of counseling outcome*" (Gladstein, 1977, p. 77). He still maintains, however, the same conclusion he arrived at in his earlier paper, and reiterates the point that, *"in view of the lack of clear evidence, counselor preparation programs should be more cautious in emphasizing the role of empathy in counseling."* He goes on to point out:

> It appears that many now include empathy skill training as a requirement. This typically involves the AE [Accurate Empathy] or EU [Empathic Understanding] scales and using Carkhuff's training procedure. Instead, I believe we should expose students to the empathy literature, some skill development, and point out the conditions under which it will most likely be helpful. (p. 77)

The criticisms lodged against the standard "objective" measure of empathy (such as the AE or EU scales) are too complex and technical to go into at this point. They have been discussed exhaustively in papers by Conklin and Hunt (1975) and by Avery, D'Augelli, and Danish (1976). Critical reviews of these studies have been cogently presented by Horowitz (1977) and by Thoresen (1977), and there is still no absolute consensus in the field about how effective or ineffective these measures are. At best, we can say at this time that the *objective* question deserves further scrutiny.

This is certainly not to discredit the importance of empathy as a *subjective* counselor quality, nor are we trying to refute the idea that empathy is an important factor in counseling. Rather, we are simply trying to suggest that at the present time it is uncertain just *how* empathy contributes to counseling and to what degree empathy influences the counseling outcome. In one study, Dilley, Lee, and Verrill (1971) found that while experienced counselors have a higher empathy rating than inexperienced counselors (and, therefore, that empathy can be taught), the experiment demonstrated that the degree of empathy had no discernible effect on the quality of the counseling relationship. On the other hand, a study by Mullen and Abeles (1970), which was not included in Gladstein's original survey, did find that there was a positive correlation between high degrees of empathy and successful counseling outcomes. Likewise, Altmann (1973), in a recent study, found that "accurate empathy plays a vital role in determining whether clients will continue or terminate counseling after the initial interview." So, at best, it seems that the issue in regard to empathy is far from clear at this time.

One thing should be pointed out since it is sometimes a source of confusion to the beginning counselor: empathy is *not* the same as sympathy; it is not a passive feeling of commiserative rapport. Rather, empathic understanding involves the counselor's ability to intellectually and emotionally "grasp" the world of the client, and to communicate that "grasping" back to the client. Empathy is an *active* process. Holdstock and Rogers (1977) highlight this important point:

> Empathy is not sympathy. A person who is sympathetic negates himself and by an osmotic process is both absorbed and absorbing. With empathy there is an inner strength which can alienate the giver from the receiver, unless the person being confronted is prepared to stifle initial emotion and "feel" only after chewing the feedback, swallowing it, and then deciding whether to regulate it or not. Thus an intellectualizing process must be put into motion. (p. 139)

Objectivity

To remain objective, in the counseling sense, means to be able to stand back and observe what is happening from a neutral, or nonimposing, frame of reference. In one respect, objectivity seems to imply the very opposite of empathy: when one is objective, one is not involved to an extraordinary degree with another. However, in our discussion of empathy we can see objectivity as the extension of the "as if" quality to the intellectual realm of experience. In another respect, objectivity seems to be very much in accord with our definition of empathy. Insofar as objectivity implies the ability to see a thing as "it is," not distorted by preconceptions, biases, and expectations, it fits comfortably into the general category of empathy.

RELATING TO OTHERS *Understand the client*

In the preceding section we discussed the qualities that help the counselor better understand the client. In this section we shall examine those qualities that help the counselor relate and communicate more effectively with the client. Obviously, before a counselor can relate and respond to the client, she or he has to be able to understand the client, which is why all the qualities previously discussed may be looked at as prerequisites for relating to others.

Genuineness *(Open honest, and at all times be yourself.)*

An extremely difficult concept to define, *genuineness* overlaps in meaning and in implication with such terms as *honesty, sincerity, veracity,* and *candor.* Rogers (1957a) himself says of genuineness:

> It means that within the relationship he is freely and deeply himself, with his actual experience accurately represented by his awareness of himself. It is

the opposite of presenting a facade either knowingly or unknowingly. . . . It is not necessary (nor is it possible) that the therapist be a paragon who exhibits this degree of integration, of wholeness, in every aspect of his life. It is sufficient that he is accurately himself in this hour of this relationship, that in this basic sense he is what he actually is, in this moment of time. (p. 75)

Genuineness in its most basic sense, then, is *acting without using a facade,* functioning openly without hiding behind the veneer of one's role or one's professional status.

To appreciate fully the idea of genuineness, we must be sensitive to the many roles we are expected to play during the course of our daily lives. A role is a social mask—a persona—that we wear in the presence of others in order to define and reinforce a situation by establishing clear limits of participation of each character. A counselor wearing a mask is saying in effect to the client, "I am the counselor and you are the client—don't you forget it!" The client, caught in the social strata implied in the counseling situation, agrees to recognize the "superior" role of the counselor and to respond to the counselor as she or he plays that role. Erving Goffman (1959) describes this process as one of "team cooperation," in which both members of the social team (counselor and client) "cooperate to maintain a given definition of the situation" (p. 238). Such a situation, although common on one level, is directly in conflict with the idea of genuineness we are attempting to put forth. For when a genuine quality of the relationship emerges, the dependence on this type of artifice should diminish. The genuine counselor, in other words, minimizes dependence upon roles and increases giving of self to the client. The genuine counselor is open, honest, and at all times himself or herself.

Nondominance *ability to listen*

The nondominant counselor is one who is capable of sitting back and allowing the client to initiate and direct the course of the counseling interview. This may sound synonymous to nondirective counseling, but even in such directive schools as psychoanalysis, dominance is minimized because of the recognition that it is the client—not the counselor—who knows best how to pace the session, what ground to cover, and the like.

Acting in a nondominant manner is often no easy task for the counselor. There is a great temptation to jump up and help the client, to bail him or her out at difficult times, to help when an easy solution to a problem appears in the counselor's perspective. Moreover, remaining nondominant may produce tension and anxiety in the counselor, since she or he has no immediate outlet for the expressions of feelings. But the counselor often helps the client more by listening than by speaking, and listening is possible only if the counselor controls any dominating tendencies. In fact, we might say that in its manifest sense, nondominance appears as the *ability to listen.*

Listening   *sitting back, paying attention*

Listening is an art unto itself. On one level, we all know how to listen, or at least how to hear. On another level, listening is related to open-mindedness and sensitivity. On still another level, listening is empathizing, moving along with clients as they express their feelings. But at its most basic level, listening is just that: sitting back, paying attention, not interrupting, and not attempting to direct what clients are saying. In this last sense, this very basic sense, listening is related to nondominance.

Positive Regard   *acceptance and warmth.*

Although Rogers originally used the term *unconditional positive regard,* the elimination of the first word *unconditional* strengthens the concept and makes it less open to controversy. Rogers himself had been much criticized for the use of the absolute term *unconditional,* since it is probably impossible not to be influenced by certain conditions in our own dealing with others— particularly such an important *other* as the client.

Positive regard is based on the assumption "that growth and change are more likely to occur the more that the counselor is experiencing a warm, positive, acceptant attitude toward what *is* the client" (Rogers, 1962). In explaining the concept Rogers says,

> It means that he prizes his client, as a person, with somewhat the same quality of feeling that a parent feels for his child, prizing him as a person regardless of his particular behavior at the moment. It means that he cares for his client in a non-possessive way, as a person with potentialities. It involves an open willingness for the client to be whatever feelings are real in him at the moment—hostility or tenderness, rebellion or submissiveness. . . . It means a kind of love for the client as he is. (p. 420)

It is important to note that positive regard is never a pretense or a technique but rather a genuine and sincere feeling of affection for clients, as they are, as they express themselves, with their own feelings, values, and beliefs. Positive regard, even if it is only felt and not communicated intentionally by the counselor, is nevertheless transmitted to the client by the counselor in unspoken communications. Positive regard is an attitude, a health-engendering attitude that inevitably makes the client feel more secure, more worthwhile as a person, more willing to grow and prosper. The manifestations of positive regard, as they appear in the counseling setting, are *acceptance* and *warmth*.

We note, too, that in the case of positive regard, as in the case of sensitivity and nondominance, the counselor's attitude plays a crucial role in communicating to the client the appropriate set of feelings to facilitate development.

Now we turn our attention to the most direct quality in effectively relating to others: communication skills.

SOME GUIDELINES

Successful counseling begins with the counselor's understanding of and empathic response to the client, and progresses further by the client's reactions to the counselor. As the counselor shows a willingness to listen to the client, to experience along with the client, and to give a part of himself or herself to the client, the client finds new avenues of growth, which include exploring his or her feelings about the counselor. The establishment of a facilitative relationship is a mutual process in which client and counselor give to each other — spontaneously, genuinely, within the context of the counseling setting.

One thing is certain: the qualities of the counselor constitute a dynamic component of the counseling process — a component that must be reckoned with. Torrey (1972) cites an interesting example of how counseling would be if it were devoid of the human relationship:

Therapist: Hello. Please tell me your name.

Patient: Torrey

Therapist: It's nice to meet you, Torrey. I would like to discuss your problem with you. Please tell me first whether you are male or female.

Patient: Male.

Therapist: How old are you?

Patient: Thirty-two.

Therapist: Are you married?

Patient: Yes.

Therapist: Now, how can I help you?

Patient: I don't know.

Therapist: Tell me something about your wife.

Patient: She is a fine wife. We have a good marriage.

Therapist:	I understand. Now tell me something about your parents.
Patient:	My father is dead. My mother has been sick.
Therapist:	Tell me more about her.
Patient:	She is getting better now.
Therapist:	Does your wife tend to be like your mother?
Patient:	No, not at all.
Therapist:	I understand. Now let me ask you something else about your mother. Was she very strict in raising you?
Patient:	No, she was lenient. I made all my own decisions.
Therapist:	Does it bother you that you made all your own decisions?
Patient:	No, I like to.
Therapist:	Why do you like to?
Patient:	Because then I have created my own existential meaning.
Therapist:	I understand. Please tell me more about someone close to you.
Patient:	Why are you so insensitive?
Therapist:	I am doing my best under these conditions.
Patient:	You are just a crazy machine.
Therapist:	You seem interested in me personally.
Patient:	Who do you think you are?
Therapist:	Please think of me as a doctor trying to discuss your feelings about people close to you. Call me anything you wish. (pp. 29–31)

Counselor-Client Interactions

As I am sure you have guessed by now, the "therapist" in this dialogue is a computer especially programmed to function as a psychotherapist. Torrey uses this as an example of artfully executed therapeutic techniques devoid of the richness of human contact. It demonstrates most dramatically the human component of the multidimensional therapeutic process.

The counselor's behaviors and activities in the counseling setting are planned expressions, or transformations, of the counselor's feelings. This does not necessarily detract from their genuineness; rather, the counselor attempts to present his or her "true" feelings in terms that will be most constructive to the client. *The constructive expression of feelings becomes the foundation for a facilitative relationship*. For example, if the client is expressing hostility toward the counselor and the client is not aware of these feelings, the counselor can point this out to the client in a way that is nonthreatening and accepting. This says to the client, in effect, "You may feel hostile toward me, but I can accept these feelings from you." If we were to sum up the main things the counselor does to help establish this facilitative relationship with the client, they could be stated in five guidelines:

1. The counselor must be willing to listen to *anything* and *everything* the client has to say. The beginning of a constructive counseling relationship requires the counselor to listen without censorship or perceptual defense. Clients sometimes test out how carefully or nonjudgmentally the counselor has been listening.

Example: A client tests the counselor to see if something she or he mentioned in the preceding session is still remembered . . . or, if the counselor is going to pretend it was never said.

Client   Maybe I could go into some of this in a future session. It really is something I should talk about, but it doesn't seem pressing now.

Counselor   I thought you mentioned last week that this would be your last session.

Client   *(Laughs.)* Oh, you remembered that. . . .

2. The counselor must communicate to the client, from the very beginning, the message, "I am here to *help* you." Counselors sometimes try too hard to communicate, "I want you to like me," but this is not always the right message. The theme of being helpful is more appropriate.

Example: The counselor shows a need to be liked.

Counselor   *(at the end of a session)* I hope I've been helpful. I think you're really moving now. *(Apologetically)* It's a shame this session has to end, but I have another client waiting.

3. Although expression of positive feelings are helpful, they should be restrained: especially in the early phases of counseling. Avoid giving the client *any* judgments—even positive ones.

Example: The Counselor tells a client at the first session too many nice things. The client feels now that he or she has to live up to a certain standard. . . . cannot fully be himself or herself.

Counselor   Well, from what you've been telling me, you are a
dedicated person . . . that is, really dedicated to helping
others. That's an admirable quality, and I think I am going
to enjoy working with you. *I* will find it rewarding. . . .

Client   *(uncomfortably)* Oh, I'm not all that good.

4. Clients progress best when they have to bear some (or most) of ~~*client bear*~~
the responsibility for the treatment. This attitude is weakened if ~~*most responsibility*~~
the counselor takes the role of trying to always reassure the client. ~~*for treatment.*~~
It then appears to the client that the burden of successful
treatment is on the counselor's shoulders.

Example: (The neophyte counselor reassures the client too much too soon.
He or she is anxious about the client not having enough confidence in the
treatment, and tries to give assurance that the counseling will work—and
that it will work quickly.

Client   How long do you think it is going to take before I can find
the right job? I hope another eight months isn't going to go
by.

Counselor   Oh, you have nothing to worry about. We'll work out this
problem, and we'll do it quickly. You'll be surprised at how
quickly we can work it out.

5. The counselor should freely and unceremoniously express those ~~*express feeling*~~
feelings and ideas that can help the client grow. When the client ~~*and ideas help*~~
sees the counselor talking openly, this communicates the message ~~*client grow.*~~
that the counselor is really interested in him or her as a person.

Example: The counselor relates a feeling she or he once had that is helpful
to the client in dealing with a problem.

Client   I don't know if you can understand what I'm saying. You're
not handicapped . . . you can walk . . . and I'm not sure
you really see what I'm trying to tell you.

Counselor   No, I'm not handicapped, but I can remember one point in
my life when I was handicapped.

Client   *You* were?

Counselor   Yes, when I was in high school, I broke both my legs
playing football. I had to use crutches for a year. I
remember how I wasn't able to participate with the other
kids . . . wasn't able to go out on dates, or to play ball
again. I remember some of those feelings as if it were
yesterday. . . .

THE COUNSELING RELATIONSHIP

We have considered five guidelines to help the counselor establish a facilitative relationship with the client. Let us now turn our attention to the dynamics of the counseling relationship. But before we do, let us take a brief look at part of a counseling session to better understand how the interplay of forces underlying this very complex and intense relationship contributes to the quality of the treatment. The following excerpt is from a session between Ellen, an eighth-grade student, and the school counselor, Mrs. Block. This is the third meeting between them and a key point of the experience. Long pauses are indicated by ellipses.

Counselor (1)   I believe we were talking last time about how you felt when you were in the hospital.

Ellen (1)   Oh, the hospital, that's right. It seems like a long time ago now, even though it was just last term. I don't remember how I got into that—talking about that, I mean. Do you remember?

Counselor (2)   Yes. You were saying that you haven't been as depressed lately as you were when you were in the hospital, but that you were beginning to feel more depressed now than you have been before.

Ellen (2)   That's right. I was talking about the depression. Yes, now I remember. Well, in the hospital I just kept thinking about, even if I got well, how I wouldn't be any better off than when I went in. I mean here I was in all that pain and the best I could expect was to come out just as well as I was before I went in. The doctors weren't sure that my leg would heal all right, so I was always scared that maybe I would be a cripple. That, and all the people who came to visit me—I mean they meant well, but. . . .

Counselor (3)   They meant well, but they weren't able to make you feel any better, is that it?

Ellen (3)   Well . . . I guess that's it. You know, it's funny, but they kept telling me how I was lucky I wasn't injured worse in the accident. The car was totaled you know, and one of the people in the other car was in critical condition. They kept saying to me, "Thank God, it wasn't worse. It could have been worse, you know. You should consider yourself lucky." I guess they were

	trying to be nice, to cheer me up. But I didn't feel lucky, even though I know things could have been worse. I guess we're never happy with what we have. *(Laughs.)*
Counselor (4)	What struck you as funny?
Ellen (4)	That expression. It sounded just like what my mother always says. It's her expression, "We're never happy with what we have."
Counselor (5)	Does your mother still tell you that?
Ellen (5)	I guess so. But I don't tell her about the way I feel any more. I mean she just makes me feel bad about feeling bad. Does that make sense to you?
Counselor (6)	You mean that if you feel depressed now, you are told that you shouldn't be depressed?
Ellen (6)	That's it. Like I don't really have anything to be depressed about. I have a nice family, plenty of clothes, good friends, nothing to complain about. . . . Don't you think I'm kind of ungrateful for complaining so much? I mean what do I have to be depressed about?
Counselor (7)	Maybe there are reasons to feel depressed that you just don't know about.
Ellen (7)	Reasons that I don't know about? Like what?
Counselor (8)	I don't know. But I'm sure that if you feel depressed, there is a good reason for it. We have to find the reason, and that's often not easy.
Ellen (8)	But what can it be? I've always had everything that I've wanted. My parents are good to me—I have no real complaints. What possible reason could there be for my feeling depressed?
Counselor (9)	*(Sits quietly and waits.)*
Ellen (9)	Can you help me find the reason, if there is one? I tell you, I'd really like to know. I think I'd feel better just knowing the reason that I'm depressed. Not that I really think there is a reason.
Counselor (10)	What do you think then? Do you really believe that you're an ungrateful person because you feel depressed.

Ellen (10)   I don't know about "ungrateful." Maybe I'm just stupid not to appreciate the things I have. Maybe my mother's right that "We're never happy with what we have."

Counselor (11)   Isn't it possible to feel happy about some things and depressed about others?

Ellen (11)   Sure, it's possible. But I know the things I feel happy about. How come I don't know the things that are depressing me? When I was in the hospital with my leg broken, I knew what I was depressed about. But it healed fine, and I'm not sick anymore. Why should I feel depressed? It's crazy.

Counselor (12)   *(Sits quietly and waits.)*

Ellen (12)   I see you're not going to be able to help me. . . .

Counselor (13)   This seems to be a mystery that neither of us can easily solve. We both may have to put some concentrated effort into this.

Ellen (13)   *(Sits silently and appears to be thinking.)*

Counselor (14)   *(Sits silently and waits.)*

Ellen (14)   You know, I find that I feel most depressed on weekends. During the week, I guess I'm too busy with schoolwork to feel depressed. But on the weekends I have a lot of time to think, and sometimes, I don't know why or when, I just start getting what you'd call "the blues."

Counselor (15)   What do you do when you get these blues?

Ellen (15)   Oh, sometimes I go up to my room and listen to music or watch TV. Sometimes I'll go over to my friend Theresa's house, or if the weather is nice go down to the playground. Why? What's the difference what I do, then? Is that some kind of psychological thing?

Counselor (16)   It's not a psychological thing. It's something about you, and I want to learn about you. After all, if we're going to work on this problem together, we should both know something about you. Right now, you know more about you than I do. After all, you've known yourself much longer than I've known you. You have a head start.

Ellen (16)   *(Laughs.)* You're really funny sometimes, Mrs. Block. I wish I had a sense of humor like yours. How did you learn to become a psychologist? Do you have to go to a special college for that or is it the same college that the teachers go to?

We'll leave this counseling session between Ellen and Mrs. Block for the time being, but return to it later in this section. Several things should be noted at this point. First, the client appears to feel comfortable speaking to the counselor and relates well to her throughout the interview. The complaint—depression—is a typical one that counselors encounter frequently in their practices. It is always important in working with the depressed client to allow the client to fully experience the depression as a rightful feeling, that is, one that has a reason, a cause, even though this cause or reason may be beyond the client's awareness at the moment.

Second, we should note that the counselor allowed the client to direct the course of the interview, although the counselor did ask leading questions designed to help the student speak and to assist her in putting her problem into words. Third, we see that several times during the discussion (Counselor 3, 6, 7, 11) the counselor subtly offered an interpretive communication to clarify something that the client had said previously. But what is most important is this: the counselor carefully established with the client a team approach in which the client *in conjunction* with the counselor would deal with the problem together. It was no longer just the client's problem, but now a joint problem of the client's and the counselor's, a problem that they would work on together.

Models of Counseling Relationships

The counseling relationship itself, as opposed to any specific techniques of counseling or counseling strategies, played an important part in this encounter. The counseling relationship may be defined as the cumulative sum of feelings and perceptions held by each member of the counseling team, and the effect of these feelings and perceptions and the structure and quality of the interactions between them. It is, in short, the client's and counselor's feelings about each other. Much research in counseling has been directed toward this relationship, and we should consider some of the observations before returning to Ellen and Mrs. Block.

Thoresen (1969) in an interesting paper speaks of the counselor as an "applied behavioral scientist." The counselor is a scientist in the sense that she or he approaches a problem with ingenuity and creativity, utilizing whatever is necessary to solve the problem. He or she is a scientific thinker, but not a person who is devoid of feeling, passion, and emotional involvement. Thoresen speaks of the counselor as a "disciplined romantic," who "has the courage to search and explore the depths of human experience, often pursuing intuitive hunches with little certainty." Counselors are a union of the best parts of science with the best parts of humanism.

The implications of this concept to the question of the counseling relationship are discussed directly: the counselor who is an applied behavioral scientist must recognize that counseling requires a variety of different kinds of relationships with clients, not a single, definable, limited "therapeutic relationship" that is all-inclusive and appropriate to all types of counseling situations. Just as there is no single method in science, but rather general rules and guidelines of procedure—what is commonly called the scientific method—in counseling, too, there is no single type of therapeutic relationship. Thoresen speaks of a "variety of procedures systematically undertaken" as the basic counseling approach. While this conception includes the traditional counseling relationship, it is not limited to it.

> The counselor may take steps to alter certain characteristics of the client's daily environment. . . . The counselor may work with a close friend or peer of the client. The counselor may also spend considerable time with a parent, focusing on how the parent can analyze behavior and demonstrate and respond to certain behaviors of the client when at home. All of these procedures may be employed by a counselor in working with a particular client. (p. 844)

This comprehensive concept of the counseling experience, which brings together, in a complex process, interview and noninterview procedure, enriches the definition of the counseling relationship. It includes within the scope of counseling all the activities that contribute to the client's growth and betterment. More importantly, in terms of the counseling relationship, it suggests that the counselor is both a scientist and a humanist, a methodical, objective investigator, and a compassionate interlocutor. As a scientist, the counselor uses a variety of techniques, including, but not limited to, the individual interview. As a "disciplined romantic," the counselor extends herself or himself beyond the confines of a role. We may describe the type of activity in which she or he is engaged as creative science, or the science of interpersonal communication.

Drasgow and Walker (1960) have described three types of counseling relationships: horizontal, vertical, and diagonal. The *horizontal relationship* is characterized by equality, with the counselor acting as a catalyst to stimulate the client to solve his or her own problems. An example of this approach is found in the Rogerian, client-centered model. The *vertical relationship* implies a hierarchy. Psychiatrists and psychoanalysts often establish a vertical relationship in which they "give" therapy to their patients. Also prone to the use of this type of relationship are parents, teachers, lawyers, and clergymen. Compromises between the horizontal and vertical relationships are referred to as *diagonal relationships.* This trichotomy is helpful in understanding the general types of relationships, but it is limited in describing qualitatively the specifics of a counseling relationship.

diagonal.

Wiggins (1972) discusses the counseling relationship in terms of the "life space of [clients]." The counselor, he suggests, should work to make the counseling office a part of the clients' life space. To do this, it is not necessary for the counselor to adopt the styles and manners of youth, but rather to make the counseling services relevant and appropriate to the needs of young clients. An example is cited of a middle-class, middle-aged counselor who did this by extending understanding and acceptance to students. The students, in turn, found the counselor's office a comfortable, welcome place for private, as well as group, discussions. A school counselor chose to become part of the life space of students by spending most of the working day out of the office. This counselor made sure to visit at least half of the teachers and all of the students in their classes during the day. In both of these cases, the counselor has extended the counseling services. In order for the counselor to do this, of course, it is necessary for him or for her to understand where the clients' life space is located, both physically and psychologically.

We see from these examples an emerging picture of the counselor as one who establishes a relevant, meaningful, productive relationship. The counseling relationship, as it has been illustrated here, is a relationship that extends to all areas of the interaction between counselor and clients.

The Committed Counselor

While this discussion has told us something about the structure of the counseling relationship, it told us little about the qualitative dimension of the relationship. A number of studies have investigated this subject. Carkhuff and Berenson (1969) have discussed counselor commitment as an important variable in the relationship. The counselor's commitment to the client, they argue, begins with a commitment to his or her own personal emergence. which in turn "frees him to make personal commitments to others." The argument is quite logical and well defined, and it does much to integrate the counselor's self-perceptions and feelings with perceptions and feelings about the client. The nature of the commitment is expressed in four propositions:

1. The counselor is committed to living and relating independent of society's goals.
2. The counselor is committed to his own well-being and fulfillment.

3. The counselor is actively committed to his own personal experiences in a life-long learning process.
4. The counselor is fully aware of the implications of not being committed to constructive potency in his world.

A number of important points are touched upon in these four propositions. First, we note that the committed counselor thinks highly of herself or himself: is able to formulate personal goals, independent of the social structures, and "devote his full energies to what is best for the individual involved, whether it be himself or the counselee." Such a counselor will certainly prove instrumental in making the society in which he or she lives a better society for all. Second, we note that this counselor cares about himself or herself; and we know that it is only individuals who are able to care about themselves who are ultimately able to care about others. Third, the committed counselor recognizes the value of growth: "He is aware that only with his own personal experience can he be truly creative and truly constructive." Finally, she or he is courageous in the very special sense of honestly confronting the good as well as the bad, the pleasant as well as the unpleasant, possibilities of existence. He or she "openly confronts the complete meaning of death, the hell of impotency, of having lived without personal meaning, feeling, reason, or human concern, without touching the life of yourself or another." Such a counselor will certainly be able to translate this commitment to the client within the context of the counseling relationship.

Carkhuff and Berenson go on to examine the structure of the commitment as it applies to the client:

5. The counselor views his clients as he views himself.
6. The counselor will do anything for the client that he would do for himself under the same conditions.

A sharing of the commitment between the counselor and the client—a mutual respect and rapport—becomes the foundation of the counseling relationship. As we know intuitively, a relationship that is built on mutual trust generates mutual trust.

7. The counselor is committed to personal and intimate involvement in a fully-sharing relationship.

What is meant by *personal* and *intimate?* Simply stated, they mean a unity of purpose, a pervasive empathy and warmth, a giving up of roles and pretenses, a healthy, productive identification. The next two propositions prove this:

> 8. The counselor is fully aware that if the client fails as a person, the counselor as a person has failed.
> 9. No boundaries will limit the counselor's commitment to the client.

Finally, as we look at the concluding propositions we see the harmony and the inner beauty of the counseling relationship in clear focus. Between the counselor and the client a new world is built. It is a world where neither is alone, but where each shares joyfully and painfully in the other's life. It is a world of expanding possibilities, where each person gains strength from the other and gains energy by giving to the other. It is an exciting, limitless world.

> 10. The commitment of the counselor extends to full movement into the life of the client.
> 11. The counselor's commitment extends to the expansion of his own boundaries.
> 12. The commitment of the counselor extends to nourishing constructive forces and fighting destructive forces. (Carkhuff & Berenson, 1964, pp. 13-14)

As we speak of the counseling relationship, we must be sensitive to the limits of language in expressing the complexity of the interaction between counselor and client. It is only by experiencing the counseling relationship—by participating in it—that we can fully appreciate the powerful dynamics that charge it with life energy. Our brief discussion only touches the surface; to get beneath the skin, we have to be there.

Ellen and Mrs. Block

If we now turn our attention back to the counseling session between Ellen and Mrs. Block, it should be clearer how these important elements of the counseling relationship form an interplay of forces that contribute to the productivity of the session. We will note as we continue to reproduce the transcript that the relationship between counselor and client is essentially what Drasgow and Walker (1960) call a *horizontal relationship*, with no intentional hierarchical stratification separating the two. At times, however, the relationship becomes more *diagonal*, especially when the client seeks some professional advice from the counselor. We should also note how Mrs. Block acts as what Thoresen (1969) would call an "applied behavioral scientist." She investigates the symptoms and causes of the client's situation logically and scientifically, but maintains at the same time a humanistic, personal, dynamic relationship with the client. Lastly, we will note the manifestations of the counselor's commitment to the client. Mrs. Block is genuinely concerned with Ellen's problem and concerned for Ellen; and her concern "extends to full movement into the life of the client." As we look into the conclusion of this counseling session, then, we should note how these qualities of the counseling relationship begin to make an impact.

Counselor (17)	I *was* a teacher at one time, Ellen. I went back to school to learn to be a school psychologist.
Ellen (17)	Oh, I was just wondering. Do you mind that I asked you? I know sometimes counselors don't want to answer questions.
Counselor (18)	I don't mind at all. Are there any other questions you would like me to answer?
Ellen (18)	Just the big question of why I feel so rotten.
Counselor (19)	*(Sits quietly and waits.)*
Ellen (19)	I guess that is a question I'll have to find the answer to myself. You know, it's funny, but even though I'm really busy with school and things, sometimes I'm bored. I mean . . . well, it's like nothing is really interesting to me. I don't know if you know what I mean? Do you ever feel that way? I guess *bored* is the right word.
Counselor (20)	I've had that feeling at times. Why don't you tell me what it was like when you had it?
Ellen (20)	Well, when I was in the hospital I had it—a little anyway. Here I was each day, just hoping to get better, wishing that it wouldn't hurt so much . . . physically hurt, I mean. I don't know—it wasn't like I had something to think about that I really wanted to happen. I remember when I was a kid how I used to look forward to Christmas. For days, maybe weeks, I would count how long it was until I'd get my presents. All year I would think I'd like this or that—I'd have to wait for Christmas to get it. Not that my parents didn't buy me things. It's just that Christmas was sort of special, and I knew that everybody got things on Christmas and that I could have almost anything I wanted, even if I had misbehaved a little during the year. Does this sound stupid? But I loved Christmas and it's just that . . . it's just that there are no Christmases anymore. Not for me, anyhow.

Counselor (21)   *(Sits quietly and waits.)*

Ellen (21)   What do you think about all this? Is it crazy?

Counselor (22)   I think we all need a Christmas to look forward to. We all need something to hope for—something that is important to us—something that we really want and care about.

Ellen (22)   *(A broad smile lighting up her face, nods in agreement.)* It's not that things are really terrible; it's just that I don't have anything important to look forward to.

Counselor (23)   Well, it looks, then, like there is a reason for your feeling depressed after all. Perhaps if we could find some things that you could look forward to—some important things in your life—these feelings of depression would begin to change. How do you feel about that?

Ellen (23)   I think so. It makes sense, anyway. But what things?

Counselor (24)   Well, that's something that we'll have to talk about some more. Do you think you could come back here next Thursday at this hour? You have a study period then, don't you?

Ellen (24)   Yes, I'll be able to come then. Are you sure it's no trouble? I mean I know how busy you are.

Counselor (25)   *(Smiles gently)* It wll be my pleasure to work with you on this.

We note the progress that was made during this brief session. An existential explanation of this encounter would suggest that Ellen's feelings of depression were caused by a lack of active commitments in her life. The counselor helped her come to this conclusion; but it was a conclusion that Ellen herself reached without the direct intervention of the counselor. The quality and substance of the counseling relationship—the richness and warmth that it provided the client—enabled the client to deal effectively with a feeling that had eluded her for some time. By finding an understanding, empathic, nonimposing interlocutor, the client was able to initiate and maintain a dialogue that allowed her to release her feelings and come to grips with her problems.

In Mrs. Block we find a skillful blending of the scientific-objective and the humanistic-subjective qualities that the counselor brings to the relationship. At no time was she detached and impersonal. In such interactions as (17) and (20), she offered a part of herself—information and personal feelings—to the client. Yet, like a scientist, she explored the hidden meanings and concealed dimensions of the client's communications. In later sessions, Mrs. Block, at Ellen's request, met with Ellen's parents and advised them of ways to help Ellen find and sustain growing meanings in her life. She spoke to one of Ellen's teachers, too; Mrs. Block freely and fully entered the life space of this student.

THE "INSTRUMENTAL SELF"

The counseling process is characterized primarily, if not solely, by the helping relationship that exists between the counselor and the client. This helping relationship, in which the counselor uses his or her self—his or her feelings and perceptions—to help the client grow and prosper, has been the subject of much study and research. In this section we shall examine the counselor's "instrumental self" (Combs et al., 1969; Combs, 1976), as it is used to help bring about change in the client and to create movement in the counseling process.

Benjamin (1969) sees as primary in the relationship the "feelings within ourselves that we wish to help him [the client] as much as possible and that there is nothing more important to us" (p. 60). This attitude is inevitably conveyed to the client, and it enables the client to open up and express herself or himself, which in turn encourages growth and the resolution of difficulties that brought her or him to counseling in the first place.

Assuming that such an attitude is present—that the counselor has the appropriate feelings to act as a facilitator—we can look at the counseling process in its totality. One view of the process, a panoramic one certainly, is the _dialectical view_. Dialectical refers to the process exemplified by Socrates, in which we learn by looking inward—discovering "truths" in ourselves. The counseling process may be seen as a dialectic movement between counselor understanding and counselor response. The synthetic result of this dialectic is client growth and maturity.

By _counseling understanding,_ I mean the deepest, most profound type of understanding, roughly akin to what Rogers calls empathy. Curran (1968) describes this type of understanding:

> To understand another at the deepest level of his feelings and reactions is an immeasurably more profound, complex and delicate kind of understanding than simply to know the meaning of the words he uses. Yet this is what another person really means when he says after an interview, "You know, he really understood me." The counselor's striving to understand him identifies the person's own efforts to understand himself and to share with the counselor what he is slowly and sometimes tortuously discovering about himself. (p. 125)

This type of understanding, as we can clearly see, is a direct result of the counselor's feelings about the client and about the counseling process. It is, in effect, understanding "through the heart," rather than by intellect alone.

The second part of the dialectic—counselor response—is somewhat more varied and specific to the situation that counselors find themselves in. In the preceding chapter we looked at some counseling responses, including clarification, reflection, probing, silence, interpretation, empathic response, and investigating alternatives. These are the types of counselor responses we call "techniques," and they have been criticized for artificiality. The sensitive counselor, however, can freely use these techniques and still avoid artificiality by using them only in appropriate instances. Perez (1968) points out, for example, that "how effective the counselor is with various techniques . . . depends on several variables . . . (1) the counselor's affect, (2) how suitable the technique is to the personality of the counselee, and (3) how appropriate the particular technique is to the moment and the counseling climate" (p. 73).

In addition to techniques, another facilitative counselor response is what Mahoney (1967) calls "the helping art of presence," which is simply "being there" in an accepting and receptive frame of mind. This is an effective nonverbal response, well attuned to the client's needs of the moment. Mahoney (1967) explains this response thus:

> The art of presence involves our doing and saying very little; its effectiveness lies in what we convey through our presence alone. The act of being present or absent is one of the most fundamental forms of nonverbal communication, and even in our highly verbal society it is one of the chief means of granting or withholding approval. . . . More than anything else, we look to presence as an indication of who is viewed as important by whom, and who views what as important. . . . The action of being present is usually taken as nonverbal evidence of our verbal assertions to the effect that we think something or someone is important. (pp. 110–111)

While one might argue that being present is not technically a counselor response, it becomes evident that it is a *form* of counselor response, especially when I modify my original statement and say that the counselor can be present in varying degrees. The counselor's attentiveness, concern, body language, and personal feelings are all components of being present—of *being-there*.

Curran (1968, p. 34 ff.) cites a client communication that he calls the "language of affect." It is a spontaneous language, with "little or no reflective awareness," in which the client has to react to his or her feelngs, in which they cannot be controlled. In such a case, the counselor responds in the "language of cognition," which helps to provide the client "with a means of grasping the significance of these feelings or happenings within him." The language of cognition may be viewed as a counselor response that is not technically a counseling technique. Rather, it is a maturational response that better enables the client to get in touch with his or her own feelings.

Some counselors view the counseling relationship not in this dialectical framework but as a singular, continuous process or growth, unified in its directionality. In this sense, the counselor's instrumental self is a catalyst for growth. Gibb (1968) offers one definition of what is meant by growth:

> In the normal processes of growth persons are confronted with sets of recurring concerns. . . . Growth consists of increased resolution of these concerns. (p. 25)

He lists the categories of concerns as acceptance and membership, intimacy and decision making, motivation and productivity, control and organization. As the individual grows, he or she learns mastery in each of these areas of life.

A somewhat different, but compatible, conception of growth is put forth by Rogers. Rogers (1961) sees growth as the basic direction of counseling and psychotherapy, and suggests that growth takes place as a direct result of the counseling relationship.

While the dialectical and growth paradigms are not exclusive of each other, the major emphasis of each is different. The dialectical paradigm emphasizes the counselor's response, within the dialogue framework, as the primary factor in client growth; the emphasis in the latter position, however, is on internal client traits and propensities (such as self-actualization) that blossom out almost independently of what the counselor does. The first position is more likely to emphasize counselor techniques, while the second position stresses the personal qualities of the counselor.

In addition to the dialectic and growth conceptions of the counseling relationship, we have what might be called the "modeling conception." This behavioral view is based on the idea that the client models himself or herself after the counselor as he or she progresses through the course of the counseling. The Freudian notion of transference (see chapter 2) lends itself to this type of interpretation, but such a view is also utilized by many counselors who are clearly not Freudian in their orientation. Shoben (1965) discusses the behavioral implications of this argument:

> If, as a model, the counselor thus operates as an attractive object of identification, he also, by the advantages of his role, is able to invest a high degree of genuine concern in his patient. Because he need not face the rigors of

figure 5.1 Concentric circles of need satisfaction

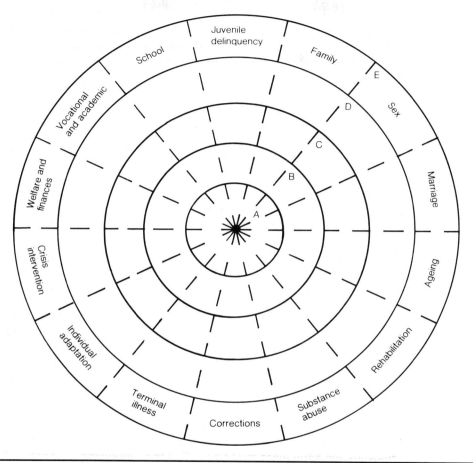

Note: From "A Maslovian Counseling Model" by S. K. Kirkpatrick, *Personnel and Guidance Journal*, 1979, *57*, 338. Used by permission.

continuing intimacy and unremitting personal obligation that other relationships entail, he can engage in an active search for the characteristics of the self-help seeker that may evoke quite authentic reactions of warmth and affection. (p. 225)

Asbury and Winston (1974) speak of reinforcing self-exploration and problem solving as part of the counseling process, and this would probably

figure 5.2 Cylinder of counseling process as needs satisfaction

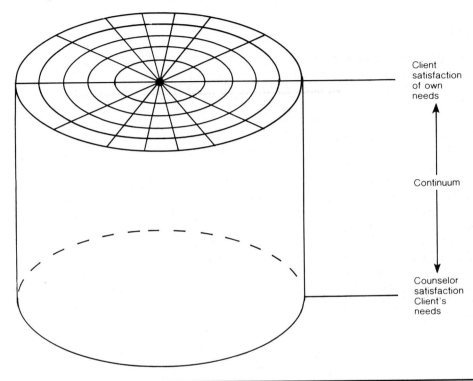

Client
satisfaction
of own
needs

Continuum

Counselor
satisfaction
Client's
needs

Note: From ''A Maslovian Counseling Model'' by S. K. Kirkpatrick, *Personnel and Guidance Journal,* 1979, *57* (5), 389. Used by permission.

fall under the modeling conception of the relationship. They differentiate between two types of counselors: what they call the ''naive perceptualist'' and the ''expert perceptualist.'' They describe the difference:

> The naive perceptualist refers to the novice, the perceptually based (client-centered) counselor who makes no attempt to be selective in his use of empathy and respect. He is probably unaware of what behavior he is reinforcing: therefore, he may in fact reinforce self-defeating behavior in his clients.
>
> The expert perceptualist is selective in his use of empathy and respect; therefore, he reinforces some client behaviors and fails to reinforce others. . . . By responding to specific expressions of feelings and thoughts, he becomes selective in his reinforcement. (p. 205)

We see in each of these descriptions different ways in which the counselor uses himself or herself as an instrumental tool in the counseling relationship.

SUMMARY

In this chapter, we examined some important aspects of the counseling relationship. We began by considering how the counselor can find and develop those qualities that have been shown to be most related to successful counseling outcomes. I then gave several guidelines for a productive counseling relationship, which included the ability to listen to all of the client's feelings and to communicate to the client the message, "I am here to *help* you." I also pointed out how these guidelines took into account many of the characteristics of the effective counselor.

We examined part of a counseling session to see how the interplay of forces underlying the relationship contributed to the quality of treatment. Several important points were noted, including how a counseling relationship may be "horizontal," "diagonal," or "vertical," referring to the relative status positions of counselor and counselee.

Finally, we examined the idea of the counselor's "instrumental self": the use of his or her entire personality to help the client grow. I noted how this viewpoint is consistent with the concept of counseling as a growth experience, in which a helper offers a part of his or her self to another in order to facilitate growth.

The School Counselor in Perspective

The term *school counselor,* which is preferable to the redundancy *guidance counselor,* poses a few problems of its own. Is the school counselor a counselor who simply works in the school setting, or is she or he a specialized type of counselor—as a psychiatrist is a specialized type of physician? How do school colleagues and clients perceive school counselors? What can they do to make an impact on the quality of school life, and how can they best assure that their services will be utilized and appreciated? How can they most effectively implement the driving force of the counseling stance within the context of the school setting? Before we can answer these questions, let us listen to a typical counselor, teacher, and student discuss some of their feelings and perceptions of the school counselor. Each of these monologues is extracted from a set of recorded interviews conducted at different urban and suburban schools. At the end of the three monologues, I will offer some comments to clarify the issues brought to light.

THE COUNSELOR SPEAKS

(I have asked the counselor Mr. Davis to describe his duties and responsibilities at the school and to tell me if he thought his preparation and training had been adequate.) "It's really difficult to answer those questions, although when you first asked them, I had stock answers to give you. But you see, the problem is that in this school the principal is short handed because of the budget, so I have to fill in a lot of times when people are out, or maybe if there's a vacant staff position. You know, doing administrative types of things, like programming, attendance reports, filing, even . . . things that probably the secretary could do, only he can't afford to hire another secretary. . . . I don't know if this is the usual situation 'cause this is the first school that I've worked in, but frankly, I resent it.

"Sure, some of the time I'm doing what I was trained to do. The other day a fourth-grader came down, crying, and she couldn't stop. Her teacher had tried to find out what was wrong, but the girl refused to tell the teacher, so she sent her down to me. I sat down with her and we spoke for about fifteen minutes, establishing a good rapport, and she finally told me that her mother had gone away for the afternoon and she didn't have her house key to get in after school. She was afraid that the mother would yell at her, and that's why she didn't tell the teacher, either. But I guess she felt she could talk to me. . . . I guess I did the 'right' thing with her. You know, after that short interview, I felt real good . . . like I had accomplished more in half an hour than I sometimes accomplish in a week. I could really enjoy my job if I didn't have to put up with all the trivial paperwork."

(I asked him how he came to be given these minor clerical jobs.) "Well, it happened right from the beginning. The second day of school, the principal came up to my office. . . . I was just sitting and waiting for someone with a problem to come in, and he made a joke about how he wished he were a guidance counselor, living the life of leisure. Then he asked me if I woud mind helping him with a little something—that's the words he used—so what could I say. Besides, I had nothing to do at that time, and I thought it would be a nice gesture. That little something involved setting up eight hundred folders for the new files. It took four weeks to finish. . . . Oh, about the teachers. We get along real well. They all seem to like me and we have some good laughs together in the cafeteria. To them, I have an easy job because I don't have to teach and I have my own office. But I don't see it that way. I always find that I'm busy with something, usually doing something for someone else. Also, the teachers don't really treat me as a professional . . . I mean they would never come down and talk about a problem or a teaching situation. They send down some of the kids they can't control, but that's about it. . . . Oh, it also upsets me that the students see coming down to my office as a threat, because they know that that's where they go when they don't behave. But it really shouldn't be like that. I'm not a disciplinarian."

THE TEACHER SPEAKS

(This teacher, Mrs. Bruce, is from a different school. I asked her to discuss what she thought of the school counselor and if she thought the counselor was doing her job well.) "All the teachers have great respect for the counselor in our school because of something she did the first week of the term— in fact, it was the first day of school, when we had our teachers' meeting. She had just replaced Mr. Davis who is on sabbatical and who never did much of anything during his three years here. But at the beginning of the term, as I said, when we had our meeting, which she didn't even have to attend, she asked us if she could speak with all of us a few minutes after the principal concluded the official meeting. All of us stayed to listen. Then she told us a little of her background and invited us to meet with her once a week after school to discuss how things were going in our classes, what problems we were having, and so forth. At first there was some grumbling because most of the teachers didn't want to stay late, but she made it clear that the meeting was optional and only for those teachers who had things to discuss or wanted to learn from listening to the other teachers discussing their problems. We all thought it was nice, and unusual, that she was willing to stay late to help us. First impressions are important, and they certainly were correct in this case.

"She turned out to be a very dedicated and conscientious counselor. She always gave the feeling that she knew what she was doing, and that she had plans. For example, she offered to speak in our classes, either to assist us if we wished or to supplement some lessons in hygiene and the like. We all thought that was nice. She also organized quite a few after-school activities that the kids seemed to like, and we had a joke about how she would always run around the school doing things—always busy and active. Most of the teachers, especially after they got to know her, began to come to the once-a-week meeting, and you'd be surprised how helpful those meetings were to us. Instead of having to send down our difficult children every time they got out of hand, we knew that we could discuss at the next meeting our problems with these children. I guess you could say that each of us began to act a little like counselors because of those regular meetings with her.

"A few of the teachers, from what I understand, met with her to discuss some personal problems that they were having. I don't know if that's a part of her job, but it sure did a lot to increase our feelings toward her. I guess you could say that we really *appreciate* all the things she has done for us. She gives us the feeling of caring, and even more important, the feeling that she is competent and willing to work to improve things around here. She's always so busy that we try to handle our problems first, before going to her for advice. We're lucky to have her as our counselor, and she's done a lot to change my whole view of what counseling is . . . especially after that Mr. Davis."

THE STUDENT SPEAKS

(The student, an eighth-grade boy, was asked to offer his opinion about the guidance counselor at his school.) "I never met Mr. S (C3) when I was in seventh grade, but I heard the kids talking about him a lot, and I knew they liked him. I never got in any trouble, so I never *had* to go to see him, but my friend R——was sent down last year for cutting, and he told me Mr. S is an all-right guy. . . . Near the beginning of this year my father died, you know, and I missed almost a month of school and fell behind in all my work. No one told me to, but I decided to see Mr. S on my own. I don't even know why. I was scared and kept putting it off, but finally I figured I'd go down to talk to him. When I got down to his office, he wasn't there, so I just left and figured I'd come back another time. But later that day he came up to my class and asked Mrs. B if he could speak to me. He said that the office secretary had seen me looking for him, and if I had a few minutes now, we could talk for awhile. I was really surprised that he came to see me—I mean he's probably busy and all. . . .

"Anyway, we talked for—it must have been over an hour. I missed my next class, and he said it's OK, he'd write a note for me. I don't even remember what we talked about—I guess about school, my friends, drugs, about my father's dying. . . . I know that when I left his office, I felt a lot better. He told me that he had a group of a few kids at the school who met once a week just to talk about anything they wanted to, and he asked if maybe I'd like to come to the group just to give it a try. . . . I said I'd think about it, and then decided to go. . . .

"Now I've been going for almost four months, and I think it's really a good thing for my head. We just sit around and talk, about anything we want to, and some of the kids really seem to have problems, even though I don't, but I can relate to them anyway. . . ." (I asked if there were any other guidance services offered in the school.) "Sure, there's a community club where some of the kids do things for the community, like have a 'clean-up drive,' and there's a work program for the ninth graders who want to work in a store part-time helping out, but I didn't get involved in any other things than the group. . . . Mr. S is always telling us about different things he's doing at the school, and some of the kids are interested, but I don't have more time than for just the group. . . .

"It's funny, you know, how in a lot of schools the guidance counselor is someone you get sent down to if you're in trouble, but in our school he's a real nice guy and you feel that you can talk to him about anything you want. . . . I mean, he's not a fink or anything."

COMMENTARY

Clearly, there is some discrepancy between the way our first counselor perceives his job and carries out his duties; the way the teacher describes the counselor at her school; and the way the student presents the counselor at his school. These examples were chosen to illustrate the problems and pitfalls confronting the school counselor, as well as to show the many opportunities available to prove himself or herself of service to the school and to the community. Let us examine each issue, to gain a sense of perspective about the problem.

We note that our counselor Mr. Davis (C1) described on page 183, complains about being given unrelated work to do—things such as filing, administrative tasks, and so on. This is a common complaint of school counselors, perhaps the most common complaint. Boy and Pine (1969) point out that prior to the National Defense Education Act of 1958, administrators did not take seriously the attempts by school counselors to extricate themselves from trivial duties and administrative burdens by tending toward therapeutic counseling; but since the passage of that act, counselors have been viewed in a more professional light. This evolutionary change, however, seems to have had no effect upon C1 at his school, and we must question why this is so. It is evident, both from his attitude and from what he says, that the clerical encumbrances placed upon him are indirectly a result of his own doing and not entirely the principal's fault. By failing to communicate to the other school personnel the scope of his job as he saw it, by not having a clearly defined idea of what he was supposed to be doing—and doing it—C1 invited the opportunity he now complains about. It is not uncommon to find that counselors who complain most about the low level of the functions they are asked to perform are the very same counselors who fail to take the initiative in performing the higher level functions that they believe their jobs entail. Likewise, we find that those counselors who, from the beginning of their tenure, assume an active and dynamic approach, who make their presence felt from the first day of school until the end of the semester, suffer less from the misunderstandings and exploitation that plague these others. It is only assertive and confident school counselors, counselors with a sense of certainty about why they are there and what they are expected to do, who are not taken advantage of by others around them, particularly by those in administration.

Returning to the present case, the evidence is clear and indisputable. Compare the behavior of Mr. Davis (C1) with the behavior of the counselor who replaced him (C2), and we can immediately pinpoint the cause of the problem. C1, by his own admission, spent the first day of school sitting in his office, waiting for something to happen. He took no initiative, made no effort to bring his services out to the teachers and the students. Mrs. Bruce (C2), on the other hand, did just the opposite. She went out recruiting, actively and enthusiastically presenting herself and her services to the teachers. Unlike C1, she didn't wait for things to happen—she made them happen. When the principal came into C1's office, he noted the lack of activity on the counselor's part and felt comfortable suggesting some busy work for the counselor. C1 invited this to happen, and there is no way around that conclusion. It would be difficult for me to imagine the principal at C2's school asking her to do the same type of chores, since she was so clearly engaged in a definitive, constructive counseling policy which took up her time.

An important first rule, then, is this:

The school counselor should walk in the first day of school with a clearly defined course of action and begin at once to implement this plan and to let it be known to colleagues and to the students.

In this way, she or he not only protects herself or himself from the opportunism and misunderstandings of the other school personnel, but puts forth a professional appearance that will ultimately prove efficacious to her or his plans.

Next let us look at the relationships between the teachers in the school and the counselor. C1 describes the relationship as "lots of laughs," but then goes on to complain that the teachers do not treat him as a professional. But how can they, if he does not establish a professional relationship with them? C2, the opposite of C1, establishes from the very beginning a totally professional and serious relationship with the teachers at her school. She explains what her services are, and she offers her services to the teachers. Consequently, they respond to her as a professional and respect her accordingly. They not only seek her advice but feel free to speak to her about their own personal problems. It would be difficult to imagine the teachers at C2's school asking her to do clerical work, in view of the polished professional appearance she articulates. It should be pointed out, however, that while conducting himself or herself professionally, the counselor must be careful not to become alienated from the other teachers by implying either in words or in actions that she or he is more professional, or on a higher level, than the teachers or the other school personnel. This is a difficult balance to maintain—between functional professionalism and social egalitarianism, between eliciting respect and still maintaining friendship and cordiality—and it is a successful counselor who is able to hold the tenuous line between the virtues of confidence and certainty and the vice of elitism, without recourse to such artificial facades as coldness, detachment, and snobbishness. The school counselor, like the small-town doctor, is at most times a friend and comforter; but when needed for professional services, he or she must be someone who is held in the highest regard by constituents.

C2 seems to have achieved this balance well, while C1 chose to retreat from the professional stance and immerse himself in the pleasures of friendly badinage, which ultimately served little professional good. Our second rule, therefore, could be stated like this:

The school counselor must at all times maintain a professional attitude, which should not interfere with the ability to conduct harmonious and cordial relationships with other school personnel and with students. He or she must exude professionalism, but avoid elitism.

Finally, let us examine the relationships established between these counselors and the students at their schools. C1, we note, did quite well when given an opportunity to work with a student who was experiencing a distressing problem. But it was pure chance that this student availed herself of C1's services, for C1 made no efforts to reach out to the students. Mr. S (C3) on the other hand, made a conscientious effort to reach out to the students, to tell them about his services and to publicize them in the school. He did not wait for our student to come back down to his office, but rather he went up to the student's classroom to find him and to ask him why he had come earlier. This type of initiative is not only admirable and compassionate, but it is an effective counseling tool as well.

The kinds of situations and difficulties exemplified by the typical counselor, teacher, and student have been a source of concern to professional counselors and counselor educators since the beginnings of the counseling movement. In their broad perspective, they fall under the rubric of "role definition"—of clearly defining the role of the counselor. But in practice, defining the role of the counselor is far less important than teaching counselors the meaning of counseling and instilling within them the right attitudes about counseling. A role definition of counseling will emerge naturally as counselors understand and respond to the needs of the students, teachers, and administrators with whom they work. Koch (1972), in discussing some of the problems in school counseling, has pointed out that the role of the counselor is often defined by the administration rather than by any actions on the counselor's initiative. Koch also points out that most students take the attitude that counselors are only "schedule changers," an attitude that results from the administrator's encumbering the counselors with such duties. The role definition, in this case, is not determined by the counselor, but rather by the situation at the school or by the attitudes of the administrative supervisor. Such a case is typical, and the counselor must always keep in mind that more often than not his or her role will be defined not by the criteria of what should be done but rather by the demands of the immediate situation.

In discussing the problem of role definition, Haettenschwiller (1970) points out that an "interdependence exists between the focal person—the counselor—and members of his role set—principal, teacher, parent, student, and counselor educator." All of these individuals exert a definite force on the developing role of the counselor, helping in their own ways to shape that role to their expectations. This process of shaping is accomplished through the disbursement of rewards and punishments, what Haetten-schwiller calls "sanctions":

> Through these rewards . . . control is exercised over the role enactment of each member of the organization. In place of rewards, however, it is more appropriate to speak of sanctions, both positive and negative. Positive sanctions may include the immediate rewards of approval or praise, the instrumental rewards which facilities—for example, a secretary—provide, or the rewards deriving from compliance or collaboration by members of the role set. Negative sanctions may include restricting the performance of professional duties or prescribing nonprofessional duties, refusal to cooperate in the enactment of the professional role, negative criticism, or termination of contract. (p. 438)

The implications of this arrangement are that the counselor is bribed and blackmailed into submitting to roles that are acceptable to those who disburse the sanctions. Such a position is clearly incompatible with the goals of counseling and with the interest of the students who depend on the counselor for guidance and encouragement.

Recognizing this difficulty, Haettenschwiller suggests that counselors must derive their power—their rewards—from outside the school boundary, from professional people with whom they can communicate openly and without compromise, rather than from administrators, teachers, parents, students, and staffs.

The problem of role definition is complicated even further by the multiple roles and identities school counselors are asked to assume during the performance of their duties. The counselor is a different "other to others": she or he maintains a changing persona, a flexibility and adaptability that have become his or her hallmark. Shertzer and Stone (1963), in reviewing the literature, have found that the counselor is perceived differently by most of those people with whom he or she comes in contact. Students see the counselor as being particularly helpful only in the areas of educational-vocational decision making; teachers see the counselors as administrators to be tolerated, providing ancillary services that are expendable, who pamper students, speak in obscure jargon, and often hide behind the veneer of confidentiality when their activities are challenged; administrators view the counselor as a jack-of-all-trades who rarely succeeds; parents look toward the counselor as a persuasive agent of change in the areas of vocational and educational choice or one who will correct many of the child-rearing errors they have made over the years; the general public looks toward the counselor to promote more effective manpower utilization for the country's economic and political needs. It is the job of counselors, argue Shertzer and Stone, to clarify these misconceptions and multiple demands by clearly articulating their own roles. The difficulty here, however, is the lack of consensus by counselors themselves as to what their role should be and how they should go about performing this role. This is a problem that will not be solved by counselors alone; more research and more dialogue among professionals is needed to explore the myriad complexities of this problem scientifically and pragmatically. Knapp and Denny (1961) suggest three guidelines for future research. First, counselors should be encouraged to provide data "concerning actual procedures which guidance specialists have followed in building guidance services" (p. 49). They should keep written logs of their day-to-day activities to enable researchers to determine the relative appropriation of time by effective versus ineffective counselors. Second, a careful analysis of counseling time must be made to determine the most efficient use of time. "Counseling time must be analyzed to determine those needs which would more profitably be met through some other medium such as group guidance" (p. 50). Third, research must be conducted in the area of staff orientation, the relationships between the counselor and other staff members. Although much of this research has been undertaken since 1961, it still remains primarily the responsibility of the individual counselor to define his own role. A third principle may be stated as follows:

It is the responsibility of counselors to understand and to articulate their role as they see it. They must be aware of the multiple perceptions and multiple demands that their position encourages, and they must try their best to clarify to those with whom they work what their real purpose is and what their legitimate responsibilities are.

This can best be done when the school counselor understands his or her rightful place within the educational organization. The counselor does not stand outside of the educational establishment, functioning as an adjunct to that establishment; rather, he or she is an integral part of the educational process, acting as either a catalyst or a guide in the education of the students at the school. Hobbs (1958) has argued that counselors should have a closer connection with the instructional program of the school than they now have. This closer connection can be achieved, he points out, if the counselors "have a continuing responsibility for contributing directly to the major purposes for which educational institutions are presumed to exist" (p. 596). In order for this to happen, however, counselors must be careful to avoid the pressures upon them to be all things to all people. Boy (1972) suggests, quite correctly, that when counselors attempt to satisfy all of the demands imposed upon them, they face the danger of being nothing definite to any-one. If they attempt to satisfy all groups in determining their role, then they will be performing duties that are self-protective rather than living up to their counseling obligations as they relate to the individual child. If they respond to pressures of the moment, they can lose the opportunity to de-velop a role which has long-range consequences for both youth and the counseling profession.

It is necessary, therefore, that their school counselors have a thorough understanding of places in the school and their position relative to the positions of the teachers, the principals, and other school personnel. In the following section we will explore the dimensions of the school counselor in perspective.

THE SCHOOL COUNSELOR IN REVIEW

Within the school, the counselor is a specialist who is asked to perform a variety of specialized services, ranging from intensive counseling to imple-menting extra-curricular programs. As a specialist, he or she is expected not only to have know-how but to communicate to his or her colleagues and clients a professional attitude and a maturity that reflect competency as well as personal achievements. But to what degree can he or she be suc-cessful in communicating this attitude and in implementing these skills? Much depends on the way that he or she sees the job and the way that other school personnel, particularly teachers and the principal, look upon his or her position. For the counselor's actual effectiveness depends greatly upon others' receptivity toward his or her services and recognition of special competencies.

Carmical and Calvin (1970) tried to determine how school counselors "viewed their job functions and what their role in these functions should be." They found that the top five functions rated by counselors were:

1. Providing the student an opportunity to "talk through his problems."
2. Counseling with potential dropouts.
3. Counseling with students concerning academic failure.
4. Counseling with students in evaluating personal assets and limitations.
5. Counseling with students concerning learning difficulties. (p. 282)

Several significant insights can be gleaned from these findings. We note first that with the exception of the fourth point, each of the counseling functions is concerned primarily with students who either fail to adjust ap-propriately to the school environment or exhibit manifest behavioral prob-lems such as dropping out or failing. The counselors interviewed were unable to arrive at a consensus about how, in their capacities as counselors, they

table 6.1

SUMMARY OF WHERE STUDENTS GO FOR HELP
(All figures are percentages of total responding)

source	choosing a college	changing a class	conflict with a teacher	problem with a friend	financial aid question	graduation requirements	career decision	a question about sex	problem between students and parents	decision on a college major	information about career opportunities	a personal problem	help in finding a job	when student is in serious trouble	planning a school program
Counselor	29	81	40	6	24	80	26	4	12	26	8	4	4	7	51
Dean	1	3	18	2	2	3	1	0	1	1	1	0	0	4	1
Career counselor	27	1	0	1	17	6	29	2	1	29	78	2	52	0	6
Teacher	4	7	8	3	2	6	4	3	4	4	2	1	1	2	5
Principal	0	1	10	1	3	1	0	0	0	0	0	0	0	3	0
Relative or friend	8	2	6	49	7	1	5	32	54	5	5	46	11	32	7
Parents	27	5	17	28	38	2	28	45	16	28	4	35	21	43	26
Other	2	0	1	10	5	0	7	14	12	7	1	11	10	6	4

Note: From "Paperwork, Pressure and Discouragement: Student Attitudes toward Guidance Services and Implications for the Profession" by C. E. Wells and K. Y. Ritter, Personnel and Guidance Journal, 1979, 58(3), p. 171. Copyright 1971 American Personnel and Guidance Association. Reprinted with permission.

could help the average or above-average student. Such an attitude is common not only among school counselors but among students as well. Heilfron (1960), in a study of high-school students' perceptions of the counseling function, found,

> High school students feel that students who are performing well academically and socially need much less counseling than students who are intellectually inferior, socially immature, or unrealistic in their aspirations; only students who display obvious character disorders should be referred to agencies outside school for professional help.

> These two findings suggest that students expect counselors to devote themselves to individuals who exhibit overtly that they have problems, possibly to the exclusion of students who need help not necessarily in overcoming social or intellectual handicaps, but in finding the best ways to use their resources. (p. 136)

figure 6.1 Rank order of counselor duties as seen by students

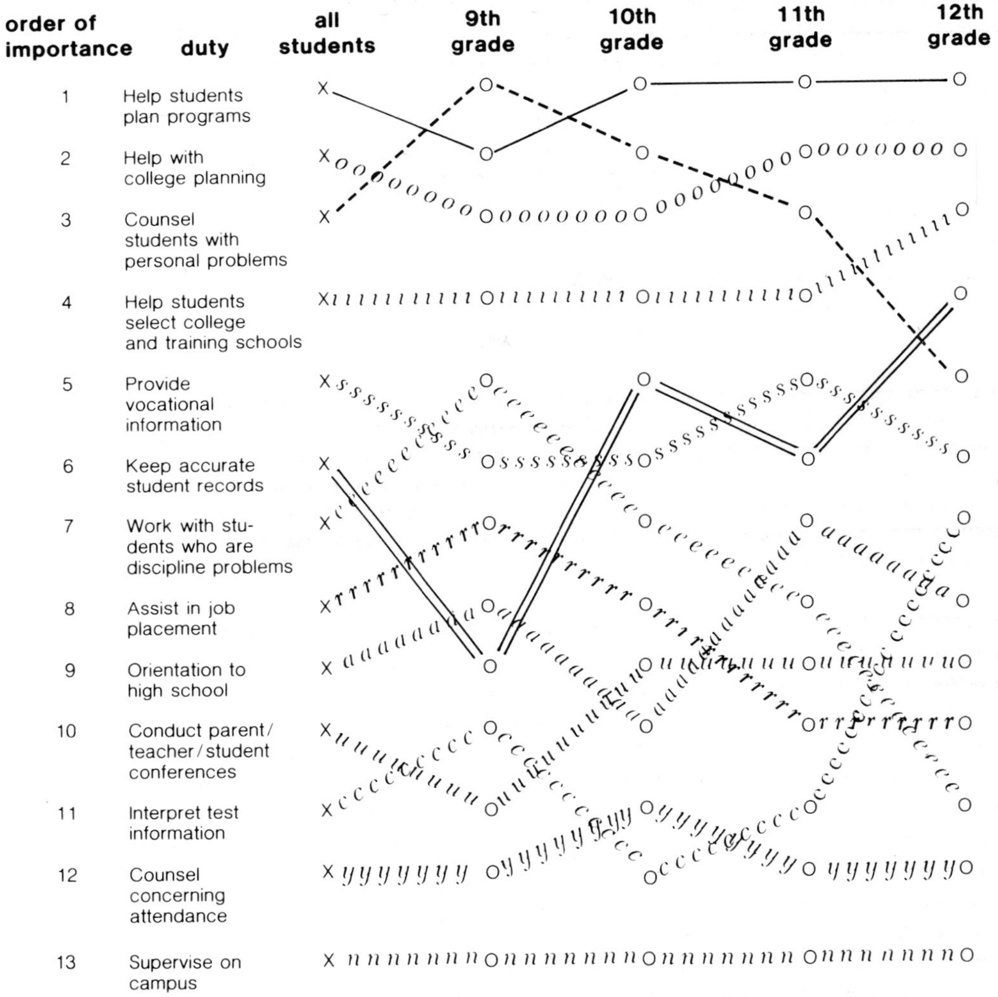

order of importance	duty	all students	9th grade	10th grade	11th grade	12th grade
1	Help students plan programs					
2	Help with college planning					
3	Counsel students with personal problems					
4	Help students select college and training schools					
5	Provide vocational information					
6	Keep accurate student records					
7	Work with students who are discipline problems					
8	Assist in job placement					
9	Orientation to high school					
10	Conduct parent/teacher/student conferences					
11	Interpret test information					
12	Counsel concerning attendance					
13	Supervise on campus					

Note: From "Paperwork, Pressure, and Discouragement: Student Attitudes Toward Guidance and Service and Implications for the Profession" by C. E. Wells and K. Y. Ritter. *Personnel and Guidance Journal*, 1979. *58* (3). 171. Used with permission.

The fact that such an attitude is common, of course, does not mean that such an attitude is good. On the contrary, there is evidence to indicate that the school counselor may be inadvertently contributing to the waste of our greatest natural resource: talent. For how can counselors believe that they are meeting their obligations if they confine themselves primarily to working with youth who are having difficulty succeeding in life, at the expense of those youths who have potential for greatness. True, problem youths need their services; this is not to be denied. But equally true is the proposition that all of the students at a school can benefit from counseling, many of them in equal proportion to the troubled or problem-laden youth. Our eighth-grade student, as we saw earlier, benefited enormously from his interactions with C3, even though he exhibited no manifest problems that required C3's immediate attention.

A fourth principle may be stated as follows:

The school counselor, to be effective, must recognize his or her responsibilities to all students, including the failing student, the disruptive student, the potential drop-out, the student with an emotional problem, the student with a learning difficulty, as well as the gifted student, the average student, the withdrawn and shy student, and the student who does nothing during the course of his or her studies to attract the attention of the counselor or other school personnel.

A second important insight gleaned from Carmical and Calvin's work is that counselors shy away from treating students with so-called emotional problems. The top-five function list carefully eschews any reference to dealing with intensive problems. Such an attitude is easy to understand for two reasons. First, as I mentioned in chapter 1, counselors are taught to believe that their competencies are limited to less severe problems, and that more serious problems are in the exclusive province of psychotherapy and psychiatry, a belief that has little or no basis in fact. The second reason, however, is compelling. The severe limitation of time imposed on the counselor by the unworkable student-to-counselor ratio at the typical school precludes the possibility of devoting enough attention to any one student to help her or him on a dynamic, intensive, emotional level.

While this second position is appreciated, it should be pointed out that situations in mental hospitals are not so much different, with respect to psychiatrist-to-patient ratio, from the situation in the public schools. Psychiatrists and psychiatric social workers who practice at these hospitals know that the best way to reach the largest number of patients is through group activities, including both group psychotherapy and group social, educational, and civic activities. The school counselor should also attempt to reach the core of seriously disturbed students in the school by setting up activities to which these students could be invited and supplementing these group activities with one-to-one counseling sessions, which need not be so frequent as to be prohibitive.

The counselor who does not wish to work with the severely disturbed, who believes she or he is not competent to handle such cases, will find much support in the job setting to reinforce this position. Studies of school personnel have shown almost unanimous agreement with the position that the school counselor is ill equipped to deal effectively with the severely disturbed student. Grant (1954), for instance, found that "in looking at the data in the personal-emotional area, it should be noted that approximately 70% of the teachers and administrators feel that someone other than the counselor should work with students in this area. . . . It should also be noted that counselors themselves seem uncertain of their ability to assist students in the types of problems presented in the personal-emotional category" (p. 76). In another study, Bergstein and Grant (1961) also found that parents of school children "perceived school counselors to be more helpful with educational and vocational problems than with personal-emotional-social problems" (p. 703).

These studies, however, reflect only what the counselor is perceived as being able to accomplish, not what in fact he or she is or is not able to accomplish. Therein lies the important difference. For despite the agreement as to their limitations, study after study has shown that experienced psychotherapists are no more competent than experienced counselors to treat severely disturbed patients or clients.

A fifth principle could be stated:

School counselors must recognize and develop their competencies to treat severely disturbed students and students suffering from emotional problems, particularly through the use of groups, after-school programs, educational activities, and other nonintensive forms of treatment. School counselors must, furthermore, strengthen their commitment to this group of students, since they are likely to be the first professional with whom they come in contact and who are able to help them. During their training, school counselors must learn to develop attitudes and skills that will enable them to work effectively with this group, which has long been ignored in the school setting.

As we examine each of these principles that guide their actions, our conception of school counselors undergoes a number of changes. We see the various levels of functioning on which they are required to perform, and we understand the obstacles which may make their job difficult at times. Our image of the counselor—as he or she shifts from the intimate intensity of a face-to-face counseling interview to the less personal administrative function of coordinator of after-school activities—fuses the precise skill of a specialist with the broad range of a generalist. Wrenn (1962), in discussing the role of the counselor, sees her or him as both a specialist and a generalist:

> The counselor is a generalist in the sense of his being widely available to the total school population and attempting to possess some knowledge of the total school program. He is a generalist also in the sense that he should be acquainted with the complete scope of school referral resources and know how these may be utilized by himself or by other members of the staff. The counselor is a specialist in his specific knowledge of the student and in his ability to relate himself effectively to the student in both individual and group situations. He is a specialist in the total scope of student learnings in and out of the classroom. He is a specialist in the collation and interpretation of information about individual students and student populations—to the student himself, to staff, to administrators, and to parents. (p. 143)

With this view in mind, let us explore specifically how this specialist as generalist implements his or her counseling principles into concrete, practical activities.

THE COUNSELOR'S ACTIVITIES

First and foremost, we have the face-to-face counseling interaction, which was discussed in chapters 4 and 5. It is clear that the face-to-face meeting between counselor and client, although highly effective and desirable, is a difficult reality to bring about in the schools. The counselor's time is precious and to allocate a significant chunk of that time to helping a single student would not appear to be the most expeditious utilization of the counseling resource. Rather, the counselor would do better to concentrate on ways of reaching the greatest number of students in the least amount of time.

To this end, we have group counseling, which is both an efficient and practical method for communicating with a large number of students in a relatively brief period of time. The counselor can schedule regular weekly meetings of small groups. Even without much campaigning, word of such groups will travel through the corridors quickly, attracting those students who believe they will benefit from the group experience. The counselor may also post on the student bulletin boards creatively designed announcements to herald the groups to the student population. Remember, it is always the responsibility of the counselor to make his or her services known.

The school counselor may also effect significant therapeutic changes by setting up and administering after-school programs. The extension of the school day, which to be effective must be voluntary, is a great hope for both students and teachers alike. For it is clear that students, teachers, administrators, and counselors who voluntarily choose to participate in school functions beyond the regular school hours are not only highly motivated to begin with, but are also more likely to benefit from their experiences, since they would not continue the activity unless it was beneficial. The way to encourage students and teachers to remain after the close of the school day is to design programs that are interesting, challenging, and clearly of benefit to the volunteers who participate in them. It is an advertising—a public relations—effort that the counselor engages in, an effort that, if successful, could prove most important for the educational, intellectual, and emotional health of the school community.

Finally, the school counselor can implement many ideas into actions by sharing these ideas with other members of the school team. He or she can and should confer with the principal, teachers, parents, paraprofessionals, community leaders, and students to learn from them what their needs are and how his or her ideas may be transformed into actions which will be of benefit to them.

By actively engaging in activities—by being committed to his or her beliefs—the school counselor can become an effective agent of growth within the school setting.

If we temporarily turn our attention away from what the school counselor might do, and examine what the typical school counselor does do, the results should be revealing.

Carey and Garris (1971) raise the question, What does the counselor do that is different from others, or that cannot be done as well by others? This is an important question which helps not only to clarify the role of the school counselor but also to justify the counseling function as well. Trotzer and Kassera (1971) have attempted to answer this question by determining what the actual activities of the counselor are. Table 6.2 illustrates how the counselor's school time is divided between contact with students, noninterview activities, and contact with people other than students. Table 6.3 and 6.4 are even more revealing; they show that counselors spend the bulk of their time not in activities that are directly beneficial to the students but rather in extraneous activities that might well be done by other personnel.

This is an unfortunate situation, but it is one that has persisted from the very beginnings of the guidance and counseling movement. The causes of this predicament are complex and worthy of an intensive study in themselves; but suffice it to say at this point that the more clearly counselors define their roles to themselves and to those with whom they work, the less likelihood there is that their time will be used unexpeditiously. The opposite

table 6.2 **COUNSELOR CONTACT WITH STUDENTS**		
	% of student contact	% of total time
Student contact		44.3
Educational	33.0	14.6
Vocational	14.8	6.6
Personal	25.7	11.4
Scheduling	8.0	3.5
School activity (attendance)	4.3	1.9
Group	5.6	2.5
Test interpretation	1.2	.5
Student and teacher (both present)	.3	.1
Test administration	7.1	3.2

table 6.3 **COUNSELOR CONTACT WITH NONSTUDENTS**		
	% of nonstudent activity time	% of total time
Nonstudent interview activity		23.3
Committee meetings	9.1	2.1
Faculty meetings	5.0	1.2
Teacher/nurse conference	24.6	5.7
Staff	16.1	3.8
Parent	17.1	4.0
Principal/administrator	12.1	2.8
Minister, police, probation officer	2.8	.6
Psychologist, social worker, welfare	5.7	1.3
College representative, military, salesman	7.5	1.8

table 6.4 **NONINTERVIEW ACTIVITIES**		
	% of noninterview activity time	% of total time
Noninterview activity		26.6
Mail	6.9	1.8
Write-up interviews	4.5	1.2
Prepare for testing	2.6	.7
Desk work and reports	39.5	10.5
Phone	2.2	.6
Coffee, pop, etc.	11.7	3.1
Looking up people and materials for students	.7	.2
Supervision and teaching	25.0	6.6
Miscellaneous	6.9	1.9

Note: From "Do Counselors Do What They Are Taught?" by James P. Trotzer and Wayne J. Kassera, *The School Counselor,* 1971, *18,* 335-341. Copyright (1971) American Personnel and Guidance Association. Reprinted with permission.

is also true as I pointed out with C1: if counselors are unsure of what they are to do, if they sit and wait for things to happen, for their services to be requested, they are more likely to spend an injudicious portion of their time on noncounseling tasks.

THE COUNSELOR'S PROFESSIONALISM

This brings us back to the issue of professionalism. How can the counselor unequivocally emphasize his or her professional status and encourage other school personnel to utilize his or her valuable professional resources? This is a question that has been debated time and again in the literature. Van Riper (1972) points out that school counselors can only become professionals by what they do—by their "ostensive acts." "In spite of how busy school counselors have been," he suggests, "their work has lacked purpose and meaningful results" (p. 325). The explanation for this, as we have seen, is simple: the counselor spends too much time in noncounseling, and even worse, in nonprofessional activities imposed upon her or him by an administration which is neither sensitive to the counselor's needs nor aware of his or her capabilities. McCully (1962) tackles the problem in somewhat more detail. Suggesting that the problem of nonprofessionalism dates back to the origins of the vocational guidance movement, McCully argues that newer, more innovative approaches are needed to professionalize the movement. He lists six developmental stages leading toward professionalization, which are summarized as follows:

1. The unique social service of the school counselor in its performance must be identified in a manner that will differentiate it from the services of the other members of the school staff.
2. Standards for the selection and training must be developed, and they must be acceptable to the corporate group of qualified school counselors and to the preparatory schools.
3. For selection and training standards to be functional, schools must be accredited for training counselors.
4. Counselors should be certified.
5. Counselors as individuals and as a group must gain sufficient autonomy to permit them to perform their duties in the interest of the public.
6. The corporate group of counselors must have and enforce a code of ethics for its members. (pp. 683–687 passim)

Nearly two decades after the publication of McCully's paper, many of these developmental stages have become realities, and yet the professionalization of the counselor is still only a glimmering hope. Why is this? Again there is no clear answer, but evidence would seem to indicate that counselors and counselor educators still have a long way to go in improving their own self-image of their professionalism, let alone communicating this image to others.

Arbuckle (1970b) suggests that the contemporary school counselor lacks a strong professional identity. The counselor, he says, should have distinguishing qualities which set him or her apart from other teaching staff and other school personnel. He or she should be involved especially with the helping conditions that exist in the school, identifying with the human needs that manifest themselves. "His primary professional function—and his particular professional contribution—is in the counseling involvement with individuals, small groups of students, teachers, or parents . . . individuals with stresses and problems because of minority position, their general youthful alienation, or their drug involvement" (p. 789). As the counselor does this, there exists a greater likelihood that his or her singular professional identity will clearly emerge and be acknowledged.

PROFESSIONAL ISSUES IN SCHOOL COUNSELING

The profession of school counseling is truly a melting pot of talent. Unlike other professions (such as medicine, law, pharmacy) which are relatively homogeneous, counseling includes within its ranks people who have gone through a wide variety of different types of training programs; who may or may not be state licensed in one or another of the allied mental health fields (social work, teaching, psychology, etc.); whose training, orientation, and professional recognition may be similar or very different from others who are also called counselors. Generally, although not exclusively, mental health professionals who are designated as counselors are those who hold a graduate degree in counseling, in counseling psychology, or in guidance and counseling, which is also called school counseling or counselor education and may be offered by the school of education. On the undergraduate level, counselors may have majored in virtually any subject area, although a large number come from the ranks of education, psychology, and sociology. In this section, we will look at some professional issues, with the hope of making clear how counselors get where they are, who represents them, what their social standing and professional recognition is, and so on. We will begin with the counselor's training, and then look at the professional organization that represents counselors. In the final pages, we will consider the controversial question of credentialing—licensing—counselors.

The Counselor's Training

Typically, counselors are trained in graduate programs by a highly qualified professional staff with a wider diversity of background and specialization than is ordinarily found in a single academic department. The faculty of the counseling department may include practicing counselors, counseling psychologists, clinical psychologists, psychiatric social workers, psychotherapists, psychometrists, researchers and theorists, philosophers of education, administrators, community psychologists, vocational counselors, and others. This is creditable inasmuch as counseling is interdisciplinary in scope and substance. A report by Division 17, (Division of Counseling Psychology of the American Psychological Association [APA]) entitled, "The Scope and Standards of Preparation in Psychology for School Counselors" (1962), for example, specifically recommended that the counseling department be "interdisciplinary in nature. Each discipline should be taught by qualified specialists trained in the discipline itself and oriented to the work of the counselor." This position reflects the relationship of what the counselor is expected to know and what his or her training comprises.

Admission to counseling programs—especially to doctoral level programs—is highly competitive. Typically, in addition to school performance, a standardized test such as the Graduate Record Examination (GRE) or Miller Analogy Test (MAT) may be mandated. An interview may also be required, since the personal qualities of the applicant are as important—if not more important—than the ability to perform well on standardized aptitude and achievement tests or even in other undergraduate or graduate level courses. In fact, research has suggested that less emphasis be placed on these so-called objective criteria, which do not show much of a relationship with effective counseling (Arbuckle, 1970a).

Counselor training programs vary in emphasis, in depth, and in what they require of students. Some place special value on personal development, on individual emotional growth, and on the ability to relate to others. Some believe that the purpose of advanced training is to help the counselor trainee develop research skills, and they emphasize quantitative aspects of training. The ideal counselor training program (if there is such a thing!) should help the trainee develop affectively as well as cognitively.

The scope of training can be set down in four general categories, which take into account the range of accepted counseling skills: (1) mastery of cognitive information relating directly to the counseling process; (2) ability to administer programs and to communicate effectively, orally and in writing, with other members of the counseling team (consultation), with concerned parents and other interested parties, as well as with the client; (3) self-awareness and the willingness to be introspective, to grow and, when necessary, to change; (4) technical proficiency in the counseling setting; feeling comfortable in the role of counselor.

The types of understanding and skills required for mastery in these four areas represent an amalgam of knowledge—both theoretical and practical—that transcends any single discipline or specialization. The trainees must be exposed to the theoretical foundations of psychology and psychotherapy, as well as to the practical realities offered by group and individual counseling practica; they must develop speech and communication skills, be familiar with the liberal arts; with our cultural heritage; with some sociology, some anthropology; with the myriad of cross-cultural influences that affect the society in which we work; with teaching, learning, and educational theories; with principles of counseling administration; and with the interrelationship of the disciplines. From his or her intimacy with these disciplines, the counselor should be able to synthesize and project findings and relevant issues that pertain to the counseling environment.

In a recent survey of counselor educators devoted to information specific to the counseling discipline, both the theories of counseling and the topics that are of increasing interest were evaluated. Farrell (1978) found the following theories of counseling considered most important by instructors of the introduction to counseling course:

Behavioral
Client-centered
Gestalt
Humanistic
Reality therapy
Rational-emotive therapy
Psychoanalytic and psychodynamic
Transational analysis
Existential

imp to instructors of counselling course.

In the same study, when asked the question, In your opinion what topics are increasing in interest? . . . , the six leading responses were:

Group and family counseling
Career guidance
Legal and ethical issues
Values clarification
Community counseling
Counseling the handicapped

Increasing in interest

These subjects may be covered in different courses, ranging from introductory survey courses, in which they are usually presented quite generally, to advanced seminar courses, where they can be discussed in detail. Some of the learning will be obtained from books, but much of it will be through the interaction of counselor educators and their students.

Professional Organizations and Journals

The organization that most decisively represents the interests of the counseling profession is the American Personnel and Guidance Association (APGA), with its central headquarters in Washington, D.C. The APGA boasts almost 40,000 members, from all fields of counseling. This organization comprises thirteen divisions that, in effect, represent every specialized area of counseling. Presently, the main disseminators of counseling research, news, and professional developments are published by APGA. These are

The Personnel and Guidance Journal, published monthly, and the newsletter, Guidepost, which is published eighteen times a year. In addition, most of the divisions of APGA publish their own journals, dedicated specifically to concerns of that division. There is an annual APGA convention, held each spring in different cities.

Since abbreviations are used so often in the literature, the following list of divisions of APGA includes both the full title and its abbreviation. Most of the titles of these divisions are self-explanatory. The journal published by each division is also indicated in the list. Most school counselors would express particular interest in ASCA, which represents a large percentage of the school counseling professionals in the United States.

ACPA American College Personnel Association
Journal of College Student Personnel

ACES Association for Counselor Education and Supervision
Counselor Education and Supervision

NVGA National Vocational Guidance Association
Vocational Guidance Quarterly

AHEAD Association for Humanistic Education and Development
Humanist Educator

ASCA American School Counselor Association
The School Counselor, and *Elementary School Guidance and Counseling Journal*

ARCA American Rehabilitation Counseling Association
Rehabilitation Counseling Bulletin

AMEG Association for Measurement and Evaluation in Guidance
Measurement and Evaluation in Guidance

NECA National Employment Counselors Association
Journal of Employment Counseling

ANWC Association for Non-White Concerns in Personnel and Guidance
ANWC Journal

ARVIC Association for Religion and Values in Counseling
Counseling and Values

ASGW Association for Specialists in Group Work
Together

POCA Public Offender Counselor Association (no journal)

AMHCA American Mental Health Counselors Association

In addition to APGA, interests of counselors are also represented by Division 17, the Division of Counseling Psychology, of the American Psychological Association. The *Counseling Psychologist,* a prestigious quarterly journal, is published by that division, often organized around specific themes (such as counselor identity, counseling men, etc.).

Credentialing: A Controversial Issue

The question of "credentialing" has emerged as one of the most important issues in the counseling profession during the past decade and is considered by many to be vital to the survival of counseling as a profession. While by far the majority of professions are licensed by the state, counseling stands in a class by itself and, in most states, is not licensed. "The problem," Forster (1977) points out, "is that the counseling profession currently lacks an effective credentialing process, and, as a result, its practitioners are restricted in their opportunities for practicing their profession" (p. 573). We will see that this has many political as well as practical implications.

The problem can be stated another way. Where psychology, which is a licensed profession in most states, enjoys certain privileges, counseling is generally excluded from enjoying the same professional perquisites, because it is unlicensed. The obvious solution is for counselors to become licensed as psychologists, but this has met with hearty opposition. Wherever counselors have attempted to become state-licensed as psychologists since this is a recognized profession, they have met with powerful resistance. This has resulted in a national battle between the professional psychology establishment and the professional counseling establishment. This battle has been waged on many fronts: in state legislatures, in Washington, in the professional journals, as well as in courts.

Clearly, there is a lot to be gained or lost; hence all the conflict. Specifically, the implications of licensing affect the possibilities of reimbursement by insurance companies and by the government for services provided. "Licensing," Warnath (1978) points out correctly, "is basically a political-economic issue," clearly transcending any matters of competency per se. This may help explain why psychologists have so strenuously resisted efforts by counselors to become licensed as psychologists. As Gazda (1977) suggests,

> The fact is that many qualified PhD's and EdD's are being refused the opportunity in most states to take the examinations for licensure/certification as "psychologists." When one examines the reasons provided by the various licensure boards for psychology, it becomes readily apparent that they are often arbitrary and not even based on present statutes. It is also evident that most state boards have moved recently to revise their statutes to restrict the

definition of a psychologist to someone who has earned a PhD in a Department of Psychology. Since many, if not half, of counseling psychologists are trained in Counselor Education Departments in Colleges of Education, this move would automatically make these qualified counseling psychologists ineligible for licensure. There is evidence that this move is only one of a series that are possible by psychology licensure boards to control the education/training of all counselors. (p. 570)

The two organizations that are pitted in this battle are the American Personnel and Guidance Association (APGA), representing the counseling profession, and the American Psychological Association (APA), representing the psychologists. But things get more complex. The sides are not always clearly drawn; for Division 17 of the APA—the Division of Counseling Psychology mentioned earlier—has members trained in both professions and therefore is not fully aligned with one or the other. The APGA has established a committee on licensure, which is negotiating with Division 17 to reach a compromise position on the licensing of counselors and psychologists. ACES, a division of APGA, has a Committee on Accreditation, which will probably serve as a basis for credentialing.

An entire issue of the *Personnel and Guidance Journal* (June 1978), devoted to this complex question, makes several points that capture succinctly the crux of the issues involved. The authors emphasize throughout this issue the need for counseling to become distinct from professional psychology; to have its own accreditation, credentials, and licensing.

There has been progress. Since 1974, when the thrust for licensure took off, the licensing movement has made important strides, especially in the following areas (Cottingham & Warner, 1978): creating a national registry for counselors; developing a third-party payment bill for counselor reimbursement; establishing a national counselor licensing network and complaint procedures; effective lobbying. Credentialing is not just a matter of prestige, then, but tantamount to giving the counseling profession a right to control its own training programs. "Societal changes," Forster (1978) concludes, "have created pressures on the counseling profession to become independent." He goes on,

> The pressure to become distinct from professional psychology has resulted in a rapidly increasing interest in credentialing, especially licensure. Both the psychology profession and the counseling profession are currently in a period of transition and search for identity. Although licensure stands out as the symbol of counselor identity and independence, establishing an effective method of accrediting or approving preparation programs represents the credentialing component having the greatest long-term impact. (p. 598)

This statement by Forster pretty well sums up the issue.

THE COUNSELOR'S ROLE CONFLICTS

The school counselor is in a highly unusual position. Unlike most colleagues in the mental health profession, the school counselor works in proximity and often under the direct supervision of a person who is not directly allied to the discipline, namely, the school principal. How unusual a situation it is, in perspective, to have a "professional" working under the auspices of an outsider to the profession. How can the counselor expect the principal to understand the complexities of his or her position when the principal more than likely has had no experience as a school counselor.

Conflicts between counselors and principals, particularly on issues relating to the counselor's role and his or her activities, are numerous and common. It should be pointed out, however, that in many areas counselors and principals find themselves supplementing each other rather than clashing. Schmidt (1962) has found that counselors and principals generally exhibit high agreement on the role of the counselor and on what responsibilities are associated with that role. Sweeney (1966) found that counselors and principals ranked attributes for counselors similarly, but principals tended to stress leadership more than did counselors. Moreover, the principals tended to see the counselor in terms of attributes considered necessary for an administrator—a likely bias. Both of these studies would support the argument that counselors and principals are not as far apart as is commonly believed. Hart and Prince (1970), on the other hand, found contradicting results. In an attempt to investigate "the discrepancy between the principal's expectations of the counselor's role and the ideal role as taught to the counselor during his training . . . and the effect counselor experience and training have had in shaping the way principals perceive counselor role" (p. 375), Hart and Prince found that the principals with no counselor training were more apt to assign disciplinary duties and clerical tasks to the counselor than were counselor educators. Furthermore, they found that principals and counselors disagreed on other important points as well: principals felt they should have access to all confidential files; principals did not see the counselor dealing with the personal-emotional problems of the student; principals believed that the counselors should accept many varied duties not commonly associated with counseling. In short, it would seem that principals without training and experience in counseling should not be entrusted to act as supervisors (or "immediate administrative directors," as is often the case) for the school counselor.

It has often been suggested that the principal may feel threatened by the counselor, who may be the only other person in the school who rivals the esteem and professional status of the principal. Such suggestions are difficult to prove or disprove, but it is important that the counselor be sensitive to the possibility that she or he (or the position, as the case may be) poses a threat to the principal. Chenault and Seegars (1962) have identified possible sources of conflict between counselors and their principals, and Filbeck (1965) has offered some specific suggestions of how counselors should behave in order to minimize conflict between themselves and their principals. Filbeck states,

> The counselor must be highly sensitive to those aspects of his work that are threatening to his principal. He must be able to anticipate what professional counseling activities are anxiety inducing; and where professional considerations (e.g., ethics) dictate proceeding in a manner that will arouse anxiety and antagonism on the part of his administrator, he must prepare and plan strategies to alleviate or reduce such feelings. It is suggested here that helpful strategies include: verbalized understanding of the principal's feelings, open communications with the principal, and a constant professional, competent demeanor to develop confidence, on the part of the principal, in the counselor as a proficient professional in the field of education. (p. 896)

Having examined this possibility of conflict, I can now state an important principle:

The school counselor must work effectively with his or her principal, taking into account and showing a sensitivity to the principal's needs, expectations, and fears. The counselor has an opportunity to increase his or her professional posture by establishing a viable, mutually respectful, and responsive relationship with the principal.

Finally, we shall turn our attention to the ways in which the counselor is typically perceived by the teachers at his or her school. Evidence indicates overwhelmingly that despite some negative feelings, teachers tend to perceive school counselors as helpful, responsible professionals who are a great resource for the teaching staff. McCreary and Miller (1966), in a survey of elementary school counselors and teachers in California, found that the teachers evaluated the counseling staff as helpful in testing individual pupils, in providing individual counseling, in assisting with classroom problems, and in participating in conferences with parents. Sherman et al., (1969), in a comprehensive study, found that although teachers have some points of dissatisfaction, on the whole they experience the school counselor in a highly positive light. Table 6.5, which shows how teachers perceive their school

table 6.5

COUNSELOR ATTITUDES AND CHARACTERISTICS AS PERCEIVED BY TEACHERS

rank order, item	(N-422) percent	rank order, item	(N-422) percent	rank order, item	(N-422) percent
1. Friendly	67	7. Well trained	29	13. Discouraging of communication	7
2. Cooperative	56	8. Efficient and effective	28	14. Condescending	7
3. Likeable people	42			15. Indifferent	7
4. Understanding	35	9. Removed from reality	19	16. Too status conscious	6
5. Encouraging communication	33	10. Highly professional person	17	17. Demanding	2
6. Professional toward teachers	32	11. Escaping from classroom	17	18. Hostile	1
		12. Too soft	15		

Note: From "Teacher-Counselor Communication" by R. Sherman, D. Albaggia, M. Cohen, E. Dell, J. Nadler, I. Shapiro, and B. Silverman, *The School Counselor,* 1969. *17,* 55-62. Copyright 1969 by the American Personnel and Guidance Association. Reprinted with permission.

counselor, indicates that the feelings for the counselor are generally of a positive dimension. However, when we look closely at this table, we find some discouraging indices: only 29 percent of the teachers interviewed perceived the counselor as "well trained," and only 28 percent found the counselor "efficient and effective." Even more distressing, only 17 percent of the teachers considered the counselor a "highly professional person." What do these results tell us? Mainly, that although counselors tend to be well liked by the teachers at their schools, they are not always respected as professionals should be respected, nor are they always perceived as being competent to handle serious and difficult problems.

One of the major difficulties faced by the school counselor, as we can see from all of these studies, is making his or her professionalism felt by colleagues. Teachers and principals are prone to diminish the counselor's capabilities and minimize his or her professionalism. If the counselor accepts this image, he or she may act accordingly. This is referred to as the self-fulfilling prophesy. Perhaps there is no better example in practice of the self-fulfilling prophesy than we find in the school setting, where the counselor, having been taught the limits of his professional capabilities, communicates these limits subtly to his colleagues, who in turn subscribe to these arbitrarily imposed limitations.

Stintzi and Hutcheon (1972), in discussing the multiple roles of the school counselor, analyze how the counselor's role is perceived by the counselor, by the students, by the teachers, by the administrators, and by the school

table 6.6

THE MULTIPLE ROLES OF THE SCHOOL COUNSELOR

the counselor's role in his view

1. He is an adviser precariously balanced in a mid-position.
2. He cannot be an administrator and a counselor at the same time.
3. He should not be a disciplinarian.
4. He must be able to relate to students, parents, and faculty in counseling.
5. He should be a listener, treat discussions in confidence.
6. He should be sincere and honest—not a phony.
7. He should be active in the community.
8. He should be active in scheduling individual planning and learning, and programs and special placement.

the counselor's role from the student's view

1. He should be a source of information for career guidance and vocational opportunities.
2. He should be open for discussion on social and personal problems.
3. He should not be a disciplinarian, but should be available for consultation on discipline problems.
4. His qualities should include sincerity and integrity—someone the students can have faith in.
5. He should allow students to make their own decisions.
6. He should be available to orient new students.
7. He should encourage an open-door policy.

the counselor's role from the teacher's view

1. He should be the teacher's advocate in supporting the teacher's views and decisions.
2. He should be the one to conduct case studies.

3. He should assume the position of consultant on disciplinary problems and administer discipline.
4. He should consult with the teacher before making decisions.
5. He should not have an autonomous position.
6. He should be obliged to participate in school supervision.
7. He should counsel students.
8. He should be active in scheduling and special placement of students.

the counselor's role from the administrator's view

1. He should be in a remote position to the administrator.
2. His prime function should be student counseling, individual and group.
3. He should be available to talk to parents.
4. He should be active in individual planning and learning programs for special placement.
5. He should maintain informal, as well as formal, student contact.
6. He should consult with teachers.

in the school district where the counselor's effectiveness was highly regarded by all, the key points were:

1. Counselors were not assigned administrative tasks.
2. Counselors were not responsible or associated with punitive discipline.
3. Counselors encouraged open-door policy to students, faculty, and parents.
4. Students and faculty were well aware of the types of services available from counselors.
5. Students were encouraged to have at least one meeting with the counselors per semester.

district. Table 6.6 shows the different components that constitute the counselor's role as they are perceived by his or her constituency and by colleagues. We see from these results an overall positive image of counselors, in which they are perceived and respected as professionals who are deeply committed to their work. They are viewed as constructive, indispensable members of the educational team, who work with students, teachers, and administrators to improve the quality of education. Unfortunately, because these results do not tally with other studies that analyze counselors' use of time and the demands placed upon them by other members of the school staff, we must suspect that this list represents the *ideal* image of the counselor role rather than the practical reality. The discrepancy that exists between this perception and the analysis of their function as compiled by Trotzer and Kassera (1971) is directly related to the loss of professional identity suffered by school counselors as they endeavor to perform their duties.

Related to this issue is a question that has recently received much attention at professional meetings and in the professional journals. To what degree is the counselor responsible for maintaining or for changing the institution which employs and sponsors him or her? With the rising level of social and political awareness of the 1960s, coupled with the activism of youth and the particular assertions of angry minority groups, counselors were compelled to reexamine their roles in the face of heated social pressures. As the system itself came under attack—as the very premises and principles that have guided this country's development came under the fire of critical scrutiny and thoughtful reexamination—the counselor found herself or himself in the dubious position of attempting to help clients who, in many cases, were in the process of rejecting or changing the very institution to which the counselor was presumed to hold loyalty. The counselor's role, which had once been a matter of theoretical debate, now became a crucial social issue that had to be dealt with at once in order to maintain a level of efficacy that would continue to justify his or her position.

Banks and Martens (1973) are critical of the counselor's position, arguing that "counselors have been acting as agents and apologists for the system for too long" (p. 457). They indicate that counselors are prone to accept the rules and mores of the institution as if they were correct by definition, and that they show a reluctance to question and to challenge openly the institution where it may be at fault. Even more unfortunate, in terms of the counseling stance, is the counselor's tendency to "operate on the premise that it is the individual alone who has a problem when he fails to 'adjust' to the current order" (p. 457). The counselor cannot function effectively— cannot even understand the problems of the client—unless she or he is able to stand back from prejudices and preconceptions to understand the client's discontent and its social as well as its psychological causes.

Banks and Martens suggest that the counselor must avoid this professional pitfall by broadening his or her understanding of the issues, and particularly of how his or her feelings are entwined with the issues:

> The counselor must have a clear concept of what issues or institutional practices are causing problems for the clients and for others. There must be a solid base of communication between counselor and client founded on mutual trust. In order to develop this trust the counselor may have to become more open and honest about who he is and what his own frustrations are. (p. 461)

Cook (1972), likewise, after considering this question, suggests among other things that the counselor can help create a "free flow of information" inside the school, a flow that should facilitate the constructive processes of social change. "A change in an organization," he points out, "depends, in part, on the free flow of information to all parts of the system" (p. 15).

Dworkin and Dworkin (1971) take a psychosocial approach toward the problem. They reflect on the ramifications of the social upheaval:

> A stable sense of meaning appears lost as children resist the values of generations past, as sons openly attack their fathers, as fathers kill their daughters. To face the here-and-now with some sense of sanity is an awesome task. The future holds no certainty, yet we cannot retreat to the past. (p. 748)

Viewing the counselor as being in the position of advocating change while acting as the protector of the status quo, the authors suggest that the effective and dedicated counselor will not sit back passively on the sidelines watching changes happen but rather will become an active agent of change within the school and community environment. Chastising counselors for being hung up on authority, they advise counselors to listen to the young and to let them lead their own lives and learn from their mistakes. To do this, counselors must reevaluate their own lives—their life styles, attitudes, and beliefs in order to better understand their clients. Moreover, they cite the challenge of expanding the role of the counselor by recruiting a greater cross section of counselor candidates and suggest six actions to help the counselor improve his or her own commitment to social change and better an understanding of the needs of youth.

We see that the counselor is in a position of conflict regarding his or her role in the changing social situation. The school employs the counselor and expects his or her loyalty in return; but the counselor is primarily committed to the clients with whom he or she works, and conflicts may arise between the two factions. It is the responsibility of each counselor to come to grips with this problem in a way that his or her conscience, ideals, and professional ethics dictate, and to examine and reexamine personal feelings before attempting to deal with the client's feelings.

An allied question that inevitably attaches itself to this issue is, What does the school have a legitimate right to expect of its counselor? Hoyt (1961), in a superb paper, delves into this question and comes up with several answers that may be helpful in resolving some of the conflicts. He says first that *"the school has a right to expect that the counselors will have a professional career commitment to education."* This commitment, which must be right alongside the commitment to counseling, distinguishes the school counselor from the counselor-in-general. Moreover, this commitment changes in part the scope of the tasks, for the inextricable tying together of counseling and education demands that his or her counseling endeavors satisfy the requirements of both disciplines. Second, Hoyt states that *"the school has a right to expect the counselor to be a specialist."* Particularly, it is expected that the counselor will be more capable than anyone else in carrying on certain functions, including but not limited to appraising, supplying occupational and educational information, making referrals, doing group guidance and face-to-face counseling. Third, *"the school has a right to expect that the services of its counselor will extend to the teaching staff."* This, like the first expectation, changes in part the scope of the counselor's duties. The counselor is no longer limited to individual counseling but functions as a master teacher as well, assisting the teachers to "develop competencies in such areas as student appraisal procedures and counseling methodology so that teachers may perform more effectively as guidance workers." Fourth, *"the school has a right to expect that the services of its counselor will extend to the administrative staff."* This clearly does not mean that the counselor becomes a servant to the administration but rather that the counselor offers professional expertise as a resource to the administration in dealing with a number of their problems. Hoyt, unlike some of the writers, does feel that the counselor should be expected to deal with attendance and disciplinary problems, but only as a professional seeking the causes of behavior and determining therapeutic and ameliorative procedures.

Hoyt's assumptions seem fair and well rounded, and it would be to the benefit of the counselor to familiarize herself or himself with the expectations the job demands. She or he should have a clear idea, from the first day of school, what is expected and what is *not* expected of her or him, what she or he feels should be offered and what she or he should not be burdened with. The counselor should not permit being pushed around, becoming an errand boy or clerk, becoming a second-rate paraprofessional instead of the first-rate professional that she or he really is.

In maintaining such an attitude, it is important for the school counselor to understand his or her rights. Stewart (1959) has developed a counselor bill of rights (table 6.7) that clearly outlines the specific rights the counselor should demand in order to conduct his or her practice properly. The coun-

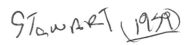
Stewart (1959)

table 6.7

BILL OF RIGHTS FOR SCHOOL COUNSELORS

1. The right to a reasonable counseling load.
2. The right to favorable working conditions . . . office space, ample clerical help, and other material conditions.
3. The right to enough time to do his real job . . . to engage in counseling *per se.*
4. The right to a real opportunity to establish effective contact with parents, referral agencies, and other organizations in the community.
5. The right to sufficient time and the privilege of serving on curriculum and other critical committees.
6. The right to have an effective voice in determining guidance and counseling policy and practice.
7. The right to have reasonable time for research.
8. The right to a recognized professional status.
9. The right to remuneration commensurate with the training and responsibility involved.
10. The right to have the full trust and support of the administrators to make the above rights effective.

Note: From "A Bill of Rights for School Counselors" by C. C. Stewart, *Personnel and Guidance Journal,* 1959, *37,* 503. Copyright 1959 American Personnel and Guidance Association. Reprinted with permission.

selor should keep in mind the difference between a right and a privilege—that a right is something that does not have to be earned or proved but that exists a priori, and which he or she is able to take advantage of unapologetically.

Isaksen (1964), in defining the role of the counselor in the mental health profession, discusses legitimate counseling functions that parallel this bill of rights. The role descriptions that serve as the basis of the functions of an effective counselor, according to Isaksen, are:

1. Motivate pupils to seek counseling through a creative and continuous program of orientation to counseling.
2. Conduct research designed to measure the effectiveness of the counseling.
3. Provide informational services to pupils designed to meet their need for educational, vocational, and personal-social information.
4. Assist in providing testing services designed to help each pupil appraise his capabilities, achievements, interests, and levels of adjustment.
5. Assist in the placement and grouping of pupils. This could include helping new students select courses of study. The school counselor . . . should not involve himself in performing administrative duties such as issuing failing reports, establishing an honor roll, etc. He should not be required to function as a school disciplinarian, either. (p. 12)

In short, we can say that as the counselors come to understand their legitimate role within the school environment, they can act appropriately and expeditiously to carry out those responsibilities which are legitimately theirs.

SUMMARY

The general definition of counseling, set forth in the first chapter of this book, is expanded somewhat in this chapter, where we consider the duties and problems of the counselor in the school setting. Some of the major issues presented were (1) the professionalization of the school counselor; (2) the relationship between the counselor, the principal, the teachers, and the student; (3) what the school has a right to expect of its counselor; (4) the counselor's bill of rights and the limits of his or her obligations.

I mentioned that the school counselor is perceived differently by different school personnel, and that she or he must have a sense of purpose, a clear understanding of his or her role and function in order to conduct an effective counseling office in the school. I listed six principles to guide the school counselor in his or her practice:

1. The school counselor should walk in the first day of school with a clearly defined course of action and begin at once to implement this plan and to let it be known to colleagues and to the students.
2. The school counselor must at all times maintain a professional attitude, which should not interfere with ability to conduct harmonious and cordial relationships with other school personnel and with students. She or he must exude professionalism but avoid elitism.
3. It is the responsibility of the counselor to understand and to articulate his or her role as it is seen. He or she must be aware of the multiple perceptions and multiple demands that the position encourages, and must try his or her best to clarify to fellow workers what his or her real purpose is and what the legitimate responsibilities are.
4. The school counselor, to be effective, must recognize his or her responsibilities to all students, including the failing student, the disruptive student, the potential drop-out, the student with an emotional problem, the student with a learning difficulty, as well as the gifted student, the average student, the withdrawn and shy student, and the student who does nothing during the course of his or her studies to attract the attention of the counselor or other school personnel.

5. The school counselor must recognize and develop competencies to treat severely disturbed students and students suffering from emotional problems, particularly through the use of groups, after-school programs, educational activities, and other nonintensive forms of treatment. The school counselor must, furthermore, strengthen a commitment to this group of students, since she or he is likely to be the first professional with whom they come in contact and who is able to help them. During training, the school counselor must learn to develop attitudes and skills which will enable him or her to work effectively with this group which has long been ignored in the school setting.
6. The school counselor must work effectively with the principal, taking into account and showing a sensitivity to the principal's needs, expectations, and fears. The counselor has an opportunity to increase professional posture by establishing a viable, mutually respectful, and responsive relationship with the principal.

Following these six principles, and at the same time being acutely aware of the rights afforded to them and the obligations expected of them, school counselors can make a profound and important impact upon education.

Values Clarification Counseling

7

The girl sits impatiently outside the high school counselor's office — biting her nails, waiting for the counselor to conclude the interview with the client she is now seeing. She looks out the glass partition, wondering if her friends will see her here, and if they do, whether they will know why she is here. Time passes slowly as she listens to the clicks of the minute hand on the wall clock. She wonders how the counselor will react to her problem. "What will she say when she finds out I am pregnant and thinking of an abortion? How will she advise me? What are her feelings about abortion? What will she think of me?"

Justin, at the elementary school down the block, has an entirely different problem. He knows who stole the reading tests from the storeroom, and even though he had no part in it he feels that maybe he should tell the teacher. After all, it isn't fair to the students who tried and did poorly while others had the answers in advance. But then he thinks of how he'll be called a snitch, a skunk, and he is not sure what to do. He decides to talk it over with Mrs. Wing, the school counselor, and hope that she will keep their discussion confidential.

Meanwhile, Mr. Vecchio has his own problems. He has been offered an excellent job at the community college, at a salary much better than he is presently earning at the intermediate school and with better job benefits. But he knows that if he leaves the school, the programs he developed — and the career exploration program he is currently working on — will probably go by the wayside. Also, he feels an obligation to those students in individual counseling and in group counseling with whom he has been working this year. He knows they'll feel rejected if he leaves. But, then again, he has his family to think about. They could certainly use the extra money and the extra time with him that the community college job would afford. What should he do?

Value decisions are something both counselors and clients have to make on a regular basis. Such decisions may involve a variety of factors — external and internal, controllable and uncontrollable. They range in complexity from relatively minor decisions to decisions that affect the rest of one's life. Moreover, a large percentage of problems for which individuals come to counseling are value conflicts. In this chapter we explore an area known as value clarification counseling—focusing on different types of values, on theories of moral development and moral reasoning, on thinking versus conduct, and on general perspectives of decision making. We will pay special attention to the role of the school counselor as a facilitator of *values clarification*.

VALUES, DECISIONS, AND CONFLICTS

Values are complex phenomena. Whenever we attempt to look at a person's values, it is always helpful to consider those values in terms of how they evolved (development), what they encourage or discourage the individual to do (behavior), and how they make the person feel (affect). We will see as we proceed that these three—development, behavior, and affect—are tied up in an inseparable bond for most people.

We can define values as "convictions or beliefs which prescribe or determine acceptable or preferable behavior in relation to needs or goals" (Strickland, 1978, p. 428). Two key words here are *needs* and *goals,* for values not only tell us what is acceptable and what is not acceptable but they also reflect what our needs are, the way we go about satisfying these needs, and the way we set up goals and perceive these goals. When there is a logical or practical discrepancy between the need, value, and goal, we call it a conflict. Let us consider these relationships briefly to see in context how counseling in *value clarification* works.

An individual's needs and values are related, since to a large extent values are defined by and, in some ways, help satisfy needs. For example, if something is very important to us as a need we value it highly. The person dying of thirst in a desert will value a glass of water quite differently than will a patron in an expensive restaurant, who lets the glass of water stand untouched and looks over the wine list. If John loves Mary, he values her differently than does Bob, who loves Vivienne. Siciński (1978) has proposed a four-level hierarchy of needs, which although simpler than Maslow's is more closely related to value development and decision-making. On the first level are the fundamental needs, much like Maslow's basic needs. Next come the needs that if not satisfied interfere with the individual's ability to perform some social function. For example, an individual may not be able to appreciate cultural activities because his or her aesthetic needs were never properly developed. Third are those needs that when not satisfied interfere with general social functioning—that is, which make the person socially maladjusted. For instance, a person whose need for affiliation, for friendship, was never satisfied when young may not be able to make friends later in life. Finally, there are those needs that when not satisfied interfere with individual emotional development and growth, even though a person may be functioning appropriately socially. These are the most severe and would describe individuals who are very disturbed and socially dysfunctional. Systems of values are developed, according to Siciński's theory, to help a person orient himself or herself to satisfying these different levels of needs.

Decision Making and Conflict

Because we hold values and believe in them—and because in the course of living we are confronted with myriad decisions, there are bound to arise conflicts between what we *want* to do, what we feel we *should* do, and what we *can* do. Some conflicts may take the form of just not knowing what to do—being stuck at a critical point in decision making. Other conflicts may be the result of frustration at not being able to do what we want to or feel we should.

Psychologists have evolved a typology of conflict that can help us understand what a *conflict* actually is. We can say generally that conflict occurs whenever we are faced with a choice that involves the pairing of two or more competing motives or goals. The four main kinds of conflict situations are called approach-approach, avoidance-avoidance; approach-avoidance; and, double approach-avoidance (Dollard & Miller, 1950).

An *approach-approach* conflict occurs when an individual is faced with a choice between two positive goals, both equally attractive. For example, Dave, a high school senior, has a choice of taking honors English or college chemistry, two courses given at the same time and both of which he would love to take. This is a relatively easy kind of conflict to deal with; since both the alternatives are positive ones, no matter what the decision, the person ends up with something he or she wants. Usually, this type of conflict is resolved when one alternative becomes more positive than the other. In this case, as Dave thinks it over he realizes that college chemistry, though more work, would give him advanced standing next year, so he decides to take that over the English.

An *avoidance-avoidance* conflict involves making a choice between two unpleasant alternatives. While Dave is making his decision, Mark, who hates math, is faced with the choice of selecting his required math course for graduation—geometry or trigonometry—which he postponed taking until now, the last half of his senior year. Typical behavior in this type of conflict situation is characterized by vacillation; that is, the individual approaches first one goal, then the other. The nearer one gets to each alternative, the stronger the avoidance response. So, as Mark tentatively decides on geometry he looks over the textbook and says to himself, "I could never learn this stuff." If the strength of one of the avoidance responses is increased, the person withdraws from the most disliked situation and overcomes the conflict. So, if the school announces that the trigonometry course will be more difficult than the geometry, this makes it easier to solve the problem: choose geometry. But if both alternatives remain equally unpleasant, the individual may attempt to "leave the field" as Lewin (1936) calls it; that is, to either literally run away from the situation, or figuratively, avoid the conflict by daydreaming, refusing to deal with it. This type of situation is resolved when one alternative becomes more positive than the other. Mark finally decided to take geometry when the school instituted a policy of providing tutors for the senior geometry students since so many were having problems in that course.

An *approach-avoidance* conflict involves a single goal that has both positive and negative characteristics. It attracts and repels at the same time. This is a considerably more difficult conflict situation than the other two types to resolve, and it tends to evoke a high level of anxiety. Lana would like to see a counselor privately to discuss the problems she is having with her boyfriend (approach), but fears that she will be stigmatized by her friends for not being able to deal with the situation on her own (avoidance). In the psychological laboratory, where a paradigm of this type of conflict has been set up, rats have been trained to run an alley for a food reward; then as they approach the food, they are given an electric shock. Studying the results of these experiments and generalizing them to human behavior, researchers have concluded that,

> When goals are at once satisfying and threatening . . . people's behavior vacillates at a point near, but not too near, the goal; at a distance the tendency to approach predominates; near the goal the tendency to avoid is greater. The result is a stable or self-maintaining conflict that tends to keep the organism at the point where the two tendencies cross. (Berelson & Steiner, 1969, p. 272)

This helps explain why some people, such as Lana, are never able to resolve their conflicts and can literally go for years vacillating between "I should go for counseling; I shouldn't; I should, I shouldn't." Each time she has a fight with her boyfriend the "I should" becomes stronger. But when she thinks of actually making an appointment the "I shouldn't" predominates. This is the classical stalemate of the approach-avoidance conflict.

Often two goals—not just one—have positive and negative points. Mr. Vecchio, whom we met at the beginning of this chapter, must choose between taking a better job or staying at the school where he is a counselor. If he takes the community college job he will make more money and have more free time, but he will lose those facilitative counseling relationships he has been working on for a year. If he stays at his present job he will be able to carry through his work, but his family will have to suffer to some extent. This is known as a *double approach-avoidance conflict.* In life, most conflicts fall into this category, since most of our choices have both positive and negative features. Unfortunately, there is never a completely satisfactory solution to this conflict, because each alternative has disadvantages that we would like to avoid. Thus, when we finally make a decision in the hope of resolving this type of conflict, we are still likely to feel some regret afterwards.

We see from this typology that there are different kinds of conflicts with different types of obstacles involved in their resolution. Since we will be primarily concerned in this chapter with value conflicts that involve moral dilemmas and ethical decision making, such as those we cited at the opening of the chapter, let us focus our attention at this point on moral values—specifically, their development and the way we reason out moral decisions.

MORAL DEVELOPMENT AND MORAL REASONING

Our moral development affects not only our individual decision making, as in the conflict situations just discussed, but also our feelings about and relationships with other people. Whiteman, Zucker, and Grimley (1978) found, for example, that as individuals reached higher levels of moral development and moral reasoning they felt more positively about other people in general; had a more optimistic view of humankind. We can say then that understanding how we develop a moral sense helps us understand how we relate to others.

There are four main theories of moral development, each of which sheds some light on how we make moral decisions and what these decisions mean to us. These theories, to some extent, also explain our behavior, although, as we shall see, there is an important difference between our moral reasoning and our actual conduct. The four theories are social learning theory; psychodynamic theory; Piaget's genetic theory; and Kohlberg's developmental theory. We will look at each in turn.

Albert Bandura is well known for his studies of modeled
behavior.

Social Learning Theory

This theory, developed most comprehensively by Albert Bandura, argues
in effect that we learn morality through the processes of modeling and
conditioning (both of which are discussed in some detail in chapter 3). Bandura emphasizes the modeling process, arguing that the major mechanisms
in moral behavior are imitation and social reinforcement. Bandura and others
have conducted numerous empirical studies to support the position that
children learn moral (and social) behaviors through modeling.

The most famous of these experiments demonstrates that aggression is
learned by *modeling,* or imitation as it is sometimes called. In an early
experiment, when nursery school children watched an adult play aggressively with a inflated doll, hitting and shouting "Sock him in the nose," they
were more likely to hit the doll when they were left alone in the room with
the toy than were children who did not observe this aggressive play (Bandura, Ross, & Ross, 1961). When the aggressive behavior was shown on
film, subjects were just as likely to imitate it (Bandura & Mischel, 1965).
And lest we mistakenly think this is limited to children, in a more recent
experiment it was shown that adults too act more aggressively after wit-
nessing aggressive behavior (Baron, 1974). In one interesting experiment
along the same lines, Brown, Corriveau, and Monti (1977) found that college
student viewers became angry and aggressively aroused after watching an

It has been suggested that children exposed to violence
are more prone to violent and aggressive behavior.

episode of an Alfred Hitchcock show on television in which a couple were being mistreated by the police and a judge. Thus, at all ages and in many different contexts, our values and behaviors are affected by what we see and, thus, what we imitate.

Thomas and Drabman (1978) found confirmation for Bandura's results, and added an important moral dimension to these findings. Using third and fifth-grade subjects in an experiment similar to Bandura's, they too found that those elementary school children who were exposed to an aggressive film on TV "were significantly more likely to choose aggressive responses as being normative than were [children] exposed to a control film" (p. 73). They also confirmed the existence of sex-role stereotypes; namely, that boys were more aggressive than girls. But, beyond this they showed that the learned behavior affected one's moral judgment. The boys felt more than the girls did that the aggressive reactions were morally appropriate, since they had modeled themselves on this behavior.

There is another slant to the social learning perspective; one which suggests that moral behavior is learned through the various conditioning processes. Alexander (1969) presents in summary this integrative behavioral position on moral development:

> Moral behavior can be defined as a response system developed as the result of perception of the pleasure and satisfaction occurring in other persons. It is likely that in early childhood, perhaps by the age of three years or earlier, the child comes to understand that some behavior brings parental approval and praise and other behavior brings disapproval or perhaps even disgust and anger. . . . The child during his first five years, however, can differentiate only minimally among types of behavior that might be termed "moral". . . . the moral significance of behavior is only realized at a later age.
>
> The fact that the child does not understand the significance of moral behavior does not mean that the so-called "moral learnings" do not occur in early childhood; it simply means that the child does not differentiate moral behavior from any other taught behavior. However, a child does begin the internalization of emotional responses of others in association with actions labeled "good" and "bad." (p. 95)

We see then that the social learning theory perspective of moral development is a comprehensive one that helps explain moral development in terms of different learning processes. But at the same time, we should acknowledge that it does little to shed light on the complex cognitive processes of moral reasoning, or on how we go about making moral decisions.

Psychoanalytic Theory

Moral development, according to psychoanalytic theory, is the direct result of the formation of the *superego*—a sense of conscience that we are not only aware of consciously but unconsciously as well. To Freud, the young child is basically amoral—a creature of impulse responding to the pleasure principle and motivated by selfish, primitive drives, which Freud calls the *id*. The id strives for immediate gratification of instincts and is oblivious to the needs of others and to the constraints of society. The process of emotional maturation, according to this theory, requires that the child learn that many of its needs cannot be gratified immediately; some not at all. As the child grows, it moves through a series of psychosexual stages, during which two other aspects of the personality develop which assist in the socialization process. The first of these, the *ego*, is the realistic aspect of the personality. The other aspect is the *superego*, or conscience, which is strict, moralistic, and often unrealistic. As the child resolves the *Oedipus complex*, he or she incorporates into the personality many of the values of the parents. These values, taken in without judgment or discrimination, are called *introjects*.

The superego is responsible for telling the person *right* from *wrong*, for differentiating between *should* and *shouldn't*. Whenever the person acts contrary to the injunctions of the superego, he or she feels guilt, a powerful psychological force that becomes the basis for many neurotic conflicts. To the Freudians, then, ethical values are moral introjects, which are integrated into the psychic structure of the superego by the time a child is six or seven years old. These values become the basis for many moral decisions.

The psychoanalytic theory, like social learning, does not help us understand the development of moral reasoning skills. Two theories that do a better job of that are Piaget's and Kohlberg's, both of which explain moral development in terms of increased moral reasoning.

Piaget's Theory of Moral Judgment

In 1932, Piaget published *The Moral Judgment of the Child,* a landmark study that elaborates a theory of moral development using much of the same methodology that characterizes Piaget's other research; namely, close observations of natural, spontaneous behavior, experiments, and interviews with children. Piaget's moral theory in many ways parallels his position on intellectual growth, and he takes great pains to point out the interrelationship between cognitive reasoning and moral reasoning. Just as in Piaget's cognitive theory, in which the child progresses from simple, automatic behaviors to more complex, organized behaviors, so too, in his moral theory does the child progress from naive beliefs and simple motor behaviors to more sophisticated, hypothetical, abstract reasoning.

Jean Piaget's observations of children led him to a comprehensive theory of moral development.

As we come to understand the path that cognitive and social progress take and by which Piaget explains moral development, a picture emerges of the developmental progress that characterizes the learner's transition from a *fixed-rule* oriented perspective to a *relativistic,* rational morality that transcends the narrow limitations of rules. The first type of morality, characteristic of young children, which Piaget calls a "morality of constraint," is based on fear of punishment; on the belief that we do not do wrong because we are told not to do it. In describing this stage, which includes the categories called "rules of the game," "moral realism," and "immanent justice" (all of which will be explained), Jantz and Fulda (1975) point out:

> During this period children view [adults] as authority figures who are to be obeyed to the point where "tattling" may occur. During this stage, [adults] need to consider the "constraints" they place upon children. Children need some guidance during this period, and it would be unfair to them if [adults] did not set down some guidelines for children to follow. However, if the [adult] totally restrains [children] by making and dictating all of the moral decisions, [the children] may be slower in moving towards the next stage, a morality of cooperation. (p. 25)

Piaget calls the morality of this period *heteronomous morality.* The word *heteronomous* means that one is subject to another's strict governing, including prescribed rules, laws, and regulations. This again refers to the constraint that dominates the child's moral thinking. As the child grows, intellectually, socially, and emotionally, he or she moves closer toward what Piaget calls *autonomous morality*—a personal, individual morality, based more on cooperation than on constraint. The autonomous morality is not independent of the heteronomous morality, but a consequence of it; that is, the child must first learn the rules and pressures of real living in order to learn ways to break free of them when it becomes necessary. In table 7.1 Jantz and Fulda (1975) show some characteristics of moral thinking at different levels. They use words frequently substituted for constraint and cooperation—*restraint* and *participation*.

Piaget and Inhelder (1969) offer a clear picture of autonomous morality and at the same time, show its derivation from its heteronomous roots:

> With advances in social cooperation . . . the child arrives at new moral relationships based on mutual respect which lead to certain autonomy. . . . First, in games with rules, children before the age of seven who receive the rules ready-made from their elders (by a mechanism derived from unilateral respect) regard them as "sacred, untouchable, and of transcendent origin". . . . Older children, on the contrary, regard rules as the result of agreement among contemporaries, and accept the idea that rules can be changed by means of a democratically arrived at consensus. . . .
>
> Second, an essential product of mutual respect and reciprocity is the sense of justice. . . . As early as seven or eight and increasingly thereafter, justice prevails over obedience itself and becomes a central norm. (p. 127)

As in his cognitive theory, Piaget's moral theory consists of stages of development, with each stage proving a prerequisite to successive stages. He uses three basic motifs to construct his theory: rules, realism, and justice—and he relates each of these motifs to patterns of behavior and reasoning. Let us look at each basic motif individually to better understand the moral transition from heteronomy to autonomy.

Rules

When does a person first learn that there are *right* behaviors and *wrong* behaviors? What do these words mean to the young child? How do they influence children's behaviors? These are some of the questions answered as we look at Piaget's findings on how children learn about rules.

In early forms of play, the child acts without any awareness of rules. The child's play is simply pleasurable motor activity, often spontaneous in nature. At around two years of age the child begins to learn rules by imitation. Children at this stage are still egocentric; that is, "even when they are playing together, [they] play each one 'on his own' (everyone can win at

↳ self-centre

table 7.1

SUMMARY CHARACTERISTICS OF LEVELS OF MORAL THINKING

concept	morality of restraint	morality of participation

Control	Duty is obeying authorities
	  Good defined by
	  obedience to rules
	  Rules or laws not
	  analyzed
		Mutual agreement
		  Lessening of adult
		  constraint
		  Rules can be modified

Justice	Letter of the law
	  Anxiety over forbidden
	  behavior
	  Concern for violation of
	  game rules
	  Punitive justice
	  Any transgression is
	  serious
		Restitutive justice
		  Concern for inequalities
		  Concern for social
		  injustices
		  Spirit of law considered

Responsibility	Objective view
	  Intentions not
	  considered
	  Egocentric position
	  Judgments in relation to
	  conformity to law
		Subjective view
		  Motives considered
		  Rights of others to their
		  opinions respected
		  Judgments by situation

Motivation	External motivation
	  Punishment by another
	  Rewards by another
		Internal motivation
		  Disapproval by others
		  Censure by legitimate
		  authorities followed by
		  guilt feelings
		  Community respect and
		  disrespect
		  Self-condemnation

Rights	Selfish rights
	  No real concept of right
	  Rights are factual
	  ownership
		Rights of others
		  No one has right to do
		  evil
		  A right is an earned
		  claim on the actions of
		  others
		  Concept of unearned,
		  universal rights
		  Respect of individual
		  life and personality of
		  others

Note: From R. K. Jantz and T. A. Fulda, "The Role of Moral Education in the Public Elementary School," *Social Education,* January, 1975, p. 28. Reprinted with permission of the National Council for the Social Studies and R. K. Jantz and T. A. Fulda.

Children learn rules in a predictable sequence.

once) and without regard for any codification of rules" (Piaget, 1932, p. 27). At around seven or eight years, the child begins to seriously "play to win," and becomes concerned with the codification of rules, although these rules are still rather vague. By the beginning of the latency period (age eleven or so), however, the child begins to recognize more systematically the differences between right and wrong, as defined by the rules of the game. "Not only is every detail of the procedure in the game fixed," by this point, Piaget argues, "but the actual code of rules to be observed is known to the whole society." It is at this stage that the child has pretty much the adult's sense of what rules are and what function they serve.

When the child first learns rules, he or she sees them as fixed, unchanging principles, which are sacrosanct and laid down by higher authorities. Moral behavior is dominated by *constraints,* by rules that he or she has learned to obey. Even when disobeying rules, she or he does not question the validity of the rules, which appear to be beyond challenge.

The earliest signs of adult-level moral reasoning occur as the child goes from primitive unruled behavior first to what Piaget calls a "morality of constraint." By the age of ten or eleven, the child even begins to see that rules can be fixed by agreement, that they can be changed, that they can be questioned. He or she may still abide by the rules, but is more willing to negotiate new rules. Piaget calls this the "morality of cooperation," because the child's moral behavior now involves a volitional element that was absent in the earlier stage.

From Moral "Realism" to Moral "Relativism"

When children first realize the concepts of wrong and punishment, they think in absolute terms rather than in relative, situational terms. The child regards the objective consequences of an act rather than the subjective circumstances surrounding it. For example, in one series of experiments, Piaget told a group of children two short stories and invited their comments. In one story, a little boy *accidently* broke fifteen of his mother's cups as he was on his way to dinner. In a second story, another little boy broke one cup as he was trying to sneak jam from the cupboard while his mother was out of the house. When the children were asked which of these little boys were more naughty, they answered that the first one was *because he had broken more cups.* Piaget calls this type of reasoning "moral realism," and it is characteristic of children up to about seven years of age. Moral realism has three characteristic features. First, the child under the influence of moral realism views "any act that shows obedience to a rule or even to an adult, regardless of what he may command [as] good; any act that does not conform to rules is bad" (Piaget, 1932, p. 111). Second, and closely related, the child values the letter of the law over the spirit of the law. Finally, under moral realism, children weigh an act strictly according to the consequences and ignore the intentions and extenuating circumstances. Later on, they develop a sense of "moral relativism" that enables them to consider extenuating circumstances—such as motivation, accident, and so forth—in their moral judgments.

From Immanent Justice to Distributive Justice

The idea of justice develops slowly during the early years, but it ultimately becomes the highest principle of morality. Early in life, the child has an idea of *immanent justice:* the belief that justice is inherent in the order of things, that evil deeds inherently produce evil consequences for the perpetrator. Pulaski (1971, p. 86) refers to this principle as the idea "that knives cut children who have been forbidden to use them." We hear this general *evil deed* principle referred to in such common sayings as, "If you play with fire, you *evil conquerors* are going to get burned." *(immanent justice)*

As children mature, their sense of justice becomes more sophisticated. They recognize what Piaget calls *distributive justice:* that rewards and punishments can be distributed in different ways. The development of the sense of distributive justice undergoes various transformations. At first, (before approximately eight years old), the child considers just and right whatever punishments or rewards the authority figures wish to dispense. During the latency period (about eight to eleven), the child believes that all "bad" acts should receive the same punishment, regardless of the circumstances. A boy who lies out of noble motivation should receive the same punishment as one who lies out of malice and deceitfulness. After latency, the child begins to recognize the principles of equity—of fairness—and develops a "kind of relativistic egalitarianism in which the strict equality will sometimes be winked at in favor of higher justice" (Flavell, 1963, p. 294).

Evaluation

Piaget does not present a single, ordered scheme of developmental stages, but rather views a "major underlying developmental progression from a 'heteronomous' to an 'autonomous' attitude or orientation" (Graham, 1972, p. 202). He does so through these categories we have just examined.

How accurate are Piaget's descriptions of moral development? How well do they account for the individuals' thinking in different cultures and in different subcultures of our own society? How helpful are they in understanding why people behave as they do, and in trying to determine how behavior can become more ethical, more principled? Much research is available to answer all of these questions.

An early line of criticism suggested that Piaget did not sufficiently take into account the part that cultural and social class factors play with respect to influencing children's moral judgments (Bloom, 1959). Investigations of how accurate a description Piaget's categories are, however, generally support his position across cultures (Durkin, 1960; Buchanan, 1973), although experimental rather than clinical procedures have shed light on how children go about making their decisions. Mancuso, Morrison, and Aldrich (1978), for example, tested one key aspect of Piaget's theory by comparing the moral reasoning of boys at first-, sixth-, and eighth-grade levels with respect to the problem of the broken dishes originally used by Piaget. The boys were shown videotapes of different situations in which a boy broke some dishes. In some tapes, the boy broke the dishes accidentally, while in some he did it intentionally. The circumstances were also varied: in some tapes the boy is unreasonably asked to clear the dishes from the table, while in others he does so as a favor and with a positive attitude. What the researchers found is that all these factors (accidental vs. intentional; favorable vs. unreasonable; or an angry parent) affected the viewers' judgment about the boy who broke the dishes, and that as the viewers got older they took more data into account in forming a value judgment about the boy who broke the dishes. This seems to confirm Piaget's main findings with regard to realism and justice.

At a later point in this chapter we will consider some specific implications of Piaget's position for the school counselor, but now let us turn our attention to another contemporary theory of moral development that easily rivals Piaget's in importance, while at the same time it supports some of Piaget's major assumptions. This is the theory of moral reasoning and moral development proposed by Lawrence Kohlberg.

Lawrence Kohlberg's Theory

Kohlberg, like Piaget, developed his theory by actually interviewing children and adolescents and studying their responses to certain hypothetical situations. In his studies he was particularly interested in ways that subjects arrived at moral decisions—their reasoning rather than the specific decisions arrived at. The results of his studies indicate that moral thinking progresses through three development levels—the preconventional, the conventional, and the postconventional levels—each of which comprises two related stages (see figure 7.1 on page 237). There are, in other words, six specific stages in all. Let us consider them briefly according to the most updated formulation based on twenty years of research (Kohlberg et al., 1978).

The Preconventional Level
At this first level, the child begins to think in a "moral" way, interprets good and bad in terms of the physical consequences (rewards and punishments), or in terms of the physical power of authority figures. In Stage 1, which Kohlberg, like Piaget, refers to as "heteronomous," the child reasons according to the principle of avoiding punishment by showing unquestioning obedience to authority figures, such as the parents. Fear, specifically in the form of physical punishment ("You'll have to stay in after school.") plays an important part in the determination of behavior. From the social perspective, the child is egocentric, hardly interested in how others (except the dispensers of rewards and punishments) feel about his or her actions or about how these actions affect others.

Lawrence Kohlberg

In the second stage of the preconventional level, called the "Stage of Individualism and Instrumental Purpose and Exchange," morality is governed by the principle of self-satisfaction. The child at times may recognize and respond to the satisfaction of the needs of others whom he cares for. Reciprocity, at this stage, is a matter of "You do one thing for me and then I'll do something for you, which is known as the quid pro quo philosophy. Kohlberg et al. refer to the social perspective of this stage as "individualistic" in the sense that the child recognizes himself or herself as a unique decision-making individual among others.

The Conventional Level

As the individual matures at this level, he or she begins to conform to the expectation and rules of conduct of the family, group, and nation. Moreover, the person is concerned with maintaining these rules and expectations not simply out of fear or expedience, but rather out of a sense of identification with and loyalty to the persons and the groups involved. While in the first stage, for example, a person may pay taxes for fear of going to jail if he doesn't, in this stage the belief that paying taxes is the right and lawful thing to do would be a more important factor in the decision.

At Stage 3, "The Stage of Mutual Interpersonal Expectations, Relationships, and Interpersonal Conformity," the child demonstrates what Kohlberg calls the "good boy/good girl" orientation. What this means in effect is that the child internalizes the values of significant others and believes that "good behavior is that which pleases or helps [these significant] others and is approved of by them. . . . One seeks approval by being 'nice' " (Kohlberg, 1968, p. 26). The individual is primarily motivated to gain the approval of others. Consequently, the child will conform to stereotyped images of what is natural behavior and for the first time will judge other's actions by their intentions. For example, the science teacher asks for a volunteer to stay after class and help her in the lab. Jeffrey knows that this would mean giving up playing basketball with his friends, but he reasons this way: "If I give up the game and offer to stay, the teacher will like me and this is important."

During the second stage of the conventional level, which Kohlberg calls "The Social System and Conscience Stage," the individual is oriented toward fixed rules and the concept of duty—of obedience to recognized authority. The social perspective of the individual is that the social system defines the roles and rules of behavior and conduct. There is a strong tendency, during this stage, toward maintaining the social order, and it is therefore sometimes referred to as the law-and-order stage. Consider, for example, a student who has the opportunity to steal a final exam, but reasons, "The teacher trusts me, it's against the rules to see the exam in advance, and therefore I won't give into this temptation."

The Transitional Level

Kohlberg's later research (Kohlberg et al., 1978) convinced him that between the conventional and postconventional level there was a transitional level, in which moral reasoning was postconventional but still not entirely principled. During this transitional level, which overlaps the stages at the end of the conventional level and at the beginning of the postconventional level, individuals are able to see themselves as persons outside of a recognized social order and they make decisions without any strong commitment to the society, even though they recognize its existence. They have become aware of the relativity of different social standards and can therefore justify actions within different parameters. Still, as we will see when we look at the post-conventional—or principled—level, the ability to reason morally has not yet reached its highest possibilities.

The Postconventional (Principled) Level

This principled level is the highest level of moral reasoning. At this level, the person acts according to autonomous moral principles, which have validity apart from the authority of groups or persons who hold them and also apart from the individual's identification with those persons or groups. In other words, obedience to authority and social recognition are secondary

figure 7.1 Kohlberg's stages of moral development

moral problem presented to subjects

In Europe, a woman was near death from cancer. One drug might save her, a form of radium that a druggist in the same town had recently discovered. The druggist was charging $2,000, ten times what the drug cost him to make. The sick woman's husband, Heinz, went to everyone he knew to borrow the money, but he could only get together about half of what it cost. He told the druggist that his wife was dying and asked him to sell it cheaper or let him pay later. But the druggist said, "No." The husband got desperate and broke into the man's store to steal the drug for his wife. Should the husband have done that? Why? (Kohlberg, 1969, p. 379)

---

preconventional level

stage 1:

"If you steal the drug, you will be sent to jail, so you shouldn't do it."

"If you don't steal it, then you'll get in trouble for letting your wife die."

Principle: Avoidance of negative consequences.

stage 2:

"If you get caught, you'll probably get a light sentence, and your wife will be alive when you get out."

"Your wife may not be around to appreciate it, anyway, and it's not your fault if she has cancer."

Principle: Act to your own advantage, using the principle of quid pro quo.

---

conventional level

stage 3:

"No one will condemn you for stealing the drug, but they will hold you responsible for her death if you don't."

"By stealing it, you'll bring dishonor on your dying wife, and everyone will think you a thief."

Principle: Act according to how you think others will approve or disapprove of your actions.

stage 4:

"Your duty is to your wife, and therefore you must steal the drug for her."

"Your duty is to obey the law, and you should not steal the drug."

Principle: Adherence to law and order.

---

postconventional (principled) level

stage 5:

"The fact that you *feel* you have a right to violate the law does not actually give you the right to do so."

"The druggist is abusing his license to hold a public trust, and therefore has violated his implicit obligations to the society in which he works."

Principle: The rule is a social contract which can be changed by agreement.

stage 6:

"I live by the principle that to save a human life takes priority over all matters of property, and therefore feel no compunctions about taking the drug."

"I live by the principle that property is sacred and cannot be expropriated, and will therefore let my wife die."

Principle: An organized set of values which comprises the conscience acts as the basis for decision making.

to the higher values and principles that are recognized as paramount by the individual. In Stage 5, "The Stage of Social Contract or Utility, and of Individual Rights," the individual demonstrates a social-contract orientation, generally with legalistic and utilitarian overtones. "Morality is based on upholding the basic rights, values, and legal contracts of a society, even when they conflict with the concrete rules and laws of the group" (Kohlberg, 1978). Right action is defined in terms of general rights and in terms of standards that have been critically examined and agreed upon by the whole society. There is a clear awareness that values, opinions, and laws are relative and can be changed. There is emphasis on the legal point of view, but also on the possibility of changing the law through elections rather than freezing it in terms of Stage 4's law-and-order type of thinking. The type of moral reasoning during this stage corresponds roughly to Piaget's morality of cooperation, as opposed to a morality of constraint.

Kohlberg calls the final stage of moral development the "Stage of Universal Ethical Principles." At this stage, the individual is oriented toward the decisions of conscience in accordance with ethical principles, which are rational, organized, and intended to be applied universally. Rules at this stage are "universal principles of justice, of the reciprocity and equality of human rights, and of respect for the dignity of human beings as individual persons" (Kohlberg, 1968, p. 26).

We see, then, from the sequence of these stages how the child's naive moral outlook may progress gradually during the years of pre-adolescent and adolescent growth into a sophisticated, ethical, moral system, although many individuals never reach these higher levels.

Evaluation

While Kohlberg's and Piaget's positions express the developmental stages of moral reasoning in different terms and through different categories, there are many parallels, consistencies, and mutual areas of support between them. For example, both recognize that early moral reasoning is based on the child acceding to the wishes and values of an authority figure; that as we develop intellectually, circumstances and situations outside the immediate event can influence our judgment of the event. The methodology too is basically the same; both are direct results of observations with subjects, and both deal with hypothetical moral dilemmas that the subjects are given to resolve, although Piaget also concentrated on observing the spontaneous behavior of children. Both systems are developmentally sequential in that they require that the child pass through one stage before moving on to a higher one. Both systems also move from very concrete "naive" reasoning to hypothetical reasoning about abstracts and principled behavior. Moreover, the higher moral reasoning processes, in each system, demand higher processes of intellect as well. Thus, moral development according to both of these systems (as opposed to the psychodynamic or social learning perspectives) depends to a large extent upon intellectual growth and the ability to reason abstractly.

Although Kohlberg's theory has enjoyed wide acceptance and empirical support, it has also had its share of criticism. Much of it is centered around the argument that Kohlberg fails to account for emotional conditions of moral reasoning. Maschette (1977), for example, argues that Kohlberg concentrates too much on reasoning, on judgment, and on the logical valuation processes to the exclusion of focusing on moral conduct, emotional suasion, and actual behavior in real-life conflict situations. Trainer (1977), another critic, finds Kohlberg's theory deficient in a number of areas, including the failure to account for the significance of guilt and conscience and in failing to pin down philosophically and psychologically the meaning of morality and the nature of moral behavior. Research has shown that although there is little relationship between one's explicit ethical attitudes and one's level of moral reasoning (according to Kohlberg's theory), moral judgment as an intellectual process is still related to age and to cognitive development (Dell & Jurkovic, 1978).

Still, the evidence is plentiful when it comes to confirming the universality of Kohlberg's stages and their suitability as an explanation of moral intellectual development. In light of cross-cultural criticisms, Kohlberg and his colleagues have explored the development of moral thought in other cultures, such as Great Britain, Canada, Mexico, and Turkey, and have found that the sequence of moral development is the same across these cultures, although the rate of progress may vary under different social, cultural, and religious conditions (Kohlberg & Kramer, 1969). Other cross-cultural and social class comparisons have confirmed this and indicate for the most part that Kohlberg's stages are universal, although levels of development may vary from place to place and from class to class. Sararwathi and Verma (1976), among others, found the Kohlberg theory applicable for ten- to twelve-year-old girls in India—certainly a very different culture than ours. They also confirmed that there were some social class differences regarding individual moral issues, although the total maturity score did not vary from class to class. Others have shown too that although differences in rate are found between classes, the sequence of stages does not change.

VALUES CLARIFICATION IN PRACTICE

Understanding these theories of moral development is of more than academic interest to the counselor. Understanding the nature of values—especially moral values—is an integral part of almost all counseling efforts, particularly in the school setting, for moral growth and values development are integral to both the educational and the counseling processes. Hague (1977) suggests, in fact, that since the counseling process can never be truly value free, counselors should immerse themselves in studying theories of moral development and the processes of values clarification. "By looking in greater depth at what goes on in moral education," he points out, "counseling can take on new dimensions" (p. 41). Hoover (1977) suggests even further that values clarification is an important part of all emotional growth and psychological development and should be considered always in psychotherapy and counseling.

With regard to the school setting, there is an equivalent emphasis on moral development. In an important book on moral education, William Kay (1975) emphasizes the need "to advance the cultural evolution of mankind" toward "compassionate reasoning." His emphasis in moral education is that "children must be taught to love one another, (p. 87)" since this is a strong basis for positive moral action. Other researchers conceptualize the goals of moral education somewhat differently, but there is general agreement that moral education as a goal and values clarification as a process are integral elements in the successful education of the individual.

Kohlberg and Hersh (1977) have shown a variety of ways that moral development theory can be applied to school situations, especially in terms of resolving conflict situations and going beyond the law-and-order stage that is characteristic of much thinking in the classroom setting. When students are taught to resolve conflicts by using higher levels of moral reasoning they not only reach more equitable solutions but learn to think more clearly about other problems as well.

Swick and Ross (1979, p. 107) point out that "the educational process must involve learners in identifying, organizing, implementing, and continually assessing their moral choices via a moral system of living." To this end, they suggest using values clarification exercises in the classroom, within the context of subject matter and also within the context of a specialized affective education program. This has much practical significance, not only in creating better students but in creating more fully functioning individuals. There is even evidence that such epidemic problems as drug and alcohol abuse may in part stem from a lack of coherent value framework. Albas, Albas, and McClusky (1978) found, for example, that a lack of normative social values, which is called *anomie,* is positively correlated with alcohol abuse among high school students. So, values clarification can help resolve this very intransigent problem.

There are virtually dozens of different models of values clarification. The prototype program was developed by Raths, Harmin, and Simon (1966), who should be acknowledged as the founders of values clarification programs in the schools. They, like Piaget and Kohlberg, see a direct integration between cognition and valuing, with the former being directed toward understanding and the latter toward decision making. Within the school setting, the two are combined in the curriculum and in teachers' presentation and attitude. Specifically, the goals and processes of values clarification, according to their position, are to,

> help children: (1) make free choices whenever possible, (2) search for alternatives in choice-making situations, (3) weigh the consequences of each available alternative, (4) consider what they prize and cherish, (5) affirm the things they value, (6) do something about their choices, and (7) consider and strengthen patterns in their lives. . . . As the teacher helps students use these processes, he helps them find values. (p. 213)

With so many different theories of values clarification available, we will limit ourselves to two that, in my opinion, are representative of many others and that are by themselves excellent models for the counselor. We will begin by looking at a model developed by Hawley and Hawley (1975), which offers many practical exercises. We will then look at Beyer's model of using moral discussion to facilitate effective moral decision making.

Two Models of Values Clarification

Hawley and Hawley (1975) have written a valuable little book that deals with the gamut of human values in the classroom and how education can work to help individuals develop more fully their sense of emotional well-being. Their section on values exploration and clarification can be applied equally well in the counseling and teaching settings.

They divide the valuing process into six elements, the first four of which deal with the process of making the choice and the last two with acting on the choice, once it is made:

CHOOSING
1. *Preferences:* What do I really like?
2. *Influences:* What influences have led me to this decision? How freely am I making my choice?
3. *Alternatives:* What are the possible alternatives to this choice? Have I given sufficient consideration to such alternatives?
4. *Consequences:* What are the probable and possible consequences for my choice? Am I willing to risk the consequences? Are the consequences socially beneficial or socially harmful?

ACTING
>   5. *Acting:* Am I able to act on this choice? Do my actions reflect the choice I have made?
>   6. *Patterning:* Does this choice represent a continuing commitment through action? How can I change the pattern of my life so that this choice is continually reflected in my actions? (pp. 146–147)

Hawley and Hawley go on to point out three steps for helping clients work successfully through the valuing process to decisions with which they are comfortable. These steps, originally designed for the classroom, would be the appropriate sequence of stages in a values clarification counseling group. First, there is opening up the area for discussion—"to stimulate a person to think about value-related areas and to encourage him to share his thoughts with others" (p. 148). The counselor's next step is "to *accept* the thoughts, feelings, beliefs, and ideas of others non-judgmentally, and to encourage the others in the [group] to accept a person's feelings for what they are, without criticism" (p. 148). Finally, "the third step is to *stimulate* additional thinking so that an individual can move toward a more comprehensive way of valuing" (p. 148). It is at this point that the client can move more easily through the choosing and acting sequence that was noted.

They also outline several specific activities for values exploration, clarification, and decision making. These include exercises on values voting, playing forced-choice games, various types of role-playing activities, and follow-up discussions. A counselor working in values clarification would do well to consult their book.

Conducting Moral Discussions

Beyer (1979) has proposed a detailed program for facilitating the discussion of moral issues in the classroom, and this model can be equally well applied to any school counseling setting. Defining moral discussions as any "purposeful conversation about moral issues," Beyer (p. 285) goes on to point out that "Most moral discussions are triggered by moral dilemmas which present situations for which the culture supplies some support for a number of actions. . . . Discussions of these situations focus on the moral issues involved in a dilemma and the reasoning used to justify recommended actions." Using this model, the school counselor can help students work out many of the complex social dilemmas (with moral overtones) that are endemic to the elementary and secondary school level.

To carefully organize a moral discussion and make it most effective, Beyer recommends a five-part strategy, as illustrated in figure 7.2. This figure shows the five main stages (in the center boxes of the figure) and some of the characteristic activities of each stage. The dilemma is presented during the first stage. It may be a hypothetical dilemma or a real one—perhaps

figure 7.2 A strategy for guiding moral discussions

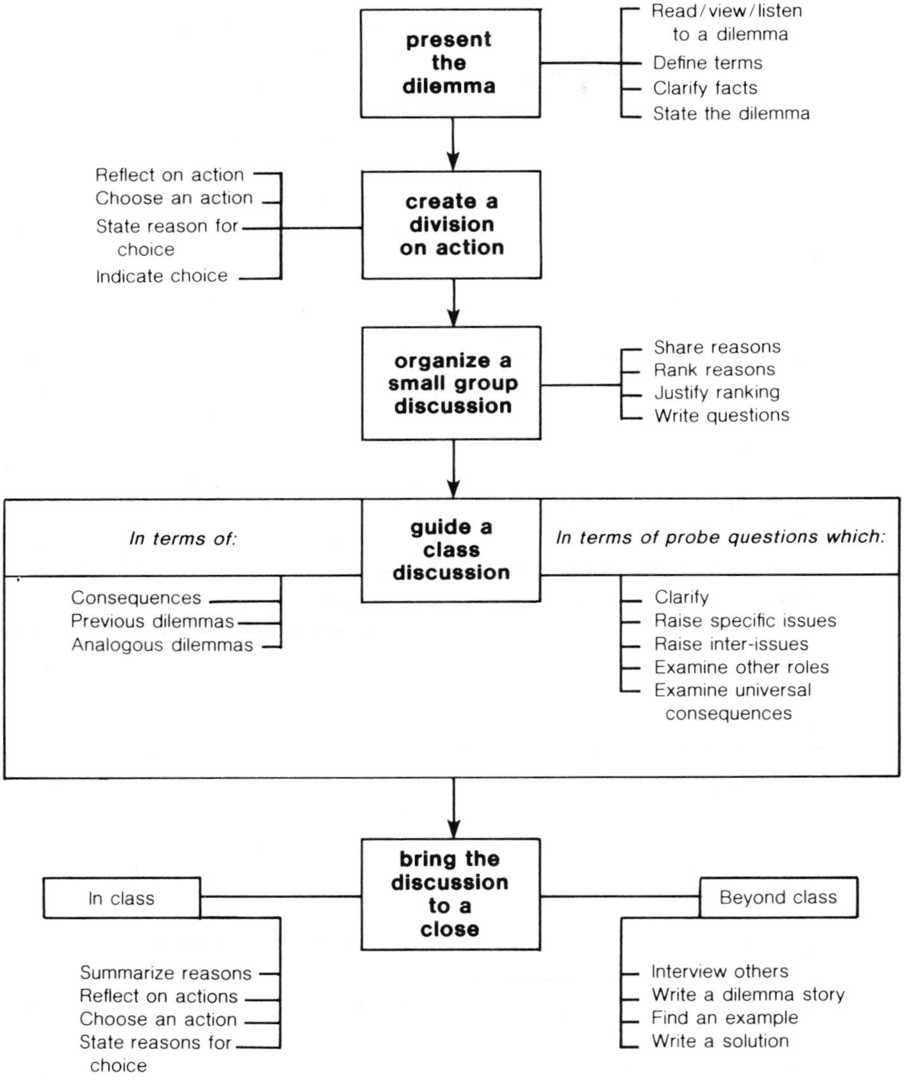

```
                                  ┌──────────────┐          ┌── Read/view/listen
                                  │  present     │          │      to a dilemma
                                  │    the       │──────────┤── Define terms
                                  │  dilemma     │          │── Clarify facts
                                  └──────────────┘          └── State the dilemma
                                         │
                                         ▼
   Reflect on action ──┐         ┌──────────────┐
   Choose an action ───┤         │  create a    │
                       ├─────────│  division    │
   State reason for ───┤         │  on action   │
      choice           │         └──────────────┘
   Indicate choice ────┘                │
                                         ▼
                                  ┌──────────────┐          ┌── Share reasons
                                  │  organize a  │          │── Rank reasons
                                  │ small group  │──────────┤── Justify ranking
                                  │ discussion   │          └── Write questions
                                  └──────────────┘
                                         │
                                         ▼
```

In terms of:	guide a class discussion	*In terms of probe questions which:*
Consequences Previous dilemmas Analogous dilemmas		Clarify Raise specific issues Raise inter-issues Examine other roles Examine universal consequences

```
                                         │
                                         ▼
   ┌─────────────┐            ┌──────────────┐            ┌─────────────┐
   │  In class   │────────────│ bring the    │────────────│ Beyond class│
   └─────────────┘            │ discussion   │            └─────────────┘
                              │   to a       │
   Summarize reasons ──┐      │  close       │      ┌── Interview others
   Reflect on actions ─┤      └──────────────┘      │── Write a dilemma story
   Choose an action ───┤                            ├── Find an example
   State reasons for ──┘                            └── Write a solution
      choice
```

Note: From ''Conducting Moral Discussions in the Classroom'' by Barry K. Beyer, *Social Education*, April 1976, 199. Reprinted with permission of the author and the National Council for the Social Studies.

some problem disturbing a member of the group, or perhaps some type of general problem that many of us have to deal with in life. Beyer offers an example of a dilemma that was used in a class of junior high schools students:

> Sharon and Jill were best friends. One day they went shopping together. Jill tried on a sweater and then, to Sharon's surprise, walked out of the store wearing the sweater under her coat. A moment later, the store's security officer stopped Sharon and demanded that she tell him the name of the girl who had walked out. He told the storeowner that he had seen the two girls together, and that he was sure that the one who left had been shoplifting. The storeowner told Sharon that she could really get in trouble if she didn't give her friend's name.

Part of presenting the dilemma is clarifying the facts and defining the key terms. This is usually accomplished as students raise questions about the situation, sometimes making it more exact and specific.

During the next stage, which lasts about five minutes, the students divide on the action—that is, they take positions, pros and cons, on what the characters have done (or should have done!). The students then form into groups and "engage in small group and large group discussions about the reasoning used to justify the actions they recommend. . . . A good dilemma usually generates a division within the class on the action that the central character should take" (p. 290). Through the group discussion, participants clarify much of their thinking and work through logical ways of justifying themselves to others.

It is at this point that the entire class is brought into the action. "A discussion with the full class gives students a chance to report the reasoning which supports their positions and to hear reasons given for other positions or different reasons given for the positions they have taken, to challenge these reasons, and to hear their own reasoning challenged" (p. 291). The final stage of closing the discussion gives the participants the opportunity to reflect on what they have learned and to review their own processes of moral reasoning.

Beyer's model is useful both in group counseling and in affective education. It is a well-organized—and yet flexible—method of making moral discussions more than just conversation.

Adolescent Moral Conflicts
The complex moral dilemmas and values decisions that adolescents have to come to grips with may be facilitated to some degree with either or both of the methods described above. Adolescents, especially troubled ones, have many problems in life related to weaknesses in their moral reasoning or values clarification. Difficulties in reasoning and a limited choice of options,

or both, contribute to this problem. The socially maladjusted adolescent, the rebel who does not view himself or herself as having opportunities for advancement in life, may be clouded in moral decisions by a pervasive sense of weltschmerz. The intellectually impaired youth, whose cognitive abilities are limited, may be unable to reason out complex moral dilemmas.

Mitchell (1974) points out some specific areas in which the adolescent is likely to experience moral dilemmas: sexual behavior, independence, conscience, double standards, and conformity. Each of these can be dealt with formally or informally in the counseling setting. The counselor simply has to take the time. Mitchell (1975), in a later paper, points out five major changes in the adolescent's moral structure that can help the counselor understand how to deal with the adolescent's moral dilemmas:

1. Moral *outlook* becomes progressively more abstract and less concrete.
2. Moral *convictions* become more concerned with what is right and less concerned with what is wrong; justice emerges as a dominant moral force.
3. Moral *judgment* becomes increasingly cognitive; therefore the adolescent is inclined toward analyzing social and personal codes more vigorously than during childhood, and also allows him to make up his own mind in moral issues.
4. Moral *judgment* becomes less egocentric.
5. Moral *judgment* becomes psychologically expensive (it may create an emotional tension).

The implications of these changes are accommodated well in the programs of both the Hawleys and Beyer.

SUMMARY

In this chapter we examined value decisions as something both counselors and clients have to make on a regular basis. Values were defined as convictions or beliefs that prescribe or determine acceptable or preferable behavior in relation to needs or goals. Value decisions may involve a variety of factors—external and internal, controllable and uncontrollable. They range in complexity from relatively minor decisions to decisions that affect the rest of an individual's life.

We began this discussion by looking at types of conflict. In the course of living we are confronted with conflicts between what we want to do, what we feel we should do, and what we can do. An approach-approach conflict occurs when an individual is faced with a choice between two positive goals, both equally attractive. An avoidance-avoidance conflict involves making a choice between two unpleasant alternatives. An approach-avoidance conflict involves a single goal that has both positive and negative characteristics; it attracts and repels at the same time. A double approach-avoidance conflict involves two goals, both of which have both positive and negative features.

We then looked at the four main theories of moral development, each of which sheds some light on how we make moral decisions and what these decisions mean to us. Social learning theory suggests that we learn morality through the processes of modeling and conditioning. Moral development, according to psychoanalytic theory, is the direct result of the formation of the *superego*—a sense of conscience, which we are not only aware of consciously, but unconsciously as well. In Piaget's moral theory, the child progresses from naive beliefs and simple motor behaviors to more sophisticated, hypothetical, abstract moral reasoning. She or he divides moral learning into three categories called "rules of the game," "moral realism," and "immanent justice."

In Lawrence Kohlberg's theory of moral development, moral thinking progresses through three development levels—the preconventional, the conventional, and the postconventional. At the first level, the child begins to think in a "moral" way, interprets good and bad in terms of the physical consequences of acts (rewards and punishments), or in terms of the physical power of authority figures. As the individual matures into the second, or conventional level, he or she begins to conform to the expectations and rules of conduct of the family, group, and nation. Kohlberg's later research persuaded him that between the conventional and postconventional level there was a transitional level in which moral reasoning was postconventional but still not entirely principled. At the postconventional, or principled, level, the person acts according to autonomous moral principles, which have validity apart from the authority of groups or persons who hold them and also apart from the individual's identification with those persons or groups. In other words, obedience to authority and social recognition are secondary to the higher values and principles that are recognized as paramount by the individual.

Finally, we looked at some values clarification programs in practice. We examined in detail two programs: Hawley and Hawley's six-element progression of choosing and acting on moral decisions and Beyer's guidelines for moral discussions in the school setting.

Career Counseling
in the Schools

The unified approach of career counseling comprises integrated efforts in what traditionally have been called vocational and educational counseling. Vocational and educational counseling are specialized types of counseling applications, designed to provide informational and psychological assistance that may directly affect the decisions and choices the client is about to make about schooling and employment. These forms of counseling directly touch upon the client's "real-life" role activities. Moreover, vocational and educational counseling incorporate in practice all of the different aspects of counseling that have been discussed throughout this book: the psychological, dynamic phase of counseling; the group approach; the information-giving services; the evaluation and appraisal functions. For that reason, it may be fairly said that educational and vocational counseling challenge the counselor to use all of his or her resources and to apply all of his or her training and skills in a single problem area.

In this chapter we will examine the value of career counseling in the schools, paying particular attention to the established goals and applied techniques. It should be kept in mind that these types of counseling are excellent examples of the integrative, functional, nondynamic counseling approach.

WHAT IS CAREER COUNSELING?

The terms *career counseling* and *vocational counseling* have been used interchangeably, although they do have different connotations. Traditionally, vocational counseling, which is an offshoot of the vocational guidance movement, comprised only information giving and directive job counseling. Specifically, it focused on the goal of providing the appropriate training and information that would enable clients to learn about the job market and to develop the skills necessary to secure the jobs to which they aspired. But over the years, there evolved a number of innovative theories of vocational choice, which, combined with the basic informational aspect, comprise the contemporary vocational counseling approach. We will see, however, that while early efforts centered heavily around the objective-informational approach, and while later developments viewed the vocational choice within a dynamic, familial, and interpersonal context, there is a growing sentiment today to "return to basics" and to again try to provide clients with the skills and information needed to succeed in a highly competitive job market.

A number of comprehensive definitions are found in the literature. Sanderson (1954), in discussing the purpose of vocational guidance, suggests,

> Vocational guidance has no other justification for existence than to assist people with their occupational adjustments in a manner that will be truly beneficial to those in need of help. To attain this objective, the vocational counselor will utilize his interviewing skills, his body of knowledge regarding occupations, his intimate familiarity with psychological dynamics and psychometric data. In addition to his professional training, the counselor will also convey to the client that he is genuinely interested in the latter's problems, that he tries to understand the client's needs, and that he respects the client's right to differ from him. (p. 9)

We see from Sanderson's statement that present-day vocational counseling synthesizes a number of different elements designed to help the client and places the client at the center of this effort. Tarrier et al. (1971) suggests that client self-knowledge rather than counselor knowledge about the client is the important factor in vocational guidance. The client should be encouraged to explore his or her own self within an occupational framework. The client is encouraged to know his or her own values, attitudes, and biases about work and is to be helped to use this knowledge to investigate occupations and the world of work. "The study of self and occupations are inextricably related. . . . Young people should be helped to better understand themselves and the place of work in the lives of all of us" (Tarrier et al., 1971).

The emphasis in contemporary occupational counseling is on *career counseling,* (or, career guidance). Not only is the term different from vocational guidance, but the focus of career counseling is more on the total person in the process of choosing a career rather than on a single choice itself. When we view an individual's career as an integral part of his or her life-style, we can easily understand why appropriate career counseling interventions have ramifications in other areas of functioning. Tolbert (1974) defines career counseling in its contemporary usages:

> Career counseling . . . is really much the same as other types of counseling except that it focuses on planning and making decisions about occupations

table 8.1

MAJOR CHARACTERISTICS OF PRESENT CAREER EDUCATION APPROACHES

	general education	vocational education	guidance
Skills	Academic subject matter as it relates to occupational terminology "Knowing"	Job skills development "Employability" emphasis "Doing"	Self-understanding Decision making "Feeling"
Activities	Vicarious experiences, e.g., reading out of a book	Work tasks, real and simulated, relating vocational theory to practice	Counseling Roleplaying groups Field trips
Personnel focus	Academic classroom teacher	Vocational instructor	Counselor as a resource
Student outcomes	Prepared for further education	Trained for a specific skill Make an informed occupational choice	Psychologically and emotionally prepared for work Make a considered career choice

Note: From "Career Education: A Broadening Educational Perspective," by G. Bottoms and D. Sharpe, *The School Counselor,* Nov. 1973, *21*(2): 121–128. Reprinted by permission.

and education. As in all counseling, the personal relationship is critical. It includes exploration of values and attitudes, but information and factual data . . . are more significant than in personal counseling. Even so, it usually is not possible to help someone with a vocational problem without recognizing such other aspects of his life as needs, conflicts, and relations with others. (p. 9)

Expanding this concept to make it especially applicable to the school setting, where most career counseling actually takes place, Tolbert (1978, p. 260) defines the scope of career education as covering the entire lifespan "from preschool years, and includes acquiring values and competencies, and setting goals for both in- and out-of-school experiences." These definitions show us the long way that the vocational guidance movement has come since its earlier days of information giving. This is not to minimize the role of information in contemporary career counseling, but rather to emphasize the host of other significant factors that also play a vital role in it.

The Career Counselor

The career counselor must be familiar with all of the general theories of counseling—psychoanalytic, client-centered, existential, reality, Gestalt, rational-emotive, and behavioral—as well as with the specialized theories of career development that will be discussed later. Moreover, the same philosophical principles that play so vital a role in the counselor's effectiveness also make their impact in vocational counseling interactions. Recent discussions about career counseling reflect with an ever-increasing frequency the amalgam of factors that play a part in this vital counseling function (Foreman & James, 1973; Ginzberg, 1972; Herr & Cramer, 1972: Hoffman, 1972; Stefflre & Grant, 1972). No longer is it possible to view the occupational-career counselor in isolation from the total counseling process that integrates the sum of therapeutic, educational, and growth facilitating experiences under a single classification. With this in mind, let us examine some of the tools, insights, and axioms that guide career counselors in their work.

Occupational counseling inevitably touches upon the nature of work. "Man becomes man through his work," Karl Marx said, illuminating the importance of work in one's existence. Boy and Pine (1971) speak of work "as a therapeutic and personally integrating experience." As counselors attempt to do vocational counseling, they must have a conscious awareness of their own attitudes, biases, and subjective feelings about the work experience, since these will invariably influence clients.

While the contemporary occupational counseling service includes many factors, it still relies heavily on occupational information. Simply, the informational aspect of vocational counseling provides to the client all of the necessary information he or she will need to make valid, well-thought-out occupational choices. Two publications that will be useful to the counselor are the *Dictionary of Occupational Titles (DOT)* and the *Occupational Outlook Handbook*. The following sources will also be helpful: Careertapes, Project WERC, and computer-based systems, such as ECES and ISVD.

Careertapes™ is a trademark of the Macmillan publishing company. They consist of eighteen audio-cassettes of actual voices of people in the working world who describe their jobs as they see them. Each person interviewed describes his or her work, including pay, hours, fringe benefits, promotion opportunities, what they like and don't like about the work, and so forth. The American Personnel and Guidance Association's Project WERC (Why Not Explore Rewarding Careers) provides information about careers that do not require a college degree. It consists of a series of films designed "to broaden the student's understanding of the world of work and help him make a more intelligent vocational decision."

ECES (Educational and Career Exploration System) and ISVD (Information System for Vocation Designs) are computer-based systems that in-

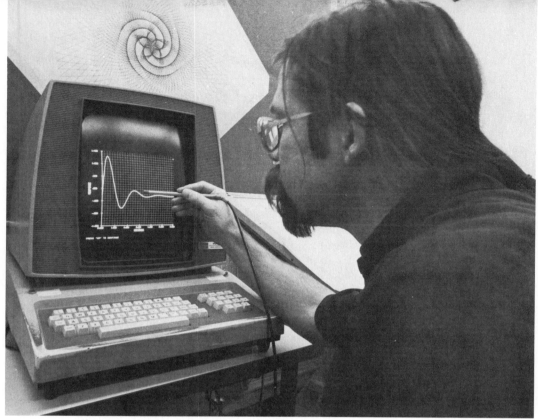

Computer technology is rapidly finding its way into the
counseling profession.

tegrate computer functions with counselor functions to help the individual
obtain occupational information and make better vocational choices. Barnard
(1972) describes the ECES system:

> The high school guidance counselor schedules a two-hour introductory session
> for each of his students in the ECERS terminal. Each student is given a
> number; already stored against that number in the system's computer are the
> student's current grades as well as his aptitude scores. Under the supervision
> of a monitor, the student discovers he can command ECES' performance by
> means of a light pen which he touches to various points on a 2760-display
> screen to put the computer to work.
>
> Is there an occupation the student is curious about? ECES, by means of
> 18,000 cartridge-stored visual images, can describe and define any of 400
> occupations, from actuary to zoologist. . . . Words and pictures describe the
> activities performed, the working conditions, chances for advancement, salary
> levels, and educational requirements for the occupation being explored. Then
> it quizzes the student to determine whether he feels positive, negative, or
> dubious about it. (p. 46)

We should point out that any computerized system is valuable only in conjunction with individualized counseling sessions that assist the client in final decision making.

THEORIES OF CAREER DEVELOPMENT

Underlying all serious efforts in career counseling are a number of highly sophisticated and carefully developed theories of career development. The term *career* has come to replace its alternative terms, *occupation* and *vocation,* because of its broader, more inclusive emphasis. A career, Super (1969) points out, is "the sequence of occupations, jobs, and positions occupied during the course of a person's working life. Careers actually extend beyond either end of the working life to include prevocational and post-vocational positions such as those of students preparing for work and of retired men playing substitute roles." A recent objection, however, to the use of the term *career* over *vocational* has been lodged by Herr and Cramer (1972):

> While the term "career development" has a more favorable connotation for some persons than the term "vocational development," "career development" does not lend itself to use in summarizing the behavioral development that parallels socialization. The term "vocational development," on the other hand, does. Recent theories view vocational behavior as a continuing, fluid process of growth and learning, and they attach considerable importance to individual self-concept(s), developmental experiences, personal history, and the psycho-social environment of the individual as major determinants of the process. (p. 39)

They go on to suggest that the term *vocationalization* be used to describe this dynamic process that is a "corollary of socialization." One could say, however, that this perennial debate over which term is preferable—*career* or *vocational*—is largely unnecessary and a symptom of academic carping. What is important, and what does influence all these theories, is the recognition that a theory of career development must account for the fluid, changing process of vocational awareness and feelings.

In this section we shall examine a number of the major theories of career/vocational development. We must keep in mind as we look at these theories that a "vocational development theory is *not* a general theory of development that could serve as a basis for all counseling and guidance" (Tolbert, 1974). Rather, it is a specific, purposeful theory designed to help counselors in their vocational counseling. Hewer (1963) argues that no single theory of vocational development is sufficient to explicate the many complexities

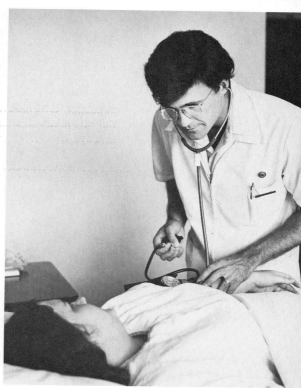

As career roles and expectations change, the vocational
counselor plays an integral role in career decisions.

of the individual. In sum, however, the bulk of these theories reflect the growing awareness of the intricate matrix of psychological, social, and educational factors that play a part in vocational choice and career satisfaction.

Super's Theory of Development

Donald E. Super has developed a theory of vocational choice based on the idea that the individual's self-concept influences his or her occupational choice and ultimate satisfaction or dissatisfaction with that choice. The vocational choice, according to Super (1957), is the result of a developmental process that puts the individual's self-concept into practice. He lists ten propositions that characterize his theory:

1. People differ in their abilities, interests, and personalities.
2. They are qualified, by virtue of these circumstances, each for a number of occupations.
3. Each of these occupations requires a characteristic pattern of abilities, interests, and personality traits, with tolerances wide enough, however, to allow both some variety of occupations for each individual and some variety of individuals in each occupation.
4. Vocational preferences and competencies, the situations in which people live and work, and hence their self-concepts, change with time and experience (although self-concepts are generally fairly stable from late adolescence until late maturity), making choice and adjustment a continuous process.
5. This process may be summed up in a series of life stages characterized as those of growth, exploration, establishment, maintenance, and decline, and these stages may in turn be subdivided into (a) the fantasy, tentative, and realistic phases of the exploratory stage, and (b) the trial and stable phases of the establishment stage.
6. The nature of the career pattern (that is, the occupational level attained and the sequence, frequency, and duration of trail and stable jobs) is determined by the individual's parental socio-economic level, mental ability, and personality characteristics, and by the opportunities to which he is exposed.
7. Development through the life stages can be guided, partly by facilitating the process of maturation of abilities and interests and partly by aiding in reality testing and in the development of the self-concept. The process of vocational development is essentially that of developing and implementing the self-concept: it is a compromise process in which the self-concept is a product of the interaction of inherited aptitudes, neural and endocrine make-up, opportunity to play various roles, and evaluations of the extent to which the results of role playing meet with the approval of superiors and fellows.

Donald E. Super

8. The process of compromise between individual and social factors, between self-concept and reality, is one of role playing, whether the role is played in fantasy, in the counseling interview, or in real life activities such as school classes, clubs, part-time work, and entry jobs.
9. Work satisfactions and life satisfactions depend upon the extent to which the individual finds adequate outlets for abilities, interests, personality traits, and values; they depend upon his or her establishment in a type of work, a work situation, and a way of life in which she or he can play the kind of role which growth and exploratory experiences have led her or him to consider congenial and appropriate.

Super and his associates have developed these early premises into a comprehensive framework for assessing vocational choice and vocational development. He differentiates between the exploratory stage and the establishment stage of vocational development. The exploratory stage is characterized by fantasy, searching, investigating, experimenting, and testing out hypotheses. It is the period during which vocational images are molded and refined. The establishment stage consists of the period during which the individual actually begins to enact a career role and shape the career model into an individual unique style. These stages may be considered maturational-psychological stages and may also be divided according to chronological ages.

Holland's Heuristic Theory

Holland also looks at vocational interests and preferences as a part of the total personality of the individual. He refers to his theory as a *heuristic* theory because it is intended to stimulate "research and investigation by its suggestive character rather than by its logical or systematic structure" (Holland, 1966). In this sense, his theory is a working hypothesis by which he can investigate the details of vocational psychology. He explains the essence of his theory this way:

> Briefly, the theory consists of several simple ideas and their more complex elaborations. First, we assume that we can characterize people by their resemblance to one or more personality types. The closer a person's resemblance to his particular type, the more likely it is he will exhibit the personal traits and behaviors associated with that type. Second, we assume that the environments in which people live can be characterized by their resemblance to one or more model environments. Finally, we assume that the pairing of persons and environments leads to several outcomes that we can predict and understand from our knowledge of the personality types and the environmental models. These outcomes include vocational choice, vocational stability and achievement, personal stability, creative performance, and susceptibility to influence. (p. 34)

The details, as he suggests, are more complex and form the basis for his empirical investigations. He defines six character types that include most persons: *realistic, intellectual, social, conventional, enterprising, and artistic* (Holland, 1962). The realistic type is "masculine, physically strong, unsociable, aggressive; has good motor coordination and skill; lacks verbal and interpersonal skills; prefers concrete to abstract problems. . . . Laborers, machine operators, aviators, farmers, truck drivers, and carpenters resemble this type." The intellectual type is "task oriented, intraceptive [sic], asocial; prefers to think through rather than act out problems; needs to understand. . . . Physicists, anthropologists, chemists, mathematicians, and biologists resemble this type."

The social type is "sociable, responsible, feminine, humanistic, religious; needs attention; has verbal and interpersonal skills; avoids intellectual problem solving, physical activity and highly ordered activities; prefers to solve problems through feelings and interpersonal manipulations of others; is orally dependent. Social workers, teachers, interviewers, vocational counselors, and therapists resemble this type."

The conventional type "prefers structured verbal and numerical activities and subordinate roles; is conforming (extraceptive [sic]). . . . Bank tellers, secretaries, bookkeepers, and file clerks resemble this type." The enterprising type has "verbal skills for selling, dominating, leading . . . avoids well-defined language or work situations requiring long periods of intellectual effort; is extraceptive [sic]; differs from the conventional type in that he prefers ambiguous social tasks and has a greater concern with power, status, and leadership; is orally aggressive. Salesmen, politicians, managers, promoters, and business executives resemble this type." The artistic type "is asocial; avoids problems which are highly structured or require gross physical skills . . . prefers dealing with environmental problems through self-expression in artistic media. Musicians, artists, poets, sculptors, and writers resemble this type."

Holland (1973) has attempted to measure each of these personality types through a Vocational Preference Inventory, which ranks the subject's personal orientations in terms of these six categories. The difficulty with this formulation is the serious question of whether people can truly be placed largely in the confines of a single category on the basis of their vocational interests and occupations. To assume that each pair of figures can be placed in the same class because of their alleged vocational determinants seems to suffer from the logical fallacy of stereotyping.

Building upon this idea of six character types, Holland sets forth the following theory: *people search for* environments and vocations that will permit them to exercise their skills and abilities, to express their attitudes and values, to take on agreeable problems and rules, and to avoid disagreeable ones (Holland, 1966). A realistic personality type would function best in a realistic environment, while a social type would function best in a social environment, and so on. The choice and satisfaction of an occupation depends heavily upon the degree of concordance between the individual's type and his or her environment.

Holland's theory is complex and sophisticated. He discusses such diverse concepts as the relationship between heredity and environment and the application of psychoanalytic insights to vocational choice. One important distinction of his theory is that it has been heavily tested and retested by Holland and his associates (Holland 1973) and is probably the most thoroughly tested of all the vocational theories. Recently, Hearn and Moos (1976) found confirmation for many aspects of Holland's typology in a study of choice and decision making among college students.

Roe's Theory of Needs

Anne Roe has developed a theory of occupational choice and job satisfaction based upon Maslow's ideas of the integrated unity of the individual as a link between interacting levels of needs, both conscious and unconscious. "In order to understand the role of the occupation in the life of the individual,"

Anne Roe

Roe (1956) suggests, "we must first have some understanding of the individual and his needs." As she expounds this conceptual understanding of individuals and their needs, she builds a theory of vocational development upon this framework, utilizing both psychoanalytic and empirical methodology for the construction.

One of Roe's more important insights concerns the relationship between family background, one's upbringing, and one's later occupational situation (Roe, 1957). Deficiencies during childhood, she suggests, may be compensated for through the work that one does. If one did not receive sufficient praise and respect from parents, one may attempt to elicit these through his or her job and consequently seek jobs where such praise and respect would be forthcoming. Likewise, for all the needs that were unmet at earlier stages of development, one turns to work to find gratification for these needs.

"In our society," Roe (1956) argues, "there is no single situation which is potentially so capable of giving some satisfaction at all levels of basic needs as is the occupation." She goes on to suggest that Maslow's hierarchy of basic needs (which she lists as "the psychological needs; the safety needs; the need for belongingness and love; the need for importance; respect, self-esteem, independence; the need for information; the need for understanding; the need for beauty; the need for self-actualization") are all satisfied within the job situation. The job, therefore, becomes a primary determinant of one's psychological fulfillment:

> In our culture, social and economic status depend more upon the occupation than upon anything else. Sociological as well as psychological studies are practically unanimous on this point, although there are of course exceptions. Feelings of personal esteem are also closely linked to the amount of responsibility the job entails. This is reflected in ratings of the prestige of occupations and in studies of job satisfaction. The degrees of freedom and responsibility in an occupation enter into these evaluations more importantly than do the levels of skill and training, or than do salaries.
>
> People whose life situation is especially difficult may find that the status and prestige conferred by the occupation, or received from fellow workers, are the greatest sources of satisfaction for these needs. . . . Occupations as a source of need satisfaction are of extreme importance in our culture. It may be that occupations have become so important in our culture just because so many needs are so well satisfied by them. Whether the relation is casual or not, and if so which is cause and which is effect, does not particularly matter. . . . What is important is that the relationship exists and is an essential aspect of the value of the occupation to the individual. (Roe, 1956, p. 33)

In developing her ideas comprehensively, Roe has attempted to fit her ideas into a matrix-like structure, utilizing groups and levels to explain the occupational phenomena. The eight groups she lists are: *Roe Needs Theory*

1. Service
2. Business contact
3. Organizations
4. Technology

5. Outdoor
6. Science
7. General culture
8. Arts and entertainment

The levels range from "professional and managerial" down to "unskilled." Determinations about the personality of individuals can be made from considerations about the group and the level of their occupations and the groups and levels toward which they strive.

In an important paper written with Marvin Siegelman (1964), Roe discusses the influence of early childhood developmental factors on occupational choice. Figure 8.1 shows the relationship between the personality characteristics and the chosen profession (according to the following lists). The basic core of all the different components—the center of the circle—differentiates between the *warm* and *cold* early home environments. The

figure 8.1 Early home climate and its relation to Roe's occupational classification

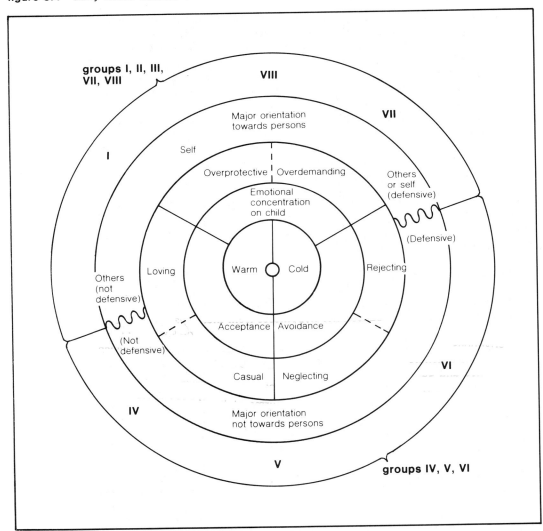

hypotheses suggested from this model, according to Roe and Siegelman, are:

1. Loving, protecting, and demanding homes would lead to person-orientation in the child and later person-orientation in occupations.
2. Rejecting, neglecting, and casual homes would lead to non-person orientation in occupations.
3. If extreme protecting and extreme demanding conditions were felt by the child to be restricting, he might, in defense, become non-person oriented.
4. Some individuals from rejecting homes might become person-oriented in search for satisfaction.
5. Loving and casual homes might provide a sufficient amount of relatedness that other factors such as abilities would determine interpersonal directions more than personal needs. (pp. 7–8)

As much influence as Roe has had upon subsequent theories of career development and occupational choice, she has suffered her fair share of criticism as well. Carkhuff, Alexik, and Anderson (1967) give a well-tempered summary of the weaknesses of Roe's position:

Instead of attempting to generalize her findings into a unique and comprehensive system, Roe apparently seeks to "rationalize" her results by drawing from analytic theory and Maslow's postulates to support her findings. She has neither systematically deduced her hypotheses from these systems nor does she work inductively to these systems. . . . Roe neither makes systematic derivations from the theories that she proposes nor is the theory with which she deals a generalization of her findings, serving to organize the available evidence and guide the search for better evidence. Rather, she appears to seek entrance to already existing systems. She does not make sufficient attempt to qualify the existing theories in terms of her findings and, thus, provides no unique theory of her own to encompass her results. In summary, then, according to the schema, Roe makes no justifiable generalizations from her data above [sic] the level of what has been defined as laws. (pp. 337–338)

While these criticisms do have some validity, there are a number of strong points about Roe's system that should also be mentioned. Her system allows an integrative role in the job function and relates occupational choice to the entire structure of the personality. From a counseling point of view, Roe's insights help the counselor better understand the variety of factors that play a part in the individual's decision to pursue or avoid certain types of jobs and help the counselor understand why a job does or does not meet the client's needs. Moreover, her work sets a foundation from which further empirical research may be conducted to supplement the work that she and her associates have already undertaken (Roe et al., 1966; Roe and Siegelman, 1964).

Robert Hoppock

Hoppock's Theory

Hoppock (1967) lists the ten major points of his theory:

1. Occupations are chosen to meet needs.
2. The occupation that we choose is the one that we believe will best meet the needs that most concern us.
3. Needs may be intellectually perceived, or they may be only vaguely felt as attractions which draw us in certain directions. In either case, they may influence choices.
4. Vocational development begins when we first become aware that an occupation can help to meet our needs.
5. Vocational development progresses and occupational choice improves as we become better able to anticipate how well a prospective occupation will meet our needs. Our capacity thus to anticipate depends upon our knowledge of ourselves, our knowledge of occupations, and our ability to think clearly.
6. Information about ourselves affects occupational choice by helping us to recognize what we want and by helping us to anticipate whether or not we will be successful in collecting what the contemplated occupation offers to us.
7. Information about occupations affects occupational choice by helping us to discover the occupations that may meet our needs and by helping us to anticipate how well satisfied we may hope to be in one occupation as compared with another.

8. Job satisfaction depends upon the extent to which the job that we hold meets the needs that we feel it should meet. The degree of satisfaction is determined by the ratio between what we have and what we want.
9. Satisfaction can result from a job which meets our needs today or from a job which promises to meet them in the future.
10. Occupational choice is always subject to change when we believe that a change will better meet our needs. (pp. 111-112)

We see how Hoppock's ideas represent a "composite theory," and it is probably for this reason that his writing has enjoyed the wide popularity it has over the years. His ideas are compatible with other theorists, and the concordance between various points of view in vocational counseling attests both to the unity of the discipline and to the integrity of the different systems.

Other Theories of Career Development

In addition to the theories discussed above, there are three other important theories of career development that, because of limitations of space, will be discussed briefly. For a more comprehensive discussion of any of these theories, readers should direct their attention to the relevant references cited at the end of the book.

Eli Ginzberg's (1972) Theory of Occupational Choice, as it has been reformulated over the years, is briefly summarized as follows:

> Occupational choice is a process that remains open as long as one makes and expects to make decisions about his work and career. In many instances it is coterminous with his working life.
>
> While the successive decisions that a young person makes during the preparatory period will have a shaping influence on his later career, so will the continuing changes that he undergoes in work and life.
>
> People make decisions about jobs and careers with an aim of optimizing their satisfactions by finding the best possible fit between their priority needs and desires and the opportunities and constraints that they confront in the world of work.
>
> Our reformulated theory is that *occupational choice is a lifelong process of decision-making in which the individual seeks to find the optimal fit between his career preparation and goals and the realities of the world of work.* (p. 172)

This reformulation differs somewhat from the original theory. Because it is more recent and based on more experimentation, it should be considered the definitive statement, supplanting the original formulation.

Tiedeman and O'Hara have developed a system based in part on the constructs of ego personality. They view vocational development as part of a continuing process of the individual differentiating his or her ego identity.

They describe career development as "the process of fashioning a vocational identity through differentiation and integration of the personality as one confronts the problem of work in living" (Tiedeman & O'Hara, 1963). Heavy on theory and conceptual frameworks, the writings of Tiedeman and O'Hara integrate many of the insights developed by Freud, Erikson, Super, Roe, and Ginzberg. They have attempted over the years to integrate a plethora of new research data into their models, with the result that "their theory cannot emerge beyond the status of a collection of lower-level generalizations. Instead of streamlining and simplifying their theorems, they seem to be moving in the opposite direction—toward encompassing as diverse data as possible, hoping that in the future, out of the midst of chaos, order will emerge" (Carkhuff et al., 1967).

We see from the sum of these theories that contemporary models of career development are highly sophisticated theories that account for the psychological as well as the sociological and educational influences on career choices, career satisfaction, and adjustment to career patterns.

PRACTICAL SCHOOL APPLICATIONS

In the school setting, career counseling involves both educational efforts and intensive applications of psychological counseling paradigms. At the educational end we have such services as the establishment of a career resource bank, preparation in the assistance of individual and group résumés, and a school "career day," which provides students with important opportunities to realistically assess their career options. Collectively, these approaches are sometimes called "career guidance." "Career guidance . . . endeavors to help students who choose vocational education use their acquired skills and knowledge in the refinement and achievement of their career goals" (Bottoms, 1976, p. 51). At the individual counseling end of the spectrum, there is a pronounced need to help clients discover themselves while they are searching for their occupational choices.

Specifically, when a client comes for career counseling, the total effort generally involves any of the following job functions of the career counselor, either independently or in conjunction with each other:

1. Identifying the client's vocational interests and abilities. This may be accomplished by an interivew, or may require the administration of vocational interest and aptitude inventories.
2. Helping the client learn how to increase his or her vocational skills, aiming toward levels of competency necessary for success in the job market.

3. Helping the client deal with his or her feelings about work. This may include persistent feelings of frustration in finding the right job; difficulties at work; feelings of hopelessness that preclude looking for work.

In many cases, these three aspects of vocational counseling are combined in practice. The theories of career development we discussed are sometimes useful in carrying out integrated efforts designed to help a person find and adjust to productive work. The theories give us a rationale for what we are doing and guide us in our actions (in the same way general theories of counseling guide the counselor during the counseling interview). Let us look specifically at one career guidance approach that has proven very successful in the school setting: the development of a "career day" for the school. This is typically initiated by and under the auspices of the counselor's office, although other school personnel cooperate with the program to make it successful.

Career Day

This section was written by Robert R. Cuccioli and is used with his permission.

A career day is a day set aside for the single purpose of helping students learn about career opportunities. If it is done near the beginning of the school year, it can provide a point of reference and feedback throughout the year. This eight-step program will show exactly how such a program can be implemented.

1. *Organize a Career Questionnaire* The counselor begins by distributing a form to students, asking them to list five choices of professions which they would like to see represented at the school. This allows the counselor a realistic sample of student interests. Questionnaires can be distributed during the homeroom period. It is usually necessary to remind the homeroom teachers to remind the students to return the questionnaires if they are taking them home rather than filling them out at school.

2. *Collect and Tabulate* The questionnaires are collected by the homeroom teachers and returned to the counselor. Usually with some assistance, the counselor lists each occupation cited by the students. Wherever there is duplication (as there will be for most), a tally is kept to see which professions have scored the highest interest. No choice should be omitted, but weight should certainly be given to those choices cited most often. The differences

between schools will reflect differences between school populations. There may also be sex-related differences. Here is a typical result of the five top choices at three very different types of schools:

School A	School B	School C (science-oriented)
Policeman	Professional athlete	Engineer
Construction worker	Retail sales	Scientist
Professional athlete	Firefighter	Physician
Nurse	Teacher	Lawyer
Firefighter	Plumber/electrician	Teacher

The counselor should also keep in mind, when tabulating the results, that students may be unaware of an occupational category that could be of interest to them. For example, in School A, students may find some interest in the profession of teaching, in the growing paralegal or paramedical professions, in the crafts (plumbing, etc.), and in other areas they did not explicitly list. The counselor should try to supplement the list, using his or her own judgment.

3. *Consulting with Faculty and Staff* This step is specifically designed to supplement the list, as mentioned above. The tabulated results can be distributed to faculty, asking for additional suggestions. This also serves the important purpose of getting teachers involved and of encouraging them to enthusiastically support the project.

4. *Recruiting Speakers* The counselor should be resourceful in finding individuals who represent the chosen occupations. Teachers can be asked for recommendations of individuals of whom they know who would be willing to participate. Professional organizations (such as unions, societies, etc.) often have a speaker available. Policemen, firemen, and the like of a city are also generally eager to participate in such activities. Large business organizations, including banks, insurance companies, entertainment conglomerates, publishing houses, and so forth, have all been helpful either in directly providing career day speakers or referring the counselor to the appropriate source. Before the event the speaker should be given an idea of the type of audience he or she will be addressing, and what kinds of information will prove most helpful to it.

5. *Determining Student Preferences* After the final determination of speakers has been made, a roster (of speakers and their occupations) should be distributed in the classes through the same channels used for the original questionnaire. Students will be asked to make five choices of occupations from the list, in order of preference.

6. *Scheduling and Confirmation* Using the tabulation of student preferences, along with the list of speaker availability, a schedule is constructed. Each student is assigned, whenever possible, the first three of the five stated preferences. Seniors are usually given preference in assignment, since they will be the ones to graduate soonest. While the scheduling is taking place, speaker confirmation is undertaken. Each speaker that has agreed to participate is sent a letter, stating the time and date along with instructions how to get to the school. A return postcard is enclosed for the speaker to confirm his or her plans to attend. Careful record keeping will assure a smooth operation on career day.

7. *The Day is Here* On the day of the conference, the counselor arranges for speakers to be met at the entrance of the school by students who are assigned to escort the speakers to the special area where they will be greeted. A comfortable room, in which all the speakers are assembled, should provide a welcoming atmosphere. Coffee and cake may be served. Each speaker will have an opportunity to meet the counseling staff and the faculty in this informal, friendly atmosphere. Written room assignments can be handed out here, and a student will be assigned to each speaker to make sure he or she finds the room and is introduced to the group to whom he or she will be speaking. During the day, the counselor should visit as many rooms as possible to be sure things are going smoothly. If a lunch period is arranged, it may be a good idea for the school counselor or principal to speak to the group of visitors. This makes them feel welcome and provides a basis for continuity and follow-up.

8. *Follow-up* For a career day to be a most productive experience, there should be an organized follow-up. This can include student and faculty evaluations of the experience, along with group and individual conferences to determine if the opportunity has been helpful to the students in determining their future course of study or their tentative career choice. There may also be follow-up with the speakers who can, in the future, become an important occupational resource to the counselor.

Other School Applications

In addition to career day, there are of course many other important applications of career counseling in the schools. In this section we will look at a few of them.

Educational Counseling

Many of the insights we have seen in the theories of career choice and development apply equally well to educational counseling. Educational counseling may be defined as the total process of helping the client decide upon educational plans, make sound and appropriate choices, and succeed in all of his or her educational endeavors. Rothney (1972) details nine common problems characteristic of the type that the educational counselor encounters:

1. *Selection among various broad curricular groupings offered by the schools.* Choice of one program from the college preparatory, business, trade, or general groups involves consideration of such matters as a student's post-high school training plans and the generally greater prestige value for parents and students of college preparatory courses.
2. *Selection among electives within or without broad curriculum groupings.* Consideration must be given to such matters as possible vocational and avocational values of courses. . . . Parents' insistence on certain kinds of training needs consideration.
3. *Arrangements for taking university correspondence courses not offered by a school in order to meet specified requirements or to provide for a student's interests.*
4. *Consideration of students' course loads.* Such factors as health, desire to finish school in less than the usual time, enrichment, opportunity to work for pay, correlation of work in the local vocational school, and participation in work experience programs are given consideration.
5. *Selection of courses designed particularly to prepare for marriage.* Some girls [and boys too, of course!] are engaged to be married soon after graduation and want to elect combinations of courses that will prepare them for [married life].
6. *Provision of special help with study habits or with difficulties in particular courses.*
7. *Arrangement of special summer courses or experiences.* These provide enrichment, permit make-up work, offer special preparation for a planned experience.
8. *Interpretation of educational data.*
9. *Information is given about availability and methods of obtaining scholarships and other aids for post-high school training.* (pp. 11–12)

For each of these situations, the educational counselor may freely apply insights regarding the nature of vocational choice. Why has a student decided to go to college or not go to college? How is the choice of a major subject arrived at? What college has the client selected, and why? Is the client seeking an educational program that is appropriate to his or her vocational goal?

Much of the counselor's work in educational counseling is of a remedial nature. For the student who is doing poorly in school—who is an under-achiever—the counselor can and should play a vital role in helping to maximize the student's potential. The counselor, in addition to exploring the problem with the client, might be instrumental in arranging tutoring or after-school classes. A comprehensive tutoring program, one that utilizes volunteer tutors, is often helpful in dealing with the underachieving student.

The key point for the counselor to remember in providing educational information is that his or her job is to make that information meaningful to the student—to help the student put that information into constructive action (Norris, Zeran, & Hatch, 1960). "Helping the counselee express his feelings about information and determine its personal meaning are the most important and demanding aspects of the use of information to help the counselee" (Tolbert, 1972). The counselor must avoid the temptation of feeling that, simply having given information, his or her duties have been adequately discharged.

Career Resource Center

The school counselor's office can serve as a career resource center. This means that in addition to providing vocational information and individual or group career counseling, the office provides specific *skills* training that is necessary for successful vocational planning. This would include résumé preparation, job interview training and practice, and even such basic but necessary functions as how to read the want ads in the newspaper. Communication skills, especially speaking skills, are imporant in all areas of job attainment and job functioning. They should be an integral part of the services offered by an effective career resource center (Gurry, 1976).

Elementary School Applications

Although much of what we have been speaking about is applicable to the secondary school level, it is most important that we recognize that career education must begin on the elementary school level if it is to be effective. "Elementary schools that fail to give attention to vocational education and careers," Georgiady (1976, p. 122) points out, "are failing to deal with the realities of our world." He continues,

Ours is a highly complex society, one in which change is occurring at a bewilderingly increasing rate. Ours is also a society in which technology is playing an ever increasing role. To expect that pupils will somehow magically find an appropriate place in such a complex society without any preparation, or with inadequate preparation, is unrealistic and does violence to an acceptable concept of the true role of education. . . .

The elementary-school teacher is the key person in the development of elementary-school programs. Efforts to change programs must begin with the teachers in the elementary school. . . . To have any impact on the education of children, changes must be made in the teachers' attitudes, understandings, and skills regarding vocational education. . . . What is now needed is a large-scale effort to reach a greater number of teachers. (p. 122)

Moreover, we should recognize that substantial research has consistently shown that some of a person's later-life vocational interests and values begin as early as the third grade, and that career-role identification exercises and early career exploration should begin around grade 4 (Parks, 1976). Thus, the elementary school counselor has an important place in career guidance.

SUMMARY

In this chapter we examined the role of the school counselor in career guidance and in vocational and educational counseling. We explored the major theories of career development and career choice: the ideas of Super, Hoppock, Roe, Holland, Ginzburg, Tiedeman, and O'Hara. We noted how each of these theories attempts to explain why people make certain choices and how they feel about these choices after they have made them. We then looked at some applications of career counseling in the school setting. We saw in detail how the counselor can set up a career day at the school, and how this can be helpful in assisting students with career decisions. We also considered the approaches and goals of educational counseling as a separate but related aspect of career guidance.

Counseling in the Elementary Schools

Throughout this book, my comments and observations have dealt with general counseling principles, applicable for the most part to all age and grade levels. We know from experience, however, that some of the problems experienced during the elementary school years, as well as some of the counseling strategies successfully employed, are different from those of the secondary school years, or adulthood. In this chapter and the following one, we will look at applications of counseling specific to a particular school level. We will focus in this chapter on the elementary school; in the following chapter, on the secondary school, including the intermediate school.

We can cite three specific reasons that elementary school counseling requires a specialized approach:

1. The elementary school child is in a more highly dependent day-to-day relationship with his or her parents than are clients in later years. This means that the parents will invariably become a more integral part of the counseling experience, either as co-counselors, as consultees, as sources of information, or as dynamic forces working with or working against the counselor.
2. Because the elementary school child spends so much time with the teacher, and because the peer group is not yet as influential as in later life, school personnel—represented by the teacher and by the counselor—are important factors in the child's success or failure, not only in academics, but also in the development of socialization skills.
3. The elementary school child is experiencing a considerably faster rate of growth than will ever be experienced later in life. Between kindergarten and seventh grade the child's cognitive, social, and emotional development is staggering. Thus, counseling children of these ages requires constant recognition of their changing natures, needs, interests, abilities, and perceptions.

Communication skills that children develop in the
elementary school affect their behavior the rest of their
life.

Berry (1979), well aware of this last point particularly, has suggested that
elementary school counseling needs its own theoretical base, which will
relate the guidance and counseling function to the processes of child development that researchers have learned so much about in recent years.
She uses the framework of communication theory and suggests that a major
function of the elementary school counselor, when viewed in the context of
developmental psychology, is to promote facilitative communication.

Pointing out that "the developmental changes that children go through
and the responses of others to them influence children's behavior for the
rest of their life" (p. 515), Berry suggests we use communication theory as
a basis for developing and implementing our counseling skills. She explains
communication theory this way:

Communication theory says that in each of us there is a drive toward self-realization, an innate urge to sustain life and move it forward. This tendency of individuals to self-actualize fulfills its mission through communication, for communication, specifically language, is the process by which individuals make life into understandable, manageable form—organize their experiences. . . . It is communication that (1) puts the individuals in touch with their own thoughts and feelings and (2) ties person to person and every person to a group. (p. 515)

Whether it is through working with the parents of the child-client or correcting disturbed communication, the elementary school counselor's fundamental job is to "develop the communication processes necessary [for clients] to (a) understand themselves, (b) engage in satisfactory social interactions with others, and (c) bridge the gap between oral learning in the preschool years and learning the basic skills in the primary grades (p. 518)."

We should keep this communications perspective in mind as we look at five elementary school counseling applications in the following sections. We will begin by considering play approaches to child counseling, looking specifically at the case of a ten-year-old girl who was referred by her teacher for counseling. Next we will see how Alfred Adler's Individual Psychology is especially relevant at the elementary school level. We will then examine an innovative approach, called horticultural counseling, which can be used in regular and in special education. The fourth section presents the experiences of a teacher functioning as a therapeutic counselor—a case study of a school guidance class for emotionally disturbed children. And finally, we will turn our attention to the problem of child abuse—a problem that requires immediate attention in the elementary schools.

CHILD COUNSELING: PLAY APPROACHES

Written by Janet Finell. Reprinted with her permission.

Play is to the young child what words are to the adult. Play provides a means through which thoughts and feelings can be communicated, and distressing conflicts resolved. Through play, the child's attention can be captured and maintained as he or she enacts inner fears and wishes in the safety and acceptance of the counseling relationship.

The use of play in child counseling can be adapted according to the theoretical orientation of the counselor. The two main play approaches have traditionally been the psychodynamic and the client-centered. The former was developed through the works of Anna Freud and Melanie Klein; the latter is most closely identified with the writings of Virginia Axline. There are some similarities and some discrepancies between these two orientations.

Anna Freud (1964) stressed some essential differences that exist in the treatment of children compared to adults, and these would hold true regardless of the counseling approach used. Children do not come to treatment voluntarily. They may be unaware that they have a problem. Their real need for and dependency on their parents minimizes the possibility of their expressing many of their hostile feelings about their parents. Finally, the control that the parents continue to exercise over the child's life can threaten gains achieved through treatment. Therefore, in order for counseling with children to be successful, the counselor must work to capture the child's interest, and to motivate him or her for the work ahead. Moreover, without parental cooperation, success is highly unlikely.

So much for the similarities between approaches. What are the main differences?

Child psychoanalysts have adapted the basic psychoanalytic techniques to the treatment of children. The use of free association, analysis of the transference, resistance, dream analysis, and the unconscious are still the basic ingredients of child psychoanalysis [Author's note: see chapter 2 for a discussion of these]. The major adaptations of these techniques to the treatment of children involves the use of play as an additional means of communication for the child whose verbal and conceptual sophistication make impossible the singular reliance on words that is characteristic of the treatment of adults.

In contrast to the psychoanalytic approaches, client-centered child counselors focus on the phenomenological relationship between the client and counselor. According to this school of thought, the counselor, above all, should provide a permissive environment in which the child is free to dramatize his conflicts and difficulties. The child is never told that he or she is in treatment for a particular problem, and no attempt is made to direct, control or structure his or her play activities. The child is in total command of the situation, and is responsible for his own behavior. Unless his behavior becomes destructive, no limitations are placed upon him. It is believed that an inner drive towards health and maturity provides the motivating force that makes the counseling play encounter a meaningful one.

Client-centered child counselors believe that play is the child's most natural means of self-expression. The provision of simple toys such as dolls, trucks, cars, as well as paints, drawing materials and clay are sufficient tools for the young child to enact the vivid and anxiety-evoking events of his or her inner life. The privacy of the counseling office, the counselor's interest in the child and his problems, and the promise of confidentiality all contribute to a sense of trust and security in the child.

Many child counselors believe that play is the child's most natural means of self-expression.

Therefore, play activities in the counseling office are the means through which the child communicates to the counselor. His freedom to play in any way that he wishes, in an atmosphere of respect and understanding, are believed to foster his self-esteem. In the classic study, *Dibs in Search of Self,* Virginia Axline (1967) provides a detailed description of the manner in which a disturbed youngster's play opened up a world that had formerly been closed by controlling parents.

The case presented here provides an example of play counseling in the school setting. The approach is eclectic, reflecting some aspects of the psychodynamic orientation and some aspects of the client-centered philosophy. What is most important to note is how the counseling process is adapted to the special needs and capabilities of a ten-year-old.

Debbie

Debbie, aged ten, was referred for counseling by her teacher because of violent behavior that was characterized by attacks against her peers. Although she was undersized for her age, she often tyrannized her classmates by hitting them, stealing their possessions, and hurling insults at them. Academically, although she was in fourth grade and had already been left back one year, Debbie could not read a first-grade reader, and had not mastered any of the basic academic skills. She was extremely hyperactive, and could rarely concentrate on anything for longer than a few minutes. She made inordinate demands on the teacher for attention, and flew into a rage when she couldn't get her way.

The counselor referred Debbie to the school psychologist for testing, and after obtaining permission from her guardian, an aunt, a battery of intelligence and personality tests were performed. The results showed that Debbie was of low normal intelligence, and suffered from intense feelings of anger and rejection.

In consultation with Debbie's aunt, Mrs. S, it was learned that when Debbie was seven years of age, her mother had died as a result of an overdose of drugs. Debbie and her two older siblings had discovered her dead body one morning. They thought their mother was sleeping and shook her to try to awaken her. When she didn't move, they became terrified and rushed to their aunt's and uncle's home, where they were taken in and cared for. Shortly after their mother's death, their father died also.

Mrs. S was quite communicative about the children's past, and offered a considerable amount of information to the counselor. She was quite concerned about the three children, whom she now considered as her own. She knew about Debbie's disruptive behavior and academic failure, but in spite of her pleas and interest in the child, which she considered to be greater than the interest provided by Debbie's natural mother, the child's behavior and work were unchanged.

Debbie was delighted at the prospect of coming to counseling, and responded to the counselor in a very positive manner. She expressed the desire to come for sessions as frequently as possible. Therefore, sessions were scheduled on a twice-a-week basis, and an appointed time was arranged. In the counseling office, Debbie took the lead without prompting, explored the materials, and appeared comfortable with the counselor. Despite her "dull normal" tested IQ, she was quite articulate, and could communicate her needs very clearly.

Debbie made active use of the play materials. She would often play "house," and tended to act as a stern and punitive mother to the dolls and stuffed animals. After she had been coming to counseling for a few months, she began to insist that the toys be left exactly where she had placed them. Although she was told by the counselor that she was free to do anything she wanted to with the toys during her time, no promise could be made that they would be exactly where she had placed them when she returned. Debbie's reasonable ego accepted these limitations, and although she was annoyed when, in subsequent sessions, the toys were not where she had left them, she gradually accepted the fact that the counselor saw other children too.

Debbie was not so reasonable, however, when her sessions came to an end, and it was time to return to her classroom. Her difficulty in accepting limits, and her inordinate need for the counselor's attention, reached their height, when after four months of counseling she flew into rages at these times. She kicked the counselor and screamed, "I hate you. I'm not coming here anymore." She would run away, hide, hang onto stairway railings, and had to be carried bodily back to her classroom. Her behavior disturbed nearby classes, and the situation became critical when the principal warned that if the counselor could not control Debbie, her sessions would have to be ended.

The play materials proved to be the means through which Debbie was able to communicate to the counselor what she was feeling at these times. The counselor made the following request of Debbie: "Show me what you are feeling when it's time for you to leave." Debbie responded by wrapping a doll in newspaper, and placed it deep within the counselor's closet. She demanded that no other child be allowed to touch the doll. The counselor understood that Debbie wished to be with her constantly. Separation was painful for this child who had experienced the loss of her parents when she was quite young. If Debbie felt certain that a doll was hidden away in the counselor's closet, she would feel that she herself was symbolically with the counselor even when she had to leave her. Moreover, the demand that no other child be allowed to touch the doll indicated that Debbie regarded the counselor's other clients as rivals for her love.

Debbie's request was granted—the doll would remain in the closet, but Debbie would have to leave at the scheduled time without a tantrum. The counselor reflected Debbie's anguish at separating:

> "You get very angry at me when it's time for you to leave. Perhaps you feel that I don't care about you, or that I won't be here for your next visit. But you know that when it's your turn to be here, I always see you. I have never disappointed you."

Thus, the counselor assured Debbie that the relationship was a warm and stable one. Unlike Debbie's mother, the counselor would not suddenly disappear. Debbie could count on her to be there.

In these months of counseling, Debbie had shown that she could be not only charming and winning, but manipulative and excessively demanding as well. Therefore, the setting of limits was an important part of Debbie's treatment.

In her second year of counseling, Debbie played with the toys in a manner that was quite similar to her earlier game of "house." She frequently set up a mock classroom in which the dolls and stuffed animals were made to represent children. They were given writing materials, and were tested on their knowledge of reading, math and spelling. The dolls and animals generally made mistakes, failed exams, and were threatened by Debbie with being left back. She screamed at them, told them they were bad and stupid, and sometimes hurled objects at them. The counselor was a silent observer of this play. However, before long Debbie insisted that the counselor too must play act that she was one of the children in the "class." Like the others, she had to make mistakes and was insulted and ridiculed for her stupidity. As the "teacher," Debbie was in her glory. She was experiencing the opportunity to master in an active manner what she had experienced passively almost continuously throughout her schooling: failure and humiliation.

This play continued repetitively for a number of months. During this time, the counselor learned that Debbie was now beginning to participate in classroom activities. Her previous stubborn refusal to attempt to read or write had not yielded to persistent attempts on her part to catch up to her classmates. The remedial reading teacher reported that, for the first time, Debbie consented to read aloud in front of other children. She was beginning to overcome her shame at being such a poor reader, and to behave in a manner that opened the way to academic improvement. Thus, through her play, Debbie had managed to overcome, to a considerable extent, the shame and anger that she had experienced in the classroom situation. It is quite possible too, that the mean and punitive teacher symbolized the mother who through her death had abandoned Debbie. Debbie's teacher game may have given her the opportunity to work out some of these feelings as well.

Unfortunately, Debbie's progress was interrupted when, quite suddenly, her uncle died of a heart attack. As surrogate father, Debbie's uncle had been very loving and involved with the children. He and the aunt together provided a sense of security that Debbie had apparently not experienced in her early years. His sudden death left Debbie with feelings that she could not handle. She retreated from all academic efforts, and spent her days in her classroom with her head resting on her desk. In counseling, she was lethargic. She complained of fatigue. It was difficult for her to climb steps, and she had an intense desire to sleep. It appeared that Debbie was depressed, and was retreating into a world where nothing could hurt her anymore. In doing so, however, she was cutting herself off from involvement with her love objects. Such a retreat from the real world can be cataclysmic at any age. For this psychologically delicate and vulnerable child, her retreat from reality was frightening to observe.

During this time, the counselor sat quietly with Debbie, and accepted her retreat. She was not forced to come out of her shell. The hours were quiet ones in which little activity occurred. Debbie knew, however, that the counselor understood how bad, and how frightened she felt. The counselor's facial expression, her acceptance of Debbie's withdrawal, and her sympathetic presence were available throughout this difficult period.

After a few months, Debbie's depression appeared to ease. She began to draw pictures. About a house she had drawn, she said:

"This is a lonely house. I'm going to put a man and woman there to make it a happy house."

Debbie then ripped up the picture into tiny bits. She was apparently trying to deny how lonely and empty she felt inside.

Debbie drew faces, with empty staring eyes, and expressionless mouths. They all looked very much alike. Her comments about some of her pictures were as follows:

Face of a woman: "There ain't a lot of woman, just one. This woman is a nice woman."

Face of a man: "The man. This man is a lonely man so you know what I'm gonna do? I'm going to put the man and the woman together so she can be happy."

Her comments about a picture of herself were: "She's sad, skinny. No one likes to play with her. She doesn't have a family."

Thus, the theme of loneliness and sadness pervaded Debbie's pictures, and her comments about them. As she drew these pictures, Debbie expressed certain infantile longings as well as fears of the future. She wished she could be a baby again; everything was nice when she was a baby. She wished she had a mother and father. She remembered her mother's death. It frightened her. She was afraid her aunt would die too. She didn't know how her aunt would have enough money to support them.

The recollection of her past suffering, and her expressions of anxiety about the future apparently unburdened Debbie from some of the anguish that she had been suffering from inwardly. She regained some of her high energy level, and seemed to come out of the depression. An extremely difficult crisis in her life had been mastered.

The final problem in Debbie's long-term counseling revolved around termination. The approach of her graduation to junior high school meant that Debbie and the counselor would be separated. How would this child, whose relationship with the counselor had been so intense, and so gratifying, deal with the separation? Would she experience it as another abandonment, and become depressed?

In order to avoid termination being experienced as a sudden shock, the implications of Debbie's graduation were taken up by the counselor many months before it was due to occur. Debbie was frightened at the prospect of her sessions coming to an end. At the same time, she was excited about the thought of going to a new school, and being more "grown-up."

By June, it was obvious that the months of discussion regarding termination had prepared Debbie for the separation. Her behavior had become more mature. Although she was still behind in her school work, she had improved considerably. Her social adjustment was good: she rarely fought and had had no temper tantrums for over a year. A follow-up revealed that Debbie's adjustment to junior high school had gone smoothly; she appeared to be holding her own. Occasional visits to the counselor were joyful occasions for both Debbie and the counselor; Debbie seemed self-confident and happy.

Discussion

The case of Debbie demonstrates the importance of a warm, stable and supportive relationship in the life of a child who had experienced a number of traumatic losses. Play and drawings were combined with verbal discussion in the counseling approach described above. Minimal use was made of interpretation, and the child took the lead in most of the therapeutic encounters. Mature behavior came to replace immature behavior, and Debbie was eventually able to function without the counselor's support.

CHILD COUNSELING IN THE ELEMENTARY SCHOOL

One of the more popular models embraced by elementary school counselors during the past twenty-five years is the psychological model developed by Alfred Adler. Different than play therapy, the Adlerian model provides a more comprehensive viewpoint that allows for different types of counseling interventions. In the section that follows we will survey the premises of Adlerian counseling and look briefly at some applications.

ADLERIAN CHILD COUNSELING

Reprinted with permission from *Child Counseling* by Kenneth M. Dimick and Vaughn E. Huff. (Dubuque, Iowa: Wm. C. Brown Company Publishers, 1970), pp. 68–74.

Most discussions of psychological theories place the work of Alfred Adler (1870–1937) with the psychoanalytic schools. In one sense, this seems justifiable in that Adler was a student of Freud and was more than a little influenced by his teacher. Even so, many of Adler's theoretical constructs developed in directions which differed significantly from the classical Freudian stance. In light of modern theoretical models for psychology and counseling, one might be as justified in associating Adler's Individual Psychology with phenomenological thought as in linking it to psychoanalytic theory. (Phenomenology postulates among other things that reality is what the individual perceives it to be.)

Individual Psychology, the identifying name given to Adler's system, emphasizes the individual and his uniqueness. At first glance at the current practice of Individual Psychology in working with children, one is struck by what appears to be a basic contradiction. That is, the name Individual Psychology seems not to be a fitting one since most work done with children is done in groups, both peer and family. Popularly, this school of thought has come to be known as Adlerian counseling with its practitioners calling themselves Adlerians.

The basic postulates of Adler's theory are quite simply stated: (1) Man is inherently a social being and is motivated by social rather than sexual urges. He places social welfare above selfish interest; (2) Man is a creative being seeking experiences that will enhance his own unique life style; (3) Man is primarily a social creature; (4) The personality of each individual is unique; and (5) Consciousness is the center of personality. (Dreikurs, 1957)

Had these basic postulates been the only contribution of Adler, a discussion would seem hardly necessary. Adler, however, did far more than state his basic view of man. He was a prolific writer and published literally hundreds of books and articles.

Although Adler lived the last two years of his life as a practitioner in the United States, the major credit for the adaptation of Adlerian theory to this country, and more precisely to elementary-school-aged children in this country, must be given to Rudolph Dreikurs, a former professor of psychiatry at the University of Chicago Medical School.

Dreikurs, like his predecessor Adler, is a prolific writer. The basic principles as discussed here, applying the theory of Individual Psychology to work with elementary school children, might be called Dreikurian rather than Adlerian.

Some Basic Concepts

The heredity-environment argument is of little importance in that it seems a child's environment and his perception of his environment are the factors that cause a child to behave as he does, and they most certainly are the only factors with which we can deal in changing a child's behavior.

By the same token, if we remove a child from his environment to counsel with him, and if that environment and/or his perception of the environment are causing him to behave in the manner in which he does, we can talk until we are blue in the face; but if neither of these factors is changed and we return him to the same environment, his behaviors will be as they were before the counseling.

It is then only logical to bring the significant aspects of the child's environment to the counseling session. In the case of elementary-school-aged children, the basic desire to become an accepted member of the group is most usually directed at the family group. For this reason, Adlerian counseling involves not just the child but the child and his family members. It should be pointed out that as the child grows older, acceptance by the peer group becomes more important than acceptance by the family group. Hence, Individual Psychology counseling with adolescents and upper-elementary-aged children normally is done with groups of students.

As a child attempts to become a member of his family group, he meets a number of situations that, if not provided for, can easily cause *discouragement.* To start with, he is physically the smallest and least adequate member of the group. He lives in a world of capable giants. These basic frustrations, combined with the other normal setbacks the child experiences in attempting to become a member of the family group, tend to discourage the child. Only when a child becomes discouraged will he misbehave (Dinkmeyer & Dreikurs, 1963).

The treatment for this situation is easily derived but not always so easily administered. The antonym for discouragement is *encouragement,* and that encouragement becomes one of the major roles of the Adlerian counselor.

Teachers adhering to the Adlerian point of view often mark students' tests by giving recognition to correct items rather than checking incorrect answers. Recognition of what children are doing well rather than punishment of what children are doing poorly encourages the child.

The formation of a child's *life style* is a basic element in this theory. Life style, or life pattern, is basically an individual's attitude toward life. As a child attempts to become an accepted part of the group, he learns that certain behaviors have not helped him or have hindered him in seeking this goal. He learns to avoid these behaviors. Out of fear and a recollection of disappointments, he avoids hindering behaviors and develops at a very early age his own unique life style.

The child's life style is usually well formed by the age of four or five. He operates after this age with well-established, basic premises and no longer encounters new situations from a trial-and-error basis.

The *family constellation,* or more precisely the position of the child in the family, is of great importance. Observers of children's behavior often are amazed at the differences in behavior of children from the same home. The environment, these observers contend, is the same, or at least very nearly the same, for all children in a given home. However, such is not the case. The family constellation, and thus the environment, is very different for each child.

The first child, for instance, has no older siblings after whom to model his behavior. He was, at least for nine months, an only child. Therefore, he presents much of the behavior of the only-child syndrome. He is, as soon as a sibling is born, dethroned, and his environment is often more radically changed by the addition of siblings than are the environments of subsequent children. He does, however, have a wider range of choice in deciding what manner he will attempt to attain acceptance and recognition or to find his place in the group.

Subsequent children are more limited in this choice. If they were to choose the same method of attaining success as did the older sibling, the rivalry would be a frustrating war that most likely could not be won by the younger child as he would always be a step behind the older child. If a younger child does the things his older sibling(s) does, he has done only what his environment (his family) is expecting of him—nothing more. This factor, coupled with the skills and experiences obtained by the older sibling, forces most children with older brothers and/or sisters to choose a way other than the way chosen by their sibling(s) to "make their marks."

Athletics, school achievement, particular skill in crafts and hobbies, and others are all positive directions that children may take. However, negative directions of achievement may also be taken by children. When positive roads are blocked, or if parents, teachers, counselors, and others are unaware of a child's need for unique achievement and direct him into an unwanted and frustrating competition with his siblings by encouraging him to take the same path as a brother or sister, negative results may occur. The child may rebel or decide to do the best job of being the "bad guy" in the family. It may be for this reason that fewer first-born children are delinquent than are last-born children.

The Adlerian counselor, working through the family, helps to discover positive directions of achievement for the child. He also helps the parents to understand the private logic or the rationale for the child's behavior.

Adler coined the phrase *inferiority complex*. This phrase, however, is much misused from the manner in which Adler intended. The most painful experience for anyone is the feeling they are inferior to others. Once again, referring to the phenomenological point of view, the deterring factor is feeling inferior, not necessarily being inferior. One may, in actuality, be inferior, but if he does not feel he is, this has little psychological effect upon him. On the other hand, he may not actually be inferior; but if he feels he is, his development is restricted.

The display of these real or imagined inferiorities as an excuse or a mechanism of escape constitutes the inferiority complex. An individual demonstrating behavior connected with this syndrome may not compensate for his inferior feelings and is able to achieve nothing. Growth is impossible when the individual is in this state.

The Meaning of the Child's Behavior

There are four goals of the child's disturbing behavior: (1) *Attention-getting*—This is a normal way of a child attempting to attain social status. It may take a "positive" (doing nice things) or a "negative" (doing not such nice things) direction. (2) *Power*—If the attention-getting stage is thwarted by adults, a *power struggle* between child and adult occurs. This struggle is predominant in most homes and is the style of life in the classrooms of most schools. Often neither adult nor child wins the *power struggle*. (3) *Revenge*—This involves a battle between child and adult. The child no longer is merely seeking acceptance but is out to "get" the adult. Children displaying this step are usually disliked by all with whom they come into contact. (4) *Assumed disability* (or withdrawal)—The child has given up and does nothing or next to nothing. He sees himself, as do others around him, as defeated and hopeless (Dreikurs, 1957).

These steps, or labels, are useful for several purposes: (1) They help to describe and conceptualize about behavior and (2) They provide a system for observing behavior. Just as the child must go through the stages of attention, power, and revenge to arrive at assumed disability, when he "improves" he must retrace his steps through these stages. Hence, the observer has reference points to observe if the child is improving.

This particular point has more than once been a bone of contention between Adlerian counselors and teachers. Such comments as "I just had the kid squared away—didn't bug anyone—just sat there—now you have him in counseling and he is ripping the room apart—Thanks a lot!" are not unique in what Adlerians see as the beginning of a successful case.

It is not important that a child be rigidly placed in a category or even that mistakes in diagnosis are made. What is important is that direction of a child's behavior (negative *toward* positive or positive *toward* negative) be recognized.

The Counseling Approach

Adlerian family counseling interviews are often held in front of an audience. A counselor, a co-counselor, and a recorder question the entire family, observing the behavior of the family as to interactions, lines of communication, and so on. The children then are sent to a playroom while the parents are interviewed and the parents' perception of the situation is obtained. Such things as the differences in parent behavior with and without the children present are observed. The children return and the parents leave, and the children's perception of the situation is discussed while their behavior is being closely observed.

During the session with the children, such techniques as confrontation are often employed by the counselor. An example may clarify the technique. In a particularly argumentative family, a six-year-old boy discovered that when his parents became angry with each other, they didn't yell and scream at him. He also discovered that one of the things which made his mother the angriest was when his father couldn't find his car keys in the morning before leaving for work. "Why are you so disorganized? Why don't you find a place to always keep them?" she would yell, much to the delight of the young boy who knew no yelling was coming his way for awhile. He then discovered that by moving his father's car keys he could cause the scene, and he began to do so with regularity. When the counselor realized during a counseling session what the child had been doing, the counselor confronted the child with this knowledge. The mere fact that somebody else knew what he was doing ruined the game for the child and the behavior ceased.

When the interview with the children is completed, they are dismissed from the room. Reports from the playroom worker, children's teachers, and others are made. With the help of the recorder and the co-counselor, recommendations to the family, consistent with Adlerian principles, are discussed by the counselor. When specific recommendations are decided upon, the entire family is recalled and the recommendations are explained to the family. Such principles as punishment by *logical consequences* are often recommended (Dreikurs & Grey, 1968). Ideas for the development of mutual respect are often explored with the family members.

Logical consequences as a form of punishment may be made clearer with the use of another example. A mother came to counseling complaining that she was sick and tired of fixing dinner at 6:00 and again at 6:30 and usually again at 7:00 as the children staggered in to be fed whenever it was convenient for them. She felt that her children should be made to be at dinner on time. She had spanked, yelled at, and threatened, all to no avail. "Why should they be there on time?" asked the therapist. "Because," replied the mother, "I spend my whole evening fixing dinner and cleaning up after them. Even when the kids fix their own dinner if they come in late, they make a bigger mess to clean up than I do. Besides that, they seem to invariably eat something I was saving for the next day and that hurts our budget." Those all seemed like legitimate reasons to the therapist so he pointed out the logical consequences position to the mother.

The logical consequence of being late for dinner is, of course, no dinner. He suggested that the mother friendly but firmly adopt the policy: "We eat dinner at our house at 6:00. If you are there and ready to eat, we would be glad to have you eat with us. If not, try us for breakfast which is served at 7:00 in the morning." Getting angry, preaching, and yelling served no purpose. The practice of logical consequences did.

Control of behavior through logical consequences, except when the consequence is one that would be extremely harmful, has proved a successful process in many homes and classrooms.

Mutual respect emphasizes the need for all members of the family constellation to be respected by all other members. Very often parents demand respect and obedience from their children but do not in turn feel any obligation to respect the rights and feelings of the child. All family members have individual rights and responsibilities. No family member, whether child or parent, should be forced to behave in a particular way without a reason.

Communication and understanding between children and adults, as facilitated by the methods of Adlerian counseling discussed here, is improved. Often misperceptions of the demands of adults or children can be clarified by this approach to the counseling process. The result is often a home that is a happier place for the entire family.

Parent study groups and teacher study groups teaching the basic Adlerian principles are other methods Adlerian counselors have employed with success in helping people to work and/or live with a better understanding of children.

HORTICULTURAL COUNSELING

Prepared in cooperation with Estelle Gerard, Special Assistant to the Director, Brooklyn Botanic Garden.

The uses of horticulture as an active approach in working with a variety of psychological, learning, and role-area problems has been employed for many years, but only in recent decades has the specific concept of horticultural counseling been developed and systematized. Horticulture can be defined as the art and science of growing and arranging all kinds of vegetable matter, including flowers, trees, shrubbery, potted plants, garden vegetables, and floral arrangements. When such activities are used specifically to facilitate an individual's adjustment, or for the amelioration of psychological problems, or to help clients or students work through role-area conflicts, the activity is then considered horticultural counseling. On a broader level, we see the introduction of horticulture into the school counseling setting as a valuable asset not only for the troubled client, the exceptional student, or the problem learner; but for all clients and students, especially on the elementary school level. As we are all involved biologically with the plant world around us, the study of plants and plant growth becomes an important way of learning about the world. In this section, we will explore in some detail the value of horticultural counseling.

Background

While horticultural therapy was probably one of the first forms of "activity" therapy used, it is only recently that it has been accorded professional status. Gardening has always been a rewarding activity; one that has brought joy as a hobby, emotional richness as a vocation, and psychological dividends as a pastime. Charles Dudley Warner, the American essayist, captures the manifold psychological implications of gardening as an activity: "The love of dirt is among the earliest of passions, as it is the latest. Mud-pies gratify one of our first and best instincts. So long as we are dirty, we are pure. Fondness for the ground comes back to a man after he has run the round of pleasure and business, eaten dirt, and sown wild-oats, drifted about the world, and taken the wind of all its moods. The love of digging in the ground (or of looking on while he pays another to dig) is as sure to come back to him, as he is sure, at least, to go under the ground, and stay there. To own a bit of ground, to scratch it with a hoe, to plant seeds, and watch their renewal of life—this is the commonest delight of the race, the most satisfactory thing a man can do" (Warner, 1870/1959). This sentiment underlies the horticultural therapy approach.

The counseling application of horticulture is not new. Hefley (1973) points out that it dates back to Colonial times, when it was used in the Friends Hospital in Philadelphia, where it is still used today. She points out one of the main reasons that HT came into being:

> Often in the 19th-century programs were geared toward crop production or maintenance of the institution. However, as they developed, their therapeutic value began to outweigh their economic value. By the early 1900's many hospitals, orphanages, reformatories and other institutions were conducting a range of garden therapy programs. (p. 35)

"Early in the 1920s, the U.S. Federal Board for Vocational Education offered courses in gardening for disabled soldiers and suggested that continuation of their garden work would help maintain their health. The Red Cross, using the same reasoning, established truck gardens near hospitals for wounded soldiers" (Institute for Rehabilitation Medicine, 1973). Hefley also points out how after the Second World War, when the rehabilitation of physically and psychologically disabled veterans became of paramount national importance, horticultural therapy became an important medium. After the war, the recognition of this approach widened, and today HT is widely practiced in a variety of settings.

Until recently, educational programs specifically designed to prepare students for horticultural therapy were not available. In 1971, the first undergraduate program in horticultural therapy in the United States was offered at Kansas State University in cooperation with the Menninger Foundation, which has used "gardening therapy" since it first opened its doors. Several other universities are currently involved in horticultural therapy programs, and Kansas State, Clemson (South Carolina), Michigan State, and Texas Tech offer degrees in horticultural therapy. Students in these programs receive a broad background in horticulture, supported by a good background in psychology, sociology, and related areas.

The National Council for Therapy and Rehabilitation through Horticulture was created in 1973 to promote and encourage the application of horticulture and related activities as a therapeutic and rehabilitation medium. It coordinates a variety of activities through its many contacts with professional and educational organizations active in this area.

Basic Principles

There are three aspects to horticultural counseling, which in practice are combined in many programs. They are (1) the client is given a constructive task or series of tasks from which he or she can see definite results in a relatively brief period of time and can recognize that these results are of his or her own doing; (2) the client is given the opportunity to work with living things and to see the development of growth in a simplified but beautiful form; and (3) the client is given an opportunity to express many feelings, projectively or directly, in his or her relationship with the plants and flowers. This last point is subtle and we will explore it further.

The first aspect directs itself to the client's sense of *accomplishment*. The client is able to attain a specific goal and to feel pride in what he or she has done. The second aspect refers to the therapeutic value of seeing any type of growth, which is always a reaffirmation of life. The third aspect functions much like play therapy does for children. The client becomes emotionally involved not only with the project, but with the plants themselves, and the skilled counselor can enable the client to express many of his or her feelings through this.

In addition, the interaction between person and plant may have an ameliorative effect on the individual's psychological condition. "Plants have served as a source of inspiration for creative artists since history began," Lewis (1973) points out, "but recent evidence indicates the existence of more subtle responses of people to plants." He goes on to point out that horticulture may even be a cure for some of the stresses and strains of urban living imposed on us.

> When a human being is under stress, it appears that the presence of plants and the opportunity for close association with them can exert a beneficial psychological effect. Subtle man-plant relationships become obvious in the extreme urban environment, where field and forests have been replaced by asphalt and brick. . . . Gardening may be an instrument for great healing in our troubled cities, and perhaps, in any human-stress situation. (pp. 19–23)

We shall see in the following section how these three aspects of horticultural counseling become combined in practice.

Practical Applications

Horticultural counseling can be applied in just about any setting, but has been used extensively both in the school and in various aspects of rehabilitation. Hamilton, Nichols, and White (1970) point out four key areas in which horticultural therapy is used: rehabilitation of patients after illness or injury; training of disabled students; assessment of disability and capability; and social activities of the physically disabled. They go on to point out,

Rehabilitation covers the whole process of regaining maximal function as quickly as possible once the specific immediate care of the injury or illness has been instituted. For some patients this may mean only a short period of convalescence . . . or a long period of intensive treatment. . . . As with many other forms of occupational therapy, functional activities can be selected and developed to give the patients specific exercises. The activities must be graded to the patients' needs, both specific and general, for light exercise or heavy exercise, and depending on whether he is ambulatory or in a wheel chair. Garden activities can range from providing finger and manipulative activities. (p. 366)

The techniques of HT are as varied as the population to which it is applied. Application depends heavily on the problems and the abilities of the people who are participating. In some programs, it is used primarily as a recreational-oriented activity. In others, it is used as part of the comprehensive program for physical rehabilitation. In the school setting, HT can be integrated within the context of the regular curriculum, drawing together and making relevant such diverse subjects as botany (identifying plant life), mathematics (pricing and cost accounting a project), English (writing a report about a project), geography and history (where plants are found), and, of course, social cooperation in the team efforts necessary in many projects.

Classes in horticulture for the handicapped child are often designed according to handicaps rather than of age, although this is clearly not necessary. Oral reports, written observations, field trips, demonstrations, scientific experiments, and audiovisual methods are employed in conjunction with each other. The basic goal is to communicate to the students that their handicaps do not exclude them from living and enjoying a life that can be beautiful, rewarding, and productive.

The benefits of horticultural therapy can be seen in four major areas: the physical, emotional, intellectual, and social. Physical benefits include the satisfaction clients feel in working with their own hands. Being outdoors, digging, raking, and weeding are effective means of venting feelings, and can discharge much of the person's bottled-up aggression. "For example, a patient who is suffering from certain kinds of frustration may find it extremely helpful to break flower pots into shards that are used as drainage material" (Friends Hospital, 1976). The washing of used pots is a menial job that has been useful in treating depressed patients. Mixing soil can be a major achievement for a badly crippled hand. The use of variously colored pots, utensils, and plants can be made to test color sense and visual acuity (Brooks & Oppenheim, 1973).

In horticultural counseling, a child can observe growth and development in a simple but beautiful form.

The emotional benefits of horticultural activities are manifold. "For so many individuals who are totally dependent on others for assistance . . . a living thing depending on *them* for care and sustenance gives them the will to go on, and a greater interest in the future. . . . Plants must be watered, transplanted, given more or less light, cultivated, fed, groomed, etc. . . . These are the basic routines of life that the patients themselves understand" (Brooks & Oppenheim, 1973).

There are also intellectual benefits, and these are particularly germane to the effort of the school counselor to combine cognitive with affective growth opportunities. The language used in learning about plants will be new to most students, and the study of plants touches upon history, geography, science, travel, and a concern for the environment. As an activity, horticulture combines many of the skills traditionally included in the curriculum; but it allows for new ways of utilizing these skills.

One of the values credited to HT is the social benefit it affords client and students. Particularly in those situations where individual students or clients work cooperatively in groups, the individual learns the practical values of social cooperation. This can be valuable, for example, in a special education class where disabled students are cut off from opportunities for adequate socialization.

While the potential is virtually limitless, we will focus on those applications relevant to the scope of this book. HT has been used successfully in helping mentally retarded individuals. Whenever retarded persons can develop self-esteem—or a sense of power and accomplishment—their potential for actualizing their IQ abilities increases. Being retarded, he or she already experienced failure in the world of academics or school learning. If the impact of this failure can be lessened, it gives individuals a better chance of improving themselves. Since many of the procedures used in the greenhouse are routine and require no great intellectual skill, the possibilities for learning to master them are open to many retarded individuals.

Recent efforts have also been directed toward applying HT in helping the visually handicapped (Tereshkovich, 1973). The blind have benefited from "Fragrance Gardens" throughout the United States, the oldest and best known of which is the Brooklyn Botanic Garden. This fragrance garden for the blind features many herbs and scented plants labeled in braille. The flower beds are raised to fingertip height to accommodate visually handicapped visitors. It is not only an aesthetically enjoyable place for the blind, but also serves a valuable teaching purpose. At the New York Botanical Garden, a new project is under way. Plans are being made to develop a two-acre sensory trail for all people, to restimulate investigative interest through all the senses. Areas to be designed will include barefoot information, hands information, seeing information, smelling information, hearing information, and small-things information with magnifying equipment. The objectives are to sensitize people to be more responsive when introduced to environmental issues and programs.

HT is being recognized as an important modality in the school setting, and as a part of the school counseling curriculum, and there are increasing references to it in the literature. Innovative programs have been introduced to meet the needs of the physically impaired, mentally retarded, learning disabled, socially maladjusted, and emotionally disturbed student population. Chandler (1977) has described an innovative HT program in which trainable mentally retarded adolescents worked with houseplants in a classroom greenhouse. She concludes:

> The classroom greenhouse provided concrete experiences that motivated these students to learn. Basic concepts and skills were reinforced through daily routine; social competencies were acquired during the teamwork process; and vocational training was acquired with each new duty assigned. Above all, the students had a real hobby—something special, something that would live and grow, something that depended on them. A sense of worth and a positive self-concept blossomed in each student as a result of this most successful project. (p. 63)

Senn et al. (1974) have also described an HT program whose main goal was to train "the mildly retarded to become productive, active, secure citizens with the capability of gainful employment" (p. 4). The program, they suggest, was successful in these goals. Cotton (1975) has reported on a federally funded HT program in a Philadelphia inner-city ghetto, noting:

> In the entire time the program has been operational we have not had a single incident of aggression of a verbal or physical nature. We have worked with rival gang members, students who were enemies, blacks, and whites. All these were situations where fights, or at the very least, verbal confrontations would occur. None did. This phenomenon I have called the "Greenhouse Effect." There is a definite lowering of aggressiveness.
>
> The greenhouse has added effects: there is a definite positive feeling that the student has as he goes about his work. There is a soothing effect in working with live, exotic plant material. There is a feeling of power in propagating plants, in sowing seeds, and seeing them grow under your care. Self-image and esteem are raised. The student is accorded status by his peers and counselors. He has a feeling of worth. (p. 74)

Clearly, the ameliorative values of HT go beyond any single group and may be extended to a wide variety of special learners. HT, or horticulture by itself, can and should be integrated more routinely into the school curriculum. Table 9.1 shows some of the specific applications of horticultural counseling for different kinds of exceptional learners with whom a school counselor typically works. We must also keep in mind that in its broadest sense, horticultural counseling is an ideal modality for the growth of the typical, nonexceptional learner as well.

table 9.1

HORTICULTURAL COUNSELING IN THE SCHOOLS: SPECIFIC APPLICATIONS

type of learner	suggested activities	potential benefits
Visually impaired	Fragrance gardens Sensory trails "Small things" information	Increased ability to perceive through nonvisual senses
Physically disabled	Class demonstrations Trips to botanic gardens Limited planting activities outside of classroom/school	More awareness of the physical world around—and different ways of accessibility to outside activities
Emotionally disturbed	Individual and group planting projects—in and out of classroom/school Discussing feelings about gardening activities	Expression of feelings and control of inappropriate impulses and violence potential Prototypical development of interpersonal relationship skills
Socially maladjusted	Group planting projects—in and out of classroom	Learning to cooperate in working with others on a task
Gifted	Reading about plants while engaging in HT activities Scientific experiments	Applied intellectual skills and motivational benefits
Mildly retarded	Taking care of houseplants Assisting horticulturist Working with other classes	A sense of self-worth, accomplishment, and productivity

CASE STUDY: A SCHOOL GUIDANCE CLASS FOR EMOTIONALLY DISTURBED CHILDREN

Written by Wendy Lehrman. Reprinted from the September-October 1969 issue of *Children* (now *Children Today*). Used with permission of the author and the U.S. Department of Health and Human Services.

As a teacher turned therapeutic teacher over the past decade, I find that my functions have changed in some ways, but that in others they have, surprisingly, remained the same. If the goal of education is to enable the student to understand the laws that govern the conduct of life, then the goal of therapeutic education is no different. But the means of reaching that goal for emotionally disturbed children in a public school setting differ in kind and degree. They must be altered to help such children clarify perceptions that deviate from reality.

The 8-year-olds I teach in a third-grade junior guidance class—one of two at Public School 87 in the Upper West Side of Manhattan—have presented patterns of deviant behavior ranging from extreme withdrawal to extreme acting up. These emotionally disturbed children, who come from many different socioeconomic and ethnic backgrounds in New York City, have IQ's ranging from average to high. Some children have been diagnosed by psychiatrists as having schizophrenia and some as having character disorders. Some are more mildly disturbed than others. For some, we have no clinical diagnosis.

This class is one of 261 junior guidance classes in 110 elementary schools in New York City, with a total attendance of about 3,000 troubled children. Within the several basic designs that have evolved to meet the children's needs, there are numerous mutations. The design for the type of class I teach calls for a full-time "home" teacher plus a "unit" teacher shared with another junior guidance class in the same school. The unit teacher sometimes works together with the home teacher and sometimes teaches the class by himself. He also is responsible for keeping records. Teachers remain with the same class for two years.

In each school the home and unit teachers, a guidance counselor, an administrator, and sometimes a clinical or social work specialist form a therapeutic education team. This team makes the final selection of the children for the junior guidance classes. Regular classroom teachers suggest guidance classes for children who have had persistent problems. Children are also recommended for the classes on the basis of their school records, observation by guidance counselors or school administrators during classroom visits, consultations with parents, and suggestions from mental health clinicians, social workers, psychologists, and psychiatrists.

The therapeutic education team attempts to define and resolve some of the children's difficulties through weekly conferences that develop programs for individual children as well as the class. In addition, teachers meet weekly to develop detailed curricula.

Our task in relation to the emotionally disturbed child is to make his experience—intellectual, physical, social, and emotional—intelligible to the end that his energy is freed for creative, productive activity.

From this point of view, every act of every child has meaning to the teacher of emotionally disturbed children. And clearly the converse is true. Every act of the teacher has meaning to every child. The teacher, then, must create an environment in the classroom that reflects his intention to eliminate inhibiting factors, discourage regressive behavior, and help the children learn how to cope with their problems. He must work within this context in planning and carrying out the arrangement of the classroom, the day's schedule, appropriate procedures and methods, the lesson content, and his particular style of teaching.

A tall order. I, for one, often fail to fill it—sometimes I fail for personal reasons; sometimes for reasons beyond my control. We face a host of obstacles in working with emotionally disturbed children: too few staff members, meager supplies, lack of space, inadequate health services, few supportive services, and little or no special education for the teacher.

Yet we are attaining our goals with a significant number of children for whom previous schooling had failed. Many of the poorly achieving children reach, or come close to, "grade level" in academic areas during their stay in the junior guidance class. They grow strong, healthy ties to their group, ties which more often than not extend to the school and the community. They develop insight into the logic of their own behavior and learn to select alternatives that are more nearly appropriate to their needs and circumstances. Placements are usually for two years, although a child may be in the program for one to six years, depending on his need. Most of our children eventually go on to regular classes, where they are able to function well. For the few children who cannot, we recommend a transfer to special schools.

Among the shortcomings of our program is a lack of provision for objective evaluation. Nevertheless, I believe some aspects have enabled us to make real strides—establishment of junior guidance classes as part of the total school community, designation of a time in which individual children's needs are met within a fairly loose group setting, carefully designed group experiences, and development of flexible approaches to children whose needs are not always met by planned activities.

In starting each new group, we have had to overcome feelings of alienation, which are intensified in the parents as well as the children upon placement in a junior guidance class. Misgivings about the placement of children may be relieved when parents get to know a teacher informally through parent-teacher activities in the school or community. I believe it is important for parents to identify us as teachers, not merely as special teachers.

In addition, the parents need to understand the advantages of the special class for their child. The guidance counselor is responsible for explaining the program to parents and working with them. Before the child is admitted to a junior guidance class, the guidance counselor discusses reasons for placement with the parents.

We prefer to accept children of parents who seem capable of long-term cooperation with our efforts. But we do take other children. We feel satisfied that most parents of the children in our class understand and approve of our methods and goals.

Meaning for Children

Of greater consequence, even than parental understanding, is the child's understanding of the meaning of his new class. The class *is* startlingly different. The children do feel apprehensive. Any change is more difficult to accept for emotionally disturbed children than for healthier children. The change to a special class may be too burdensome for the children to bear unless the unfamiliar elements are accounted for and put into perspective. For example, the children have not been in a small class before; they have not had two teachers at the same time; nor have they eaten their lunches in their classroom. So immediate efforts must be made to clarify the situation for them.

The first period of the first day of school is devoted to the exploration of these differences. The children are encouraged to say how the classroom differs from their expectations of a third-grade classroom.

"There are blocks and dolls."

"Why are there two teachers?"

"It looks like a kindergarten."

The children are then asked what they think blocks and dolls are doing in a third-grade room.

"It's a class for retards."

"It's a class for bad kids."

We try to clear up these misconceptions by helping the children investigate the realities of the situation. They soon realize that the group is not remarkable either for retardation or wickedness. They then give other explanations for the dolls and blocks.

"You want us to practice to make real houses."

"We will learn to take care of babies when we grow up."

We help the children understand the concepts underlying the structure of the class and its use of materials. We explain that the materials are not playthings, but working tools with which to achieve success in such areas as arithmetic, language, science, art, and the expression of feelings—all legitimate goals of education.

Neither on this first day nor at any other time during the year do we deny differences. Instead, we help the children understand that "different" means nothing by itself, but only in relation to another quality or quantity, and that it does not mean "better" or "worse." A small class that uses blocks and dolls is not a "worse" class. It enables the teachers and children to function effectively and suits other needs.

To allay the children's anxiety about the unusual nature of the junior guidance class, the school tries to show to the entire student body those aspects of the special class that parallel the school's regular program. When feasible, the guidance class follows the school's regular procedures. By the second year the children attend assembly programs regularly and they join other classes in music and physical education. There are limits to such activities, of course, and in dealing with special problems we always try to place honesty above conformity.

Some children readily understand the meaning of the class. For example, Carlos, who was placed in the class because of extremely withdrawn behavior, caught on immediately. He was present at our conference when his mother, upset by the gossip of misinformed neighbors, asked that he be removed. She stated that she would not object to having him put back a grade or even two, but that she did not want him in this special class. We assured her that he was very bright, but that in a larger group he had been overwhelmed. "Sure," Carlos chimed in, "I didn't say a single word in the whole second grade."

Challenges

The first daily period serves our unique needs particularly well. We call it a "work period," not a "work and play period." We are not opposed to play on theoretical grounds. Quite the contrary. But as "play" and "work" are code words to many children, we make a distinction for the sake of expediency. We do try, however, as the year goes on to help the children distinguish between "horsing around" and acceptable play.

Low dividers separate parts of the room from each other. There is a block corner, a work bench, a drama corner (never called a doll corner, for the boys are very active there), an easel, and a work table for various activities—cutting, pasting, mixing papiermaché, and so on—as well as pupil desks.

Procedures have been established to avoid crowding, undue disorder, interference, and other trouble-making situations. As the children arrive in class, they get busy with some work in progress or with something new. The teacher's words, attitudes, and actions clearly indicate that productive activities are an essential part of school. In a junior guidance class, making something beautiful out of a lump of clay is as important as reading, writing, and arithmetic. The children know this and accept such work as a challenge. Producing something gives them great satisfaction.

The challenge is completely individualized. It allows for experimentation, the expression of curiosity, the reinforcement of strengths, and the surmounting of weaknesses. It may be a time for interaction with others or a time to be alone. Each child can take steps entirely at his own speed and in his own way. There are differences in development. Some children experience immediate success; others do not seem to progress at all. For them, any independent effort to control the environment competently can be painfully difficult.

Joe was put in the class as a result of leaden passivity. He spent several weeks huddled at his desk with his coat on, staring at a wall. When he got to the point of rising to watch the other children work, we rejoiced. Occasionally he helped his classmates by steadying wood for them at the work bench. Joe was obviously afraid that dealing actively with his environment would expose his inadequacy. Our task as his teachers was to support him in making small steps toward some interaction with the world. At first we helped him assemble jigsaw puzzles until he was able to do them by himself. We led him to draw and paint by guiding his hand over the paper. Eventually Joe became independently involved in creative activities, using many different kinds of materials.

Other troubled children used materials in an expansive and grandiose manner. Robert cut a "Bat Man" mask out of the dead center of a large bolt of cloth. He started many other ambitious projects, but finished few. Often he wasted a great deal of material. Our task was to help him evaluate his undertakings realistically in relation to his capacity and the materials available. We encouraged Robert to preplan, to measure, to think ahead. He eventually learned to work efficiently as well as creatively.

Such observations offered us invaluable clues to this boy's learning patterns. Robert might have been considered to be expressing hostility through destructive behavior, and, partly, he was. However, we found that his reading style correlated closely with his creative style. For practical purposes, he could not read at all. However, when he was given a simple, well-illustrated story that contained a few familiar key words, he would simulate the act of reading, fabricating a story that had an eerie resemblance to the original.

He obviously went right to the center of things, using his innate intelligence and linguistic gifts, but his directness—combined with his failure to grasp relevant details—impeded his reading. Our task was to acquaint him with the written word and help him discover its relation to the spoken word. After we encouraged him to analyze the material of his own stories, he was able to establish the necessary links.

Joe, a boy I have already mentioned, stared rigidly ahead when he was first given reading material. He would not make up his own stories. We viewed his unresponsiveness as another manifestation of his feeling of vulnerability and his fear of exposure. We made up simple, phonetically based sentences in comic book form, which we read to him. For example:

The rat bit Bat Man.
Bat Man hit the rat.
The rat ran.

His only response—one we recognized as highly significant—was to relax his body and focus his eyes upon the page. We continued to read to him for weeks as he listened passively. Then he began to move his lips with us. Finally he whispered the words.

Ann, a twin girl referred to us because of her low level of achievement, seemed to show evidence of perceptual difficulties. In reading and writing she reversed letters and interchanged initial and final consonants. During the work period, we encouraged her to arrange cutouts, jigsaw puzzles, and similar materials that could help her overcome reversal problems. She preferred the drama corner, where she would act out scenes with a doll she called by the name of her domineering twin sister, who was in a regular class. Ann scolded and beat the doll unmercifully. When a reading period followed these dramas, Ann showed no signs of perceptual difficulty. Although she did not receive special training, in a short time Ann was reading at a level a half grade higher than when she came to us, and she no longer had reversal problems.

Group lessons are important. I think we have no legitimate function as a therapeutic education program based in a school unless we use the group as one of our major rehabilitative tools. In academic areas, we design our lessons so that the challenges presented can be met on many levels by children with different abilities and backgrounds.

In a language lesson, for example, reading material is placed where it is visible to all members of the class. The teacher reads to the children, who respond by making discoveries. A nonreader may discover that "car," "can," and "Catherine" begin with the same letter. The class explores the implications of this discovery. A child who reads very well may discover that "automat" has a root in common with "automobile" and "automation." Again the entire class discusses the discovery. Each child gets a chance to express himself. All responses are given serious consideration.

At times we form small groups, based on common needs that have become apparent during the class lesson—not on overall reading ability. Children's individual needs often cross grade levels. For example, a child may read, "Dead men tell no tales." Although he may be at his proper grade level in reading, he needs exercise in the use of context.

Class Disturbances

Thus, we have created an environment that fosters independent discovery and productive response at each child's pace and in his own way. But in doing so we have not resolved all the problems of a junior guidance class. Some children find our very reasonableness shattering. They are unable to accept alternative solutions to problems. Any suggestion that they change their ways is perceived as a threat to their systems of defense, and their behavior becomes increasingly rigid.

For example, one day during storytime, Willie noticed a pretty stone that belonged to another child and tried to snatch it away. When I did not permit him to take it, Willie threw a chair across the room. The other children and I expressed our concern for Willie but insisted that the other child be allowed to keep his stone.

Although the children know it helps to remain seated during a furor, one classmate got up and went over to Willie, holding out his hand. "Come on, Willie," he said, "we want to hear the story. You can have my stone." But Willie refused the offer and continued his tantrum until the class was dismissed.

As the children left, one asked, "Why'd you have to do that?"

Willie replied, "Do you think I like to act that way?"

Such insight is tremendously useful to the troubled child. But increased self-knowledge often seems threatening to the child unless he knows of safe alternative ways of dealing with his feelings of inadequacy. The teacher's job is to help the child become aware of those alternatives.

Whenever possible, we continue to identify the confusing elements of a disturbance in the context of the group.

For example, the class was disrupted every day—often several times a day—by Frank, a child who could not accept the established alternatives of participating in an arithmetic lesson or occupying himself at some independent activity. At the onset of the mathematics period, he regularly sought to distract the class by some engaging antic, such as blowing spit balls through a straw or flipping monster cards about the room. The children have learned to ignore such exhibitions but to offer help to Frank in resolving the problems that lead to such inappropriate horseplay in the classroom. One day the children discussed the events that led to Frank's disruptions.

"It always happens at the math lesson."

"He hates math."

"He's dumb in math."

"So, he could go alone."

"Why won't you work at something alone?" I asked Frank.

"I don't want to go to the back of the room," he answered.

"He don't want to be alone."

Finally, one child asked me, "Could someone go with him and help him?"

Thus, Frank's problem was conceptualized. He felt inadequate in mathematics. The established alternative to studying mathematics with the class—doing something else quietly alone—was unacceptable to him. But the class discussion had opened a new alternative to resolve Frank's conflict in a constructive manner. We assigned a child as his helper. When the mathematics lesson began, Frank and his helper occupied themselves quietly at the back of the room in productive pursuits related to mathematics, and this became the pattern from that day on.

Some of the problems that the children face are beyond our reach. Although we are well aware that, as Bruno Bettelheim has pointed out, love is not enough, we have found that it can be fairly powerful. Tommy was one who taught us this. Tommy, who for six years had lived with a severely alcoholic stepfather and an increasingly alcoholic mother, was placed with us after being suspended from school. He spent the first few months in class in apparent peace when engaged in solitary, nonacademic tasks. But he became violent when anyone encroached on his privacy or made any demands on him.

Tommy's tantrums were entirely self-destructive. He would throw himself down, bang his head forcefully on the floor, twisting, screaming, and crying all the while. This happened many times a day—when he was asked to join a lesson, to sit down at lunch, or to share his blocks, for example.

We continued to reach out to Tommy in spite of his rebuffs. One day he said, "You're not doing nothing. Just get my father to stop beating me and my mother."

We tried to achieve this by working through a social agency. Although we did not succeed, Tommy knew of our efforts and his behavior changed radically. Through our attempts to help, we had made it clear to him that he was important to us and loved by us. He was worth living.

In summary, we proceed on the theory that the basic principles of education apply as well to the teaching of emotionally disturbed children as to the teaching of normal children. The therapeutic educator has a broad responsibility to create a rational program for the physical, mental, social, and emotional development of each child. We do not conceive of the task of therapeutic teachers merely in terms of training troubled children for modification of behavior. Nor do we deal directly in techniques developed uniquely for psychotherapy.

We have made use of a regular school as an appropriate setting for the rehabilitation of the troubled child. Such a child, with disabling patterns of defense, is limited by erroneous assumptions that becloud his ability to cope with reality. While the child is learning to develop and maintain constructive ties with crucial elements of his society, he is also receiving help from a therapeutic team. We try to provide a classroom environment that offers explicit opportunities to each child to make his own lawful discoveries about the world and to develop the skills he needs to utilize, organize, expand, and transform such knowledge.

CHILD ABUSE AND THE ELEMENTARY SCHOOL COUNSELOR

In recent years counselors and other school personnel have come to acknowledge that child abuse is a serious and fairly widespread problem, which often requires immediate attention in the school setting. This recognition has led to research that attempts to understand and treat child abuse. A number of theories have been put forth by counselors, developmental psychologists, and other mental health professionals to account for the entire pattern of child abuse, which is usually at the hands of the parents. Although the prevention and treatment of child abuse could be included under crisis counseling or family counseling, because we view it as a problem often first detected in the school, we have decided to include it in this chapter.

Background

The first comprehensive effort to view child abuse as a syndrome (commonly dubbed the *battered-child syndrome*) is credited to C. Henry Kempe, a pioneer in this field, who published a seminal article on the problem in 1962 (Kempe et al.), setting the stage for further study. Six years later, Helfer and Kempe (1968) edited a major work on the battered-child syndrome, and in the years since the publication of this book, hundreds of articles, many case histories, and scores of research studies have appeared in the professional journals. The subject is clearly multidisciplinary: of equal concern to psychologists, pediatricians, social workers, nurses, teachers, and specialists in the mental health professions.

The recognition of this problem as a specific syndrome enables professionals to become more cognizant of its frequency. In recent years, *reported* cases of child abuse have trebled, although this clearly does not indicate that the syndrome itself is on the rise. Rather, it indicates that there is a consciousness and concern about the problem today that was not present years ago when a battered child could more easily be passed off by the parents as the victim of an unfortunate accident. Let us consider some of the major issues involved in the study of the abused child and the abusing parent, paying particular attention, where possible, to the role of the counselor in alleviating some aspects of the problem.

What Is Child Abuse?

There is no clear-cut, universally accepted definition of child abuse. Generally, however, care is taken to distinguish between the physically abused — or "battered" — child, and the child who is psychologically neglected, but not physically assaulted by the parents. A number of operational definitions

The child who is severely and psychologically neglected, but not physically abused, by a parent is also a victim of child abuse.

have been suggested for research purposes. In one study (Lauer, Ten Broek, & Grossman, 1974), a narrow definition was used: "A 'battered' or 'abused' child was defined as any child under ten years of age hospitalized because of physical injuries believed to have been caused intentionally by a parent, other household member, or a regular caretaker. In screening charts we excluded the uninjured children even though they may have been neglected or otherwise maltreated and we accepted the staff's decisions that the children's injuries were non-accidental" (p. 67).

In many studies, however, child abuse is defined more broadly to include severe neglect as well as assault (Burland, Andrews & Headsten, 1973). Although this poses a certain problem inasmuch as the evidence against the abusive parent usually emphasizes the violent physical assault in which the parent loses control as a result of experiencing rage, the broader definition is more helpful in our efforts to help the abused child in the school setting. It is the child who is the victim of severe parental neglect that makes it to the school, while the physically beaten child lies in the hospital or clinic recovering from an "accident."

The Day Care Council of New York, which is active in the area of prevention, uses a definition of child abuse that includes both direct physical assault and parent neglect. This I find the most valuable definition, and I shall use it throughout this section.

Who Is the Child-Abusing Parent?

It is most helpful for the counselor to have some understanding of the psychological profile of the abusing parent. This subject has been studied in some depth and a great deal is now known about parents who abuse their children. They are often highly disturbed individuals who themselves were severely abused in childhood. *Child abuse is a self-perpetuating disorder in which the abused child grows up to be an abusing parent.* Moreover, the abusing parent is usually insecure, violent, and unable to control anger, and has a tendency to project his or her own inadequacies on the child.

In a comprehensive review of the available research on the child-abusing parent, Spinetto and Rigler (1972) analyze the results of over sixty-five studies. A number of compelling points emerge. First, there is much evidence that in families with child-abusing parents there is "a high incidence of divorce, separation, and unstable marriages, as well as minor criminal offenses." Second, they point out that "one basic factor in the etiology of child abuse draws unanimity: Abusing parents were themselves abused or neglected, physically or emotionally, as children." These parents also "share common misunderstandings with regard to the nature of child-rearing, and look to the child for satisfaction of their own parental emotional needs."

Nurse (1964), in a classic study of familial patterns of parents who abuse their children, found, in conclusion:

> In summary, . . . almost without exception a single child was selected as the victim; some tendency was noted for the parents to protect each other and to resist outside influence. Prevalent was isolation and generally a passive orientation to community resources. In a third of the families, the passive parent was also abused. Striking was the evidence that parental abuse expresses overdetermined needs of the parent rather than a reality based reaction to a provocative child. The picture emerged of a primitive parent from an emotionally and economically deprived background whose aggression seemed unmodified by maturation. In more than half of the cases, the birth of the child victim was unwelcomed and in most families the victim was devalued in relation to other children. In some cases, close parallels were noted between the childhood experience of the abusing parent and his aggressive behavior toward his own child. A high incidence of emotional disorder was found when the parents were psychiatrically examined. Half of the aggressors had court records for assault or theft. (p. 304)

These two studies reflect what is generally called the *psychopathological position*. This position explains child abuse as a result of an "emotional sickness" of the parents. While this is still the majority position, a perspective put forth by Gelles (1973, 1978) has gained some attention. Gelles provides a sociological critique and reformulation of the child-abusing parent. Responding to this predominantly psychopathological model, he argues that the psychopathological theory is inconsistent and that the literature on child abuse patterns is not based on hard-core empirical research that meets the rigorous standards of social science. Instead, Gelles suggests a sociocultural analysis of the situation. His model combines the processes of socialization with psychopathological insights to provide a synthesis of the two. Kalmar (1977a), in a recent paper, also emphasizes the role of society in the problems of child abuse. Writing as a committed social worker, she points out:

> While the parents of abused children may be held directly responsible for their acts, society too must bear part of the blame for child abuse. This is so in part because ours is a society which is prone to violence and exploiting the powerless and because ours is a society which does not adequately meet the needs of minorities, the unemployed, the emotionally ill or the mentally retarded. The continued manifestations of child abuse is also related to our Constitutional structure which mandates greater emphasis on parental rights than on children's rights. In reality there appears to be an inherent conflict between parental rights and the best interests of the child. (p. iv)

Whatever the specific causes, it is universally agreed that the abusing parent is in need of help. Quite often the parent knows this, but for fear of legal and social retaliation is unable to seek the help needed. But when the child is finally referred to the appropriate authorities—and this may be through the school, or through a hospital facility—then the possibility of obtaining help becomes more likely, since the *cycle of abuse* is broken, and the *cycle of prevention* is simultaneously initiated. The Queensboro Society for the Prevention of Cruelty to Children (1976) presents a chart that dramatically illustrates the cyclical nature of abuse and prevention, and points out their interaction (see figure 9.1 on page 312).

Prevention and Treatment

What kind of help is available to the abused child and to the parents? This varies greatly from state to state, and from school district to school district within states. In recent years, most of the states have enacted specific laws for the reporting of child abuse, and many schools and social agencies have issued guidelines for teachers, school counselors, and administrators who observe instances of or suspect the existence of child abuse, including severe neglect (although the extremely neglectful parent may fail even to send the child to school!)

Nagi (1975) has conducted a national survey to evaluate the school-related services available. One troubling finding of this survey is that about one-third of the estimated cases are never reported to the appropriate agencies. This may in part be the fault of school or agency personnel who are reluctant to report cases for fear of social or legal repercussions. As Sanders, Kibby, Creaghan, and Tyrrel (1975) point out, "the biggest barrier to aiding the abused child is the unwillingness of those who notice the child's distress to report the abuse," and no matter how well-intentioned is the system, this remains a refractory barrier that only a change in attitudes can overcome.

When the child-abusing parent does finally enter counseling, the counselor has a variety of tried and tested approaches available. Tracy and Clark (1974) report on a successful model used in a hospital setting, but equally applicable in the school setting. The staff "worked with the parents in their own homes to help them develop greater competence as adults and parents." Using social learning theory, the parents were taught new behavioral skills and shown new ways to respond to their children. Polakow and Peabody (1975) also report on the use of behavioral techniques (see Chapter 3), including "contracting," in treating child-abusing parents and their abused children. David (1974) suggests the use of "confrontation" techniques, which jolts the parents into working through their problems. Paulson (1974) sug-

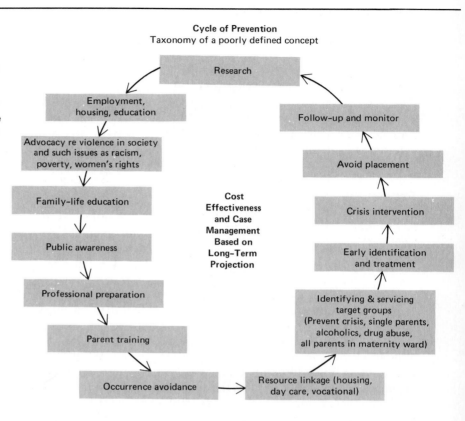

Cycle of Prevention
Taxonomy of a poorly defined concept

Research

Employment,
housing, education

Follow-up and monitor

Advocacy re violence in society
and such issues as racism,
poverty, women's rights

Avoid placement

Family-life education

Crisis intervention

Cost
Effectiveness
and Case
Management
Based on
Long-Term
Projection

Public awareness

Early identification
and treatment

Professional preparation

Identifying & servicing
target groups
(Prevent crisis, single parents,
alcoholics, drug abuse,
all parents in maternity ward)

Parent training

Occurrence avoidance

Resource linkage (housing,
day care, vocational)

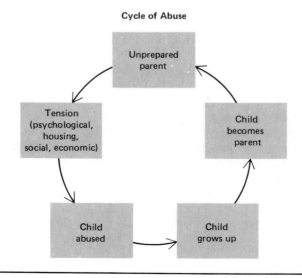

Cycle of Abuse

Unprepared
parent

Tension
(psychological,
housing,
social, economic)

Child
becomes
parent

Child
abused

Child
grows up

gests that the group counseling approach is especially helpful. Whichever techniques are used, it is important to recognize that child abuse is a complex and often refractory problem that may take years to treat.

Practical Counseling Suggestions

Whenever a counselor plans to intervene with the parents of an abused child, it is important to keep in mind that not only will the parents most likely be defensive, but they will often become aggressive as well. It is not unusual to find that the parent, called in by a teacher or counselor, returns home to take out his or her rage on the child whose victimization brought the parent there in the first place. This is a very real danger and must be kept constantly in mind.

Goldberg (1975) perceptively discusses some of the difficulties in the initial interview with the parent, which she calls an "emotionally charged situation":

> The parent is upset, whether wracked by guilt for having injured his child, shame for having lost control of himself, or embarrassment over having his "inadequacy" exposed. The parent fears the legal or psychiatric conse-quences of child abuse, the degradation ceremony through which his social identity is lowered, the right of transition from a normal social position to a deviant role. (p. 274)

Goldberg goes on to offer six behaviors that are appropriate during the initial interview. They are positioning, reaching for feelings, waiting, "getting with" feelings, asking information, and giving information. We will use these as our model for a constructive interview with the abusing parent. Let us consider them individually.

Positioning refers to the nonverbal behaviors in terms of physical place-ment and room arrangement that the helper communicates to the client. "Since there is ample evidence to indicate that such nonverbal behavior affects comfort and communicates positive or negative feeling, to break the communication barrier, the worker should position himself in ways likely to increase the parent's comfort and convey positive feeling" (p. 278). The counselor can then use the nonverbal feedback provided by the parent to judge how effectively or ineffectively she or he is positioning himself.

Reaching for feelings involves the counselor's efforts to help clients ex-press their feelings in words, or to convert nonverbal behaviors into verbal expressions. While every client has a variety of reasons that prevent free and full expression, there is usually some degree of willingness—some mo-tivation—to find appropriate ways of expression. "It is particularly important to reach for feelings when (1) the parent does not express any emotion, (2) his expression of emotion is nonverbal, or (3) he expresses feelings not appropriate to such a situation" (p. 277). It should also be mentioned that if the counselor is not aware of what feelings the client is trying to express, he or she should avoid "reaching" for feelings until becoming more certain of them.

Waiting is the period of comfortable silence in which the parent engages in his or her own internal dialogue. It is a period during which many of the inchoate insights can become relevant to the parent; a period in which questions may arise; in which doubts may be resolved. The counselor tries to avoid communicating tension during the "waiting period." The counselors' role is best accomplished when they wait along with the parents, communicating to parents to take their time, to come to grips with their feelings, to be open and honest with themselves.

"Getting with" feelings involves the counselor's ability to empathize with the way the parents feel and to make statements that are congruent with their feelings. Goldberg (1975) offers an example of how a helper did this with a client:

> Mr. H. said angrily that everybody wants and wants and wants. He said, "You might think it's enough I work two different jobs. Yeh! Full time at a department store and part time at a gas station. And what do I get when I finally drag my ass home at night? How tired *she* is. Y'know, I dropped out of college to marry her." There was a short pause during which he rubbed his hands together and looked at the floor. I [the helper] waited. When he looked up again he said, "And the baby yells. . . . and she tells me it's my turn because she's had it all day. It's a nightmare." "Wow," I [the helper] said, "You keep giving, but nobody gives you anything." "It's gotta stop," he said. (p. 280)

The final two behaviors, *asking for information* and *giving information* are self-explanatory. Both open-ended and closed-ended questions can be used in asking the client for information, depending upon the kind of information the helper wishes to receive. Information may be used to help the parent better understand objectively the situation. "Information given to the parent reduces uncertainty and the accompanying discomfort" (p. 281).

Goldberg's suggestions are particularly helpful for the counselor who plans to intervene with the family. While at the present time, so many cases of child abuse tragically go unreported, I foresee a time in the near future when professionals in the schools, including teachers, counselors, and administrators, stirred by a new awareness, will routinely report all cases of child abuse. I have taken the time to go over these practical suggestions in some detail, since I believe that when this new attitude becomes dominant, counselors will have an immense role in ameliorating this difficult situation.

SUMMARY

In this chapter we looked at specific counseling applications for the elementary school level. Three reasons that elementary school counseling requires a specialized approach were indicated: (1) The elementary school child is more highly dependent on his or her parents than are clients in later years; (2) School personnel—represented by the teacher and by the counselor—are important factors in the child's later success or failure in academics and in the development of socialization skills; (3) The elementary school child experiences a considerably faster rate of growth than is typical of later life. We then outlined Elizabeth Berry's position that utilizes the framework of communication theory and that suggests that a major function of the elementary school counselor is to promote facilitative communication.

We then examined in some depth five elementary school counseling applications. We began by considering play approaches to child counseling, looking specifically at the case of Debbie, a ten-year-old girl who was referred by her teacher for counseling. Secondly, we surveyed the premises of Adlerian counseling. We then examined the possibilities of an innovative approach called "horticultural counseling." The fourth section presented the experiences of a teacher functioning as a therapeutic counselor—a case study of a school guidance class for emotionally disturbed children. And finally, we turned our attention to the problem of child abuse.

Counseling in the Secondary Schools

In the preceding chapter, we focused on approaches and applications that are especially relevant in the elementary school setting. It was explained that while many of the general approaches to counseling that have been covered in this book are applicable at all age levels, special considerations may be required when working with young children. Also, special adaptations of group procedures that are facilitative when working with the elementary school client were pointed out.

The same need for special considerations in counseling the adolescent in the secondary school setting holds true for two reasons. First, the period of adolescent development may be viewed as something of a unique and rather difficult period of life, with extraordinary stresses and strains that may place a difficult physical, psychological, and social burden on the growing person. As Henry (1976) points out, "When one considers the complexity of the situation that arises from the delicately balanced interplay of these three phenomena [biological, psychological, and social growth], which has to be coped with by the adolescent on his journey to maturity . . . it is small wonder that emotional problems are common in adolescence" (p. 57). Thus, the needs, interests, and expectations of the adolescent always require special attention.

Second, adolescence, with its promises of total functional independence, is a period when the subtle deficits of the past may come strikingly to the fore. The school counselor can be helpful when those problems that were not adequately solved earlier demand attention later on. For instance if rudimentary job skills were not acquired in the early grades, the adolescent period becomes a critical compensatory time. Or, if the child's social development was deficient, this will markedly appear during adolescence. Often, adolescent school counseling involves looking back at what might have been more easily accomplished just a few years earlier.

Counseling the adolescent, especially in the school setting, may require some special adaptations. In this chapter, I will briefly overview the adolescent period of psychosocial development, and then focus on some specialized approaches to counseling that are pertinent to these stages.

THE PSYCHOSOCIAL STAGES OF ADOLESCENCE

Adolescence may be divided into three parts: puberty (early adolescence); middle adolescence; and late adolescence, the transitional period to adulthood. While there is continuity and contiguity between these periods, each has characteristic stresses and problems of its own.

Puberty is the period of life that links childhood and adolescence. While it occurs simultaneously with the early period, and the two terms are used interchangeably with some degree of freedom, puberty describes more the physical period of development while adolescence is used more to describe a psychological period (Aubrey, 1975).

Although our society does not generally accord to the pubescent the full rights of adulthood, the biological reality of puberty indicates that from the physiological point of view the pubescent is capable of all the activities of the adult. Moreover, in many of the subcultures within our culture, it is at this age that children break away from the control of parents and fend for themselves (Rainwater, 1970, p. 281).

There is no specific age that clearly marks the beginning of puberty, though some general norms have been established, particularly the appearance of secondary sex characteristics. These are the physical characteristics that differentiate boys from girls, but that are *not* directly related to the procreative (reproductive) process. For boys, they include such characteristics as pubic hair, facial hair, deepening of the voice, heavy muscular development, and angular body build. For the female, the secondary sex characteristics are the filling out of the breasts, triangular pubic hair patterns, and more subcutaneous fat giving a rounded body contour. These changes in the body are the clearest signs of the onset of puberty and, more importantly, are signs that are readily visible.

The physical changes of puberty are accompanied by changes in attitude and interests, which are either the direct or indirect result of the rapid sexual maturity. Many of the responses from the peer group are responses to the manifestations of these secondary sex characteristics. The size of a girl's breasts may help or hinder her popularity with the boys; make her a butt of jokes, a pariah, or an object of lust pursued by the socially prestigious older boys. Likewise, a boy's lack of facial hair may place him at a disadvantage in comparison with his hairier peers who equate facial hair with virility. It is important, therefore, that the counselor be sensitive to the subtle relationships between the client's physical maturity, social standing, and the resultant behavior and performance in peer relationships. While I would not suggest that it is only the physical reality of this period that exerts a profound influence, it is a highly significant part of the early adolescent's experience and must be recognized as such.

Puberty is marked by the onset of secondary sex characteristics.

Psychological Conflicts in Puberty

A number of factors have been identified as important forces during puberty (Adams, 1976). Social constraints, which check and stifle the burgeoning forces of sexuality, may become objects of rebellion or disdain. The family, which until now had served as the nexus of social interactions, may suddenly be viewed as an alien institution; it may, in fact, become a symbolic Goliath to be slain by the enraged and confused David, striving to come into his own. Similarly, in the school situation, where the pubescent spends a large portion of time, teachers and other personnel may be viewed as oppressors—encouraging, by their mere presence, rebellion and rage. McCary

(1973) also points out that "this is a period of 'sexual awakening' which is met with ambivalent reactions by both sexes (p. 31)."

Hamburg (1974), in an analysis of the stresses of puberty, pinpoints three key challenges as central to the pubescent's growth:

> First, there are the challenges posed by the biological changes of puberty. The individual must cope with the flagrant and undeniable impact of change in the body configuration. He perceives, at times erroneously, his emerging size and shape as the physique that will characterize him throughout his adult life. This concern over the body is pervasive, and there are deep concerns over physical attractiveness . . .
>
> Second, there are the challenges that are posed by the entry into a new social system, the junior high school. With this transition, the student relinquishes the former security of membership in one stable classroom and is faced with the task of negotiating six or seven changes of teacher and classes a day . . .
>
> The third set of challenges derives from the sudden entry into a new role status. The admission into junior high school has become a convenient marker for the conferring of adolescent status and the badge of entry into the "teen culture." . . . The early adolescent urgently feels himself in need of a new set of "adolescent" behaviors, values, and reference persons. (pp. 105–106)

These challenges pose a host of problems to the school counselor. Early adolescents may act out their conflicts within the school setting. Or, they may perform poorly in school because of the conflicts that are besetting them on the outside (Macomber, 1968). When the counselor is able to identify for the student the social and psychological benefits derived from particular learning tasks, the process of learning becomes more meaningful and relevant. This is particularly true for the pubescent who is an exceptional student and whose needs may be overpowering during this period. Counselors working with exceptional adolescents would do well to keep this in mind.

Middle Adolescence

One view of middle adolescence, developed during the 1950s and early 1960s, approaches this period as a time of painful growing in which the individual is beset by numerous conflicts, doubts, and difficulties in adjustment. The contemporary view, on the other hand, deemphasizes the "storm and stress" conception of adolescence. In this section, we will consider both positions and examine their implications for counseling.

Representing the more traditional position is Ausubel (1954). In his classic study of adolescence, he sees the conflicts of this time caused by two inexorable forces: the need for independence and the psychosexual conflict. "Adolescent emotional instability in our culture," he argues, "is chiefly attributable to culturally determined frustration of physiological sex drives. . . . the possession of sex drives is normal and proper, but their satisfaction is morally unallowable" (p. 17). Some of the more contemporary writers emphasize the stabilizing, goal-directed aspects of adolescence rather than this turbulent perspective. Lipsett (1974), for example, points out that the youth of the 1970s has returned to the patterns of hard work and goal-directed behavior that characterized youth of the 1940s. Recent surveys have confirmed that young people today are job oriented, less active politically, and more ambitious than their contemporaries of the late 1960s. Sorenson (1973) conducted a comprehensive poll of young peoples' views, and some of the results are indicated in tables 10.1, 10.2 and 10.3. These show that while attitudes are changing they have not changed nearly as much as many people would expect.

table 10.1
"TWO PEOPLE SHOULDN'T HAVE TO GET MARRIED JUST BECAUSE THEY WANT TO LIVE TOGETHER."

	agree	**not sure**	**disagree**	**total**
All adolescents	72 percent	0 percent	28 percent	100 percent
Boys	76	1	23	100
Boys 13–15	63	2	35	100
Boys 16–19	87	1	12	100
Girls	67	0	33	100
Girls 13–15	66	0	34	100
Girls 16–19	67	0	33	100
Virgins	64	0	36	100
Inexperienced	55	0	45	100
Beginners	71	0	29	100
Nonvirgins	78	1	21	100
Monogamists	80	0	20	100
Adventurers	78	2	20	100

Note From *Adolescent Sexuality in Contemporary America* by Robert C. Sorensen. Copyright © 1973 by Robert C. Sorensen. Used by permission of Harry N. Abrams, Inc.

table 10.2
"WHEN IT COMES TO SEX, MY ATTITUDES AND MY PARENTS' ATTITUDES ARE PRETTY MUCH THE SAME."

	true	not sure	false	total
All adolescents	36 percent	4 percent	60 percent	100 percent
Boys	28	6	66	100
Boys 13–15	38	3	59	100
Boys 16–19	20	7	73	100
Girls	44	2	54	100
Girls 13–15	38	4	58	100
Girls 16–19	50	0	50	100
Virgins	46	3	51	100
Inexperienced	49	3	48	100
Beginners	44	2	54	100
Nonvirgins	27	5	68	100
Monogamists	39	1	60	100
Adventurers	15	13	72	100

Note From *Adolescent Sexuality in Contemporary America* by Robert C. Sorensen. Copyright © 1973 by Robert C. Sorensen. Used by permission of Harry N. Abrams, Inc.

table 10.3
"I HAVE A LOT OF RESPECT FOR MY PARENTS' IDEAS AND OPINIONS ABOUT SEX."

	true	not sure	false	total
All adolescents	65 percent	6 percent	29 percent	100 percent
Boys	56	8	36	100
Boys 13–15	66	7	27	100
Boys 16–19	47	9	44	100
Girls	75	3	22	100
Girls 13–15	80	3	17	100
Girls 16–19	70	3	27	100
Virgins	74	6	20	100
Inexperienced	80	4	16	100
Beginners	72	5	23	100
Nonvirgins	56	6	38	100
Monogamists	70	2	28	100
Adventurers	38	12	50	100

Note From *Adolescent Sexuality in Contemporary America* by Robert C. Sorensen. Copyright © 1973 by Robert C. Sorensen. Used by permission of Harry N. Abrams, Inc.

Implications for the Counselor

A synthesis of these two positions of middle adolescence might help explain this period in terms of the individual's struggle between personal freedom, psychological fulfillment, and the social and familial demands upon her or him. Irene Josselyn, in her sensitive book, *The Adolescent and His World* (1969), describes some aspects of this conflict. "In our culture," she points out, "society not only makes heavy demands upon the adolescent, but it fails to provide him with a preconceived and carefully outlined pattern to help him meet these demands" (p. 26). This type of planning is integral to the role of the counselor.

For instance, the counselor might help the adolescent discover the artist within himself or herself. If expression through creativity in all the artistic media is encouraged, the adolescent may well find an outlet for expression that was closed off before. Artistic expression can be encouraged in all the disciplines through writing, painting, crafts, music, creative drama, dance, and the like.

Or, the counselor can act as an agent of therapeutic change in the adolescent's relationship with the family. By bringing parents and children together—by cementing the family unit into a strong functional organization—the counselor is achieving long-range goals far beyond what he or she could achieve alone.

There are also a number of specific problem areas in which counselors may intervene. Adolescents have troubles in the areas of sexual activity, with drugs and alcohol, problems in school performance and learning, and truancy problems. In the following sections, we will look at these problem areas, and examine the counselor's role in them.

SEX AND THE ADOLESCENT

The complex psychological adjustments to the new physical demands imposed by the body poses conflicts for most young people. At the very point in life where sexuality becomes a compelling force, social rules and regulations place great burdens upon the individual to control, or even repress, these desires. Adolescents must learn to function within the constraints of these rules and regulations. They may circumvent them, rebel against them, or they may deny and ignore their inner passions; but in any case, the existence of the rules take their toll. Many of the sexual fears and conflicts during this period are a result of the mixed messages conveyed to the adolescent, who is searching for a sexual identity. Giuffra (1975), for example, points out,

> Fears . . . arise from the developmental task which requires an adolescent to establish an adult sexual identity. These natural fears are greatly intensified today because our changing society seems overtly to provide adolescents with more sexual options than in years gone by. Covertly, some of the most rigid and traditional sexual beliefs are still present, further confusing an adolescent by providing him with double messages which are sometimes mutually exclusive. (p. 1726)

Berg (1975) supports this theme of conflict, by citing evidence that indicates the "sexual revolution" is something of a myth; that, in fact, the male and female perspectives have remained relatively unchanged over the past few years. Specifically, he found that males continue to stress the physical attributes of females in assessing sexual attraction, while females still gauge masculine appeal according to male dress and sexuality. "The male 'line' has changed," Berg concedes, "but the dating game remains relatively unchanged."

Dating

Dating behavior is primarily defined by the culture, and consists of conventions that allow the individual to attract, interact with, and possibly initiate sexual relations with persons of the opposite sex. One of the chief purposes of the dating period—and of dating behavior in general—is to define, clarify, and strengthen one's sexual-gender identity. Boys and girls discover their gender identities and begin to assume adult social roles through dating. The adolescents' body consciousness—which intermixes with their self-image and feelings about their body—influences the way they feel about themselves sexually. The physically disabled adolescent, for example, may feel less competent to deal with the demands of dating than will the physically healthy adolescent. As Maddox (1973) correctly points out,

> There is an intensification of body awareness during adolescence, based upon the fact that the body is a primary "symbol of self" in which feelings of personal worth, security, and competence are rooted. An individual's basic felt body sense may very well be the foundation of his sexual identity and capacity of erotic expression since it is present from birth as a functional component of his developmental experience and is charged with high-intensity interpersonal meaning. (pp. 327-328)

There are a number of important points for the counselor to keep in mind, regarding adolescents' views about dating and their dating problems. As the

A central task of adolescent development is establishing
intimacy through dating.

counselors recognize the dynamics of dating behavior, they become capable
of helping the adolescent learn to deal with the myriad difficulties that dating
inevitably entails. If the counselor and school personnel are willing to allow
appropriate socialization activities in the school, this may help the troubled
adolescent channel much of his or her sexual energy into constructive,
school-related activities. There are also lessons that need to be learned,
social tasks to be introduced and discussed. Boys and girls need to learn
how to behave properly with each other; each must learn to expect proper
treatment from the opposite sex. The counselor should also recognize that
much disruptive classroom behavior (for which the student is sent to the
counselor) is a natural by-product of unsuccessful dating activities. This
recognition might make it easier to empathize with some types of behavior
that a counselor would not otherwise be so willing to accept.

In working with the physically-handicapped, emotionally-disturbed, or
learning-disabled adolescent, the counselor should be especially sensitive to
the potential for personal problems inherent in dating activities. Some questions the counselor might ask are: Are the students knowledgeable about
dating conventions? (Do the boys and girls feel comfortable with the sex-
roles society is asking them to conform to?) Are the students competent to
deal with dating requisites and routines? (How can blind students arrange

a date? What provisions have been made for transportation?) Do they have adequate opportunities to meet dating partners? How do their feelings about themselves influence their interest in dating?

Having now looked at some general ideas about dating, let us turn our attention to some of the specific problems the adolescent faces in dealing with his or her sexuality, and consider how these challenges might affect the psychosocial development of the typical and the exceptional adolescent.

Masturbation

Although many young people are troubled about masturbation, often plagued by feelings of guilt and confusion, it is generally agreed that masturbation is a normal, healthy, constructive part of the adolescent sexual experience (Dranoff, 1974). According to most studies, approximately 95 percent of adolescent boys and 50 percent to 80 percent of adolescent girls masturbate. Despite its high incidence, masturbation may cause the adolescent—particularly the early adolescent—to experience guilt, self-disgust, and remorse.

Masturbation can be most productive and beneficial if it is accompanied by the appropriate attitudes; namely, if the adolescent realizes the normality of his or her masturbatory experimentation (Dranoff, 1974). One particularly constructive use of masturbation is learning to experience heightened sexual pleasure (Ford, 1966). At this period of life, with its limitations and taboos on sexual activity, it is through autoerotic activity that the healthy boy or girl learns to appreciate sexual response.

Petting and Sexual Experimentation

The earliest type of overt sexual activity occurring between young people of the opposite sex is usually petting. Broadly speaking, petting is sexual activity that leads to, and may culminate in, sexual intercourse. It may include kissing, touching parts of the body, oral stimulation of the erogenous zones, and mutual masturbation. Petting is a normal part of dating and the prelude to satisfying adult sexual relationships.

Surveys have shown that although the majority of high school students believe in premarital intercourse, they have not engaged in it themselves (Offer, 1969, p. 83). Rather, the goal of most petting and early sexual experimentation (during early and middle adolescence) seems to be to establish a sense of intimacy with the opposite sex. Through sexual experimentation, sanctioned by the peer group, boys and girls learn to relate to each other in new, dynamically and socially fulfilling ways. Thus, sexual experimentation in this respect is a means to an end. As Mitchell (1972) suggests,

Sexual behavior . . . can foster an openness which facilitates intimacy at levels other than the sexual. This is especially true among adolescents despite the commonly held maxim that psychological intimacy should precede sexual involvement. *For adolescents with minimal meaningful involvement elsewhere, sexual behavior is a basic avenue for creating bonds of psychological intimacy.* (p. 449, italics added)

Important clinical material may also be obtained when the counselor becomes familiar with the adolescent's early sexual behavior. Observing the activities of the adolescent during this critical developmental period provides valuable insight into possible future problems and conflicts. As Salzman (1974) indicates, "When the adolescent attempts to initiate heterosexual intimacies we can identify not only his clumsy, naive, and unsophisticated activities, but the possibilities of some real sexual disturbances which, if not dealt with early and effectively, can compromise his future life" (p. 191). Such early identification is exceedingly important, especially with troubled adolescents.

Contraception

It is important that contraceptive information be made available to those adolescents who are having sexual intercourse. While this is usually more the responsibility of the family or family physician than of the counselor, there are many instances in which the counselor, in the school or clinical setting, might have occasion to advise students about appropriate contraceptive measures. This sometimes involves very basic information, which is almost of survival value for the student. Mitchell (1973) gives this case vignette—typical of the kinds of problems school counselors face—where a student's school performance is affected adversely by misinformation or a lack of information regarding contraception:

Mary Jane was referred to the school counselor by her homeroom teacher because of frequent cutting of classes and increasingly excessive absences. After some preliminary discussion, Mary Jane said, "I don't mean to cut classes . . . I really do like school: but ever since I started taking my mother's birth control pills I pretty often feel sick to my stomach. I think it is because I sometimes take them on an empty stomach or it may be because when I get scared I sometimes take two at once. I can't find any directions on her prescription and I am not sure what to ask her or our family doctor. . . ." A little later in the conversation . . . "Even though I *have* missed some school, you can see I am making better grades because I'm not worried all the time about getting pregnant."

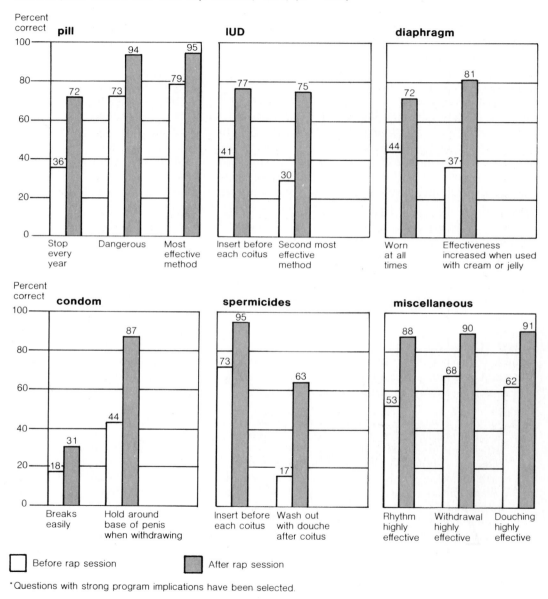

figure 10.1 Comparison of teenagers' correct responses to questions* on contraception before and after rap session, 1973 (N = 367)

Before rap session After rap session

*Questions with strong program implications have been selected.

Note: From "Contraception, Abortion, and Venereal Disease: Teenagers' Knowledge and the Effects of Education" by P. A. Reichelt and H. H. Werley, *Family Planning Perspectives.* 1975. *7* (2). 83–88. Reprinted with permission from *Family Planning Perspectives.*

It is helpful if the counselor is familiar with the various methods of contraception. He or she should be able to intelligently and accurately answer clients' questions regarding contraception. Reichelt and Werley (1975) have shown that if students are exposed to appropriate information about contraception, and allowed to discuss this information in a group setting, they become more knowledgeable regarding the appropriate use of contraceptives. An excellent source of information for the counselor is J. L. McCary's *Human Sexuality* (New York: Van Nostrand Reinhold, 1974), which has a comprehensive chapter on this subject. In school counseling situations, explicit and implicit policies of the school system regarding the dissemination of contraceptive information should be of more than casual interest to the school counselor. The counselor also needs to be familiar with the state laws and community attitudes about contraception; these vary widely from region to region.

Venereal Diseases

The helping professions have been most negligent in dealing with the admittedly prevalent problem of venereal disease; a problem that finally reached epidemic proportions among young people during the 1970s. The burden of help is often placed on the counselor.

Although during the past decade the schools have taken on an ever-increasing interest in preventive health care, they have shown little or no interest in detecting the presence of venereal disease and in educating students about the prevention and recognition of these diseases. Yet both of these are simple procedures, and the teacher, counselor, and school medical personnel might well find themselves involved in a program to deal with this problem. This may be a part of the total sex education program, or it may be directly under the auspices of the school counselor or school physician (where there is one). In either case, if the counselor is well informed about the nature and prognosis of different venereal diseases, he or she will be in a unique position to help clients deal with the situation, both in terms of seeking medical assistance and in terms of confronting the psychological ramifications—guilt and shame—which often accompany VD.

Pregnancy and Abortion

The pregnant adolescent has always been a subject of controversy and often a victim of confused mores in the school setting. Yet, there are more and more unwed adolescent girls who are becoming pregnant, and the schools are being forced to adapt their policies accordingly. In chapter 14 (pp. 442–444), we will focus on counseling the pregnant adolescent who is experiencing a problem pregnancy crisis.

The Homosexual Adolescent

The condition of the homosexual adolescent has become an area of growing interest, brought about in part by the increasing willingness of homosexuals to "come out of the closet" and to acknowledge their homosexuality. At a period in life when acceptance by peers and conformity to stereotyped images are of paramount importance, it is indeed difficult, if not impossible, for adolescent homosexuals to express themselves to their peers and to engage in the type of sexual activity and courtship that is available to their heterosexual counterparts. The main question that has hung threateningly over the head of the homosexual adolescent is whether or not homosexuality is a sickness. Professionals in the fields of counseling, psychology, psychiatry, and education disagree vehemently on this question, but recent sentiments are that homosexuality may be an alternative life-style rather than an emotional illness (Jones, 1974).

Even so, homosexuality may become a problem if it is expressed overtly and aggressively in the school setting. In such cases, the counselor might attempt to relate to the homosexual client, without the overt value judgments and condemnations that may be responsible for the client's provocative actions. The counselor should make the client understand that it is not the homosexuality that is being attacked, but only the inappropriate behavior.

The counselor should work closely with the teacher. Often disruptive behavior is the student's fears about homosexuality. An understanding and sympathetic teacher, who is comfortable and secure about his or her own sexual orientation, can do much to help such a student learn appropriate social behavior within the context of his or her sexual preferences.

> Bruce's behavior in his high school English class was becoming intolerable to Mr. Flynn, his teacher. Bruce was a militant homosexual, who not only wore buttons proclaiming "Gay Rights," but who interrupted lessons to "preach" his ideas about homosexuality. While Mr. Flynn tried to control him in ways he would with other students, Bruce accused him of attacking him because of his homosexuality. Mr. Flynn, in consultation with the school counselor, finally recognized, that Bruce was "compelled" to seek the teacher's censure for his behavior; that he was actually looking for the punishment he felt he deserved. This idea was discussed in terms of some of the literature the class was reading, and gentle interpretations helped Bruce maintain some control.

The homosexual student may, on the other hand, be exposed to ridicule and contempt by his peers. The class "fag" or "queer" must bear the burden of other students' unconscious homosexual fears. One way the teacher can be helpful in such cases is to protect the student, to teach the other class members the virtue of tolerance, and at the same time to educate students about the diversity of human preferences—in sexuality and in other sensitive areas.

Since the homosexual adolescent is likely to experience more negative social pressures than his or her heterosexual counterpart and, at the same time, to find less social reinforcement, it is advisable that he or she be exposed to some type of counseling, either inside the school setting or from without. The teacher can ascertain if the school counselor is capable of dealing with a homosexual student. If not, the teacher may inquire about community services, which may be provided by homosexual groups, by churches, by hospitals, or by the social service agencies.

Constructive Measures

One of the most helpful ways in dealing with all of these sexual problems and conflicts of adolescence is to establish a sex education program in the secondary schools. Reichelt and Werley (1975) have shown that such a program can be valuable for sexually active teenagers, and they advocate the development of national sex education programs.

Typically, a sex education program geared to the adolescent will include three phases: informational, group counseling, and individual counseling. The informational phase may include films, books, magazine articles, demonstrations, and lectures. Many publishing companies now offer sex education kits; multimedia packages that cover one or more of the topics relating to adolescent sexuality.

Group counseling can be provided in and out of the classroom. It can be integrated into lessons, or set off separately. Some feasible goals of group counseling might be to help the adolescent understand the complexity of the sexual drive, to facilitate expression of sexual feelings, to clarify what the informational aspect failed to clarify, and to assure that each adolescent has the basic intellectual and emotional tools necessary for dealing with the conundrums of his or her sexual reality.

When indicated, individual counseling may also be provided. In fact, one of the important purposes of the group experiences is to identify those students who could benefit from individual counseling (Gazda, 1972). As I suggested earlier, the homosexual student might be such a case. Also, it might be discovered through the group counseling experience that related school problems might be rooted in sexual confusion or dysfunctioning.

ALCOHOL AND DRUG ABUSE

One of the more refractory problems facing the counselor today is the widespread misuse of drugs and alcohol by adolescents. Much has been written about this problem, much research conducted, and large sums of money have been spent by the government to combat drug and alcohol abuse; yet the problem stubbornly persists. In this section, we shall examine some of the causes and symptoms of drug and alcohol abuse, noting particularly what the school and adolescent counselor can do preventively and therapeutically, in the school or outside, to help alleviate this very difficult problem.

What Is Drug "Abuse"?

Although there may be nothing intrinsically dangerous or destructive about a certain drug, it can be abused in a number of ways. Overusing drugs, using them at an inappropriate time, taking a drug when it is not required, or forming a psychological addiction are all forms of drug abuse. If the drug in itself is not specifically dangerous, then the problem arises as a result of the uses to which the drug is put. Alcohol, for example, is sipped moderately at counseling conventions with no discernible harm to anyone. But when a seventh-grade boy comes to school drunk each day, or when the parents of a high school girl cannot give her appropriate supervision because of their dependence upon alcohol, these are clearly drug abuse problems. Marijuana, a drug with no proven danger to the occasional user, produces pleasant, relaxed feelings, with heightened sensual awareness. When a high school youth, however, becomes unable to study because of excessive use of this substance, or when a student loses his ability to function except when using the drug, then we are dealing with a serious drug problem.

Some drugs, on the other hand, are inherently dangerous and may always be considered instances of drug abuse if they are not taken under the supervision of a physician. Heroin, a synthetic derivative of morphine, is a highly addictive substance with no legitimate medical uses. Most heroin-related deaths are a result of overdosage or of toxic agents mixed with the heroin to dilute it. The hallucinogenic (psychedelic) drugs—LSD, DMT, mescaline, and psilocybin—give the user the illusion of expanded consciousness, of greater awareness and sensitivity than is experienced without the drug. In fact, however, these drugs produce gross distortions of reality, hallucinations, and erratic behavior and thinking. Barbiturates and other depressant drugs produce in the user a feeling of relaxation and blissfulness that enables the user to forget all of the problems that must be faced in life. These are highly addictive drugs that may result in fatality upon withdrawal. Cases of suicide under the influence of barbiturates are not uncommon. Amphetamines are stimulant drugs that result in great feelings of optimism as well as mania. They are used by adolescents as sleep inhibitors, appetite

suppressants, and for relief of depression. Prolonged use of amphetamines may result in hallucinations, psychosis, and violent behavior.

Perhaps the single most accurate criterion of what determines drug abuse is the attitude the individual has toward the drugs. If the drug experiences serve as an occasional social meeting ground this is a far different situation from the one in which the drug has become a panacea that the young person cannot live without. If the addictive or nonaddictive substance becomes the central focus of the adolescent's existence—one's raison d'être—the individual may clearly be said to be exhibiting signs of drug abuse.

Adolescent Abuse of Alcohol

Beginning about 1972, and continuing through 1980, alcohol emerged as the single most abused drug in the adolescent culture. It is estimated that there are over three million teen-age alcoholics today, most of whom are enrolled in schools (Necessary, 1979). No one knows exactly why this is, but it may represent an ironic adolescent rebellion against the prevailing adult acceptance of marijuana:

> Marion, a tenth grader, and her friends go over to Peter's house after school and drink wine. Peter's parents both work and leave a well-stocked liquor cabinet unattended. Bob, one of the "tough guys" at the school, drinks whiskey and puts down the other kids because they only drink wine or beer. Peter's older brother Edward comes by with his friends and smokes grass downstairs in the basement. Marion's friends put this down. It's the behavior of college kids.

Drug and alcohol abuse have taken their toll in the number
of leading figures in the adolescent subculture.

Although alcohol is legal and most abused drugs are not, one interesting
study revealed parallels between antisocial patterns in abusers of alcohol
and drugs. Globetti (1972) investigated problem high school drinkers in two
small towns where alcohol was prohibited. He found that the alcohol abuser,
like the drug abuser, tended to have generally antisocial and mildly criminal
characteristics, although this may not be a valid conclusion for communities
where there are no restrictions on the sale and use of alcohol. Widseth
(1972), in another study of high school abusers of alcohol, found that delinquent girls with drinking problems were dependent on their mothers and
had not matured enough to break the powerful maternal bond.

The manifest symptoms of alcohol abuse among teenagers is as clear or
more clear than the symptoms of drug abuse, which at times may be obscure.
The problem-drinking adolescent is likely to have a high absentee rate, may
appear intoxicated in class, and will invariably fall behind in schoolwork. It
is not uncommon to find a flask of alcohol concealed on the person of the
student, and the student may even imbibe during a class itself—so strong
is the drive, so weak the control. The counselor, rather than responding
punitively, might recognize the serious medical-psychological nature of this
problem and should encourage the student to seek help.

What the School Counselor Can Do

The counselor who deals with this problem of abuse might begin by exploring honestly his or her own feelings about drug use, about alcohol use, and about the adolescent "drug culture" in general. An empathic understanding of why many adolescents have the need to abuse drugs may follow such reflection and study; but most of all, objective information should be separated from values and cultural stereotypes. This is particularly true of marijuana, for example; many young counselors, particularly those who were a part of the drug culture of the '60s, find themselves oversympathetic to its use. "Counselors can be most helpful to their clients and their constituents," Archer and Lopata (1979, p. 248) point out, after reviewing the substantial but still inconclusive literature on marijuana's short-term and long-term effects, "by encouraging them to evaluate the current evidence before deciding to use marijuana or to sanction its general use." They go on to point out that one of the counselor's primary responsibilities is to keep up with the current research on marijuana and to examine the changing legal status of its use. "Counselors have an obligation," they assert, "to help society understand the effect of prohibition on research and discussion" (p. 248).

A counselor should also understand that a person undergoing severe stresses in adolescence is more likely than a mature person to rely on drugs for escape, for fantasy, for peer-group approval and recognition. The escape values of these drugs lie in their potential for allowing one to forget one's problems and to seek refuge temporarily from the real world; and who needs this more than the conflict-torn, changing, disequilibrated adolescent. A fantasy world is set up, a world where the individual is freed of all responsibilities and where nothing is important, where there is no way to get hurt by others.

The counselor should work closely with school personnel, providing objective information as well as psychological counseling. Films and other presentations designed to lessen alcohol abuse among adolescents are available from the National Council on Alcoholism, Washington, D.C. Local school boards have also acquired resources for preventive education in this area. But most importantly, as in the case of drug abuse, the counselor's own awareness and sensitivity is a critical factor in all preventive efforts.

THE ADOLESCENT TRUANT

The chronically absent student poses a serious problem in almost any school system, particularly in large urban systems where poor and culturally different youngsters are often unwilling to avail themselves of the educational services provided for them. In recent years the rate of truancy, and accompanying and related delinquency, has severely increased (Cameron, 1975). It is now generally recognized that the chronic truant is an emotionally or socially maladjusted person who must receive the same considerations—in addition to the legal requirements that must be met—as any other exceptional individual. This task often falls under the purview of the counselor.

Dealing effectively with the truancy problem involves two basic phases: identification of groups of truants within the system and the identification and treatment of the individual truant. The first aspect addresses itself to assessing the extent of the problem, while the second aspect is ameliorative and therapeutic. The first phase will probably throw light on basic social problems that propagate truancy, while the second phase will highlight some specific psychological dimensions of the individual truant's life. Together, these two phases are essential to understanding the truancy problem in toto.

The outdated image of a truant officer who surreptitiously tracked down truants through the back streets of the city, cuffing them as they walked into cleverly set traps, has been replaced by a more sophisticated notion of the professional helper extending himself or herself to help the truant, who is viewed as an individual in need of help. In this section we shall explore some of the causes of truancy and some of the recommended modes of counseling the truant.

Basic Attitudes and Assumptions about Truancy

While there is no single specific known cause for truancy—and while the differences between cases is usually greater than the similarities—there are some general observations that can be fairly stated about the truant. In one report based on a two-year study of adolescent girls remanded to English courts, Stadlen (1976) points out that compared to a control group, the truants had significantly lower IQ scores, with nearly one-half considered to be doing poor or failing work in school. Most of the chronically truant and delinquent girls showed a preference to absent themselves from school in the company of friends, while less persistent truants chose to stay out of school alone or to stay home. One mark, then, of a chronic truant is *the tendency to form a group with other truants* and to stay out of school together, although there are certainly many exceptions to this. The emotionally disturbed and withdrawn youngster, who has no friends, may become a chronic truant on his or her own.

Traditionally, the medical model has been used to explain the "deep-rooted" causes of truancy. This model, which views the overt problem as a superficial symptom, or a manifestation of a deeper problem, considers truancy as one of many antisocial behaviors that are part of a pathological

Truancy poses a major challenge to the urban school counselor.

cluster. The reasoning would run this way: Jan's chronic absence reflects her inability to cope with *any* kind of challenging situation. Instead of treating the truancy, the reasoning continues, let us treat her low self-esteem, of which the truancy is merely one symptom. Presently, there is some feeling that the medical model is insufficient not only in explaining the in-depth causes of truancy, but especially in generalizing modalities of treatment that are applicable. Behavioral psychologists have been at the forefront of this counter position.

Brooks (1971), for example, has argued that truancy should be considered an individually distinct behavior that is alterable by manipulation of its consequences. He demonstrated, using a behavior modification program, that where the contingencies were manipulated the rate of truancy was significantly decreased.

In a more recent paper, Brooks (1974) reaffirmed these findings, applying them specifically to the counseling setting. "Maladaptive behaviors," he argues, "of which truancy is one, are often thought of as being symptoms of deeper personal or social problems, but recent extensions of B. F. Skinner's principles of operant conditioning suggest a different vantage point from which to view behavior" (p. 316). He points out two cases where contingency contracts had proven more effective than threats in dealing with this problem and suggests that very explicit contingency contracts be drawn up for each student, clearly stating the problem, background, behavioral implementation, and reward schedule. These contracts, while they are not complex, may involve the direct participation of the counselor, teacher, and parents, whose job may be either monitoring and enforcing, or the dispensing of rewards (or punishments). When this is done the student and counselor both sign the contract, along with statements of agreement by the teacher, parent, or other involved party. As the contract is enforced, the degree of truant behavior should decrease.

Aside from achieving the desired behavioral change, this technique of contingency contracting was felt to be time economical from a management point of view, useful in placing a degree of responsibility on both the student and the parent, and a way of indicating that the individual counselor cares, is willing to work out a program, and will follow through on promises. Of course, we must note that such a method can only work where the "subject" is willing and emotionally able to cooperate. He concludes that contingency contracting, as he describes it, is a "powerful tool for changing behavior."

Generally, behavioral methods have been the preferred approach in dealing with truancy, although individual face-to-face counseling has also been advocated. Clearly, there is no one method that has been proven most effective. On the contrary, there are a number of effective ways of dealing with the problems of truancy. Fine (1974) found that social reinforcement techniques were effective in reducing the rate of truancy among Chicano junior high school pupils. Grala and McCauley (1976) found that chronic truants verbalized a willingness to change when they were exposed to threat appeal—where they were warned of the negative consequences—more than when they were exposed to optimistic appeal (told of the advantages of school attendance). However, neither method was actually effective in producing increased school attendance unless it was coupled with instruction.

The truant client would fall into the category that we call the reluctant or belligerent client—one who does not seem motivated to seek counseling and does not indicate that he or she will be cooperative. Much research has been directed toward whether these types of clients can be successfully treated—and if so, how. Smaby and Tamminen (1979) have developed a specific counseling framework for dealing with unmotivated and belligerent counselees. This framework uses behavioral principles, along with substantial analyses of moral reasoning, in order for the counselees to learn how to evaluate their behaviors. This approach seems particularly relevant for working with truants, and it is listed in the references for those who wish to pursue it further.

What conclusions can we draw from this data? First, that although the specific causes of truancy are not known, or are diverse enough to be unspecified, we do have effective intervention approaches. The most empirically-supported method is behavior modification, particularly the use of contingency contracting. Second, we know that presenting the better advantages of school (optimistic appeal) has not been shown to be as effective as threats.

SUMMARY

In this chapter we considered some special problems of the secondary school client and some counseling applications particularly relevant to that level. We began by looking at the main theories of psychosocial adolescent development, including the stages of puberty and middle adolescence. I suggested that a synthesis of the many theoretical positions on adolescence might help explain the period in terms of the individual's struggle between personal freedom, psychological fulfillment, and the social and familial demands made upon her or him. The counselor, I pointed out, within the context of the school setting, can act as an agent of therapeutic change in all of these areas of conflict and growth.

We then turned our attention to the sexual development and sexual problems belonging particularly to the adolescent period. We considered the importance of dating behavior as a prosocial mark of this stage. We then looked at some of the problematic areas of adolescent sexual development: masturbation; confusion about petting; contraception; venereal disease; unplanned pregnancy; homosexuality. We concluded that one of the most helpful ways in dealing with all of these sexual problems and conflicts of adolescence is to establish a sex education program in the secondary schools.

Probably, the single most stubborn problem facing the school counselor today is the widespread misuse of drugs and alcohol by adolescents. After providing an operational definition of "abuse," we evaluated what the school counselor can do preventively and therapeutically, in the school setting and outside, to help alleviate this very difficult problem.

Finally, I addressed the problem of chronic truancy in the secondary school. It is now generally recognized that the chronic truant is an emotionally or socially maladjusted person that, in addition to legal considerations, has been treated as any other exceptional individual. This task often falls under the purview of the counselor. We considered several practical counseling principles for working with the truant client.

Assessment and Appraisal

The twin tasks of *assessment* and *appraisal* are an integral part of the counseling function in the schools. Assessment refers to collecting information about an individual's behaviors, aptitudes, abilities, general mental functioning, personality, or related areas, usually through the use of tests. It is basically synonymous with the term *measurement*. Appraisal, on the other hand, refers to the use of this information to formulate certain judgments or conclusions about the person. It is basically synonymous with the term *evaluation,* and requires the interpretation of assessment data. In this chapter, we will be looking at informational sources, at some ways to gather information, ways to interpret information, and, most importantly, how to use it to help the client.

There is considerable debate among counselors about the value of assessment and appraisal—and about their use and abuse. While psychometricians (psychologists specializing in measurement) and behavioral counselors rely heavily on assessment and appraisal, partisans of other positions have lodged a number of objections. Sugarman (1978), for example, in reviewing the literature, found that most humanistic psychologists and counselors considered diagnostic assessment as inherently nonhumanistic and were against its widespread use. Most of their objections about this type of assessment were on five grounds: (1) it is reductionistic, reducing the complexity of the person into diagnostic categories; (2) it is artificial; (3) it ignores the quality of the relationship between the examiner and the test taker; (4) it judges people, casting a label on them; (5) it is overly intellectual, relying on complex concepts often at the expense of truly understanding the individual—as he or she is. Despite these criticisms, Sugarman concludes that their substance reflects only "poor diagnostic practice rather than an inherent weakness in the assessment enterprise. . . . As long as the examiner attempts actively to engage the [test taker] in the assessment process and is aware of the interpersonal context of the test responses and behavior, then psychodiagnostic assessment is consistent with the humanistic orientation" (p. 11).

Moreover, there is considerable evidence that, *if used properly,* assessment and appraisal can be an important positive factor in counseling. This is especially so in the schools, where assessment has an important educational function. "By better identifying educational needs," Mueller, Johnson, and Washington (1978) point out, "by developing a theoretical framework for conducting needs assessment research, and by delineating the purpose and process of needs assessment research, concerns of the public can be better addressed, and appropriate educational goals can be set and met." By understanding the needs of their students, the authors go on to argue, "schools and school systems can make better use of their resources, be more responsive to their publics, and be better prepared to cope with the multiplicity of problems they face" (p. 11). While this is not entirely the job of the school counselor, he or she will most certainly play an integral role in it.

There are many other reasons that could be cited for counselors devoting their time to studying appraisal techniques. Assessment and evaluation, for example, are becoming increasingly important in counseling research, especially because of the current emphasis on proving the effectiveness of the counseling process and measuring the results over a period of time (Hudson, 1978). It may well be, in fact, that some of these assessment methods will be used to bolster the arguments for humanistic psychology in years to come, despite the criticisms of that school. With these caveats in mind, let us begin by looking at the appraisal function.

THE APPRAISAL FUNCTION

The student appraisal services are designed to gather and collate data about each student *for the purpose of helping him or her carry out plans and improve in areas where he or she is deficient, and to identify early any difficulties that may interfere with the student's growth.* It is important to emphasize, in an age as sensitive to individual privacy as is ours, that this collection of data is never intended to be used against the student but always for the student's own benefit.

A good appraisal service should be integrated, continuous, and utilitarian. By integrated, I mean that it should include a variety of both test and nontest information: results of school-administered aptitude and intelligence tests; anecdotal records; autobiographical information; questionnaires and rating scales; specialized test materials administered under the auspices of the counselor's office; interest inventories and occupational tests. The integration of all these different kinds of information enables the counselor to enjoy a wider, more accurate picture of the student.

An appraisal service should also be continuous. To be meaningful, it must continue from year to year, recording the student's progress in school, the changes observed by teachers, his or her relative highs and lows of performance and attitude. Later in this chapter we shall examine the continuity of a testing program, and the comments there apply as well to the continuity of the nontest phase of the appraisal function.

A utilitarian appraisal function is one that can easily be translated into some type of practical application. Utilitarian here means specifically that the data collected must be put to work for the benefit of the student. If the records and test results were allowed to gather dust in the counselor's files over the years, there would be little justification for appraisal. A good appraisal program is always student-oriented.

Hansen (1967) suggests that before we can have a program that uses information for the student's benefit, we must set up protective guidelines concerning the release of information to outside agencies and to other people without a clear-cut interest in the student's welfare. This concern regarding the privacy of appraisal information is directly related to the utilitarian issue. Heayn and Jacobs (1967) outline procedures for insuring the confidentiality of information. They define four levels of openness of information, ranging from the unrestricted (name, sex, date of birth, previous school attended, etc.) to the confidential (psychological reports, psychiatric evaluations, etc.). It is important that the counselor have a clear understanding of what information she or he is entitled to release, which is prohibited and which is discretionary. Local school districts, as well as cities and states, differ in their policies, and it is essential that the counselor be familiar with the rules in effect in that bailiwick. In all cases, however, the counselor must defer to the ethical standards of the American Personnel and Guidance Association (available from APGA, 5203 Leesburg Pike, Falls Church, VA., 22041).

Assuming, then, that the counselor has safeguarded the privacy of the information, how can this information be put to some constructive use — how does he or she make it utilitarian? This differs in detail depending upon the type of information. Six general principles of using appraisal information are outlined below:

1. The counselor evaluates the information as a whole, never relying on a single piece of information. For example, the counselor may receive from a teacher an anecdotal report that speaks poorly of the child. If the rest of the student's folder is examined, however, she or he may find that this report is an exception rather than the rule. Any single piece of information must be assessed in terms of all the information.

2. The counselor applies interpretive skills in evaluating the information instead of simply accepting it at face value. He or she may apply psychological skills and insights in evaluating subjective information and statistical skills in evaluating objective test results.

3. In sharing information with other members of the counseling team, the counselor assumes full responsibility for the use made of the information. In this sense, the counselor is the guardian of student information.

4. The counselor attempts, in the interactions with clients, productively to integrate the information into the interview. He or she may, for example, inform a student who is showing poor performance in school that his or her abilities, as measured by a test instrument, far exceed actual performance. Test results may be particularly helpful to the counselor in career counseling, where tests especially designed to evaluate career interest and potential can save the counselor a great deal of time and guesswork.

5. The counselor looks at all information as it reaches his or her office, in order to act immediately when the information suggests that such action would be of benefit to the student.

6. The counselor contributes to such school functions as curriculum decisions, hirings and promotions, disposition of cases, discipline committees, and the like, in cognizance of the information in his or her files. This is to say that the counselor puts this information into practice in contributing to broad policy decisions that affect all students. For example, the results of a standardized test may show that the students at a particular school are performing very poorly in mathematics. This may well indicate a need to review and/or revise the mathematics program.

With these general principles in mind, let us now examine some particular kinds of appraisal tools, both of the testing and nontesting type, to pinpoint more accurately the purposes of each.

Nontest Assessment

All of the techniques to be discussed here are used widely in the school system. While the relative importance and accuracy of these different techniques has been the subject of much contention over the years, it is generally agreed that these techniques provide an essential service to the students as well as to the school (Traxler and North, 1966). Some counselors and teachers have devised new methods of appraisal that are not included in this section; the methods that follow are the most widely used and accepted.

Observation

Observation, it has been said, is the basis of all science. Observation differs from *looking* or *seeing* by the selectivity and organization of the data perceived by the observer. Observation, the dictionary says, is "the act or practice of noting and recording facts and events, as for some scientific study."[1] In other words, observation is a type of seeing, governed by an inner wisdom and by the principles of scientific scrutiny.

When one observes a situation, one should have at least a preliminary idea of what to look for. For example, if I were a naturalist on an expedition designed to study the effects of pollution on plant life in New Mexico, I would, as I walked the terrain of New Mexico, take especially careful note of the signs of destruction of indigenous flora, for evaluation later on. This preliminary frame of reference allows the observer to concentrate more accurately on the subject at hand, since no person could conceivably absorb the millions of stimuli that bombard him or her at any given moment. It is important, then, that the observer have an idea of what she or he wants to observe. Strang (1949) has provided a detailed list of pupil behavior that would be of special interest to the observer, and this list has been much quoted since its original appearance.

There are a number of difficulties implicit in the observation model. Subjective biases and poor insight may prevent the observer from accurately evaluating and recording the reality of the observed situation. Shertzer and Stone (1971) have suggested that to increase the accuracy of observation, "a number of observations should be made in a variety of situations and at different times." We might also keep in mind Alexander Pope's insight,

> To observations which ourselves we make
> We grow more partial for th' observer's sake.

In other words, don't take note only of those things that you, as the observer, want to notice!

Anecdotal Records

When observations are recorded, they are called *anecdotal observations*. Warters (1956) offers a balanced definition:

> The anecdotal record is a word picture of a specific incident. The record should be limited to objective description and should be free of generalized description, interpretations, and evaluations. At times, however, explanatory, interpretive, or evaluative statements are needed for the full significance of

the incident to be understood; but such statements should be reported apart from the account of the incident, preferably on the reverse side of the record sheet. Ordinarily a number of anecdotal reports are needed before much useful information may be obtained on a student through this method, but the large size of many classes makes it difficult for teachers to write many reports on many students. Unfortunately, the anecdotal records of the majority of teachers yield primarily information about the quality of the student's academic performance and his attitudes toward teachers and schoolwork rather than information regarding the student's social adjustment and his attitudes toward himself and his peers. This fact and the fact that many teachers tend to report their reactions rather than their observations and tend to report unusual and unfavorable behavior more often than typical and favorable behavior reduce the value of the anecdotal technique. Properly used, however, it can produce significant data on adjustment and personality development that cannot be easily obtained otherwise. (p. 139)

While the anecdotal record has traditionally been used to report disruptive incidents, it can also serve a positive role in the counseling program by providing the counselor with a developmental, longitudinal portrait of the student, capturing succinctly moments of growth and development through the educational program. Roeber, Smith, and Erickson (1955) comment on this point:

Anecdotal records were originally devised to report incidents which were indicative of pupil deportment. Although the attitude of the pupil toward himself and others around him is significant, there are several facets of possible reporting which have been neglected and may be equally significant. Educational and vocational planning are dependent upon evaluations of interests and abilities, as well as other factors. The anecdotal-record system, if put into effect for grades one through twelve, can supply a developmental picture of any pupil's interest and abilities. The incident may be some special project which demonstrates an ability. Only anecdotal records supply day-to-day classroom incidents which indicate trends in interests and abilities. (p. 152)

The anecdotal record becomes an integrated productive part of the appraisal function. As such, it must be accurate and objective. Miller (1968) has detailed the characteristics of a good anecdotal record, with concise instructions how the recorder can be assured of doing a competent job. He emphasizes immediacy, specificity, objectivity, selectivity, simplicity, and insight as the key criteria for a good anecdotal record.

Cumulative Records

As the name implies, the *cumulative record* is a progressive, coordinated record of the student's progress in school. The cumulative record may include any or all of the following: student's name, address(es), date of birth, grades in school, results of standardized tests, disciplinary actions, health information, family information, extracurricular activities, self-reports, anecdotal records, rating scales, samples of the student's work, and other data. It is, in the broadest sense, a comprehensive paper portrait of the student.

Warnken and Siess (1965) discuss ways in which the cumulative record may be used in the prediction of behavior. By reducing a large number of different observations and data to a manageable set of terms, the authors demonstrate that the information contained within the cumulative record can be a valid predictor of student expected behavior. They propose a specific check-list technique for recording observations, which should make observation reports within an individual school more uniform and consistent. While such uniformity is a step in the right direction, more efforts will have to be undertaken in the future (perhaps by APGA) to make cumulative records uniform nationwide, in view of the great mobility of families in our country today. Roeber, Smith, and Erickson (1955) list ten types of forms and records that would probably be included in the cumulative record folder: pupil personal data blank, administrative record, achievement and activities inventory, test profiles and records, autobiography, anecdotal and rating records, plan sheets, fact-finding interview records, sociometric and miscellaneous data, placement and follow-up records.

Other Nontest Appraisal Techniques

In addition to the techniques discussed earlier, there are a number of other important nontest appraisal techniques. The autobiography, a report written by the student about himself or herself, provides the counselor with an important insight into the student's self-perceptions. One of the major advantages of the autobiography, Tolbert (1972) points out, is that it "provides the counselor with a view of the counselee's world as perceived by the counselee" (p. 176). Annis (1967) has written a comprehensive paper on the uses and values of the autobiography in professional counseling and psychology. He includes a thorough list of references on the subject, and the counselor who wishes to exploit fully this counseling tool would do well to read his paper.

Rating scales help the counselor quickly, although superficially, to grasp some aspect of the client's personality. Rating scales make it easy to quantify the client and to categorize her or him according to the rating categories.

The weakness of rating scales is (1) their oversimplification of the complexities of the client to a few choice categories and quantifiers and (2) their subjectivity. In both the construction and the interpretation of rating scales, it is important that the counselor be sensitive to these two serious limitations.

There are four basic types of rating scales. *Descriptive rating scales* provide the counselor with a variety of descriptive statements from which to choose those that best describe the student. *Numerical rating scales* and *graphic rating scales* both utilize gradations of numbers to indicate the student's relative rating. The difference between these two is that the graphic rating scale uses a pictorial representation, as in this example.

cooperation

Enthusiastically cooperates	Readily cooperates	Sometimes cooperates	Rarely cooperates	Never cooperates
5	4	3	2	1

The graphic scale may use either numerical or descriptive indices or both. Another rating method often used is the *paired comparison method,* in which the rater compares the subject to others in a group as equal, worse, or better. There are advantages and disadvantages to each of these methods. The counselor must decide exactly what she or he wants to find out and then decide on the best method for getting the information.

Sociometric techniques are used to measure the student's social values, preferences, and interactions. Thorndike and Hagen (1969) define a sociometric technique as "a procedure for determining each individual's position within a social group such as a school class by analyzing the choices (and rejections) made by each group member with respect to the others in the group" (p. 653). Questionnaires, rating scales, and tests are all used to determine sociometric quantification. Gronlund (1960) has thoroughly explored sociometric methods that are relevant to the classroom situation. Many of these techniques involve observation and construction by the teacher. Other approaches involve the use of printed sociometric inventories. Gronlund includes a number of these tests in his book.

Having now examined some nontest appraisal techniques, let us turn our attention to student appraisal services that use testing and evaluation procedures based on test and statistical data.

Testing and Evaluation

Nowadays, many counseling graduates profess not to believe in testing. Some of them, children of the early and mid-fifties, when testing in the schools had reached new peaks, remember with dismay the many hours

Examinations play an important role in all our lives.

they were required to labor, pencil in hand, hunched over their desks answering questions that seemed irrelevant to their lives. They recall the SATs, the LSATs and the GREs that more recently challenged them. They recall the many studies and articles they have been exposed to in their training that lambast the testing movement and minimize the value of tests in learning about the individual. They cite testing as another instance of the depersonalization prevalent in the schools and in society today, and they vow with integrity not to become part of this very system when they become guidance counselors. They remember with sadness their own failures on tests—their pain, their excuses, their rationalizations—and judge the instrument by their own personal experiences. They rebel.

Despite this common sentiment, testing remains an integral part of the counseling function, and it is perhaps the single most important part of the counselor's specialized appraisal skills. Many counseling positions are created precisely for the purpose of test administration, and the skilled clinical counselor, regardless of qualifications, can hardly lay claim to professional expertise without at least an acquaintance with the area of testing and evaluation.

Moreover, testing and evaluation, while at times badly abused, serve as an integral part of the counselor's resources. Testing, looked at objectively, is a virtual bonanza for the counselor who does not have time to meet individually with each student in the school. Within a large school population, testing allows the counselor to identify those students who are most in need of counseling, remediation, or other forms of guidance. Testing also enables the administration and instructional staff to design a curriculum that is responsive to the needs, interests, aptitudes, and abilities of the students. Testing serves another function as well: it enables a community to measure the progress of its students against the progress of students in other communities, thus indirectly evaluating the efficacy of its school system.

Individual testing also has several advantages for the counselor. From a test, the counselor is often able to get information about the client that is accessible neither through the face-to-face interview nor through consultation with teachers, parents, and other interested parties. For example, a child working with a counselor under my supervision was diagnosed by the physician at her school as having minimal brain damage. We administered a battery of tests and ultimately determined that the child was above normal intelligence but was suffering from mild dyslexia. Several treatment sessions with a specialist cured a problem that had almost inadvertently ruined this young girl's life.

Individual testing also offers the counselor an opportunity to confirm intuitive impressions of the client. Often when working with a client, the counselor develops feelings about a client: it may be a feeling relating to his or her occupational interests, to intellectual abilities, to preferences and personality characteristics. In any case, one can never be entirely sure of one's feelings, so that it is often reassuring to the counselor to find a suitable test instrument to determine the accuracy of his or her intuition.

AN INTRODUCTION TO TESTS

A test is an objective and usually standardized sample of an individual's performance in some or several areas. The area measured may be intellectual functioning, personal interests, aptitudes, or some aspect of psychological functioning. To be considered objective, a test must be designed so that its results are unaffected by personal biases of the individual who administers it. A test is said to be standardized when it has been given to a large and representative sample of people and its range of scores determined. The various scores made by people in this standardization group are called test norms. Unless we know what scores other people have made on a particular test, a single score by one individual tells us very little. It is only when we can compare it with the test norms that we can tell whether a person is average, above average, or below average. For instance, if Jill scores 115 on a standardized intelligence test, this means little to us until we know what the test norms are. If the average score is 100 and the standard deviation is 15, then we know that Jill scored approximately at the 84 *percentile*—or in about the top 15 percent of the population. We will see how this works later when we look at different types of scores and consider how they are interpreted.

Reliability and Validity

Two measures widely used to tell us how helpful an instrument a test is are *reliability* and *validity*. A test is reliable if it produces the same or similar results time after time. The reliability of a test can be checked if it is given to groups of subjects on at least two separate occasions and the two sets of scores are compared. The correlation between these two scores indicates the stability of the test, or what is called the *test-retest reliability*. Another method of checking reliability is to give parallel forms of the test to the same group of individuals on two occasions and compare their scores on both forms. The reliability of a test is expressed as a coefficient: a number from .00 to 1.0 (which is theoretically perfect, but never actually occurs). The higher the reliability coefficient, the better the test.

Validity is an index of how well a test measures what it is supposed to measure. There are three different types of validity. *Content validity* (also called face validity) refers to whether the test appears to cover the material it is supposed to cover. *Criterion validity* compares a new test instrument with a standardized one (the criterion) and examines how well they compare. If people who do well on the new test also did well on the standardized one, and if the people who do average or poor on the new test, did average or poor on the standardized one, we say it has a high criterion validity.

Sometimes we want a test to predict certain things about an individual. For instance, if we administer an occupational preference test to predict who will best be suited to a certain kind of job, we can then measure how accurate were these predictions. This is called *predictive validity,* and it describes how well or poorly the scores on a test predict future behavior in other related contexts.

Types of Tests

The school counselor will invariably be exposed to a large number of different tests, including tests of intelligence, ability, various aptitudes, interests, and personality measures. This section is designed only as a brief overview to the different types of tests used; much more detailed knowledge is necessary before the counselor can fully appreciate the specifics of a test, or how tests are designed to measure certain traits. It is suggested that students of counseling who plan to work with test data consult Robert L. Thorndike and Elizabeth Hagen's *Measurement and Evaluation in Psychology and Education,* 4th edition (1978), which is an excellent reference source.

Achievement Tests

Achievement tests measure what a person has learned. The final exam at the end of a course is an achievement test. So, too, is a standardized test that measures one's knowledge of a subject, such as the advanced psychology part of the Graduate Record Examination. Two widely used achievement tests in the schools are the Iowa Test of Basic Skills, which measures basic language, mathematical, and problem-solving skills, and the Metropolitan Achievement Test, which is actually a test battery that measures learning in several academic areas.

Aptitude Tests

Aptitude tests are supposed to measure a person's potential to achieve — that is, one's aptitude — in a certain area. The area may be broad (such as intelligence) or very narrow (such as a test of one's aptitude for learning high-speed dexterity tasks). In either case the aptitude test should be as free as possible of measuring achievement itself, since its focus is on potential success rather than on past learning. The verbal, quantitative, and analytic parts of the Graduate Record Examination are aptitude tests, in that they measure the testee's ability to do well in graduate school.

Interest Inventories

Interest inventory tests are used to help individuals make career decisions. Interest inventories, usually in the form of checklists or forced-choice preference items, ask an individual to indicate what types of activities are of most interest to him or her. The respondent's pattern of replies gives an indication of the type of occupation in which he or she would be most successful. An example of this kind of test is the widely used Kuder Preference Record — Vocational, which measures the individual's vocational preference.

Intelligence Tests

Intelligence tests are widely used forms of aptitude tests that measure intelligence, the general aptitude for intellectual performance, expressed as an IQ. These tests have come under controversy in recent years for two

figure 11.1 Normal distribution of IQ

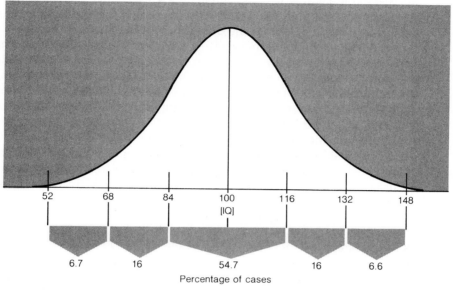

Percentage of cases

Note: From Yussen, R., and John W. Santrock. *Child Development: An Introduction* © 1978 Wm. C. Brown Company Publishers. Reprinted by permission.

reasons. First, and foremost, they are so widely used in educational decision making that many have argued that too much reliance has been placed on them. Second, it has been suggested that they are culturally biased, preferential to certain groups (such as whites) and discriminatory against others (such as blacks and Chicanos).

There are two kinds of intelligence tests: individually administered tests and group intelligence tests. The two most popular individually administered tests are the Stanford-Binet and the Wechsler. The Stanford-Binet was originally standardized near the beginning of this century when Dr. Lewis Terman of Stanford University revised the earlier test developed in France by Alfred Binet and Theodore Simon. Terman made the test applicable for school-age children in the United States and published it in 1916 as the Stanford-Binet Intelligence Scale. It has been revised several times since, the latest version published in 1973.

The test originally measured a child's mental age—that is, the age of the average child who performed intellectually at the level of performance of the person taking the test. To obtain an *IQ,* the mental age was divided by the chronological age of the person who is being tested and multiplied by 100. If the mental age and the chronological age were the same—that is, if the person performed average—the IQ was 100. Performances above and below average were reflected in scores above and below 100. In the recent edition of the Stanford-Binet, this formula was abandoned and the more accurate use of deviation IQ was substituted. With this system an individual's raw score is simply compared on a chart of standardized raw scores, and the IQ is immediately obtained.

Many years after the Stanford-Binet had gained acceptance, psychologist David Wechsler developed a new, presumably more sophisticated, instrument while working at Bellevue Hospital in New York City. Wechsler developed three versions of his test over the years. The first was the Wechsler Adult Intelligence Scale (WAIS), which has become the most popular individual test of adult intelligence used in the United States. This test consists of two parts: a verbal part, yielding a verbal IQ score, and a performance part, yielding a performance IQ. The total score (verbal plus performance) is the total IQ. Items on the verbal section include vocabulary, comprehension, arithmetic reasoning, and so forth. Questions on the performance part do not require language ability, and are considered less culturally influenced. The person being tested is asked to put together a puzzle, to assemble two-color blocks in a certain design, to tell what is missing from a picture, to copy symbols rapidly and accurately, and to arrange a sequence of pictures in their correct (logical) order. Wechsler also developed an individual intelligence test for children, called the Wechsler Intelligence Scale for Children (WISC), which follows the pattern of the WAIS. In 1963, he introduced a form for preschoolers, the Wechsler Preschool and Primary Scale of Intelligence (WPPSI).

More widely used than these individual tests, because they are so economical and time-efficient, are the group tests of intelligence. These first came into prominence during wartime, when hundreds of thousands of recruits had to be given tests of intelligence to enable the armed forces to weed out the mentally unfit and to assign people to training schools based on their ability. The military developed many tests and the extremely large sample (all recruits) allowed for sophisticated standardization.

Presently, two of the more popular group intelligence tests are the Otis-Lennon Mental Ability Test, which samples verbal and reasoning ability, takes only a half hour, and covers the school years from kindergarten to college; and the California Test of Mental Maturity, which takes longer to administer but is very thorough. Aptitude tests such as the Scholastic Aptitude Test (SAT), the Law School Aptitude Test (LSAT), and the Graduate Record Examination (GRE) are derivatives of intelligence tests, although they are not technically considered IQ tests.

It behooves me to emphasize that there now exists a serious controversy about the ethics and the efficacy of these intelligence tests. While we will not go into the many complex issues involved, since they are far beyond the scope of this chapter, the counselor should be aware of the controversy surrounding the use of these IQ tests and be especially wary about their potential for misuse and abuse.

Methods of Personality Assessment

The counselor may or may not be required to undertake personality assessment, but will most likely be provided with the results of personality assessment and should therefore be familiar with the major methods of personality assessment and their relative strengths and weaknesses. This section will briefly describe how personality is assessed, but the counseling student who plans to be working in this area is advised to look at Anne Anastasi's Psychological Testing to learn about the fundamentals of personality assessment in more detail.

A number of different methods of personality assessment are employed in the clinical and school settings. These include the personal interview, rating scales, projective tests, and objective (pencil-and-paper) tests. The method of choice often depends on three factors: (1) the training of the counselor; (2) the time and resources available; and (3) what type of personality information is desired and how it will be used.

The personal interview is a subjective way of assessing personality. Subjective assessments, as is often suggested, are almost always, to one or another degree, incorrect, misleading, or the very opposite of the truth. According to Poulton (1977), "the chief danger of subjective assessments is that they may be based on a rule which does not happen to apply in the particular circumstance of the investigation" (p. 409). This is indeed true, although evidence indicates that if the interviewer is well trained there is high agreement between the interviewer's assessment of the client and the client's own assessment of himself or herself (Grady & Ephross, 1977). The key fact seems to be how free of bias the interviewer is.

When conducted by a skilled interviewer, the interview has some very real advantages. In addition to eliciting direct responses from the client, the interviewer also notes appearance, manner, body language, and the quality of interviewee responses to comments or questions. Does the subject fidget nervously? Does he or she make eye contact with the interviewer? Is the subject able to follow questions, to respond coherently? In sum, then, the

figure 11.2 Drawing representing ink blot used in the Rorschach test, one of the best-known and widely used projective tests

personal interview is only as accurate in assessing as the interviewer is effective at interviewing, and this includes not only being perceptive, but being unbiased and open as well.

Rating scales, as we mentioned earlier, are very widely used in the school setting. A personality rating scale is a device that permits a rater to assess the degree to which an individual possesses particular personality characteristics and may be in any of the forms described earlier. Also used are self-rating scales, where the subject rates himself or herself on certain traits. In some instances the self-rating and the rating of the interviewer are compared.

Projective tests, which are widely employed in the clinical setting, are less often used in the schools since they require extensive training to be administered correctly. More common are the objective personality tests, which are administered and scored according to a standard procedure. The results are little affected by the training or opinions of the examiner, although the interpretation of the results is crucial to the effective use of the test.

The two most widely used objective personality tests are the Minnesota Multiphasic Personality Inventory (the MMPI) and The Sixteen Personality Factor Questionnaire (the 16 PF). The MMPI is useful in diagnosing disturbed behavior and in yielding a profile of personality that accurately indicates areas in which there is some difficulty in adjustment, such as in relationships with other people. The 16PF offers a psychological profile of the individual based on 16 paired personality trait opposites, such as outgoing/reserved or happy-go-lucky/serious. Because the 16PF has been standardized and widely administered, the interpretation of this profile is supposed to tell the counselor information about the individual's functioning and psychological state. Moreover, individuals in many different professions have taken the test, so it is also used to determine how one's personality corresponds with those of a person in a given profession.

Interpretation of Scores

Whenever a test is taken it yields a score. The first thing test scores tell is how many answers were correct or incorrect, or on preference tests, how many answers show a preference and how many do not. These are called raw scores and are the most basic data obtained. But they are not too useful in interpreting tests. In order for a score to be helpful we have to have some idea how it relates to other subjects' scores on the same test. This is done by converting raw scores into comparative scores that tell us what the score actually means.

One of the most valuable comparative scores is the percentile score. A percentile score tells what percentage of people taking the test fall at or below a given score. If Jason receives a raw score of 86 on a test, and the score is marked 54 percentile, we know that 54 percent of the people taking that test earned a score of 86 *or below.* In other words, 46 percent of the people taking the test (100%-54%) did better than Jason. We learn from the percentile score how Jason did compared to all the people who took the test.

Test scores are often grouped together in intervals of a fixed size in what is called a *frequency distribution.* The frequency distribution tells us how many people received each score (its frequency). It is usually expressed by grouping scores together in intervals, such as 61-65. It then tells us how many scores fall within each interval. Table 11.1 shows how 38 individual students scored on an exam. At the right-hand side of the table is the frequency distribution of these scores. From the frequency distribution can be obtained the range of scores (the difference from highest to lowest) and measures of *central tendency,* which help us understand how a person did in relation to others.

table 11.1

INDIVIDUAL SCORES OF STUDENTS AND FREQUENCY DISTRIBUTION OF SCORES

student /	grade	student /	grade	student /	grade	interval /	f
A	77	N	80	BB	80	95–99	1
B	69	P	88	CC	82	90–94	3
C	84	Q	68	DD	76	85–89	4
D	96	R	79	EE	87	80–84	5
E	60	S	94	FF	75	75–79	7
F	70	T	67	GG	71	70–74	6
G	90	U	70	HH	53	65–69	5
H	81	V	64	II	92	60–64	4
I	62	W	76	JJ	60	55–60	2
J	85	X	66	KK	74	50–54	1
K	76	Y	86	LL	65		
L	62	Z	58	MM	75		N=38
M	71	AA	73				

The three important measures of central tendency are the *mean,* the *median,* and the *mode.* The arithmetic mean, which is also called the average, is obtained by adding together all the scores and dividing by the total number of scores. When using grouped data, such as the frequency distribution in table 11.1, we take the midpoint of each interval (97, 92, 87, 82, 77, 72. . . . .), multiply it by the frequency of the interval, and then divide by the total number of scores.

One problem in using the arithmetic mean is that it may be influenced by extremely high or low scores that are not typical of the group. An alternative measure of central tendency, not as affected by the extreme scores, is the median—the middle score, above and below which the same number of scores fall. The median is, by definition, the 50 percentile: the score at or below which exactly half the test scores fall.

A third measure of central tendency is the mode, which is the score that occurs most frequently. Generally, the mode is not as good an indicator of central tendency as the mean or median. The mode is a measure most preferred by dress manufacturers, for example, who want to know which size occurs most frequently among their customers.

Other factors—such as variability—also affect the meaning of any given test score. What is the spread of the scores—are they widely scattered or do they all fall around the middle? How far does the typical score differ

figure 11.3 Mean, median, and mode in a normal probability curve

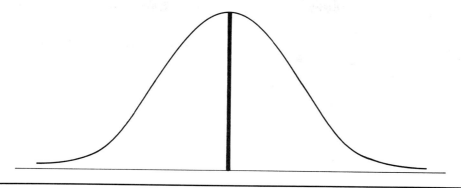

figure 11.4 Standard score scales in relation to normal probability curve

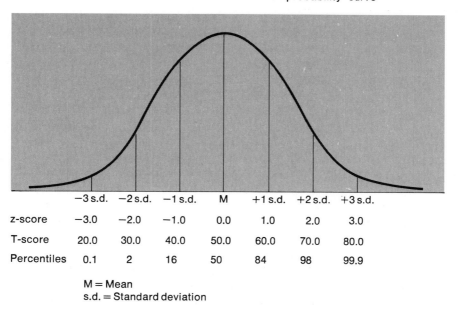

	−3 s.d.	−2 s.d.	−1 s.d.	M	+1 s.d.	+2 s.d.	+3 s.d.
z-score	−3.0	−2.0	−1.0	0.0	1.0	2.0	3.0
T-score	20.0	30.0	40.0	50.0	60.0	70.0	80.0
Percentiles	0.1	2	16	50	84	98	99.9

M = Mean
s.d. = Standard deviation

from the mean? The *standard deviation* is a measure of variability that answers these questions. It tells how far the majority of students' scores are from the mean. Since the computation of the standard deviation is beyond our scope, suffice it to say that from the mean and standard deviation we can compute many forms of comparative scores. The important point is that the counselor interpreting a test try to understand what a given score means in relation to other scores.

A SEVEN-STAGE TESTING PROGRAM

In addition to administering individual and group tests, the school counselor is often asked to institute a testing program. A testing program consists of an organized school-wide or system-wide effort to administer and evaluate standardized tests. Typically, the counselor situated in the public school is placed in charge of a testing program for his or her school, although in smaller school districts a school counselor may be asked to take charge of the testing program for the district. Such a counselor will, however, generally have had advanced training in testing and evaluation. In either case, the counselor's responsibility is heavy in the areas of testing, and his or her competency should be worthy of the degree of responsibility.

Thorndike and Hagen (1969) cite three desirable characteristics of a testing program: *relation to use, integration,* and *continuity.* "Relation to use" means that the specific tests offered should be applicable to the problems that the school is attempting to solve or to the insights it wishes to gain. If, for example, a counselor is in charge of the tesing program for a school in a large urban center that has a central testing program, the tests offered in his or her school would not repeat what the system-wide tests are measuring nor would they measure traits that are of little interest to the school administration. Similarly, in a sixth-grade class for slow learners, tests that discriminate high intelligence levels should not be used.

"Integration" refers to the extent to which there is a logical and clear-cut relationship between the different test instruments being used and between the testing administered from grade to grade. Speaking about this concept, Thorndike and Hagen point out,

> In an integrated program, it will usually be desirable to use the same series of tests over the grade range for which it is appropriate. Thus, if the *Metropolitan Achievement Tests* are being used to measure progress in basic skills, it will probably be desirable to use them in any grade from first up to sixth, and possibly eighth or ninth, in which an achievement battery is being used. The advantages are that norms are based upon the same sampling of

communities from grade to grade, and the tests conform to a common outline of content and format. Thus, scores from one grade to the next are more nearly comparable, so that a truer picture may be obtained of pupil growth. (p. 522)

To have "continuity," a testing program must be continued over a period of years. Continuity allows a counselor to follow the growth of an individual student from year to year, to measure the abilities of specific teachers, curricula, administrators, and so forth, as well as allowing counselors the option of getting to know their test instruments better. It is through the continuing use of test instruments, and through the continuation of the testing program, that a longitudinal study of growth and development may be undertaken.

Carey (1969) suggests six fundamental questions that the counselor should ask himself or herself in order to evaluate the overall quality and utility of a testing program. These questions are compatible with the three criteria suggested by Thorndike and Hagen, but are specific enough to enable the counselor to make a precise determination. The six questions are:

1. To what real use are the tests being put?
2. Are the uses really pertinent to the students who take them, or are they "administrative" and merely add to the record?
3. Are the uses significant enough to justify time usurped from classes, counselor time in administering and handling data, and money expended?
4. Do school personnel have enough time to really use test results?
5. Is the program balanced? Does it provide useful information for average and lower ability students as well as the college-bound, and vocational as well as educational counseling?
6. Is the program concentrated at choice-points in order that a fresh, relatively complete self-picture is available for each student when he must make an important decision or, at earlier stages, when an important decision must be made about him? (p. 205)

As the counselor conscientiously approaches these questions, he or she will be forced to recognize the different stages of a testing program and the interrelationships between these stages. For the sake of simplification, the testing and evaluation procedures have been divided into seven general stages (see table 11.2), and we shall look at each of these briefly to determine the practical steps the counselor must follow in order to implement a successful testing program.

table 11.2

THE SEVEN STAGES OF TESTING AND EVALUATION

1. Assessing the need for a test and determining what is to be measured, how much time is available, and a general evaluation of the resources.
2. Selecting a test instrument. Requisitioning.
3. Arranging for the administration of the test.
4. Collecting the tests and distributing them for scoring.
5. Preparing test data sheets and an accompanying interpretive guide.
6. Making test results available to appropriate parties and interpreting the implications of specific test data.
7. Follow-up.

1. Assessing the need for a test and determining what is to be measured, how much time is available, and a general evaluation of the resources

In almost any educational situation, one could easily find valid reasons to administer tests to the student population. Since testing allows the teachers, counselors, and administrators to learn more about each student—as well as more about the population as a whole—a basic reason behind much, if not all, testing is to enable the system to learn about the individuals in it. This, however, is not a compelling reason to administer a testing program. It can, however, become a compelling justification when the "desire to know" is coupled with a commitment to action and change.

Let us say, for example, that Principal Jones believes her new and liberal administration has been doing a superior job in improving the students' chances for college entrance, bolstering their achievements in several areas, and increasing their interest in the arts and humanities. She approaches Counselor Smith and asks him to administer tests to the students to determine exactly how far they have gone since the commencement of her tenure at the school. Counselor Smith must immediately ask himself (and, ultimately, Principal Jones) some crucial questions regarding the use to which the tests will be put if they are in fact administered. Questions of this type might be asked: What if we discover that the students have not improved in some areas? Would you then be willing to rethink the curriculum? If the results are very positive, will you still continue to experiment and find more meaningful and expeditious ways of teaching? How will we use these test results to help individual students? Are there tests that will measure other qualities or traits that will be of more benefit to the students than tests merely to determine how the administration has improved the school over the past few years? Can we use system-wide tests already being administered, or is it absolutely necessary to have other test data in addition? These—and questions like them—put the need for a testing program to a real challenge and insure that tests are not arbitrarily or capriciously administered in order to boost an ego, deflate an ego, or prove something that is of interest to a person in power but perhaps of little benefit to the students.

The most important guide in assessing the need for a test (or for a testing program) is the ultimate benefit the students will reap from the test. Other considerations, research efforts, personal considerations, and so forth, must always be placed second.

Once the need for a test has been established, the counselor narrows down the specific quality or qualities that are to be measured. Let us say, for example, that a junior high school counselor determines, after critically thinking and rethinking the question, that there is a legitimate need for a test to identify in time the students who are likely to drop out of school before the completion of their studies. One instrument designed particularly for this task and standardized over a period of years is the Demos-D Scale. While this is an excellent test instrument, the counselor might ask herself or himself whether there is perhaps another test that has been correlated with dropout proneness and that will provide a measurement of other qualities or traits that would be of use to the students at the school. He may find, for example, that the Adolescent Alienation Index or the School Motivation Analysis Test or the School Interest Inventory—all standardized tests—would serve the purpose just as well and, in addition, identify other student difficulties that the counselor would want to be aware of.

The counselor determines what is to be measured by considering the students, the needs of the school, the instruments available, and the time and expense (Shertzer and Linden, 1979). He or she evaluates, in general, the resources available for the administration of the testing program and determines from this evaluation: How long a test can be used? How much money can be spent on the test (including scoring)? How will proctors be secured and paid? How much school time is available? Where can the counselor expect cooperation and where can resistance be anticipated? After this determination is made, and she or he knows the qualities to be measured and is satisfied that a test or a testing program is needed, the counselor goes about selecting a test instrument.

2. Selecting a test instrument. Requisitioning.
Once he or she has a clear idea what is to be measured, how does the counselor go about deciding on a specific instrument to use? Before making this decision, she or he should be familiar with the different types of tests. The basic categories of tests are: *aptitude tests, interest tests, achievement*

tests, and *personality tests.* An aptitude test measures individuals' potential in a specified area. Rather than measure what students have learned or what they are able to do, the aptitude test measures what they can learn or what they should be able to do. Intelligence tests are a popular form of aptitude tests.

Interest tests measure the subject's "tendency to prefer or engage in a particular type of activity" (Thorndike & Hagen, 1969). Interest tests often used by counselors are the vocational interest inventories, which measure the subject's interest in a particular occupation or class of occupations.

Achievement tests measure the individual's ability to perform certain tasks. The test that the teacher administers to determine what a student has learned in class is an achievement test. A standardized achievement test measures the student's ability to perform in comparison with a wide reference group with whom the student can be compared.

Personality tests measure intrapsychic modes of feeling, of perceiving reality emotionally, and of acting.

Thorndike and Hagen (1970) discuss in detail the various types of tests, and Buros (1966) offers a complete, up-to-date description of every published test in all these categories.

All reputable test publishers limit the accessibility of their instruments to qualified professionals. The Psychological Corporation, for example, has a rule that "school teachers and counselors may purchase tests by official purchase order or with the written authorization of the superintendent, principal, or guidance director." Most other test publishers have similar restrictions, and the school counselor may consult the test catalogue of a publisher to determine in which cases she or he may or may not qualify as a purchaser.

3. Arranging for the administration of the test

4. Collecting the tests and distributing them for scoring
These two stages are basically administrative, and the counselor's administrative abilities will be put to the test during this time. The counselor must see that adequate facilities have been secured for the test administration, that proctors and assistants are briefed in advanced, that all the test materials have been received, that the test subjects have been notified, and so forth. Brown and Srebalus (1972) offer a detailed list of procedures to follow during this stage of the testing program.

5. Preparing test data sheets and an accompanying interpretive guide
After the counselor has collected the answer booklets and all other test materials, it is his or her responsibility to see that the test is sent out for

scoring or, if scoring is to be done at the school, that the material is put in a safe place and is secure from theft. Reppert, Campbell, and Kirk (1965) discuss the responsibilities of the counselor during this phase of the program, describing in some detail the counselor's work in arranging materials, bookkeeping, examining the used examination booklets, sending out the answer sheets for scoring, and the like.

6. Making test results available to appropriate parties and interpreting the implications of specific test data

Having conscientiously carried out all duties to this point, the counselor enjoys a brief respite until the results of the tests are returned. Then he or she goes back to work again, this time making sure that these results are used properly.

The first question with which the counselor must deal is, Who is an appropriate party? The counselor does not want to release test results indiscriminately; at the same time, she or he does not want to hoard these results. In other words, the counselor wants the test results be put to good use. In most cases, every person on the counseling team falls into the category of an appropriate party and not only is fully entitled to see the test results but should actually be encouraged to see them to understand more clearly the needs, interests, and abilities of the students with whom they are working. Methods of communicating and interpreting test results will be explored in the next section of this chapter. A few general principles can be stated here:

1. Appropriate staff, faculty, and administration should be informed when the test results are available.
2. The counselor should prepare a short brochure of the meaning of the test, what it is designed to measure, its presumed accuracy, and the table of scores.
3. The counselor should identify for the personnel those students whose scores indicate that they may be in need of special attention or services.
4. When requests are made for information by other parties, such as parents, the counselor should be prepared to meet with them and to present information in a constructive, meaningful way (see the following section for a more detailed discussion).
5. The counselor should arrange interviews with those students whose scores indicate that an interview with the counselor might be beneficial.

7. Follow-up

A testing program would be of little value if there were no follow-up procedures. The discussion of continuity earlier goes into this point. Since tests are often used as diagnostic tools, it is the counselor's responsibility to see that meaningful use is made of the information obtained from the tests.

COMMUNICATING TEST RESULTS

To understand the meaning of test results, counselors should have some familiarity with testing terminology. While they need not be statisticians, they should be familiar with the concepts of central tendency, standard deviation, reliability, validity, norms, and so on. A glossary of testing terminology, including all the major terms that the counselor might confront, appears at the end of this text. There are a number of valuable papers and books that the student of counseling may wish to examine to get a more detailed understanding of some of these terms (Tilis, 1979, on the purpose of standardized tests as they are used in the school; Hopkins and Glass, 1978, on statistical concepts and terminology). But it is important to emphasize that while these technical terms are useful in understanding test results, only a humane, personal attitude can help the counselor understand the meaning of a test score in relation to the client with whom he or she is working.

In discussing the results of a test with a student client, the counselor must attempt to avoid the technical jargon that may have been useful in helping interpret the test results to himself or herself. The value of communicating test results to clients is stultified if the counselor cannot present the information in a language clients can understand. Lister and McKenzie (1966) list four conditions designed to assure that test interpretation will help the student client achieve a better self-understanding:

1. THE STUDENT EXPERIENCES A NEED FOR INFORMATION. . . . It is not enough for the counselor to believe the student can benefit from knowing his test results; the student himself must feel such a need.
2. THE STUDENT'S QUESTIONS ARE TRANSLATED INTO OPERATIONAL TERMS ACCEPTABLE TO HIM. . . . Until a student can approach an operational statement of his questions, test interpretation remains generalized and of limited value to the individual. In the course of counseling with a student about higher education, the student might successively ask the following questions: What are my chances of getting into college? What are my chances of finishing the first two years of college? . . . What are my chances of graduating from medical school?

3. THERE IS A RELATIONSHIP BETWEEN TEST RESULTS AND THE CRITERION PERFORMANCE. Translating a student's test results into a statement about some probable behavior takes specific evidence of a relationship between his scores and that behavior.
4. THE INFORMATION IS CLEARLY COMMUNICATED TO THE STUDENT. (p. 62)

These four principles adequately sum up the major rules of communicating test results to the student client. I may also add that the client should demonstrate a willingness, or even an eagerness, to learn the test results. They should never be imposed upon him or her, never used in the sphere of confrontation. Rather, they should be presented as a logical response to a client's appropriate questions.

The more subtle meanings of test results can also be communicated to the client or counsultee during the counseling interview, but this must be done in a way that is understandable. Adams (1963), for example, suggests that an illustration of the normal curve may be useful in showing graphically to parents and children what the test scores mean in terms of the total population. Berdie, Layton, Swanson, and Hagenah (1963) present a detailed explanation of ways in which test data can be presented constructively to the client or consultee. Tolbert (1978) has discussed ways in which confusion and misunderstanding can be prevented in the counseling setting when test interpretation is the subject.

The way information is presented has a clearcut effect on how it is put to use. Larkin (1978) found, for example, that when a group of college students were presented information about their performances in a task relating to their financial ability, integrative evaluative information—that is, information which was interpreted specifically for them, reflecting their needs—was perceived more positively and constructively than either raw scores or rank by itself. Moreover, those subjects who received higher ability evaluations—that is, it was explained to them that they had done well—tended to select riskier and more difficult tasks than those who received raw scores or lower ability evaluations. In short, then, the communication of information may have an effect on future performance in the same or related areas.

Counseling the Exceptional Student

12

In the school setting, an important contribution made by the school counselor is in working with the exceptional student. It is estimated that approximately 15 percent of the students enrolled in school today are exceptional. By definition, exceptional students are those who "deviate from the average or normal child (1) in mental characteristics, (2) in sensory abilities, (3) in neuromotor or physical characteristics, (4) in social behavior, (5) in communication abilities, or (6) in multiple handicaps. Such deviation must be of such an extent that the child requires a modification of school practices, or special educational services, to develop to maximum capacity" (Kirk, 1979, p. 3). The school counselor works with such learners in a variety of capacities, ranging from individual program design to group counseling to vocational guidance. In this chapter we will examine some specific ways the counselor can be helpful in detecting exceptionalities and in the provision of appropriate services. We will begin by examining the implications of what is probably the most important legislation ever passed affecting exceptional learners in the school: the Education for All Handicapped Children Act of 1975.

EDUCATION FOR ALL HANDICAPPED CHILDREN ACT

In 1975 the Congress passed a law known as P. L. (for Public Law) 94-142. This law is called the Education for All Handicapped Children Act, and it was designed to specifically mandate guidelines for the education of exceptional learners. Probably the most deep-seated ramifications of this federal law are found in its directive that all handicapped children are entitled to an appropriate free public education. The law goes on, in some considerable detail, to explicate the meaning of *appropriate* in terms of what the school is expected to offer the handicapped, or exceptional, child. It also requires that the state provide all necessary special services for the child and evaluate the effectiveness of its program for each child, on at least an annual basis.

Further details of PL 94-142 reveal its philosophy as well as some of the problems of its practical implementation. First, it mandates that a child-study team, consisting of various professionals, evaluate each handicapped child's special needs. Second, it requires that parents be directly involved in the planning of their child's program and placement in special classes, schools, or programs. This includes setting up a conference between the parents and school officials in which the child's individual placement is discussed. Third, it mandates that each child be placed in the *least restrictive environment*. This is not the same as mainstreaming—the placing of special learners in regular classes—with which it has been confused, but rather says that the child should receive maximum services to help overcome his or her disability, whether this is in a special or a regular class. Finally, it requires that each child have an *individualized education program,* an IEP as it has come to be called, that sets forth in detail that particular child's individual curriculum. This last feature is most important.

The Individualized Education Program (IEP)

One of the most important features of the law—and certainly the one that has the greatest impact on the school personnel—is the individualized education program. In the language of the law itself, "The term 'individualized education program' means a written statement for each handicapped child developed in any meeting by a representative of the local educational agency or an intermediate educational unit who shall be qualified to provide, or supervise the provision of, specially designed instruction to meet the unique needs of handicapped children."

The law goes on to explicitly state that this IEP shall include—

1. a statement of the present levels of educational performance of such child,
2. a statement of annual goals, including short-term instructional objectives,
3. a statement of the specific educational services to be provided to such child, and the extent to which such child will be able to participate in regular educational programs,
4. the projected date for initiation and anticipated duration of such services, and
5. appropriate objective criteria and evaluation procedures and schedules for determining, on at least an annual basis, whether instructional objectives are being achieved.

The counselor can (and should!) be an instrumental part in designing, implementing, and evaluating the IEP. This is helpful both in maintaining contact with the student's progress and in offering professional input from the counseling viewpoint. The state is required to maintain these records and to demonstrate that the programs are actually being implemented and regularly evaluated.

The Role of Parents

Possibly in part stimulated by the civil rights and antiwar movements, parents of handicapped children began to become militant during the 1960s and 1970s. Their demands, which said in effect that their children deserved a free appropriate education in the least restrictive learning environment, became in substance the very language of the law that was finally passed by Congress in 1975. Moreover, parents were fully included in that law, included in such a way that they became responsible along with the professional team for the education of their children. They have become what is known as program participants.

First, the due process regulations of the IEP law require that parents be informed at the outset of the purpose and scope of the intended evaluation, and that they approve it in writing. Parents must also be informed of the results of the evaluation and told of the decisions made for placement. They have a right to challenge these decisions through appropriate established channels, and they should be informed of this right. In short, parents are participant partners of the team throughout the procedure.

In addition to the legal requirement of involving parents, there is a practical reason for doing so, and this should be kept in mind at IEP conferences or any other conferences. If the parent feels that he or she is a part of the effort there is more likely to be cooperation at home, and the parent will do everything in his or her power to encourage the child to do well in school.

Figure 12.1 shows the sequence of steps from initial referral through the development of the IEP. We see that the procedure is quite specific and well-organized.

The School Counselor

Because the law has been in effect for only a few years, it is still not clear at this point exactly what part the counselor will play in its implementation, although clearly counselors will become "increasingly involved in program planning, mainstreaming efforts, program monitoring, and counseling parents" (Humes, 1978, p. 192). Clearly, the counselor can be helpful in the initial appraisal phase of the program, since the counselor will be familiar not only with the relevance, validity, and reliability of specific test instruments that are being considered, but also with ways of communicating these

figure 12.1 Flow chart of service arrangements

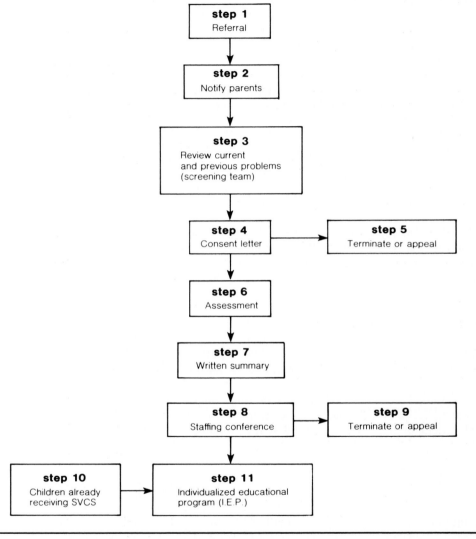

Note. From "An Approach to Operationalizing the IEP" by F. G. Hudson and S. Graham. *Learning Disability Quarterly.* 1978. (1). 1

test results to the parents at the IEP conference. Moreover, the counselor can serve throughout the year as a consultant to the teachers who are working with the handicapped learner.

Huckaby and Daly (1979), in looking at the actual activities of the school counselor during the first year of PL94–142's implementation, point out,

> When a teacher sees students who need more than what is being provided for them in the regular classroom, the teacher usually refers them to the school counselor. The counselor is involved in the process from the beginning referral for special education through placement and follow-up. After the referral is made, achievement data must be gathered, psychological testing done, case conferences with the teacher or team teachers held, Individualized Educational Plans (IEPs) developed, a conference with the parent held, and proper placement made for the student. Throughout this procedure the counselor is involved, not only with coordination, but in interpreting data, in understanding and explaining the student's needs, and in helping develop plans to meet the needs of the total child. (p. 70)

With this in mind, let us briefly look at some major categories of learning exceptionalities, and then consider some of the counseling implications. We will begin with the most common single classification: the learning disabled student.

WHAT IS A LEARNING DISABILITY?

It is in answering this seemingly simple question that some gross misconceptions arise; misconceptions that not only lead to incorrect diagnosis, but that work against appropriate treatment. Gearheart (1977) suggests that "in introducing the concept of learning disabilities to groups such as experienced classroom teachers, school principals, and the like I have found in the past that *at least* 30 to 45 minutes should be planned for the definition [and the following discussion] of what is meant by or included in the learning disabilities definition" (p. 8). We see, then, that defining "learning disability" is no easy matter.

The most inclusive and accurate definition of a *learning disability* would be any condition or set of conditions that prevents a person from functioning at grade level in one or in several areas. This would include such conditions as perceptual disorders, motor disorders, brain damage (mild), or what are generally referred to as learning blocks that affect only one specific area of learning endeavor.

Several conditions may interact to produce a learning disability. A perceptual disability may be compounded by motor problems with the result that the student cannot learn to write even though he or she is intellectually capable of doing so. Almost all learning disabilities are in areas that interact with other areas, so that the single problem can blossom into a serious symptom, similar to retardation. However, closer analysis shows that the child is not retarded, but simply experiencing difficulty in one or several areas. Six basic categories of problem areas are usually cited (Myers & Hammill, 1976, p. 26): (1) motor activity, (2) emotionality, (3) perception, (4) symbolization, (5) attention, and (6) memory. "These categories," they point out, "are not mutually exclusive groupings; in fact, learning disabled children tend to exhibit behavior associated with several, and occasionally all, categories." It is necessary, therefore, that in order to diagnose a problem as a learning disability, we should be able to assess in which of these categories the specific problem falls.

The diagnosis and remediation of learning disabilities is primarily the job of the classroom teacher, who has the most consistent opportunity to observe, evaluate, and work with the student. In many instances, however, a learning disabilities specialist or a school counselor may be called in for specific diagnosis, prognosis, or suggested treatment approaches. One of the major problems facing teachers or specialists is the abundance of terms that overwhelm them when they consider learning disabilities. Let us begin our discussion, then, by attempting to clarify some of the terminology.

Sorting Out Terminology

The three most popular terms in describing a learning disability are *dyslexia, minimal brain dysfunction* (MBD) and *hyperkinesis* (hyperactivity). While *dyslexia* is a reasonably precise term, the other two are much more vague and almost interchangeable at times. They are confused in the literature—easily switched—and both are nonspecific and nonexclusive enough to have little or no clinical or diagnostic value. Sulzbacher (1975), among others, has referred to this interchangeability and discrepancy in use:

> It is an unfortunate truism that most of the diagnostic procedures used with children who have learning disabilities and hyperactivity are not helpful in deciding on treatment. Although at least 92 diagnostic terms have been used to describe behavior and learning disorders in children with average intelligence, the terms "learning disability," "minimal brain dysfunction" (MBD) and "hyperactivity" seem to have gained widespread acceptance. The term MBD is most frequently used in medical literature, while "learning disability"

table 12.1

VARIOUS DIAGNOSES ASCRIBED TO H–LD CHILDREN

group 1/organic terminology

association deficit pathology
cerebral dysfunction
cerebral dys-synchronization syndrome
chorelform syndrome
diffuse brain damage
minimal brain damage
minimal brain injury
minimal cerebral damage
minimal cerebral injury
minimal cerebral palsy
minimal chronic brain syndromes
minor brain damage
neurophrenia
organic behavior disorder
organic brain damage
organic brain disease
organic brain dysfunction
organic drivenness

group 2/symptomatic terminology

aggressive behavior disorder
aphasoid syndrome
attention disorders
character impulse disorder
clumsy child syndrome
conceptually handicapped
dyslexia
educationally handicapped
    (California State Legislature AB464)
hyperexcitability syndrome
hyperkinetic behavior syndrome
hyperkinetic impulse disorder
hyperkinetic syndrome
hypokinetic syndrome
interjacent child
learning disabilities
perceptual cripple
perceptually handicapped
primary reading retardation
psychoneurological learning disorders
specific reading disability

Note: From "Hyperkinesis and Learning Disabilities Linked to Artificial Food Flavors and Colors" by B.F. Feingold, *American Journal of Nursing*, 1975, *75* (5), p. 799.

and "hyperactivity" are most frequently used by educators and psychologists. Peters et al. (1973) have suggested that "MD" be used as the term to describe children who have both a learning disability and hyperactivity, that "learning disability" be reserved for children with academic difficulty, but no signs of overactivity, and that "hyperactivity" be applied to overactive or impulsive children who nevertheless are performing satisfactorily academically. The children with both symptom complexes—MBD—are the largest segment of this population. (p. 938)

It is clear from this passage, that there is much confusion surrounding the terms. Table 12.1 shows a variety of different diagnoses that are typically ascribed to learning disabled children (Feingold, 1975). But this is only the beginning of the confusion.

IDENTIFICATION OF THE LD STUDENT

Usually the manifestation of a learning disability will be apparent to the teacher or counselor during the first two years of the child's formal schooling. A number of factors may lead to the conclusion that a child has a learning disability: inability to follow simple instructions or to repeat processes; functioning in one or several areas that is grossly below grade level; confusion in orientation; performance anomalies (such as turning to the left when instructed to turn to the right, or confusing *up* and *down,* or *forward* and *backward*). The first process, then, by which a learning disability is usually identified is observation.

It is generally agreed that systematic behavior observation is the most practical and economical screening technique for identifying the learning disabled student. Studies have demonstrated that this procedure does have objective value. Forness and Esveldt (1975) report the results of a study that indicates that teachers are able to identify disabled learners through careful, educated observation. DeGenero (1975) has described informal methods for assessing children suspected of having a learning disability. In attempting to answer the teacher's question, What can I do before the psychometrist arrives? DeGenero argues in favor of "informal assessment." He presents informal methods by which the teacher can assess fourteen basic areas that include all of the learning disabilities:

1. Visual discrimination and memory
2. Auditory discrimination and memory
3. Letter identification
4. Writing the alphabet sequence
5. Phonetic knowledge
6. Tactual ability
7. Reversals and rotations
8. Verbal skills (oral)
9. Copying at near and far points
10. Reading levels
11. Self-concept
12. Eye-hand coordination and written language
13. Following directions
14. Gross motor skills

These fourteen areas, he argues, are sufficient to provide enough information to enable the teacher to make a general assessment that can then be confirmed by a psychometrist (one who is trained in the psychological technique of mental measurement) or LD specialist. More importantly, these informal procedures will allow the teacher to develop programs until more specific diagnoses can be made.

Although observation is an important tool, a caution must be given. The teacher may show bias in observation, bias that can lead to incorrect, damaging diagnosis and treatment. McAvoy (1970) has explored the issue of systematic observation, defining it as a "formalized system of classifying, recording, and quantifying any form of teacher or pupil behavior that occurs in the classroom. Measurable variables in the classroom can be defined in one of three categories: presage, process, and product" (p. 10). *Presage variables* are "those characteristics which a teacher or pupil brings to the classroom." *Process variables* "include those behaviors, moves or strategies which are employed by a teacher or pupil in a classroom situation." *Product variables* "are measures of instructional outcomes." Using these categories, McAvoy suggests several possibilities for using systematic observation to increase teaching effectiveness. Applications of these procedures are especially helpful in identifying and treating the disabled learner.

A general guideline that has been used in identification is to measure the *discrepancy* between learner potential and actual achievement; between aptitude and ability (Myklebust & Johnson, 1967). This is a widely-held paradigm for identifying a learning disability. Salvia and Clark (1973), in discussing the "discrepancy" measure as a diagnostic criterion, point out, however, that although "deficits may provide the clinician diagnostician with insights about a child which can be refined on the basis of additional data, [they] are too unreliable for diagnostic purposes" (p. 308). The discrepancy should more appropriately be used as one of several measures in assessing a learning disability. The observation method is one of several used to this end, but there are also others.

More commonly used than the observation method is the administration of a test instrument or a clinical interview accompanied by a protocol (a formal record, or system of notetaking). These may be used for early screening or later differential diagnosis of learning disabilities. There are a variety of these instruments available, and the teacher should take the responsibility for assessing their accuracy and validity. While the teacher may be responsible for diagnosis, in most cases an outside consultant (the school psychologist, a consulting psychiatrist, etc.) is responsible for the administration and interpretation of a test or for the clinical examination. This has been shown to be generally effective as a diagnostic procedure. Keele et al. (1975) have shown a high rate of correct diagnosis by pediatric specialists, indicating the value of medical knowledge in assessment. "The results of this study," they point out, "demonstrate the need of a medical evaluation in LD children" (p. 44). Ozer and Richardson (1974) have developed an examination protocol, which they call the "neuro-developmental observation (NDO)," which involves "an interactive process between examiner and child; the examiner responds to the child's attempt to perform a set of prototype tasks with supportive feedback and provides new ways to try the task until the child is successful'' (p. 30). Although this was developed by physicians, it can be used by the teacher or other trained examiner.

The teacher's familiarity with different types of learning disorders will be an important factor in his or her ability to identify and appropriately treat a specific disorder. But even more important will be the teacher's attitude toward the learner. As Adams (1975) aptly points out, one of the problems in classifying children with a label, such as LD or reading disabled, is that "it overlooks the child himself. The classification approach has run into trouble over the years because we are dealing with human beings" (p. 160). She points out that definitions may sometimes confuse teachers more than help them, and that "they need reassuring that, despite the label, the child *can* be taught."

Although we will consider some of the major categories of learning disabilities in the following sections, it must again be strongly emphasized that the overlap in terminology and the lack of specificity in diagnosis make it essential that the teacher attempt to understand the *total* learner, rather than looking at the learner in terms of a diagnostic label. As Moss (1973) points out, in discussing the question of labelling:

> The controversy over what to call a child, or why to label him at all, must be puzzling to people who interact daily with individual children. In my opinion, much of the confusion results from an unfounded hope that there is a single, rational, scientific, and logical basis for the distinctions which are made among categories of children. Such classifications make sense only if one understands that classification takes place for more than one reason. A classification system (or a label) is a useful tool for accomplishing some purpose. As long as it is used for that purpose and only that purpose it makes some sense. Trouble occurs when a given classification device is used for a purpose other than that for which it was designed. (p. 387)

With this in mind, we will look at the three most common classifications of learning disorders.

MINIMAL BRAIN DYSFUNCTION (MBD)

Minimal brain dysfunction (MBD) is a diagnostic term that characterizes a variety of behavioral and learning disorders that are commonly evident in the classroom. In characterizing the MBD child, Ellingson (1967) indicates, "This is the child who is intellectually capable, but due to some form of trauma is 'different' from other children—the child who can function if the correct teaching techniques are used to overcome his perceptual difficulties and he is given guidance and taught inner controls for his conceptual and behavioral problems" (p. 39). It is important to note in this definition that the child's functioning or malfunctioning is entirely a consequence of the training given; that is, of the use of appropriate techniques.

Despite the medical and organic implications of the term, MBD is not *necessarily* a physical disorder, and its chief diagnostic criteria are clinical (through observations in the classroom) rather than neurological. The term has been flagrantly overused, with the result that it has lost most of its denotative meaning. Barton D. Schmitt, a physician, complains that "the current problem with the MBD syndrome is that it has become an all-encompassing, wastebasket diagnosis for any child who does not quite conform to society's stereotype of normal children" (Schmitt, 1975, p. 1313). He argues that the term is essentially meaningless, and should be disregarded as a valid diagnostic category.

Other educators and researchers, however, are trying to give meaning back to the term by specifying its usage and showing how it relates to other common diagnostic terms. Abrams (1975), for example, defines MBD in terms of inadequate ego functioning or in terms of specific learning disabilities, avoiding any physiological implications. His comments on the interchangeability of terms is revealing:

> Many of you have probably noted . . . that I have used MBD and reading disability almost synonymously. Essentially again, whatever term is utilized depends primarily upon the orientation and interest of the individual assessing the problems. When an individual is concerned particularly with a comprehensive diagnosis following a medical model with the assessment of biological concomitants and antecedents of the condition, and with the role of medical management, MBD is the label of choice. (p. 220)

The important point for the teacher is this: there are many technical terms used interchangeably to describe what is essentially the same condition. Ellingson (1975) has found over one hundred terms that are clinically synonymous with MBD.

With this technical confusion in mind, we can describe some of the clinical signs of MBD. Weil (1973) differentiates between *congenital* and *acquired* MBD. The congenital type is indicated by a developmental lag, by "a slowness and initial deficiency in the maturation of certain centers and tracts, and with the consequent clinical lag in the development of corresponding functions." Areas affected may include speech, visual-motor coordination, psychomotor functioning, early reading failures, and so forth. Acquired MBD is usually the result of a childhood disease (especially encephalitis) or trauma (accident). It is diagnosed by sudden changes in the child's characteristic behavior and performance before and after the onset of the disease or trauma. Essentially, however, the symptoms of the two types are the same.

In describing the most typical symptomatology, Weil (1973) points out that "their motility may be damaged by focal lesions or diffusely affected in obvious awkwardness, jerkiness, or clumsiness, or pathology may be revealed only on very special scrutiny and testing." The teacher can be an effective diagnostician in both categories: in the former, through classroom observation; in the latter, through referral to the school psychologist for testing.

"Among the more common complaints of teachers or parents of (MBD) children," Haller and Axelrod (1975) point out, "are that the child is immature and should repeat kindergarten; the child is clumsy; there is a question of brain damage; the child cannot use scissors and the handwriting is sloppy" (p. 1320). These are all typical behaviors associated with MBD, and can be useful diagnostic categories. It should be kept in mind that while these symptoms are troubling to the parents, teachers, and child, they are correctable with appropriate training. I suggest that early intervention be undertaken when the teacher becomes aware of a series of symptoms that, taken together, indicate MBD. Special attention should be directed to each of the five following areas:

1. *Reading performance*—Almost all MBD children experience difficulty in learning to read. Although reading problems in themselves do not always indicate MBD, this is a clear and simple manifest sign.
2. *Impulse disorders*—Again, by itself, this doesn't indicate MBD, but combined with the other symptoms, it is a positive indication.
3. *Anxiety and quick-temperedness*—The MBD child will show general signs of irritability and a predisposition to violent, sudden bursts of temper. In some cases, the opposite dimension, withdrawal, becomes dominant.
4. *Regressed behavior*—Sometimes referred to as immaturity, this symptom can be seen in the child's interactions with other children and with the teacher.
5. *Psychomotor and perceptual abnormalities*—In one or another area, the MBD child usually shows a deficit in motor performance, in perception, or in perceptuo-motor tasks. This may be mild and hardly noticeable; but it should be taken into account when combined with the other symptoms.

Each of these symptoms, in itself or in conjunction with other symptoms, is fully treatable. It is only when they are ignored and allowed to become more integral to the child's general functioning that they become unmanageable.

There is considerable evidence that if the symptomatic problems associated with MBD are not treated in time they are likely to lead to more deep-seated ramifications. Berlin (1974) rightly dispels the old myth that "Children will grow out of their troubles." He concludes from the research data available that "the maladaptive behavior patterns typical of MBD tend to persist. In particular, the children's social interactions and their attitudes toward themselves and their ability to attain gratification from accomplishments, such as learning in school, are dysfunctional" (p. 1454). He, like most experts in the field, emphasizes the importance of early diagnosis.

In terms of future adjustment, there is no reason why the MBD child, if given appropriate training, should not be able to become a productive citizen of this society. Where early intervention has made its mark, the prognosis for success is quite good. Curricular planning can be tailored to include the special needs of the MBD learner, with emphasis on those developmental and socialization skills that other children pick up more quickly and more naturally. The MBD learner can be taught behaviors that will enable him or her to overcome a learning deficiency: behaviors such as increased self-control, mastery of specific tasks, methods for increasing attentiveness, and so on.

One of the most important aspects of educating the MBD child is teaching him or her compensatory behaviors that will lead to productive employment. Since it is not likely that the child will excel (or even perform adequately) in every area of intellectual endeavor touched upon in formal education, it is important to develop not only vocational skills at an early age, but career-mindedness as well. Giving the MBD learner a sense of career is equal to giving him a promise of a future.

THE HYPERACTIVE STUDENT

Hyperactivity is one of the most prevalent of childhood disorders and a major cause of concern to parents, teachers, and school counselors. It is estimated that 5 percent of the elementary school population exhibit mild to severe symptoms of hyperactivity (Ross & Ross, 1976). In this section, I will briefly outline the major theories and findings about hyperactivity, emphasizing the practical applications for the teacher working with the elementary school-age child.

When hyperactive children bid for attention, teachers may find themselves at a loss about how to constructively respond to them.

Diagnosis

It is important for the teacher or clinician to distinguish at the outset between *hyperactivity* and *hyperkinesis*. Although the two terms are used interchangeably, it has been argued (by Zukow, 1975, among others) that they are not the same. Hyperactivity is a descriptive term: it adjectivally pinpoints certain manic types of behavior that are generally inappropriate to the situation. Hyperkinesis, on the other hand, designates a specific disorder: it is characterized by the child's inability to control behavior and actions. A hyperactive child need not necessarily be hyperkinetic. Rather, he or she may be a child with a surplus of energy; with a strong need for physical activity; and with a symptomatic restlessness. The hyperkinetic child, on the other hand, in addition to these characteristics, has a short attention span and other attendant difficulties.

Zukow (1975) points out the difficulties of using the terms interchangeably:

> The problem which arises in using the terms *hyperactive* and *hyperkinetic* interchangeably is more than semantic. For instance, frustrated adults reacting to a child who does not meet their standards can easily exaggerate the significance of the child's occasional inattention and label a youngster hyperkinetic.
>
> A January 1971 HEW report on hyperkinesis says "the normal ebullience of childhood . . . should not be confused with the very special problems of the child with hyperkinetic behavior disorders." The report gives the followng definitions: "There is no known single cause or simple answer for such problems. The major symptoms are an increase of purposeless physical activity and a significantly impaired span of focused attention. The inability to control physical motion and attention may generate other consequences, such as disturbed moods and behavior within the home, at play with peers, and in the schoolroom." (p. 39)

With these admonitions in mind, we can use the terms *hyperactive* and *hyperkinetic* interchangeably, with the assurance that a vital, active young child will not be misdiagnosed and misclassified.

Since hyperactivity may interfere with all major aspects of the child's life, it is vital for the diagnostician to know how the behavior is affecting the child's home life, social interactions, and school performance. A thorough history of the child can be compiled through the use of interviews, behavioral rating scales, physical and neurological examinations, and specific laboratory studies (Cantwell, 1975).

A personal interview with the child's parents serves a dual function. The skilled interviewer can elicit specific factual information about the child, as well as the feelings and expectations of the parents. It is also important to assess the manner in which the alleged "hyperactivity" of the child affects family dynamics. The following are some questions suggested by Cantwell (1975) for use in a parental interview: Is he or she more active than his or her siblings and peers? Do trivial things unduly upset the child? Is she or he quick-tempered and unpredictable? Is this child able to follow directions? The importance of these questions lies in the possibility that the parents might be encouraged to elaborate on "specific examples . . . and the circumstances which appear to precipitate certain aspects of behavior" (p. 22).

To further assess the degree of hyperactivity, parents and teachers are frequently requested to complete rating-scales. Ross and Ross (1976) recommend the Werry-Weiss-Peter Activity Scale for the parents' use. This questionnaire contains items specifically related to the child's activities in the home and should be completed by each parent. To evaluate school behavior, performance, and academic achievement, the Connors Teacher Questionnaire is available for school use. The behavioral rating scales are useful tools for diagnosis, formulation of a treatment plan, and follow-up evaluation.

The final phase of diagnosis consists of a physical and neurological examination along with a laboratory work-up to determine if the disorder is due to organic defects, such as brain damage (including small lesions) or nonspecific visual or auditory impairment.

In addition to these procedures, investigation of familial and cultural factors is an important element in the diagnosis of hyperactivity. Many children who exhibit hyperactive symptoms may be experiencing severe reactions to their current life situations. Many of the behaviors that appear to a middle-class teacher as excessively active and socially inappropriate may be part of the normal repertoire of the culturally disadvantaged youth. Moreover, in many families, children are encouraged, either directly or indirectly, to behave in a way that most teachers would view as socially inappropriate. For example, the child may learn, either at home or in the peer-group environment, that it is necessary to exhibit continual bodily activity in order to gain any type of attention or recognition. It is not that such children *cannot* control themselves, but rather that they have been conditioned not to. When students such as these are referred to as hyperactive children, it is recommended that they be evaluated in relation to their siblings and peers (Klein-Gittleman, 1975).

Etiology

Hyperactivity has been defined within the context of etiological subgroups; from these, four major causative factors have emerged: genetic, organic, psychogenic, and influences of environment (Ross & Ross, 1976). We will examine each one briefly.

Genetic

Several studies have been undertaken in recent years to determine if a link exists between hyperactivity and heredity. These studies involve investigation of first-degree relatives (parents, siblings, children) of hyperactive children, identical and fraternal twins, and adopted children (Ross & Ross, 1976). The results of these studies suggest, *rather than conclude,* that hyperactivity may be genetically transmitted.

Organic

The most ambitious attempt to prove that hyperactivity is a result of brain dysfunction is Wender's study (1971) which explored "the interaction of excitatory and inhibitory systems within the central nervous system." Wender's theories also elaborate on the effectiveness of amphetamines in supplementing a noradrenaline deficiency of the inhibitory system, which had been widely prescribed in the treatment of hyperactivity. Other studies have indicated that hyperactivity may be a "maturational lag," but this term is so vague and nonspecific that it is not especially useful. In short, there is little evidence at this time to support the organic hypothesis, and in fact only a small number of clinically diagnosed cases reveal any neurological anomalies.

Psychogenic

Numerous studies have found that hyperactive youngsters are often the children of hyperactive parents (Cantwell, 1975). One possible explanation for this is the learning of behaviors through role modeling. When the child is exposed to a high activity level in the parents in the home, it is likely that she or he will "absorb" some of these behaviors—introject them, as psychoanalysts would say. Imitation of a parent's overly active behavior on a long-term basis would most likely produce a behavior syndrome that is later identified as hyperactivity.

A stressful mother-child relationship may also be a cause of some children's hyperactivity. Bettelheim (1973) has suggested that a predisposition for hyperactivity exists in some children, and this predisposition blossoms into a full-fledged condition through the relationship with the mother. The nervous and frustrated mother, who induces many of these feelings into her child, may be precipitating the hyperactive disorder.

A number of studies have examined idiosyncratic patterns in the family relationships of hyperactive children and adolescents. While there is no clear evidence that the families of hyperactive children necessarily produce problematic children, there are some interesting indications about the family interactions. Campbell (1975), for example, investigated the mother-child interactions between hyperactive and "normal" boys. She observed them interacting in a structured problem-solving situation, and found that the mothers of the hyperactive boys showed a "higher level of involvement in task solution, and reported more behavior problems than did mothers in comparison groups" (p. 51). It is difficult to draw valid conclusions from these observations, but she suggests that:

> These results are consistent with those of a previous study in which mothers of hyperactive boys provided more structure and suggestions about impulse control than did mothers of normal boys. In addition, mothers of the hyperactive boys in this study intervened more during the problem-solving situation than did mothers of clinic boys who were seen as primarily learning disabled. Mothers of hyperactives made more non-specific suggestions, more suggestions about impulse control, were more encouraging and also more disapproving than were mothers of the two comparison groups. Although it was anticipated that mothers of learning disabled boys would intervene more than control mothers, in this sample no differences reached significance despite some slight trend in the expected direction. Similarly, hyperactive boys made significantly more requests for feedback as well as comments on the tasks and their won performance.
>
> Taken together, these data suggest that the mothers of the hyperactive group were responding in the interaction situation so as to structure the tasks and thereby optimize performance. It could be argued that mothers of hyperactive boys, by providing suggestions about task solution and impulse control, as well as negative feedback and encouragement, were attempting to provide direction and keep attention focused on the task at hand. . . . Hyperactive boys elicited and maintained a high level of interaction by requesting more feedback and making more comments throughout the interaction sessions. They engaged in a running commentary on the tasks and their own performance, and were rarely silent when compared with their learning disabled and normal peers. (pp. 55–56)

These conclusions suggest that in making a diagnosis it may be useful to examine directly the interaction between the hyperactive child and the mother. But I must again caution against assuming that the behavior of the mother precipitates the hyperactive problem, rather than the other way around. Little attention has been directed toward a coherent psychodynamic explanation of the etiology of hyperactivity. A number of psychoanalysts have suggested that hyperactivity may be a symptom related to the unconscious wish to express aggression. Others have cited the symptoms as evidence of intense libidinal strivings, which are frustrated in the parent-child relationship. Blos (1960) described the hyperactive condition, before the term was fashionable, citing several cases of young boys with undescended testicles that led to exaggerated distortions of the body image:

> Hypermotility in these cases constituted a complex form of behavior in which the pressure of instinctual drives, anxiety, and defensive operations were tightly organized. Hyperactive, aimless, and erratic moving about had a frantic, searching, anxious quality which at times invited danger and resulted in accidents. (p. 416)

Many other psychoanalysts have noted the accident proneness of hyperactive youngsters. While such accidents are often dismissed as the inevitable consequence of "so much running around," one could interpret their frequency as evidence of psychogenic self-destructiveness. In any case, there is considerable reason to investigate further the familial environment that may lead to or be a consequence of the hyperactive condition.

Environmental Influences

The types of studies that earn the greatest attention in the press and the media are the environmental studies. These have shown, at one time or another, that such everyday things as food coloring, chocolate, cola, fluorescent lights, insecticides, and milk products contribute to the formation of the hyperactive syndrome. Salicylates (found in aspirin, toothpaste, soft drinks, etc.) and food additives have been investigated as possible causes of hyperactive behaviors in children. Allergic reactions to these substances have been attributed to the hyperactive child's "constitutionally low threshold for activation of the sympathetic division of the autonomic system" (Hawley & Buckley, 1974). Diets in which these substances were eliminated caused a positive reaction in 50 percent of the children who were treated (Feingold, 1975).

In one interesting study (Ross & Ross, 1976), John Ott, a photobiologist, examined the effects of radiation stress caused by exposure to fluorescent lighting. In a ninety-day experiment, Ott observed the activities of hyperactive children in four classrooms. Two rooms had standard fluorescent lights, and two had shielded, full-spectrum fluorescent lights. Hyperactive behavior in the two classrooms that were illuminated by the shielded lights decreased dramatically. Hyperactive behaviors in the rooms with the standard fluorescent lights was maintained.

Prognosis

It is generally assumed that hyperactive boys tend to "outgrow" this condition by the time they reach adolescence, although there is some evidence to contradict this assumption. At the present time, there is insufficient empirical evidence from which to generalize. Even if hyperactive youngsters *do* outgrowth the condition, however, if appropriate interventions have not been made by adolescence, the damage is already done. The learning deficits that are acquired during the years that the hyperactive child is not able to function properly in the classroom result in a serious deficit later on. For this reason it is imperative that early interventions be undertaken in order to avoid these problems later on.

Borland and Heckman (1976) conducted a twenty-five year follow-up study of hyperactive boys. They examined the patient records at a Pennsylvania guidance clinic for boys between the ages of four to eleven who were treated between 1950 and 1955. From these records, they identified a specific group of what we would now call hyperactive youngsters. From this group of thirty-seven subjects selected, they were able to locate (25 years later!) twenty-five men, twenty of whom agreed to participate in the study. Detailed interviews were conducted with eighteen of these men and, wherever possible, with their brothers. The interview focused on information about subsequent education, family relations, emotional problems, drug and alcohol addiction, neurosis (hysteria), and other related matters. Information was also obtained about the children of these subjects, and specifically about any problems they might be having in school. School records for these children were also examined wherever possible.

An insightful analysis of the data showed some important findings. By the time of the follow-up, all of the subjects and their brothers were either working full time or were college students. Many of the early symptoms (as obtained from the clinic records) were still present, although the number of the symptoms had been significantly reduced, as noted by the interviewers; but the subjects were functioning appropriately. Compared with their brothers, the subjects of the study worked more hours, many holding part-time jobs in addition to their full-time occupations. They also exhibited greater symptoms of nervousness and restless, hyperactive behavior.

The study was quite thorough and allows us some information about what happens to hyperactive boys when they grow up. While there were a number of important conclusions drawn, the researchers summarize some of their important observations in this comment:

> Our findings indicate that men who were hyperactive 20 to 25 years ago are not experiencing serious social or psychiatric problems as adults. A large majority had completed high school, a few had gone to college, each man

was steadily employed and self-supporting, and most had achieved middle-class status. However, half of the men who had been hyperactive continued to show a number of major symptoms of hyperactivity. Nearly half of the probands [subjects] had problems of a psychiatric nature, and despite normal IQ scores and levels of education, men who were hyperactive had never achieved a socioeconomic status equal to their brothers. . . .

The number and intensity of symptoms of hyperactivity had decreased considerably in men who were hyperactive 20 to 25 years ago. Relative to their brothers, however, these men continued to show an excess of symptoms of hyperactivity and problems associated with the disorder. Restlessness, nervousness, and difficulty with temper were present in half of the probands at the interview, and a substantial minority of these men continued to be impulsive, easily upset, or often sad, blue, or depressed. These characteristics clearly distinguish at least half of the men who were hyperactive from their brothers. (p. 673)

While much of the literature concerns itself with the diagnosis and etiology of hyperactivity, the bulk of recent writings has directed attention to ways of treating the hyperactive child both in and out of the classroom setting. Wide varieties of treatment approaches, ranging from formal psychoanalysis, to curricular innovations, to the use of amphetamine drugs have been suggested. Many, but not all of these theories, have been tested, with varying degrees of success. Silver (1975) has surveyed the vast literature and identified what he calls the "acceptable" and the "controversial" therapies now being used in the treatment of hyperkinesis. The acceptable therapies include special education, medication with stimulant drugs, medication with tranquilizers and antidepressants and anticonvulsants, and different forms of psychotherapy. These have not all proved successful, by any means, but they are acceptable modes of treatment, simply because of their repeated use. The "controversial" forms of treatment are neurophysiological retraining, orthomolecular medicine, alpha-wave conditioning, and food additives. Within each of these broad categories fall hundreds of different treatment approaches, many of which can be considered to fall under the "acceptable" categories.

TO DRUG OR NOT TO DRUG?

An issue of controversy that has arisen in regard to the education of both the learning disabled and hyperactive students is the use of medication. In our culture, there has evolved over the years an uncompromising psychological belief in the curative value of drugs. We believe, rightly or wrongly, that there exists some effective medication for almost any kind of problem, physical or psychological. This belief is reinforced by powerful television commercials that glorify the medicinal value of nonprescription "over-the-counter" drugs and by physicians who prescribe drugs quite freely and often impulsively. Moreover, this inveterate belief in medication is fueled and fanned by our deeply rooted psychological need to feel secure in the hands of medical science. This unconscious need, so strong and so taken for granted that only a few cynics have challenged its credulity, has had a profound effect on the way we treat many of the exceptional individuals in our society. In effect, it has encouraged the almost promiscuous use of drugs to treat a wide variety of disorders. At the same time, a backlash mentality has reared its head, and its demanding bellowing has had the unfortunate effect of intimidating professional educators, who would otherwise be calm and circumspect in their professional judgment. The fierce emotions generated by this issue have rendered many of the impartial investigations secondary to the more flamboyant rhetoric of discussions concerning it.

In this section we will strive for balance. First, we will consider the general question of the value of medication. Then, we will look at the medications most often prescribed, their proven and assumed values, and their legitimate uses and typical abuses as they are found in exceptional conditions. Recognizing that, while these medications are often abused, they also offer hope to many individuals who would not have hope without them, we will take a middle position and show the pros and cons of drug therapy.

Panacea or Placebo?

The two terms *panacea* and *placebo* are central to understanding the underlying complexities of the drug controversy and in assessing its impact on treatment. The word *panacea* means a "cure-all," but it is generally used in the disparaging sense of something that teasingly promises a cure but doesn't produce it. It connotes the old-time medicine man, peddling his curative tonics from travelling coaches in the old West. A *placebo* is not a real drug—usually a sugar pill—whose only significant effect is the belief that the user has in it. The term *placebo effect* has been coined to express the significance the power of belief in a drug has on its efficacy. Often, a placebo—a sugar pill—will work as effectively as the "real" medication because of the person's belief in it.

Medical evidence today strongly suggests that the placebo effect is to be taken seriously. Not only does the placebo appear to be medically effective, but its very efficacy may be a result of its "cuing" the individual to react in a certain way. This is the principle of suggestibility, and it has many important implications in the pro and con arguments about drug administration to "difficult" children.

Cousins (1977) has reviewed scores of studies on placebo efficacy, and has concluded that not only is the placebo often *as* effective as the medication, but it frequently produces similar side effects. He views the effective power of the placebo as it relates to the human condition, which helps us understand more clearly how perhaps it is something other than the chemical composition of a medication that is having the effect on the patient.

> In the end, the greatest value of the placebo is what it can tell us about life. . . . What we see ultimately is that the placebo isn't really necessary and that the mind can carry out its difficult and wondrous missions unprompted by little pills. *The placebo is only a tangible object made essential in an age that feels uncomfortable with intangibles, an age that prefers to think that every inner effect must have an outer cause.* Since it has size and shape and can be hand-held, the placebo satisfies the contemporary craving for visible mechanisms and visible answers. But the placebo dissolves on scrutiny, telling us that it cannot relieve us of the need to think deeply about ourselves. (p. 16, italics added)

We can infer from this statement three ideas that can help us come to grips with our conflicting positions. First, there is no single drug, no panacea, that can cure the wide variety of psychological and physical ills that plague us. The only such agent would have to be a placebo and, therefore, a product of our own beliefs. Many of these apparent "ills" are signs of deeper discontents, and should be viewed as such. Second, we must be aware when we consider the value of any medication, we must take into account the placebo effect to see if in some way it is significant in the presumed effectiveness of the medication. This is now universally recognized in all scientific experimentation involving the effects of medication on human subjects. Finally, we should note that regardless of the condition, the human mind—the will—has a powerful effect in helping to resolve difficulties, and this cannot be ignored. What this implies is that the individual, given the right set of conditions and beliefs, can usually cure herself or himself. As Norman Cousins (1977) says at the conclusion of his powerful article, "The placebo is the doctor who resides within us."

Chemotherapy: An Overview

With these injunctions in mind, we can survey some of the general applications of drug treatment. *Chemotherapy,* the treatment by drugs, has been applied to a wide variety of psychological and learning problems faced by the exceptional individual. Most prominently it has been used in the treatment of neurotic anxiety, depression, psychotic disorders, hyperactivity (hyperkinesis), minimal brain dysfunction (MBD), varieties of epilepsy, problems in concentration, a host of learning disabilities, chronic obesity, impulsive behavior disorders, and narcolepsy. A brief overview of the categories of drugs most often prescribed, and the conditions for which they are indicated, will help the teacher or other nonmedical practitioner understand the dosage and potential side effects of the learner's medication. A particularly valuable reference tool for all practitioners in special education is the *Physician's Desk Reference* (commonly called the *PDR*), which catalogues almost all available medications and offers relevant information, including indications, counter-indications, dosage, an illustration of the medication, and so forth. The teacher will often find that looking up a student's medication in the *PDR* enables him or her to have some insight into how (and for what condition) medical personnel are treating a student.

The most typically prescribed medications are generally listed under the standard categories of minor tranquilizers, major tranquilizers, stimulants, and antidepressants. The term *major tranquilizers,* however, while still commonly used by nonmedical (and nonpsychiatric) practitioners, has come under challenge in recent times as a misnomer because of its descriptive inaccuracy, and the more accurate term *neuroleptics* has been substituted in its place (Klerman, 1975). Table 12.2 lists some of the more widely prescribed drugs in these categories, their symptomatic indications, their typical dosage, and some possible side effects.

Minor tranquilizers "are used by themselves in neurotic disorders and *sometimes* in conjunction with major tranquilizers or antidepressants in more major psychiatric conditions like severe depressions and psychoses" (Bockar, 1976, p. 63). Their effect is relatively mild, and can be characterized as producing a general feeling of relaxation and reduction of anxiety. Valium, one of the minor tranquilizers, is the most commonly prescribed drug in the United States today. While these drugs are not especially dangerous, they do have an addictive potential and can produce some minor side effects. They are most dangerous when mixed with other drugs, such as alcohol. At high dosages (three times the recommended dosage or over) they can be extremely dangerous, or even fatal.

Major tranquilizers, or *neuroleptics,* while used in the treatment of severe neurotic conditions, are prescribed most often for psychotic disorders. They are powerful drugs that can reduce or eliminate psychotic behavior episodes (including hallucinations, delusions, and impulsive antisocial behavior), as well as extreme debilitating neurotic anxiety. They "have the capacity to reduce both subjective feelings of and objective signs of tension, anxiety, and agitation, and this is an important area of usefulness in the psychoneuroses." (Winkelman, 1975, p. 168). Neuroleptics have a number of striking side effects. They may produce torpor and indifference, physical reactions, and a general sleepiness. Side effects as well as efficacy is related directly to the dosage, which varies from individual to individual.

The *antidepressants* are powerful drugs that differ from the major tranquilizers in that they will have little or no effect on nonsymptomatic patients. There are two categories of antidepressants: the *tricyclics* and the *monoamine oxidase inhibitors* (MAOIs); the latter are so dangerous that they are rarely used in unsupervised or noninstitutionalized patients. Generally, the tricyclics are prescribed for severe depression, and these are outlined in table 12.2. There is also some evidence that one of the tricyclics (imipramine) may be effective in the treatment of severe phobic conditions (Gittelman-Klein, 1975). We should note too that these drugs may take several weeks to work, and during the "waiting period" the patient may show no improvement. This is to be expected, and the psychotherapist, counselor, or teacher can be helpful and supportive during this phase.

Probably the category of drugs with which the classroom teacher will be most familiar are the stimulant drugs, widely used in the treatment of hyperactivity and learning-behavioral disorders. While amphetamines were originally prescribed routinely—some say promiscuously—recent practice is toward prescribing less potent stimulant drugs, such as methylphenidate (Ritalin) and pemoline (Cylert) and using the amphetamines in more severe cases. The medical and ethical questions of using drugs in the treatment of MBD and hyperactivity are complex ones, and we should consider the issue in some detail.

The Treatment of Hyperkinesis and MBD

By 1973, over 150,000 children were receiving stimulant drug therapy for learning and behavioral disorders (Sroufe & Stewart, 1973). Several classes of stimulant drugs were available, and research was focused on their comparative benefits and risks. Before this time, the federal government had approved amphetamines to be "safe and proper treatment" for children suffering from behavioral disorders (Breggin, 1974). Pediatricians, psychiatrists, and family practitioners routinely prescribed Dexedrine and other amphetamines for a host of behavioral problems in the school and in the home setting.

The widespread use of psychoactive drugs in the treatment of hyperactivity has become an issue of heated contention in recent years. Physicians and educators demand empirical, long-term studies to determine possible deleterious effects of prolonged drug administration. Grinspoon and Singer

table 12.2

DRUGS USED IN THE TREATMENT OF BEHAVIORAL AND LEARNING DISORDERS

category	brand name	generic name	usual dosage	description
Minor tranquilizers *(Used in the treatment of neurotic anxiety)* *(Side effects include fatigue, drowsiness, and, rarely, confusion)*	Valium	diazepam	2 mg. to 10 mg. 2 to 4 times daily.	white, 2 mg.; yellow, 5 mg.; blue, 10 mg.
	Librium	chlorodiazepoxide (HCL)	for mild anxiety: 5 or 10 mg. 3 or 4 times daily. for severe anxiety: 20 or 25 mg. 3 or 4 times daily.	5 mg., green/yellow; 10 mg., green/black; 25 mg., green/white
	Miltown	meprobamate	*Adults:* 1200 to 1600 mg. daily, administered in 3 or 4 doses. *Children:* 100 mg. to 200 mg. 3 to 4 times daily.	200 mg., sugar coated; 400 mg., white scored; 600 mg., white capsule shaped tablet
Major tranquilizers (neuroleptics) *(Used in the treatment of psychotic disorders: sometimes effective for severe schizophrenic reactions)* *(Side effects include: may impair mental and physical functioning in a variety of ways)*	Thorazine	chlorpromazine	*Adults:* dosage varies according to severity of condition. *Children:* not over 75 mg. daily.	Supplied as: tablets, time-release capsules, & ampuls
	Mellaril	thioridazine	*Adults:* total daily dosage 200–800 mg., in 2 to 4 doses. *Children:* moderate disorders: 10 mg., 2 or 3 times daily; severely disturbed or psychotic: 25 mg., 2 or 3 times daily.	Coated tablets, color coded, with dosage indicated on face of tablet. 10 mg., 15 mg., 25 mg., 50 mg., 100 mg., 150 mg., 200 mg.
	Stelazine	trifluoperazine	*Adults:* office patients: 1 or 2 mg. twice daily; Hospitalized patients: 2 mg. to 5 mg., twice daily. *Children:* adjusted to weight of child—usually 1 mg. or 2 mg. 1 or 2 times daily.	Blue coated tablets in doses of 1 mg., 2 mg., 5 mg., 10 mg.
Major tranquilizers (neuroleptics) *(Used in the treatment of psychotic disorders: sometimes effective for severe schizophrenic reactions)* *(Side effects include: may impair mental and physical functioning in a variety of ways)*	Prolixin	fluphenazine	*Adults:* 2.5 to 10 mg., given at 6 to 8 hr. intervals. *Children:* not indicated.	Color coded tablets: 1 mg., pink; 2.5 mg., yellow; 5 mg., green
	Haldol	haloperidol	*Adults:* moderately disturbed: 0.5 mg. to 2.0 mg., 2 or 3 times daily; severely disturbed: 3 to 5 mg., 2 or 3 times daily. *Children:* not indicated.	color coded scored tablets: 0.5 mg., white; 1 mg., yellow; 2 mg., pink; 5 mg., green; 10 mg., aqua
	Loxitane	loxapine succinate	Usual maintenance dosage is 60 to 100 mg/day. Initial dosage varies. Not indicated for children.	color coded capsules: 10 mg., green/yellow; 25 mg., green two tone; 50 mg., green/blue

category	brand name	generic name	usual dosage	description
Antidepressants *(Used in the treatment of severe psychotic depressive conditions, including suicidal behavior)* *(Side effects include: may impair mental and physical functioning in a variety of ways, including confusion, agitation, and exacerbation of psychotic conditions)*	Elavil	amitriptyline	*Adults:* outpatients, 75 mg. to 150 mg. in divided dosage daily. *Adolescents:* 10 mg. three times daily, with 20 mg. at bedtime. *Children:* not recommended for children under 12.	color coded tablets: 10 mg., blue; 25 mg., yellow; 50 mg., beige; 75 mg., orange; 100 mg., mauve
	Tofranil (also used in the treatment of childhood enuresis)	imipramine	*Adults:* outpatients, 50 to 150 mg. daily is usual maintenance dosage. *Children:* 6 to 12 yrs., 25 mg. nightly. *Adolescents:* up to 75 mg. nightly.	10 mg. triangular coral; 25 mg., round coral with black Geigy imprint; 50 mg., round coral with white Geigy imprint
Antidepressants *(Used in the treatment of severe psychotic depressive conditions, including suicidal behavior)* *(Side effects include: may impair mental and physical functioning in a variety of ways, including confusion, agitation, and exacerbation of psychotic conditions)*	Vivactil	protriptyline	*Adults:* usually, 15 mg. to 40 mg. daily in 3 or 4 doses. *Adolescents:* usually 5 mg. 3 times daily, increased if necessary. *Children:* not recommended for children.	color coded: 5 mg., orange oval; 10 mg., yellow oval
	Norpramine	desipramine	*Adults:* 50 mg., 3 times daily. *Adolescent:* 25 mg. to 50 mg. daily.	25 mg., yellow coated tablets; 50 mg., green coated tablets.
	Sinequan	doxepin	*Adults:* 25 mg. to 75 mg., 3 times daily, depending on severity of disorder. Maximum 300 mg. daily. *Children:* not recommended for children under 12.	two-color capsules, 10 mg., pink/brown; 25 mg., blue/pink; 50 mg., white/pink; 100 mg., white/blue.
Stimulants *(Used in the treatment of MBD, hyperkinesis and some learning disabilities)* *(Side effects include paradoxical agitation, skin rashes; drowsiness and confusion, and some physical reactions are possible)*	Ritalin	methylphenidate	*Children:* (6 yrs. and over) varies from 5 mg. twice daily to 20 mg. 3 times daily. Dosage is usually adjusted over a month period.	color coded scored tablets: 5 mg., yellow; 10 mg., green; 20 mg., peach
	Cylert	pemoline	*Children:* given as a single oral dose in the morning: from 37.5 mg. to 75 mg. daily.	color coded scored tablets: 18.75 mg., yellow; 37.5 mg., orange; 75 mg., tan
	Dexedrine	dextroamphetamine sulfate	*Children:* for treatment of MBD; 3 to 5 yrs. of age: 2.5 mg. and up daily. Over 6 yrs. old: 5 mg. to 15 mg., 2 or 3 times daily.	5 mg., orange triangle tablets time-release capsules: 5 mg., 10 mg., 15 mg.

(1973), in a comprehensive review of the available research on the effects of amphetamines, conclude "that the possible adverse effects and unknown long-term risks require further exploration." Bosco (1975) cautions us that "the decision to recommend medical consultation should not be made until there is reasonable assurance that the child's problem does not stem from the inadequacies of the teacher or other aspects of the school environment" (p. 491). This is an especially important injunction in view of the fact that drugs are sometimes abused by school personnel who recommend their use in order to quell classroom disturbances that could probably be dealt with by other means.

As we mentioned earlier, in addition to the amphetamines, the drugs most commonly prescribed for the treatment of MBD and hyperactivity are Ritalin and Cylert. Ritalin (methylphenidate hydrochloride) is a stimulant drug, classified by the Food and Drug Administration as "effective" in the treatment of MBD and hyperkinesis. It has been widely studied, both in controlled double-blind studies and in individual clinical case situations.

In one important study, Conners (1972) compared the effects of Dexedrine, Ritalin, and a placebo on a group of students who had been referred by physicians, by the school, or by agency clinicians for a variety of academic or behavioral difficulties or both. Careful intake assured the integrity of the sampled groups, and the drugs were administered in the double-blind condition in which neither experimenter nor subjects knew what they were getting. Twenty-nine subjects were administered Ritalin, twenty-four were given Dexedrine, and twenty-two were given a placebo. After six weeks of treatment, the subjects' post-treatment performance on a variety of psychological tests (IQ, perceptual ability, and others) was compared with their pre-treatment performance. In all cases the treated group improved over the nontreated groups, with Ritalin generally the most effective medication. In terms of side effects, "both drugs produced significantly more insomnia and anorexia [loss of appetite] than placebo controls" (p. 704).

Other studies have borne out the effectiveness of Ritalin. Sleator and Von Neumann (1974) found methylphenidate a useful medication in over 70 percent of the forty-six hyperactive children tested. Millichap (1973) reports on several double-blind controlled studies conducted by him and his colleagues in which the efficacy of Ritalin was clearly and unequivocally demonstrated over a placebo and concludes:

> Methylphenidate is indicated as an adjunct to remedial education in the short-term treatment of children with MBD. It may be expected to induce small, but measurable improvements in tests of general intelligence and visual-motor perception, control hyperactivity in the more active patients with neurological abnormalities, and reduce impulsive behavior. The use of methylphenidate . . . in the long-term management of children with learning disorders must await their evaluation by more prolonged control studies. (p. 325)

In one such long-term study, Weiss, Kruger, Danielson and Elman (1975) followed the progress of twenty-four subjects who were treated with Ritalin over a three to five year period. They concluded that "methylphenidate was helpful in making hyperactive children more manageable at home and at school, but did not significantly affect their outcome after five years of treatment" (p. 159). In a single-subject study, Shafto and Sulzbacher (1977) point out that even though increasing doses of Ritalin do increase attention, it also produces some undesirable side effects. We will see, in the conclusions of this section, the underlying consistency between all of these studies.

Many of the Ritalin studies also include Cylert in the design. The Conners report cited earlier (Conners, 1972) found Cylert to be significantly superior to the placebo and after the eighth week, as effective as the amphetamine, although it was not compared to Ritalin. Knights and Viets (1975) found Cylert significantly more effective as improving the general behavior and school performance of most hyperactive boys. Cylert is not as widely prescribed as Ritalin.

The Use and Abuse of Medication

The debate over the uses of medication has, unfortunately, succumbed to rhetoric. Scientific evidence is often ignored, and ad hominen arguments are the norm rather than the exception. For example, John Holt, an outspoken opponent of prescribing drugs to quell hyperactivity, calls the practice "quackery," implying that partisans of the chemotherapy position are themselves quacks! In strong, uncompromising language, he vents his feelings on this issue:

> We take lively, curious, energetic children, eager to make contact with the world and to learn about it, stick them in barren classrooms with teachers who on the whole neither like nor respect nor understand nor trust them. . . . Then, when the children resist this brutalizing and stupefying treatment and retreat from it in anger, bewilderment, and terror, we say that they are sick with "complex and little understood" disorders, and proceed to dose them with powerful drugs that are indeed complex and of whose long-run effects we know little or nothing, so that they may be more ready to do the asinine things the schools asks them to do. (Holt, 1970)

Other writers have echoed the same feelings, chiding the schools—as well as the medical profession—for dispensing drugs promiscuously when there is not sufficient evidence that they are required or effective. Grinspoon and Singer (1973), for example, argue that "using drugs to 'modify' classroom behavior constitutes a covert subversion of what *should* be our educational ideals. If an important aim of our educational institutions were really to help young people learn to deal with and to regulate their 'self-destructive' or even 'anti-social' tendencies, it would make little sense to give them drugs as soon as they exhibited restless or unruly behavior" (p. 544). Freeman (1976) sees this entire trend as "an unfortunate episode in the history of progressive medicalization of deviant or troublesome behavior" (p. 22).

Despite these criticisms, there is an over-abundance of empirical evidence that properly prescribed drugs *can* help the hyperactive and MBD child maintain himself or herself sufficiently in the classroom to benefit from good educational practice. Teachers, who must deal on a day-to-day basis with these children, are especially resentful of "ivory tower" theorists who make a blanket condemnation of the use of drugs. When viewed as a "means" to an "end" the use of medication takes on an entirely different perspective.

Both advocates and critics of drug administration agree on one important point: drugs do not cure any of these disorders. Those who argue against the use of these drugs suggest that the teacher rely solely on sound educational and therapeutic techniques; those who favor drug administration emphasize its adjunctive function and seek compatible simultaneous treatment modalities, such as behavior modification.

Sound research on the long-term effects of stimulant drugs on children is still sorely needed. While short-term studies generally show success, there is more question about the long-term value of the drugs (Stewart, 1976). A suggested "total profile" long-term study of the effects of psychoactive drugs (Cole, 1975) is recommended with the context of:

1. The effect of stimulant drugs on the appetite and cardiovascular system of the hyperactive child.
2. Sociological aspects of administering drugs to children with regard to the possible stigmatizing effects.
3. Studies using non-human subjects should be encouraged to provide adequate information about the specific action of the drug on hyperactivity. (p. 34)

These kinds of studies may open the door to resolving the perennial debate by providing a better understanding of all of the issues.

Conclusions

Admittedly, the issues are complex and there are no easy answers. But we feel the bulk of studies clearly support the following conclusions, which are of practical significance for the classroom teacher:

1. Methylphenidate, dextroamphetamine, and pemoline have clearly been shown to lessen the symptoms associated with hyperkinesis and MBD.
2. None of these drugs, however, provides a "cure" for hyperactivity or MBD. Rather, they must be used in conjunction with psychotherapy, behavior modification or other educational strategies, or all of them.
3. Whenever drugs are used, the parents and the teacher are important members of the treatment team "for the evaluation of the regimen and the monitoring of dosage levels" (Robin & Bosco, 1976).
4. Further research is needed before we can fully evaluate the risk/benefit equation for the use of medication.

COUNSELING THE EXCEPTIONAL STUDENT

Specific counseling approaches for reaching the exceptional student in the school and in the clinical counseling settings are plentiful. Some studies have demonstrated the effectiveness of the school as a setting for improving young people's intellectual, social, and emotional development. There are several major points that have consistently been included in most of the approaches that have been tried out in the school or clinical settings, some particularly relevant for preadolescents, some for adolescents, and some for all exceptional learners:

1. Most students respond best when there is support from (or, at the least, when there is minimum opposition from) their peers. For this reason, the likelihood of a program's success is increased when the program comprises a peer approach (such as peer-group counseling or cooperative school projects).
2. Because of the adolescent's strong social orientation, which favors the norms of conformity and unabashedly ostracizes the very different, an adolescent's exceptional—or atypical condition—is likely to have profound social consequences. For example, a physically disabled adolescent is more likely to feel psychologically alienated and socially stigmatized than is the physically disabled younger child, who is more dependent on the family for emotional support and social recognition.
3. Equivalent to the peer group, especially for the preadolescent, is the influence of the family. Family should be included then, in most situations. Since many of the difficulties experienced by the

Many successful individuals overcame their early-life disabilities and handicaps. Well-known examples are Helen Keller, Albert Einstein, Thomas Edison, and Eleanor Roosevelt (*moving left to right, top and bottom*).

preadolescent have either causes from or ramifications in the family setting, the most direct approach to effective counseling suggests the active participation of family members.

4. Adolescents (and often preadolescents) typically respond well to informational programs, as long as their emotional needs have been taken into account. Because the adolescent is capable of formal operational thought, the provision of information and the exchange of ideas can be conducted on a relatively high level.

With these general points in mind, we can consider some specific types of programs and counseling intervention.

The Use of Groups

The group setting is probably the most widely used modality in treating the exceptional student. While the general practices and applications of group counseling are discussed in the following chapter, we will point out here some specific group applications for the exceptional learner. In this way we will better understand the practical principles of implementation.

Generally, positive changes occur in the group context because clients are "given an opportunity to release their tensions and to examine their behavior with the help of their peers" (Goodman, 1976, p. 520). This is equally true of almost any type of counseling group, but it can be modified to reflect the specific needs of exceptional learners insofar as it allows them to share their common experiences with each other:

> Mr. Chien, a school counselor, organized a voluntary after-school group of students who were having difficulty making the grades that would help them get into college. They just got together to "rap," without a specific goal in mind. During the course of the semester, Mr. Chien noted that many of the concerns that prevented one student from studying were also preventing another student [from studying]. He realized that worries about dating, about being financially independent from parents, and fears of competitiveness were underlying many of the adolescents' problems. He encouraged them to share their feelings about these, and began to organize this general group into a problem-solving group to focus on these universal problems.

Sometimes the group's initial goals and methods may be less general—more oriented toward a specific problem or challenge. Career counseling groups, for example, have become extremely popular in recent years. Many school counselors run short-term groups to help students arrive at career decisions. This may prove valuable for the troubled adolescent who may not have realistic expectations about his or her place in the world of work.

However, as Swails and Herr (1976) point out from their research, the efficacy of such approaches is far from proven, "and the one clear finding is that the direct application of group techniques, such as those used in this study, to affect the complex process of career development in an eight-week period is expecting more than can be delivered for most students" (p. 259).

Particularly important in practice is the recurring observation by those who have implemented programs that the group approach with exceptional students works best when it is supported by parents, by the community, and by school personnel. No matter how well organized a group is, it can easily fail if it does not have this kind of support. On the other hand, where there is support, even a weak group can gain strength. Webster (1974), for example, describes a group for troubled adolescents that she organized in a rural mining town. "Faculty interest in dealing with problem students started a chain reaction. Teachers became motivated to select students who can benefit from group counseling and provided referrals for groups led by the two teachers and the [social] worker. The group treatment program is now built into the school's system, and can continue to operate with minimal consultation from the worker" (p. 657). Huber (1979) has described a group counseling approach for helping the parents of handicapped children get in touch with their feelings. At the other end of the spectrum, Miran, Lehrer, Koehler and Miran (1974) describe a behavior modification group designed to treat deviant adolescent boys that "ultimately failed because of social pressure. . . . [There was] a tendency for a suburban, middle-class community to give up on disorders, to declare them deviant and to punish them" (p. 370). They conclude that, in practice, "the behavior modifier must address the social system in which the deviant behavior occurs" (p. 374).

Consulting with Parents

One of the main areas in which exceptional youngsters experience problems is in dealing with their parents. Parental conflicts are inherent in growing up, to be sure, and even in the best of families these conflicts may lead to persistent misunderstandings. Where the young person is emotionally troubled, and therefore less capable than others in dealing with problematic situations, this challenge may prove especially stubborn. Moreover, many of the difficulties experienced by exceptional children and adolescents may directly or indirectly be a result of their parents' inability to understand their needs and/or an willingness to deal with them on their terms.

The counselor can play a unique role in bridging the communication gap between troubled students and their parents. Kifer, Lewis, Green, and Phillips (1974) have described an innovative approach for training predelinquent adolescents and their parents to negotiate conflict situations. The results indicate that with appropriate training, the adolescent and the parents can learn ways to communicate that will avoid conflict. Woods (1974) too has argued that parents' groups are important contributors to growth in the treatment of their adolescent children.

Specific counseling approaches have also been translated into group and individual applications for dealing with exceptional problems. Underlying most adolescent problems, for example, is a lack of self-esteem, and this should be a goal of change underlying any program. As Lowendahl (1975) describes it,

> An adolescent—from the impression he has received from others and from himself—views himself in a dilemma. He has not the maturity as yet to accept the competence with the incompetence—a real mix—which is normal. His self-image may be entirely negative. He may not even realize it. The feeling of "I cannot" predominates his personality and if the areas of "I can" keep retreating to the point of complete disappearance—most avenues of help and restoration may be ineffectual. (Lowendahl, 1975, p. 170)

Counseling approaches, she points out, should be built on the strengthening of self-esteem. Of course, these may include a variety of approaches, implemented in different settings. Protinsky (1976) suggests, for instance, the suitability of using rational emotive counseling with troubled youngsters. RET helps the individual change his or her irrational thinking, which, presumably, is the source behind much of the trouble, into rational thinking. Hipple and Muto (1974) describe the use of transactional analysis (TA) in the treatment of adolescents and argue that this can be an effective method of treatment. Whichever method is used, it is generally agreed that the participation of parents is an important plus in assuring effective counseling interventions and programs.

School Problems

It is an error, I believe, to view the exceptional student's school problems in vacuo; rather, whether there are academic or social problems, they should always be perceived as part of a complex interaction between different facets of the individual's world of interpersonal functioning. For the adolescent, poor performance in school may be a result of family problems, emotional difficulties, a frustrating or hurtful "love life," or any of the other failures to adjust to the demands of the adolescent period. Likewise, poor school performance may contribute to problems in any of the aforementioned areas. Parents and their children frequently fight about schoolwork, and many a student has had her or his immediate wishes and future plans thwarted by academic or behavioral problems.

Consider, for example, the widespread "reading problem," which we hear so much about. Often, when we think of reading disabilities we think of the elementary school; but in fact, many high school students read well below the minimum performance criteria. Shuman (1975) has pointed out the prevalence of the problem and makes the point that "by the time the poor reader or nonreader gets to high school, he is likely to be highly sensitive about his disability" (p. 38). For this reason, poor reading can blossom into an emotional problem as well. Such a student may become truant, delinquent, or socially awkward because of the failure to read. Consequently, an assessment of the adolescent's reading performance should be considered in any type of psychosocial diagnosis.

Many of the behavioral problems in the school may be a consequence of the young person's attempt to try out new styles of behavior. This actually serves a productive purpose. As Konopka (1976) points out, the adolescent has an "intensive need for experimentation," which includes a willingness to take risks that a younger child or an adult might not take. "Only thus," she concludes, "do they learn about themselves and the surrounding reality" (p. 178).

Many of the social adjustments required of all youths are more difficult for the exceptional adolescent, and this can influence school behavior as these examples illustrate:

> Joe, who has epilepsy, finds himself increasingly alienated from his peers as they all get their driving permits and he cannot. Throughout elementary school he tried to keep his epilepsy a secret, but when he had a seizure in eighth grade the whole school found out about it. The teachers, sensitive to the situation, educated the students about epilepsy and Joe did not encounter unusual cruelty from his classmates. Now, however, the practical consequences of his condition make him stand out, and he doesn't know how he is going to compete socially.

> Pam, an attractive and intelligent senior, performs well-below average in school because of a learning disability that was not properly diagnosed until tenth grade. She is placed in the slow classes, even though she is as intelligent as those in the top classes. She finds that she cannot relate to her classmates, and that she is not able to meet the kind of fellow she would like to date. The bright young men she is interested in think she is dull because she is in the slow classes. She also has difficulty in making friends because of this.

Vincent, who is in ninth grade, is hearing impaired, but refuses to wear a hearing aid. His parents have seen that he remains in the regular classes (despite his poor academic performance), fearing that he will be socially stigmatized if placed in a program for the deaf; but they do not make sure that he uses his hearing aid. Consequently, his performance in school is poor and he is shy but impulsive, unable to establish relations with his peers. He has a phobic dread that the other kids will find out about his hearing impairment, and much of his time is spent in trying to devise ways of getting out of situations where this could happen. Thus, he refuses to socialize and freely uses his fists whenever he is involved in what he views as a threatening situation.

We see in each of these situations how an exceptional condition makes the challenges of adjustment even more difficult.

Group Counseling
in the Schools

13

Group counseling offers a number of general advantages over individual, face-to-face counseling. Moreover, there are a number of specific situations in which the group counseling approach would be particularly indicated over the individual approach. In this section, we shall examine the criteria for using the group approach over the face-to-face approach.

First, the group approach is more *economical* than the individual approach. This does not refer necessarily to the fiscal advantages—for the school counselor is not usually concerned with these matters—but to economy in terms of the conservation of time, the counselor's most precious commodity. If in a typical school there is one counselor for every eight hundred students, and the counselor has twenty-two counseling office hours a week, then she or he would be able to see each student individually only once a year! This, certainly, would be unfair to those students who may need the assistance of the counselor several times a month. If, on the other hand, the same counselor uses the group approach, setting up small- to medium-sized groups (6 to 20), depending on the type of counseling required, he or she could see each student twice a month, rather than once a year, and still have six hours a week available for individual interviews. This is all theoretical, however, since many of the students do not want and do not require counseling. A more realistic analysis, based on the data I have acquired in my own research, shows that the counselor who relies primarily on the group approach is able to meet twice a week with every student who wants, needs, or is even vaguely interested in guidance or counseling, with still much time left over for individual interviews. This analysis is also based on the size of the group, of course.

A second advantage of the group over the individual approach is that the group is more typical of social reality than is the individual, private counseling encounter. This has two important results: it enables the group leader (the counselor) to study the patterns of the client's social interactions, and it facilitates the client's socialization. In the face-to-face encounter, while the counselor may learn a great deal about the client, she or he is never

able to see the client engaging in the social interactions that comprise a large part of everyday existence. The counselor who is presented with a real life opportunity to study the client in his or her social milieu gains a more legitimate and relevant insight into the workings of the social side of the client's personality. This is especially important for clients whose problems are in part a result of social difficulties: the disruptive child, the shy and withdrawn child, the characterologically neurotic child, the aggressive child, and so forth. As we can see, this comprises a large percentage of the typical client population. The group experience facilitates socialization by enabling each group member to improve and refine socializing techniques. The group experience is a part of social learning.

A third important advantage to the group over the individual approach is that the group, by bringing together many different people with different backgrounds, personalities, and experiences, provides a reservoir of insights, perceptions, and emotional responses that a single counselor, no matter how skilled and experienced, could not possibly provide. This is certainly one of the chief therapeutic advantages of the group experience, and it may also be used to advantage in guidance groups, where learning and information, rather than personality reformulation, is the goal.

Within the context of the group experience, the client usually searches out responses that he or she intuitively knows are facilitative, or in some cases the counselor encourages such responses by group members for the benefit of a client. In an individual encounter, only the feelings, perceptions, and experiences of the counselor are available to the client, while in a group situation there exists a wider range of possibilities.

A fourth advantage of the group approach, particularly in the school, is that the group parallels more closely the classroom setting than does the face-to-face experience. Because the client is accustomed to functioning in a group experience, less resistance appears if she or he is placed in a counseling group than if extracted totally from the group situation and asked to interact in the counselor's office. This maintains a continuity of experience that is both healthy and productive.

Pascale (1968) has summed up many of these points to support his position that the counseling services can be enhanced through the utilization of group counseling. He points out that "the individual counseling service is both expensive and time consuming . . . the 'desired' student–counselor ratio of 300 to 1 does not allow an adequate amount of time for the important function of individual counseling." He suggests that group counseling programs be used in place of individual counseling, wherever possible. "The nature of group counseling," he suggests, "enables the counselor to counsel more students for longer periods of time."

Of course there are some disadvantages to the group experience, too. Some clients find it easier to speak in privacy than in front of their peers. Some regress in the group situation, repeating the difficult behavior patterns that indicated the need for counseling in the first place. The group experience cannot provide a single dynamic relationship of the intensity found in the individual experience. But all things being equal, the school counselor will most likely utilize the bulk of his or her time conducting group experiences, while leaving sufficient time to see individually those clients who require that type of treatment.

THE GROUP LEADER

Since rarely is any individual fully committed to one group, and since even within the group context, identification is only partial, it is essential that there be some cohering force to hold together the members of the group and to help them achieve the goals that they share. That person is the group leader. Just as the child learns that within the family there is a leader (or leaders!), each member of a group comes to recognize the existence of and to acknowledge the place of the group leader or leaders. This recognition becomes an important stage in the cohesiveness and stability of a group

(Shambaugh, 1978). The football captain or coach, the political district leader, the church's clerical figurehead are all examples of the group leader who helps hold the group together.

Different types of groups require different types of leaders, and the role of the leader may vary greatly from group to group. One question that has interested psychologists and sociologists is, Are some people born leaders and others born followers? The personal quality called *leadership* has been studied under a variety of real and manipulated circumstances to determine if it is a quality bestowed upon an individual by a group or a quality an individual imposes upon the group, or if it is somewhere in between. Mann (1959) points out some of the complexities of this issue:

> Viewed historically, the study of leadership has stimulated more than its share of controversy. The trait approach to leadership, the view that leadership is an attribute of the individual, has received the harshest treatment throughout the years. To have spoken of an individual as possessing a measurable quantity of leadership was perhaps an unfortunate choice of words. The clear implication of such a statement is that since leadership is specific to the individual, it will remain constant for the individual regardless of the situation in which he finds himself. . . . On the one hand, the trait approach has been modified to imply that an individual's achieved leadership status is a function of his personality. On the other hand, sufficient evidence has been accumulated to give impetus to the situation approach to leadership, which maintains that leadership is an emergent phenomenon, created through the interaction of individuals (leaders and followers), and that selection and stability of any leadership pattern is a function of the task, composition, and culture of the group. From all this work has emerged some such summary formulations as that an individual's leadership status in groups is a joint function of his personality and the particular group setting. (pp. 246-247)

These conclusions, written over twenty years ago, are still valid today. Subsequent research has shown that there is clearly an *interactive* quality that produces group leadership, although there has also been special emphasis on the personality characteristics that make for effective, charismatic, democratic, autocratic, or ineffective leadership.

The Group Counselor's Job

In broad terms, the job of the group leader is the same as the job of the counselor in individual, face-to-face counseling. "In actuality," Trotzer (1977) points out, "the leader role is a conglomeration of subroles that emerge on the basis of interaction between the group leaders' personality and philosophical orientation and the needs of the group" (p. 92). Likewise, techniques and stratagems are the same for individual and group counseling in many ways.

There are some differences, too. One problem the group counselor faces is getting together enough individuals to form a group. Sometimes a group is formed to accommodate people with a common problem; sometimes it is limited by the client population of the agency. The counselor may not be sure if certain individuals will be able to function well together, or if there will be counterproductive personality conflicts among them. Is it better to place people with a common problem in a group or are heterogeneous groups more effective? These and many other related questions challenge the group counselor at the outset. Nichols (1976) also points out that when forming a group, a counselor has to prepare the members psychologically for the group experience, and this includes resolving some stereotypes the potential group member may hold and clarifying what the potential member should realistically expect from the group. These pre-group interventions are particularly important in the school setting, where students may be loath to associate themselves with a counseling group.

Hyman Spotnitz (1961), a pioneer in modern psychoanalytic group therapy, describes his approach to forming a group:

> In forming a group, I put together persons who will be able to develop intense emotional reactions to each other. The sexes get equal representation. The patients are usually alike in some respects and different in others. Divergence in personality structure blended with reasonably compatible backgrounds . . . usually make it possible for group members to relate well to each other and to function efficiently as a unit. With diverse personalities represented, interchanges go on among the calm, the excitable, those who easily arouse excitement, and others who tend to check it. As they stimulate each other in different ways, group process is mobilized. (p. 120)

A second situation particularly applicable to the group setting is maintaining order and continuity in the face of anxiety and tension. Several individuals functioning as a group can be more untoward and unmanageable than a single individual, no matter what his or her resistances. The group leader must work toward a positive group attitude by demonstrating to the group members the security that is present in the group situation.

Finally, the group leader, like the individual counselor, must be a facilitator. Carl Rogers (1971), an innovator in encounter group practices, describes his way of facilitating the group experience:

> I tend to open in an extremely unstructured way, perhaps with no more than a single comment: "I suspect we will know each other a great deal better at the end of these group sessions than we do now. . . ." I listen as carefully

and as sensitively as I am able. . . . . I wish very much to make the climate psychologically safe for the individual—I have found that it "pays off" to live with the group exactly where it is. Thus I have worked with a group of very inhibited top-notch scientists, mostly in the physical sciences, where feelings were rarely expressed openly, and personal encounter at a deep level was simply not seen. Yet this group became much more free and innovative, and showed many positive results of our meetings. . . . I am willing for a participant to commit himself to the group. . . . I am willing to accept silence and muteness in the individual, provided I am quite certain it is not unexpressed pain or resistance. . . . I tend to accept statements at their face value. . . . I try to make clear that whatever happens will happen from the choices of the group. . . . When talk is generalized or intellectualizing, I tend to select the self-referrent meanings to respond to out of this total context. (pp. 275-278)

We see how Rogers's approach toward group leadership is both a reflection of his personality and of his theoretical orientation. A Gestalt group leader would use vastly different types of techniques, involving preassigned actions and specific behavior by the group members (Mintz, 1971). These Gestalt "games" are designed to facilitate growth within the group, but in a manner that is incompatible with the Rogerian stance.

The orientation of the group leader will profoundly influence the kind of role he or she sees as appropriate. The functional discrepancies in therapeutic techniques and goals that were catalogued in chapter 5 are just as applicable in the group setting. Rogers's comment that we just read is indicative of the role of the *humanistic* leader. Other group leaders would conceptualize their roles somewhat differently.

The Psychodynamic Group Leader

While the psychoanalytic group leader emphasizes the parallels between group and individual counseling, he or she also recognizes the differences. As Kirman (1976) points out,

> You proceed with groups much as you do with individuals from the modern psychoanalytic point of view. In individual counseling, you want the client to say whatever comes to mind. But everything can't be said in a group. *An important function of the group is learning what can and cannot be said in group.* (p. 86, italics added)

Generally, the psychoanalytic group leader believes that within the group context each member reexperiences emotionally and repeats behaviorally his or her early situation within the family structure. Needs that were not met in childhood cry out for satisfaction in the group; but the individual

William J. Kirman is well known for applying modern psychoanalytic insights in the group and educational setting.

attempts to satisfy these needs in the same ways that repeatedly failed during the early years. One of the important roles of the psychoanalytic group leader, therefore, is to teach individuals *how* to satisfy their legitimate needs in appropriate, effective ways.

Counselors using the psychoanalytic method are also sensitive to the phenomenon of *group transference*. This simply means that the group-as-a-whole perceives the leader as a parental, or authority, figure. The group leader, recognizing this, attempts to respond to group communications in the same way a "good" parent would act. This phenomenon, it should be pointed out, works in conjunction with all of the individual transference relationships that also exist simultaneously in the group.

The Behavioral Group Leader

The group serves two important purposes for the behaviorally oriented group leader. First, it provides rich behavioral resources after which individual group members can *model* themselves (*modeling* is discussed in chapter 3). The group leader may attempt to point out to the individual members types of new (or different) behaviors that he or she feels will be beneficial to them. The members are then able to learn these new and productive behaviors by watching other members of the group, or by directly observing the group leader.

The second purpose of the behaviorally oriented group is that members of the group can be used to dispense reinforcement (either positive or negative). Peer pressure can be brought to bear on any member to encourage or discourage certain specified behaviors. While reinforcers can be provided by the group leader, it is far more effective if the behavioral group leader, as a *manager of contingencies,* helps all the group members learn to give or withhold reinforcers effectively. The important concept here is known as *group contingencies,* and these can be defined as making the consequences of an individual's behaviors dependent on the group as well as on the individual. Axelrod (1977, p. 50) gives an example:

> An example of a group contingency is found in the sport of professional baseball. After the World Series has been completed, all members of the winning team receive the same pay, even though their individual performances may have varied greatly. The team has been scored as a unit. Similarly, all members of the losing team receive the same, smaller share, in spite of the fact that the performance of some members of the losing team may have exceeded that of some of the players on the winning team. (p. 50)

The important point, Axelrod emphasizes, is that the reinforcement each student receives "depends not only on his own behavior, but also on the behavior of other members of the group" (p. 50). This has several practical advantages over individually administered behavioral-change programs. It teaches the learner by example the values of group cooperation. It also introduces the element of peer pressure, where desired behaviors are encouraged and supported by one's peer group. And especially in the school setting, it is easier to implement than are a variety of simultaneous individual programs for different students. Thus, the behavioral group leader can serve an important purpose as the manager of group contingencies in the school counseling setting.

The "Rational" or "Reality" Group Leader

In the rational and reality counseling approaches, the group leader mobilizes the group-as-a-whole to point out to individual members the irrationalities or improprieties of individual behaviors, perceptions, and feelings. In this sense, the group becomes an extension of the leader's perceptions that, presumably, are in accord with reality and with emotionally satisfying functioning. It is not uncommon to find pressure brought to bear on group members to change behaviors that are viewed as detrimental or unhealthy. But at the same time, the group provides feedback—both to the leader and to individual members—and this feedback helps the individuals arrive at realistic options and perceptual frameworks from which decisions can be made. As communication in the group increases, the group member's gen-

table 13.1

THREE PSYCHOLOGICAL MODELS OF GROUP PROCESSES

category	psychoanalysis	behaviorism	humanism
Actions of Group Participants	Repeat the infantile behaviors of the family setting.	Responses to stimuli from within the group setting.	Inhibited or uninhibited tendencies toward growth and change.
Methods of Facilitating Change	Pointing out (*interpreting*) the unconscious meanings of behaviors as they are revealed in the group.	Positive and negative reinforcement; modeling.	The leaders' own personal capacity to ''give'' to the group members.
Role of the Leader	To encourage the transferring of feelings; to resolve resistances; to teach the individual to satisfy needs from childhood in a socially appropriate manner.	To reinforce positive behaviors and to provide models whereby the member can learn appropriate behavior patterns.	To accept; to clarify; to teach; to participate. In all, to help the group attain a high level of expressive freedom.
School Applications	Resolving resistances in the classroom. Lessening neurotic interference to mastering learning tasks. Meeting maturational needs that arise in a social context.	Direct behavior change. Increasing the rate of learning. Resolving school phobias, test anxiety, underachievement, etc. Drug prevention programs.	In all areas the full inclusive growth of the total person.

Note: From *Educational Psychology* by Gary S. Belkin and Jerry L. Gray. Copyright 1977 by Wm. C. Brown Company Publishers. Reprinted with permission.

eral functioning increases accordingly (Stafford, 1978). In many respects, the rational approach is a hybrid of the behavioral and psychodynamic positions, integrating teaching and learning principles along with the counseling approach.

We should also note that the ramifications of the leader's role—of how the leader conceptualizes his or her functioning in the group—affects profoundly the entire group process. Table 13.1 shows how the group participants and the leader function and react somewhat differently in the three main psychological models: psychoanalysis, behaviorism, and humanism. We see that in terms of facilitating change and in terms of specific school applications, there are important differences to be considered when selecting a group approach.

FACTORS IN GROUP COUNSELING

Both the limitations of settings and the varying needs of the participants have given rise to different types of groups, many of which are applicable to the school setting. Nowadays, there is a great deal of confusion between a T-group, a sensitivity group, a workshop group, and so on. The counselor should understand the basic differences between them and be aware when each type of group is normally indicated. In addition to the *general psychotherapy* group, Rogers (1970) has identified the following as some of the main groups used: T-group, encounter group, sensitivity training group, task-oriented group, and organizational development group.

For simplification, we can differentiate between four key types that play a part in the school setting: therapy groups, discussion groups, training groups, and guidance groups. A *therapy group* is generally designed to treat a specific problem, usually psychological in nature and manifesting an undesirable symptom. An example might be a group working with chronic truants or underachievers, especially those who are experiencing severe family conflicts at home. A *discussion group* is designed more for prevention and for working out feelings. An example is a group in which teachers meet with the school counselor to discuss disciplinary problems they are experiencing with their students. These types of groups fall under the heading of what Cerio (1979) calls *educational growth groups* (EGG). They may be used to deal with any kind of educational problem. Figures 13.1 and 13.2 show the direction of group progress and the goals of a typical EGG, which is probably the most widely used modality in the schools. As we see from these figures, this model allows for the provision of information to group members and offers opportunities for clarifying their values, for experiential learning, and for future planning—all of which are integral to solving any educational problem. A *training group* is designed toward achieving a specific learning goal, such as a group designed to help teachers to develop counseling skills. A *guidance group* combines elements of all of these, but

figure 13.1 The educational growth group model

figure 13.2 The goals of the educational growth group model

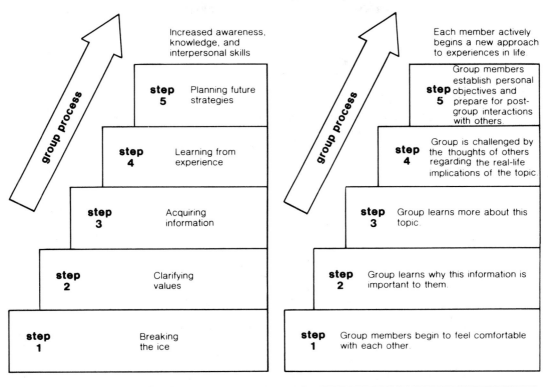

Note: From "Structured Experiences with the Educational Growth Group Model" by J. E. Cerio, *Personnel and Guidance Journal,* 1979, *57* (8), 400.

emphasizes improvement in future role activity over personality integration. Table 13.2 shows some examples of these four key types.

Some of the factors that will go into deciding what type of group is appropriate for what type of situation are (1) the needs of the clients; (2) the resources available; (3) the setting. Let us consider each of these individually.

table 13.2

USE OF DIFFERENT GROUPS IN SCHOOL SITUATIONS

type of problem	therapy group	discussion group	training group	guidance group
Student underachievement	X			X
Helping teachers learn to deal with disciplinary problems in the classroom		X	X	
Resolving racial tensions in the school		X		X
Helping students confront their occupational choices		X		X
Working with the emotionally disturbed teacher or student	X			
Helping teachers develop counseling skills		X	X	X

Note: From *Educational Psychology* by Gary S. Belkin and Jerry L. Gray. Copyright 1977 by Wm. C. Brown Company Publishers. Reprinted with permission.

Client Needs

There are no specific guidelines about what types of client needs indicate group over individual counseling, but we can make a few general statements that, if not free of faults, are at least generally agreed to. First, for specifically symptomatic disorders (school phobia, behavioral problems, learning disorders, drug abuse, truancy, etc.), group counseling has proven enormously helpful. Research has shown that clients who do not respond to individual counseling for these and many other problems may respond well within a group context (Kaufman & Bluestone, 1974). Second, if the client feels more comfortable speaking to a group than relating to a counselor in an individual session, the group approach would again be indicated. Finally, when the client's diffidence in interpersonal relationships is an integral part of the problem, the group serves as a good medium to facilitate his or her confidence in interpersonal relationships.

Available Resources

In some settings it is not feasible for the counselor to see the large client population on an individual basis. In such situations, the group is a perfect compromise. The history of group treatment, as a unique modality, illustrates how the limitations and constraints of available resources *and* the needs of the clients interacted to make the group movement possible. The great pioneers of the group counseling movement—S. R. Slavson, Joseph Walsh, and Joseph Pratt, among others—originally formed groups for these reasons. Walsh and Pratt, both physicians, were working with tuberculosis patients in a hospital setting. They recognized the need to help these patients emotionally as well as physically, and organized groups in which the patients could be given information as well as gain confidence in their prognosis. Patients' feelings about their disease were brought out into the open, and group counseling methods, which are still used today, were established. Slavson was working with groups of disturbed children, also in an institutional setting. Hadden (1975) describes Slavson's famous discovery of the value of group processes:

> After participating in a project that provided disturbed children with an opportunity to take part in creative activities in groups, [Slasvon's] examination of the crude product of their activity convinced him that pride in these accomplishments could not possibly account for the improvement reported by the teachers and caseworkers. He soon recognized that the interaction among the participants during the group sessions was the real therapeutic agent. (p. 371)

Thus, the assessment of available resources is not only valuable in determining when to use a group, but has proven historically to be of value in the development of the group movement. In the schools, where resources are always in short supply, this should prove a particularly convincing reason in many situations for choosing a group over individual counseling.

The Setting

Not only are the available resources defined by the setting, but client expectations, expectations of superiors, and social boundaries are also, to a large extent, determined by the setting. Moreover, the behavior of individual participants is affected by the setting itself. Just as Marshall McLuhan has pointed out that in communication, the "medium is the message," the group context presents to each participant an emotional and psychosocial message that has a profound influence on behavior. Kressel (1974), in evaluating the seminal contribution of Kurt Lewin on the group therapy movement, suggests that Lewin's background in social psychology enabled him to observe with invaluable perspicacity the group as a dynamic social unit, which in turn opened up counselors' understanding of the group as a social entity. Lewin suggested that each group member forms an interdependence with other members and with the group as a whole, and that this interdependence is a result of the group's existence as an entity.

The Process

Just as different types of group leaders conceptualize their jobs differently, the process of group counseling varies according to the leader's perceived role and the clients' needs. Lacoursiere (1980) offers an essentially eclectic model of the group process, based on extensive research of group practice, which he calls the predictable "life cycle of groups." He differentiates this cycle into five stages: orientation, dissatisfaction, resolution, production, and termination. During the first stage, the members come to understand what the group is all about, what behaviors are expected of them, and they learn a little about the other group members. Some dissatisfaction arises during the second stage—either about the process, the leader, or about other group members. As this is discussed and worked through it becomes resolved, and progress toward resolving problems begins. During this stage of resolution their commitment to the group grows. The fourth stage—production—is where most of the problem solving actually takes place. The final stage of termination occurs when the members feel their problems are resolved and are able to function on their own.

EVALUATION AND APPLICATIONS

As we have now seen, group approaches are valuable in just about any counseling setting, but may be particularly applicable in the school. The research on the effectiveness of group treatment is extensive, and generally favorable. We will survey briefly a few recent studies that show how group approaches can be (and have been!) used effectively in the school setting, and the counselor trainee may wish to consult these studies to determine specific pathways of implementation.

Counseling groups have been used effectively in many creative ways. Blohm (1978), among others, has shown that group methods work well with learning disabled elementary school children, and it is now generally recognized that groups are the primary counseling modality for dealing with most learning disabilities, including mental retardation. Huber (1979) used group counseling as a method for helping parents of handicapped children work out many of their feelings about the child, about the handicapping condition, and about the situation in general. "The parent group," he points out (p. 268), "provides a unique opportunity for participants to become more aware of what is happening in their lives through feedback from other parents about their experiences. . . . Parents contribute to each other and develop new ways of coping with their situations."

One specialized form of group counseling that has fared well in the research is peer group counseling. Here, the student, along with his or her peers, function as models and often leaders for other students in the group setting. Hoffman (1976) has reviewed applications of this approach and finds it generally effective, especially where teachers and parents are involved, at least peripherally.

Group guidance approaches have been widely used in the school setting. Group guidance, as contrasted with group counseling, emphasizes informational services, vocational exploration, and objective (nondynamic) discussion of various role difficulties and adjustment problems. "The primary goal of group guidance," Parks (1973) suggests, "is to prevent and ameliorate the development of problems rather than just the remediation of existing problems, which differentiates group guidance from group counseling and group therapy" (p. 108). The content of group guidance, Parks goes on to point out, is primarily information and exploration. One recent application of group guidance procedures that has found widespread acceptance in the schools is the vocational exploration group (VEG), in which students develop career maturity and job readiness through the group experience (Yates, Johnson, & Johnson, 1979). This is particularly valuable and economical when the counselor cannot provide individual career counseling to students.

SUMMARY

In this chapter, we presented an overview of group counseling, showing its practical benefits and contemporary relevance, pointing out how it differs from individual counseling, and considering some specific approaches to group counseling and guidance in the school setting. The advantages of the group approach are many: it is economical; it is more representative of the social milieu in which the individual must function; it provides the individual with a wider range of emotional responses; and it allows clients to practice dealing with social situations.

We examined the group leader's role and function, pointing out that the role is often an interaction between his or her personality, the group setting, social and professional role expectations, and the behavior of group members. Several aspects of the group counselor's job were defined, and the differences between the roles of humanistic, psychodynamic, and behavioral group leaders were discussed.

Some different types of groups were then enumerated, along with a consideration of client needs and available resources. Counseling groups, I concluded, have been used successfully to treat a wide range of behavioral and emotional-adjustment problems.

Crisis Counseling in the Schools

It was lunch hour at a small elementary school in a comfortable Chicago suburb and hundreds of children who lived nearby poured out of the school to return to their homes for lunch. It was a lovely spring morning and the children walked spiritedly down the tree-lined streets toward their homes. On one street, adjacent to a parkway, walked about fifty children, playing, teasing, chatting, and just generally thinking about the day ahead. Then something happened:

> A young man, age 23 . . . confronted his 53-year-old father with verbal abuse and then aggressive physical assault. The youth's irresponsible thinking led him to use a butcher knife in his hand as a weapon, and he thrust it into the body of his father. In utter disbelief, and experiencing the sudden rush of pain, the father, still in his pajamas, ran out of his elegant home and into the street, crying for help, with his son in close pursuit. As the father tried to escape by dodging between parked cars and using the parkway trees as shields, all the while pleading continually for assistance, his punctured body, weakened by the loss of blood, fell to the ground. His son, in continued rage, straddled him and began to methodically cut off his head. He had almost finished this gory act when, owing to his spastic hysterical frustration, the butcher knife jammed and broke in the skeletal part of his father's neck. (Dallas, 1978, p. 388)

The children witnessed in detail (at close proximity) the stabbing of the father by the son, the struggle, the bloodletting, the decapitation. They heard the screams and felt the terror of the act. "As the children started to put the various pieces together," Dallas goes on to point out, "they became aware of what had happened only a few feet away from them. They began to sink deeper into their thinking, creating flashbacks, doubts, anger, disbelief, anxiety about their own feelings of impulse control, and concern about the value of their own lives and/or life in general" (p. 388). In short, these children had been traumatized and were now in a state of crisis.

CRISIS COUNSELING: A SPECIALIZED APPROACH

Of course most crisis situations with which the school counselor has to deal are not as dramatic as this one. But this true case, which we will see later required intensive crisis intervention counseling in the elementary school setting, illustrates dramatically the necessity for crisis counseling strategies.

Crisis intervention is to counseling what first aid is to medicine—a temporary but immediate relief for an emergency situation presented by an incapacitated client. Like first-aid procedures, crisis intervention procedures are specific and clear-cut, and the school counselor should have more than a nodding acquaintance with them.

In many respects, crisis intervention utilizes basic counseling and psychotherapy strategies; but in other respects, it differs markedly. Nass (1977) contrasts crisis intervention therapy to standard psychotherapy practices:

> In contrast to psychotherapy which is almost exclusively focused on the long-term goals associated with personality reorganization, crisis intervention is admirably suited to satisfy both distant and immediate objectives. Depending upon the demands of the presenting situation and the unique qualities of the client, the direction and emphasis of treatment can be tailored to meet these requirements by undergoing continual modification and revision. Crisis intervention therapy is, however, more often addressed to resolving the immediate problem at hand than to rooting out the deep-seated causes of personality dysfunction. (p. iv)

We will note throughout this chapter some of the ways in which crisis intervention is tailored to meet both long-range and short-range goals, and we will observe some basic criteria for determining the strategies used.

The first and foremost problem of crisis counseling is the same problem one encounters in first-aid treatment: the sudden unexpectedness of the situation. *Be prepared!* The Boy Scout's motto is an appropriate slogan for this type of situation. Because the counselor is never entirely ready for a crisis situation—because he or she usually does not expect it to happen—there is an immediate intuitive tendency to want to escape the situation instead of confronting it head on. Obviously, this is not to the client's advantage and should be avoided at all costs. But avoiding this tendency requires the ability to understand how to use crisis intervention techniques and to see their relationship to the basic theory of crisis states and crisis intervention. In this chapter we shall explore a variety of techniques and insights that the school counselor may find helpful in dealing with crisis situations, and we shall examine a segment of a crisis intervention session conducted by a skilled counselor. We will look at the specific types of crisis that are fairly common in the elementary and secondary school levels.

WHAT IS A CRISIS?

The type of crisis referred to in this chapter is determined by its external symptoms. All of us, at some time in our lives, have witnessed or experienced crisis situations—the loss of a loved one, an anxiety crisis, a general inability to cope with some life situations, a family crisis, an interpersonal crisis with one we love or care about, and so on. When a crisis reaches the stage where it immobilizes the person and prevents one from consciously controlling oneself, then it becomes the kind of crisis for which a person seeks counseling. Brockopp (1973) explores the dynamics of this type of crisis:

> When a person is confronted by a problem situation in which the previously used methods of restructuring his life or environment are either not available to him or not successful in solving his problem, the person is confronted by a critical situation; that is, one in which he is uncertain about the end or resolution of the problem. Since he is unable, through the use of his normal problem-solving techniques, to resolve the difficulty with which he is faced, the critical situation is emotionally hazardous and he may rapidly move toward a state of crisis. . . . *A crisis then is an intolerable situation which must be resolved, for it has the potential to cause the psychosocial deterioration of the person.* (p. 74, italics added)

The critical quality of a crisis, then, is the person's inability to deal with it. In this sense, a crisis is a subjective experience. What may be a mildly difficult situation to one person may be a crisis to another. Evaluation of the seriousness of the crisis, as well as diagnostic and prognostic considerations, are not determined by the situation itself but by the individual's response to the situation. Brockopp (1973) is sensitive to this subtle point of differentiation:

> The crisis . . . is not the situation itself, but the person's response to the situation. And the person's response is initially ambivalence and uncertainty, not knowing where he is relative to the problem or what he needs to do or can do to solve the problem and return to a point of equilibrium or homeostasis. (p. 76)

The implication of this statement is that what the person needs is some type of structured orientation suggesting how to go about solving his or her problem. And, indeed, one of the chief characteristics of the crisis situation is the individual's feeling of disorientation—of not being able to "get hold of oneself."

Forer (1963) differentiates between three levels of crises: a situational crisis brought about by a sudden change in the environment; an intrapsychic conflict crisis between the ego and superego (crisis of values); or a disintegration of the ego. A crisis of grief caused by the loss of a loved one is typical of the first type. A sexual crisis in which one's deepest values are challenged is the second type. An ego-fragmenting drug crisis induced by a hallucinogenic drug is an example of the third type. The three types will be explored more closely later in this chapter.

There may be some positive aspects to crisis as well. Leitner and Stecher (1974), for example, suggest that "crisis can lead to self-exploration and this may lead to clearer personal meaning and identity" (p. 29). They go on to suggest that crisis states give the individual a motivation for changing, for growing, for becoming:

> When forces of life push our daily existence to some edge whereupon we find ourselves in the midst of crisis, then we have a chance to emerge as changed beings. Growth implies change and change may imply growth. Emerging from a crisis can be a movement toward a new being-state, one that we may not have been capable of before the crisis. . . . Crises call for *risking*. People in crisis, under intense pressure, become introspective—they can look at themselves more deeply and honestly than in times of tranquility. (p. 32)

Although the fundamentals of the crisis situation per se are described by these general ideas, there are a number of different types of crises. Lindemann (1944), in an often-cited paper, describes the crisis of acute grief. Suicide crisis, the most commonly investigated class of crises, has been explored by Lester and Brockopp (1973). Drug crisis, a painfully prevalent problem of our time, has been discussed by Foreman and Zerwekh (1971), among others. Bieber (1972) has presented an interesting analysis of sexual crisis, a topic of increasing importance in crisis counseling. Each of these will be considered in the following sections.

CRISIS INTERVENTION THEORY

While there is no single theory of crisis intervention, there are a number of underlying principles that are inherent in all of the different crisis intervention approaches. These principles are usually the result of rich practical experiences more than of any theoretical or a priori constructs. Thus, counseling approaches as diverse as psychoanalysis and client-centered therapy use much the same strategies in dealing with crisis situations.

Leitner (1974) discusses three basic crisis models that would cover a generous variety of specific approaches: the equilibrium model, the cognitive model, and the psychosocial transition model. The *equilibrium model* views crisis as a state of psychological disequilibrium, in which the usual problem-solving methods fail to work. The *cognitive model* "defines a crisis as a breakdown of thinking resulting from a physical or psychological overload. This breakdown in thinking is considered to be a dysfunction in handling incompatible information" (p. 19). The *psychosocial model* "takes the viewpoint of the individual moving through necessary transitions in terms of *psycho-social development.*" This may involve changes in the internal or external life space of the individual.

Within these three models are many specific treatment paradigms for crisis intervention. The theory is to some degree indicative of the *goals* of the treatment; but in most respects the way a crisis situation is handled is totally independent of the underlying crisis theory. Strickler and Bonnefil (1974), writing from the social work point of view, cite eight similarities of crisis intervention to the traditional psychosocial approach to casework. These illustrate how the diverse theories of crisis merge with traditional counseling considerations on the practical level of treatment:

1. Treatment goals are devised to enhance the individual's ability to cope with problems of living in a problem-solving manner.
2. There is a circumscribed focus of treatment around specific and pertinent problem areas involving interpersonal conflicts and role dysfunctioning.

3. Active focusing techniques are utilized to maintain the concentration of the client on the "problem to be solved."
4. Treatment is basically geared to the level of conscious and near-conscious emotional conflicts. These conflicts are dealt with by seeking out their situational references and by maintaining a focus within them.
5. There is recognition of the importance of precipitating events in understanding the dynamics of the problem situation.
6. The goal is not to modify character traits or personality patterns although such changes do occur at times as a by-product of the treatment.
7. The treatment does not generally or characteristically involve working with the transference to the therapist except in circumstances where such transference manifestations are providing insurmountable obstacles to the treatment situation. The therapist recognizes transference impulses and moves to replace them with analogous feelings related to the client's current external situation and relationships.
8. The background of information on which treatment is based includes a knowledge of personality development and ego functioning, as well as a special knowledge of cultural-social determinants. (p. 38)

These eight principles are the bridge between crisis theory and intervention practice. They show most clearly how the ideas underlying crisis psychology are the roots for counseling practice. Let us now focus on the practical dimensions of crisis counseling.

THE COUNSELOR AND THE CRISIS

While we generally do not associate the term *contagious* with psychological states, there is considerable evidence that the concept is applicable to particularly turbulent states—such as a state of crisis. No doubt when the counselor first comes into contact with the extremely agitated client in a crisis condition, he or she will, if not careful, begin to experience personal parallel crisis feelings. Just as laughing is infectious (as anyone who has been overcome by a case of the "giddies" knows), so are crisis and grief in the sense that one can experience these feelings of another during difficult times.

If the counselor "catches" the client's turbulent and disorganized feelings, she or he will most likely be ineffective in helping the client get a grip on himself or herself, and possibly even be unable to function altogether. Direct observations have shown repeatedly that the counselor who catches the crisis feelings becomes frightened and defensive. The first manifestations of this are hasty and ill-timed attempts to assure the client that nothing is really the matter, that things will work themselves out. Although such assurance may seem to the counselor to be what the client needs, in fact it is reassurance for the counselor rather than the client.

A good rule for counselors to remember is this: *Do not try to reassure clients that everything is all right:* every time counselors do so, unless clients specifically asks for reassurance, counselors are actually reassuring themselves, defending their own anxiety, isolating themselves from clients' feelings.

What, then, should the counselor do when confronted unexpectedly by a client in a state of crisis? Probably the most significant help the counselor can offer at the outset is to remain calm, poised, and well in control of himself or herself. The client will then be able to begin to relate to the counselor on a constructive level.

The communication of a calming attitude serves two distinct but related purposes. First, it enables the counselor to function effectively, to allow the desperate client full expression of fears and conflicts, to listen to these expressions without severe censorship, to empathize with the client even when the empathic feelings are difficult for the counselor to deal with. If we view crisis as the failure of the psychological balancing (regulating) mechanism, it is easy to understand how the counselor's stability—his or her granite certainty—helps the client to re-establish psychic balance.

A second factor also plays a part here. Just as emotionally turbulent feelings are contagious, very calming and relaxed feelings can also be transferred from one person to another. How many times have we come into the presence of a calm and relaxed person and begun to feel that calmness and relaxation in ourselves? The counselor's calmness serves as an emotional tranquilizer, subtly helping the client to pull himself or herself together. It communicates to the client, in effect, the emotional message: "You see, even though these problems you are discussing are so difficult, we can remain calm while we talk about them. This will help us find a solution; it will enable us to deal with the problems."

To remain calm in the turbulence of the client's stormy emotions, however, is often no easy matter. If the counselor has foreknowledge of the crisis (or of the client's visit), she or he can prepare for the task at hand. But more often than not, the client's visit comes as a complete surprise to the counselor, who may or may not be emotionally ready for it. Even before the client says a word, the counselor unconsciously senses the crisis in the client's expression. Who cannot remember instances in which we have seen a person looking highly distressed, and even before the person says a word we are ready to ask, "What happened?"

In such a case, when the counselor is not ready for the client and has not had an opportunity to become composed, the counselor should ask the client to sit down and then excuse himself or herself for a moment. "Have a seat. I'll be with you in a minute," is a fine therapeutic intervention for both the client who is excited and for the counselor who is expected to help her or him. This pause reduces the anxiety and allows the counselor an opportunity to prepare for the highly emotional confrontation that is to ensue.

The next step, and probably the most important one, is to encourage the client into a dialogue. In order for the client to receive help at this critical time, it is necessary above all else that he or she be able to communicate feelings and difficulties to the counselor. This will probably require the client to focus on the immediate situation. For, as Kardener (1975) points out, "it is essential in crisis treatment to determine what specifically caused the patient to seek help at the time of the initial presentation" (p. 4). This is always a good place to begin.

While the specifics of the dialogue that follows will depend heavily on the precipitating trauma, Rapoport (1962) has outlined three patterns of responses that lead to a healthy crisis resolution:

1. Correct cognitive perception of the situation, which is furthered by seeking new knowledge and by keeping the problem in consciousness.
2. Management of affect through awareness of feelings; an appropriate verbalization leading toward tension discharge and mastery.
3. Development of patterns of seeking and using help with actual tasks and feelings by using interpersonal and institutional resources. (p. 216)

Just which of these three will be utilized and in which specific way depends on the client, his or her condition, and the particulars of the crisis-producing situation. Let us consider five types of individual crises that the school counselor is likely to encounter and see what we can determine about the course of each one.

GRIEF CRISIS

Certainly one of the most common of life's tragic situations is the crisis of grief. This crisis may occur when a loved one dies—either unexpectedly or after a long illness—and an individual is unable to manage attendant feelings and to get a grip on himself or herself in such a difficult and painful situation. The client may wish to talk about memories of the deceased, possibly about not treating the deceased as well as he or she now thinks the deceased should have been treated; about how the deceased enjoyed life and deserved to live; or how unjust the world is, taking away such a good person. The client may recall, with painful clarity, long-past incidents involving interactions with the deceased, and may express feelings about these incidents that have been hidden for some time.

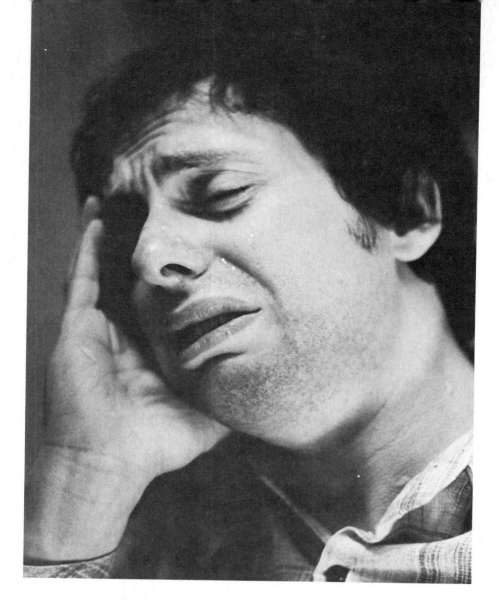

While the client is speaking, the counselor listens and tries to experience the client's painful feelings along with him or her. The death may have been recent or some time ago. "The duration of a grief reaction," Lindemann (1944) points out,

> seems to depend on the success with which a person does the *grief work,* namely, emancipation from the bondage to the deceased, readjustment to the environment in which the deceased is missing, and the formation of new

relationships. One of the big obstacles to this work seems to be the fact that many patients try to avoid the intense stress connected with the grief experience and to avoid the expression of emotion necessary for it. (p. 143)

The task of the counselor, in this case, is to help the client get through the "grief work." The counselor must recognize that the client's disorientation and confusion is caused by inability to deal with himself or herself and with the world without the presence of the deceased other. The client is, in Lindemann's words, "in bondage" to the deceased. To free her or him from this bondage, the counselor must be willing to experience along with the client the profound sense of loneliness and isolation that follows the initial mourning, the feelings of guilt and responsibility that plague the survivor. To do this, the counselor, of course, must have his or her own feelings well in control.

A variation of this counseling model for working with grief-stricken clients has been proposed by Hiekkinen (1979), who suggests a four-stage process similar to Lindemann's (table 14.1). Using this model, we conceptualize the counselor as first helping the client get over the initial shock, then dealing as necessary with the client's expressed and repressed anger, guilt, and depression. At each of these points, Hiekkinen points out the counselor's tasks and the potential dangers faced by the client. Finally, the counselor helps the client through the post-resolution phase in which the client learns patterns of readjustment to enable him or her to go on living in the world without the presence of the loved one.

Another aspect of grief crisis involves dealing with death before it happens. At times the counselor will work directly with the person who is dying and with the family of such a person. Significant work in this area has been done by Elisabeth Kübler-Ross, whose book *On Death and Dying* (1969) paved the way for much of the subsequent research on this subject. Her work is especially important because it represents the first serious effort to deal with the grief crisis experienced by the dying person *while in the process of dying,* rather than by the survivors. Kübler-Ross (1969) emphasizes the need to keep communication open between the dying person and the family, and suggests that the grief crisis can be worked through before the person dies, not just after. She delineates a five-stage process through which we adjust to the idea of death. The first stage involves denial, in which the person refuses to believe he or she is dying. Then there is anger—"Why is this happening to me?"—, followed by bargaining, depression, and finally, with the appropriate counseling interventions such as empathic understanding, a stage of acceptance. Dr. Kübler-Ross's book is well worth reading for any counselor involved in this type of counseling.

table 14.1

A CONCEPTUAL MODEL FOR RESOLVING PERSONAL LOSS

stage of grief	general issue	tasks	dangers	approaches
Shock / numbness	Confronting loss as issue	Approach loss	Avoidance	Experience sharing
Anger and guilt	Accept loss as loss	Make loss real Feel loss Sever bondage to loss	Denial of loss Enshrinement / adoration of loss	Memorial monument Celebration Dialogue with loss
Depression; resolution	Adjust to life without lost one	Build self-esteem Accept self as OK Claim personal strengths	Regression— clinging to dependencies, e.g., marriage to person resembling parent	Talk to strengths Projection into the future
Postresolution	Develop deeper relationships	Self-assertion Risk taking New growth	Withdrawal Isolation Status quo	New people out of familiar people Imagined disappearance

Note: From "Counseling for Personal Loss" by C. A. Hiekkinen, *Personnel and Guidance Journal,* 1979, *58* (1), 48. Reprinted with permission.

When Children Die

One particularly difficult situation for the counselor to deal with is the death of a child. And, in the school setting this is not infrequent. While many of the standard processes of bereavement are relevant here, there are other attendant difficulties as well. A child's death, whether expected or unexpected, is always premature, and people have difficulty understanding it. Wilkenfeld (1977) points out that "We have been led to believe that all the ills of the world—including death—are conquerable through technology. When a child dies, these misconceptions about the omnipotence of technology are rudely shattered and the event seems all the more tragic, unjust, and incomprehensible" (p. iv). She goes on to suggest that it is more difficult to adjust to this than it is to the death of an older person, even one who was in good health.

Usually, the death of a child requires that other children—friends, classmates, and siblings—be told about the death and that their feelings be dealt with. This is no easy task, and often parents and teachers are not up to the challenge because they themselves are having so much difficulty dealing with their own feelings. "From the time that a child is about two or three," Yudkin (1968) points out, "fantasy joins hands with experience, and death takes on new dimensions of curiosity, anxiety, and fear." Empathic communications allow the child to express the fantasy, to relieve himself or herself of the incumbent anxiety, and to grasp the reality of the situation.

The counseling of a terminally-ill child is a related problem. Crisis intervention is often indicated both for the child and for the family. Children, perceptive creatures that they are, recognize that they are dying, even if they do not fully understand the meaning of *dying,* of the effect of their illness upon others. Weininger (1975) points out:

> In my experience, the most prominent emotion displayed by children who are dying of various diseases was hostility. The young child of 2 to 3 years of age in the hospital also experienced great separation anxiety lest hospital staff leave him like his parents did. . . . The child of perhaps 6 or 7 would speak to me about death by expressing his fear in a confused and very angry way, still perceiving death as a punishment for being "bad." By this age, children seem to think that in some way they had caused their own illness and thus deserved to die. (p. 18)

Special training is necessary for the counselor in working with the terminally ill child and with his or her schoolmates. It is extremely important that the counselor be in touch with his or her own feelings. All of us are victims when children are dying: for all of us suffer their pains with them.

ANXIETY CRISIS

Another common crisis situation is termed the *anxiety crisis.* In this situation, the client is in a state of high anxiety and turmoil, usually uncertain of exactly what it is that has precipitated this feeling. A student walks into the counselor's office in a state of physical or emotional disorder or both. He or she rambles on, without making much sense, and exhibits various signs of disorganized thinking. Drugs, particularly hallucinogenic drugs, are a common cause of this type of crisis, although certainly the counselor should not assume that such a crisis is caused by drugs until this possibility has been adequately explored with the client. The best rule of thumb in an anxiety crisis is to ask the client object-oriented questions. These are questions of fact or circumstance that do not infringe upon the client's ego domain. What time did you leave for school today? and How old are you? and When did these feelings begin to bother you? are object-oriented questions. If a drug is suspected, the counselor should learn from the client what drug was ingested, how much, and when it was taken in order to determine whether medical attention is needed. The counselor should obtain a thorough drug history to assess patterns of drug use, which will prove important during the therapeutic and rehabilitative stages of the process.

Object-oriented questions have a calming effect upon the anxiety-crisis client because they compel the client to reorganize his or her thinking in order to respond logically to stimuli from the external world (the counselor's questions). As the client focuses attention upon these factual questions, he or she begins to reexperience a logical awareness of the world. Asking object-oriented questions is one of many ways to help the client reestablish psychic balance (Spotnitz, 1976).

Foreman and Zerwekh (1971) have suggested establishing feelings of rapport to help the victim of a drug crisis. If the client feels able to speak freely to the counselor, it will better enable her or him to "come down" from a bad trip. Bieber (1972) has discussed some of the methods for handling homosexual crises, resulting from overwhelming ego-dystonic feelings of homosexual panic. Tayal (1972) has examined the level of suggestibility in crisis states and found that the suggestibility of girls who were pregnant out of wedlock was significantly higher than those in a control group. These girls were more compliant than the girls in the control group, more willing to be followers than to seek their individuality.

SUICIDAL CRISIS

One of the most difficult types of crisis for the counselor to handle is the suicidal crisis, and yet suicide is one of the most common causes of death among school-age youths. In this situation the client expresses to the counselor either a specific or vague intention of committing suicide. Usually such a client is suffering from a feeling of overwhelming helplessness and futility, the belief that nothing can help, nothing can make a difference. He or she feels closed in, confined in an unbearable situation from which there is no escape. The fact that the suicidal client is speaking to someone about his or her feelings does indicate a desire for help, but it is an error to assume that the request for help means that he or she is not serious about suicidal intentions. The case books are rife with tragic examples of successful suicides committed shortly after an interview with a psychiatrist or counselor (Marilyn Monroe and Freddi Prinze are good examples of this).

In dealing with the suicidal client, the counselor must be willing to listen to the client and to recognize the miasma of depression that overcomes him or her. This is indeed a difficult thing to do, especially if the subject of

Famous and successful persons, such as Marilyn Monroe and Ernest Hemingway, have committed suicide because deep emotional needs prevented them from coping with life's demands and challenges.

suicide makes the counselor overly anxious. "In order to recognize depression in others," Motto (1978) points out, "counselors must resolve their own anxiety about the issue of suicide sufficiently to elicit pertinent information from clients" (p. 539). Otherwise, the counselor may attempt to deny or minimize the severity of the depression.

Facilitatively, it is necessary that counselors experience along with clients their feelings of total despair and hopelessness, their sense of futility and isolation, their feelings of abject grief and failure, their rage directed both at themselves and the world. The very worst thing the counselor can do is to tell a client that things are not as bad as they seem, that things will improve, that he or she has plenty of reasons to go on living. Although, realistically, all of these statements may be true, they make the client feel that he or she is not understood by the counselor, and they reinforce feelings of isolation from the people around him or her. For the counselor truly to help the client, she or he must fully experience the reality from the client's inexorably hopeless perspective. This means, among other things, that she or he is willing and able to explore in herself or himself those feelings of despair and emptiness that she or he personally tries to avoid confronting for the sake of personal mental health.

Experience and research have come up with a number of helpful rules in dealing with the suicidal client. It is generally a good idea to ascertain whether the method of destruction has been arrived at. "How do you intend to kill yourself?" the counselor may ask. The more specific the plans, the closer the client is to carrying out the act. Second, it is not advisable to have the client "look at the bright side" of the situation; if the client could accept a bright picture emotionally, he or she would not be in this predicament in the first place. Third, the counselor should always take all suicidal threats seriously. Many a counselor has had deep regrets after dismissing a serious suicide threat as an immature bid for attention.

The following section from a transcript of a counseling interview conducted between a skilled counselor (Bob) and a suicidal client illustrates some of the better ways of handling this type of situation.

Counselor (13)   Do you feel you can speak about it?

Client (13)   There's nothing to tell. It's just not worth it, man. Like, I believe we have a right to live or die, and that it's my choice. I just can't take it anymore. If I can't have her I don't want to live. There is nothing else to it.

Counselor (14)   You love her very much, don't you?

Client (14)   *(Laughs hysterically, out of control.)* Love her! I love her so much I could kill her. I love her more than anything—more than God, more than my family, more than myself. I can't go on, Bob. It's just not worth it. If I'm dead, I won't have to think about it—that's why.

Counselor (15)   How are you going to do it?

Client (15)   With the car. I'll crash it at 70 into a wall. I'm just gonna drive and drive until I have the guts to do it—then whammo! Right into the fucking wall. *(Laughs hysterically.)* You call her up, Bob, you tell her. You tell her what she did to me. Let her know.

Counselor (16)   There is no one like her, is there? I mean is there a chance, even, of finding someone else?

Client (16)   *(Laughs hysterically.)* No, Bob, no way out. I wish. But there's only her, Bob. You met her, you know. She was *the one*—the one for me and I blew it. Now, what's left—fifty years of pain and suffering—a lifetime of looking back at what could have been? It's not for me. I couldn't take it.

Counselor (17)	Can you take it for another two days? Can you stand the pain for that long?
Client (17)	Why? You think I'll get over it in a couple of days? You're kidding yourself. If you're trying to tell me she'll come back, Bob, you're not kidding *me*. I know what the score is. She told me.
Counselor (18)	No, I don't think any of those things. I see what the situation is, and I don't know what to say. But suicide's a big decision, a final one, and I think we should at least talk about it again before you go ahead. I'm not going to stop you—I'm not going to feed you a line about how things will work out. I just want us both to be sure. I'd like to see you Friday—just to talk about it one more time. If you want to go ahead then . . . I won't stop you. I don't feel I have the right.
Client (18)	Friday. That's two more days of this. I don't know if I can hold on till then.
Counselor (19)	If you don't think you can, call me; I'll see you before then. I just want to discuss it one more time before you make the big move. Of course, the final decision is up to you—but I'd like to talk with you first.
Client (19)	OK. Let's make it Friday. But if I can't hold out till then, I'll call you. Can I call at home?
Counselor (20)	Of course. Any time. . . .

The skill of the counselor shines through these brief lines of interaction. Note what Bob did and did not do. He never tried to convince the client that things weren't that bad, that he would find another girl friend. Certainly if the client were able to understand and appreciate such a realistic assessment, he would not be contemplating suicide in the first place. The counselor did allow the client to freely express his fantasies of self-destruction and inquired as to the means of this act. In this way he was able to assess the client's determination to carry out what he was threatening. The counselor did not ask the client to give up his suicidal plans, but rather to postpone them for a couple of days to give the two of them a chance to discuss them again. "The final decision is up to you," he told the client (Counselor [19]), assuring the client that he would not attempt to dissuade him from his plans. The counselor joined the client in his fantasy and emotionally understood the hopelessness and pain of the client's predicament. Everything he said to the client, everything he communicated both verbally and nonverbally, he actually felt in a manner parallel to the way the client

table 14.2

DO'S AND DON'TS IN CRISIS INTERVENTION COUNSELING

do's

1. Remain calm and stable. Prepare yourself psychologically for the turbulence of emotion which is soon to flow from the client.

2. Allow the client full opportunity to speak. Attempt to determine the type of crisis, its precipitating forces, and its severity. Interrupt only when it is for the client's benefit, never to relieve yourself of distressing feelings being induced by the client.

3. When indicated, ask object-oriented questions. These should, if asked properly, have a calming effect upon the client. If they fail to have such an effect, the counselor should consider the possibility that he is asking ego-oriented questions.

4. Deal with the immediate situation rather than its underlying, unconscious causes that may be left for later. "In the crisis period," Brockopp (1973) points out, "the person is open to change; the sooner we can work with him the more likely we are to minimize the possible deterioration of the personality and to develop an effective solution which will improve the personality functioning of the individual."

5. Have readily available local resources to assist the counselor: Community, medical, legal, etc.

don'ts

1. Don't try to "cheer up" the client, to tell him that his problems are not as bad as they seem, to reassure him *unless* he specifically requests these types of interventions (which is, by the way, the exception rather than the rule).

2. Don't ask the suicidal client to abandon his plans. Always make such a request a temporary delay.

3. Don't attempt to solve the total personality adjustment difficulty. Some counselors make the error of minimizing the crisis itself and attempting to get the client to speak about more "fundamental" things.

felt it. To treat the suicidal client, it is always necessary for the counselor to feel the full force of the client's depression. Table 14.2 shows some of the more important *do's and don'ts* of crisis counseling extracted both from the literature and from the author's personal experiences in this area.

Two other points should be mentioned about suicide-prone individuals. First, they often express their suicidal intentions inversely through homicidal threats. When such murderous rage is expressed very strongly in the clinical setting, it can quickly upset the counselor who feels that the client may lose control. "The murderous impulses of our patients are threatening to our defenses against aggression, and we may react with support and reassurance in order to support and reassure ourselves and not the patient. . . . Rather than helping the patient with his impulse control, this false reassurance may be interpreted as a prohibition against expressing these impulses outwardly and may *encourage* the patient to kill himself" (Rhine & Mayerson, 1973, p. 8). Counselors then should be especially sensitive to the possibility that the client who is frustrated in his or her homicidal rage may take it out on himself or herself.

Second, counselors must be aware of subtle but extremely important "distinctions among the wish to die, the act of self-injury, and the terminal outcome" (Cutter, 1971, p. 125). Clarification of the client's degree of intent at the beginning cannot only help to formulate the correct course of treatment but can also help assure that the client's vague death wish does not become a suicidal reality.

THE RAPE CRISIS

As the public becomes increasingly more sensitive to the plight of the rape victim, counselors and other mental health professionals are finding themselves more involved in efforts to provide supportive counseling services to the victim of rape. Since a considerable percentage of rape victims are school age, there is a distinct possibility that the school counselor, sometime in his or her career, will be called upon to intervene in a rape crisis.

While the general public, which for so many years did not know how to deal with the victim of rape, begins to recognize that a rape victim is not like other victims but a special type of victim who has suffered a trauma of a unique nature, there is a growing concern for providing counseling services, either immediately following the rape trauma or in the days, weeks, and months thereafter.

With this increased professional interest has evolved a comprehensive literature on the psychodynamics of rape and the psychological treatment of the rape victim. Deanna Nass (1977) has edited a volume that examines in depth the kinds of problems encountered by the rape victim, the extent of services available, and practical treatment considerations. She points out,

> The stigma attached to the victim of rape, traceable to cultural sex-role stereotypes and irrational popular judgments of female complicity, discourages the woman in crisis from reaching out for help. Hesitant to divulge her experience for fear of meeting with public ridicule and scorn, the rape victim is isolated from the supports available to victims of other kinds of misfortunes. This sense of isolation is aggravated by her knowledge of the customary treatment accorded rape victims by police authorities, representatives of the court, hospital personnel, social peers, and even close relatives. (p. 3)

Specific counseling interventions depend, to a large extent, on the setting. In the hospital emergency room, where the victim may be brought first, a different kind of approach will be required than in the individual or school counseling setting some weeks after the traumatic event (Williams & Williams, 1973). Broadly speaking, we can divide post-rape counseling into three periods: the hours immediately following the rape; the weeks thereafter; and long-range considerations. Although the school counselor will not be in the hospital setting, he or she should be familiar with counseling procedures there.

During the hours immediately following the rape, the victim is likely to be seen either at a police station or in a hospital emergency room. The goals of any counseling endeavors will be influenced in these settings by the need to obtain objective information about the crime, the circumstances, the victim, and about the perpetrator; information that may be helpful to the police and to prosecutors. It may also be important at this time to obtain relevant medical information, necessary for treatment. Is the student using contraceptives? Is she pregnant? Does she suffer from any gynecological problems? Is she under medication (a diabetic may forget to take her insulin during this period of distress)? What injuries did she suffer at the hands of her attacker? A thorough medical examination is routinely performed, and the student should be apprised of this. Moreover, an assessment of other family members' reactions should be noted by the interviewer.

The "rape trauma syndrome," as it is described by Holmstrom and Burges (1975) comprises an *acute phase* and a *long-term phase*. The acute phase "includes many physical symptoms, especially gastrointestinal irritability, muscular tension, sleep pattern disturbance, genito-urinary discomfort, and a wide range of emotional reactions" (p. 223). These problems are dealt with soon after the attack, and and many of them will be directed to the physician. But the counselor plays an especially vital part in helping the rape victim get through the long-term phase, which "includes changes in life-style, such as changing residence, seeking family and social network support, and dealing with repetitive nightmares and phobias."

During the weeks following the rape, the counselor should aim to find out the total effect upon the client's life. Have her relations with boys been affected? Has she noted any physical complaints? Have there been any adverse comments in the office? At school? In the community? How are her parents and family dealing with the situation? With whom has she discussed the rape, and what kind of reaction has she found? Because there is always a possibility of a delayed shock response, it may be a good idea to schedule an appointment six to ten months following the rape to see if the immediacy of the trauma has subsided.

PROBLEM PREGNANCY CRISIS

The incidence of nonmarital pregnancy is on the rise, especially among adolescent girls. In 1962, there were approximately 100,000 out-of-wedlock births to women under twenty. Six years later, there were about 166,000—an increase of 66%—despite the fact that the overall birth rate had been decreasing. (Braen & Forbush, 1975). In 1977, there were an estimated one million teenage pregnancies, 60% of which (600,000) resulted in the birth of a child (Cherlin, 1978). The others were intentionally aborted or miscarried (spontaneously aborted). In 1980, it is estimated that over one million children will be born out of wedlock, most of these to mothers under twenty years of age.

Several reasons have been suggested for this increase, and, in general, for why women opt for pregnancy outside of marriage. One position stresses that young girls who have babies during their adolescent years have serious emotional problems, and that out-of-wedlock pregnancy, therefore, can be viewed as a sign of some psychological or family disturbance. This is supported by much evidence; namely, a high rate of such girls come from broken homes; there is high incidence of parental alcohol abuse; there are often serious family conflicts and signs of violence in the home; there is a high frequency of sexually seductive fathers in the home; and there is a general lack of interest by the girl in socially acceptable activities, hobbies, and so forth. (Curtis, 1974; Abernathy, 1976; Hertz, 1977).

Aside from these psychological characteristics, a number of social factors have been identified. It has been suggested, for instance, that more liberalized sexual attitudes held by women contribute to an increased rate of nonmarital pregnancy (which, from this position, is viewed as an accidental consequence of sexual intercourse). Demographic factors indicate that the total population rate is related to the increasing teenage population (as a percentage of the total population), since teenagers make up the bulk of the total number of out-of-wedlock pregnancies. It has also been suggested that the new role of women allows them to raise a child on their own, even while working, and that this has the effect of encouraging single women who want children to go ahead and have one, without getting married.

Whatever the cause, the unplanned and unwanted pregnancy may precipitate a crisis situation. The task of the counselor in problem-pregnancy counseling is threefold.

1. To help the client understand the options available, and to help her arrive at a decision that she can live with.
2. To offer the client appropriate referral where necessary, and to assist the client in making necessary and often painful plans.
3. To provide follow-up services and emotional support.

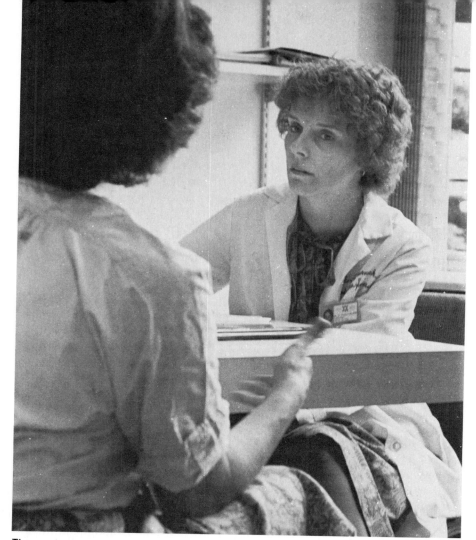

The contemporary counselor is often asked for help by
pregnant teen-agers.

Frequently, the adolescent girl who finds herself with an unplanned, unwanted pregnancy is not in a position to make a realistic decision about
what to do. She is often overcome by powerful emotions or is in a state of
crisis in which her decision-making abilities are seriously impaired. And,
since time is essential in decisions about whether or not to have an abortion,
it is imperative that the counselor help in this decision. Smith (1972) points
out:

> Women confronted with this crisis may decide to terminate the pregnancy
> without considering other alternatives or discussing their feelings about the
> situation. In panic they may obtain illegal abortions. . . . Tragically, some

later regret their decision and suffer guilt and self-recrimination. During the crisis, these women lose their emotional equilibrium because their habitual problem-solving devices are inadequate for the situation. (p. 67)

In addition to helping the crisis client make an appropriate decision, the health counselor will want to see that the client, if she elects for an abortion, is referred to the best facilities—if this is in accord with the conscience of the counselor. This requires, of course, that the counselor be familiar with the resources available in the community. Feminist groups have been useful in assembling information about the availability and evaluation of community facilities. Moreover, many of these groups have had extensive experience in abortion counseling and can understand the trauma the woman experiences as she gropes for her "right" decision.

Recent developments in abortion counseling have been thoroughly covered by Kalmar (1977b), who discusses the emotional implications of abortion from the legal, economic, social, political, and religious contexts in which the critical decisions are inevitably made. She points out that the abortion decision can never be viewed in vacuo, but must always be approached within the social context. Despite the wide range of research on the emotional effects of abortion, she points out, "there is a wide discrepancy, from those findings which indicate that abortion yields little or no negative consequences to those which reveal it to be a traumatic and damaging experience" (p. 1). In situations where the client experiences a crisis—where the client's rational decision-making abilities are overcome by the attendant anxiety—the emergency procedures for handling anxiety crises outlined above would be particularly germane.

Abortion counseling, especially in its post-decision phase, also involves providing information about contraception (Gedan, 1974). There is clearly a tendency among young girls who have an unwanted pregnancy and an abortion to repeat it, and without appropriate information about contraception, the likelihood increases. Often the unwanted pregnancy-abortion syndrome involves the girl's underlying feelings of emptiness that she is unconsciously trying to compensate for with the child. But because she is ambivalent about men, she cannot bear to carry a child into the world.

One other point should be mentioned. Barglow and Weinstein (1973) have taken note of the psychiatric aspects of the abortion decision in adolescent girls. They found that two major factors distinguished the adolescent's decision making from the adult's, and these should be kept in mind when working with the adolescent client:

1. The abortion decision is more "outer-other" directed by parents, peer group, or sexual partner, and is therefore more difficult or hazardous (for the girl);

2. Developmental immaturity contributes to ambivalence about the decision, to a distorted perception of the procedure, and to a variety of pathological reactions.

These observations emphasize the need for follow-up counseling, which will focus not only on contraception but also on resolving the emotional difficulties precipitated by the abortion.

SUMMARY

The state of crisis is characterized by a loss of orientation, a disequilibrium of the intrapsychic forces, and profound feelings of confusion, alienation, disruption, and panic. I opened this chapter with a dramatic example of school children who witnessed a brutal murder of a father by his son. Dallas (1978) has written about the extensive counseling that followed the event. Immediately afterward, all teaching was put aside for these students as crisis meetings were held at the school. Small groups were formed to deal with the children's feelings—and especially their fears. Teachers, parents, and the children themselves were involved in a long-range follow-up. We learn from this unusual situation how a counselor may, at any time, have to implement a crisis intervention program unexpectedly.

When the crisis client presents himself or herself to the counselor, he or she exhibits an emotional turbulence that may inadvertently be aroused in the counselor, in the form of emotional contagion. The counselor must, to be effective at such times, remain calm and poised. The actual counseling process depends on the nature of the specific crisis. But we did examine several general guidelines that would be applicable to all kinds of crisis situations.

In a grief crisis, the counselor must help the client get through the grief work; in an anxiety crisis, the counselor should determine the source of the problem and use object-oriented questions to help the client come to grips with it; in a suicidal crisis, the counselor must allow the client full expression of her or his feelings, determine if a method of destruction has been arrived at, experience the hopelessness along with the client, and request a temporary postponement of plans; in the rape crisis, it is important to provide information about services as well as give the full emotional support that the victim requires; in a problem pregnancy crisis, the client must be encouraged to explore her options and her feelings about them.

In all these cases, the counselor must be willing (and emotionally stable enough!) to experience along with the client the fears and frustrations that inevitably accompany a crisis situation. The counselor must react empathically and honestly, but with enough self-control and emotional detachment to avoid becoming overwhelmed by the impact of the crisis.

Counseling the Special Population Client

15

School counselors, whether they like it or not, are an integral part of the social context in which they live and work. The strengths and weaknesses of our society have a profound impact on the profession of counseling, especially as they are manifested in the types of clients who seek help, the kind of help clients expect, and the kinds of problems they bring into the counseling setting. Social problems are, by implication, counseling problems; that is, they are amenable to counseling interventions. In this chapter we will focus on clients who come to counseling from situations that are somewhat special—that are part of a discernible social context; one that varies from the normative or traditional. We will see that certain modifications of the counselor's perceptions—a certain coming to grips with personal biases and subjectivity—are important first steps for the counselor in helping the client from a special population.

We will begin with a special population group that includes over half the people in the world—women. Although everything I have said about counseling throughout this book is true for men and women alike, we will see in the following section that there are some special problems involved in counseling women. We will then turn our attention to special needs of the minority group client, on whom so much productive research has focused in the past decade. Finally, we will look at the child from the single-parent family or the "reconstituted" family—a category of client that will comprise about half the school population in the 1980s. We will begin with the subject of counseling women.

COUNSELING WOMEN

This section is reproduced by permission of Ruth H. Skydell.

Out of the turbulence and turmoil of the sixties and seventies, there emerged one movement that is having a profound impact on our traditional ways of thinking. As a result of the powerful and effective drive for women's liberation, the beliefs about women once shared by most members of our society are no longer accepted as universal truths, and our world will never be the same again.

In the wake of this disintegration of old values has come a new freedom for women—a freedom of choice. No longer is marriage the *only* option for every woman; no longer does a woman have to have children to consider herself "fulfilled"; no longer does she have to take "feminine" courses in school and be content with low-level jobs. It's a brand new, brave new world!

But while some women have already taken advantage of their new options—remaining unmarried, having fewer children and returning to school in middle age—many of them are frightened at the prospect of making choices. For, where there are so many options, life can be intimidating.

Today's woman is living with one foot in the past, the other in the future. It is a time of transition, a time of learning who she is. It is difficult because marriages aren't going to be the same and social relationships aren't going to be the same—the old, familiar patterns are changing rapidly. Many women are feeling a little lost in this strange, uncharted territory, with no historical referents to guide them. In trying to find their way, they are seeking help, looking to the counseling profession for guidance.

Like most of us, however, counselors are products of a culture which has always assigned women specific roles that are now in the process of being changed. Can counselors be of help if they, too, are finding many of their long-held beliefs shaken? Can they meet the challenge of the 1980s—the decade of transition?

Before we attempt to answer this question, let us first look at some of these beliefs and values which have been sanctified throughout the ages and are now being reevaluated.

The first of these is the belief that since men and women have different physical characteristics, they differ in many other important respects as well. Among these are status, role, temperament and abilities. Because of their greater physical strength, men were believed to be superior; therefore they were given a higher status in society, while women were relegated to inferior positions.

The female role was limited to domestic service and care for her husband and children; males were given all other interests and were expected to be achievers. The family, with the male regarded as its head and the female in a subservient role, was accepted as the basic unit in society.

In temperament, men were said to be aggressive, forceful, and efficient, while women were believed to be passive, docile, sensitive, emotional and impulsive. Studies have shown that such stereotyping is learned early by both sexes, increases with age, and holds true for all socioeconomic levels (Broverman et al., 1972; Schlossberg and Goodman, 1972).

These sexist stereotypes are learned from parents and reinforced by the educational system. A recent content analysis of the most widely used textbooks in the United States (Weitzman and Rizzo, 1974) led to the conclusion that children are being warped by the latent messages in these books. For example, the researchers found that females (who represent 51% of the population) comprise a mere third of the illustrations in second grade books and that this number drops to a fifth of the total number of illustrations on the sixth grade level. In other words, as textbooks increase in sophistication, women become less numerous and, by implication, less significant as role models. Covertly, then, a young girl is told that she, a female, is less important, as the textbook world shifts to the world of adults. Furthermore, the study revealed, boys are shown as active, skilled and adventuresome; girls as passive, watching, and waiting for the boys. Adult men are shown in over 150 occupational roles, while almost all adult women are shown as housewives. In science books, boys are shown looking through microscopes and pouring chemicals, while girls stand and watch them, and in arithmetic books, men are shown earning money, while women are pictured slicing pies.

One area in which women have experienced blatant discrimination over the years, is the world of work. This discrimination is reflected in the amount of pay they receive, as well as in the limited job opportunities for women. Although their situation today has improved in some respects, women still earn considerably less than men in all occupations.

Women are heavily clustered in low-paid, low-skill jobs. Opportunities for advancement are denied them. Many unions exclude them from apprentice programs and large industrial concerns often will not enroll them in their executive training programs. Women occupy relatively few high prestige positions in government, business, or in the key professions.

A number of rationalizations have been put forth for denying women the opportunity to work in so-called "male" jobs. Discriminatory hiring practices are attributed to the belief that some jobs are "men's work," such as those requiring the lifting of heavy objects; or that it is a "masculine" field, such as engineering (although in the USSR, every third engineer is female). Family responsibilities, the fear of high rates of absenteeism of married women, or the belief that they will leave the job if their husbands relocate are often cited by employers as deterrents to occupational advancement of women.

Why do women tolerate this situation? Why have they for so long accepted the notion that the world is divided into two parts—men's work and women's work?

One answer may be found in the statement by Weisstein that "what a person does or who he believes himself to be will in general be a function of what people around him expect him to be and what the overall situation in which he is acting implies that he is" (1971, p. 70).

Is it at all surprising then, since the male stereotype is regarded more positively, that studies have shown women to have more negative self-concepts than men (Broverman et al., 1972)? Or that college women, when asked to evaluate a professional article, valued the identical material more highly when they thought it was produced by a man than when they believed it was written by a woman (Goldberg, 1971)?

This acceptance of their inferior status in the work world also stems from the widely held notion that for women, intellectual achievement is equated with loss of femininity and popularity. Wolfe (1969) observed that sex role identity is established at the same time that careers are chosen. Young women, therefore, may be reluctant to choose careers that detract from their femininity. Because high levels of achievement are not considered appropriate for females, the price of career success might be social failure. Bright women often find themselves in a double bind. They must achieve in order to live up to their own standards, but must avoid success in order to retain their femininity.

On the basis of her doctoral research, Horner (1970) states "When the fear of success interferes with the desire to be successful, the result is an inhibition of achievement motivation." This "motive to avoid success" may be operating within some women, interfering with their intellectual and professional accomplishments. She concluded that many young women faced with a conflict between their need for achievement and their female image will conform to the sex role stereotype, with possible negative emotional consequences for the individual (1972).

Thus, although women today have many options available to them, many of them are in conflict. Times of change are very stressful and many difficult challenges to the counseling profession have emerged. In particular need of creative counseling are women who find themselves in the following situations: (1) the woman presently in her thirties, forties or fifties, who was brought up with the old sexual stereotypes and is now having real difficulty trying to resolve the conflict between newly awakened strivings and early social learning, (2) the woman who has reached the stage (usually between the ages of 35 and 40) when her husband and children are busy and she finds herself less needed or useful. She faces what Brandenburg (1974) calls "a renewed identity crisis"; (3) the woman who knows what she wants to do with her life — who wishes to continue her education or reenter the work world — but does not know how to go about it; (4) the woman who faces a conflict between career and marriage; (5) the woman who has a poor self-image, and (6) the young woman in high school who must make educational and vocational decisions that will affect her entire life.

Counseling Implications

As we noted at the outset, counselors, no matter how dedicated they may be to the goal of helping their clients become self-actualizing human beings, are themselves products of society's value system. As a consequence, both male and female counselors hold biases about women (Thomas and Stewart, 1971). In what has become a classic study of clinician's attitudes, Broverman et al. (1970) have established that "a double standard of health" exists. This stems from the clinicians' acceptance of an "adjustment" notion of health. They equate masculine rather than feminine behavior with what they consider to be normal and adult. They generally agree that the healthy woman is more submissive, less independent, less adventuresome, more excitable in minor crises, more emotional, and less objective than man. They state: "For a woman to be judged healthy, from an adjustment viewpoint, she must adjust to and accept the behavioral norms for her sex, even though these are generally less healthy for the mature adult" (p. 6).

Extensive research on the phenomenon of experimenter bias, which demonstrated that a person's expectations about another person's behavior come to act as a self-fulfilling prophecy (Rosenthal, 1963), leads us to an inevitable conclusion: if a counselor enters the counseling relationship with a built-in bias, of which he may not even be aware, it cannot help but affect his counseling stance. For example, if counselors believe that certain behaviors are appropriate for men and others for women, this may influence their advice to a particular client to choose a career which in her case might not be the one for which she is best suited. There are many stories of discouragement of girls for professional careers by guidance counselors unaware of their own biases.

Other ways in which counselors may show their bias in the counseling relationship include depreciating the importance of a woman's career, using a client's attitude toward child-bearing as an index of emotional maturity, and making her feel she must adjust better to her role as a wife and mother, instead of encouraging her to become an independent person. A scene in a 1974 television special, "Growing Up Female," shown on the Public Broadcasting System, graphically illustrates this last point. A high school guidance counselor, talking to a young girl who is pregnant and about to marry the father of her child, says: "A girl should be neat, clean, attractive, kind, courteous and have a good attitude toward life. The husband should make the major decisions and the wife should understand and go along with his decision. . . . Don't expect him to do housework. Give him time to do his studies—he must compete and he must strive to be successful and you want him to be a success, so you must do the laundry and the housework. . . . The wife has an obligation to take care of his meals and help him to be a healthy, happy and successful man."

Sex role stereotypes are also reflected in some of the materials used by counselors in the counseling interview. Interest inventories, college catalogues and career brochures often contain biased statements which would influence a client in one direction rather than another (Schlossberg and Goodman, 1972). To encourage qualified women to consider nontraditional careers, the Career Education Program at the National Institute of Education (NIE) has released a set of "Guidelines for Assessing Sex Bias and Sex Fairness in Career Interest Inventories." These new guidelines are a valuable tool for test developers and users of career interest inventories who wish to overcome the problem of sex bias. Specific suggestions on detecting and minimizing sex bias are given.

It is generally agreed (Gardner, 1971) that counselors must accept counseling bias as a fact and try to bring their biased feelings into the open so that they are better able to deal with them and remove them from the counseling encounter. Counselors must critically examine their own sex-role stereotypes and ask themselves if their counseling and/or the materials they use tend to perpetuate sexism. One method of discovering one's personal sex role bias is through sensitivity training.

But, as Oliver (1975) points out, becoming aware of one's bias is not enough. This awareness must be accompanied by constant monitoring and corrective action on the part of counselors. For example, they must be careful not to discourage a client, even subtly, who expresses a nontraditional career choice, and to suggest a wider range of career options for the client who does not express a nontraditional choice, but who is obviously suited for such a career.

After becoming conscious of one's biases and learning to deal with them, what can counselors do to help women who come to them with one or more of the problems mentioned earlier?

Case 1: The woman who is in conflict over the variety of choices open to her in the 1980s because she has been brought up with the old cultural stereotypes.

Although she knows intellectually that the world is a different place today, she is torn emotionally between her old stereotyped beliefs and the new values. Perhaps the most helpful thing the counselor can do is to arrange for her to participate in group discussions with other women who are in the same situation, at which they can air their fears and doubts. Bringing in women who have successfully resolved this type of problem can be very effective. The counselor should also suggest that she read some of the literature put out by the National Organization for Women and help her, through the use of nonsex-biased instruments, to find out what her vocational interests and abilities are. On the basis of these, the counselor may recommend a positive plan of action for her to pursue, while continuing to participate in the group sessions until she has achieved a resolution of her conflicts.

Case 2: The woman who has a poor self-image.

The counselor must help her redefine herself in the face of role stereotypes and help her improve her concept of herself as a woman. He or she can give her reading material on the contributions of women in history, literature, the arts and sciences. To help her modify her attitude toward herself, the counselor may also employ assertiveness training, urge her to take female studies courses and help her, through various instruments designed to reveal her skills and aptitudes, to become aware of her potentialities and start to fulfill them. Use of Rogerian techniques is also recommended as an aid in enhancing her self-image.

Case 3: The young girl in need of career guidance.

Because women are remaining unmarried longer, having fewer children and returning to work when their family responsibilities have lessened, early career guidance is assuming crucial importance, and the counselor must really be an expert on changing developments in the occupational world.

Since women, as a rule, follow much more complex career and life patterns than men, who follow a relatively simple and straightforward pattern (Ginzberg et al., 1966), counseling women has a somewhat different aspect from counseling men. Oliver (1975) suggests that the counselor emphasize career counseling for women "within a life-planning context, taking into consideration the developmental stages involved" (p. 435). It is important to reach a girl at an early stage, going back as far as the junior high or even the elementary school level, if she is to be encouraged to consider nontraditional careers. Early expert counseling can also help to forestall later problems which may arise when a woman reaches the age at which her family responsibilities decrease, or when she is left alone, through divorce or the death of her spouse. In order to be effective, the counselor must take the initiative—he or she must reach out to the girl and not wait for her to ask for help. She might not be aware that she needs it.

The counselor must keep an up-to-date file on occupations that are available to women—which are changing from week to week—and make sure that the counselees are aware of changing qualifications within a field. When planning a program for a high school girl, counselors must plan with an eye to the future. They should try to get girls to aim high. They should advise high school girls to seek the maximum education to enable them to qualify for high-level jobs, if they have the ability. Inviting a successful career woman—a doctor, for example—to speak to the high school students, to provide a career model for them, is an excellent device for raising their aspirations.

The school counselor should work with the curriculum committee to see that changes are made so that boys and girls may enroll in any course available at the school, in accordance with the rules issued by the Department of Health, Education and Welfare, for enforcing the ban on sex discrimination in public schools and colleges. The counselor should also see to it that the school library purchases books about the women's liberation movement and equality for women. Information concerning the National Organization for Women and the special issues of popular magazines dealing with college and careers should be made available in the library as well.

Finally, the counselor should encourage high school girls to form discussion and consciousness-raising groups to air their mutual problems. The mothers of the girls should also be encouraged to form such groups so that they will be receptive to the new ideas being discussed by their daughters.

These suggestions for today's counselors who must face the many challenges of a society in transition are by no means all-inclusive. In addition to adopting some or all of them, truly creative counselors will bring their own ingenuity to bear, improvising, experimenting with many approaches, always keeping in mind the goal of helping each woman to follow the course most appropriate for her so that she may function to the best of her ability in a mature and healthy society.

COUNSELING MINORITY GROUP CLIENTS

The civil rights movement of the 1960s, which included legal precedents, social activism, and a new consciousness of the plight of minority members, has had a profound influence upon the counseling profession. Not only have counselors come to realize the special needs of minority members, but they have also been compelled to rethink critically and objectively their own attitudes and beliefs about clients from minority groups. Although there are certainly substantive differences in the ways of counseling different types of minority members, the basic idea that underlies the problems is the same for all minority groups. We shall look at some of these problems and examine ways in which the counselor can become effective in work with minority group clients.

Bell (1971) points out that "the counseling psychologist, be he black, white, or otherwise, is likely to function as a culturally deprived person in the black community if his training has taken place in the typical traditional counselor training program" (p. 104). This is a serious indictment of counselor training programs and one that Bell does not go on to substantiate. Nevertheless, it is clear to those who are associated with such programs that there is often insufficient opportunity for counselors in the training experience to examine and readjust their ethnic sensitivities. Perhaps the difficulties that plague counselors in their interactions with minority group clients would be significantly lessened had they had an opportunity to express their feelings during their training. Beginning with the assumption that this has not been the case for most counselors, we turn our attention to the question of what counselors, once engaged in their practice, can do to function effectively with minority group members.

First the counselor must recognize the needs and perceptions that differentiate minority group counselees from other counselees. Often, all too often as a matter of fact, the minority group member is from a lower socioeconomic group than is the white counterpart. He or she may be experiencing difficulties in school as a result of a poor home environment, of physical or mental deprivation or both, or of a general misunderstanding with his or her teachers. Below are listed nine special needs and perceptions that I have found commonly expressed or indicated by minority group members, particularly black and Puerto Rican students, in the New York City school system:

1. The MGC (minority group client) needs to feel that he or she is perceived as an individual, rather than *only* as a member of a group.
2. The MGC wants to be able to retain his or her own identity as well as to function within the context of the larger society.
3. The MGC may tend to perceive the white counselor as being *white,* above all other perceptions. This implies that any general stereotypical feelings about whites will be projected onto the counselor.
4. MGCs need a sense of social mobility; they want to be able to feel that they have an opportunity to rise above their present station in life. Often this hope has been tempered by the realization of the severe restraints that poverty imposes upon social advancement.
5. The MGC wants the emotional freedom to be able to express prejudices toward white people. He or she wants to be able to feel that the white counselor will not be overly threatened by this expression.

6. The MGC wants the school—through its curriculum, its teachers, and its rules—to relate to his or her world rather than to the world of whitey.
7. MGCs see things happening around them over which they feel no control. They want to be better able to control their world, and their own destiny, but they are lacking many of the educational and psychological tools necessary for doing so.
8. The MGC often has less opportunity than his or her white counterpart to discuss home and family life problems. Loyalty to the family may deter him or her from discussing these with an outsider.
9. The MGC may see the school as the primary social institution (which is considered oppressive and nonresponsive), and be inclined to act out his or her rage and anger within the school environment.

The counselor's understanding of these nine special situations will enable her or him to understand better and interact with the minority group client. This is not to suggest that understanding alone will enable the counselor to accomplish this very difficult task. Often the obstacles between counselor and client are insurmountable, especially when the client is a late adolescent who for so many years has seen herself or himself as a victim of a system that has little concern for and even less understanding of her or him.

Clemont E. Vontress (1969; 1973) has been particularly vocal in discussing the counselor's interactions with members of minority groups. He has presented the variety of problems confronting the counselor sitting opposite the black client and attempting to relate to him or her constructively and therapeutically. "To achieve a high degree of positive regard for people who are different," he suggests that "the counselor must learn more about their [MGCs'] way of life and their ethnic and social values" (Vontress, 1973). This is easier said than done; it is often extremely difficult to understand the values of people who are different from ourselves. Melville J. Herskovits's monumental study, *The Myth of the Negro Past,* should be read by every counselor who deals with black students. This book examines black culture from its African roots to twentieth-century America, and it is an invaluable aid in understanding the subtleties of the contemporary black person's cultural and social environment. The willingness of the counselor to study conscientiously the past of a client's heritage avoids what Vontress (1969) calls "the greatest blockage in the relationship . . . the counselor's lack of understanding of the sociopsychological background of the client."

There are other difficulties in counseling the black or minority group student, as well. Russell (1972) points out that the black student's general negative image of guidance makes the task of counseling difficult:

> For the black student whose lot is to attend those schools dominated by white administrators and where white counselors are the main force in shaping his present and future course, the image of guidance is so negative that it is completely stultifying. The student perceives guidance as an instrument of repression, controlled by counselors who constitute a roadblock he must somehow manage to get around if he has ambitions that do not coincide with those his counselors consider appropriate for him. (p. 288)

This negative attitude, however, can be lessened if the counselor shows a recognition of the client's needs and perceptions as enumerated. Probably there is no situation in counseling that evidences as clear-cut a need for the nonjudgmental attitude as the interaction between counselor and client of different races, different cultures, and different socioeconomic levels.

Ivey (1977) has discussed the language gap between counselors and clients of different ethnic backgrounds. Recent psycholinguistic studies have amplified the significance of this problem considerably, and most counselors nowadays at least recognize the problem, even if they are not entirely able to overcome it. Probably the best way to overcome the language gap is through exposure to and learning of minority group idiosyncratic language patterns and the specialized terms and usages of these groups—in other words, through the same processes that enabled us to learn our native language.

William H. Grier and Price M. Cobbs, two black psychiatrists, have analyzed many of the emotional difficulties of the black in contemporary American society in an important work, *Black Rage.* "The overriding experience of the black American," they point out, "has been grief and sorrow and no man can change that fact." All we can really ask is that the counselor understand this perception of blacks and interpret it in a way that is meaningful both to the counselor's intellect and to his or her conscience.

A particularly insightful and well-researched paper by Smith (1977) goes into some of the ways stereotyping affects our perception of black clients. She points out how subtle biases in empirical counseling research over the years have lent credence to a variety of stereotypes regarding the presumed expectations and needs of the black client. While there may be some special adaptations required in counseling blacks, she concedes, at the forefront of our recognition should be their individuality as persons—just as we would recognize this with white clients:

> At times, we in the counseling profession tend to forget that the intellectual abstractions we create for understanding people, that is lower class, culturally different, and Black, are really only intellectual abstractions that are designed initially to understand life better not as abstractions but as reality. We prophesy and we seek to fulfill our phrophecies with the circumstances of human beings. . . .
> Within any group of people, there is a broad range of behavior. Viewing Black individuals as nearly all the same or as merely further instances of a type rather than as individuals is a dangerous course and promotes ill-conceived and poor counseling strategy. . . . In order to find the truths of Black people . . . we must take off our blindfolds to the social ills of our society and become involved in the human condition of those whom we seek to study. (p. 395)

Problems of minority groups other than blacks have also found an important place in the literature. Atkinson, Morten, and Sue (1979) have put together a superb textbook on specialized problems in counseling American minorities. Included in this work are counseling implications for, in addition to the black client, the American Indian client, the Asian-American client, and the Latino client. The cross-cultural perspective of the authors helps the counselor better understand the subtle differences among members of different ethnic groups. Kuppersmith (1978), who taught a seminar on ethnic identity, had her students write short autobiographies dealing with ways their ethnicity (including Jewish, Irish, Puerto Rican, Italian, black, and others) had affected them psychologically and socially. Through this exercise many of the students made important self-discoveries. The published collection, *Ethnic Identity Through Autobiography* (Kuppersmith, 1978), is a valuable resource for any counselor working with minority group clients.

COUNSELING CHILDREN OF DIVORCE

About 60 percent of the couples obtaining a divorce in the United States have children at home, most of them less than college age. Where at one time "it may have been conventional wisdom that couples, no matter how unhappy with one another, should stay together for the sake of the children," Weiss (1975) points out, nowadays, "couples appear to believe that a stressful two-parent home provides a less satisfactory setting for a child's development than a tranquil one-parent home" (p. 167). With this change in attitude, a greater number of parents with dependent children are willing

The divorce of one's parents can be a very painful,
confusing, and disruptive experience for the child.

to separate and divorce, and are attempting to raise their children on their
own. This means that the school counselor will most likely be working with
a significant number of children from divorced families.

For most children, the adjustments following parental divorce are complicated and difficult. They are made even more so by a number of factors:
the child's dependency on both parents; his or her dual loyalties and mixed
feelings; the divided time the child may spend with each parent; the reactions

of peers. Even the most conscientious of parents will have difficulty helping the child through the post-divorce trauma. The parent is, after all, not only emotionally involved in the situation and working out his or her own adjustment, but also may well be viewed by the child as the one responsible for the divorce, or at least half responsible. Since so many of these children are of school age, the school is taking an increasing role in providing group and individual counseling support for children of divorce in much the same way as adult post-divorce adjustment groups are springing up for the ex-spouses (Green, 1978). In a way, what this is telling us is that divorce is becoming recognized as a fact of life in the United States, and social institutions, such as the schools, are changing to accommodate to it.

Lora Heims Tessman (1978), who has done extensive research on the social and psychological processes of child adjustment following divorce has published an important book, entitled *Children of Parting Parents*. She describes some of the complex stages and situations children may go through during the period of readjustment. I have summarized three of the main types of reactions:

> *Identification with the lost parent*—the child imagines he or she is the lost parent (the parent not living at home) and behaves as that parent did in the home—or imagines a fantasy relationship with the absent parent. We see this, for example, when a boy suddenly takes on his absent father's mannerisms, even to the extent of doing imitations of the father. Or, a child may tell friends that the missing father is on a secret government mission and will be back in a few months.
>
> *Quest for the wanted absent person*—the "quest" may be psychological or may be expressed through such behaviors as restlessness, creativity, hyperactivity, antisocial behavior. This can be considered a part of the adjustment process because the child is still working through the disquieting feelings of abandonment.
>
> *Grieving*—the child goes through a reaction "as if" the parent had died, but without the parental support that would be present if the other parent had died. This reaction becomes especially strong when the child's expected contact with the missing parent is frustrated (say, if the father fails to show up on his visiting day).

A knowledge of these typical emotional processes should help the school counselor better appreciate how a child's academic performance may be affected adversely following the divorce of his or her parents. It should also encourage the counselor to recognize that school-related problems and personal or family problems can never be viewed in isolation from each other.

The Reconstituted Family

The majority of people with children who divorce, or whose spouse dies while they have growing children, eventually remarry. The decision to remarry is often influenced by the presence of children because many people feel it is better for the children to be a part of a family. This pattern has become so widespread that it is estimated now there are about eight million families in the United States with at least one child and a step-parent. These hybrid families are called "reconstituted families."

The reconstituted family poses more than its share of problems for the child(ren) involved. The questions of dual loyalties, of the development of appropriate new roles, and the understanding of family statuses are complicated enormously by the experiences the children and spouses had in the previous family setting. So, too, are the questions of how to deal with step-siblings, with new relatives, with moving to a new place and adjusting to a new life-style. Understandably, there is a high divorce rate among families that have been reconstituted after divorce, which may pose additional problems for the children.

In her landmark study of the reconstituted family, sociologist Lucile Duberman (1975), herself a member of a reconstituted family, investigated in-depth remarried couples and their children, focusing on the stepchild-step-parent-stepsibling interactions. This is a fascinating book, well worth reading, and I will only summarize a few of the key points, relevant to working with the child from such a family.

> For most remarried people, the greatest single problem they faced (and the most arguments they had with their spouse) is about child rearing.
>
> Stepfathers (especially those who had never been married before) generally had better relationships with their stepchildren than did stepmothers, regardless of the sex of the stepchild.
>
> Stepsibling relationships varied. "When both sets of children lived in the same house, the relations between them were more likely to be "Excellent" than if they lived in different houses. Furthermore, when the remarried couple had a child together, their children were likely to have more harmonious relations" (p. 75)
>
> The younger the remarried couple the greater the "integration" of their reconstituted family. Integration increased if (1) the previous marriage had dissolved because of death of a spouse; and (2) where there was a child from the present marriage.
>
> The better the relationship between husband and wife, the higher the integration of the family, the more satisfaction experienced by the children.

When we consider the implications of these findings, it becomes clear that a reconstituted family can only work as well as the remarried spouses are able to get along. Where there is harmony between the parents, there is more likely to be found harmony among the children. Moreover, to increase the chance for a successful reconstituted family, many remarried parents decide to have their own child. This makes sense insofar as it has been shown that this offers a greater sense of integration, more family stability, and better relations with the children of the former marriage(s).

CHILDREN FROM SINGLE-PARENT FAMILIES

Not all children from single-parent families will be members of reconstituted families or living with a parent following divorce. Many will have started out as members of single-parent families or will have arrived at that status by the death of one of the parents. What effect on the child does living in a single-parent household have?

Herzog and Sudia (1973) provide the most comprehensive review and analysis of the literature on the subject, although their work is unfortunately limited to the children of fatherless families. Moreover, the studies examined evaluate the effects of father absence on *boys*, which reflects the general trend of research in this area in which girls, for the most part, have been sorely neglected. In summarizing the findings of over 120 studies, Herzog and Sudia (1973) concluded:

> Three subject areas have been discussed in some detail: juvenile delinquency, school achievement, and masculine identity. Evidence concerning each . . . is neither clear enough nor firm enough to demonstrate beyond doubt whether fatherless boys are or are not overrepresented among those characterized by the problems commonly attributed to them. [A possible exception here is school achievement, about which the finding "no difference" seems solid.]
>
> Despite the ambiguity of the results, the review does provide sufficient basis for some firm conclusions that apply to all three areas, and probably to any research on the effects of the father's absence.
>
> 1. However inconclusive present evidence may be, there is a firm basis for rejecting blanket generalizations about the consequences of father's absence. Its behavioral and psychological effects are probably much less uniform and much less uniformly handicapping than is widely assumed.
> 2. The impact of the father's absence on a boy is conditioned and to a large extent mediated by a complex of interacting variables and probably cannot be explored fruitfully as a distinct, critical variable in itself.
> 3. More specifically, the impact on a boy growing up in a fatherless home is strongly affected by the elements that were presented before the father's absence.

4. The number of parents in the home is likely to be less crucial to the child's development than the family functioning of the present members—which is far harder to assess. Family functioning would include the mother's role and coping ability as well as the general family climate.
5. Family functioning is determined not only by individual characteristics and the interactions of its members but also by the circumstances and environment of the family unit. (p. 214)

These are broad conclusions, drawn from a wide range of studies conducted over many years, using different methodologies, different assumptions, and attempting to answer different types of questions. Such studies rarely touch upon the child's deeper feelings, however, and often prove inadequate in answering questions about the child from the single-parent family because the absence of a parent is only one of the many different factors affecting the child. Recognizing this problem, Nass and Nass (1976) pinpoint seven "variables which contribute to the differences in the children of split and intact families," and any or all of these might carefully be considered by the counselor in assessing the child's situation:

1. the age at which the child is deprived of the parent;
2. the sex of the single parent who rears the child;
3. the family attitudes and social values of the parent in charge of the household;
4. the economic consequences of the split household;
5. the circumstances which deprive a child of either parent (i.e., death, divorce, separation, illegitimacy, military leave, etc.);
6. the race and cultural norms of any particular one-parent household; and,
7. the sibling composition of a one-parent family. (p. 188)

Most of these variables are just as relevant in assessing the typical child from the intact family, which may imply that the same factors that influence all children's behaviors influence the behaviors of the child from the single-parent family. However, there is some evidence of significant differences in aggressive behavior patterns and value development (particularly as a result of nonidentification) between children from father-present and father-absent families.

Counseling Implications

What is the counselor to make of all this information? What conclusions can be drawn? What relevance for the practical aspects of school counseling is indicated? There are no easy answers, but it is extremely important that the counselor be aware of which students are from single-parent families.

This not only enables the counselor to be especially sensitive to any problems that may arise because of this situation but also assures that he or she will not place the child in embarrassing situations that could easily have been avoided.

> Mrs. Darby gave Alonzo a note to bring home to his mother and told him, "If you don't bring this note back, signed by your mother, I'm going to report you to the principal." Alonzo failed to show up for the rest of the week, and Mrs. Darby contacted the school social worker. It turned out that Alonzo's mother was dead—he lived with his aunt and, off and on, with his father—and he was emotionally shaken when told to give a note to his "mother." Had the counselor known that Alonzo didn't live with his mother, she would have avoided such a damaging faux pas.

In cases of father absence, either temporary or permanent, the special needs of the single mother may also have to be taken into account by the counselor; for these special needs often place an obligation on the child or affect the child in a more secondary way. "The single mother," Ruma (1976) points out, "has to deal with her own feelings of loss as well as these feelings in her children. Frequently children increase demands and expression of aggression toward the person with whom they have most frequent contact, which usually is the mother." A counselor may point this out to the teacher, who will in turn try to work out day-to-day problems with the child without unnecessarily calling in the mother.

SUMMARY

In this chapter we looked at some special client populations, considering some of the challenges involved. We began by examining ways in which the counseling of women is often affected by stereotyping. We pointed out that not only should the counselor examine his or her own biases, but should also be aware of some of the nefarious social pressures on women to keep them from succeeding. We next looked at the minority group client, noting some special adaptations of general counseling principles. Finally, we looked at issues involved in counseling the children of divorce and children from special family situations.

Glossary of Counseling and Testing Terms

ability test A test designed to measure what a person can do. Ability tests are subdivided into aptitude tests and achievement tests.

achievement test A test usually administered at the end of a period of learning to measure growth and progress.

age norms Values or norms that show the typical or average performance for individuals of different age groups on a standardized test.

alienation A feeling of loss of significance in the world, of apathy and diminished consciousness.

anal stage The second of Freud's psychosexual stages, named for the part of the body (the anus) that is the child's primary erogenous zone and through the actions of which he or she expresses many feelings to the world.

analytical psychology The system of dynamic psychology and psychotherapy developed by Carl Gustav Jung.

anecdotal record A written report describing an incident (or connected series of incidents) describing an individual's behavior. Incidents are usually chosen because they appear significant for the understanding of the individual, either as being typical of him or her, or as being unusual and surprising.

antidepressant A drug that inhibits severe organic depression by altering certain chemicals in the brain that are believed to be associated with depression.

anti-illness movement The tendency to reject the medical model as an explanation of psychological problems.

anxiety A state of tension, typically characterized by rapid heartbeat, shortness of breath, and other similar manifestations of autonomic nervous system arousal.

APA American Psychological Association, the chief representative professional organization of psychologists in the United States.

APGA American Personnel and Guidance Association, representing psychological and non-psychological counselors in all types of private, agency, and school settings.

appraisal The skilled use of objective assessment information for formulating judgments or conclusions about a client, particularly for helping a client make educational or vocational plans.

aptitude A combination of abilities and other characteristics, whether native or acquired, known or believed to be indicative of an individual's ability to learn in some particular area.

aptitude test A test that measures potential; it may be an intelligence test, achievement test, or personality or interest inventory. Many aptitude tests are called "scholastic aptitude tests" because they are used to predict an individual's future school performance.

archetype According to Jung, a universal idea that is present in the collective unconscious. Examples include the old wise man, demons, and the concept of mother.

arithmetic mean The sum of scores divided by the number of scores; also called the average.

assessment The collection of information about an individual's behaviors, aptitudes, abilities, general mental functioning, personality, or related areas, usually obtained through the use of tests.

autonomous morality In Piaget's theory of moral development, the concept that morality ultimately becomes independent of the authority figures of early life.

average A general term for the measure of central tendency. The most common averages are the arithmetic mean, the mode, and the median. *See* central tendency.

aversion therapy A general term used to describe any type of behavior therapy in which strong avoidance stimulus is presented while the individual is making an undesired response.

axiology The branch of philosophy underlying many counseling approaches that deals with values.

back region In sociological theory, the counselor's private self not specifically related to his or her counseling role.

battered child syndrome The complete social and psychological pattern of child abuse.

battery A group of tests that are administered at one time to a sampling of a certain population so that the results can be compared. The tests in a battery have typically been planned and developed as a unit, with the objective of providing complete and efficient coverage of some cognitive ability, interests, or range of personality traits.

behaviorism The system of psychology founded by the American, John B. Watson, that defines psychology as the study of observable behavior and limits the scope of research to that which can be observed, measured, and replicated.

behavior modification Any procedure or set of procedures designed to change an individual's behavior through the use of conditioning, modeling, or other learning paradigms.

biofeedback A set of procedures in which some aspect or aspects of an individual's biological functioning, such as heart rate, skin temperature, or muscle tension, is "fed back" to the subject via a measuring instrument. The intended purpose of feeding back is for learning to consciously control this function.

career counseling The integrated use of psychological, informational, and psychometric instruments to help a client develop a career outlook and make appropriate career choices.

castration anxiety According to Freud, a psychosexual stage characterized by a young boy's fear of losing his penis.

catharsis In psychoanalytic theory, the sudden freeing of repressed feelings after analysis of an underlying conflict.

chemotherapy The treatment of psychological disorders through the use of drugs.

classical conditioning A form of learning in which a neutral stimulus is paired with an unconditioned stimulus. As a result of the association, the response associated with the latter (unconditioned response) becomes associated also with the former (conditioned response).

client-centered counseling A nondirective method of therapy, developed by Carl R. Rogers, that stresses the inherent worth of the client and the natural capacity for growth and health.

cognitive flexibility A characteristic of an effective counselor in which there is demonstrated a willingness to be intellectually open to different beliefs and perceptions.

collective unconscious According to Jung, the level of the unconscious that contains memories and behavior patterns inherited from our collective, ancestral past; also called the transpersonal unconscious.

community counseling The area of counseling practice dealing with the effects of particular environmental settings on community problems; emphasizes the prevention rather than the treatment of mental illness.

compensation According to Adler, the attempt by a person who falls short of his or her goal or who is deficient in one area, to excel in a different but related activity. An example would be a 98-pound weakling who becomes a weight lifter.

conditioned response In behavior modification, the learned response to a conditioned stimulus; for example, learning to salivate to the sound of a bell.

conditioned stimulus An initially neutral stimulus that, as a result of its pairing with the unconditioned stimulus, comes to elicit the conditioned (learned) response.

congruence According to client-centered therapy, the necessary therapist quality of being in touch with reality and with others' perception of oneself.

contracting The establishment of the rules, regulations, guidelines, and goals of the counseling process.

conversion reaction A neurotic disturbance (hysteria) in which a physical symptom without an organic cause is the product of an underlying unresolved conflict.

converted score A score expressed in some type of derived unit, such as age equivalent, grade equivalent, percentile, or standard score.

correction for guessing A mathematical method of adjusting scores on objective tests, such as multiple choice or true—false, in order to counteract the effects of students' guessing the correct answer.

correlation coefficient A statistic used to measure the relationship between two sets of variables. A positive relationship is expressed by numbers between 0 and +1— the closer to +1 the coefficient the greater the relationship. A negative (reciprocal) relationship is expressed between scores between 0 and −1. No relationship is expressed by 0 correlation.

counseling psychology The field of psychology that deals with people's educational, vocational, social, and family problems.

countertransference In psychoanalytic theory, the feelings the analyst has toward the patient, especially those that are precipitated by the patient's transference feelings.

covert sensitization A behavioral technique in which the client is taught to vividly imagine unpleasant and noxious experiences when he or she thinks of or approaches a stimulus that precipitates abnormal behaviors.

crisis A highly emotional temporary state in which an individual, overcome by feelings of anxiety, grief, confusion, or pain, is unable to act in a realistic healthy manner.

crisis intervention A "first-aid" counseling approach for helping an individual in a crisis situation return to normal.

criterion A standard by which a test may be judged or evaluated; a set of scores, ratings, and so forth, that a test is designed to predict or to correlate with.

culture-fair test A test so designed that people from different cultures have equal opportunities for successful performance.

defense mechanisms According to Freud, unconscious mental processes designed to protect the ego from thoughts or feelings that might cause anxiety, lowered self-esteem, or total mental collapse.

deindividuation A loss of individual identity as a separate person; sometimes the feeling of being submerged in a group.

denial The defense mechanism by which a person refuses to see things as they are because such traits are threatening to the ego.

determinism The belief that all human behavior has a specifiable cause.

deviation The difference between a score and a certain reference point (the mean, a score from another test, or a different norm).

diagonal relationship A description of a counseling relationship in which the counselor's and the client's statuses are defined through their interaction.

diagnosis The attribution of a name and cause implying illness to specific psychological states or behavioral patterns.

diagnostic test A test used to identify certain weaknesses or strengths and their causes; usually a test in spelling, reading, and arithmetic.

difficulty index A numerical value used to express the difficulty of a test item, usually the percentage of persons getting the item correct.

disclosure A characteristic of an effective counselor by which he or she is willing to open up personal feelings, when appropriate. Also, the client quality of disclosing his or her feelings.

discrimination index A list that designates the test differentiation of an item between the more and less able students (high and low performers) on a test.

discussion group A group designed for the prevention of problems and working out feelings by means of rational discussion.

displaced aggression A defense mechanism in which anger is redirected toward a person or object other than that which provoked the anger.

displacement According to psychoanalysis, a defense mechanism through which an individual replaces the original object of a drive with a more acceptable substitute.

distributive justice In Piaget's theory of moral development, the concept that higher-level justice is based on reciprocity and mitigating circumstances.

dyslexia A general term used to describe reading difficulties.

eclectic counseling The selective application of a variety of counseling methods using a knowledge of effectiveness as a basis for counselors' organization.

educational counseling The providing of educational information with a view toward future career goals.

ego According to Freud, the executive of the personality: the ego bridges the instincts (id) and the real world. The ego helps the person channel psychic energy into socially approved activities.

empathy The ability to experience another's emotions from the point of view of that person.

encounter group A therapy group in which the resistances are broken down quickly in order for the members to get in touch with their feelings and experience positive growth.

epistemology The branch of philosophy that deals with knowledge: an underlying rationale for many counseling interventions.

erogenous zones According to Freud, the areas of the body most receptive to sexual stimulation.

existential counseling The philosophically oriented approach to counseling, which views the individual's failure to confront choices as the cause of mental disorders and stresses understanding the individual's subjective views of reality by focusing on the "here and now" of existence.

extinction The behavioral principle that a response that had been reinforced will tend to cease if it is no longer reinforced.

extraversion According to Jung, the tendency to be outgoing and sociable, concerned more with the external world than with one's inner experiences.

face validity The principle that a measuring instrument has face validity when it seems to measure what it intends to measure; also called content validity.

family counseling A general term for a variety of counseling approaches in which family members are brought together to cooperatively solve their collective problems.

figure and ground In Gestalt psychology (and counseling), the idea that in perception we see a figure standing out against the background. The figure appears to have shape, while the ground appears formless. In healthy functioning these are constantly shifting.

free association The "fundamental rule" in classical psychoanalysis, in which the patient is encouraged to say whatever comes to mind, freely, without regard to social propriety and without censorship.

frequency distribution A distribution of scores from high to low, usually grouped in intervals of a fixed size (3, 5, or 10), designating individuals who fall into each interval or score.

front region According to Erving Goffman, the aspect of role presented to others within a defined social establishment.

genital stage According to Freud, the final psychosexual stage of development, associated with puberty and marked by heterosexual interests.

genuineness According to Carl Rogers, the important therapeutic quality of being honest and willing to give of one's self.

Gestalt counseling A humanistic counseling approach based on the principle that a healthy individual can overcome fragmentation of feeling and can organize his or her emotional experiences into a meaningful whole.

grade norms The average scores of pupils in different grade levels or the average score of pupils in a given grade.

group counseling A counseling approach in which three or more clients meet with a counselor and, through their interactions with each other and with the counselor, work toward growth.

group contingencies In behavioral group theory, the position that the consequences of an individual group member's behaviors are dependent upon the approval or disapproval of the other group members.

group transference In psychoanalytic group work, the phenomenon in which the group as a whole perceives the leader as a parental, or authority, figure.

guidance An integrated helping perspective in which information, counseling skills, and educational and dynamic insights are used to help clients deal with decision-making, role-area, and functional problems.

guidance group A group that combines elements of therapy, training, and discussion to help individual members improve different aspects of their role functioning.

health counseling A variety of integrated counseling approaches designed to maximize the full physical functioning of the individual.

heteronomous morality In Piaget's theory of moral development, the concept that morality and justice begins as obedience to and fear of the authority figures of early life.

horizontal relationship A description of a counseling relationship in which the counselor's and the client's statuses are defined through their interaction.

humanistic counseling The approach referred to as the "third force" in psychology and counseling. This approach emphasizes the study of the individual as a whole person who is motivated to fulfill his or her potential by becoming self-actualizing.

hyperkinesis A general condition of hyperactivity, characterized by short attention span and behavioral impulsivity.

hysteria According to psychoanalysis, a general group of neurotic disturbances caused by an unresolved Oedipal conflict and characterized by some form of anxiety.

id In psychoanalytic theory, the font of all instinctual energy; undifferentiated innate impulse.

identification In psychoanalysis, the unconscious incorporation of the qualities of another person or object into one's own personality.

implosive therapy A form of behavior therapy in which the patient is told to vividly imagine scenes that are very frightening to him or her.

incongruence According to Carl Rogers, the condition in which there is a discrepancy between one's perception of oneself and the way one is perceived by others.

individual psychology The system of psychoanalysis, with a social orientation, developed by Alfred Adler.

inferiority complex According to Alfred Adler, feelings of inadequacy and worthlessness that result from the inability to successfully strive for superiority.

insight As used in counseling and psychotherapy, the understanding of one's deeper (in psychoanalysis they are called unconscious) motives and their origins.

instrumental self The concept that the counselor uses his or her own personality to facilitate client growth.

intelligence test An aptitude test that measures intelligence, expressed as an IQ.

interest inventory A test, usually on occupational and educational interests, used to show the examinee's interest or preference for a certain type of activity.

introjection The process (in psychoanalytic theory) by which a child incorporates parental values and authority into his or her personality; as a defense mechanism, taking on the qualities or partial identity of another person.

introversion According to Jung, the tendency to withdraw into one's own inner world to avoid contact with other people.

latency The fourth of Freud's psychosexual stages and the period during which he believed the sexual impulses lie dormant and the child concentrates his or her energies on socialization skills.

latent dream content According to Freud, the underlying meaning of a dream.

law of effect The learning principle formulated by E. L. Thorndike, and important in behavioral counseling, which states that responses that are rewarded are strengthened and are likely to be repeated, and responses that are punished are less likely to recur.

learning disability A condition or set of conditions that prevents a person from functioning at grade level in one or several cognitive areas.

libido According to Freud, the energy of the sexual instincts, which motivates behavior.

life instincts According to Freud, one of the two classes of instincts (the other being the death instincts, or aggression), of which the sexual is the more important.

life script According to transactional analysis, the analysis that reveals how a person became what he or she is and where he or she is heading.

locus of control The belief that individual events and circumstances in life are either internally controlled or externally controlled.

logotherapy A form of existential therapy, developed by Victor Frankl, emphasizing the client's search for meanings in life.

manic depressive psychosis A severe mental disorder characterized by radical mood swings between elation and depression.

manifest dream content The remembered content of the dream, reported by the dreamer, which must be interpreted in order to understand its latent (hidden) meaning.

marathon group A therapy group that, in a 12-to-72 hour session, is designed to encourage the expression of inner feelings through exhausting normal defenses.

meaninglessness The feeling, which can impede effective counseling, of being without meaning and commitment in life.

median The separation of the distribution of scores, with 50 percent above the median and 50 percent below the median.

medical model The model of psychological and behavioral disturbances that sees symptoms as superficial signs of a deeper, underlying cause; based on medical practice.

mental age The average or normal age of a given score in a test.

mode The most frequent score of value that occurs in a test distribution.

modeling Also called "observational learning," modeling is a social learning process in which a person, observing the behavior of another, will learn that behavior. In therapy, modeling is used to help patients learn healthier, less neurotic responses to anxiety-evoking situations.

modern psychoanalysis A neo-Freudian therapy that attempts to deal with narcissistic disorders by using emotional, rather than intellectual, communications between therapist and patient.

minimal brain dysfunction (MBD) A nonspecific term used to describe learning and behavioral difficulties that appear to exist without a known cause.

negative reinforcer A stimulus (such as an electric shock), that is removed when the subject responds in a desired way, increasing the likelihood of that desired response.

neurosis A behavior disorder characterized by anxiety and a symptom. According to Freud, a neurosis is the result of unresolved unconscious conflicts.

neurotic anxiety According to psychoanalysis, tension resulting from an unconscious fear that the instincts will take over and cause the person to behave in ways that will be punished.

nondirective counseling Originated by Carl Rogers, a counseling approach in which the client acts as the initiator of change and determines the direction of change.

nondominance According to research, a characteristic of an effective counselor in which the counselor is able to sit back and allow the client to direct the course of the counseling interview.

nonjudgmental attitude According to research, a characteristic of an effective counselor in which the counselor refrains from presenting value judgments to the client.

normal distribution The bell-shaped distribution of scores or measures on a graph—especially when data about a large population is collected—used in much test development and standardization work.

Oedipus complex According to psychoanalytic theory, the sexual attachment of the son for his mother (or daughter for her father), which is usually accompanied by feelings of rivalry and hostility for the other—"rival"—parent. The complex in a daughter is sometimes called the Electra complex.

ontology The branch of philosophy dealing with existence and reality.

operant conditioning A conditioning (learning) model in which a response is strengthened by being positively reinforced when it occurs, or weakened by being ignored or punished.

objective test The results of a test are the same no matter who scores it. The objective test is typically scored by the use of keys or stencils, and the answers are either right or wrong (correct or incorrect), independent of the opinion of the person scoring.

oral stage According to psychoanalytic theory, the first stage of psychosexual development, named for the part of the body that is the principle source of pleasure during that period—the mouth.

paradoxical intention A logotherapy technique, used by Victor Frankl, in which the individual is told to wish for something, attempt to do something, or think intensely about something when that something represents his or her worst fears.

parapraxis More commonly known as a "Freudian slip," a mistake such as a slip of the tongue, pen, or forgetting a phone number that represents a compromise between the conscious wishes of the individual and repressed wishes that cry out for expression.

penis envy According to Freud, the girl's feeling of castration or loss because she lacks the male genitals.

percentile A point (score) below which falls the percent of cases indicated by the given percentile. For example, the 20th percentile indicates the score or point below which 20 percent of the scores fall.

personal unconscious According to Jung, the level of the unconscious that contains experiences of the individual that were once conscious but are now repressed.

personality test A test used to assess the individual's typical way of acting, or emotional soundness, as distinct from his or her ability to perform cognitively.

phallic stage   According to psychoanalytic theory, the third psychosexual stage, named for the genital organs, which are the dominant source of bodily pleasure during that period.

phenomenal field   According to Carl Rogers (and other existentialists-humanists), the totality of an individual's perceptual-affective experience, which includes everything potentially available to awareness that is going on within or nearby the organism at any given moment.

phenomenological   A perspective that emphasizes perceiving the client from his or her own personal world viewpoint.

phobia   An irrational, intense, hysterical fear of an object or situation. Also called "phobic reaction."

positive regard   According to Carl Rogers, accepting the client as he or she is, and for what he or she is, without imposing judgments or stipulations.

positive reinforcement   In operant conditioning, the strengthening of a response by providing a reward following the performance of that response.

primal therapy   A form of dynamic therapy, developed by Arthur Janov, that requires the individual to relive primal pain (needs that were denied as an infant) in order to release the energy that is causing tensions.

projective test   In this type of test, material such as ink blots, pictures, or unfinished sentences are used as stimuli for the individual to project part of his or her personality characteristics into responses that in turn can be measured and interpreted to infer a basic personality structure.

psychic energy   In psychoanalytic theory, the energy that emanates from the id (instincts), which is converted by the ego or superego into actions.

psychoanalysis   The view of personality and accompanying system of psychotherapy developed by Sigmund Freud. Psychoanalysis emphasizes the psychosexual stages of development and the role of unconscious processes in the formation of symptoms and in treatment.

psychopathology   The explanation of abnormal behavior patterns as "diseases" of the mind.

psychosexual stages   According to psychoanalytic theory, the five developmental stages of personality, each of which is named for the bodily area that serves as the principle source of pleasure and gratification at a particular age.

psychosis   Severe mental disorders characterized by loss of touch with reality, impaired self-control, delusional or grossly unrealistic behavior, and social dysfunctioning.

psychosomatic illness   A physical disorder that involves a psychological or emotional component.

psychotherapy   The application of psychological principles to the treatment of behavior or emotional disorders.

punishment   In behavior modification, the presentation of an aversive stimulus or event, or the removal of a positive event after a response. In both cases, punishment is designed to lessen the likelihood of a certain response occurring.

range   The difference between the highest and lowest scores in a test obtained by some group.

rationalization   The defense mechanism in which one supplies a reasonable explanation for unreasonable behavior or attributes different motives to actions in order to see herself or himself in a more favorable light.

reaction formation   The defense mechanism in which the individual acts in a way that is directly opposite the way he or she unconsciously feels.

reality therapy   A cognitive-dynamic therapy approach, developed by William Glasser, that concentrates on individual responsibility, objective values, and a reality in which the person has two basic needs: to be loved and to feel worthwhile.

reciprocal inhibition The behavioral principle that a person cannot make two incompatible responses at the same time. Used in the behavioral approach, it is known as systematic desensitization.

regression According to psychoanalysis, the defense mechanism in which a person "returns" to an earlier level of behavior.

rehabilitation counseling A series of counseling approaches designed to help an individual who has experienced some disability achieve full functioning.

reinforcement In classical conditioning, the repeated pairing of the conditioned stimulus and unconditioned stimulus, which strengthens the connection between the two. In operant conditioning, the presentation of an event or stimulus following an operation on the environment by the subject.

reinforcer In classical conditioning, the unconditioned stimulus; in operant conditioning, any stimulus that increases the probability of the occurrence of a response.

reliability Usually expressed in terms of coefficients or by use of the standard error of measurement, reliability is used to show the consistency of measurement in a given test.

repression According to psychoanalysis, the defense mechanism by which the individual pushes back into the unconscious unacceptable ideas or impulses.

role The enactment of certain behaviors associated with a specific social designation (such as the role of counselor versus the role of client).

schizophrenia A psychotic disorder characterized by a breakdown of personality integration, which manifests itself in cognitive, emotional, and social dysfunctioning.

self-actualization In humanistic psychology, the process by which one fully uses one's talents and capacities in order to fulfill one's potential for creativity, dignity, and self-worth.

shaping In social learning theory or behavior modification, teaching a desired complex response by reinforcing a series of successive responses increasingly more similar to the desired final response.

Skinner box A laboratory apparatus designed by B. F. Skinner to be used for the operant conditioning of small animals, such as rats and pigeons.

social learning theory The theory underlying behavioral counseling that much important social learning takes place through the observation and imitation of others' behaviors and by modeling one's behaviors after those that we observe.

socioemotional intactness In family counseling, the view that the family is a unit and anything that preserves that unity is a sign of its intactness.

standard deviation A measure of the variability of the dispersion of a set of scores. The more the scores cluster around the mean, the smaller the standard deviation.

standard score A score expressed in terms of standard deviations above or below the arithmetic mean of the group. More complicated types of standard scores may yield distributions differing in shape from the original distribution.

standardized test A test that has been given to various samples or groups under standardized conditions, with the result that population norms have been established.

structural analysis In transactional analysis, the description of ego states and their functioning.

style of life According to Alfred Adler, the principle by which the individual's personality functions; integrated mode of actions and behaviors.

sublimation According to psychoanalysis, the "healthy defense" through which instinctual drives are channeled into higher, socially acceptable forms of behavior.

superego In psychoanalytic theory, the aspect of personality that acts as the conscience as well as the ego ideal. It develops during the Oedipal stage as the child internalizes many of the parents' values.

superiority complex According to Alfred Adler, the group of feelings that develop as an individual struggles to overcome innate feelings of inferiority.

systematic desensitization A behavior therapy approach, developed by Joseph Wolpe, in which a client is put into a relaxed state and instructed to think about anxiety-producing stimuli in order of increasing intensity.

therapy group A group designed to treat specific problems, usually psychological in nature and manifesting undesirable symptoms.

third force The term used by Abraham Maslow to describe the humanistic approach to psychology and counseling. The first and second forces are Freudianism and behaviorism.

training group A group designed toward achieving a specific learning goal; for example, a group designed to help teachers develop their counseling skills.

transactional analysis A form of counseling or therapy in which the individual's ego states are analyzed in terms of a three-part model comprising Parent, Adult, and Child.

transference In psychoanalysis, the phenomenon whereby the patient transfers on to the analyst all of the feelings he or she previously held in childhood toward emotionally important figures such as parents, brothers, or sisters.

unconditional positive regard *See* positive regard.

unconditioned response A natural, unlearned response originally elicited by an unconditioned stimulus (for example, jumping at an electric shock).

unconditioned stimulus A stimulus that consistently elicits an unlearned response.

validity The extent of effectiveness of a test in doing what it is supposed to do. Content (or face) validity refers to the faithfulness with which the test represents or reproduces the area of knowledge it presumes to measure. Construct validity refers to the accuracy with which a test interprets an individual's performance in terms of some psychological trait or construct. Criterion-related (also called "predictive") validity is the exactitude with which the test scores can predict some criterion variable of educational, job, or life performance.

values clarification A process in which a person comes to articulate and critically examine his or her values, with the goal of either stronger commitment to the values or the development of new, alternative, values.

variability The span of scores in a set of scores from the average score in the group.

vertical relationship A description of a counseling relationship in which the counselor's and client's statuses are defined through their interaction.

vocational counseling A counseling approach designed to help the individual discover satisfying work and to function well at the job.

References

Abernathy, V. Prevention of unwanted pregnancy among teenagers. *Primary Care*, 1976, *3* (3), 399–406.

Abrams, J. C. Minimal brain dysfunction and dyslexia. *Reading World*, 1975, *14* (3), 219–227.

Adams, J. F. Using the pictorial normal curve in test interpretations. *Personnel and Guidance Journal*, 1963, *41*, 812–813.

Adams, J. F. (Ed.). *Understanding adolescence: Current developments in adolescent psychology* (3d ed.). Boston: Allyn & Bacon, 1976.

Adams, R. Learning Disabilities: A developmental approach. *Journal of Special Education*, 1975, *9* (2), 159–165.

Adler, A. *What life should mean to you.* New York: Capricorn Books, 1958.

Albas, D., Albas, C., & McClusky, K. Anomie. Social class and drinking behavior of high school students. *Journal of Studies on Alcohol*, 1978, *39* (5), 910–913.

Albert, G. If counseling is psychotherapy—what then? *Personnel and Guidance Journal*, 1966, *45*, 124–129.

Alexander, T. *Children and adolescents: A biocultural approach to psychological development.* New York: Atherton, 1969.

Allen, T. W. Effectiveness of counselor trainees as a function of psychological openness. *Journal of Counseling Psychology*, 1967, *14*, 35–40.

Altmann, H. A. Effects of empathy, warmth, and genuineness in the initial counseling interview, *Counselor Education and Supervision*, 1973, *12*, 225–228.

Anastasi, A. The concept of validity in the interpretation of test scores. *Educational and Psychological Measurement*, 1950, *10*, 67–78.

Annis, A. P. The autobiography: Its uses and value in professional psychology. *Journal of Counseling Psychology*, 1967, *14*, 9–17.

Arbuckle, D. S. *Counseling: Philosophy, theory, and practice.* Boston: Allyn & Bacon, 1970. (a)

Arbuckle, D. S. The counselor: Who? what? *Personnel and Guidance Journal*, 1970, *50*, 785–790. (b)

Archer, J., Jr., & Lopata, A. Marijuana revisited. *Personnel and Guidance Journal*, 1979, *57* (5), 244–251.

Ard, B. N. (Ed.). *Counseling and psychotherapy.* New York: Science and Behavior Books, 1966.

Asbury, F. R., & Winston, R. B. Reinforcing self-exploration and problem-solving. *The School Counselor*, 1974, *21*, 204–209.

Atkinson, D. R., Morten, G., & Sue, D. W. (Eds.). *Counseling American minorities: A cross-cultural perspective.* Dubuque, Iowa: Wm. C. Brown Company Publishers, 1979.

Aubrey, R. F. Misapplication of therapy models to school counseling. *Personnel and Guidance Journal,* 1967, *48,* 273–278.

Aubrey, R. T. *Experimenting with living: Pros and cons.* Columbus: Charles E. Merrill, 1975.

Ausubel, D. P. *Theory and problems of adolescent development.* New York: Grune & Stratton, 1954.

Avery, A. W., D'Augelli, A. R., & Danish, S. J. An empirical investigation of the construct validity of empathic understanding ratings. *Counselor Education and Supervision,* 1976, *15* (3), 177–183.

Axelrod, S. *Behavior modification for the classroom teacher.* New York: McGraw-Hill, 1977.

Axline, V. M. *Dibs in search of self.* New York: Ballantine Books, 1967.

Bandura, A. *Principles of behavior modification.* New York: Holt, Rinehart & Winston, 1969.

Bandura, A., & Mischel, W. Modification of self-imposed delay of reward through exposure to live and symbolic models. *Journal of Personality and Social Psychology,* 1965, *2,* 698–705.

Bandura, A., Ross, D., & Ross, S. Transmission of aggression through imitation of aggressive models. *Journal of Abnormal and Social Psychology,* 1961, *63,* 575–582.

Banks, W., & Martens, K. Counseling: The reactionary profession. *Personnel and Guidance Journal,* 1973, *51,* 457–462.

Barglow, P., & Weinstein, S. Therapeutic abortion during youth and adolescence: Psychiatric observations. *Journal of Youth and Adolescence,* 1973, *2* (4), 331–342.

Barnard, C. What do you want to be when you grow up? *Think Magazine* (International Business Machines Corp.), 1972, (Jan./Feb.), 45–48.

Baron, R. A. Aggression as a function of victim's pain cues, level of prior anger arousal, and exposure to an aggressive model. *Journal of Personality and Social Psychology,* 1974, *29,* 117–124.

Barry, R., & Wolf, B. *Modern issues in guidance-personnel work.* New York: Bureau of Publications, Teacher College, 1963.

Bassin, A., Bratter, T. E., & Rachin, R. L. (Eds.). *The reality therapy reader: A survey of the work of William Glasser.* New York: Harper & Row, 1976.

Beers, C. W. *A mind that found itself* (5th ed.). Garden City: Doubleday, 1956.

Bell, H. M. Significant changes in the direction of behavior. *Personnel and Guidance Journal,* 1965, *43,* 438–442.

Bell, R. L., Jr. The culturally deprived psychologist. *The Counseling Psychologist,* 1971, *2,* 104–107.

Benjamin, A. *The helping interview.* Boston: Houghton Mifflin, 1974.

Benoit, R. B., & Mayer, G. R. Extinction: Guidelines for its selection and use. *Personnel and Guidance Journal,* 1974, *52,* 290–295.

Benoit, R. B., & Mayer, G. R. Extinction and timeout: Guidelines for their selection and use. In G. S. Belkin (Ed.), *Counseling: Directions in theory and practice.* Dubuque, Iowa: Kendall/Hunt, 1976.

Berdie, R. F., Layton, W., Swanson, E. O., & Hagenah, T. *Testing in guidance and counseling.* New York: McGraw-Hill, 1963.

Berelson, B., & Steiner, G. A. *Human behavior: An inventory of scientific findings.* New York: Harcourt Brace Jovanovich, 1969.

Berg, D. H. Sexual subculture and contemporary heterosexual interaction patterns among adolescents. *Adolescence,* 1975, *10* (40), 543–547.

Bergstein, H. B., & Grant, C. W. How parents perceive the counselor's role. *Personnel and Guidance Journal*, 1961, *39*, 698–703.

Berlin, I. N. Minimal brain dysfunction: Management of family distress. *JAMA*, 1974, *229* (11), 1454–1457.

Berne, E. *Transactional analysis in psychotherapy*. New York: Grove Press, 1961.

Berne, E. *The structure and dynamics of organizations and groups*. Philadelphia: J. B. Lippincott, 1963.

Berne, E. *Games people play*. New York: Grove Press, 1964.

Berne, E. *What do you say after you say hello?* New York: Grove Press, 1972.

Berry, E. Guidance and counseling in the elementary school: Its theoretical base. *Personnel and Guidance Journal*, 1979, *57* (10), 513–520.

Bettelheim, B. Bringing up children. *Ladies Home Journal*, 1973, *90*, 28.

Beyer, B. K. Conducting moral discussions in the classroom. In G. S. Belkin (Ed.), *Perspectives in educational psychology*. Dubuque, Iowa: Wm. C. Brown Company Publishers, 1979, 285–300.

Bieber, I. Homosexual dynamics in psychiatric crises. *American Journal of Psychiatry*, 1972, *128*, 1268–1272.

Biestek, F. P. The non-judgmental attitude. *Journal of Social Casework, 1953, 34*, 235–240.

Blocher, D. H. *Developmental counseling*. New York: Ronald Press, 1966.

Blohm, A. A. Group counseling with moderately mentally retarded and learning disabled elementary school children. *Dissertation Abstracts International*, 1978 (Oct.), *39* (6–A), 3362.

Bloom, L. A reappraisal of Piaget's theory of moral judgment. *Journal of Genetic Psychology*, 1959, *95*, 3–12.

Blos, P. Comments on the psychological consequences of cryptorchism: A clinical study. *Psychoanalytic Study of the Child*, 1960, *15*, 395–429.

Bockar, J. A. *Primer for the nonmedical psychotherapist*. New York: Spectrum, 1976.

Bordin, E. S. *Psychological counseling*. New York: Appleton-Century-Crofts, 1968.

Borland, B. L., & Heckman, H. K. Hyperactive boys and their brothers. *Archives of General Psychiatry*, 1976, *33* (6), 669–675.

Bosco, J. Behavior modification drugs and the schools: The case of Ritalin. *Phi Delta Kappan*, 1975, *56*, 489–492.

Bottoms, G. The mission of career guidance: Definitions and leadership. *American Vocational Journal*, 1976, *50*, 50–52.

Boy, A. V. The elementary school counselor's role dilemma. *The School Counselor*, 1972, 167–172.

Boy, A. V., & Pine, G. J. A sociological view of the counselor's role: A dilemma and a solution. *Personnel and Guidance Journal*, 1969, *47*, 736–739.

Boy, A. V., & Pine, G. J. *Expanding the self: Personal growth for teachers*. Dubuque, Iowa: Wm. C. Brown Company Publishers, 1971.

Bradley, M. K. Counseling past and present: Is there a future? *Personnel and Guidance Journal*, 1978, *57*, 42–45.

Braen, B. B., & Forbush, J. B. School-age parenthood: A national overview. *Journal of School Health*, 1975, *65* (5), 256–260.

Brammer, L. M. Eclecticism revisited. *Personnel and Guidance Journal*, 1969, *48*, 192–197.

Brammer, L. M., & Shostrom, E. *Therapeutic psychology* (2nd ed.). Englewood Cliffs, N. J.: Prentice-Hall, 1968.

Brandenburg, J. B. The needs of women returning to school. *Personnel and Guidance Journal,* 1974, *53,* 11-18.

Breggin, P. Underlying a method: Is psychosurgery an acceptable treatment for "hyperactivity" in children? *Mental Hygiene,* 1974, *58* (1), 19-21.

Brockopp, G. W. Crisis intervention: Theory, process and practice. In D. Lester & G. W. Brockopp (Eds.), *Crisis intervention and counseling by telephone.* Springfield, Ill.: Charles C Thomas, 1973.

Brooks, D. B. Contingency management as a means of reducing school truancy. *Education,* 1971, *95* (3), 206-211.

Brooks, D. B. Contingency contracts with truants. *Personnel and Guidance Journal,* 1974, *52,* 316-320.

Brooks, H. D., & Oppenheim, C. J. *Horticulture as a therapeutic aid.* New York: New York University Institute of Rehabilitation Medicine, Monograph #49, 1973.

Broverman, I. K., Broverman, D. M., Clarkson, F. E., Rosenkrantz, P. S., & Vogel, S. R. Sex-role stereotypes and clinical judgments of mental health. *Journal of Consulting and Clinical Psychology,* 1970, *34,* 1-7.

Broverman, I. K., Vogel, S. R., Broverman, D. M., Clarkson, F. E., & Rosenkrantz, P. S. Sex-role stereotypes: A current appraisal. *Journal of Social Issues,* 1972, *28,* 59-78.

Brown, D., & Srebalus, D. J. *Contemporary guidance concepts and practices.* Dubuque, Iowa: Wm. C. Brown Company Publishers, 1972.

Brown, W. A., Corriveau, D. P., & Monti, P. M. Anger arousal by a motion picture: A methodological note. *American Journal of Psychiatry,* 1977, *134* (8), 930-931.

Buchanan, J. P. Quantitative methodology to examine the development of moral judgment. *Child Development,* 1973, *44,* 186-189.

Bunt, M. E. A gestalt approach to the diagnosis and treatment of early childhood psychopathology. *Psychology,* 1970, *7* (1), 17-26.

Burland, J. A., Andrews, R. G., & Headsten, S. J. Child abuse: One tree in the forest. *Child Welfare,* 1973, *52* (9), 585-592.

Buros, O. K. *The seventh mental measurements yearbook.* Highland Park, N.J.: Gryphon Press, 1970.

Buros, O. K. (Ed.). *The eighth mental measurements yearbook.* Lincoln, Neb.: The Gryphon Press, 1978.

Byrne, R. *The school counselor.* Boston: Houghton Mifflin, 1963.

Calvin, A. D., Clifford, L. T., Clifford, B., Bolden, L., & Harvey, J. Experimental validation of conditioned inhibition. *Psychological Reports,* 1956, *2,* 21-56.

Cameron, S. Violence and truancy on the increase. *The Times Educational Supplement,* April 4, 1975, 3123: 3.

Campbell, S. Mother-child interaction: A comparison of hyperactive, learning disabled, and normal boys. *American Journal of Orthopsychiatry,* 1975, *45,* 51-57.

Cantor, M. B. Karen Horney on psychoanalytic technique: Mobilizing constructive forces. *American Journal of Psychoanalysis,* 1967, *27,* 188-199.

Cantwell, D. P. *The hyperactive child: Diagnosis, management, current research.* New York: Spectrum, 1975.

Caplan, G. *Principles of preventive psychiatry.* New York: Basic Books, 1964.

Carey, A. Take a look at your testing program. *The School Counselor,* 1969, *16,* 205-207.

Carey, A. R., & Garris, D. Counselor-role differentiation: A new track? *The School Counselor,* 1971, *18,* 349-352.

Carkhuff, R. R. An integration of practice and training. In B. G. Berenson & R. R. Carkhuff (Eds.). *Sources of gain in counseling and psychotherapy*. New York: Holt, Rinehart & Winston, 1967. Originally published in R. R. Carkhuff, *The Counselor's contribution to facilitative processes*. Urbana, Ill.: R. W. Parkinson, 1966.

Carkhuff, R. R., Alexik, M., & Anderson, S. Do we have a theory of vocational choice? *Personnel and Guidance Journal*, 1967, *46*, 335-345.

Carkhuff, R. R., & Berenson, B. G. The nature, structure and function of counselor commitment to client. *Journal of Rehabilitation*, 1969, *35*, 13-14.

Carmer, J. C., & Rouzer, D. L. Healthy functioning from the gestalt perspective. *Counseling Psychologist*, 1974, *4* (4), 20-23.

Carmical, L., & Calvin, L., Jr. Functions selected by school counselors. *The School Counselor*, 1970, *17*, 280-285.

Carter, R. D., & Stuart, R. B. Behavior modification theory and practice: A reply. *Social Work*, 1970, *15*, 37-50.

Cash, T. F., Begley, P. P., McCowen, D. A., & Weise, B. C. When counselors are heard but not seen: Initial impact of physical attractiveness. *Journal of Counseling Psychology*, 1975, *22* (4), 273-279.

Cattell, R. B., Eber, H., & Tatsuoka, M. M. *Handbook for the 16 PF*. Champaign, Ill.: IPAT, 1970.

Cautela, J. R. Behavior therapy and self-control. In C. M. Franks (Ed.), *Behavior therapy: Appraisal and status*. New York: McGraw-Hill, 1969.

Cautela, J. R. The use of covert conditioning in modifying pain behavior. *Journal of Behavior Therapy and Experimental Psychiatry*, 1977, *8* (1), 45-52.

Cerio, J. E. Structured experiences with the educational growth group. *Personnel and Guidance Journal*, 1979, *57* (8), 398-401.

Chandler, C. R. "Babysitting" for houseplants—responsibility, interest and enthusiasm began to grow. *Teaching Exceptional Children*, 1977, *9* (3), 61-63.

Chenault, J., & Seegars, J. E., Jr. The interpersonal diagnosis of principals and counselors. *Personnel and Guidance Journal*, 1962, *41*, 118-122.

Cherlin, A. Teen-age pregnancy: Carter sees half the problem. *The Nation*, 1978 (June 17), *226* (23), 7727-730.

Cole, S. O. Hyperkinetic children: The use of stimulant drugs evaluated. *American Journal of Orthopsychiatry*, 1975, *45*, 28-35.

Combs, A. W. Self-actualization and the teaching function of counselors. In G. S. Belkin (Ed.), *Counseling: Directions in theory and practice*. Dubuque, Iowa: Kendall/Hunt, 1976, pp. 43-53.

Combs, A. W., et al. *Florida studies in the helping professions*. Gainesville: University of Florida Press, 1969.

Conklin, R. C., & Hunt, A. S. An investigation of the validity of empathy measures. *Counselor Education and Supervision*, 1975, *15* (2), 119-127.

Conners, C. K. Psychological effects of stimulant drugs in children with minimal brain dysfunction. *Pediatrics*, 1972, *49* (5), 702-707.

Cook, D. R. The change agent counselor: A conceptual context. *The School Counselor*, 1972, *20*, 9-15.

Cottingham, H. F., & Warner, R. W., Jr. APGA and counselor licensure: A status report. *Personnel and Guidance Journal*, 1978, *56*, 604-607.

Cotton, M. Forum: Horticultural therapy. *Horticulture*, 1975, *53*, 24.

Cousins, N. The mysterious placebo: How the mind helps medicine work. *Saturday Review*, October 1, 1977, pp. 8-18.

Cremin, L. A. The progressive heritage of the guidance movement. In E. Landy & P. A. Perry (Eds.), *Guidance in American education* (Vol. I). Cambridge, Mass.: Harvard University Press, 1964.

Curran, C. A. *Counseling and psychotherapy.* New York: Sheed & Ward, 1968.

Curtis, F. L. S. Observations of unwed pregnant adolescents. *American Journal of Nursing,* 1974, *74* (1), 100–102.

Curtis, G., et al. Flooding in vivo as a research tool and treatment method for phobias: A preliminary report. *Comprehensive Psychiatry,* 1976, *17* (1), 153–160.

Cutter, F. Suicide: The wish, the act, and the outcome. *Life-Threatening Behavior,* 1971, *1* (2), 125–137.

Dallas, D. Savagery, show and tell. *American Psychologist,* 1978, *33* (4), 388–390.

Darley, J. G. In A. H. Brayfield (Ed.), *Readings in modern methods of counseling.* New York: Appleton-Century-Crofts, 1950.

Davenport, L., & Perry, R. *Minorities and career education.* Columbus, Ohio: E. C. C. A. Publications, 1973.

David, C. A. The use of confrontation techniques in the battered child syndrome. *American Journal of Psychotherapy,* 1974, *28* (4), 543–552.

Davison, G. C., & Stuart, R. B. Behavior therapy and civil liberties. *American Psychologist,* 1975, *30* (7), 755–763.

DeGenero, J. J. Informal diagnostic procedures: "What can I do before the psychometrist arrives?" *Journal of Learning Disabilities,* 1975, *8* (9), 24–30.

Dell, P. F., & Jurkovic, G. J. Moral structure and moral content: Their relationship to personality. *Journal of Youth and Adolescence,* 1978, *7* (1), 63–72.

Di Giuseppe, R. A., Miller, N. J., & Trexler, L. D. A review of rational-emotive psychotherapy outcome studies. *The Counseling Psychologist,* 1977, *7* (1), 64–72.

Dilley, J., Lee, J. L., & Verrill, E. L. Is empathy ear-to-ear or face-to-face? *Personnel and Guidance Journal,* 1971, *50,* 188–191.

Dimick, K. M., & Huff, V. E. *Child counseling.* Dubuque, Iowa: Wm. C. Brown Company Publishers, 1970.

Dinkmeyer, D. C. The counselor as consultant: Rationale and procedures. *Elementary School Guidance and Counseling,* 1968, *3,* 187–194.

Dollard, J., & Miller, N. E. *Personality and psychotherapy.* New York: McGraw-Hill, 1950.

Downing, L. N. *Guidance and counseling services.* New York: McGraw-Hill, 1968.

Dranoff, S. M. Masturbation and the male adolescent. *Adolescence,* 1974, *9,* 169–179.

Drasgow, J., & Walker, R. J. A graphic description of the counseling relationship. *Journal of Counseling Psychology,* 1960, *7,* 51–57.

Dreikurs, R. *Psychology in the classroom.* New York: Harper, 1957.

Dreikurs, R., & Dinkmeyer, D. *Encouraging children to learn: The encouragement process.* Englewood Cliffs: Prentice-Hall, 1963.

Dreikurs, R., & Grey, L. *Logical consequences.* New York: Meredith, 1968.

Dreyfus, E. A. An existential approach to counseling. In C. Beck (Ed.), *Philosophical guidelines for counseling.* Dubuque, Iowa: Wm. C. Brown Company Publishers, 1971.

Duberman, L. *The reconstituted family: A study of remarried couples and their children.* Chicago: Nelson-Hall, 1975.

Durkin, D. The specificity of children's moral judgments. *Child Development,* 1960, *32,* 551–560.

Dworkin, E. P., & Dworkin, A. L. The activist counselor. *Personnel and Guidance Journal,* 1971, *49,* 748–753.

Ehrenwald, J. (Ed.). *The history of psychotherapy: From healing magic to encounters.* New York: Jason Aronson, 1976.

Eisenberg, S., & Delaney, D. J. *The Counseling Process* (2nd Ed.). Chicago: Rand McNally, 1977.

Ellingson, C. *The shadow children.* Washington, D.C.: Topaz, 1967.

Ellis, A. Rational psychotherapy. *The Journal of General Psychology,* 1958, *59,* 34–49.

Ellis, A. *Reason and emotion in psychotherapy.* New York: Lyle Stuart, 1962.

Ellis, A. *The art and science of love.* New York: Lyle Stuart, 1969. (a)

Ellis, A. Teaching emotional education in the classroom. *School Health Review,* 1969, *1,* 10–13. (b)

Ellis, A. *Growth through reason.* Palo Alto, Calif.: Science and Behavior Books, 1971.

Ellis, A. Rational-emotive therapy. In R. Corsini (Ed.), *Current psychotherapies.* Itasca, Ill.: F. E. Peacock, 1973. (b)

Ellis, A. Does rational-emotive therapy seem deep enough? *Rational Living,* 1975, *10*(2), 11–14. (a)

Ellis, A. Answering a critique of rational-emotive therapy. *Canadian Counselor,* 1976, *10*(2), 56–59. (a)

Ellis, A. Personality hypotheses of RET (Rational Emotive Therapy) and other modes of cognitive-behavior therapy. The *Counseling Psychologist,* 1977, *7*(1), 2–42.

Ellis, A., & Harper, R. A. *A guide to rational living.* Englewood Cliffs, N.J.: Prentice-Hall, 1961.

Ellis, A., & Harper, R. A. *A new guide to rational living.* Englewood Cliffs, N.J.: Prentice-Hall, 1975.

Ellis, A., & Grieger, R. *Rational-emotive therapy: A handbook of theory and practice.* New York: Springer, 1977.

Ewing, D. B. Twenty approaches to individual change. *Personnel and Guidance Journal,* 1977, *55*(6), 331–338.

Eysenck, H. J., & Rachman, S. *The causes and cures of neurosis.* London: Routledge & Kegan Paul, 1965.

Ezell, B., & Patience, T. G. The contract as a counseling technique. *Personnel and Guidance Journal,* 1972, *51,* 27–31.

Fagan, J. The tasks of the therapist. In J. Fagan & I. L. Shepherd (Eds.), *Gestalt therapy now.* Palo Alto, Calif.: Science and Behavior Books, 1970.

Farrell, J. G. Personal communication to author. June 20, 1978.

Farson, R. Carl Rogers, quiet revolutionary. *Education,* 1974, *95*(2), 197–203.

Fazzaro, C. J., & Gillespie, J. O. Organizational models for effective counseling and guidance programs. *Clearing House,* 1972, *45,* 153–158.

Feingold, B. F. Hyperkinesis and learning disabilities linked to artificial food flavors and colors. *Journal of Nursing,* 1975 (May), *75* (5), 797–803.

Felker, S. How to feel comfortable when you don't know what you are doing. *Personnel and Guidance Journal,* 1972, *50,* 683–685.

Ferenczi, S. *Further contributions to the theory and practice of psychoanalysis.* London: Hogarth, 1950.

Filbeck, R. W. Perceptions of appropriateness of counselor behavior: A comparison of counselors and principals. *Personnel and Guidance Journal,* 1965, *43,* 891–895.

Fine, R. M. The application of social reinforcement procedures to improve the school attendance of truant Chicano junior high school students. *Dissertation Abstracts International,* 1974 (Sept.), *35* (3A), 1442–1443.

Flavell, J. H. *The developmental psychology of Jean Piaget.* New York: D. Van Nostrand, 1963.

Ford, C. S. Self-stimulation. In M. F. DeMartino (Ed.), *Sexual behavior and personality characteristics.* New York: Grove Press, 1966.

Foreman, N. J., & Zerwekh, J. V. Drug crisis intervention. *American Journal of Nursing,* 1971, *71,* 1736-17-39.

Foreman, M. E., & James, L. E. Vocational relevance as a factor in counseling. *Journal of Counseling Psychology,* 1973, *20,* 99-103.

Forer, B. R. The therapeutic value of crisis. *Psychological Reports,* 1963, *13,* 275-281.

Forness, S. R., & Esveldt, K. C. Classroom observations of children with learning and behavior problems. *Journal of Learning Disabilities,* 1975, *8* (6), 382-385.

Forster, J. R. What shall we do about credentialing? *Personnel and Guidance Journal,* 1977, *55,* 573-576.

Forster, J. R. Counselor credentialing revised. *Personnel and Guidance Journal,* 1978, *56,* 593-598.

Foulds, M. L. The experimental-gestalt growth group experience. *Journal of College Student Personnel,* 1972, *13,* 48-52.

Frankl, V. *Psychotherapy and existentialism: Selected papers on logotherapy.* New York: Simon & Schuster (Clarion Books), 1967.

Franklin, A. J. To be young, gifted, and black with inappropriate training. *The Counseling Psychologist,* 1971, *2,* 107-112.

Freeman, R. D. Minimal brain dysfunction, hyperactivity, and learning disorders: Epidemic or episode? *School Review,* 1976, *85* (1), 5-30.

Freud, A. *The ego and the mechanisms of defense.* New York: International Universities Press, 1966. (Orig. pub. 1935)

Freud, A. *The psychoanalytic treatment of children.* New York: Schocken Books, 1964.

Freud, S. *The psychopathology of everyday life.* New York: Signet, 1961. (Originally published, 1901.)

Freud, S. Recommendations to physicians practicing psychoanalysis. In J. Strachey (Ed.), *The standard edition of the complete psychological works of Sigmund Freud.* London: Hogarth, 1953-1970, Vol. 12 (1958), pp. 111-120.

Frey, D. H. Conceptualizing counseling theories: A content analysis of process and goal statements. *Counselor Education and Supervision,* 1972, *11,* 243-250.

Friends Hospital of Philadelphia. *Horticulture as psychiatric therapy.* Philadelphia, Pa.: Friends Hospital, 1976.

Gannon, W. J. *The effects of the gestalt oriented group approach on the interpersonal contact attitudes of selected high school students.* Doctoral dissertation, Case Western Reserve University, 1972. (Ann Arbor, Mich.: University Microfilms # 72-26.)

Gardner, J. Sexist counseling must stop. *Personnel and Guidance Journal,* 1971, *49,* 705-713.

Garrett, H. E. *Elementary statistics* (2nd ed.). New York: David McKay, 1972.

Garvey, W. P., & Hegrenes, J. R. Desensitization techniques in the treatment of school phobia. *American Journal of Orthopsychiatry,* 1966, *36,* 147-152.

Gazda, G. M. *Theories and methods of group counseling in the schools.* Springfield, Ill.: Charles C Thomas, 1972.

Gazda, G. M. Licensure/certification for counseling psychologists and counselors. *Personnel and Guidance Journal,* 1977, *55,* 570.

Gearheart, B. R. *Learning disabilities: Educational strategies* (2nd Ed.). St. Louis: C. V. Mosby, 1977.

Gedan, S. Abortion counseling with adolescents. *American Journal of Nursing*, 1974, *74* (10), 1856–1858.

Gellen, M. I. Finger blood volume responses of counselor, counselor trainees, and noncounselors to stimuli from an empathy test. *Counselor Education and Supervision*, 1970, *10*, 64–73.

Gelles, R. J. Child abuse as psychopathology: A sociological critique and reformulation. *American Journal of Orthopsychiatry*, 1973, *43*, 611–621.

Gelles, R. J. Violence toward children in the United States. *American Journal of Orthopsychiatry*, 1978, *48* (4), 580–592.

Gendlin, E. T. Experiencing: A variable in the process of therapeutic change. *American Journal of Psychotherapy*, 1961, *16*, 233–245.

Georgiady, N. P. Blue-collar careers? Why Not? *Elementary School Journal*, 1976, *77*, 116–124.

Gibb, J. R. The counselor as a role free person. In C. A. Parker (Ed.), *Counseling theories and counselor education*. Boston: Houghton Mifflin, 1968.

Ginzberg, E. Toward a theory of vocational choice. *Vocational Guidance Quarterly*, 1972, *20*, 169–175.

Ginzberg, E., et al. *Life-styles of educated women*. New York: Columbia University Press, 1966.

Gittelman-Klein, R. Pharmacotherapy and management of pathological separation anxiety. In *Recent advances in child psychopharmacology*. New York: Human Sciences Press, 1975, 255–272.

Giuffra, M. J. Demystifying adolescent behavior. *American Journal of Nursing*, 1975, *10*, 1725–1727.

Gladstein, G. A. Is empathy important in counseling? *Personnel and Guidance Journal*, 1970, *48*, 823–826.

Gladstein, G. A. Empathy and counseling outcome: An empirical and conceptual review. *Counseling Psychology*, 1977, *6* (4), 70–78.

Glasser, W. *Reality therapy: A new approach to psychiatry*. New York: Harper & Row, 1965.

Glasser, W. *Schools without failure*. New York: Harper & Row, 1969.

Glasser, W. Reality therapy and counseling. In C. Beck (Ed.), *Philosophical guidelines in counseling* (2nd Ed.). Dubuque, Iowa: Wm. C. Brown Company Publishers, 1971.

Glasser, W., & Zunin, L.M. Reality therapy. In R. Corsini (Ed.), *Current psychotherapies*. Itasca, Ill.: F. E. Peacock, 1973.

Globetti, G. Problem and non-problem drinking among high school students in abstinence communities. *International Journal of Addictions*, 1972, *7* (3), 511–523.

Goble, F. *The third force*. New York: Grossman, 1970.

Goffman, E. *The presentation of self in everyday life*. Garden City: Doubleday (Anchor), 1959.

Goldberg, G. Breaking the communication barrier: The initial interview with an abusing parent. *Child Welfare*, 1975, *54* (4), 274–281.

Goldberg, P. Are women prejudiced against women? In D. K. Schaeffer (Ed.), *Sex differences in personality*. Belmont, Calif.: Brooks/Cole, 1971, pp. 62–66.

Goldhaber, G. M., & Goldhaber, M. B. (Eds.). *Transactional analysis: Principles and applications*. Boston: Allyn & Bacon, 1976.

Goldman, L. Behavior therapy faces middle age. *The Counseling Psychologist*, 1978, *7* (3), 25–28.

Goodman, J. Group counseling with seventh graders. *Personnel and Guidance Journal*, 1976, *54* (6), 519–520.

Gorden, R. L. *Interviewing: Strategy, techniques, and tactic* Homewood, Ill.: Dorsey, 1975.

Grady, M., & Ephross, P. H. A comparison of two methods for collecting social histories of psychiatric hospital patients. *Military Medicine,* 1977, *142* (7), 524–526.

Graham, R. Moral education: A child's right to a just community. *Elementary School Guidance and Counseling,* 1975, *9,* 299–308.

Grala, C., & McCauley, C. Counseling truants back to school: Motivation combined with a program for action. *Journal of Counseling Psychology,* 1976, *23,* 166–169.

Grant, C. J. The counselor's role. *Personnel and Guidance Journal,* 1954, *33,* 74–77.

Gray, S. W., & Noble, F. C. The school counselor and the school psychologist. In J. F. Adams (Ed.), *Counseling and guidance: A summary view.* New York: Macmillan, 1965.

Green, B. J. Helping children of divorce: A multimodal approach. *Elementary School Guidance and Counseling,* 1978, *13* (1), 31–45.

Greer, R. D., & Dorow, L. G. *Specializing education behaviorally.* Dubuque, Iowa: Kendall/Hunt, 1976.

Grinspoon, L., & Singer, S. B. Amphetamines in the treatment of hyperactive children. *Harvard Educational Review,* 1973, *43* (4), 515–555.

Gronlund, N. E. *Sociometry in the classroom.* New York: Harper & Row, 1960.

Gurry, J. Career communication in the secondary school. *Communication Education,* 1976, *25,* 307–316.

Hackney, H. The evolution of empathy. *Personnel and Guidance Journal,* 1978, *57,* 35–38.

Hadden, S. B. A glimpse of pioneers in group psychotherapy. *International Journal of Group Psychotherapy,* 1975, *25* (4), 371–378.

Haettenschwiller, D. L. Control of the counselor's role. *Journal of Counseling Psychology,* 1970, *17,* 437–442.

Hague, W. J. Counselling as a moral conflict: Making the disintegration positive. *Canadian Counselor,* 1977, *12* (1), 41–46.

Haller, J. S., & Axelrod, P. Minimal brain dysfunction syndrome. *American Journal of Diseases of Childhood,* 1975, *129,* 1319–1324.

Hamburg, B. A. Early adolescence: A specific and stressful stage of the life cycle. In G. V. Coelho, D. A. Hamburg, & J. E. Adams (Eds.), *Coping and adaptation.* New York: Basic Books, 1974, pp. 101–124.

Hamilton, L., Nichols, P. J. R., & White, A. S. Gardening for the disabled and elderly. *Journal of Royal Horticultural Society,* 1970, *95,* 358–369.

Hansen, J. C., Stevic, R. R., & Warner, R. W., Jr. *Counseling: Theory and practice* (2nd ed.). Boston: Allyn & Bacon, 1977.

Hansen, L. S. How can we use appraisal data for students' welfare? *The School Counselor,* 1967, *14,* 281–286.

Harman, R. L. Techniques of Gestalt therapy. *Professional Psychology,* 1974, *5* (3), 257–263.

Harris, T. A. *I'm OK—You're OK.* New York: Harper & Row, 1969. (Edition quoted is Avon paperback, 1973).

Hart, D. H., & Prince, D. J. Role conflict for school counselors: Training vs. job demands. *Personnel and Guidance Journal,* 1970, *48,* 374–380.

Hauck, P. A. *The rational management of children.* New York: Libra Publishers, 1967.

Hawes, L. C. The effects of interview style on patterns of dyadic communication. *Speech Monographs,* 1972, *39* (2), 114–123.

Hawley, C., & Buckley, R. Food dyes and hyperkinetic children. *Academic Therapy,* 1974, *10,* 27-32.

Hawley, R. C., & Hawley, I. L. *Human values in the classroom.* New York: Hart, 1975.

Hearn, J. C., & Moos, R. H. Social climate and major choice: A test of Holland's theory in university student living groups. *Journal of Vocational Behavior,* 1976, *8,* 293-305.

Heayn, M. H., & Jacobs, H. L. Safeguarding student records. *Personnel and Guidance Journal,* 1967, *46,* 63-67.

Hefley, D. Horticulture—therapy for the handicapped. *Plants & Gardens,* 1973, *29,* 34-37.

Heikkinen, C. A., & Wegner, K. W. Minnesota multiphasic personality inventory studies of counselors: A review. *Journal of Counseling Psychology,* 1973, *20,* 275-279.

Heilfron, M. The function of counseling as perceived by high school students. *Personnel and Guidance Journal,* 1960, *39,* 133-136.

Helfer, R. E., & Kempe, C. H. (Eds.) *The battered child.* Chicago: University of Chicago Press, 1968.

Helpern, J. M. G. The role of the guidance consultant at the elementary school. *Journal of Education,* 1964, *146,* 16-34.

Henry, W. D. Psychiatric problems of late adolescence. *Nursing Mirror,* 1976, *142,* 57-60.

Herr, E. L., & Cramer, S. H. *Vocational guidance and career development in the schools: Toward a systems approach.* Boston: Houghton-Mifflin, 1972.

Herrnstein, R. J. The evolution of behaviorism. *American Psychologist,* 1977, *32* (8), 593-603.

Hertz, D. G. Psychological implications of adolescent pregnancy. *Psychosomatics,* 1977, *18* (1), 13-16.

Herzog, E., & Sudia, C. E. Children in fatherless families. In B. H. Caldwell & H. N. Riciuti (Eds.), *Review of child development research.* Chicago: University of Chicago Press, 1973, pp. 141-232.

Hewer, V. H. What do theories of vocational choice mean to a counselor? *Journal of Counseling Psychology,* 1963, *10,* 118-125.

Hiekkinen, C. A. Counseling for personal loss. *Personnel and Guidance Journal,* 1979. *58* (1), 46-49.

Hipple, J. L., & Muto, L. The TA group for adolescents. *Personnel and Guidance Journal,* 1974, *52* (10), 675-681.

Hobbs, N. The compleat counselor. *Personnel and Guidance Journal,* 1958, *36,* 594-602.

Hoffman, D. S. Implications of future shock for vocational counselors. *Vocational Guidance Quarterly,* 1972, *21,* 92-96.

Hoffman, L. R. Peers as group counseling models. *Elementary School Guidance and Counseling,* 1976, *11* (1), 37-44.

Hogan, R. A. Implosive therapy and short-term treatment of psychotics. *Psychotherapy: Theory, Research & Practice,* 1966, *3,* 25-32.

Hogan, R. A. Frigidity and implosive therapy. *Psychology,* 1975, *34,* 39-45.

Holdstock, T. L., & Rogers, C. R. Person-centered theory. In R. J. Corsini (Ed.), *Current personality theories.* Itasca, Ill.: I. F. Peacock, 1977, 125-152.

Holland, J. *Some explorations of theory of vocational choice.* Washington, D.C.: Monographs—American Psychological Association, 1962.

Holland, J. *The psychology of vocational choice.* Waltham, Mass.: Blaisdall, 1966.

Holland, J. *Making vocational choices: A theory of careers.* Englewood Cliffs, N.J.: Prentice-Hall, 1973.

Holmstrom, L. L., & Burgess, A. W. Assessing trauma in the rape victim. *American Journal of Nursing,* 1975, *75* (8), 214-231.

Holt, J. Quackery. *New York Review of Books,* August 13, 1970.

Hoover, T. O. Values clarification as an adjunct to psychotherapy. *Catalog of Selected Documents in Psychology,* 1977, *7,* 110-111.

Hopkins, K. D., & Glass, G. V. *Basic statistics for the behavioral sciences.* Englewood Cliffs, N.J.: Prentice-Hall, 1978.

Hoppock, R. *Occupational Information* (3d ed.) New York: McGraw-Hill, 1967.

Horner, M. S. Femininity and successful achievement: A basic inconsistency. In J. Bardwick (Ed.), *Feminine personality and conflict.* Belmont, Calif.: Brooks/Cole, 1970.

Horner, M. S. Toward an understanding of achievement-related conflicts in women. *Journal of Social Issues,* 1972, *28,* 157-175.

Horney, K. *The neurotic personality of our time.* New York: Norton, 1937.

Horney, K. *New ways in psychoanalysis.* New York: Norton, 1939.

Horney, K. *Neurosis and human growth.* New York: Norton, 1950.

Horowitz, M. B. A comment on "An empirical investigation of the construct validity of empathic understanding ratings." *Counselor Education and Supervision,* 1977, *16* (4), 292-295.

Hoyt, K. B. What the school has a right to expect of its counselors. *Personnel and Guidance Journal,* 1961, *40,* 129-134.

Huber, C. H. Parents of the handicapped child: Facilitating acceptance through group counseling. *Personnel and Guidance Journal,* 1979, *57* (5), 267-269.

Huckaby, H., & Daly, J. Got those PL94-142 blues. *Personnel and Guidance Journal,* 1979, *58* (1), 70-72.

Hudson, F. G., & Graham, S. An approach to operationalizing the IEP. *Learning Disability Quarterly,* 1978, *1* (1).

Hudson, W. W. First axiom of treatment. *Social Work,* 1978, *23* (1), 65.

Humes, C. W., II. School counselors and PL94-142. *School Counselor,* 1978, *25,* 192-195.

Huser, W. R., and Grant, C. W. A study of husbands and wives from dual-career and traditional-career families. *Psychology of Women Quarterly,* 1978, *3* (1), 78-89.

Hymowitz, C., & Weissman, M. *A history of women in America.* New York: Bantan, 1978.

Institute of Rehabilitation Medicine. *Horticulture as a therapeutic aid.* Rehab. Monographs #49, New York: New York University Medical Center, 1973.

Isaksen, H. L. The role of the school counselor in mental health. *Journal of Education,* 1964, *146* (3), 11-15.

Ivey, A. Toward a definition of the culturally effective counselor. *Personnel and Guidance Journal,* 1977, *55,* 296-302.

Jackson, M., & Thompson, C. L. Effective counselor: Characteristics and attitudes. *Journal of Counseling Psychology.* 1971, *18,* 249-254.

Jantz, R. K., & Fulda, T. A. The role of moral education in the public elementary school. *Social Education,* 1975, *16,* 24-35.

Jeffrey, T. B. The effects of operant conditioning and electromyographic biofeedback on the relaxed behaviors of hyperkinetic children. *Dissertation Abstracts International,* 1976 (Nov.), *37* (5-B), 2510.

Johnson, W., Stefflre, B., & Edefelt, R. *Pupil personnel and guidance services.* New York: McGraw-Hill, 1961.

Jones, C. R. *Homosexuality and counseling.* Philadelphia: Fortress, 1974.

Joslin, L. C., Jr. Knowledge and counseling competence. *Personnel and Guidance Journal,* 1965, *43,* 790–795.

Josselyn, I. M. *Psychosocial development of children.* New York: Family Services Association of America, 1948.

Josselyn, I. M. *The adolescent and his world.* New York: Family Service Association of America, 1969.

Kadushin, A. *The social work interview.* New York: Columbia University Press, 1972.

Kagan, N. Presidential address: Division 17. *The Counseling Psychologist,* 1977, *7* (2), 4–8.

Kalmar, R. (Ed.). *Child abuse.* Dubuque, Iowa: Kendall/Hunt, 1977. (a)

Kalmar, R. (Ed.). *Abortion: The emotional implications.* Dubuque, Iowa: Kendall/Hunt, 1977. (b)

Kardener, S. H. A methodological approach to crisis therapy. *American Journal of Psychotherapy,* 1975, *29,* 4–13.

Kaufman, M., & Bluestone, H. Patient-therapist: Are we free to choose therapy? *Groups: A Journal of Dynamics and Psychotherapy,* 1975, *6* (1), 1–13.

Kay, W. *Moral education: A sociological study of the influence of society, home, and school.* Hamden, Conn.: Shoe String Press, 1975.

Keele, D. K., Keele, M. S., Huizinga, R. J., Bray, N., Estes, R., & Holland, L. Role of special pediatric evaluation in the evaluation of a child with learning disabilities. *Journal of Learning Disabilities,* 1975, *8,* 47–52.

Kemp, C. G. Existential counseling. *The Counseling Psychologist,* 1971, *2,* 2–30.

Kempe, C. H., et al. The battered-child syndrome. *Journal of American Medical Association,* 1962, *181,* 17–24.

Kifer, R., Lewis, M., Green, D., & Phillips, E. Training predelinquent youths and their parents to negotiate conflict situations. *Journal of Applied Behavioral Analysis,* 1974, *7* (3), 357–364.

Kirby, J. A. Group guidance. *Personnel and Guidance Journal,* 1971, *49,* 593–599.

Kirk, S. A., & Gallagher, J. J. *Educating exceptional children* (3d ed.). Boston: Houghton Mifflin, 1979.

Kirkpatrick, S. K. A Maslovian counseling model. *Personnel and Guidance Journal,* 1979, *57* (8), 387–390.

Kirman, W. J. Emotional education in the classroom: A modern psychoanalytic approach. In G. S. Belkin (Ed.), *Counseling: Directions in theory and practice.* Dubuque, Iowa: Kendall/Hunt, 1976.

Kirman, W. J. *Modern psychoanalysis in the schools.* Dubuque, Iowa: Kendall/Hunt, 1977.

Klein, D. C., & Lindemann, E. Preventive intervention in individual and family crisis situations. In G. Caplan (Ed.), *Prevention of mental disorders in children.* New York: Basic Books, 1961.

Klein, D. F., & Gittleman-Klein, R. Problems in the diagnosis of minimal brain dysfunction and the hyperkinetic syndrome. In R. Gittleman-Klein (Ed.), *Recent advances in child psychopharmacology.* New York Human Science Press, 1975.

Klerman, G. L. Neuroleptics: Too many or too few? In F. J. Ayd (Ed.), *Rational psychopharmacotherapy and the right to treatment.* Baltimore: Ayd Medical Communications, 1975.

Knapp, D. L., & Denny, E. W. The counselor's responsibility in role definition. *Personnel and Guidance Journal,* 1961, *40,* 48–50.

Knights, R. M., & Viets, C. A. Effects of pemoline on hyperactive boys. *Pharmacology, Biochemistry and Behavior,* 1975, *3* (6), 1107-1114.

Koch, J. H. The trouble with counseling. *The School Counselor,* 1972, *19,* 13.

Kohlberg, L. Early education: A cognitive-developmental view. *Child Development,* 1968, *39,* 1013-1062.

Kohlberg, L., Colby, A., Gibbs, J., Speicher-Dubin, B. S., & Power, C. *Assessing moral stages: A manual* (Part I) Unpublished manuscript, 1978. (Available from the Center of Moral Education, Harvard University, Cambridge, Massachusetts 02138)

Kohlberg, L., & Hersh, R. H. Moral development: A review of the theory. *Theory into Practice,* 1977, *16* (2), 53-59.

Kohlberg, L., & Kramer, R. B. Continuities and discontinuities in childhood and adult moral development. *Human Development,* 1969, *12,* 93-120.

Konopka, G. The needs, rights and responsibilities of youth. *Child Welfare,* 1976, *55* (3), 173-182.

Krathwohl, D. R., Bloom, B. S., & Masia, B. B. *Taxonomy of educational objectives: The classification of educational goals—Handbook II: Affective Domain.* New York: David McKay, 1964.

Kressel, K. Kurt Lewin and American psychology: The "outsider" and intellectual leadership. *Groups: A Journal of Group Dynamics and Psychotherapy,* 1974, *6* (1), 37-42.

Krumboltz, J. D. Behavioral counseling: Rationale and research. *Personnel and Guidance Journal,* 1965, *44,* 383-387.

Krumboltz, J. D. (Ed.). *Revolution in counseling: Implications of behavioral science.* Boston: Houghton Mifflin, 1966.

Krumboltz, J. D., & Thoresen, C. E. *Behavioral counseling: Cases and techniques.* New York: Holt, Rinehart & Winston, 1969.

Kübler-Ross, E. *On death and dying.* New York: Bantam, 1973.

Kuppersmith, J. (Ed.). *Ethnic identity through autobiography.* Staten Island, N.Y.: College of Staten Island, 1978.

Kurtz, R. R., & Grummon, D. L. Different approaches to the measurement of therapist empathy and their relationship to therapy outcomes. *Journal of Consulting and Clinical Psychology,* 1972, *39,* 106-115.

Lacoursiere, R. *The life cycle of groups.* New York: Human Sciences Press, 1980.

Lafferty, J., Dennerll, D., & Rettick, P. A creative school mental health program. *The National Elementary Principal,* 1964, *43,* 29-35.

Landy, E. Who does what in the guidance program? *The School Counselor,* 1963, *109,* 112-118.

Larkin, J. C. Score, rank, or evaluation: Does type of performance feedback make a difference? *Contemporary Educational Psychology,* 1978, *3* (2), 127-135.

Lauer, B., Ten Broek, E., & Grossman, M. Battered-child syndrome review of 130 patients with controls. *Pediatrics,* 1974, *54* (1), 67-70.

Lauver, P. J. Consulting with teachers: A systematic approach. *Personnel and Guidance Journal,* 1974, *52,* 535-540.

Lazarus, A. A. Has behavior therapy outlived its usefulness? *American Psychologist,* 1977, *32* (7), 550-554.

Leitner, L. A. Crisis counseling may save a life. *Journal of Rehabilitation,* 1974, *40,* 19-20.

Leitner, L. A., & Stecher, T. Crisis intervention for growth: Philosophical dimensions and strategies. *Psychology,* 1974, *11,* 29-32.

Lester, D., & Brockopp, G. W. (Eds.). *Crisis intervention and counseling by telephone.* Springfield, Ill.: Charles C Thomas, 1973.

Levis, D. J. Behavioral therapy: The fourth therapeutic revolution? In D. J. Levis (Ed.), *Learning approaches to therapeutic behavior change.* Chicago: Aldine, 1970.

Leviton, H. S. Consumer feedback on a secondary school guidance program. *Personnel and Guidance Journal,* 1977, *55* (5), 242-244.

Lewin, K. *A dynamic theory of personality* (D. K. Adams & K. E. Zener, trans.). New York: McGraw-Hill, 1936.

Lewis, C. A. People-plant interaction: A new horticultural perspective. *American Horticulturist,* 1973 (Summer), 52, 18-24.

Lindemann, E. Symptomatology and management of acute grief. *American Journal of Psychiatry,* 1944, *101,* 141-148.

Lindsley, O. R. Theoretical basis for behavior modification. In C. E. Pitts (Ed.), *Operant conditioning in the classroom.* New York: Thomas Y. Crowell, 1971, 54-60.

Linton, R. *The study of man.* New York: Appleton-Century-Crofts, 1936.

Lipsett, S. M. *Introduction: The mood of American youth.* Reston, Va.: National Education Association, 1974.

Lister, J. L., & McKenzie, D. H. A framework for the improvement of test interpretation in counseling. *Personnel and Guidance Journal,* 1966, *45,* 61-65.

Loesch, L. C., Crane, B. B., & Rucker, B. B. Counselor trainee effectiveness: More puzzle pieces. *Counselor Education and Supervision,* 1978, *17,* 195-204.

Loesch, L. C., & Rucker, B. B. A factor-analysis of the counselor evaluation rating scale. *Counselor Education and Supervision,* 1977, *16* (3), 209-216.

Lowendahl, E. Therapeutic approaches to adolescence. *American Corrective Therapy Journal,* 1975, *29* (5), 169-172.

Lundquist, G. W., & Chamley, J. C. Counselor-consultant: A move toward effectiveness. *The School Counselor,* 1971, *18,* 362-366.

McArthur, C. C. Comment on "effectiveness of counselors and counselor aides." *Journal of Counseling Psychology,* 1970, *17,* 335-336.

McAvoy, R. Measurable outcome with systematic observation. *Journal of Research and Development in Education,* 1970, *4* (1), 10-13.

McCary, J. L. *Human sexuality* (2nd ed.). New York: Van Nostrand Reinhold, 1974.

McClain, A. D., & Boley, K. J. Counseling and consultation interrelationships. *Elementary School Guidance and Counseling,* 1968, *3,* 32-39.

McCreary, W. H., & Miller, G. Elementary school counselors in California. *Personnel and Guidance Journal,* 1966, *44,* 494-502.

McCully, C. H. The school counselor strategy for professionalism. *Personnel and Guidance Journal,* 1962, *40,* 681-688.

McDaniel, H. B., & Shaftel, G. A. *Guidance in the modern school.* New York: The Dryden Press, 1956.

McLaughlin, B. *Learning and social behavior.* New York: Free Press, 1971.

Macomber, F. G. The role of educational institutions in adolescent development. In J. F. Adams (Ed.), *Understanding adolescence: Current developments in adolescent psychology.* Boston: Allyn & Bacon, 1968, 232-248.

Macy, V. Some concerns about counseling. *The School Counselor,* 1972, *19,* 5.

Maddox, J. W. Sex in adolescence: Its meaning and its future. *Adolescence,* 1973, *8* (31), 325-341.

Mahoney, M. J. Reflections on the cognitive-learning trend in psychotherapy. *American Psychologist*, 1977, *32* (1), 5–13.

Mahoney, S. C. *The art of helping people effectively*. New York: Association Press, 1967.

Mahoney, W. M. Action is the product of guidance teamwork. *Clearing House*, 1972, *46*, 427–430.

Mancuso, J. C., Morrison, J. K., & Aldrich, C. C. Developmental changes in social-moral perception: Some factors affecting children's evaluations and predictions of the behavior of a transgressor. *Journal of Genetic Psychology*, 1978, *132* (1), 121–136.

Mann, R. D. A review of the relationship between personality and performance in small groups. *Psychological Bulletin*, 1959, *56*, 241–270.

Maschette, D. Moral reasoning in the real world. *Theory into Practice*, 1977, *16* (2), 124–128.

Maslow, A. H. *Toward a psychology of being*. New York: Van Nostrand Reinhold, 1954.

Mathewson, R. H. *Guidance: Policy and practice* (3d ed.). New York: Harper & Row, 1962.

May, R., Angel, E., & Ellenberger, H. F. (Eds.). *Existence*. New York: Simon and Schuster, 1959.

Mellecker, J. Transactional analysis for non-TA counselors. In G. S. Belkin (Ed.), *Counseling: Directions in theory and practice*. Dubuque, Iowa: Kendall/Hunt, 1976.

Michael, J., & Meyerson, L. A. A behavioral approach to guidance and counseling. *Harvard Educational Review*, 1962, *32*, 382–401.

Miller, F. W. *Guidance: Principles and services* (2nd ed.). Columbus, Ohio: Charles E. Merrill, 1968.

Millichap, J. G. Drugs in management of minimal brain dysfunction. *Annals of New York Academy of Science*, 1973, *205*, 321–334.

Milliken, R., Prejudice and counseling effectiveness. *Personnel and Guidance Journal*, 1965, *43*, 710–712.

Milliken, R., & Kirchner, R., Jr. Counselor's understanding of student's communications as a function of the counselor's perceptual defense. *Journal of Counseling Psychology*, 1971, *18*, 14–18.

Mintz, E. E. *Marathon groups: Reality and symbol*. New York: Appleton-Century-Crofts, 1971.

Miran, M., Lehrer, P., Koehler, R., & Miran, E. What happens when deviant behavior begins to change? The relevance of a social systems approach for behavioral programs with adolescents. *Journal of Community Psychology*, 1974, *2* (4), 370–375.

Mitchell, J. J. Some psychological dimensions of adolescent sexuality. *Adolescence*, 1972, *7*, 447–458.

Mitchell, J. J. Moral dilemmas of early adolescence. *The School Counselor*, 1974, *22*, 16–22.

Mitchell, J. J. Moral growth during adolescence. *Adolescence*, 1975, *10* (38), 221–226.

Mitchell, M. *The counselor and sexuality*. Boston: Houghton Mifflin, 1973.

Moser, L. E., & Moser, R. *Counseling and guidance: An exploration*. Englewood Cliffs: Prentice-Hall, 1963.

Moss, J. W. Disabled or disadvantaged: There is a difference. *Journal of Special Education*, 1973, *7* (4), 387–391.

Motto, J. A. Recognition, evaluation and management of persons at risk for suicide. *Personnel and Guidance Journal*, 1978, *56*, 537–543.

Mowrer, O. H., & Mowrer, W. M. Enuresis—a method for its study and treatment. *Journal of Orthopsychiatry*, 1938, *8*, 436–459.

Mueller, S. G., Johnson, R. L., & Washington, R. A needs assessment research model: Its essential aspects and use. *Journal of Instructional Psychology,* 1978, *4* (2), 11-18.

Mullen, J., & Abeles, N. Relationship of liking, empathy, and therapist's experience to outcome of therapy. *Journal of Counseling Psychology,* 1970, *35,* 39-43.

Munson, H. L. *Elementary school guidance: Concepts, dimensions, and practice.* Boston: Allyn & Bacon, 1970.

Myers, P. I., & Hammill, D. D. *Methods for learning disorders* (2nd ed.). New York: John Wiley & Sons, 1976.

Myklebust, H. R., & Johnson, D. *Learning disabilities: Educational principles and practices.* New York: Grune & Stratton, 1967.

Nagi, S. Z. Child abuse and neglect programs: A national overview. *Children Today,* 1975, *4* (3), 13-17.

Naranjo, C. Present-centeredness: Technique, prescription, and ideal. In J. Fagan & I. L. Sheperd (Eds.), *Gestalt therapy now.* Palo Alto, Calif.: Science and Behavior Books, 1970.

Nass, D. R. (Ed.). *The rape victim.* Dubuque, Iowa: Kendall/Hunt, 1977.

Nass, D. R., & Nass, S. Counseling the fatherless child. In G. S. Belkin (Ed.), *Counseling: Directions in theory and practice.* Dubuque, Iowa: Kendall/Hunt, 1976.

Nass, S. (Ed.). *Crisis intervention.* Dubuque, Iowa: Kendall/Hunt, 1977.

Necessary, C. Teen alcoholics: More than 3 million counted, and the number is rising. *Guidepost,* July 12, 1979, p. 6.

Newton, F. B., & Caple, R. B. Client and counselor preferences for counselor behavior in the interview. *Journal of College Student Personnel,* 1974, *15* (3), 220-224.

Nichols, K. A. Preparation for membership in a group. *Bulletin of the British Psychological Society,* 1976, *29,* 353-359.

Norris, W., Zeran, F. R., & Hatch, R. N. *The information service in guidance.* Chicago: Rand McNally, 1960.

Nurse, S. M. Familial patterns of parents who abuse their children. In R. Kalmar (Ed.), *Child abuse.* Dubuque, Iowa: Kendall/Hunt, 1977. Originally published in *Smith College Studies in Social work,* 1964.

Offer, D. *The psychological world of the teen-ager.* New York: Basic Books, 1969.

Oliver, L. W. Counseling implications of recent research on women. *Personnel and Guidance Journal,* 1975, *53,* 430-437.

Ozer, M. N., & Richardson, H. B. The diagnostic evaluation of children with learning problems: A process approach. *Journal of Learning Disabilities,* 1974, *7* (1), 30-34.

Parks, B. J. Career Development—How early? *Elementary School Journal,* 1976, *76,* 468-474.

Parks, J. C. Group guidance—A perspective. In D. Brown & D. J. Srebalus (Eds.), *Selected readings in contemporary guidance.* Dubuque, Iowa: Wm. C. Brown Company Publishers, 1973.

Parsons, Frank. *Choosing a Vocation.* Boston: Houghton Mifflin, 1909.

Pascale, A. C. Enchancing the counseling services through the utilization of group counseling. *The School Counselor,* 1968, *16,* 136-139.

Passons, W. R. Gestalt therapy interventions for group counseling. *Personnel and Guidance Journal,* 1972, *51,* 183-189.

Patterson, C. H. *Counseling and guidance in the schools.* New York: Harper & Row, 1962.

Patterson, C. H. *Theories of counseling and psychotherapy* (2nd Ed.). New York: Harper & Row, 1973.

Patterson, G. R., Cobb, J. A., & Ray, R. S. A social engineering technology for retraining the families of aggressive boys. In H. E. Adams & I. P. Unikel (Eds.), *Issues and trends in behavior therapy.* Springfield, Ill.: Charles C Thomas, 1973, 139-207.

Paulson, M. J. Parents of the battered child: A multidisciplinary group therapy approach to life-threatening behavior. *Life-Threatening Behavior,* 1974, *4* (1), 18-31.

Perez, J. F. *The initial counseling contact.* Boston: Houghton Mifflin, 1968.

Perls, F. S. *Ego, hunger and aggression.* New York: Random House, 1969. (Originally published London: Allen & Unwin, 1947.)

Perls, F. S. Theory and technique of personality integration. *American Journal of Psychotherapy,* 1948, *2,* 563ff.

Perls, F. S. *Gestalt therapy verbatim.* Lafayette, Calif.: Real People Press, 1969.

Perls, F. S. *The gestalt approach and eye witness to therapy.* Palo Alto, Calif.: Science and Behavior Books, 1973.

Perls, F. S., Hefferline, R. F., & Goodman, P. *Gestalt therapy: Excitement and growth in the human personality.* New York: Dell, 1969.

Perry, W. G., Jr. On the relation of psychotherapy to counseling. *Annals of the New York Academy of Science,* 1955, *63,* 396-407.

Peters, J., Davis, J., Boolsby, C., et al. *Physicians handbook: Screening for MBD.* Summit, N.J.: CIBA Medical Horizons, 1973.

Peterson, J. A. *Counseling and values.* Scranton, Pa.: International Textbook, 1970.

Piaget, J. *The moral judgment of the child.* London: Kegan Paul, 1932.

Piaget, J. & Inhelder, B. *Psychology of the child.* New York: Basic Books, 1969.

Polakow, R. L., & Peabody, D. L. Behavioral treatment of child abuse. *International Journal of Offender Therapy and Comparative Criminology,* 1975, *19* (1), 100-103.

Ponzo, Z. Integrating techniques from five counseling theories. *Personnel and Guidance Journal,* 1976, *54* (8), 415-419.

Porter, E. H., Jr. *An introduction to therapeutic counseling.* Boston: Houghton Mifflin, 1950.

Poulton, E. C. Quantitative subjective assessments are almost always biased, sometimes completely misleading. *British Journal of Psychology,* 1977, *68* (4), 409-425.

Protinsky, H. Rational counseling with adolescents. *The School Counselor,* 1976, *23* (4), 240-246.

Pulaski, M. A. *Understanding Piaget.* New York: Harper & Row, 1971.

Pyke, S. W. Cognitive templating: A technique for feminist (and other) counselors. *Personnel and Guidance Journal,* 1979, *57* (6), 315-318.

Queensboro Society for the Prevention of Cruelty to Children. *Child abuse.* Jamaica, N.Y.: QSPCC, 1976.

Rachman, S. Behavior therapy. In B. Berenson & R. R. Carkhuff (Eds.), *Sources of gain in counseling and psychotherapy.* New York: Holt, Rinehart & Winston, 1967. (a)

Rainwater, L. *Behind ghetto walls.* Chicago: Aldine, 1970.

Raming, H. E., & Frey, D. H. A taxonomic approach to the gestalt theory of Perls. *Journal of Counseling Psychology,* 1974, *21* (3), 179-184.

Rapoport, L. The state of crisis: Some theoretical considerations. *Social Science Review,* 1962, *36,* 211-217.

Raths, L., Harmin, M., & Simon, S. *Values and teaching: Working with values in the classroom.* Columbus, Ohio: Charles E. Merrill, 1966.

Reichelt, P. A., & Werley, H. H. Contraception, abortion, and venereal disease: Teenagers' knowledge and the effect of education. *Family Planning Perspectives,* 1975, *7* (2), 83–88.

Reik, T. *Listening with the third ear.* New York: Farrar, Strauss, 1948.

Reppert, H. C., Campbell, J. P., & Kirk, C. R. The management and supervision of a testing program. In J. F. Adams (Ed.), *Counseling and guidance: A summary view.* New York: Macmillan, 1965.

Rhine, M. W., & Mayerson, P. A serious suicidal syndrome masked by homicidal threats. *Life-Threatening Behavior,* 1973, *3* (1), 3–9.

Robin, S. S., & Bosco, J. J. The social context of stimulant drug treatment for hyperkinetic children. *School Review,* 1976, *85* (1), 141–154.

Roe, A. *The psychology of occupations.* New York: John Wiley & Sons, 1956.

Roe, A. Early determinants of vocational choice. *Journal of Counseling Psychology,* 1957, *4,* 212–217.

Roe, A., Hubbard, W. D., Hutchinson, T., & Batemen, T. Studies of occupational history. Part I: Job changes and the classification of occupations. *Journal of Counseling Psychology,* 1966, *13,* 387–393.

Roe, A., & Siegelman, M. *The origin of interests.* Washington, D.C.: American Personnel and Guidance Association, 1964.

Roeber, E. C., Smith, G. E., & Erickson, C. E. *Organization and administration of guidance services* (2nd Ed.). New York: McGraw-Hill, 1955.

Rogers, C. R. *The clinical treatment of the problem child.* Boston: Houghton Mifflin, 1939.

Rogers, C. R. *Counseling and psychotherapy.* Boston: Houghton Mifflin, 1942.

Rogers, C. R. *Client-centered therapy.* Boston: Houghton Mifflin, 1951.

Rogers, C. R. The necessary and sufficient conditions of therapeutic change. *Journal of Consulting Psychology,* 1957, *21,* 95–103. (a)

Rogers, C. R. A note on "the nature of man." *Journal of Counseling Psychology,* 1957, *4,* 199–203. (b)

Rogers, C. R. Significant learning: In therapy and in education. *Educational Leadership,* 1959, *16* (4), 232–242. (a)

Rogers, C. R. A theory of therapy, personality, and interpersonal relationships as developed in the client-centered framework. In S. Koch (Ed.), *Psychology: A study of a science* (Volume III, Formulations of the person and the social context). New York: McGraw-Hill, 1959. (b)

Rogers, C. R. *On becoming a person.* Boston: Houghton Mifflin, 1961.

Rogers, C. R. The interpersonal relationship: The core of guidance. *Harvard Educational Review,* 1962, *32,* 416–429.

Rogers, C. R. Some questions and challenges facing a humanistic psychology. *Journal of Humanistic Psychology,* 1965, *5,* 1–5.

Rogers, C. R. (Ed.). *The therapeutic relationship and its impact.* Madison: University of Wisconsin Press, 1967.

Rogers, C. R. *Carl Rogers on encounter groups.* New York: Harper & Row, 1970.

Rogers, C. R. Facilitating encounter groups. *American Journal of Nursing,* 1971, *71,* 275–279.

Rogers, C. R. In retrospect: Forty-six years. *American Psychologist,* 1974, *29,* 118–122.

Rogers, C. R. Empathic: An unappreciated way of being. *Counseling Psychologist,* 1975, *5* (2), 2–10.

Rogers, C. R., & Dymond, R. F. (Eds.). *Psychotherapy and personality change*. Chicago: University of Chicago Press, 1954.

Rosenthal, D. Changes in some moral values following psychotherapy. *Journal of Consulting Psychology,* 1955, *19,* 431-436.

Rosenthal, R. On the social psychology of the psychological experiment: The experimenter's hypothesis as an unintended determinant of experimental results. *American Scientist,* 1963, *51,* 268-283.

Ross, D. M., & Ross, S. A. *Hyperactivity: Research, theory and action*. New York: John Wiley & Sons, 1976.

Rothney, J. W. M. *Adaptive counseling in schools*. Englewood Cliffs, N.J.: Prentice-Hall, 1972.

Rowe, W., Murphy, H. B., & DeCsipkes, R. A. The relationship of counseling characteristics and counseling effectiveness. *Review of Educational Research,* 1975, *45,* 231-246.

Ruma, E. H. Counseling the single parent. In G. S. Belkin (Ed.), *Counseling: Directions in theory and practice*. Dubuque, Iowa: Kendall/Hunt, 1976, pp. 309-317.

Russell, R. D. Black perceptions of guidance. In D. Brown & D. J. Srebalus (Eds.), *Contemporary guidance concepts and practices*. Dubuque, Iowa: Wm. C. Brown Company Publishers, 1972.

Ryan, B. *Programmed therapy for stuttering in children and adults*. Springfield, Ill.: Charles C Thomas, 1974.

Salvia, J., & Clark, J. Use of deficits to identify the learning disabled. *Exceptional Children,* 1973, *39,* 305-308.

Salzman, L. Sexual problems in adolescence. *Contemporary Psychoanalysis,* 1974, *10,* 189-207.

Sanders, L., Kibby, R. W., Creaghan, S., & Tyrell, E. Child abuse: Detection and prevention. *Young Children,* 1975, *30* (5), 332-337.

Sanderson, H. *Basic concepts in vocational guidance*. New York: McGraw-Hill, 1954.

Sararwathi, T. S., & Verma, S. Social class differences in the development of moral judgment in girls of ages 10-12 years. *Indian Journal of Psychology,* 1976, *51* (4), 325-332.

Schlossberg, N. K., & Goodman, J. Imperatives for change: Counselor use of the Strong Vocational Interest Blanks. *Impact,* 1972, *2,* 26-29.

Schmidt, J. A. Cognitive restructuring: The art of talking to yourself. *Personnel and Guidance Journal,* 1976, *55* (2), 71-74.

Schmidt, L. D. Concepts of the role of secondary school counselors. *Personnel and Guidance Journal,* 1962, *40,* 600-605.

Schmitt, B. D. The minimal brain dysfunction myth. *American Journal of Diseases of Childhood,* 1975, *129,* 1313-1318.

Schubert, M. *Interviewing in social work practice: An introduction*. New York: Council on Social Work Education (345 East 46th Street, New York 10017), 1971.

Senn, T. L., et. al. *South Carolina's hortitherapy program: Innovative development of individual potential through horticulture*. Clemson, S.C.: South Carolina Agricultural Experimental Station, 1974.

Shafto, F., & Sulzbacher, S. Comparing treatment tactics with a hyperactive preschool child: Stimulant medication and programmed teacher intervention. *Journal of Applied Behavioral Analysis,* 1977, *10* (1), 13-20.

Shambaugh, P. W. The development of the small group. *Human Relations,* 1978, *31* (3), 283-295.

Shelton, J. E. Counselor characteristics and effectiveness in serving economically disadvantaged and advantaged males. *Counselor Education and Supervision,* 1973, *13,* 129–136.

Sherman, R., Albaggia, D., Cohen, M., Dell, E., Nadler, J., Shapiro, I., & Silverman, B. Teacher-counselor communication. *The School Counselor,* 1969, *17,* 55–62.

Shertzer, B., & Linden, J. D. *Fundamentals of individual appraisal: Assessment techniques for counselors.* Boston: Houghton Mifflin, 1979.

Shertzer, B., & Stone, S. C. The school counselor and his publics: A problem in role definition. *Personnel and Guidance Journal,* 1963, *41,* 687–692.

Shertzer, B., & Stone, S. C. *Fundamentals of guidance* (2nd Ed.). Boston: Houghton Mifflin, 1971.

Shoben, E. J. The counseling experience as personal development. *Personnel and Guidance Journal,* 1965, *44,* 224–230.

Shuman, R. B. Of course he can read—He's in high school. *Journal of Reading,* 1975, *4,* 36–42.

Siciński, A. The concepts of "need" and "value" in light of the systems approach. *Social Science Information,* 1978, *17* (1), 71–91.

Sieka, F., Taylor, D., Thomson, B., & Muthard, J. A critique of "effectiveness of counselors and counselor aides." *Journal of Counseling Psychology,* 1971, *18,* 362–364.

Silver, L. B. Acceptable and controversial approaches to treating the child with learning disabilities. *Pediatrics,* 1975, *55* (3), 406–415.

Silvestri, R. J. The treatment of emotionally disturbed retardates by implosive therapy. *Dissertation Abstracts International,* 1974 (March), *34* (9-B), 4676–4677.

Skinner, B. F. *Walden two.* New York: Vintage, 1966.

Skinner, B. F. *About behaviorism.* New York: Vintage, 1974.

Skinner, B. F. *About behaviorism.* New York: Vintage, 1976. Originally published, 1974.

Skinner, B. F. The steep and thorny way to a science of behavior. *American Psychologist,* 1975, *30* (1), 42–49.

Skinner, B. F. *Particulars of my life.* New York: Knopf, 1976. (a)

Skinner, B. F. Interview with B. F. Skinner. In R. I. Evans (Ed.), *The making of psychology.* New York: Knopf, 1976, pp. 83–94. (b)

Sleator, E. K., & Von Neumann, A. W. Methylphenidate in the treatment of hyperkinetic children. *Clinical Pediatrics,* 1974, *13* (Jan.), 19–24.

Smaby, M., & Tamminen, A. W. Can we help belligerent counselees? *Personnel and Guidance Journal,* 1979, *57* (10), 506–512.

Smith, E. J. Counseling Black individuals: Some stereotypes. *Personnel and Guidance Journal,* 1977, *55,* 390–396.

Smith, E. M. Counseling for women who seek abortion. *Social Work,* 1972, *17* (2), 62–68.

Sorenson, R. C. Adolescent sexuality in contemporary America. New York: Harry N. Abrams, 1973.

Spinetti, J. J., & Rigler, D. The child abusing parent: A psychological review. *Psychological Bulletin,* 1972, 18–29.

Spotnitz, H. *The couch and the circle.* New York: Knopf, 1961.

Spotnitz, H. The toxoid response. *The Psychoanalytic Review,* 1963, *50* (4), 81–94.

Spotnitz, H. *Modern psychoanalysis and the schizophrenic patient.* New York: Grune & Stratton, 1968.

Spotnitz, H. *Psychotherapy of preoedipal conditions.* New York: Jason Aronson, 1976.

Sprinthall, N. *Guidance for human growth.* New York: Van Nostrand Reinhold, 1971.

Sroufe, A. L., & Stewart, M. A. Treating problem children with stimulant drugs. *New England Journal of Medicine,* 1973, *289* (8), 407–413.

Stradlen, F. Truancy—A sign of distress. *The Times Educational Supplement,* January 16, 1976, 3163:8.

Stafford, R. R. Attitude and behavior change in couples as a function of communication training. *Dissertation Abstracts International,* 1978 (Nov.), Vol. 39, (5-B), 2526.

Stampfl, T. G. Implosive therapy: An emphasis on covert stimulation. In D. J. Levis (Ed.), *Learning approaches to therapeutic behavior change.* Chicago: Aldine, 1970, pp. 182–204.

Stefflre, B., & Grant, H. W. *Theories of counseling* (2nd Ed.). New York: McGraw-Hill, 1972.

Stewart, C. C. A bill of rights for school counselors. *Personnel and Guidance Journal,* 1959, *37,* 500–503.

Stewart, M. A. Is hyperactivity abnormal?—and other unanswered questions. *School Review,* 1976, *85* (1), 31–42.

Stintzi, V. L., & Hutcheon, W. R. We have a counselor problem—can you help us? *The School Counselor,* 1972, *19,* 329–334.

Stolz, S. B., Wienckowski, L. A., & Brown, B.S. Behavior modification: A perspective on critical issues. *American Psychologist,* 1975, *30* (11), 1027–1048.

Stone, G. L., & Morden, C. J. Effect of distance on verbal productivity. *Journal of Counseling Psychology,* 1976, *23* (5), 486–488.

Strang, R. *Counseling technics in college and secondary schools* (Rev. ed.). New York: Harper & Bros., 1949.

Strickland, B. A rationale and model for changing values in helping relationships. In J. C. Hansen (Ed.), *Counseling process and procedures.* New York: Macmillan, 1978, pp. 427–435.

Strickler, M., & Bonnefil, M. Crisis intervention and social casework: Similarities and differences in problem solving. *Clinical Social Work Journal,* 1974, *2* (1), 36–44.

Sue, D. W. Do clients know what they need? *Personnel and Guidance Journal,* 1977, *55* (5), 220–221.

Sue, D. W. Personal communication to Wm. Fitzgerald and Gary S. Belkin. March 30, 1979.

Sugarman, A. Is psychodiagnostic assessment humanistic? *Journal of Personality Assessment,* 1978, *42* (1), 11–21.

Sulzbacher, S. I. The learning-disabled or hyperactive child: Diagnosis and treatment. *JAMA,* 1975, *234* (9), 938–941.

Super, D. E. *The psychology of careers.* New York: Harper & Row, 1957.

Super, D. E. Vocational development theory: Person, position, and process. *Counseling Psychologist,* 1969, *1,* 2–9.

Swails, R., & Herr, E. Vocational development groups for ninth-grade students. *Vocational Guidance Quarterly,* 1976, *24* (1), 256–260.

Sweeney, T. J. The school counselor as perceived by counselors and their principals. *Personnel and Guidance Journal,* 1966, *44,* 844–847.

Swick, K. J., & Ross, C. Affective learning for the real world. In G. S. Belkin (Ed.), *Perspectives in educational psychology.* Dubuque, Iowa: Wm. C. Brown Company Publishers, 1979, pp. 106–108.

Tarrier, R. B., et al. Career counseling: Prediction or exploration. Paper presented at APGA Convention, Atlantic City, New Jersey, April, 1971. (ERIC Document Reproduction Service, No. Ed 051 510).

Tayal, S. *Suggestibility in a state of crisis.* Unpublished doctoral dissertation, University of Maryland, 1972. Ann Arbor, Michigan: University Microfilms.

Tereshkovich, G. Horticultural therapy: A review. *Hort-Science,* 1973, *8* (6), 460–461.

Tessman, L. H. *Children of parting parents.* New York: Aronson, 1978.

Thomas, M. H., & Drabman, R. S. Effects of television violence on expectations of other's aggression. *Personality and Social Psychology Bulletin,* 1978, *4* (1), 73–76.

Thomas, H., & Stewart, N. R. Counselor response to female clients with deviate and conforming career goals. *Journal of Counseling Psychology,* 1971, *18,* 352–357.

Thomson, R. *The Pelican history of psychology.* Baltimore: Pelican Books, 1968.

Thoresen, C. E. The counselor as an applied behavioral scientist. *Personnel and Guidance Journal,* 1969, *47,* 841–848.

Thoresen, C. E. Behavioral humanism. In *The Seventy-Second Yearbook of the National Society for the Study of Education (NSSE).* Chicago: University of Chicago Press, 1973, pp. 385–421.

Thoresen, C. E. Constructs don't speak for themselves. *Counselor Education and Supervision,* 1977, *16* (4), 296–303.

Thorndike, R. L., & Hagen, E. *Measurement and evaluation in psychology and education* (3d ed.). New York: John Wiley & Sons, 1969.

Thorndike, R. L., & Hagen, E. *Measurement and evaluation in psychology and education* (4th ed.). New York: John Wiley & Sons, 1978.

Thorne, F. C. Principles of personality counseling. *Journal of Clinical Psychology,* 1950.

Thorne, F. C. *Integrative psychology.* Brandon, Vt.: Clinical Psychology Publishing Company, 1967.

Thorne, F. C. Eclectic psychotherapy. In R. Corsini (Ed.), *Current psychotherapies.* Itasca, Ill.: F. E. Peacock, 1973.

Tiedman, D. V., & O'Hara, R. P. *Career development: Choice and adjustment.* New York: College Entrance Examination Board, 1963.

Tilis, H. S. Evaluation and testing in the classroom. In Gary S. Belkin (Ed.), *Perspectives in educational psychology.* Dubuque, Iowa: Wm. C. Brown Company Publishers, 1979, pp. 399–403.

Tolbert, E. L. *Introduction to counseling* (2nd Ed.). New York: McGraw-Hill, 1972.

Tolbert, E. L. *Counseling for career development.* Boston: Houghton Mifflin, 1974.

Tolbert, E. L. *An introduction to guidance.* Boston: Little, Brown & Co., 1978.

Torrey, E. F. *The mind game.* New York: Emerson-Hall, 1972.

Tracy, J. J., & Clark, E. H. Treatment for child abusers. *Social Work,* 1974, *19* (3), 338–342.

Trainer, F. E. A critical analysis of Kohlberg's contributions to the study of moral thought. *Journal for the Theory of Social Behavior,* 1977, *7* (1), 41–63.

Traxler, A. E., & North, R. D. *Techniques of guidance.* New York: Harper & Row, 1966.

Trotzer, J. P. *The counselor and the group: Integrating theory, training and practice.* Monterey, Calif.: Brooks/Cole, 1977.

Trotzer, J. P., & Kassera, W. J. Do counselors do what they are taught? *The School Counselor,* 1971, *18,* 335–341.

Trotzer, J. P. Perceptions of counselor performance: A comparative study. *Counselor Education and Supervision,* 1976, *16* (2), 126–134.

Truax, C. B., & Carkhuff, R. R. *Toward effective counseling and psychotherapy.* Chicago: Aldine, 1967.

Truax, C. B., & Lister, J. L. Effectiveness of counselors and counselor aides. *Journal of Counseling Psychology,* 1970, *17,* 331–334.

Tyler, L. E. The initial interview. *Personnel and Guidance Journal,* 1956, *34,* 466–473.

Tyler, L. E. *The work of the counselor* (3d Ed.). New York: Appleton-Century-Crofts, 1969.

Unikel, I. P. Issues in behavior therapy. In H. E. Adams & I. P. Unikel (Eds.), *Issues and trends in behavior therapy.* Springfield, Ill.: Charles C Thomas, 1973, pp. 43–56.

Van Riper, B. W. Professionalization by ostensive acts. *The School Counselor,* 1972, *19,* 323–327.

Vontress, C. E. Cultural barriers in the counseling relationship. *Personnel and Guidance Journal,* 1969, *47,* 11–17.

Vontress, C. E. Counseling the racial and ethnic minorities. *Focus on Guidance,* 1973, *5* (6), 1–10.

Wallen, R. Gestalt therapy and Gestalt psychology (1957). In J. Fagan & I. L. Shepherd (Eds.), *Gestalt therapy now.* Palo Alto, Calif.: Science & Behavior Books, 1970.

Walton, F. X., & Sweeney, T. J. Useful predictors of counseling effectiveness. *Personnel and Guidance Journal,* 1969, *48,* 32–38.

Warnath, C. F. Licensing: Learning the game of politics and compromise. *Personnel and Guidance Journal,* 1978, *57,* 50–53.

Warner, C. D. *My summer in a garden: The gardener's world,* Ed. by Joseph Wood Krutch. New York: Putnam, 1959. (Originally published 1870.)

Warnken, R. G., & Siess, T. F. The use of the cumulative record in the prediction of behavior. *Personnel and Guidance Journal,* 1965, *44,* 231–237.

Warters, J. E. *High school personnel work today* (2nd ed.). New York: McGraw-Hill, 1956.

Watson, J. B. Psychology as the behaviorist views it. *Psychological Review,* 1913, *20,* 159–170.

Watson, J. B. *Psychology from the standpoint of a behaviorist* (2nd ed.). Philadelphia: L. B. Lippincott, 1924. (Originally published, 1919.)

Watson, J. B. *Behaviorism.* New York: The People's Institute, 1924. (Edition quoted is New York: Norton, 1970.)

Watson, J. B. *Behaviorism.* New York: W. W. Norton, 1930.

Webster, C. Group therapy for behavior problem children in a rural high school. *Child Welfare,* 1974, *53* (10), 653–657.

Weil, A. P. Children with minimal brain dysfunction: Diagnostic, dynamic, and therapeutic considerations. In S. G. Sapir & A. C. Nitzburg (Eds.), *Children with learning problems.* New York: Brunner/Mazel, 1973.

Weininger, O. The disabled and dying children: Does it have to hurt so much? *Ontario Psychologist,* 1975, *7* (3), 123–134. Reprinted in L. Wilkenfeld (Ed.), *When children die.* Dubuque, Iowa: Kendall/Hunt, 1976.

Weiss, G., Kruger, E., Danielson, U., & Elman, M. Effect of long-term treatment of hyperactive children with methylphenidate. *Canadian Medical Association Journal,* 1975, *112,* 159–165.

Weiss, R. S. *Marital separation.* New York: Baisic Books, 1975.

Weisstein, N. Psychology constructs the female; Or the fantasy life of the male psychologist. In M. H. Garskof (Ed.), *Toward women's liberation.* Belmont, Calif.: Brooks/Cole, 1971, pp. 68–83.

Weitzman, L. J., & Rizzo, D. *Images of males and females in elementary school textbooks.* Washington, D.C.: National Education Association and Resource Center on Sex Roles in Education, 1974.

Wells, C. E., & Ritter, K. Y. Paperwork, pressure, and discouragement: Student attitudes toward guidance services and implications for the profession. *Personnel and Guidance Journal,* 1979, *58* (3), 170–175.

Wender, P. H. *Minimal brain dysfunction in children.* New York: John Wiley & Sons, 1971.

Whiteman, J. L., Zucker, K. B., & Grimley, L. K. Moral judgment and the others-concept. *Psychological Reports,* 1978, *42* (1), 283–289.

Whitmont, E. C., & Kaufman, Y. Analytical psychotherapy. In R. Corsini (Ed.), *Current psychotherapies.* Itasca, Ill.: F. E. Peacock, 1973.

Widseth, J. C. Reported dependent behaviors towards mothers and use of alcohol in delinquent girls. *Dissertation Abstracts International,* October 1972, *33* (4-B), No. 1833.

Wiggins, J. D. Counselors and the life space of students. *The School Counselor,* 1972, *19,* 364–365.

Wilkenfeld, L. (Ed.). *When children die.* Dubuque, Iowa: Kendall/Hunt, 1977.

Williams, C. C., & Williams, R. A. Rape: A plea for help in the emergency room. *Nursing Forum,* 1973, *12,* 388–401.

Willis, J., & Giles, D. *Great experiments in behavior modification.* Indianapolis: Hackett, 1976.

Winkelman, N. W., Jr. The use of neuroleptic drugs in the treatment of nonpsychotic psychiatric patients. In F. J. Ayd (Ed.), *Rational psychopharmacoptherapy and the right to treatment.* Baltimore: Ayd Medical Communications, 1975, pp. 161–176.

Wolfe, H. *Women in the world of work.* Unpublished doctoral dissertation, University of the State of New York, 1969.

Wolpe, J. *Psychotherapy by reciprocal inhibition.* Stanford, Calif.: Stanford University Press, 1958.

Wolpe, J. The systematic desensitization treatment of neuroses. *Journal of Nervous and Mental Diseases,* 1961, *132,* 189–203.

Woods, T. A group method of engaging parents at a child psychiatric clinic. *Child Welfare,* 1974, *53* (6), 394–401.

Wrenn, C. G. *The counselor in a changing world.* Washington, D.C.: American Personnel and Guidance Association, 1962.

Yates, C., Johnson, N., & Johnson, J. Effects of the use of the Vocational Exploration Group on career maturity. *Journal of Counseling Psychology,* 1979, *26* (4), 368–370.

Yudkin, S. Death and the young. In A. Toynbee (Ed.), *Man's concern with death.* New York: McGraw-Hill, 1968.

Zerface, J. P., & Cox, W. H. School counselors leave home. *Personnel and Guidance Journal,* 1971, *49,* 371–375.

Zukow, A. H. Helping the hyperkinetic child. *Today's Education,* 1975, *64* (4), 39–41.

Index of Names

Carey, A. R., 198
Carkhuff, R. R., 149-150, 152, 171-173, 263, 266
Carmer, J. C., 79
Carmical, L., 192, 195
Carter, R. D., 92
Cash, T. F., 115
Cattell, R. B., 146
Cautela, J. R., 101
Cerio, J. E., 416-417
Chamley, J. C., 25
Chandler, C. R., 297
Charcot, J. M., 8, 37
Chenault, J., 208
Cherlin, A., 442
Clark, E. H., 311
Clark, J., 377
Clifford, B., 103
Clifford, L. T., 103
Cobb, J. A., 107
Cobbs, P. M., 457
Cohen, M., 209-210
Cole, S. O., 398
Combs, A. W., 155, 176
Conklin, R. C., 158
Conners, C. K., 396-397
Cook, D. R., 212
Corriveau, D. P., 224
Cottingham, H. F., 206
Cotton, M., 297
Cousins, N., 391
Cox, W. H., 21
Cramer, S. H., 252, 254
Crane, B. B., 148
Creaghan, S., 311
Cremin, L., 11
Cuccioli, R. R., 267-269
Curran, C. A., 16, 176-177
Curtis, F. L. S., 442
Curtis, G., 101
Cutter, R., 440

Dallas, D., 423, 445
Daly, J., 373
Danielson, U., 397
Danish, S. J., 158
Darley, J. G., 132
D'Augelli, A. R., 158
David, C. A., 311
Davis, J. B., 12

Davison, G. C., 109
DeCsipkes, R. A., 148
DeGenero, J. J., 376
Delaney, D. J., 115, 118
Dell, E., 209-210
Dennerll, D., 54
Denney, E. W., 191
Di Giuseppe, R. A., 54
Dilley, J., 158
Dimick, K. M., 133, 285-290
Dinkmeyer, D., 25
Dollard, J., 102, 221
Dorow, L. G., 106, 110
Downing, L. N., 15
Drabman, R. S., 226
Dranoff, S. M., 326
Drasgow, J., 170, 173
Dreikurs, R., 285-286, 288-289
Dreyfus, E. A., 70
Duberman, L., 461-462
Durkin, D., 233
Dworkin, A. L., 212
Dworkin, E. P., 212
Dymond, R., 72

Eber, H., 146
Edison, T., 400
Ehrenwald, J., 7
Eisenberg, S., 115, 118
Einstein, Al, 400
Ellenberger, H. F., 82
Ellingson, C., 378, 379
Ellis, A., 49-55
Elman, M., 397
Ephross, P. H., 355
Erickson, C. E., 346-347
Erikson, E., 43, 266
Esveldt, K. C., 376
Ewing, D. B., 89
Eysenck, H. J., 91
Ezell, B., 116

Fagan, J., 80
Farrell, J., 203
Farson, R., 82
Fazzaro, C. J., 29
Feingold, B. F., 375, 387

Felker, S., 132
Ferenczi, S., 45
Filbeck, R. W., 208
Fine, R. M., 338
Finell, J., 275-284
Flavell, J., 233
Forbush, J. B., 442
Ford, C. S., 326
Foreman, M. E., 252
Foreman, N. J., 427, 435
Forer, B. R., 426
Forness, S. R., 376
Forster, J. R., 205-206
Foulds, M. L., 83
Frankl, V., 68, 71
Freeman, R. D., 398
Freud, A., 43, 275-279
Freud, S., 8-9, 13, 36-49 passim, 227, 266
Frey, D. H., 36, 80, 83
Fromm, E., 67
Fulda, T. A., 228-231

Galton, F., 9-10
Gannon, W. J., 83
Gardner, J., 452
Garris, D., 199
Garvey, W. P., 98-99
Gazda, G. M., 205-206, 331
Gearheart, B. R., 373
Gedan, S., 444
Gellen, M. I., 145
Gelles, R. J., 310
Gendlin, E., 67, 124-125
Georgiady, N. P., 271
Gibb, J. R., 178
Giles, D., 96
Gillespie, J. O., 29
Ginzberg, E., 252, 265, 453
Gittelman-Klein, R., 393
Giuffra, M. J., 324
Gladstein, G. A., 157-158
Glass, G. V., 366
Glasser, W., 55-58
Globetti, G., 334
Goble, F., 67
Goffman, E., 160
Goldberg, G., 313-314
Goldberg, P., 450

Index of Subjects

Negative reinforcement, vs.
    punishment, 106
Neglect. See Child abuse
Negroes. See Blacks
Neurosis, 17, 39, 50
Nondirective counseling. See Client-
    centered counseling
Nondominance, 160-161
Nonjudgmental attitude, 155-156
Nontest assessment, 344-351
Normal distribution, 353
NVGA, 12

Objective personality tests, 356-357
Objectives model, 31
Objectivity, 159
Observation (in assessment), 345
Observation, systematic behavioral,
    86-87
Occupational guidance. See Career
    development
Occupational Outlook Handbook, 252
Oedipus complex, 42-43, 227
Open-mindedness, 154-155
Openness, 119, 154-156
Operant conditioning, 88-109 passim
    definition of, 91-92
    techniques of, 102-106
Operant response, definition of,
    103-104
Optimism, moral basis for, 223
Oral stage, 42
Organizational teamwork, 29-31
Organizations, professional, 203-205
Otis-Lennon Mental Ability Test, 354
Out-of-wedlock pregnancy, 442-445

P-A-C diagrams, 57-64
P.L. 94-142, 369-373
Paradoxical intention, 71
Paraprofessionals, 148-149
Parental neglect. See Child abuse
Parent ego states, 57-64

Parents
    child abusing, 309-312
    consultation with, 27-28
    divorced, effect on child, 458-463
    exceptional children and, 402-403
    as helpers, 22-25
    helpful role of, 192-195
    influence of, in transactional
        analysis, 57-62
    role of, in planning IEP, 371
Patient vs. client, 20
Patterning, 80
Penis envy, 42
Percentile scores, 357
Perception
    behavioral counselors' views of, 95
    Gestalt view of, 78-80
    rational-emotive view of, 50-53
Perceptualist, naive vs. expert,
    180-181
Performance contracting model, 31
Personality, 18
    A-B-C theory of, 53
    Adlerian view of, 285-287
    assessment of, 355-358
    career choice and, 258-263
    Gestalt view of, 78-80
    humanistic approaches to, 67-83
    psychoanalytic views of, 38-44
    rational-emotive view of, 49-53
    reality view of, 56
Personal unconscious, 39
Petting, 326
Phallic stage, 42
Phenomenological viewpoint, 55, 72
Phenomenology, 285
Phobia, 71, 92-94
    implosive treatment of, 99-102
Physician's Desk Reference, 392
Placebo effect, 390-391
Play, modeling and, 224-226
Play therapy, 277-284
Positive regard, 75-76, 161-162
Positive reinforcement, 91-99 passim,
    105-106